TRANSITION AND ECONOMICS

Comparative Institutional Analysis

Transition and Economics

Politics, Markets, and Firms

Gérard Roland

The MIT Press

Cambridge, Massachusetts · London, England

This book was set in Melior and MetaPlus by Windfall Software using ZzTEX and was printed and bound in the United States of America.

Library of Congress Cataloging-in-Publication Data

Roland, Gérard, 1954–
    Transition and economics : politics, markets, and firms / Gérard Roland.
      p. cm.
    Includes bibliographical references and index.
    ISBN 0-262-18203-3
    1. Economic history—1990– 2. Post-communism—Economic aspects.
  3. Economics—Political aspects I. Title.
    HC59.15 . R65 2000
    338.9171′7—dc21   00-028246

To Heddy, Elsa, Florence, and Juliette, and to my parents

Contents

Acknowledgments

Transition and Economics: Politics, Markets, and Firms provides an overview of academic research on the transition processes. It emphasizes the new issues for economics that were raised by transition processes when economists had no ready answers from economic theory. It should be of interest not only for researchers working on transition economies but also for the economics profession at large. The research covered intersects with the fields of political economics, development, public economics, corporate finance, and, more broadly, microeconomics and macroeconomics. It can be used as a graduate textbook on transition, and most of the material can be used in advanced undergraduate courses.

In the academic year 1997–98, I was asked to give full Ph.D. courses on transition in Oslo, Stockholm, Brussels, and Gerzensee. That same year, I was asked to give two shorter courses at the summer schools of the European Economic Association and at Central European University in Budapest. It is out of the notes for those lectures that this book has grown. The invitation to Mathias Dewatripont and myself to write a survey paper on the economics of transition for the 1995 World Congress of the Econometric Society in Tokyo had provided a prior opportunity to think about the structure of the exposition. During the academic year 1998-99, I benefited from a fellowship at the Center for Advanced Studies in Behavioral Sciences at Stanford, where I wrote a first draft. Without that fellowship and the unique environment of the Center, this book would have taken much longer to write.

I must express here my deep intellectual debt to Mathias Dewatripont. It was only when he came back to Brussels after earning his Ph.D. at Harvard and a stay at MIT and when we started working together on the political economy of transition that I was put in direct contact with modern applied economic theory and with the network of researchers practicing it at the frontier. My intellectual debt to Mathias thus goes far beyond our research collaboration on the political economy of reform. Mathias also created a unique intellectual environment at the Université Libre de Bruxelles with the establishment of the European Center for Advanced Research in Economics (ECARE) when Patrick Bolton came to Brussels. I also owe an enormous intellectual debt to Patrick Bolton, from whom I also learned much about frontier research when we started working together on privatization policies in transition economies. Patrick also contributed greatly to the unique intellectual environment at ECARE. The ECARE lunches to which Patrick invited us at the Matignon restaurant were a constant opportunity to discuss economics and exchange ideas on work in progress. From the very start, the research environment at ECARE was characterized by a very cooperative and friendly spirit that encouraged intellectual exchange among ECARE researchers and between ECARE fellows and the numerous visitors. It is thanks to that cooperative environment that I started working at ECARE with other colleagues (Erik Berglöf and Khalid Sekkat) and students (Micaël

Castanheira and Frédéric Pivetta) on joint projects reported in this book. I am very grateful to them for these collaborations.

Outside ECARE, I owe a lot to joint work with Yingyi Qian, with whom I have had a deep and long-term collaboration on various projects on transition in the last five or six years. We both share a long-term intellectual interest in the transition process and a sense of its general relevance for economics. Our joint discussions during our long working days together have always been and continue to be for me a great source of inspiration for my thinking on transition. I also owe a lot to Thierry Verdier, with whom I also have had a long-term collaboration on several transition projects since the early 1990s and with whom I also share an intellectual affinity in many domains. I am also very grateful to all my other coauthors on transition research reported in this book: Irena Grosfeld, Lawrence Lau, Eric Maskin, and Chenggang Xu. I have learned a lot from all of them in our collaboration and also via numerous, long intellectual exchanges, especially with Chenggang Xu, that go much beyond these joint collaborations.

In all my research on transition, I benefited from interactions with Philippe Aghion, George Akerlof, Alberto Alesina, Ron Anderson, Masa Aoki, Anders Åslund, Chongen Bai, Abhijit Banerjee, David Begg, Marek Belka, John Bennett, Daniel Berkowitz, Olivier Blanchard, Tito Boeri, Giuseppe Bonnano, Maxim Boycko, Jorge Braga de Macedo, Laszlo Bruszt, Bruno Biais, John Bonin, Michael Burda, Nauro Campos, Wendy Carlin, Juan Carrillo, Daniel Cohen, Simon Commander, Fabrizio Coricelli, Francesca Cornelli, Jacques Crémer, Alex Cukierman, Jean-Michel Dewaele, Michel Devroey, Avinash Dixit, David Ellerman, Saul Estrin, Raquel Fernandez, Jan Fidrmuc, Guido Friebel, Roman Frydman, Stanislav Gomulka, Roger Gordon, Brigitte Granville, Avner Greif, Denis Gromb, Roger Guesnerie, Sergei Guriev, Laszlo Halpern, Oliver Hart, Haizhou Huang, Athar Hussain, Barry Ickes, Marvin Jackson, Samir Jahjah, Claus Kastberg, Iannis Katsoulacos, Patrick Kehoe, Michael Keren, Grzegorz Kolodko, Jozef Konings, Janos Kornai, Jean-Jacques Laffont, Patrick Legros, Mark Levin, David Li, Wei Li, John Litwack, Bentley Macleod, Dalia Marin, Jacek Mercik, Paul Milgrom, Ron McKinnon, Tracy Lewis, John McMillan, Janet Mitchell, Peter Murrell, Jacques Nagels, Damien Neven, Mario Nuti, Marco Pagano, Torsten Persson, Jean-Philippe Platteau, Joan Pearce, Enrico Perotti, Thomas Piketty, Jean Pisani-Ferry, Viktor Polterovich, Richard Portes, Ailsa Roëll, John Roemer, Dariusz Rosati, Jacek Rostowski, Andrew Rose, Howard Rosenthal, Ratna Sahay, David Sappington, Gilles Saint-Paul, André Sapir, Mark Schaffer, Paul Seabright, Claudia Sénik-Leygonie, Andras Simonovits, Hans-Werner Sinn, Georges Siotis, Andrei Shleifer, Mark Schankermann, Enrico Spolaore, David Stark, Oren Sussman, Pekka Sutela, Jan Svejnar, Jo Swinnen, Ariane Szafarz, Guido Tabellini, Kathy Terrell, Jacques Thisse, Jean Tirole, Daniel Treisman, Henri Tulkens, Frantisek Turnovec, Sveder van Wijnbergen. Chris Woodruff, E-Lu von Thadden, Jean Waelbroeck, Yijiang Wang, Shang-Jin Wei, Philippe Weil, Barry Weingast, Wing Woo, Charles Wyplosz, Joseph Zeira, Katia Zhuravskaya, and many others.

I have received many very helpful comments on a first draft from Philippe Aghion, Daniel Berkowitz, Olivier Blanchard, Patrick Bolton, Micaël Castanheira, Daniel Daianu,

Mathias Dewatripont, Guido Friebel, Irena Grosfeld, Jozef Konings, Janos Kornai, Dalia Marin, Enrico Perotti, Yingyi Qian, Alexander Repkin, Anouk Rivière, Mark Schaffer, Monika Schnitzer, Andrei Shleifer, Jan Svejnar, Guido Tabellini, Daniel Treisman, Wei Li, Chenggang Xu, and Xiaokai Yang.

Special thanks go to Anouk Rivière, who also kindly read the first draft with meticulous care from the first page to the last and indicated multiple mistakes in formulas as well as in the text. I am also very grateful to the graduate students at the Leuven Institute for Central and Eastern European Studies (LICOS) who have provided very useful feedback to improve the pedagogical exposition in various chapters. The very numerous and varied comments I have received from so many colleagues, students, and friends have helped me to substantially improve the final manuscript. I am of course solely responsible for any remaining errors in the final draft.

I benefited from research assistance by Guido Friebel and Gyongyi Loranth in the framework of ACE projects. Nancy Demunck has provided wonderful secretarial assistance in the preparation of the book. She also prepared most of the figures. Throughout these years, I have benefited from outstanding secretarial assistance from Romy Genin. Without her efficient help on innumerable administrative matters, the time I could have devoted to research would have been considerably more brief.

I would like to thank Terry Vaughn of MIT Press for his support.

Finally, I must thank my wife, Heddy, and my three daughters, Elsa, Florence, and Juliette, for having put up with me, especially at the end of 1999 in the last stages of finishing the book.

INTRODUCTION: TRANSITION AND ECONOMICS

WHY DO RESEARCH ON ECONOMICS OF TRANSITION?

Since the fall of the Berlin wall in the fall of 1989, a sizable group of economists has been studying the process of transition from socialism to capitalism in former socialist economies. The field is called transition economics, or sometimes transformation economics. This group includes some of the most prominent macroeconomists and microeconomists from the best universities in the world.

Interest in research on transition has grown over time, but the focus of interest has changed. The first wave of interest in transition was mostly dominated by policy papers that attempted to influence various aspects of transition policies. The policy excitement in the West has abated somewhat after the first years. Nevertheless, academic research in the area, both theoretical and empirical, has kept increasing, as witnessed by an impressive flow of publications in academic journals (including top journals), numerous sessions at congresses of the American Economic Association and the European Economic Association, and many specialized conferences. In Europe, the Center for Economic Policy Research (CEPR) has set up a research program in transition economics together with its traditional programs in such areas as international macroeconomics, industrial organization, trade, public policy, finance, and labor. Various economics institutes have been set up with the main objective of undertaking research on the transition process: the William Davidson Institute at the University of Michigan, the Stockholm Institute for Transition Economics (SITE) at the Stockholm School of Economics, LICOS at Katholieke Universiteit Leuven, the Center for Economic Research and Transition (CERT) at Heriot-Watt University in Edinburgh, the Center for Economic Research and Graduate Education–Economics Institute (CERGE-EI) in Prague, the Russian-European Center for Economic Policy (RECEP) and the New Economic School in Moscow, and others.

This growing interest in the transition process within the economics profession can be explained both by its policy importance and by its relevance for economic theory.

THE POLICY IMPORTANCE OF TRANSITION

The transition process affects the lives of about 1.65 billion people.[1] The comprehensive transformation of the economic institutions of the countries concerned has brought about a complete change in the economic conditions of the population. It is surely one of the most important economic events of the twentieth century, along with the transition from capitalism to socialism and the Great Depression. Economic historians of the future will most probably remember the twentieth century (apart from the tremendous technological progress it has witnessed) for the specific contest that took place between the socialist and the capitalist economic systems, and for the defeat of the former by the latter. It will also surely be remembered for several important failures of the capitalist system, the Great

[1] *This figure should be seen as a lower bound given the likely underestimation of Chinese population statistics.*

Depression being the most important, and for the attempts, successful and unsuccessful, to improve the system or to prevent depressions.

Despite its victory over socialism and its important successes, capitalism has not been introduced successfully everywhere. At the beginning of the third millennium, there still remains the major challenge of bringing about prosperity and growth via well-working market institutions in the poorest (and highly populated) continents, countries, and regions in the world. By introducing capitalism in former socialist economies, the objective, one hopes, is to bring these countries, within an appropriate period of time, to levels of prosperity comparable to those of the most advanced industrialized countries.

Such an objective is by no means assured for countries having undertaken the transition process. Developments in the former Soviet Union, for example, have been increasingly worrying since the beginning of transition. In August 1998, seven years after the failed putsch against Gorbachev that precipitated the end of the communist regime in the former Soviet Union, an unprecedented political crisis, against a background of economic disaster (continued decline in output, high inflation, fall of the ruble, lack of fiscal revenues, proliferation of organized crime, generalized asset diversion, and capital flight), made international stock markets plunge and shiver for several months when fears of an international crisis were looming large. The observed output stagnation, the lack of institutional stability, and the absence of rule of law in transition economies like Russia pose important risks that could lead that big country to prolonged economic stagnation, and even underdevelopment. Devising transition policies that deliver successful capitalist development in former socialist economies is thus an important task.

The results of policy advice given to transition countries have been particularly humbling for economists, to say the least, and remain a subject of controversy. The titles of some books on Russia (*How Russia Became a Market Economy,* Åslund, 1995; *The Coming Russian Boom,* Layard and Parker, 1996; *The Success of Russian Economic Reforms,* Granville, 1995) suggest the exaggerated optimism about Russia that still existed a few years ago. Transition policies have delivered unexpected failures (Russia being one of the most spectacular ones) as well as unexpected successes (China being the best example). The large-scale institutional changes involved in transition are among the most complex economic and social processes one can imagine. Given these complexities and the important stakes at play for hundreds of millions of people, economists cannot claim to know the right answers a priori. Open debates and serious research are of fundamental importance to help formulate adequate policies for a successful transition to capitalism.

THE IMPORTANCE OF TRANSITION FOR ECONOMICS

Policy advice, however elaborate, is not delivered in a vacuum. It is based on theory and representations about the way economies and societies function and react to reforms and large-scale transformation. In the beginning of transition, much of the policy advice was derived from basic textbook economics, the so-called Washington consensus, with strong emphasis on (1) liberalizing prices, (2) tight monetary policy and balanced budgets to stabilize the macroeconomy, and (3) privatizing state-owned enterprises in order to induce profit-maximizing behavior. The experience has revealed important shortcomings in that vision of transition. Liberalization mostly did not yield a positive supply response; it led to a major unpredicted fall in output. Organized crime has sprung up faster than markets in some transition countries. Stabilization attempts were stubbornly unsuccessful in various countries, and the soft budget constraints of enterprises have lingered on and taken various forms even when enterprise subsidies were slashed (bad bank loans, tax arrears, barter chains). Mass privatization has often led to massive asset stripping and plundering by incumbent managers.

These various surprises have further contributed to a change of focus in thinking about economics and have very much reinforced the institutionalist perspective, emphasizing the importance of the various institutions underpinning a successful capitalist economy. Successful institutions of capitalism are already present in advanced economies, and we tend to take them for granted when reasoning about economies in transition or about developing economies where such institutions are absent. If anything, the experience of transition shows that policies of liberalization, stabilization, and privatization that are not grounded in adequate institutions may not deliver successful outcomes. Much of this change of focus toward the institutionalist perspective had already been taking place with the development of contract theory, political economy, law and economics, regulation theory, corporate finance, and other areas in applied economic theory. However, the transition experience has helped to accelerate various changes of focus in the way we think about economics. Thus, there is a shift of emphasis from markets and price theory to contracting and the legal, social, and political environment of contracting. Transition has not only helped to reinforce this change of focus in economic thinking. It has also renewed interest in thinking about the interplay and complementarities between the various constitutive institutions of capitalism. Finally, transition has forced us to think about institutions not in a static way but in a dynamic way. To understand transition, one must understand the dynamics of large-scale institutional change: how momentum for reform is created and how institutions can evolve, but also how momentum can be lost and how one can get stuck in inefficient institutions. In that sense, transition has reinforced what I would call the evolutionary-institutionalist perspective, insisting on the institutional environment of agents at any moment in time and also on its evolution.

The word "transition" itself can be misleading in various ways. It may give the impression that transition is "simply" a short-run policy issue that should take a few years at most, analogous to stabilization policy where a new government can make all the hard decisions early in its tenure, then reap the benefits before the end of its mandate and hope to get reelected. In reality, nobody can tell for sure how transitional the transition is or whether the countries engaged in this process will end up transformed into successful capitalist economies. It is useful to draw a parallel here with development. Development policies were formulated decades ago with the objective of helping underdeveloped economies catch up with the industrialized countries. Some countries, like the East Asian tigers, have been successful in their development, but other countries, in particular in Africa, have not been catching up and have even undergone a process of further impoverishment. The transition from socialism to capitalism is a process whereby there is a given coherent set of institutions as starting point. Formulating specific objectives for the end point (like adopting the U.S., Swedish, or German model) is no guarantee that such an end point will be reached, however much one exhorts policymakers to be bold, just as was the case with development. Institutions of other countries cannot so easily be copied or imitated, and attempts at imitation may yield unintended outcomes. These outcomes are strongly dependent on the initial set of institutions that form the starting point of transition. The starting point cannot be neglected because any process of change must take that starting point and the initial economic behavior and expectations of agents as given. This statement implies that there is not necessarily an institutional shortcut whereby institutions of successful capitalist economies are simply copied. Russia copied many successful laws from Anglo-Saxon countries in the domain of corporate governance, but these laws could not be enforced (Black, Kraakman, and Tarassova, 1999; Stiglitz, in press). On the contrary, it may be necessary to devise "transitional institutions" as necessary steps towards more successful institutions. China in its pragmatic reform process developed specific transitional institutions such as dual-track liberalization and township and village enterprises (TVEs) in a far from perfect institutional context where the rule of law is basically absent (Qian, in press). Nevertheless, the question is raised whether "transitional institutions" represent stepping-stones toward better institutions or whether they create vested interests that block further institutional transition.

Seen from the institutional perspective, research on transition can help to improve (1) our understanding of capitalism as an economic system and (2) our understanding of large-scale institutional change.

A Better Understanding of Capitalism as an Economic System

The rise and fall of centrally planned economies probably constitute not only one of the greatest events of the twentieth century but also one of the most important failed economic experiments in human history. Even though it is clear with hindsight that the advent of central planning and its intellectual support were based on a wrong understanding of the costs and benefits of the coordination role of markets and on a strong overestimation of the coordination capacity of hierarchical organizations, the relative role of market coordination and coordination in hierarchies remains a fundamental question in economic theory. Hayek's (1945) vision, more than forty years before the demise of central planning, of the informational limitations of planning and of the capacity of market prices to convey decentralized information has proved truly prophetic. The coordination role of markets and hierarchies has been the object of important advances in formal theory (Weitzman, 1974; see chapter 4 in Milgrom and Roberts, 1992) and in economic history (Chandler, 1962). The question of the boundaries of the firm and the costs and benefits of vertical integration have also been at the forefront of economic theory in recent decades (see, e.g., Williamson, 1975; Grossman and Hart, 1986). Capitalism is composed of markets and organizations that operate within those markets and of complex interactions between both that depend on the constitutive building blocks of capitalism.

Despite the important advances in economic theory of the second half of the twentieth century, we still do not understand well the interactions between the constituent elements of capitalism as an economic system. Thanks to general equilibrium theory, we now understand the interaction between interdependent markets rather well, but we still need to improve our understanding of various other important interactions between systemic elements of capitalism.

The Link between Incentive Structures and Markets   What happens in an economy where prices are liberalized but the incentives of enterprises are different from profit maximization (and where enterprises are subject to soft budget constraints, for example)? This question is of direct relevance for transition economies where price liberalization takes place in an environment of state-owned enterprises (SOEs) accustomed to the incentive schemes of the centrally planned economy. The question, however, is also extremely relevant in the context of modern capitalism, where in most big corporations there is separation of ownership and control, a fact that has been the object of scholarly research at least since the 1930s (Berle and Means, 1932). In that context, understanding the incentives of enterprise managers is a key issue, especially since the private interests of managers may differ from those of the shareholders.

Managers operate according to incentive schemes set by the shareholders. Managerial behavior depends on these formal incentives schemes but also on other variables such as the financial situation of the firm (in particular the degree of indebtedness) (Jensen, 1986; Grossman and Hart, 1982; Hart and Moore, 1994), career concerns (Holmström, 1982; Dewatripont, Jewitt, and Tirole, 1999a, 1999b), and other factors. There is thus a relationship between managerial incentives and enterprise decisions or market behavior (see, e.g., Aghion, Dewatripont, and Rey, in press, on the link between managerial incentives and growth). In many sectors of a capitalist economy, private firms coexist with state-owned firms. Not only do state-owned firms pursue different objectives from private firms, but the coexistence of both affects the behavior of private firms as well (see, e.g., Crémer, Marchand, and Thisse, 1989).

The Relation between Property Rights and Incentives   Stating that the difference between private and state ownership has a key effect on the incentives of the firm seems a commonsense proposition, but it is by no means an uncontroversial proposition in economic theory. Indeed, why can't one mimic the incentives of private firms inside state-owned enterprises? In the context of transition economies, such an ability would mean that, once communist political regimes collapsed, there would be no urge and even no need to privatize SOEs, since the new democratic promarket governments could set up the appropriate incentive schemes for managers to behave in a profit-maximizing way. Needless to say, this position met with a lot of skepticism in transition countries. However, it is also fair to say that few logically convincing reasons were put forward to explain why the incentives of private firms cannot be mimicked inside SOEs. If this is the case, what then are the irreducible differences between them?

Until very recently, the role of ownership played no role whatsoever in economic theory. According to general equilibrium theory, there is no difference between private and state-owned firms as long as they maximize profits. *Mutatis mutandis*, there is no difference between capitalism and market socialism as long as markets are perfectly competitive. Most incentive theory is done in the context of complete contracts. With complete contracts, ownership is not a relevant issue, since the same incentive schemes can be applied in a private or a state-owned firm. Provided all the other conditions facing the firm are the same, economic behavior should be the same and should not depend on ownership per se.

It is only with the introduction of incomplete contract theory (Grossman and Hart, 1986; Hart and Moore, 1990; Hart, 1996) that the role of ownership has started to play a central role in economic theory. If contracts are incomplete, ownership gives residual rights of control that will affect enterprise decisions. Finding theoretical foundations to explain why contracts are incomplete is currently an important challenge for economic theory and the object of many research efforts among economic theorists (see, e.g., Maskin and Tirole, 1999; Segal, 1999; Hart and Moore, 1998).

The Relation between Legal Arrangements and Social Norms Are legal arrangements necessary to guarantee given norms of behavior? Are legal arrangements sufficient to guarantee given norms of behavior? Are legal arrangements and social norms substitutes or complements? These are important questions for an understanding of social systems.

More specifically, will laws be enforced against social norms? Can existing legal codes be introduced overnight, as has been argued by various policy advisers in the transition context? As stated earlier, the transition experience has raised considerable doubt about such a proposition. More generally, the question is raised of why law is enforced in some countries and not in others. This is also a very important question.

Important scholarly work has shown that the introduction of the rule of law—in particular, of credible legal guarantees against predation of private property rights by the sovereign—played a fundamental role in explaining the early and successful development of capitalism in England (North and Weingast, 1989; North, 1990). In contrast, in continental Europe such legal guarantees were absent, and there were no real limits to royal despotism. These conclusions have been implicitly challenged by Weitzman and Xu (1993), who, in the context of transition in China, have pointed to the fact that, despite the absence of clear legal arrangements, economic development in the Chinese countryside has been extremely successful, even spectacular, with the phenomenon of township and village enterprises. This Chinese puzzle raises questions with respect to the relative role of social and cultural norms, on one hand, and legal norms, on the other hand, in the establishment of a successful capitalist system. Weitzman and Xu emphasize the role of cultural norms and advance the hypothesis that Western individualism requires solid legal arrangements to foster cooperation, whereas Asian values, which are more collectivist, can rely more on the reputational effects associated with social norms.

Clearly, much research is still required on these issues to better understand the role of culture and social norms in economic development.

The Relations between Government and Economic Agents   In any capitalist economy, government activity is deemed indispensable, even though there has always been a lot of controversy as to what its size relative to the private sector should be. Governments generally have a monopoly over the use of violence that they use to enforce laws. On the one hand, government power, everywhere and always, creates the scope for possible abuses of power. From the economic point of view, such power can be used to prey on the private sector and on economic agents. On the other hand, anarchy, or the absence of government, destroys legal guarantees for the protection of private property and paves the way for unbridled organized crime and racketeering, violent competition between competing Mafias, and general insecurity of property rights. In order to have successful growth and development, the dilemma, as stated by B. Weingast (1997) is to have a government that is not too strong, so as to make credible the absence of predation on private agents, but that is still strong enough to enforce the rule of law.

These questions are of immediate and practical relevance in the transition context. When transition starts with inherited communist government structures, as in the case of China, the Soviet Union during the Gorbachev years, or reformist Hungary, private sector development is hampered by fears of predatory taxation or of policy reversals that will lead to the spoliation of private economic agents. These fears were not unfounded, since private enterprise was never officially tolerated and had to be called by other names, such as "cooperatives" in the Soviet Union. At the other extreme, with the collapse of communist regimes, especially in the former Soviet Union, government structures usually also quasi-collapsed, leading to absence of law enforcement and to the emergence of Mafias.

Weak governments not only allow the emergence of organized crime, but they may also divert the efforts of economic agents from productive activity to rent-seeking activities, especially under initial conditions where markets are repressed. This will be the case in particular if the return to influence activities and rent-seeking behavior is higher than the return to productive activities. The question is then, What institutional conditions and what forms of organization of government are needed in order to encourage productive rather than rent-seeking activity?

The Relations between the Political System and Economic Interest Groups   The relationship between political systems and economic interest groups is a very important topic that has been the subject of important research in the field of political economy, now more and more often called political economics. What is the sustainability of given legal and economic arrangements under various political systems, given the relative strength of interest groups that have an interest either in the continuation or in the reform or reversal of given arrangements? How good are various political systems at getting efficiency-enhancing reforms adopted, and at overcoming the resistance of interest groups who have an interest in the status quo?

These are key questions in the context of transition. One popular question was whether the early introduction of democracy in Central and Eastern Europe, compared to China, which has remained a dictatorship, has made economic reforms more difficult to get through or not, and whether or not it contributed to economic stability. Quite opposite answers have been formulated to that question.

In thinking about various political systems, one must not only distinguish between dictatorship and democracy, but also between the various kinds of dictatorships (see, e.g., Rodrik, 1992) and various kinds of democracies, such as presidential and parliamentary systems (see, e.g., Persson, Roland, and Tabellini, 1997), different electoral systems, and so on.

All these questions pertaining to the understanding of capitalism as an economic system can be seen from a positive as well as from a normative angle. From the positive point of view, we may simply try to understand better the internal mechanics of the capitalist system. The normative angle is never absent, however. Indeed, a better understanding of the capitalist system may help us improve it and adjust institutions in various countries in order to move to more efficient institutions.

Naturally, the preceding questions, though of obvious relevance for transition, are general questions about capitalism as an economic system and are equally relevant in many other contexts. What can be the specific contribution of transition economics?

In transition economies, the constitutive parts of the capitalist system are instituted at various speeds, in different variants, in varying order and different initial conditions. The economic observations from these economies are not generated from a system that is already in steady state but from a system that is emerging. By observing systems that are not yet in steady state, we may better understand the system itself, the interactions between various constitutive parts, and the relative importance of various elements in the system in generating outcomes. In a way, transition can be compared to a controlled experiment where the action of some variables is suppressed to better understand the interaction of other variables. Of course, the transition process is not a conscious experiment in social sciences, and much of the process itself is spontaneous rather than controlled. Nevertheless, the unique historical process of transition generates "out of steady state" observations, reflecting different initial conditions and policies in different countries. Such observations should tell us more about the interaction between the constitutive parts of the capitalist system.

Understanding Large-Scale Institutional Change

Throughout history, economic, social, and political systems have developed, evolved, and died or been replaced by other systems. History has many discontinuities: prolonged periods of slow changes or even stagnation are followed by short periods of very rapid changes, often changes on a very large scale that deeply affect the economic, social, and political spheres alike. These periods of rapid change, which often last less than a generation, sometimes less than ten years, may exert a decisive influence on future periods, even in the very long term. The reign of the first Chinese emperor Qin Shi Huang lasted only eleven years after he unified China (221–210 B.C.), but in those eleven years he built the Great Wall, standardized the writing system, unified the money and measurement systems, and created a centralized administration with uniform taxes, law codes, a sales monopoly (to collect salt taxes), and a central army. Similarly, the short periods of the American Revolution and of the reign of Napoleon in France had a lasting effect on the institutions and the history of those countries. These examples and many others show us that there is a strong path dependency from such periods of large-scale institutional change. Therefore, it is of crucial importance to gain a better understanding of the dynamics of such changes: When and why do they come about? What are the factors or conditions in the economic environment driving change and opposing change? What are the social forces pushing for change and those resisting change? How do the forces of change organize to overcome the forces in favor of the status quo? Are the new institutions that are set up just one equilibrium among many possible others, or is the observed equilibrium uniquely determined or selected among a very narrow range of equilibria?

Politics plays an important role in large-scale institutional change and the pro- and antichange forces organize to achieve their goals within legislatures, in elections, through lobbying, and sometimes by violent means that may even lead to civil wars. The politics of reform is most often a dynamic game: decisions made today affect tomorrow's balance of power between conflicting groups. Therefore, the setting of agendas for today's decisions involves most often a strategic dimension that forward-looking players understand reasonably well. Important strategic issues are the speed of reforms and their sequencing, that is, the order in which they are adopted. The political dynamics of large-scale reform processes, though crucial, has been underresearched until recently. Under what circumstances does reform sequencing create vested interests to block further reform, and when does sequencing on the contrary build momentum for further reforms and unblock situations of stalemate and paralysis of decisionmaking? The transition process has brought these issues to the foreground, and in the first part of this book we formulate a comprehensive exposition of the dynamic theory of reform politics.

Understanding large-scale institutional change obviously goes beyond the understanding of the dynamical political process in which those who have stakes in reform and those who have stakes in maintaining the status quo oppose each other. Understanding why and under what evolving circumstances political, legal, military, social, religious, cultural, and family institutions decay and are replaced by others is a fascinating issue that has motivated generations of researchers and undoubtedly will in the future until we better understand the fabric of social sytems and how they evolve and change.

TRANSITION AND ECONOMICS

One question often asked in the profession is whether transition economics is or not a "field." There are usually considered to be three types of fields in economics.

The first type of field is defined by its focus on a particular methodology defined by particular questions—for example, game theory. Though it covers most of contemporary economics and, beyond that, important parts of political science and sociology, it asks, What are the outcomes of interactions between rational agents with possibly conflicting objectives, given their information, endowments, and possible restrictions on strategies? Similarly, fields like decision theory and various subfields in econometrics are defined essentially by an abstract methodological focus with a wide range of possible applications in various domains.

The second type of field is defined by particular real-world domains, also focusing on a limited set of questions. Such fields include labor, public finance, general equilibrium, finance, and macroeconomics. Labor economics focuses only on one market. Finance asks questions about arbitrage between assets of varying characteristics. These domains have a relatively abstract focus in the sense that the questions asked are independent of a given geographical and historical context, often claiming validity for all, or many, geographical and historical environments.

The third type of field is institutional economics, where the geographical, historical, or particular institutional context plays an important role. This is clearly the case for the fields of development and economic history. If transition is to be defined as a field, it clearly belongs to this group. Transition, however, is clearly narrower and can even partly be seen as a subset of those fields. Transition is history in the making[2] and will sooner or later become a subfield of economic history. At the same time, transition can be seen as a subfield of development with specific initial conditions, compared to other development contexts: generalized state ownership and strong state power, overindustrialization, a relatively high level of human capital and of economic development, and a low initial income inequality.

Seen that way, transition would seem to be a rather narrow subject. I would also claim that research on transition cannot develop successfully purely as a field of its own and must develop in interaction with various other fields of economics to benefit from the various angles provided by the different fields of specialization.

Should research on transition then simply be broken up into the appropriate fields of specialization: macroeconomics, industrial organization, finance, trade, and so on? I don't think so. I think it is important to develop specific transition research programs and to bring together the community of economists working on transition. The main reason, and this is also my main reason for writing this book, is that the group of scholars interested in transition have come up with research issues that are extremely relevant in the context of transition and that simultaneously represent a contribution to economics at large. Let me give one example: the issue of soft budget constraints, that is, the bailout of financial losses of enterprises or agents. The concept of soft budget constraints was coined by Kornai (1980) in the context of the socialist economy. It was later modeled by Dewatripont and Maskin (1995) in the context of sequential game theory. The soft budget constraint problem has now been nearly universally recognized as an important economic phenomenon that applies not only to socialism and to the transition process at large but also to other contexts like important bank bailouts (the S&L crisis in the United States in the 1980s) or in other banking crises like in Sweden in the early 1990s. It is also relevant today to understand the East Asian crisis and the complex interaction that

[2] This observation does not imply any significant methodological difference between transition and economic history. Economic agents, in the past as well as in the present, face uncertainty regarding the future when forming their expectations and making decisions. Only historians know how uncertainty was resolved ex post. This benefit of hindsight may lead to an underestimation of the role of uncertainty when studying history. The causal link between the Treaty of Versailles and Auschwitz is relatively obvious with hindsight. In 1918 it surely was not.

existed between firms, banks, and government in a country like Korea, or even Japan. Yet, research on soft budget constraints has been developed mainly by economists working on transition. This is thus clearly an area of expertise where the group of scholars working on transition has made contributions that go beyond the study of transition. If all research on transition had been discouraged or suppressed, such developments would not have taken place. A large group of scholars, both senior and junior, has invested time and effort since the early 1990s to address the issues raised by transition in Eastern Europe and China in both theoretical and empirical work (the latter obviously with a lag). This group is much larger than the former group of comparative economists who studied socialist economies. Moreover, it comprises both leading economists in the profession and junior scholars with strong Ph.D. training in the best American universities. These scholars study issues that are not only very relevant for China, Eastern Europe, and other places but are also very relevant beyond transition itself and are at the frontier of research in economics. One example is the political economy of reforms. Another example is the difference between private and public ownership, a fundamental issue in economics that has only started to be grasped since Oliver Hart's pathbreaking work on incomplete contract theory. It is not a coincidence that many famous microeconomists and corporate finance people have been attracted to transition.

In general, I think good research on transition economies should always yield more general lessons for economics. This statement is true mostly because good models are built in such a way that they can be applied to many different situations, but also because economists have common tools that form a common language to analyze different situations. There is no reason to believe that the variety of economic interactions analyzed in the context of transition is completely disconnected from other contexts of economic interactions.

My objective in writing this book is to make research on transition better known and recognized in the academic community by showing that the policy issues of transition from communism to capitalism have raised new questions for economics and generated serious and innovative research that is relevant beyond transition itself.

OUTLINE OF THE BOOK

In thinking on how to write this book, I could have decided to mechanically list all research issues raised in the various fields and subfields of economics. This approach would have presented a complete but perhaps somewhat tedious picture. In many cases indeed, research on transition consists simply—and rightly so—in applying existing theories and methods to transition countries, just as they could be applied, say, to Europe or Latin America. I chose instead to focus only on areas where research on transition had, in my view, contributed to bringing new topics to economics. I also chose to abstract largely from the huge quantity of policy papers on transition to concentrate on papers contributing to the theory of transition or to our empirical knowledge of the transition process.

The objective is to give in the book as much as possible a unified exposition of the most interesting aspects of this research in transition economics. Three aspects will be emphasized that are very relevant for transition but carry simultaneously a more general message for economics: (1) the political economy of reforms, (2) the dynamics of large-scale sectoral reallocation, (3) changes in the governance of firms and, to a lesser extent, of government agencies.

The book is thus divided in three parts:

1. Political Constraints and Reform Strategy

2. Allocative Changes

3. Governance Changes

The logic of the exposition is to go from the "forest" to the "tree." This organization in three parts is aimed not only at "collecting" results of research in these three areas but also at combining a comprehensive view of the transition process integrating politics, markets, and firms with more detailed analysis of specific issues. This approach reflects the view that transition necessarily must lead to complementary and consistent changes in these three areas and that they are interrelated. Kornai (1992, 1998) emphasizes five building blocks of economic systems: (1) the political system, (2) the dominant ownership structure, (3) the dominant mode of economic coordination, (4) incentives, and (5) market situations. Part One emphasizes all blocks viewed from the first block. Part Two deals with blocks 3 and 5, and Part Three with blocks 2 and 4. Like Kornai, I believe that the sustainability as well as the transformation of economic systems cannot be separated from the political sphere. Economic interests as shaped by incentive structures and allocative mechanisms translate, through the political system, into political coalitions that either sustain existing arrangements or lead to their transformation. Since these various spheres of economic systems are interrelated, we should of course aim for integrated theories and model all the relevant interactions between politics, markets, and firms. For reasons of tractability, we cannot achieve so much most of the time. Therefore, one needs models to understand the "forest" where our description of "trees" is at most sketchy and unsatisfactory but yields insights that are deemed sufficiently robust in comparison to ones that would be derived from more complex and full models. Similarly, our models of "trees" can, in many respects, abstract from the "forest" or represent it in an overly simplified way but yield relevant and robust insights.

At a very general level, transition deals with large-scale institutional changes. The first part of the book treats political economy aspects of transition and focuses on how these large-scale changes are decided dynamically via the political process. As the analysis concentrates on dynamic political processes, the economy is modeled in rather abstract and simple terms, giving generality to the analysis. The main questions addressed are the effect of political constraints on the speed and sequencing of reforms, dynamic trade-offs between efficiency and costs of compensating losers, and trade-offs between acceptability and irreversibility of reform programs.

The second part looks at the general equilibrium and macroeconomic effects of these changes. It focuses on the effects of different policies of liberalization, on the dynamics of sectoral reallocation, and on the macroeconomic effects of the large allocative changes induced by large-scale reforms and institutional change. The main questions addressed are the optimal speed of sectoral reallocation, the speed of price liberalization, and the output fall early in transition as well as coordination problems in law enforcement and their economy-wide effects.

The third part looks at enterprise adjustment to changes. It deals with changes in incentives and economic behavior of firms from state ownership under socialism to private ownership. Changes in organization of government and enterprise governance of public enterprises are also analyzed (such as TVEs in China) as well as the effect of different privatization policies and financial reforms.

In each part and in each chapter, theory will be presented and motivated first. Applications of the theory to the reality of transition will be discussed. Failures of the theory will be discussed as well as shortcomings (aspects of reality that are not covered by theory). Application of the theory to other contexts will be discussed too, as well as the relevant empirical literature for each chapter. I will only cover a small part of the empirical literature. Much empirical research in transition has been done without theoretical background or with the goal of testing well-established theories. Also, there is always an obvious lag between the production of theoretical models and their empirical verification. I hope the theoretical expositions in the book will be useful in generating further empirical research.

The formal exposition in each part and each chapter will be covered as much as possible with a unified model. The emphasis will be on substance and ideas generated by the models.

UNDERSTANDING TRANSITION

1.1   LITTLE PRIOR KNOWLEDGE BEFORE TRANSITION

In his essay on economic policy and the political process, Avinash Dixit (1996) quotes Alan Blinder's "Murphy's Law of Economic Policy" (1987, p. 1): "Economists have the least influence on policy where they know the most and most agree; they have the most influence on policy where they know the least and disagree most vehemently."

This statement, its second half at least, seems to be especially valid for the economics of transition. Rarely have economic advisers played such a prominent role in policy debates as has been the case since 1990 in Central and Eastern European economies. Jeffrey Sachs, for example, has attracted worldwide attention for his forceful advocacy of the "big bang" approach to transition. These views were endorsed by one part of the profession and criticized vehemently by another part. Controversies focused very quickly on the speed of transition. Advocates of big bang arguing for a simultaneous and quick introduction of all reforms included Lipton and Sachs (1990a), Åslund (1991), Berg and Sachs (1992), Boycko (1992), Murphy, Shleifer, and Vishny (1992), Sachs (1993), Frydman and Rapaczynski (1994), and Woo (1994). Advocates of gradualism emphasizing the need for a given sequencing of reforms included Svejnar (1989), Portes (1990, 1991), McKinnon (1991), Roland (1991), Dewatripont and Roland (1992a, 1992b, 1995), McMillan and Naughton (1992), Murrell (1992), Aghion and Blanchard (1994), Litwack and Qian (1998), and Wei (1993). Others emphasized the need for big bang along certain dimensions and gradualism along other dimensions. This was the case for Kornai (1990), Blanchard and colleagues (1991), and Fischer and Gelb (1991).[1] This early polarization, along with the surrounding controversy on transition strategies, can surely be seen as a sign of unpreparedness of the economics profession for the tasks of transition.

No preestablished theory of transition existed before the fall of the Berlin Wall. The ratio of theory to policy papers in transition economics has nevertheless been surprisingly low. The early literature on transition was largely verbal in style, aiming essentially

[1] *Many other economists remained skeptical about whether economic theory has or should have anything to say at all about the transition from socialism to capitalism.*

at giving advice on transition policies. The theories with which Western advisers were probably best-equipped were those concerning macroeconomic stabilization. However, existing theories of stabilization assume a market environment. It was not clear a priori how stabilization policies would work in an initial environment without markets. More importantly, most economists will agree that stabilization is only one of the dimensions of transition. Other very important aspects relate to the necessary large-scale institutional changes: the creation and development of markets, including financial markets, the institution and enforcement of property rights, and other legal and political changes along with enterprise privatization and restructuring. The difficulty of transition is that all these complementary changes need to take place without creating too many economic disturbances, as the economy must continue to function and the various needs of the population must continue to be fulfilled.[2] To make things even more complex, because of the magnitude of the changes implied by transition, political support needs to be continuously maintained during the reform process to avoid policy reversals.

There were no preexisting theories in some of the most crucial areas of transition, such as

- The effects on sectoral reallocation and general output performance of different methods of liberalization in a socialist economy where there were no preexisting markets or market networks, let alone capital and labor markets.

- How to harden budget constraints and achieve efficient restructuring in existing enterprises.

- The effect of political constraints on general reform strategies and specific reform policies.

- How to privatize socialist enterprises.

Even though practice has shown a general inferiority of state firms over private firms, no good theory existed to explain the difference in performance between private and state firms.

1.2 SURPRISES OF TRANSITION

Theoretical knowledge on how to achieve the changes listed in the preceding section was scarce before transition. Moreover, the only major experience prior to 1989 was that of China, where the political and economic circumstances differ strongly from those of Europe. Countries like Hungary, Yugoslavia, and Poland had only limited experience of partial reform within the socialist system. In almost every case, the lack of prior knowledge of the transition process has led to surprises.

[2] An analogy to this difficulty would be the task of changing the engines of a plane while it keeps flying!

Economists did not expect the huge output fall observed after price liberalization and stabilization. As acknowledged by Kornai (1993), most economists who had been thinking about transition before 1989 did not predict the output fall. Many economists had expected a sluggish supply response to price liberalization. Many others had expected a mild economic slowdown, a "transformational recession" to use the words of Kornai, with the transition from a shortage economy, characterized by a generalized excess demand on most markets, to a market economy, with mostly buyers' markets (excess supply) rather than sellers' markets. The observed double-digit output fall was quite unexpected.

Moreover, while most Central European countries were recovering from this important output fall, for most countries of the former Soviet Union, including Russia, transition has led to an abysmal plunge in output that has all the appearances of a huge negative permanent output shock.

The outcome of privatization policies was also unexpected to many. As a rule, privatization of former SOEs benefited mostly the "insiders"—that is, managers, and sometimes also workers, who were inside the firm before transition started. Many, if not most economists, would have expected outsiders (foreign investors and new private entrepreneurs) to play a much bigger role. Indeed, the skills of socialist managers are not necessarily the same as those of managers of capitalist enterprises. Socialist managers had to learn to be good at coping with a shortage economy and dealing with planning agencies. Because of excess demand and planned deliveries, they never had to worry much about selling their products and competing with other firms offering comparable products. Also, in the previously centrally planned economies there was no market for managers, and the allocation of managers to specific firms was not necessarily done on the basis of productive efficiency. One of the objectives of privatization was precisely to achieve a better allocation of managers to assets. The fact that insiders benefited much from privatization raises suspicions about the efficiency of some of the privatization policies followed, especially the policies of mass privatization. Indeed, as we will see later in the book, many studies tend to show that privatized firms, especially firms privatized to insiders, do not perform better than nonprivatized SOEs. At a positive level, the question is raised of why insiders were able to benefit so much from privatization, especially in Russia.

However, there were good surprises of restructuring inside SOEs. Many economists advocated fast privatization, sometimes fast privatization at any cost—that is, at the cost of efficiency—because of the fear that the alternative of no privatization, or slow privatization, would be so much worse. The fear was that managers of SOEs, being in an "endgame situation," would start dissipating the assets of SOEs to their private benefit, leading to inefficient squandering of productive assets. Privatization was much slower than expected in many countries, Poland being the best example. Nevertheless, doomsday predictions about the effects of slow privatizations did not materialize. Very early in transition, evidence started to be produced that SOEs were restructuring. In a paper published in the *Brookings Papers on Economic Activity* in 1993, Marek Belka, Stefan Krajewski, and Brian Pinto gave evidence of restructuring of SOEs in Poland. At the same time, privatization did not seem to prevent asset dissipation. A few years after mass privatization, there is increasing evidence of diversion of assets privatized through vouchers in the Czech Republic (Weiss and Nikitin, 1998) and through mass privatization in Russia (Black, Kraakman, and Tarassova,1999). This massive asset stripping points to the absence of appropriate legal structure, mostly absence of law enforcement and government collapse.

This observation leads us to another surprise of transition: the spectacular growth of organized crime, and especially the so-called Mafia phenomenon in Russia. On the ruins of communist government, organized criminal groups, specializing in racketeering, prostitution, smuggling of drugs and of the spoils of the former Soviet nuclear arsenal, and the like, started to emerge at an amazing speed. The Russian Mafia has become so important that the FBI, Interpol, and other international law enforcement agencies have started monitoring this phenomenon because of the obvious spillover effects outside Russia. This organized crime came as an unpleasant surprise to economists who had predicted the emergence of private enterprise. The Mafia phenomenon obviously has a negative effect on private-sector development because of racketeering in private business, uncertainty related to Mafia wars, the absence of the rule of law, and the general breakdown of government and its replacement by corruption and stealing.

Another big surprise was the breakup of countries. At the beginning of transition, Yugoslavia broke up, followed soon by the USSR and Czechoslovakia. After the fact, many explanations were offered of the inevitability of such breakups, but before they happened, few observers had predicted that there would be so many breakups and that they would happen so fast.

Electoral backlash was also an important surprise to many observers. A few years after the communists had been evicted from power by the democratic revolutions of 1989, former communists came back to power via the ballot box in Lithuania (1992), Poland (1993), Hungary (1994), Bulgaria (1994), and Latvia (1994). In Russia, the Communist Party in 1995 gained 22 percent of votes, giving it a dominant position in the Russian parliament, the Duma. In the case of "accession countries"[3] like Poland and Hungary, the communists had transformed themselves into European-style social democrats, as the Italian communists had done many years before, but this was certainly not the case in Russia. The breakup of Czechoslovakia itself can be seen as a form of political backlash, since there was, at the moment of the breakup, wide divergence of views about how transition should proceed, the big bang approach being more favored in the Czech Republic under Vaclav Klaus, whereas in Slovakia, where there was heavy concentration of former military industry of the Soviet bloc, expectations about transition were much more lukewarm.[4]

Last and not least, the most positive surprise is probably the success of Chinese economic reforms. Between the beginning of its reforms in 1978 and 1998, China's GDP per capita has more than quadrupled, growing at an average annual rate of 9.5 percent. The transition strategy in China was also very different from the big bang approach advocated in Central and Eastern Europe. The Chinese success came unexpectedly for several reasons. First of all, because of the gradualist approach, partial reforms in some areas co-

[3] Accession countries are countries expected to become members of the European Union in the medium term. In 1998 official negotiations for accession started with Poland, Hungary, the Czech Republic, Slovenia, and Estonia.

[4] However, in many cases, governments led by former communist parties tended to lose the subsequent election, suggesting that Central and Eastern European populations tend to be discontented with all governments, left and right.

existed with the socialist status quo in other areas. Because reforms are complementary, the Chinese approach was criticized for being half-baked and inconsistent (Woo, 1994). However, as stated earlier, the successful development of the nonstate sector, especially the township and village enterprises (TVEs), came as a surprise because of its unclear property right structure. It was not clear whether TVEs were pseudoprivate firms or firms owned by local governments. Price liberalization did not follow the big bang approach either. Prices were liberalized only at the margin with planned production and deliveries frozen at a given level and all output liberalized in excess of those planned obligations. This dual-track system was criticized for creating output diversion. China's successful growth came during a period where SOEs were not the object of restructuring and where privatization was still taboo. Despite important criticisms of the Chinese transition strategy in the 1980s, the Chinese experience appeared to be extremely positive, compared to the transition experience of Eastern Europe. China did not experience an initial output fall, and its continuous growth record appeared impressive compared to the Eastern European situation. Despite the Tiananmen massacres and the lack of democratization, there was no backlash against economic reforms that brought prosperity and increased incomes to hundreds of millions, despite the associated increase in income inequality. Any normative evaluation of the evolution of China cannot ignore that it is the world's largest dictatorship and also one of the few remaining ones. This fact, however, should not distract us from making a sober assessment of Chinese transition and recognizing its huge economic success.

All these surprises show that economists were not really prepared to face the tasks of transition. Our knowledge and understanding of transition processes remain limited and happen mostly "after the fact." In the rest of this chapter, we first give a rough description of the main features of the socialist system before transition and then lay out the objectives and constraints of transition. Against that background, we describe what we think are the main stylized facts of transition so far and what questions these stylized facts have raised that we need to understand.

1.3   THE INITIAL SITUATION BEFORE TRANSITION

A large body of knowledge has been generated by several generations of Sovietologists and comparative economists who have been studying the socialist economy. The scholarly knowledge developed by that literature is impressive compared to the caricatural description of socialism that one often finds in the transition literature. Nevertheless, many important questions related to the functioning of the system remain unanswered today. In this section, we only roughly describe the main features of the socialist economy and of partial reforms under socialism and focus essentially on features that are relevant to understanding transition.

TABLE 1.1 SECTORAL ALLOCATION OF LABOR IN OECD AND CPES
(PERCENTAGE SHARES)

	Agriculture	Industry	Services
(1) OECD, 1991			
Eight richest countries	5.5	29.8	64.7
Eight middle countries	5.8	30.4	63.9
Eight poorest countries	17.9	29.5	52.6
(2) Centrally planned economies (CPEs, 1989)			
GDR	10	44.1	45.9
Czechoslovakia	11.6	46.8	41.6
Hungary	17.5	36.1	46.4
Poland	27.2	36.3	36.4

Source: *OECD.*

First of all, the price system and markets were completely absent under "classical" socialism. Allocation of goods and services was done by the planning administration that organized production and exchange. Enterprises were told what to produce, from whom to purchase, and to whom to sell. The only existing markets were those of the shadow economy, which were illegal and operated at the margins of the system.

The production structure was distorted compared to market economies. The two most important distortions were (1) a relative overdevelopment of heavy industry and underdevelopment of services and (2) a bias toward big firms and against small firms. This distortion is clear from Tables 1.1 and 1.2. From Table 1.1, it appears that the sectoral bias is relatively independent of the level of development measured in terms of income per capita, since the same conclusion obtains if one compares East European countries with richer or relatively poorer OECD countries. From Table 1.2, one sees that German industry tends to be more concentrated than French and Italian industry, but the comparison between East and West shows clearly a bias toward large firms in the East.

Heavy industry was overdeveloped because of the requirements of the arms race. Before its demise, the Soviet Union was the biggest producer of steel in the world. One reason why services were underdeveloped is that, following Marx, services were viewed as "unproductive": transforming a good physically was considered to add value, but bringing it to the buyer was not. The bias toward big firms was explained mostly by the fact that it was easier to plan output for a small number of large firms than for a big number of small firms, and also by a desire to exploit economies of scale. Managers of enterprises

TABLE 1.2 DISTRIBUTION OF EMPLOYMENT IN INDUSTRY BY SIZE OF FIRMS
(PERCENTAGE SHARES)

	0–100	100–500	500 and more
West Germany	14.1	23.9	62
France	22.5	24.9	52.6
Italy	32.3	27.3	40.4
GDR	1	11.1	87.9
Czechoslovakia	0.1	3.4	96.5
Hungary	4.5	16.3	79.3
Poland	1.4	18.2	80.4

Source: *OECD. Data for West Germany, France, and Italy are from 1987,
for the GDR from 1988, and for the other countries from 1989.*

also pushed to increase the size of their enterprise in the expectation that they would then get more attention from central planners. These distorted structures are important to mention because they imply that transition requires important sectoral reallocations and a substantial entry of small firms. In many of the transition debates, there has been an excessive focus on the privatization of the existing large SOEs but insufficient attention to the entry of small firms and the organic development of capitalism from below by the new entrepreneurs. From the point of view of sectoral reallocation, much of the "destruction" must take place among the existing large SOEs, whereas much of the "creation" is the task of newly entered firms.

Enterprise incentives were characterized by large bonuses for fulfillment of the planned output target and smaller bonuses based on a percentage of overfulfillment of the plan. This system led enterprises to distortions in product mix and quality so as to maximize the plan indicators. For example, when glass was planned in tons, it tended to be too heavy. When the measurement of glass output switched to square meters, glass became too thin and fragile (see Nove, 1958). Since managerial rewards depended mostly on these output targets, there were few incentives to save on costs. One plan indicator, the *val* (*valovaia produktsiia*) aggregated enterprise output using prices calculated on a cost-plus basis. This system led enterprises to bias their output mix in a cost-maximizing fashion. Moreover, whenever enterprises lacked the financial means necessary to achieve their output target, they would always be refinanced in order to achieve that goal. This practice is the phenomenon of soft budget constraints conceptualized by Kornai (1980). Because there was no cost consciousness, wages were kept under centralized control to prevent any drift in wages at the enterprise level.

An important fact about socialism is that there was not really a consistent plan at the level of the economy. Consistent plans were developed for a disaggregated nomenclature of between 40 and 200 categories of goods. In reality, the Soviet economy had about 12 million different types of goods. The mathematical planning literature of the 1950s and 1960s attempted to find "decomposition algorithms" that would allow the calculation of consistent plans for a disaggregated nomenclature from the consistent plan of an aggregated nomenclature (Kornai and Liptak, 1965; Malinvaud, 1967; Arrow and Hurwicz, 1960; Weitzman, 1970). Central-planning practice, however, remained very far from those algorithms. Computer capacities were by far insufficient to cope with the complexity of such calculations, as Hayek (1945) had predicted.[5] Already in the early 1960s, Montias (1962) had understood that the method of material balances used to compute plans did not produce consistent plans. Material balances are like balance sheets with two columns where all planned demands for a given good are listed in one column and all planned supplies for that good are listed in the other column. Planners would readjust planned supplies and demands for a given good until total demand and supply would be equalized. The problem is that material balances were not mutually consistent. For example, the planned supplies of a steel factory could be adjusted upward to equalize the material balances of, say, a given type of machine, but this adjustment would not lead to an increase in the input requirements for that factory on other material balances where its inputs figured on the demand side. The real puzzle of socialist economies was thus how, in the absence of markets and consistent plans, total chaos did not result! In reality, the problem was less dramatic than it appears. First of all, Montias (1962), Manove (1971), and others showed that the system of material balances could lead to some convergence, despite the absence of the input-output methodology, at the disaggregated level. Also, planning was not only an iterative process but also a cumulative one. The point of departure for the plan in period $t + 1$ would be the achieved level of production in period t. Planning should thus be seen as an incremental process, known as "planning from the achieved level" (in Russian *planirovanie ot dostignutogo urovniia*, Birman, 1978). The required consistency to achieve a general equilibrium in the economy was thus limited to output *increments*, since existing output *levels* were equilibria—though not necessarily desirable equilibria. Note that with the increasing complexification of the economy, it became increasingly difficult to plan important deviations from previous production paths. Indeed, it is easier to plan a 2 percent increase in all goods than to expand some sectors by, say, 20 percent, while shrinking others by comparable amounts. This fact led to an important bias toward the status quo. This bias is ironical because one of the claimed strengths of central planning over the market was its capacity to organize large deviations from existing production patterns, especially in the presence of nonconvexities.

These incremental adjustments were done at the level of economic ministries, which were thus the spinal cord of the economy and played a key role in coordinating production and adjusting to unexpected disequilibria. In most socialist economies, with the exception of China and Yugoslavia, the planning administration was organized along a functional principle with branch ministries: ministry of steel, ministry of coal, ministry of machine-building industries, and so on.[6] Ministries had aggregate output

[5] *Throughout the twentieth century, there was a big debate, starting with Barone (1908), von Mises (1920), and Lange (1938), about the theoretical possibility of central planning that culminated in the two fundamental welfare theorems showing the equivalence of central planning and competitive market equilibrium. Hayek, however, emphasized that, even if central planning was theoretically conceivable, in practice it could not be operational because of the complexity involved in gathering all the relevant information to compute consistent and efficient plans.*

plan fulfillment objectives and relied on the enterprises under their jurisdiction to achieve these goals. Ministries not only played a crucial role in planning the yearly outputs and inputs of their enterprises, but also intervened constantly in enterprise activities. In general, these interventions were responses to perceived shortages by enterprises. Ministries would often use their influence with central planning authorities to try to reroute specific deliveries in response to such shortages.[7] They would also readjust enterprise plans in response to shortages. Enterprises unable to meet their plan often had their plan lowered, while enterprises with more slack or more productive capacity had their plan increased.[8] Overall, interventions of ministries could be seen as various forms of input and output substitutions in response to shortages, leading to improvement of the aggregate output target of the ministry (Powell, 1977; Roland, 1990). Such mechanisms played a key role in preventing general output collapses in the absence of markets.

The general situation was one of perceived shortages. For enterprises, overproduction or excess supply was never seen as a problem, whereas shortage or excess demand was. Indeed, because of incentives for plan overfulfillment and soft budget constraints, any above-plan production was always easily sold. However, any shortage was likely to lead to plan underfulfillment and was perceived as a serious threat. Perceptions of shortage led to all sorts of behavior like hoarding (Weitzman, 1991), including hoarding of labor, or "forced substitution," substituting an available input or material for an unavailable one, leading to possible quality deteriorations or further distortions of output mix (see Kornai, 1980, for a comprehensive treatment of economic behavior under shortage).

Shortages in markets for consumer goods meant that producers did not have to worry about quality or lack of consumer demand. Shortages were a nightmare for consumers who lost hundreds of hours each year in queues and were forced to buy lower quality goods and make forced substitution. However, the sellers' market created by shortages gave workers important bargaining power toward management of enterprises. The threat of unemployment was therefore virtually nil, and labor discipline was extremely poor (see, e.g., Moskoff, 1984; Roland, 1988). Authoritarian and repressive campaigns to impose labor discipline under Stalin or under Andropov always failed after a temporary surprise effect. Voluntary mobility was also high as dissatisfied workers could easily find work elsewhere. Managers could only use positive incentives (rewards) to motivate and attract workers. Given the soft budget constraints, they were tempted to increase wages for that purpose. Central authorities resisted this kind of move under central planning by centralizing wage funds and denying firms any autonomy in wage setting. Managers had to use indirect tricks to motivate workers such as declaring secretaries to be managers and unskilled personnel to be skilled. One particularly popular way of attracting workers was to have in-house shops where workers could buy food and basic goods. It is also for this reason that social services, such as day-care centers, were frequently developed inside enterprises. Enterprises could thus use their clout in the central planning system to short-circuit the retail system and assure that "their" workers would not face shortage and would have decent enough conditions of living so as not to quit. In periods of more acute shortage, goods would disappear from shop shelves, but

[6] China and Yugoslavia were organized along regional lines with planning done at the level of regions or provinces. Khrushchev attempted to introduce a regional organization of planning in the early 1960s (the so-called sovnarkhoz experience), but these attempts were undone when Khrushchev was overthrown.

[7] Ministries also lobbied hard to have their own delivery administration that they could manage directly in order to reroute supplies between enterprises of their jurisdiction. For example, the steel ministry would be able to use its own delivery network to reroute coal from steel factory A to steel factory B.

[8] In the former case, plan adjustments were needed for incentive reasons. Enterprise managers lost all their bonuses if they did not fulfill the plan. Once the plan target was out of reach, it was not worthwhile putting up effort to increase output, since managers were indifferent between, say, 5 percent and 10 percent underfulfillment. Ministries were not indifferent because enterprise output contributed to their own plan target and therefore reduced plan targets in response to shortages in order to elicit effort. The corresponding plan increase in enterprises with more slack had an obvious adverse incentive effect, leading to attempts to hide slack as much as possible.

the refrigerators of workers' households were never empty. Because the labor market was a sellers' market and because social services were so concentrated inside enterprises, it is no wonder that enterprise restructuring under transition would be perceived as the most threatening reform to workers. Worker resistance and political constraints to restructuring could thus easily be predicted before the beginning of transition, especially in countries like Poland where they had had the opportunity to organize themselves.

The economic literature on socialist economies also discovered the existence of investment cycles under central planning. This was an interesting paradox, since one of the proclaimed goals of central planning was to eliminate the business cycle. Theories of the investment cycle (Bauer, 1978; Kornai, 1980; Simonovits, 1991) were based on central planners' macroeconomic adjustments to shortages. In a situation with less than normal shortages, planners would approve a larger number of investment projects than usual. Enterprises had all sorts of tricks to get their investment project approved: underestimation of costs, low first-year budget, and so on. After a while, the number of unfinished construction projects would accumulate, as well as the information on increased shortages. Given soft budget constraints, unfinished projects would never be abandoned and would ultimately be completed.[9] As a result, planners would halt the approval of new projects and inject funds as a priority to finish existing projects until perceptions of shortage would decrease, leading to a new investment boom, and so on. Econometric evidence tended to confirm the existence of such cycles and adjustment mechanisms (Grosfeld, 1987; Roland, 1987; Ickes, 1990; see, however, the book by Mihalyi, 1992, containing a comprehensive review of the literature while advocating a less deterministic approach to investment cycles).

Despite a general perception of shortages at the microeconomic level, it was not clear that the "classical" centrally planned economy was in a state of excess demand at the aggregate level. At the macroeconomic level, planners had various instruments to balance aggregate supply and demand, like central control over wages. A whole literature developed to test disequilibrium models of the macroeconomy on socialist economies (Portes and Winter, 1980; Portes et al., 1987) suggesting that there was little evidence of systematic states of macroeconomic excess demand, except for Poland, which was no longer a "classical" centrally planned economy but a reformed socialist economy.[10]

Certain socialist economies indeed had a history of market-oriented reforms before the fall of communism. Hungary abolished mandatory planning in 1968, and Yugoslavia introduced self-management in 1965. Poland underwent similar reforms in the early 1980s, followed by the USSR under Gorbachev. The typical reform in a socialist economy consisted in measures increasing enterprise autonomy substantially. One of the inefficiencies of planning is that enterprises tried to bargain for plans that were as low as possible and attempted to hide as much slack as possible in order to achieve that goal. Communist leaders thought that if enterprise managers had more autonomy in determining their output mix and prices, they would show more profit awareness and increase enterprise performance and that the result would be increased flexibility. However, the most immediate consequence of such reforms was wage drift. Enterprises started distributing most of the value added in the form of wages. Because soft budget constraints

[9] As we will see in Chapter 9, such behavior is not necessarily specific to the socialist economy. At the heart of the soft-budget-constraint syndrome is the sequential rationality of bailing out existing projects and incurring sometimes substantial cost overruns in order to finish given investment projects.

[10] Empirical work by Chawluk and Cross (1997) suggested a substantial monetary overhang in the case of Poland.

prevailed, enterprises under reform socialism or under Yugoslav self-management indeed started bargaining for more resources for wages and investment. These increased pressures from below led to a further weakening of the planning system and to a weakening of the central authorities, who yielded to enterprise demands. These increases in enterprise demands started leading to serious macroeconomic imbalances that the "classical" socialist planning system had been able to prevent. The consequence was increased foreign borrowing or increased shortages and forced savings. Countries with a history of reform prior to transition, like Hungary, Poland, Yugoslavia, and the USSR, tended to start transition with serious macroimbalances, requiring a stabilization package, whereas countries that had no prior history of reform, like the GDR, Czechoslovakia, and Romania, did not have such a stabilization problem at the beginning of transition.

1.4   OBJECTIVES AND CONSTRAINTS OF TRANSITION

Given the initial conditions of the socialist economy (with or without a history of reforms), what are the tasks involved in transforming the economy toward a well-functioning market economy? In this section, we provide a brief description of the main objectives of transition and of the constraints in achieving those objectives. There has not always been a consensus among economists on these objectives and constraints. We indicate the issues that are more controversial.

In terms of objectives, the following are broadly agreed upon:

1.   Improving allocative efficiency by correcting the distortions of socialism through the introduction of flexible relative prices and the creation of a competitive market environment open to the world economy.

2.   Stabilizing the macroeconomy, which is necessary for a correct functioning of the price system.

3.   Providing better incentives and corporate governance arrangements to make firms respond to market signals. Privatization at a large scale is a key component of such changes, but so is encouragement of entry of new private firms and the creation of an entrepreneurial class.

4.   Creating government institutions "adequate" for a market economy. Economists have different views of what the "adequate" government institutions are, but there is a relative consensus on (a) the need for political and institutional stability and (b) the need to protect private property rights from encroachment (by government but also by the Mafia) and to protect taxpayers from rent-seeking behavior of pressure groups toward government.

While economists tend to agree on the preceding objectives, it is also crucial to stress the constraints facing the transition process:

1. Uncertainty of outcomes, at both the aggregate and the individual levels, is a key feature of transition. Economists sometimes diverge in their appreciation of the importance of uncertainty. Implicit in many policy analyses on transition is the idea of a clearly defined goal, usually the analyst's pet blueprint for an ideal economic system. To be honest, however, one must acknowledge that the model of capitalism toward which transition economies should converge is not necessarily clear. Existing controversies among economists on the role of government in a market economy transpose quite naturally to debates on transition. More importantly, even if there is a clear goal of transition, there is no accepted theory of how to get there. Can our economic theories tell us whether the outcome of the transition in Central and East European economies will be closer to the West German miracle or the Weimar Republic, not to speak of former Yugoslavia? Thus there is huge aggregate uncertainty about outcomes, and the experience so far in these countries has not reduced the perception of uncertainty. Indeed, as stated earlier, the important output fall early in transition was not expected. Since then, some countries, like Poland, have been recovering very well while others, like Russia, have not and seem to be sinking further. It is quite possible that, as a consequence of transition, Russia will suffer a permanent shock to its income level and remain economically fragile for a very long time. Worse scenarios can also be imagined. In 1999, at the moment of writing, the uncertainty concerning Russia's future has not yet been resolved. Aggregate uncertainty is thus very important. One must also add that economic agents and policymakers act and make decisions taking as given this aggregate uncertainty. Because the transition process is the result of decisions made by individuals and policymakers facing important uncertainty of outcomes, a theory of transition must integrate this relative ignorance in modeling the process of transition. A theory of transition must also integrate the experimentation and learning process that must take place during transition.

2. Another important constraint is related to the complementarities and interactions between reforms. One obtains a wrong picture of transition by focusing on individual reforms. There are, for example, evident complementarities between privatization and price liberalization. Profit incentives in distorted markets lead to resource misallocation, and free prices alone do not deliver optimal allocative outcomes if firms do not face incentives for value maximization. Macroeconomic stabilization programs also require different instruments if prices are liberalized than if they are not. Economists all tend to agree on these complementarities but not necessarily always on their implications. Some think that complementarities are a sufficient argument to justify a big bang approach to reform, while others do not. We will see in the next chapter that the latter view is correct and that complementarities may even be a necessary condition for the optimality of gradualist strategies.

3. Finally, political constraints are of crucial importance, because transition is an economy-wide process involving winners and losers, even if aggregate welfare is enhanced. These political constraints are particularly relevant in the countries of Eastern Europe where political reform—the move to democracy—has preceded economic reform—the move to the market. Political constraints matter ex ante, to convince voters to start a (possibly uncertain) reform process and ex post, to avoid reversal of this process (Roland, 1994). It is important to emphasize the central role of political constraints in large-scale economic reforms such as transition and the importance of not separating the economics and politics of reform. In the past, economists have too often blamed (ugly) politics for messing up (elegant) economics. This tendency goes back to the Pigovian tradition and to welfare economics whereby economics is endogenous and the object of analysis whereas politics is exogenous and the object of policy recommendations by economists. As noted by Weingast (1997) in referring to that tradition, "an ironic aspect of the economists' position is that they want individuals to pursue their self-interest in markets but not in politics." Indeed, what economists had too long ignored until relatively recently is the economics underlying the politics. Politicians and interest groups are rationally worried about their potential losses from economic reforms. There is no reason for economists to ignore the implied political constraints, just as they cannot ignore budget constraints or incentive constraints.

Even though agreement on the ultimate goal of reform exists, important policy disagreements have surfaced concerning the speed and sequencing of reforms. It is important to trace down the sources of these disagreements, in terms of the constraints that are stressed and also in terms of the internal logic of the arguments.

It is a challenging and complex task to try to integrate aggregate uncertainty, complementarities, and political constraints simultaneously in a single theoretical model. Such complexities may partly explain why relatively little theoretical work has been produced on transition. Indeed, any theory of transition will run the risk of being irrelevant if transition is not seen as a process of institutional change at a large scale, including the components that we have listed, and there are many other unsolved problems in economic theory to work on that can be more focused and still relevant. As an area of economic research, transition faces the well-known problem of the drunken man who had lost his key in front of the doorstep but was searching under the streetlight because it was the only place where there was light. Theorists know that the goal of theory is to select key features from this complex reality and to analyze their interaction in a tractable framework. Tractability can be a very important constraint. We can only deal with this problem by making compromises. We start Part I of the book, in Chapter 2, with a model incorporating complementarities, aggregate uncertainty, and political constraints. This has the advantage of comprehensiveness and yields results that we think are crucial to understanding transition strategies and transition processes. The drawback is that for the sake of tractability, these features must be modeled in a relatively abstract way, with little institutional and economic flesh. But we think it is better, when dealing with transition, to see the forest before seeing the tree. In later chapters, the analysis is more detailed and specific, focusing on particular aspects of transition, while abstracting from others.

1.5 STYLIZED FACTS ABOUT TRANSITION

We already mentioned some of the main unexpected aspects of transition. We now turn to a brief description of the stylized facts about transition that economic theory should try to explain.

1.5.1 DIFFERENCES IN REFORM PATHS AND STRATEGIES

Using the word "strategy" when talking about transition can in some sense be misleading. It may give the impression that conscious plans were elaborated at the beginning of transition and that those have been followed like a road map. First of all, because of aggregate uncertainty, there is nothing like a road map in transition. Therefore, actual paths of reform can also turn out to be very different from the initial strategies. Transition paths can be as much improvised responses to unexpected events and pressures as conscious forward-looking choices under uncertainty. We nevertheless think it is useful to talk about strategy when discussing the initial choices of reform paths. Even though such rationalization may tend to overestimate the degree of foresight and strategic thinking of reformers, it is nevertheless useful in understanding the logic behind the dynamics of reform in various countries. Talking about strategies does not mean that the choice set was the same in all countries nor that policies were simply a matter of choice. Differences in initial conditions and in political constraints in the various countries played an important role. Therefore, one should be cautious especially when making comparisons across countries. We should not conclude, however, that there was no choice at all between various strategies in each individual country nor that the strategies chosen were necessarily optimal. Even though the choices made can be rationalized in the specific contexts in which they were made, there is no reason to exclude errors of judgment and wrong representations of reality, not to speak of capture by specific interest groups.

Table 1.3 gives a rough overview of the speed and sequencing of reforms in selected transition economies. We chose the timing of the start of given reforms and indicated whether given reforms like liberalization, privatization, and restructuring were introduced gradually or by a big bang. In some cases, even though laws were enacted, little enforcement followed. In all cases, we tried to give the year where a given reform started to be really implemented.

Table 1.3 shows differences as well as similarities in the transition strategies in various countries. First of all, there are countries that have mainly followed a gradualist strategy: China, Hungary, and Slovenia. An interesting observation is that those countries tended to start reforms earlier than the other countries: China in 1978, Hungary in 1968, and Slovenia in 1965 inside the former Yugoslavia. Moreover, the sequencing of

TABLE 1.3 THE SPEED AND SEQUENCING OF REFORMS

	Political Reform	Liberalization	Stabilization	Tax Reform	Entry	Privatization	Enterprise Restructuring	Bankruptcy Reform	Banking Reform
China	1978	1984 (dual)	1994	1980	1978	1995 (gradual)	1995 (gradual)	—	—
Hungary	1989	1968 (gradual)	1995	1988	1982	1990 (gradual)	1992 (gradual)	1992	1991
Vietnam	—	1989 (big bang)	1989	1990	1979	1989 (gradual)	1989	1993	1991
Poland	1989	1990 (big bang)	1990	1992	1990	1990 (gradual)	1993 (gradual)	1992	1993
Czech Republic	1989	1991 (big bang)	Not relevant	1993	1991	1992 (mass)	1993 (gradual)	1993	1991
Slovakia	1989	1991 (big bang)	Not relevant	1993	1991	1992 (gradual)	1993 (gradual)	1993	1991
Slovenia	1989	1965 (gradual)	1990	1990	1965	1993 (gradual)	1989 (gradual)	1989	1993
Russia	1991	1992 (big bang)	1995	1995	1992	1993 (mass)	1992 (gradual)	1993	1992
Ukraine	1991	1994 (big bang)	1995	1992	1992	1994 (gradual)	1995 (gradual)	—	1995
Romania	1989	1990 (big bang)	1994	1993	1991	1991 (gradual)	1993 (gradual)	1995	—
Bulgaria	1989	1991 (big bang)	1991	1994	1993	1994 (gradual)	1991	1994	1997

Source: *European Bank for Reconstruction and Development, author's evaluations.*

reforms follows definite patterns. Policies to encourage entry of the small private sector tend to start early on, and privatization and restructuring occur later in the transition process. In those countries, liberalization and privatization also tend to be gradual.[11] Stabilization, when it occurs, usually takes place in the middle of the transition process, not in the beginning. Even though Vietnam introduced liberalization and stabilization in a big bang way in 1989, it had encouraged entry and market activities since 1979. The "contract system" in agriculture was close to the Chinese responsibility system, and dual pricing was strongly present before 1989. By 1989 when radical reforms were introduced, the private sector in agriculture and manufacturing occupied 60 percent of GDP and 85 percent of the labor force. Privatization is, if anything, gradual, in Vietnam. The sequencing of reforms in Vietnam is thus quite close to the one observed in China, even though there are important differences in timing.

The other countries can be considered roughly to have followed big bang strategies, a statement which we must qualify. The best example is Poland, where most policies started in 1990. Nevertheless, in Poland, privatization proceeded de facto in a gradual way after mass privatization (fast privatization via giveaway of assets through a voucher scheme) was blocked politically between 1991 and 1995 and had lost momentum by then. The Czech Republic is the next-best example of a big bang policy with liberalization, stabilization, and privatization all occurring between 1991 and 1992. It is also the first example of privatization achieved through a voucher scheme, started in 1992. Nevertheless, a certain sequencing of reforms can be observed in the Czech Republic with restructuring being delayed until the end of the privatization program. Restructuring was more gradual than in Poland and Hungary with in particular a very soft bankruptcy law and an accumulation of bad loans in the banking sector after privatization (Anderson and Kegels, 1997). Slovakia follows closely the pattern of reforms in the Czech Republic except for the fact that privatization policies switched to a gradual one after the split of the country. Russia can also be considered to have followed, partly at least, a big bang strategy. Liberalization, stabilization, and privatization were all launched in 1992. Stabilization policies failed to gain political support, and it was only in 1995 that some significant progress could be made on stabilization. Mass privatization was achieved quickly, as in the case of the Czech Republic.

The Russian experience illustrates a case that is to a certain degree equally or even more valid in other countries like Romania, Bulgaria, and certainly the Ukraine and other countries from the former Soviet Union: countries starting the transition process later are less successful in implementing them. Attempts to pass radical reforms do not pass through the political process and are blocked. Ukraine could only seriously start its transition in 1994 and 1995 despite false starts since its independence in 1991. Since then, the reform process has seriously stalled. Policy reversals are also more frequent in countries that started later. Bulgaria has experienced reversals of price liberalization, starting in 1992, and has experienced enormous resistance to privatization. Price liberalization has been undone in Russian "red belt" regions. Romania has also experienced setbacks with its privatization program and could never give momentum to plans for

[11] *Liberalization in Hungary accelerated substantially from 1989 onward.*

mass privatization. Countries starting later have in general also been less successful with stabilization.

Liberalization happens mostly in a big bang way, with the exceptions of gradualist countries. In China, dual pricing was introduced comprehensively in 1984. Prices were liberalized in all sectors at the margin, maintaining planned prices for planned output.

In all countries, enterprise restructuring tends to happen at later stages of transition, never in the beginning, and is always gradual: money-losing enterprises are never closed in one stroke; the process of redundancies is spread out across time. Interestingly, plans for mass privatization faced strong political resistance in Poland and Romania, with only the Czech Republic and Russia able to achieve swift implementation of mass privatization.

Traditional economic thinking would take these policies and strategies as given and simply evaluate their economic effects, a task that is clearly important to undertake. It would, however, not ask how these differences and similarities between strategies come about. For example, the less obvious success (and often outright failure) of countries liberalizing later (and in a more piecemeal way) has been interpreted by the World Bank and other economists as suggesting that faster liberalization yields better stabilization results and faster growth (World Bank, 1996; Åslund, Boone and Johnson, 1996; and others). This interpretation views policy decisions as exogenous and does not take political constraints into account. An alternative explanation is that countries starting transition later were facing stronger resistance to reforms and thus faced stronger political constraints in implementing reform policies. This view is consistent with the observation of stalled reforms and partial policy reversals in those countries. In that case, being told that faster liberalization will yield better economic results is not very helpful, from the policy point of view, when delay and incompleteness in reforms result from political constraints.

1.5.2 DIFFERENCES IN MACROECONOMIC PERFORMANCE AFTER LIBERALIZATION

After having reviewed the differences in transition paths and strategies across countries, it is useful to look at the difference in terms of macroeconomic performance. Figures 1.1 through 1.5 show the evolution of real GDP in selected transition economies in the years following liberalization.

We clearly see different and diverging time patterns of output performance after liberalization. Figure 1.1 highlights five patterns for output response to liberalization. China shows a continuous, smooth, and strong growth after liberalization.[12] All other countries have experienced an initial output decline. Some have started recovering after a few years of output fall. Poland is the best example of such a pattern. Similar countries are grouped in Figure 1.2 (Poland, Hungary, Slovenia, Czech Republic, Slovakia, Croatia, and Estonia). Another group of countries has experienced an uncertain recovery with further output fall after an initial recovery. Bulgaria and Romania belong to that group, illustrated in Figure 1.3. Other countries still have experienced a very severe output

[12] *We took 1984 as the year of liberalization because this is the year dual-price liberalization was introduced widely in industries. If we had taken 1978, the year of decollectivization and liberalization in agriculture, the growth trend would have been even stronger.*

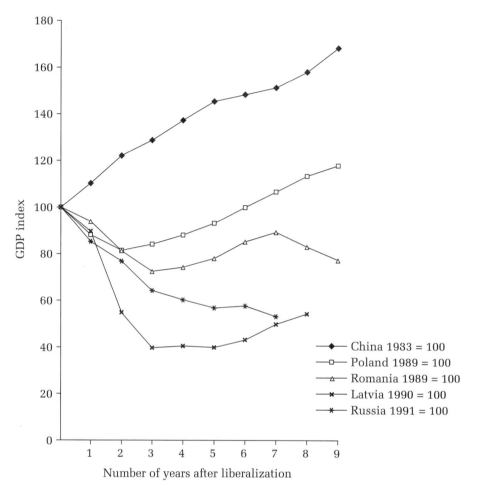

FIGURE 1.1 REAL GDP TRENDS IN TRANSITION ECONOMIES AFTER LIBERALIZATION

fall and are far from having reached a full recovery of the initial output fall (Latvia and Lithuania, Figure 1.4), while a last group of countries (Russia, Ukraine, and Belarus) have experienced a continuous output fall since liberalization with few signs of recovery (Figure 1.5). The apparently permanent, huge negative output shock in this last group of countries constitutes not only one of the most bitter surprises of transition, but also a terrible economic drama that is likely to have important yet unmeasured consequences far into the twenty-first century. The registered output fall of roughly 50 percent in many former Soviet republics must however be corrected by estimates of the hidden economy. Using data on electricity consumption, Johnson, Kaufmann, and Shleifer (1998) estimate the share of the unofficial economy in Russia and Ukraine, respectively, to be 27 and 26.4 percent in 1990–93 and 41.6 and 46.9 percent in 1995, indicating both a high share and a sharp increase. Countries in the former USSR that have experienced the strongest

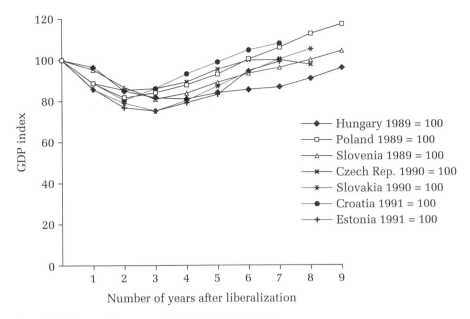

FIGURE 1.2   COUNTRIES RECOVERING AFTER AN INITIAL OUTPUT FALL

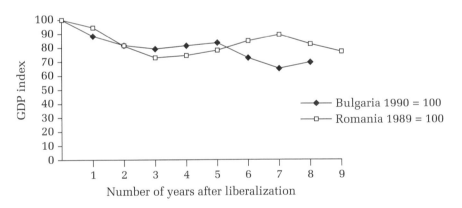

FIGURE 1.3   COUNTRIES EXPERIENCING AN INITIAL OUTPUT FALL AND UNCERTAIN RECOVERY

output fall have also seen the most dramatic increase in the share of the unofficial economy. Given the important inefficiencies associated with operating in the hidden economy with no rule of law and security of property rights, the increase in the share of the latter does not compensate for the big output loss but makes it appear less apocalyptic. Understanding why the economy goes underground in some transition countries is an important question to raise.

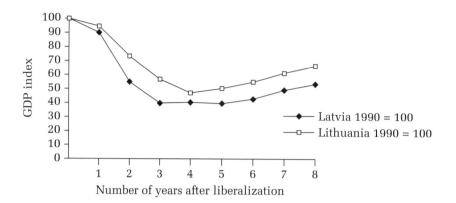

FIGURE 1.4 COUNTRIES EXPERIENCING A VERY STRONG OUTPUT FALL AND A SLOW RECOVERY

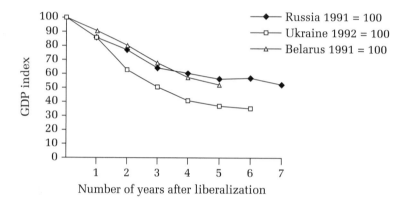

FIGURE 1.5 COUNTRIES EXPERIENCING A CONTINUOUS OUTPUT FALL

In a way, Figure 1.1 is an illustration of the aggregate uncertainty we were referring to earlier in this chapter. Few observers (if any) would have expected either that we would observe output falls of such significant magnitudes or such a divergence in output patterns across transition economies. It is therefore important to have theories able to explain both the sharp output fall in some countries and the differences between, say, China, Poland, and Russia.

Other key indicators of transition are summarized in Table 1.4. One phenomenon observed in transition countries is a decrease in life expectancy. This is clearly the case in Russia and Ukraine, slightly less the case in Romania and Bulgaria. Inequality has increased in all transition economies, but the increase has been much stronger in Russia and Ukraine. This increase has been relatively mild in Central European countries, where the Gini coefficient generally remains below 30. Figures for GDP per capita in 1989 should

TABLE 1.4 SUMMARY INDICATORS FOR SELECTED TRANSITION ECONOMIES

	Life Expectancy at Birth		Inequality (Gini Index)		GDP per Capita (constant 1995 $)	
	1989	1997	1987–89	1993–97	1989	1997
Russia	69.2	66.9	21.9	51.8	3,900	2,240
Ukraine	70.5	67.4	23	47.3	3,500	1,490
Poland	71	72.7	26	28	3,050	3,650
Hungary	69.5	70.6	20.7	22.9	4,820	4,540
Czech Republic	71.7	73.9	19	27	5,730	5,110
Slovenia	72.7	74.7	22.9	22.3	8,270[a]	10,160
Romania	69.5	69	23	29	1,680	1,400
Bulgaria	71.8	70.7	23	34	1,730	1,270
China	70	70	36	41.5	340	670
Vietnam	66	68	n.a.	35.7	202	314

Source: *World Bank, Milanovic (1998, 1999).*

[a]*1992.*

be taken with extreme caution for Central and Eastern European countries. The figures for 1998 show an important difference in income across transition economies with Vietnam at $314 on one hand and Slovenia with $10,160 on the other hand.

1.5.3 DIFFERENCES IN ENTERPRISE PERFORMANCE IN RESPONSE TO CHANGES IN OWNERSHIP AND CORPORATE GOVERNANCE

A number of different ownership and corporate governance structures have emerged in transition economies. The obvious distinction is between state-owned and private enterprises, but reality has shown that within these categories there has been substantial variation of performance. As stated previously, the big surprise in Chinese reforms has been the growth of the township and village enterprises (TVEs), which have been the main source of growth of the Chinese economy in transition (see, e.g., Byrd and Qinsong, 1990). TVEs are not pseudo-private enterprises but enterprises owned and controlled by community governments in rural China (Che and Qian, 1998a). How can we explain the superior performance of TVEs compared to SOEs? Another major surprise, as stated earlier, has been the observation of SOEs restructuring before privatization. Similarly, among privatized enterprises, whether they were privatized through mass privatization or by sales, whether privatized to insiders or to outsiders, the nature of the outsiders (dispersed shareholders, investment funds, or foreign multinationals) does seem to make a difference in terms of performance.

There is an important empirical literature emerging, based on firm-level data, trying to identify the effects of ownership and corporate governance on enterprise performance. Such an exercise is not an easy one because of endogeneity and selection effects. Regressing measures of enterprise performance on ownership form may be misleading because performance and internal characteristics of the firm may have an effect on the form of privatization itself. Results so far from that literature, which we will review in Chapter 10, suggest that insider privatization, privatization to dispersed owners, or privatization via voucher only or to voucher investment funds only, yields inferior performance compared to outsider privatization.

The growing empirical evidence calls for theories allowing a comparison of various ownership and governance structures and a finer understanding of the various links between restructuring and privatization. It is important to understand the specific channels through which state ownership and various forms of private ownership affect managerial incentives in firms.

1.5.4 SUMMARY

We have come up with three important sets of questions raised by the transition experience: (1) How do we understand differences in transition strategies, given the initial conditions faced in each country? (2) How do we understand differences in macroeconomic performance after liberalization? (3) How do we understand differences in enterprise performance depending on the changes in ownership and corporate governance? Each of the three parts of the book will address each set of questions in turn.

POLITICAL CONSTRAINTS AND REFORM STRATEGY

CHAPTER 2

THE POLITICS OF REFORMS UNDER UNCERTAINTY

2.1 THE IMPORTANCE OF POLITICAL CONSTRAINTS

On one hand, economists are often criticized by policymakers for formulating policy advice without taking political constraints into account. On the other hand, economists often blame politicians for failing to act decisively or for deciding on half-baked reforms. Whether or not economists should take political constraints into account when formulating policy advice is still a matter of debate among academic economists, but in the reality of political decisionmaking, political constraints cannot be ignored. They certainly cannot be ignored in research on economic reforms.

Political constraints appear to have played a major role in the actual transition process. In Russia, the former parliament blocked stabilization plans in 1992 and 1993, and successive parliaments have shown strong opposition to market reforms since 1992. Continued stalemate over key issues of reform has been a characteristic of reform politics in Russia. Political constraints have also played a major role in decisions on reforms. The best known example is the design of the Russian privatization plan. Boycko, Shleifer, and Vishny (1995) have argued that the main justification for the giveaway of state assets in Russia was not economic but political and that any privatization plan other than the one chosen would have been rejected at the time by the political process.

In Poland, political constraints have played an important role with respect to privatization and restructuring. The Polish mass privatization plan, based on voucher privatization and the institution of mutual funds, was blocked for at least three years in Parliament and was only adopted in April 1993 after numerous revisions, amendments, and modifications. When the plan reached the implementation stage, it had lost momentum.

In Czechoslovakia, political constraints to privatization and restructuring were more geographically concentrated. They were more important in Slovakia than in the

Czech Republic, and this difference played an important role in the breakup of the country.

In Hungary, one has observed political constraints with respect to privatization. The setting up of the State Privatization Agency was partly a reaction to fears of public opposition to spontaneous privatization (Dervis and Condon, 1994).

In all transition countries, political constraints have also played an important and varying role in blocking parts of the restructuring process. Plans to drastically cut subsidies to state-owned enterprises often could not materialize. Fiscal subsidy cuts to firms, required by the IMF, were often transformed in hidden subsidies taking the form of bank credit and interenterprise arrears. One has noted heavy worker resistance to closing inefficient state enterprises, as witnessed by the example of the URSUS factory in Poland and many other examples in all transition economies.

These examples are not exhaustive, and one can think of numerous other political constraints in economies in transition.

In this chapter, we develop the analysis of the effect of political constraints on the optimal speed and sequencing of reforms under uncertainty. In section 2.2, we introduce the concepts of ex ante and ex post political constraints, which are important for analyzing the dynamics of reforms processes and the resistance to reforms under uncertainty. In section 2.3, we analyze reform strategies when there is only individual uncertainty on reform outcomes and show that the big bang approach to reforms generally dominates. In section 2.4, we analyze the trade-off between big bang and gradualism under aggregate uncertainty. Aggregate uncertainty can make gradualism optimal by giving flexibility in reform experimentation. In section 2.5, we analyze issues of optimal sequencing of reforms in cases when gradualist strategies are optimal. Sections 2.6 and 2.7 elaborate analytically on some dimensions of reform strategies within the framework of the chapter. Section 2.6 looks at the endogenous interactions between the (foreign) investment response, reform strategies and outcomes, and political risk. Section 2.7 further develops the analysis of reform experimentation by comparing the effect of the differences in the East European (Soviet-style) and Chinese organizational forms of central planning, showing that the latter provided more possibilities than the former for experimentation with reforms. Throughout the chapter we concentrate the analysis on the comparison between big bang, gradualism, and the sequencing of reforms in the latter case. We do not analyze issues of designing transfer schemes to compensate losers from reform, an issue that will be analyzed at length in the next chapter, where we will study the effect of political constraints on reforms without uncertainty.

2.2   EX ANTE AND EX POST POLITICAL CONSTRAINTS

It is useful, when discussing political constraints, to distinguish between ex ante and ex post political constraints. Following Roland (1994), we define ex ante political constraints as feasibility constraints that block decisionmaking and ex post political constraints as constraints of backlash and reversal after decisions have been made and outcomes observed. Ex ante and ex post political constraints must be dealt with differently. Ex ante constraints imply either that compromises must be made on reform plans, that credible compensations for losers must be devised, or that decisions on radical programs must be delayed. Ex post political constraints are dealt with by trying to create irreversibility.

Ex ante and ex post political constraints will be the same in a deterministic world. They may, however, substantially differ if there is uncertainty resolution along the reform path. This point was first shown formally by Fernandez and Rodrik (1991). They did so in the framework of a trade liberalization model[1] but the basic argument applies quite generally and can be expressed very simply.

Assume an infinite horizon with discount rate δ. Individuals face a reform where they all have the same ex ante probability p of gaining from reform and getting a net-present-value payoff of $g > 0$ and the probability $1 - p$ of losing from reform and getting a net present value payoff of $l < 0$. Uncertainty is purely individual so that, with a large enough population, because of the law of large numbers, p is also the percentage of ex post winners from reform. The status quo payoff is assumed to be 0. At $t = 0$, individuals vote on whether or not to implement the reform. At $t = 1$, they can vote on whether or not to implement the reform if it was accepted at $t = 0$. In that case, they incur a cost ξ. We assume that $l < -\xi$ so that losers always prefer to reverse the reform.

If $p > 1/2$, a majority will favor reform ex post and oppose any reversal to the status quo at $t = 1$. However, assuming risk neutrality, if $pg + (1 - p)l < 0$, the reform will be rejected ex ante by all. Indeed, since they know that the reform will not be reversed once it is decided, it will never get decided as soon as the expected payoff is negative even though a majority would benefit ex post. It is thus quite possible that reforms benefiting a majority ex post are rejected ex ante. However, if $p < 1/2$, a majority will always want reversal ex post. So, even if $pg + (1 - p)l > 0$, as soon as the reversal cost is higher than the expected one-period payoff, that is, as soon as $\xi > (1 - \delta)[pg + (1 - p)l]$ (which is always true for $\delta \longrightarrow 1$), the reform will not be adopted either. Indeed, people will know that the reform will be reversed with probability 1, so the net payoff from reform is $(1 - \delta)[pg + (1 - p)l] - \xi$, which is worse than the status quo payoff of 0. For reforms to take place, they must satisfy *both* the ex ante and the ex post political constraint. In all other cases, reform is not adopted. It is for this reason that what Fernandez and Rodrik call a *status quo bias* against reform exists. It is not necessary to assume risk aversion to get this simple but important result. All that is needed is uncertainty resolution over time during the reform process.

What is important to note is that uncertainty resolution shifts majorities in favor of and against reform over time. In the case with $pg + (1 - p)l < 0$ and $p > 1/2$, 100 percent of voters are against reform ex ante, but more than 50 percent would be in favor ex post. As we will see in subsequent sections, this property of shifting majorities is very important in determining the optimal sequencing of reforms.

[1] *In a model with a similar spirit, Rodrik (1995) looks at a restructuring policy that receives initial support for reform among state-sector workers and that later in transition suffers backlash from state-sector workers.*

2.3   GRADUALISM AND THE INTERIM STATUS QUO BIAS

We now look at a case with two reforms. Our goal in the rest of this chapter is to analyze the trade-offs between a big bang strategy where both reforms are proposed simultaneously and a gradual approach where one reform is proposed first and the second reform is proposed one period later, after uncertainty resolution on the first reform. Under gradualism, the expected outcomes and the realization of reforms will also depend on the sequencing of reforms.

Throughout the chapter we assume complementarities between reforms. We can think of several examples of such complementarities. First, assume reform 1 is the development of a small private sector and reform 2 is reform in the state sector. Following Murphy, Shleifer, and Vishny (1992), to which we will come back in Chapter 6, we can say that both reforms together will create entry and competition and increase output supply as well as allocative efficiency. However, the development of the small private sector without a reform in the state sector may lead to inefficient diversion of inputs from the state sector if the private sector can bid up prices for inputs and SOEs are not allowed to do so. This inefficient diversion may induce collapses of production chains in the state sector and create a situation that is worse than the status quo from the point of view of social welfare. Alternatively, we can think of the reform package as privatization. Reforms 1 and 2 may refer, for example, to two sectors of the economy, light and heavy industry. Partial privatization is not optimal because each sector needs the other one to function efficiently. Assume for example that sector 1 requires output contraction whereas sector 2 requires output expansion. If sector 1 is privatized and not sector 2, sector 1 may shed labor, whereas sector 2 may fail to seize the opportunity to hire labor to expand its activities. This failure may be due to lack of appropriate incentives or to absence of financing possibilities (if the government abstains from investment because of stabilization policies or if the private sector is reluctant to inject money in nonprivatized firms). In any case, the outcome of partial privatization in sector 1 will then be inferior to what it would be if sector 2 had been privatized simultaneously. We can think of many other examples of complementarities. Van Wijnbergen (1992) and Boycko (1992), for example, have modeled complementarities in price liberalization. Gates, Milgrom, and Roberts (1993) have modeled complementarities in liberalization and incentive changes, Bennett and Dixon (1995) between privatization and competition policy (see Friedman and Johnson, 1996, for a model of complementarities in reform). In reality, the exact extent of complementarities will depend to a great extent on the specific reforms being considered, on the details of design and implementation of each reform, and on the initial conditions in the country considered.

The type of uncertainty and learning during the reform process plays a key role in the comparison between reform strategies. In particular, under aggregate uncertainty, we will see that a gradualist strategy can be a way of overcoming the status quo bias because of its flexibility and experimentation value. In contrast, when uncertainty is purely individual or idiosyncratic as in the Fernandez and Rodrik (1991) model, gradualism is always dominated by the big bang approach. Not only does it not overcome the status quo bias, but it also creates an additional status quo bias, the interim status quo bias whereby particular vested interests can block the reform process.[2] We first develop the case of pure individual uncertainty.

We thus extend the Fernandez and Rodrik framework to two reforms. Reform 1 brings a net present value gain $g_1 > 0$ to a proportion p_1 in the population and a net present value loss $l_1 < 0$ to a proportion $(1 - p_1)$. Similarly, reform 2 brings $g_2 > 0$ to a proportion p_2 and $l_2 < 0$ to a proportion $(1 - p_2)$. Call ξ the reversal cost of both reforms and ξ_1 the individual reversal costs of reform 1 in a gradualist strategy. We assume that in the latter case the reform process starts with reform 1. Reforms are assumed to be statistically independent. Therefore, when both reforms have been adopted, whether gradually or simultaneously, the distribution of gains and losses is as follows:

Payoff	$g_1 + g_2$	$g_1 + l_2$	$l_1 + g_2$	$l_1 + l_2$
Proportion	$p_1 p_2$	$p_1(1 - p_2)$	$(1 - p_1)p_2$	$(1 - p_1)(1 - p_2)$

Assume without loss of generality that $g_1 + l_2 > l_1 + g_2$. As in the one reform case, the first thing to note is that, since uncertainty is idiosyncratic and not aggregate, one knows in advance with probability 1 whether there will be reform reversal or not if reforms are adopted. If there is reversal, no reforms will be adopted, as seen previously, as soon as the reversal cost is big enough or if $\delta \longrightarrow 1$. Reforms will thus be adopted only if there is no reversal.

Let us then take the big bang strategy where both reforms are implemented simultaneously. There will be no reversal if a majority gains from reform. Assume $p_1 < 1/2$ and $p_1 + (1 - p_1)p_2 > 1/2$ so that the median voter gets $l_1 + g_2$. In that case, if $l_1 + g_2 > -\xi$, reforms will never be reversed. Note that once both reforms are implemented, whether the initial strategy was big bang or gradualism is irrelevant for the decision whether or not to reverse reforms. Coming back to the big bang case, reforms will be decided upon if

$$p_1 g_1 + (1 - p_1)l_1 + p_2 g_2 + (1 - p_2)l_2 > 0 \tag{2.1}$$

Let us now look at gradualism. We model complementarities by assuming that the expected outcome of reform 1 is lowered by γ. We also capture the idea of complementarities by assuming that

$$g - \gamma < -\xi_1 \tag{2.2}$$

that is, that reversal to the status quo is always preferrable to maintaining partial reform. If reforms never get reversed, the expected outcome under gradualism is

$$(1 - \delta)[p_1 g_1 + (1 - p_1)l_1 - \gamma] + \delta[p_1 g_1 + (1 - p_1)l_1 + p_2 g_2 + (1 - p_2)l_2] \tag{2.3}$$

---

[2] In the next chapter we will see that without any forms of uncertainty, the big bang approach does not necessarily dominate, and there are trade-offs between big bang and gradualism.

It is obvious, from equation (2.3) that the expected outcome under gradualism with no reversal is strictly worse than that of big bang. Indeed, due to complementarities, there will be interim suffering after the implementation of reform 1 alone $[p_1 g_1 + (1 - p_1)l_1 - \gamma < 0$ from equation (2.2)]. Moreover, big bang that has a positive expected outcome is delayed.

Because of complementarities, the choice after the implementation of period 1 is whether to go ahead with the remaining reforms or to go back to the status quo. We now show that it is possible that gradualism is a less favorable option under the same assumptions on ex ante and ex post payoffs. Indeed, since $p_1 < 1/2$, the pivotal voters for reversal or adoption of reform 2 are those who experience a loss l_1 from reform 1. It is thus quite possible that for that group the expected continuation value of reform is smaller than the payoff from reverting to the status quo; that is, it is quite possible that $l_1 + p_2 g_2 + (1 - p_2)l_2 < -\xi_1$ while equation (2.1) is still satisfied. One checks that this will be the case if $p_1(g_1 - l_1) > \xi_1$. In that case, gradualism will always be reversed but not big bang, making the former also less attractive from the ex ante point of view.

Assuming $\delta \longrightarrow 1$ to discard any discounting effects, the only relevant variable in the comparison will be differences in reversal. Since for different parameter values of p_i, g_i, and l_i, there can never be more reversal under big bang than under gradualism, but since there can be more reversal under gradualism than under big bang, big bang is never dominated by gradualism, and in some cases strictly dominates gradualism. Indeed, there are three possible cases:

1. There is no interim reversal under gradualism, in which case, its payoff is identical to that of big bang when $\delta \longrightarrow 1$.

2. There is interim reversal under gradualism and reversal after two reforms, in which case none of the reforms will be tried anyway.

3. There is interim reversal under gradualism but no reversal after two reforms, in which case gradualism is dominated by big bang when the latter has a positive expected outcome.

Because uncertainty is only individual, the probability of reversal is always either 0 or 1. When there is no interim reversal and when big bang has a positive expected outcome, gradualism will be strictly dominated by big bang because of interim suffering and delay of big bang. When there is interim reversal and when big bang has a positive expected outcome, gradualism implies an interim status quo bias that is absent under big bang, which makes the latter strictly preferrable to the former. An important advantage of big bang over gradualism under individual uncertainty is that, while it is never dominated by gradualism, it moreover allows reforms to be bundled together to prevent status quo bias associated with individual reforms.

2.4 AGGREGATE UNCERTAINTY

We now introduce aggregate uncertainty and show that there will be trade-offs between big bang and gradualism and that the latter can dominate the former.

2.4.1 THE TRADE-OFFS BETWEEN BIG BANG AND GRADUALISM

We follow the general model of Dewatripont and Roland (1995, 1997). For simplicity, we assume in this section a representative agent framework. Many results can indeed already be derived within a representative agent model with only aggregate uncertainty. We introduce individual heterogeneity in section 2.5. Apart from that, the model in this section is rather general. A simplified version of the model will be used in section 2.5.

Consider two reforms, $i = 1, 2$ with uncertain outcomes that depend on the respective realized states of nature $O_{1j}(j = 1, 2, \ldots, J)$ and $O_{2k}(k = 1, 2, \ldots, K)$. Remember from Chapter 1 that aggregate uncertainty is an important component of transition. It is not clear whether the outcome of transition will be closer to the West German miracle or the Weimar Republic, not to speak of the former Yugoslavia. Analysts of transition too often implicitly assume that the final outcome will be a version of the West German miracle. More generally, the assumption of aggregate uncertainty reflects to a great extent our ignorance of the transition process itself as well as the ignorance of agents involved. This ignorance is well reflected in the title of a recent book on the political tactics of Russian reform by Shleifer and Treisman (2000): *Without a Map.* The assumption of aggregate uncertainty may also reflect the fact that such a process of large-scale institutional change involves a lot of coordination among economic agents. This typically implies multiplicity of equilibria, and nobody knows in advance the equilibrium that will be selected. The assumption of aggregate uncertainty is not valid and fruitful only in the transition context. It can also apply to other contexts where there is genuine uncertainty about the outcome: the introduction of the single currency in Europe, the accession of Central European countries to the European Union, or the process of European integration itself. One can also readily think of other non-European examples.

When both reforms have been implemented ("full reform"), the net-present-value payoff for the representative agent is $F(O_{1j}, O_{2k}, t)$ under realizations O_{1j} and O_{2k}. When only reform i has been implemented ("partial reform"), the net present value payoff for the representative agent is $P(O_{im}, t)$ under realization O_{im}.

For simplicity, assume that the payoff is time-invariant when both reforms have been implemented: $F(O_{1j}, O_{2k}, t) = F(O_{1j}, O_{2k})$ and $P(O_{im}, t) = P(O_{im})$ for all t. Also assume that the flow payoff at any given time is also time-invariant and given by $f(O_{1j}, O_{2k}) = \frac{F(O_{1j}, O_{2k})}{1-\delta}$ and $p(O_{im}) = \frac{P(O_{im})}{1-\delta}$.[3] For simplicity, $F(O_{1j}, O_{2k})$ is assumed to be independent of sequencing. It remains the same, whether reform 1 or reform 2 is implemented first. There are thus by assumption no path-dependency effects associated with sequencing. This simplifying assumption represents a clear limitation of the analysis

[3] *The latter assumption is clearly a simplification, and the welfare effect of partial reform is likely to deteriorate over time. We assume that the lower welfare level is reached immediately. By doing so, we make partial reform and gradualism look worse than they really are.*

provided in this section. The reader should keep it in mind. We will see in later chapters that the outcome of reforms may depend on speed and sequencing effects. However, this assumption is useful for now in identifying analytically the main political trade-offs between big bang and gradualism.

The complementarity of reforms is modeled by assuming that $P(.) << F(.,.)$. We assume it takes one period to observe $F(.,.)$ and $P(.)$. An important point to note is that despite complementarities, implementing a single reform gives information on $F(.,.)$ through the observation of $P(.)$. Indeed, since $P(O_{im})$ is assumed to be certain given O_{im}, observing $P(.)$ means observing a partition on the O_{im}'s. The payoffs from partial reform may thus potentially give information about the likely payoffs from full reform, and the precision of learning will depend on how fine the partition is. This partition can include a single element ($N_i = 1$). In that case, there will be no learning at all on the prospects of full reform. However, the partition may include up to J or K elements for reforms 1 and 2, respectively ($N_i = J$ or K), in which case there will be full learning of O_{im}. In reality, depending on whether the partition is fine or coarse, there will be more or less learning.[4] We assume N_i given. Varying N_i is thus left to comparative statics analysis. For N_i given, call S_{in} an element of the partition. The variable S_{in} can be seen as a "signal" observed when implementing reform i. This is quite a general formulation, since the relevant partitions of the states of nature may be characterized by various indicators such as the volume of investment started, the number of new private enterprises, foreign trade results, and so on. To come back to our example with the development of the small private sector, even though that reform may lead to input diversion, its implementation may reveal information that is useful in order to assess the prospects of full reform. For example, it may reveal the degree of entrepreneurial spirit in the economy, even though that entrepreneurial spirit leads to adverse effects in the context of partial reform.

Let us rank signals in terms of the expected payoff of full reform:

$$n > n' \Rightarrow \underset{jk}{E}\left[F(O_{1j}, O_{2k}) \mid S_{in}\right] \geq \underset{j,k}{E}\left[F\left(O_{1j}, O_{2k}\right) \mid S_{in'}\right]$$

The "default payoff" is normalized to zero, and represents, in reduced form, the evolution of the economy when the reform package under consideration is not enacted (but an alternative one can be). Since $P(.)$ and $F(.,.)$ may be negative, reversing reforms can be optimal. After a reversal of the reform package, the economy is back at its "default payoff." So, for example, take the case where "insider privatization" is a failure because managers start dissipating the assets they control instead of using them optimally. This behavior may be due to incompetence, fear of takeover, or fear of policy reversal. Insider privatization may then have to be reversed in order to stop the dissipation and try a better privatization policy.

Call ξ_i the cost of reversing reform i when it has been implemented alone. To take the example of insider privatization, reversal is costly because the government has to reclaim control over the assets in order to try another privatization method (like giving control to concentrated external investors) or to maintain state ownership. Similarly, ξ is the cost of reversing both reforms. Reversal costs are borne by the representative agent. Assume

[4] We could assume that the partition becomes finer over time. This assumption would be an interesting extension of the model.

$0 < \max \{\xi_1, \xi_2\} < \xi \leq \xi_1 + \xi_2$, which means that reversing one reform is less costly than reversing both. Reversing insider privatization in two sectors is intuitively more costly than reversing it in a single one. Coming back to another example developed earlier, it seems obvious that it is less costly for the population at large to experience a crackdown on the small private sector in an otherwise unreformed economy than it is to reinstate price controls, renationalize, and so on. This assumption on reversal costs of partial and full reform will play an important role in the further analysis.

The idea of complementarities of reforms is again also captured by assuming that $P(O_{im})$ is always more negative than the reversal payoff $-\xi_i$ so that partial reform is never attractive per se. At a more general level, this assumption reflects the idea of "no third way" between capitalism and socialism, an idea that has been expressed by many scholars of transition (see, e.g., Kornai, 1998). Again, to what extent partial reform is unviable in the long run will depend on many institutional details. For now, we simply assume partial reform to be unviable in the long run.

Let us now turn to the analysis of the model. Given the reversal option after uncertainty resolution and the assumption that learning takes place after one period, we can define the "big bang" payoff BB obtained when implementing both reforms simultaneously:

$$BB = (1 - \delta) \underset{j,k}{E} F\left(O_{1j}, O_{2k}\right) + \delta \underset{j,k}{E} \max \left\{-\xi, F\left(O_{1j}, O_{2k}\right)\right\} \tag{2.4}$$

Outcome $F(O_{1j}, O_{2k})$ is thus experienced for one period, after which one can decide whether or not to abandon the reform package.

Under gradualism, reform 1 is tried for one period. After learning $P\left(O_{1j}\right)$, there can either be a reversal to the status quo or a move to implement reform 2. Remember that partial reform is dominated by either of these options. Once both reforms are implemented, they can also be reversed one period later, just as in the big bang case. Call this strategy and sequencing GR_{12}.[5]

Assume reform 1 has been implemented first and signal S_{1n} has been learned. The continuation payoff $R_2(S_{1n})$ is then

$$R_2\left(S_{1n}\right) = (1 - \delta) \underset{j,k}{E} \left[F\left(O_{1j}, O_{2k}\right) \mid S_{1n}\right] + \delta \underset{j,k}{E} \max \left\{-\xi, F\left(O_{1j}, O_{2k}\right) \mid S_{1n}\right\} \tag{2.5}$$

Since the expectation of $F(.,.)$ is increasing in n, define $\tilde{n}$ such that $R_2(S_{1n}) \geq -\xi_1$ if and only if $n \geq \tilde{n}$. That is, reversal takes place only for signals worse than $S_{1\tilde{n}}$. The ex ante payoff of a gradualist package starting with reform 1, GR_{12}, is then

$$GR_{12} = (1 - \delta) \underset{j}{E} P\left(O_{1j}\right) + \delta \operatorname{Prob}(n < \tilde{n})\left(-\xi_1\right) + \delta \operatorname{Prob}(n \geq \tilde{n}) \underset{n \geq \tilde{n}}{E} \left[R_2\left(S_{1n}\right)\right] \tag{2.6}$$

where, if p_n represents the probability associated to a signal S_{1n}, with $n = 1, \ldots, \tilde{n}, \ldots N_i$ we have $\operatorname{Prob}(n < \tilde{n}) \equiv \sum_{n=1}^{\tilde{n}-1} p_n$ and $\underset{n \geq \tilde{n}}{E} \left[R_2\left(S_{1n}\right)\right] \equiv \sum_{n=\tilde{n}}^{N_i} \frac{p_i}{p_{\tilde{n}}+\ldots+p_{N_i}} R_2\left(S_{1n}\right)$.

[5] Note that other strategies are dominated. For example, "cycling," i.e., implementing a reform, reversing it, going back, and so on, is wasteful because reversal costs are incurred each time. For a similar reason, a strategy of reversing reform 1, than trying reform 2 is worse than GR_{12}.

We can rewrite the expression for GR_{12} by noting that

$$BB = \text{Prob}(n < \tilde{n}) \underset{n < \tilde{n}}{E} [R_2(S_{1n})] + \text{Prob}(n \geq \tilde{n}) \underset{n \geq \tilde{n}}{E} [R_2(S_{1n})] \tag{2.7}$$

We then get

$$GR_{12} = (1 - \delta) \underset{j}{E} P(O_{1j}) + \delta BB + \delta \text{Prob}(n < \tilde{n}) \left\{ -\xi_1 - \underset{n < \tilde{n}}{E} [R_2(S_{1n})] \right\} \tag{2.8}$$

There are three terms on the right-hand side of equation (2.8) that allow us to compare big bang and gradualism. The first term is $(1 - \delta) \underset{j}{E} P(O_{1j})$, which is always < 0. This is the interim suffering in the first period under gradualism due to the strong complementarities between reforms. The second term is possibly costly delay in comparison to big bang. Delay is bad if $BB > 0$ but not so if $BB < 0$. These two elements were already present in the analysis of idiosyncratic uncertainty. The most interesting term is the third one, which represents the option value of early reversal. If $\tilde{n}$ exists, $\{-\xi_1 - \underset{n < \tilde{n}}{E} [R_2(S_{1n})]\}$ is > 0. Indeed, by definition of $\tilde{n}$, $R_2(S_{1n}) < -\xi_1$ for $n < \tilde{n}$. It is thus easy to see that $\underset{n < \tilde{n}}{E} [R_2(S_{1n})] < -\xi_1$. If $\text{Prob}(n < \tilde{n}) > 0$, the option value of early reversal will be strictly positive.

Equation (2.8) allows us to see when big bang or gradualism can be the optimal strategy as well as the trade-off between both, seen from the criterion of maximization of the ex ante expected payoff of transition. Big bang can be optimal in circumstances where there is a sufficient combination of (1) too much interim suffering $[\underset{j}{E} P(O_{1j}) << 0]$; (2) no learning from partial reform ($N_i = 1$), in which case trivially the option value of early reversal is equal to zero, or there may still be learning but no option value of early reversal ($\nexists n < \tilde{n}$); and (3) an expected outcome of the big bang package that is positive and large. However, gradualism can be optimal in circumstances where there is a sufficient combination of (1) $BB < 0$, (2) an option value of early reversal that is high enough, and (3) $\underset{j}{E} P(O_{1j})$ that is not too negative. Note that if $\delta \longrightarrow 1$, then $GR_{12} > BB \Longleftrightarrow 0 < \text{Prob}(n < \tilde{n}) < 1$.

Gradualism has an option that big bang does not have, namely, the option of early reversal at a lower cost. Under big bang, one has the choice of either maintaining the status quo or of learning the full reform outcome. The latter, however, can be very costly to reverse in case of a bad aggregate outcome. Under gradualism, there is an additional option, namely, that of experimentation or partial learning, and of possible early reversal if the prospects for full reform look bad enough after an initial partial reform. This high reversal cost under big bang may be seen as an advantage from the point of view of ex post political constraints, because it reduces the reversibility of enacted reforms. From the point of view of ex ante political constraints, high reversal costs may make the big bang approach unattractive or even unacceptable compared to the status quo. Because gradualism has this additional option of early reversal after partial uncertainty resolution, it may make reforms easier to start.

For gradualism to be optimal, the first reform has to be informative: the probability of early reversal [Prob $(n < \tilde{n})$] has to be smaller than 1 (otherwise the status quo is optimal) and greater than zero (otherwise gradualism is dominated by a big bang strategy). The finer the signals as a partition of states of nature, the higher the chance the first reform will be informative in the sense discussed previously.

Gradualism will be preferrable to big bang if and only if the condition of informativeness is fulfilled, in case learning is fast enough, that is, if δ is close enough to one.[6] Otherwise, big bang cannot be dominated. Note that with fast enough learning, a necessary condition for informativeness is that early reversal is less costly than full reversal. It is easy to see that if $\xi_1 = \xi$ with $\delta \longrightarrow 1$, it is never costly to learn first about the outcome of full reform before deciding any reversal, in which case big bang, the natural way of learning the full outcome, is undominated. The analysis suggests that in the presence of reversal costs and aggregate uncertainty, a key determinant in the choice of big bang or gradualism is less the outcome of partial reform than its degree of informativeness about future outcomes. Whether this condition of informativeness is present in reality may depend on the kinds of reform packages one is looking at. For example, even though privatization between sectors can be seen as complementary, implementing a privatization program in one sector may reveal much about the expected outcome of the program if implemented in all sectors. One can also easily think of cases where complementarities are so strong that partial reform is not informative at all.[7]

It is worthwhile to spell out some of the implications of the analysis. First of all, because the option value of early reversal raises a wedge between the ex ante expected payoff of a gradualist program and that of a big bang strategy, it is possible to have $GR_{12} > 0 > BB$. In other words, for a given default payoff, gradualism may be ex ante attractive, but big bang may not. Therefore, a gradualist strategy can be a useful way of overcoming the status quo bias of reform! This conclusion stands in contrast to the result of the previous section where gradualism only creates additional status quo bias when there is only idiosyncratic uncertainty.

This case also has interesting implications in terms of the timing of transition programs. If one assumes that the default payoff declines over time, then an initial situation with $GR_{12} > 0 > BB$ leads us to predict that (1) a gradualist program will start earlier and (2) big bang programs will tend to be observed in countries where crisis perceptions are greater (after missed opportunities for gradualism). Both predictions are consistent with the observation that gradualist programs in Hungary and China started earlier than big bang programs in Poland and Russia that started under greater crisis perception.

Note that if $GR_{12} > BB > 0$, then welfare maximization would obviously lead to the choice of gradualism over big bang. This would be the decision of a benevolent social planner and this is also the advice an economist would give on welfare grounds. If, however, one assumes that the politician who has the power to propose the reform package is a reformer whose objective is to minimize reversal of reforms subject to their acceptability, then he would choose big bang over gradualism because it implies more irreversibility than gradualism. Indeed, under big bang, reversal will only take place if $F(O_{1j}, O_{2k}) < -\xi$, whereas under gradualism, there will be reversal if $R_2(S_{1n}) < -\xi_1$. Replacing $R_2(S_{1n})$ by its expression and assuming for simplicity $\delta \longrightarrow 1$,

[6] *Remember that in the context of our model where net present values are fixed, $\delta \longrightarrow 1$ means that the length of the learning period becomes arbitrarily small.*

[7] *Many kinds of gradualism can of course be completely stupid and self-defeating and would never be considered by serious policymakers. A joke that circulated under the communist regime was the following: Polish leaders wanted to study the success of British car traffic. After sending a mission to the United Kingdom, they decided on a gradual approach to car traffic reform. In a first step, half the drivers of Warsaw would drive on the right and the other half would drive on the left.*

we get $\underset{j,k}{E} \max \{-\xi, F(O_{1j}, O_{2k}) \mid S_{1n}\} < -\xi_1$. One sees immediately that it is possible to have states of the world O_{1j}, O_{2k} consistent with signal S_{1n} where $F(O_{1j}, O_{2k}) > -\xi$ but where $\underset{j,k}{E} \max \{-\xi, F(O_{1j}, O_{2k}) \mid S_{1n}\} < -\xi_1$. In other words, in all states of the world where there will be reversal under big bang, there will also be reversal under gradualism, but there will be states of the world for which there will be reversal under gradualism but not under big bang. This outcome is possible because $\xi > \xi_1$, which, to repeat, is what makes the option of early reversal valuable.

This discussion suggests that there is a possible ex ante/ex post trade-off between big bang and gradualism, with gradualism having a higher ex ante acceptability but a lower ex post irreversibility than big bang. Thus any window of opportunity will be used by a reformist politician to get big bang reform packages through in order to create irreversibility. Big bang strategies will be preferred by such policymakers whenever they are ex ante feasible, precisely because the option of early reversal disappears. The idea of using windows of opportunity (or periods of "extraordinary politics") to get big bang packages through has been expressed frequently in the policy literature (Lipton and Sachs, 1990a; Balcerowicz, 1995). The formal discussion in this chapter shows the rationale behind such choices of reform strategy. We will come back to the trade-off between ex ante acceptability and ex post irreversibility in section 2.5 when discussing questions of optimal sequencing.

Our formal discussion also suggests that more irreversibility under such windows of opportunity can sometimes be more of a curse than a blessing. With high reversal costs of reform, one may get blocked ex post in an economically inefficient situation, whereas lower reversal costs would make it possible to undo a reform that has proved unsuccessful and then try something else in its place. For example, it is sometimes argued by Russian policymakers that Russian privatization, despite its economic failure, is a political success because it has not been reversed. It is not clear at all, in the Russian context, that this irreversibility is to be seen as a success according to the welfare criterion. As this example suggests, more irreversibility is not necessarily associated with higher welfare for the population and may be associated with lower welfare.

The preceding model was developed in a representative agent framework where the probability distributions associated with various aggregate outcomes are known to agents. We could imagine an alternative framework where agents have different subjective beliefs about the likelihood of given aggregate outcomes and where there is Bayesian updating. Thus "reformers" would have optimistic beliefs about reform and associate very low subjective probabilities with bad aggregate outcomes, whereas "conservatives" would have more pessimistic beliefs and associate high subjective probabilities with low aggregate outcomes.[8] Reformers would prefer big bang and conservatives the status quo. If reformers have the power to propose reforms but approval of conservatives is necessary, say, because they form a majority, a situation encountered in several countries during important periods (in China and Russia certainly), then conservatives would never vote for big bang. Reformers may, however, want to convince conservatives to engage in the reform process by proposing a gradual reform. One can conjecture that conservatives

[8] *Such an assumption sounds reasonable but is not easy to defend on theoretical grounds; see Aumann (1976).*

may have reason to accept a gradualist package rather than reject it. Indeed, they may want to vote for gradualism to convince the existing reformers to adopt more pessimistic beliefs in order to secure a more conservative majority in the future. This could be an interesting extension of the framework.

Beyond transition, the flexible approach to reforms provided by gradualism, because of the costs of trial and error in the presence of aggregate uncertainty are smaller, may explain why politicians so often take a gradual approach to large-scale reforms even when there is strong complementarity of reforms. The process of European unification, where there are complementarities between various reforms such as the single market, the single currency, and political integration, would obviously be a good example.

One application of the gradual approach to reforms provided by the Dewatripont-Roland (1995) model is the concept of "flexible integration" (Dewatripont et al., 1995). Flexible integration in the context of the European Union means that a subset of members of the union would have the right to go ahead and implement a further stage in European integration without other members necessarily being obliged to participate. At the same time, nonparticipants would not necessarily have the right to exercise a veto over such reforms. The European Monetary Union was implemented in this way because the United Kingdom, Denmark, and Sweden deliberately withdrew from participation. Flexible integration indeed allows the subset of countries that are the most eager to adopt the next stage of European integration to bear the costs of experimenting with the new stage of integration while the more skeptical countries wait to learn about the outcome of the reform and can decide to join after uncertainty has been resolved. Flexible integration provides a way to get around ex ante political constraints created by the unanimity rule in the European council because it eliminates the veto power of individual countries. At the same time, it preserves the rights of sovereign countries participating in the union by not imposing direct majority rule on them and allowing them to "opt out" of integration steps they do not agree to.

The same framework can be applied to the accession of Central and Eastern European countries to the European Union. This is a major challenge in European construction because of the greater heterogeneity it introduces between member countries of the European Union. As indicated by Baldwin (1995), the accession of Central European countries is likely to modify the balance of power within the EU in favor of smaller and poorer countries within the existing institutions. By starting accession only with a subset of five countries (Hungary, Poland, the Czech Republic, Estonia, and Slovenia), the EU will experiment and test its (by then reformed) institutions and prevent any irreversible move that could result from accession of a set of countries that is too large.

2.4.2 THE ROLE OF COMPLEMENTARITIES AND REFORM MOMENTUM

The formulation of the preceding model is quite general and holds with complementary reforms in particular. Remember that we have assumed that a single reform is never attractive per se, so that it is always followed either by a second reform or by a reversal to the default payoff. Complementarity of reforms thus does not prevent gradualism from being potentially optimal. The reason is that the first-period loss associated with partial reform, because of complementarities, may be outweighed by the informativeness of partial reform. What happens if we drop the assumption of complementarity? If we do so, we will realize that complementarity of reforms can actually be a necessary condition for gradualism to be optimal!

To see this point, following Dewatripont and Roland (1995), it is useful to simplify the preceding framework by assuming

$$F\left(O_{1j}, O_{2k}\right) \equiv O_{1j} + O_{2k} \quad and \quad P\left(O_{im}\right) \equiv O_{im} - \gamma \qquad \text{(2.9)}$$

This assumption of complementarity implies that γ must be sufficiently large so that the following condition holds: $O_{im} - \gamma < -\xi_i$. Assume instead that there are no complementarities and that reforms are separable (that is, $\gamma = 0$) as well as statistically independent. In that case, gradualism will never be optimal. Each reform can now be assessed independently, and will be tried either immediately or never. Thus, the only possible optimal strategies are status quo, big bang, and partial reform, but gradualism cannot be optimal. So, for example, if reform 2 looks unattractive ex ante, that is, if $\underset{k}{E}\left(O_{2k}\right) < 0$, at most reform 1 will be tried, but reform 2 will never be implemented.[9]

However, under complementarities, with $P(O_{im}) = O_{im} - \gamma < -\xi_i$, gradualism can be optimal, as shown earlier. In that case, reform 2 can be adopted after reform 1 if $R_2(O_{1j}) > -\xi_1$. Developing the expression for $R_2(O_{1j})$, putting and distributing $-\xi_1$ on the left-hand side, we find that reform 2 is decided upon after reform 1 if

$$(1 - \delta)[O_{1j} + \xi_1 + \underset{k}{E}\left(O_{2k}\right)] + \delta \max\{-\xi + \xi_1, O_{1j} + \xi_1 + \underset{k}{E}\left(O_{2k}\right)\} > 0 \qquad \text{(2.10)}$$

The thing to note about equation (2.10) is that even if the second reform looks unattractive ex ante, that is, if $\underset{k}{E}\left(O_{2k}\right) < 0$, under complementarities reform 2 can still be chosen as long as $O_{1j} + \xi_1 + \underset{k}{E}\left(O_{2k}\right) > 0$. Two effects are at play here. A first reason to adopt reform 2 is to keep the gains from the first reform if uncertainty resolution proved to be favorable (a high positive O_{1j}). Indeed, since partial reform is dominated by either reversal or further development of reforms because of reform complementarities, the only way to keep the "sweet pill" of reform 1 is to swallow the "bitter pill" of reform 2. The second reason to adopt reform 2 is that doing so saves on reversal costs of the first reform. Again, because of complementarities, the only two alternatives to weigh against each other are reversal and continuation of the reform process. When reforms are separable, these elements do not enter into consideration in deciding whether or not to adopt reform 2. Complementarities thus allow gradualism to sustain a momentum for further reform in situations where such momentum would be absent under separable reforms.

In his informal analysis of the politics of partial reforms, Hellman (1998) implicitly assumes that reforms are separable. He argues that partial reforms create large concentrated gains to a minority of winners, whereas they create dispersed transitional losses to a majority of losers. Such gains are related to rents that can be earned from partial

[9] *Of course, if reforms are not statistically independent but are instead correlated, gradualism can still be optimal because of a learning effect similar to, but less general than what we have seen. A positive outcome of partial reform may thus lead to predicting a better outcome for reform 2, leading to implementation of the latter in the second period.*

reforms, such as monopoly rents from price liberalization without competition policy. He points to the fact that partial reform tends to be adopted more often in countries where governments have longer tenure and are less accountable to voters. The minority of winners from partial reform will then be more able to capture governments that are more insulated from voters, influence them to decide partial reforms instead of big bang, and veto continuation of reforms so that reforms get stuck in the middle of the reform process. Instead, in countries where governments are closer to voters, big bang policies will tend to be more favored than partial reforms.

In the preceding framework, however, Hellman's analysis implicitly suggests that in Central and Eastern European countries, the object of his analysis, there is a strong complementarity between political and economic reforms, which suggests a sequencing of reforms where democratic reforms are initiated before economic reforms. There have indeed been strong momentum effects created by the collapse of communist political regimes in 1989. The advent of noncommunist democratic regimes, especially in the countries closest to Western Europe that suffered from being satellite states of the Soviet Union, represent welfare gains for local populations that cannot be underestimated given the democratic and national aspirations. The gains from democratic reform, along with the newly associated powers of voters, made it easier to get radical economic reform programs accepted. Accepting the transition to a market economy could be seen as a necessary condition to stabilize the new democratic regimes.

In the context of accession to the European Union, it is quite clear that both democracy and the market economy were necessary conditions of entry to the European Union. We will come back to this issue in the concluding chapter of this book, but transition had a major geopolitical component in the sense that it represented a liberation of Central European countries from Soviet Russian oppression. Entry in the European Union represents a credible sign of this geopolitical shift of Central Europe from the "East" to the "West." To the extent that Western Europe never would accept the new democracies without decisive market reforms, it was quite clear that those in Central Europe who cheered the advent of democracy and the entry to Europe would have to accept market reforms, whether they supported them or not, in order to benefit from democracy and Europe.

Independently of accession, one may argue that the emergence of a private market economy is necessary to produce the constituencies that will make democracy self-enforcing (Moore, 1966; Staniszkis, 1991). Here again, those who deeply desired the stabilization of the new democratic regimes would have to accept the economic reforms in order to have stable democracy. To summarize, a strong case can be made for the complementarity between democracy and market reforms.[10]

A clear example of momentum effects under gradualism is the success of decollectivization in China, which created support for complementary reforms such as price liberalization and enterprise reform. Decollectivization in agriculture started with the December 1978 plenum of the Central Committee of the Communist Party. The percentage of rural households participating in the "household responsibility system," that is, a

[10] *To avoid any misunderstanding, this issue is partly orthogonal to the question of whether a market economy can coexist with a dictatorial political regime. We are indeed talking about the complementarity between market reforms and democracy, not between the market economy, once it exists, and democracy, though there are also obvious complementarities there.*

return to family farming, went from 1 percent in 1979 to 45 percent in 1981 and 90 percent in 1984. Agricultural output increased by 56 percent between 1978 and 1984 (Lin, 1992). Because of this success and the support of the rural constituencies who had gained from the first phase of reforms, reformers were able to push through a second phase of reforms in 1984 that was meant to create a support for reforms in urban areas (Naughton, 1995). This was the dual-track price system, which we will analyze in more detail in Chapter 6. More comprehensive reforms would not have met the ex ante feasibility constraints. The success of the dual track itself created constituencies for further reform, and it was only in 1993 and 1994 that political support could be found for the next stage of reforms, which included restructuring of SOEs with significant layoffs as well as privatization (see Qian, in press, for a comprehensive overview of the Chinese transition process).

In the literature on European integration, the idea of complementarities of reforms and possible momentum effects has been taken up by what is called in the circles of the European Commission the *bicycle theory* of European unification, according to which the process of European integration can be compared to a bicycle ride: one can either move ahead or fall, but one cannot stay in the same spot. Momentum effects have played an important role in the history of European unification. Two experiments of supranational institutions have coexisted in recent decades in Europe: the European Free Trade Agreement (EFTA) and the European Union. While the former was purely a free trade agreement, the six countries that started the European Communities (France, Germany, Italy, Belgium, the Netherlands, and Luxemburg) had higher objectives (the founding fathers of Europe such as Robert Schumann wanted to build supranational institutions that would prevent another war between European countries) but started by building a common market when they signed the Treaty of Rome in 1957. The initial success of the Common Market led both to a widening and to a deepening of the union. The United Kingdom, Denmark, and Ireland joined in 1973, followed by Greece in 1981, Spain and Portugal in 1986, and Sweden, Finland, and Austria in 1995. Five Central European countries have started negotiations for accession: Poland, Hungary, the Czech Republic, Estonia, and Slovenia. Other transition countries would also like to enter the union. The success of the Common Market also led to a deepening of market integration with the Single Market Act in 1987 and European Monetary Union (EMU) in 1999. Possible success of the EMU may lead countries like the United Kingdom to join at a later stage. Implementation of EMU has raised questions about fiscal harmonization and economic policy coordination. The process of European integration may still deepen, but it may also unravel. It is unlikely to stay in its current state.

Momentum effects created by a first reform immediately raise questions about the sequencing of reforms: Given two reforms, which one should we start with? The examples of transition and European integration suggest that it may be good to start with a reform having a high likelihood of bringing benefits to a majority, in order to build support for further more difficult reforms. We will come back to this topic in formal terms in section 2.5.

2.4.3   THE ROLE OF REVERSAL COSTS

What happens if there are no reversal costs, that is, if $\xi = \xi_1 = 0$? It is easy to see that big bang will always dominate. Indeed, replacing the reversal costs by 0, the expression for big bang becomes

$$BB = (1 - \delta) \underset{j,k}{E} F\left(O_{1j}, O_{2k}\right) + \delta \underset{j,k}{E} \max \left\{0, F\left(O_{1j}, O_{2k}\right)\right\} \tag{2.11}$$

which for $\delta \longrightarrow 1$ is always ≥ 0. By the same logic, we know that the continuation payoff under gradualism $R_2(S_{1n})$ is also ≥ 0, implying that the option value of early reversal is always equal to zero because $\nexists \tilde{n}$ with $n < \tilde{n}$ for which $R_2(S_{1n}) < -\xi_1$. Indeed, when there are no reversal costs, there are no costs of learning, and thus never any advantage to early reversal. Big bang, which involves more (or faster) learning, can thus not be dominated by gradualism when there are no reversal costs.

A similar result will hold when the benefits of learning are large relative to the costs. This is the case with the learning model of Bertocchi and Spagat (1997). They look at the problem facing a government that wants to remove subsidies in the state sector but that fears unnecessarily high induced unemployment. In the absence of uncertainty on the rate of absorption of the unemployed in the private sector, the path of subsidy removal is gradual and in pace with private sector employment creation. In the presence of uncertainty, a higher initial pace of subsidy removal is optimal in order to learn more about the rate of absorption in the private sector. If this absorption rate turns out to be low, the government may in the next period increase again the level of subsidies in order to reabsorb some of the unemployed in the state sector. The only costs of going fast are thus the temporary unemployment costs associated with learning, since there are no reversal costs in the model. If irreversibility is introduced so that initial subsidy cuts cannot be undone because of the irreversibility of enterprise closures, then learning effects will be dampened. This analysis points again to the crucial role of reversal costs as costs of learning to be weighed against the benefits of learning. If reversal costs are important for large-scale reform experiments, uncertainty will lead to slowing down reform. Otherwise uncertainty can lead to accelerating it.

The discussion in this chapter is reminiscent of earlier debates between political philosophers on reform. Philosophers like Edmund Burke, Michael Oakeshott, and Karl Popper had argued against radical societal change and in favor of piecemeal reform on the basis of the enormous costs associated with reform experimentation, given the uncertainty of outcomes. Murrell (1992) builds on the work of those philosophers to make an evolutionary argument for gradualism, in the spirit of evolutionary economics. Note that the emphasis on aggregate uncertainty goes in the direction of such evolutionary thinking, which emphasizes the process more than the destination. Indeed, because of the assumption of aggregate uncertainty, one has little to say about the end point of transition, and one will emphasize more the process of learning about possible outcomes through the transition strategy chosen.

There is also an important ethical question involved. Economists who advise policymakers tend to be advocates for particular policy solutions and try to convince political decisionmakers of their point of view. They thus typically underplay the uncertainty associated with policy solutions, in particular the ones they propose. This will be even more the case when, as is usual, advocates of other policy options are equally adamant at presenting only the good sides of their preferred reforms. As academics, however, economists are always more cautious and are less biased in recognizing uncertainty of outcomes given the scientific standards of the academic profession. The rhetoric of policy advice, intended to convince rather than simply to convey scientific evidence or arguments, may thus give the misleading impression that the range of policy options and outcomes is more narrow than it really is. However, if we take aggregate uncertainty seriously, we should be cautious in advocating excessively fast radical policies that create irreversibilities, and we should put more emphasis on the value of experimentation.

2.5 OPTIMAL SEQUENCING

Now that we have analyzed the trade-off between gradualism and big bang under aggregate uncertainty and complementarities, we can discuss issues of optimal sequencing of reforms in circumstances under which sequencing is relevant, that is, under conditions where gradualism dominates a big bang strategy. Sequencing of reforms is then crucial to ensuring the soundness and quality of gradualist reform programs.

Three things are important to get a "correct" sequencing of reforms: (1) The unbundling of a reform package in given sequences should not lead to losing the property of informativeness discussed earlier. (2) The sequencing should be done so as to make the reform process ex ante acceptable. (3) Sequencing should aim at building constituencies and momentum for further reform and satisfy ex post political constraints.

Concerning the first objective, it is difficult to go further in the analysis with the abstract model of this chapter. In order to understand the differential effects of various approaches to the unbundling of reform packages, one must have more detailed and precise economic models of complementary reforms. In what follows, we will simply assume that the property of informativeness holds. Recall that this is a necessary condition for gradualism to dominate big bang.

The second and third objectives may conflict with each other in determining an optimal sequencing of reforms. Indeed, as with the comparison between big bang and gradualism, there may be a trade-off between ex ante acceptability and ex post irreversibility. As we will see, it is also possible that the two objectives do not conflict with each other.

The analysis in this section follows Dewatripont and Roland (1995). To make the comparison between various sequencings of reforms as simple as possible, we assume (without any real loss of generality)[11] that each reform generates only one of two out-

[11] *The more abstract formulation of section 2.4 primarily allows us to see the effect of informativeness in a precise way.*

comes. Reform i has a good aggregate outcome $G_i > 0$ with probability p_i and a bad aggregate outcome $L_i < 0$ with probability $(1 - p_i)$. Define

$$E_i \equiv p_i G_i + (1 - p_i) L_i \qquad \qquad \textbf{(2.12)}$$

and assume

$$R_i(G_j) > -\xi_j > R_i(L_j) \qquad \qquad \textbf{(2.13)}$$
$$R_j(G_i) > -\xi_i > R_j(L_i)$$

The last two conditions mean that reform i and j are each informative. Adapting the model of section 2.4, we find that

$$BB = (1 - \delta)(E_i + E_j) + \delta \max\{-\xi, E_i + E_j\}$$

Similarly, given that reforms are informative we have

$$GR_{ij} = (1 - \delta)(E_i - \gamma) + \delta p_i R_j(G_i) - \delta(1 - p_i)\xi_i \qquad \qquad \textbf{(2.14)}$$

where

$$R_j(G_i) = (1 - \delta)(G_i + E_j) + \delta p_j(G_i + G_j) + \delta(1 - p_j) \max\{-\xi, G_i + L_j\} \qquad \qquad \textbf{(2.15)}$$

and a similar expression is derived for GR_{ji}. One easily checks that the equivalent of equation (2.8), which gives the trade-off between gradualism and big bang, is

$$GR_{ij} = (1 - \delta)(E_i - \gamma) + \delta BB + \delta(1 - p_i)[-\xi_i - R_j(L_i)] \qquad \qquad \textbf{(2.16)}$$

If only one of the two reforms, say reform i, is informative, then one can see that the optimal sequencing is to have reform i before reform j. Indeed, assuming $\delta \longrightarrow 1$ to concentrate only on long-term effects, then $GR_{ji} = BB$, and since informativeness of reform i yields an option value of early reversal, $GR_{ij} > GR_{ji}$.

In the following analysis, we compare the sequencing of reforms that may differ in their first three moments—that is, in their expected outcome, in their riskiness, and in their skewness.

2.5.1 SEQUENCING OF REFORMS WITH DIFFERENCES IN EXPECTED OUTCOME

We first compare sequencing of reforms that differ only in E_i, their expected outcome abstracting from reversal effects. Following the discussion of section 2.4.2 on momentum, it seems intuitively better to start with a reform having a higher expected outcome.

We first assume two reforms identical in all respects except that payoffs for reform i are those of reform j translated upward by a positive constant Δ: $\xi_i = \xi_j = \xi_p$, $p_i = p_j = p$, $G_i = G_j + \Delta$, $L_i = L_j + \Delta$. Developing the expression for $GR_{ij} - GR_{ji}$ and noting that $E_i = E_j + \Delta$ and thus $G_i + E_j = G_j + E_i$, $G_i + L_j = G_j + L_i$, we get

$$GR_{ij} - GR_{ji} = (1 - \delta)(E_i - E_j) + \delta p[R_j(G_i) - R_i(G_j)] = (1 - \delta)\Delta > 0$$

The advantage of GR_{ij} over GR_{ji} is purely in terms of discounting because of a better partial reform outcome in the first period. The expected outcome for the second period is indeed independent of sequencing, since reversal probabilities and costs are identical for both reforms. Nevertheless, it is better to start with the reform that has the higher expected outcome.

One might expect a similar result to hold for two reforms that differ only in the relative probability of good outcomes: $\xi_i = \xi_j = \xi_p$, $G_i = G_j = G$, $L_i = L_j = L$, $p_i > p_j$. Developing the expression for $GR_{ij} - GR_{ji}$ and using the fact that $E_i - E_j = (G_i - L_i)(p_i - p_j)$ and that $p_i E_j - p_j E_i = L(p_i - p_j)$, we get

$$GR_{ij} - GR_{ji} = (p_i - p_j)\{(1 - \delta)[(1 + \delta)G - (1 - \delta)L] + \delta[\delta \max\{-\xi, G + L\} + \xi_p]\}$$

Again, concentrating on the case where $\delta \longrightarrow 1$, we see that if $\max\{-\xi, G + L\} > -\xi_p$, then $GR_{ij} - GR_{ji} > 0$, which confirms our initial intuition.

However, if $\max\{-\xi, G + L\} < -\xi_p$, which can be possible if $G + L$ is sufficiently negative, then the opposite result will hold. The optimal sequencing would then be the opposite. The intuition for this last result is based on the fact that the reversal probabilities change as $p_i > p_j$. These changes bring two effects into play. On the one hand, starting with reform i increases the probability that both reforms will be achieved, as our initial intuition told us. A corollary effect is that when reform i is introduced first, the probability of having to incur the first-period reversal cost is also smaller. As a result, the expected outcome of reform increases. If, on the other hand, G is realized in the first period and L in the second period, and if $G + L < -\xi_p$, people will be worse off than under the status quo payoff. A higher probability of G for the first reforms may therefore "seduce" into a sequencing with a higher probability of getting stuck in an outcome that is worse than the status quo. The latter effect tends to decrease the expected outcome of reform, other things remaining equal. Clearly, however, if $G + L > 0$, starting first with reform i is optimal.

2.5.2 SEQUENCING OF REFORMS WITH DIFFERENCES IN RISKINESS

We now investigate sequencing along the dimension of risk. Other things remaining equal, is it better to start with a riskier reform or with a less risky one? Let us assume two reforms i and j that are identical in all dimensions, except that outcomes of reform i are a mean-preserving spread of reform j: $\xi_i = \xi_j = \xi_p$, $p_i = p_j = p$, $E_i = E_j$, $G_i > G_j$, $L_i < L_j$.

To compare both reforms, it is useful to start with the following expression derived from equation (2.8):

$$GR_{ij} = (1 - \delta)(E_i - \gamma) + \delta BB + \delta(1 - p_i)[-\xi_i - R_j(L_i)] \tag{2.17}$$

with

$$R_j(L_i) = (1 - \delta)(L_i + E_j) + \delta p_j \max\{-\xi, L_i + G_j\} - \delta(1 - p_j)\xi \tag{2.18}$$

Given our assumptions, we get

$$GR_{ij} - GR_{ji} = \delta(1 - p)[R_i(L_j) - R_j(L_i)]$$
$$= \delta(1 - p)[(1 - \delta)(L_j - L_i) + \delta p(\max\{-\xi, L_j + G_i\} - \max\{-\xi, L_i + G_j\})]$$

It is easy to see that $GR_{ij} - GR_{ji} > 0$, since $L_j > L_i$ and $L_j + G_i > L_i + G_j$. The intuition is that introducing the risky reform first increases the option value of reversibility, thereby increasing the expected outcome. This is another application of the idea that increased volatility raises option values: whenever gains and losses of reform grow, the option value of reversibility grows because $R_j(L_i) < R_i(L_j)$ so that the worse expected outcome after outcome L_i can be avoided through earlier reversal. Seen in another way, if the opposite sequencing were applied, under continuation after a good outcome, one may get stuck with outcome $G_j + L_i$, which is worse than $G_i + L_j$.

Can we think of applications of this last result? In the case of European unification, one can argue for a sequencing whereby political reform of the union should have been implemented before monetary union. This topic will be discussed toward the end of the section.

2.5.3   SEQUENCING OF REFORMS WITH DIFFERENCES IN CONSTITUENCIES

We now combine idiosyncratic and aggregate uncertainty in order to derive more insights on optimal sequencing when there is heterogeneity in the population. In particular, taking into account the distributive impact of different reforms, we ask whether it is better to start first with reforms benefiting a majority, even with small gains, rather than with reforms benefiting a minority, even with large gains.

Assume that there are two reforms, reform 1 and reform 2, with statistically independent outcomes. Each reform has the same positive aggregate outcome G occurring with equal probability p and the same negative aggregate outcome L occurring with probability $(1 - p)$. Each individual reform has reversal cost ξ_p. Besides these aggregate gains or losses, the two reforms differ in their distributive effects. All individuals are identical ex ante. However, ex post, reform 1 is assumed to bring an additional positive gain g to two-thirds of the population, but the other third will be hurt and get $-2g$ on top of the aggregate outcome. Reform 2, in contrast, benefits a minority ex post, yielding $2g$ for one third of the population and $-g$ for two-thirds. When both reforms have been implemented, the reversal cost is ξ. Figure 2.1 compares the reforms.

These assumptions are such that the overall distributive effects are neutral for the median voter ex post (and for five-ninths of the population) after both reforms have been implemented. Note also that from the ex ante point of view, each reform is distributively neutral, since the expected idiosyncratic gain is zero in both cases. However, each individual reform is not ex post distributively neutral. Therefore, the sequencing of reforms may affect reform reversibility after implementation of a first reform, depending on the expected costs and benefits of reform continuation for the pivotal (here median) voter. In other words, the order or the sequencing of reforms affects the identity of the median voter at the interim stage, after one reform has been implemented.

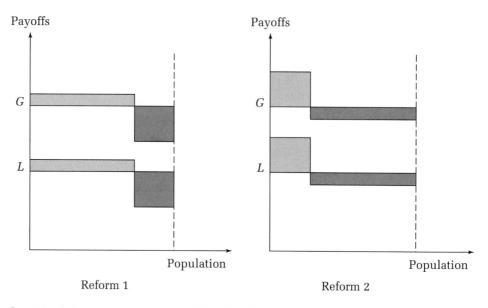

FIGURE 2.1 EX ANTE IDENTICAL REFORMS WITH DIFFERENT EX POST DISTRIBUTIVE OUTCOMES

We thus compare GR_{12} where reform 1 is implemented first and GR_{21} where reform 2 is implemented first. Assume that $G + L > -\xi > 2L$, so that the full reform package gets reversed ex post only in the worst state of nature. For simplicity, assume here immediate learning, that is, $\delta = 1$.

Under GR_{12}, the median voter has to decide whether to go ahead with reform 2 while knowing he is among the relative winners of reform 1. If outcome G is realized after the first reform, he will vote for continuation if

$$p(2G + g) + (1 - p)(G + L + g) > -\xi_p \tag{2.19}$$

If L is realized, continuation requires instead

$$p(L + G + g) - (1 - p)(\xi) > -\xi_p \tag{2.20}$$

Under GR_{21}, the median voter considers whether to go ahead while knowing he is among the relative losers of reform 2. If G is realized, continuation will be voted if

$$p(2G - g) + (1 - p)(G + L - g) > -\xi_p \tag{2.21}$$

If L is realized, continuation requires instead

$$p(L + G - g) + (1 - p)(-\xi) > -\xi/2 \tag{2.22}$$

One immediately sees that continuation is more difficult under GR_{21} than under GR_{12}. In other words, it is more likely that the reform process gets stalled after the first reform under GR_{21} than under GR_{12}. There will thus be more irreversibility if one starts with reform 1 rather than with reform 2. In particular, there are parameter values such that continuation is decided under GR_{12} if and only if G is realized, while under GR_{21}, reversal can never be avoided. In that case, GR_{12} is optimal and GR_{21} is clearly not.

2.5.4 THE POSSIBLE TRADE-OFF BETWEEN EX ANTE ACCEPTABILITY AND EX POST IRREVERSIBILITY

Note that in the case just discussed, the higher irreversibility *increases* ex ante acceptability because the suboptimal sequencing GR_{21} involves excess reversal (indeed, always reversal) whereas GR_{12} does not, but still has a positive option value of reversal, in case of a negative aggregate outcome of the first period. The inferiority of GR_{21} relative to GR_{12} comes from the "interim status quo bias" after the first reform. This can be compared to the interim status quo bias of gradualism compared to big bang when there is only idiosyncratic uncertainty, the case discussed in section 2.3.

Of course, more irreversibility ex post can be a mixed blessing, since it can reduce the option value of early reversal. Assume parameter values are such that GR_{12} would always imply continuation after reform 1 is realized irrespective of whether G or L is realized, whereas GR_{21} would yield reversal if and only if L is realized. In that case, there will be a trade-off between higher irreversibility under GR_{12} but lower ex ante acceptability. Indeed, in that case, since GR_{12} implies no reversal after the first reform, its option of early reversal has zero value. With $\delta = 1$, the ex ante expected payoff of GR_{12} will then be identical to that of big bang. Since GR_{21} has a positive option value of early reversal, it will then have a higher ex ante expected payoff than GR_{12}, yielding as optimal a sequencing opposite to the preceding one. In this case, it is precisely because GR_{21} entails more reversibility than GR_{12} or a big bang strategy that it is ex ante more acceptable.

To summarize the discussion, there may be a potential trade-off between ex ante acceptability and ex post irreversibility when one sequencing yields a positive option value of early reversal whereas the other does not. This trade-off is the same as the trade-off discussed earlier between gradualism and big bang when the former is optimal from the ex ante point of view. However, this trade-off need not exist and ex post irreversibility may well increase ex ante acceptability when one sequencing involves excess reversal and "interim status quo bias" whereas the other does not, while still having an option value of early reversal.

Note that both reform packages may be ex ante identical when, independently of the distribution of individual gains and losses, a majority always rejects reversal after the first period when no adverse aggregate shock occurs. As reform 2 is a mirror image of reform 1, the absence of reversal then makes sequencing irrelevant.

Under institutional assumptions that are different from the ones analyzed in this chapter and that focus on majority voting, one may have to target various interest groups. An obvious case is one where a powerful lobbying minority has veto power. Optimal sequencing may then lead to a different order of reforms than in the case of majority rule. The general principle, however, will remain the same, namely, to use sequencing of reforms so as to shift pivotal voters or decisionmakers toward reform continuation at the interim stage. Incorrect sequencing, on the contrary, leads to a shift of pivotal voters or decisionmakers in the direction of reform reversal.

2.5.5 EXOGENOUS VERSUS ENDOGENOUS "REELECTION" OR FUTURE SUPPORT AND RELATED LITERATURE

Going beyond our model, the case for big bang or gradualism or a particular reform sequencing may also depend on whether the probability of reelection of the incumbent government is exogenous or endogenous.

Models by Persson and Svensson (1989) and Alesina and Tabellini (1990) show the advantages of using political windows of opportunity to make decisions that constrain a potential successor government. In that framework, the occurrence of political backlash and the loss of power by the incumbent government are only the result of exogenous forces. The overriding concern is to constrain one's potential successors by choosing reforms today that will be more difficult to reverse tomorrow. An exogenous probability of reelection would thus tend to favor a big bang approach whenever feasible.

If, however, policymakers face an endogenous probability of reelection, they should strive to build constituencies by starting with more popular reforms. In that framework, political backlash may be the result of erroneous sequencing, as in the preceding examples. Aghion and Bolton (1991) have developed a political economy model of fiscal policy where the probability of reelection is endogenous (see also Milesi-Ferretti and Spolaore, 1994).

2.5.6 SEQUENCING OF REFORMS IN TRANSITION ECONOMIES

Given the discussion on the importance of sequencing, can we identify a regular pattern of sequencing in transition economies? Systematic empirical research on that topic has not been started, but one may give some illustrations of the theories developed in this chapter. Indeed, the theory sheds light on the observed regularities in the sequencing of reforms that were highlighted in Chapter 1.

First, consider the development of the small private sector in China, Hungary, and Vietnam prior to more comprehensive reforms. In China, the nonstate sector's share of industrial output increased from 22 percent in 1978 to 47 percent in 1991 and the private sector from zero to over 12 percent over the same period (Qian and Xu, 1993). In Hungary the small private sector was already producing about 10 percent of industrial output by 1990 (Hare and Revesz, 1992). Liberalizing the small private sector is a popular measure that provides a supply response in emerging markets. In China, GNP grew at an average annual rate of 8.7 percent between 1979 and 1991. Rodrik (1992) shows that (contrary to Poland and Czechoslovakia) Hungary's fall of output in 1990 and 1991 is nearly entirely due to the breakdown of the Council for Mutual Economic Assistance (CMEA) and not to an adverse domestic reaction to price liberalization. In Vietnam radical price liberalization and stabilization programs were implemented in 1989. By then, the private sector in agriculture and manufacturing already occupied 60 percent of GDP and 85 percent of the labor force. As in most countries where big bang price liberalization was implemented, Vietnamese industry experienced an output fall in 1989.

However, this fall was more than compensated by impressive growth in agriculture, thus still permitting positive growth that year (Dollar and Ljunggren, 1997). Here also, the prior existence of a small private sector made it possible to buffer the liberalization and stabilization shocks and to facilitate a supply response. Thus the development of a small private sector is observed to be one of the earlier and more popular reforms. Moreover, its introduction affects the economic outcome of further reforms. As we will see in Chapter 7, the macroeconomic effect of price liberalization depends on the prior existence of market networks.

Second, in most economies in transition, the best firms tend to be privatized first. Not only have some governments explicitly received advice to privatize the most profitable firms first (Grosfeld, 1990), but it has also been the general case in practice (see Gatsios, 1992, on Hungary; Carlin and Mayer, 1992, on Eastern Germany; and Frydman, Rapaczynski, and Earle, 1993, for all countries in transition). Recent and careful evidence from the Czech Republic gathered by Gupta, Ham, and Svejnar (1999) shows that in the Czech Republic the more profitable firms were privatized first to create support and political goodwill. Indeed, there is a profit channel at play. More profitable enterprises have a higher value when privatized. Shares of those firms distributed to Czech citizens generate more rents and thus stronger political support for privatization. Firms with the best performance in employment growth do not necessarily tend to get privatized first, which suggests that job creation is not a means of generating political support.

Third, the setting up of new institutions is one of the least costly reforms to implement and quite a popular one, given people's yearning for democracy. Note that, all over Eastern Europe, political reform has preceded economic reform. Even in China, despite Tiananmen, political crackdown has receded in the years of economic reform, as compared to the previous decade of the Cultural Revolution. The start of economic reforms in 1978 was preceded by a wave of depoliticization and relative liberalization of Chinese life. Within the confines of dictatorship, this was a very welcome change for Chinese households. This change, together with the spectacular progress of living standards under reforms, contributed to the great popularity of Deng Xiaoping. Of probably greater importance was the initial wave of decentralization of government authority. As early as 1979, China started to devolve government authority from central to local levels, empowering provinces and local municipalities by giving them fiscal autonomy and responsibility. As we will see in Chapter 11, this decentralization played a crucial role in promoting market reforms. Apart from political reforms, there are other institutional changes that are politically relatively uncontroversial and that are therefore best decided at an early stage of reforms. Fingleton and colleagues (1996), for example, have argued, explicitly using the framework of Dewatripont and Roland (1995), that competition policy should be among the first reforms to be implemented in transition economies. This conclusion agrees with what has generally been observed in practice. Competition laws have been passed rather early in the transition process, though the exact content and implementation of competition policy has varied across transition economies. It is also useful to note the danger associated with an incorrect sequencing. Privatization without effective competition policy risks developing monopolies that will have enough power to capture the state apparatus and prevent the introduction of competition policy, as well as any measure that is opposed to their interests, as we have seen with the Russian experience.

Fourth, the phase of restructuring and closing of money-losing enterprises is generally delayed. Macroeconomic figures show that early in transition, employment falls less than output, and with delay (Burda, 1993). Only in Eastern Germany have there been significant massive measures to close unprofitable enterprises right from the beginning of transition. In other countries, layoffs were more gradual and did not start right at the beginning of reforms. Clearly, restructuring involves the loss of substantial rents for well-organized groups of the population, and it requires countervailing political momentum.

While the preceding experiences (private sector development and institutional development decided early, better firms privatized first) are consistent with our results, the theory can also shed light on potential policy mistakes. For example, one can wonder whether the adverse domestic reaction to price liberalization in Russia in particular might not have been avoided if one had first sufficiently favored the emergence of a small private industrial and service sector as in Hungary. Russian reforms tended to start in that direction under Gorbachev. Cooperatives developed in the late 1980s were an embryo of small private sector development. However, that sector was still very underdeveloped when price liberalization occurred, contrary to the case of Hungary where such a sector was strongly developed by the 1980s. Second, it might have been a sequencing mistake for Boris Yeltsin not to have taken advantage of the August 1991 putsch to push immediately for further political reform (new congressional elections and a new constitution) prior to further economic reform, using the window of opportunity provided by the failed putsch. It was not until December 1993 that such changes took place, nearly two years after the beginning of economic reforms! The population had by then already suffered from the shock of liberalization. A possible "honeymoon" for reformers had already been dissipated, and elections expressed significant discontent and confusion among the population with the party of the extreme-right-wing figure Vladimir Zhirinovsky receiving an impressive number of votes.

2.5.7 OTHER APPLICATIONS OF REFORM SEQUENCING: EUROPEAN INTEGRATION

The preceding framework can be applied to areas other than transition. The framework of analysis can be applied in particular to the process of European integration where a definitive sequencing has been observed. The first phase of European integration starting in the 1960s and 1970s and reinforced with the Single Market program of 1985 was a phase of economic integration through removal of trade barriers (visible and invisible) inside Europe. The second phase, starting with the Maastricht Treaty, is that of monetary unification, and the third phase, which has not really started and may never really get started, is political integration.

In terms of sequencing, starting with economic integration makes sense because it delivers the highest expected benefits. The expected benefits of monetary union are much smaller and are even debatable. However, the question is raised whether monetary unification before political unification was a correct sequence. Political unification is clearly a more risky reform than monetary unification because it involves transfer of power from sovereign countries to the union, the outcome of which can be very uncertain and very durable. Also, it is not clear that monetary union necessarily has a higher expected benefit than political union. If it is true that political union is more risky than monetary union, then the theory in this chapter suggests that the better sequencing might be to have monetary integration after political integration. The sequencing that was eventually chosen may in that case explain important resistances to monetary union such as that reflected in the Danish referendum on the 1992 Maastricht Treaty. The reasoning applying the framework of the chapter would go as follows:

Denmark is a small country with a long tradition of decentralization of government. It can be argued that its citizens feared that accepting monetary union would "lure" them into accepting later a political union where their voice may not be heard because the reversal costs of dropping out of the European Union, including the monetary union, in case of an adverse political outcome would simply be too high. The Danish referendum could thus be interpreted as a forward-looking rejection of such a situation given the risks associated with a political union after monetary union. A sequencing with political integration first might have made Denmark less reluctant to accept monetary integration. In practice, the opt-out clause has overcome such resistance, since Denmark was not forced to enter EMU while remaining in the European Union. It may still participate in further steps in European integration in the future. This short discussion suggests that the theory of sequencing of reforms can be applied to other important areas of large-scale institutional change and refined.

The model would have to be adapted to fit these examples more closely. In particular, various players must reach agreements about decisions, and the reversal costs as well as the payoffs of given reforms are not distributed in the same way. These adaptations may be fruitful extensions of the model in this chapter.

2.6   SPEED OF REFORM AND ENDOGENOUS INVESTMENT

The model in this chapter so far has relied on the assumption of exogenous stochastic outcomes of reforms. The discussion in section 2.5 showed that the probability of reform reversal may be endogenous and may depend on a particular sequencing of reforms. Similarly, one may think that the outcomes themselves may depend to a certain extent on the design of the packages themselves. This theme will be pursued in more detail in the following chapters. In this section, following Dewatripont and Roland (1995), we look at the interactions between the speed of reforms themselves and the endogenous response of investment behavior.

We abstract again from idiosyncratic uncertainty and concentrate on the role of foreign investment, a topic much debated in economies in transition (see, e.g., Lankes and Venables, 1996). We will derive two major results. First, when the level of investment does not affect the reversal probability, the investment response under gradualism is higher before *total* uncertainty resolution and also before *any* uncertainty resolution. The reason is that the option value of waiting to invest is lower under gradualism than under big bang where the outcomes of reform are learned faster. Second, when the level of investment does affect the probability of reversal, then both gradualism and big bang may generate a higher investment response before total uncertainty resolution. In particular, gradualism will generate a higher investment response when the probability of good states is lower. However, before any uncertainty resolution, more irreversibility is created and there is a higher investment response under big bang than under gradualism.

To make things simple, assume that each reform has the same positive aggregate realization G with the same probability p and the same negative aggregate realization L with probability $(1 - p)$. Realizations are assumed to be independent. The payoff of reforms depends on these realizations but also depends positively on the amount of investment. Thus for example $O(G, L, I)$ represents the outcome of reforms with a good realization for the first reform, a bad realization for the second reform, and level of investment I. We assume symmetric payoffs; that is, a good realization in one reform and a bad one for the other yields the same payoff as a bad realization for the former and a good one for the latter. Reform payoffs are then ranked as follows:

$$O(G, G, I) > O(G, L, I) = O(L, G, I) > O(L, L, I) \tag{2.23}$$

Given that reforms are statistically independent, the probabilities to have payoffs $O(G, G, I), O(G, L, I)$ or $[O(L, G, I)]$, and $O(L, L, I)$ for any given level of investment are, respectively, $p^2, p(1 - p)$, and $(1 - p)^2$.

The payoffs of reform to the population increase positively with I. Specifically, assume that

$$O(G, G, 0) > -\xi \tag{2.24}$$
$$O(L, L, I) < -\xi$$
$$O(G, L, I) \geq -\xi \text{ for } I \geq \bar{I}$$
$$O(G, L, I) < -\xi \text{ for } I < \bar{I}$$

As in the previous sections, ξ is the cost of reversal of full reform. Reform is thus irreversible in the presence of "good news" (G, G) whatever the investment response, and will be reversed under "bad news" (L, L) independently of the level of foreign investment. We also assume, in line with the analysis in this chapter, that the first reform is informative under gradualism even for $I \geq \bar{I}$. In other words, reforms are always reversed after one reform if L is observed. However, the level of investment may matter for the reversibility of reform. Under "mixed news" $[(G, L) \text{ or } (L, G)]$, reversal is avoided only if investment has reached a minimum threshold $\bar{I}$. An investment level I costs I

by assumption, and is irreversible. Its value to foreign investors is lost under policy reversal. The gross discounted value of investment to investors is $V(I)$, assumed to be strictly increasing and concave in I.[12] To simplify calculations, it is also assumed that it takes one period for investment to become operational.

We thus compare the big bang and the gradualist strategy under the following timing:

Big bang	$t = 0$	Initial investment I_0
		Both reforms tried
	$t = 1$	Additional investment I_1
		Reversal or not
Gradualism	$t = 0$	Initial investment I_0^G
		First reform tried
	$t = 1$	Additional investment I_1^G
		Reversal, otherwise second reform tried
	$t = 2$ (if no reversal)	Additional investment I_2^G
		Reversal or not

At each date t, investment takes place after uncertainty resolution in that period. We first concentrate on the case where $\bar{I}$ is never reached (either under gradualism or big bang) under mixed news, so that foreign investors know they will enjoy the full benefit of their investment only under good news (G, G). This is a situation where the probability of reversal cannot be affected by prior investment. We show that the first-period investment response under gradualism before uncertainty resolution is unambiguously higher.

Let us see why. Given that reform is reversed in all states other than (G, G), the investment response after full uncertainty resolution I_1 under big bang and I_2^G under gradualism will be positive only under (G, G). In this case we have $I_0 + I_1 = I_0^G + I_1^G + I_2^G = I_G$, where I_G is determined by equating the marginal benefit of investment under good news (G, G) with its marginal cost, that is, by finding the solution to $V'(I_G) = 1$. Working backward, I_1^G will be positive only if the first reform generates good news G. Define then $I_{01}^G = I_0^G + I_1^G$.

Let us then compare the marginal benefits and costs of investing under both strategies *before* uncertainty realization compared to the benefits and costs of investing *after* uncertainty realization.

Under big bang, increasing investment by dI at $t = 0$ generates a net marginal benefit of $p^2 dV(I) - dI$, since, at $t = 1$, reversal will take place whenever (G, G) is not realized. Increasing investment instead by dI at $t = 1$ under good news generates $\delta p^2 [dV(I) - dI]$ measured at $t = 0$. The disadvantage is that investment is delayed by one period, but the advantage is that it takes place only under good news, which happens with probability

[12] *Dewatripont and Roland (1995) make V(I) also dependent on the realizations of the reform outcomes.*

p^2. The net gain of investing at $t = 0$ instead of $t = 1$ is then $(1 - \delta)p^2 dV(I) - (1 - \delta p^2)dI$. Equating this net marginal benefit to 0 gives the solution to I_0 determined by

$$V'(I_0) = \frac{1 - \delta p^2}{(1 - \delta)p^2} \tag{2.25}$$

Under gradualism, increasing investment by dI at $t = 1$ when the first reform was a success generates $pdV(I) - dI$ measured at $t = 1$. Indeed, at $t = 2$, reform will be maintained only under (G, G), which happens with probability p given that G has already been realized. Increasing investment instead by dI at $t = 2$ under (G, G) generates $\delta p[dV(I) - dI]$ measured at $t = 1$. Again, the disadvantage is that investment is delayed by one period, but it takes place only after good news on the second reform, which happens with probability p. The net gain of investing at $t = 1$ instead of $t = 2$ is then $p(1 - \delta)dV(I) - (1 - \delta p)dI$, which, when equated to zero, gives the solution to I_{01}^G:

$$V'(I_{01}^G) = \frac{1 - \delta p}{(1 - \delta)p} \tag{2.26}$$

Comparing both expressions, since $p < 1$, one immediately sees that $\frac{1 - \delta p}{(1 - \delta)p} < \frac{1 - \delta p^2}{(1 - \delta)p^2}$ and thus, given that $V'(I)$ is decreasing in I, we have that $I_{01}^G > I_0$. The investment response prior to uncertainty resolution is thus higher under gradualism than under big bang.

Similarly, we can derive the solution to I_0^G, the investment level under gradualism *before* any uncertainty resolution. Increasing investment at $t = 0$ yields $[p(1 - p)(1 - \delta) + p^2]dV(I) - dI$ where the first expression is the one-period benefit to investment between $t = 1$ and $t = 2$ when uncertainty resolution about the second reform has not yet been realized and decisions of reversal of full reforms have not yet been made. Increasing investment by dI at $t = 1$ yields $\delta p[pdV(I) - dI]$ measured at $t = 0$. The net gain of investing at $t = 0$ instead of at $t = 1$ is then $p[(1 - p)(1 - \delta) + p - \delta p]dV(I) - (1 - \delta p)dI = p(1 - \delta)dV(I) - (1 - \delta p)dI$. The solution to I_0^G is then determined by

$$V'(I_0^G) = \frac{1 - \delta p}{(1 - \delta)p} \tag{2.27}$$

By the same argument as before, one sees that $I_0 < I_0^G = I_{01}^G$.[13] Thus not only is the total investment response before uncertainty resolution higher under gradualism than under big bang, but it is also higher than under big bang at $t = 0$, a stronger result.

The reason for the higher investment response under gradualism is intuitive. At $t = 1$ under gradualism, since the first reform was a success, the conditional probability of (G, G) is now higher, and thus the option value of waiting is lower. Similarly, investment at $t = 0$ is higher under gradualism than under big bang because one learns less by waiting for one period under gradualism. Uncertainty resolution at $t = 1$ is only partial because the outcome of the second reform is not yet known. Reversal occurs at $t = 1$ only with probability $(1 - p)$ instead of with probability $(1 - p^2)$ under big bang. Thus the option value of waiting to invest is lower under gradualism than under big bang. The investment

[13] *The reason that I_0^G is exactly equal to I_{01}^G is that the expected one-period investment benefit in state (G, L) from an investment at $t = 0$ compensates exactly for the learning effect between $t = 0$ and $t = 1$. If the investment return in state (G, L) were lower than in state (G, G), then I_0^G would be lower than I_{01}^G but the basic result of a higher investment response would still remain. See Dewatripont and Roland (1995) for more details.*

response is thus unambiguously higher under gradualism if the level of investment does not affect the reversibility of reforms.

Results are less clear-cut when $\bar{I}$ can be reached. In that case, the incentive to invest before uncertainty resolution can be higher under big bang or under gradualism. However, there is more irreversibility and a higher investment response before any uncertainty resolution under big bang than under gradualism.

So, assume $I_G > \bar{I} > I_{01}^G$. Under big bang, increasing investment at $t = 0$ from I_0 to $\bar{I}$ to get irreversibility yields

$$(1 - \delta)p^2[V(\bar{I}) - V(I_0)] - (1 - \delta p^2)(\bar{I} - I_0) + 2p(1 - p)V(\bar{I}) \tag{2.28}$$

The first expression represents the gain from investing one period earlier the amount $\bar{I} - I_0$. The second expression represents the difference in cost of this earlier investment. By delaying it one period, it would only take place in state (G, G). The third expression is the gain in irreversibility from earlier investment given that it would make reversal happen only in state (L, L) and not any more in states (G, L) and (L, G).

Similarly, under gradualism, increasing investment from I_{01}^G to $\bar{I}$ at $t = 1$, one period before uncertainty resolution, yields

$$(1 - \delta)p[V(\bar{I}) - V(I_{01}^G)] - (1 - \delta p)(\bar{I} - I_{01}^G) + (1 - p)V(\bar{I}) \tag{2.29}$$

The three terms in equation (2.29) have a similar interpretation. We can rewrite the expression for big bang by subtracting and adding $(1 - \delta)p^2[V(I_{01}^G) - I_{01}^G]$ and get

$$(1 - \delta)p^2[V(\bar{I}) - V(I_{01}^G)] + (1 - \delta)p^2[V(I_{01}^G) - V(I_0)]$$
$$- (1 - \delta p^2)(\bar{I} - I_{01}^G) - (1 - \delta p^2)(I_{01}^G - I_0) + 2p(1 - p)V(\bar{I}) \tag{2.30}$$

Let us now compare equations (2.29) and (2.30). We know that $(1 - \delta)p^2 V'(I_0) = (1 - \delta p^2)$. So, by concavity of $V(I)$, $(1 - \delta)p^2[V(I_{01}^G) - V(I_0)] - (1 - \delta p^2)(I_{01}^G - I_0) < 0$. Obviously, $(1 - \delta)p[V(\bar{I}) - V(I_{01}^G)] - (1 - \delta p)(\bar{I} - I_{01}^G) > (1 - \delta)p^2[V(\bar{I}) - V(I_{01}^G)] - (1 - \delta p^2)(\bar{I} - I_{01}^G)$. Therefore, if $(1 - p)V(\bar{I}) > 2p(1 - p)V(\bar{I})$, which will be the case if $p \leq 1/2$, then the incentive to invest up to $\bar{I}$ will always be higher under gradualism.

The reason for this result is the following: At $t = 1$, success of one reform has already been observed. Investing up to $\bar{I}$ creates irreversibility with conditional probability $(1 - p)$ under gradualism compared to $2p(1 - p)$ under big bang. The former is bigger than the latter if $p \leq 1/2$. Second, the conditional probability of getting (G, G) is p under gradualism, after a success from the first reform, whereas it is p^2 under big bang.

However, investment up to $\bar{I}$ at $t = 0$ creates irreversibility under big bang with probability $1 - (1 - p)^2$, whereas investment under gradualism at $t = 0$ creates irreversibility only with probability $p < 1 - (1 - p)^2 = p(2 - p)$. Note also that increasing investment under big bang at $t = 0$ increases irreversibility by $2p(1 - p)$, whereas under gradualism investing more at $t = 0$ rather than at $t = 1$ does not create any extra irreversibility at $t = 0$. The optimal investment at $t = 0$ therefore remains I_0^G. Therefore, when $\bar{I}$ is chosen under big bang, that is, if $(1 - \delta)p^2[V(\bar{I}) - V(I_0)] - (1 - \delta p^2)(\bar{I} - I_0) + 2p(1 - p)V(\bar{I}) > 0$, then the investment response and irreversibility under gradualism are definitely lower.

The stronger irreversibility effect of investment under big bang than under gradualism does not automatically imply that there will be a stronger investment response under big bang. In practice, investors are facing a coordination problem that typically implies multiplicity of equilibria. The issue of coordination, however, is orthogonal to the choice between big bang and gradualism analyzed here because the coordination problem between private investors will be present under both strategies.

The general discussion of the link between political risk, investment response, and reform strategy we had in this section is valid not only for transition economies but also for the "emerging market" countries. Perotti and van Oijen (1999) present some preliminary evidence to analyze this question by focusing on the effects of privatization policies in developing countries. They examine twenty-two emerging market economies that have privatized extensively since 1987. Privatization programs tend to be gradual in these countries. Perotti and van Oijen find that privatization policies have gradually reduced political risks, in turn having a positive effect on capital flows and stock market capitalization in these countries. The direct effect of privatization on stock market capitalization is indeed relatively small compared to the total growth in market capitalization—a difference which is well explained by changes in political risks, thus confirming the importance of uncertainty resolution for investment. These authors do not test for the effect of differences in speed of privatization, but Bortolotti, Fantini, and Siniscalco (1999), in their analysis of privatization in forty-nine countries that we will discuss in Chapter 4, do not find evidence of an effect of speed on capital attracted as measures by privatization revenues. Faster privatization has no effect on privatization revenues raised, controlling for stock market liquidity.

Altomonte (1998) tests for an option value of waiting effect in determining foreign direct investment (FDI) in transition economies and finds significant evidence that progress in transition has a positive effect on FDI while variability in output has a negative effect. However, he does not test for the effect of speed of reforms.

A more general view on irreversible investment under uncertainty than the one discussed in this section can be found in Dixit and Pindyck (1994). On the theme of policy uncertainty and foreign direct investment, see also Rodrik (1991).

2.7 CHINA: THE M-FORM VERSUS U-FORM ORGANIZATION

The theory of the speed and sequencing of reforms assigns a crucial role to informativeness of reforms and to complementarities. The conditions of learning and complementarities of reforms, however, may be crucially affected by the differences in organizational structure left as a legacy from central planning. There is indeed an important difference between the organizational forms of central planning in China and in Eastern Europe as pointed out by Qian and Xu (1993). The Soviet economy was organized in specialized or functional ministries (e.g., mining, machinery, textile) regrouping similar activities organized in gigantic factories. This system is known as *branch organization* (Nove, 1980). In contrast, since 1958 the Chinese economy has been organized mainly on a geographical principle known as *regional organization* (Granick, 1990), with each province being responsible for a whole array of industries. Qian and Xu have pointed out that centrally planned economies of Eastern Europe, managed more centrally, were like U-form hierarchies (Williamson, 1975; Chandler, 1962), whereas China had a more decentralized structure, very much like an M-form hierarchy.

One of the disadvantages of the Chinese planning system is that it led to duplication of industries, as provincial authorities were striving to get "their" steel industry, "their" textile industry, and so on, whereas in the East European U-form type of central planning, it was possible to exploit economies of scale and to expand the division of labor in the economy. However, in the context of reform, the Chinese organizational structure provided much more flexibility for experimentation. Indeed, introducing reform in one region made it possible to gain great benefits from learning (compared to introducing reform in the whole of China) with substantially lower reversal costs. In the Eastern European planned economies, the U-form hierarchy made regional reform experiments impossible because of the stronger interconnectedness of firms. Any experiment of liberalization at the level of big state-owned enterprises had to take place at the economy-wide level.

This idea has been modeled by Qian, Roland, and Xu (1998) in an organization-theoretic context with application to Chinese reforms. Consider the basic model of this chapter with several modifications and extensions. One important extension is that the status quo payoff in case of reform failure is now derived endogenously because it will differ in the M-form and in the U-form.

Assume an economy with two regions A and B and two reforms 1 and 2. Without reform, the net-present-value status quo payoff *without reform* is 1/2 in each region. As before, there is aggregate uncertainty about reform outcomes, but the uncertainty is related to reform blueprints. Some blueprints for reform may be workable, but others may give bad results that are not known in advance. As before, this lack of knowledge reflects ignorance of the transition process and the related unintended consequences of large societal reform projects. It is assumed that one (and only one) blueprint of a reform program is made available each period. With probability p the blueprint is a good one, and with probability $(1 - p)$ it is a bad one. For simplicity, the net present value of a bad blueprint is assumed to be 0 when it is tried out. What is important is that it is worse than the status quo without reform. After a reform failure, another blueprint may be tried in the next period. So, for example, if a given privatization method is proving to be a visible failure, another privatization method may be tried out. The reversal payoff is thus modeled more explicitly than in section 2.4.

Blueprints for reform that become available over time are stochastically independent. It is assumed that if a blueprint is good, it will remain good in any region in the future. However, when a blueprint is intrinsically good, it may still not give good results because of bad coordination in the implementation of the reform blueprint. The analysis encompasses organizational coordination, an obviously important though neglected dimension in transition. Because of the importance of coordination, it is assumed that success is not necessarily guaranteed even when a blueprint has proven to be good and thus could be applied to another region, because good coordination cannot be copied. Coordination in implementation is still necessary before a successful outcome can be achieved.

Given the emphasis on coordination, the analysis assumes extreme complementarity in the coordination of reforms. This is based on a concept of coordination called *attribute matching* inspired by Milgrom and Roberts' (1992) concept of "design attributes." The analysis has rather general applications, in particular to business organizations. Applying the framework to transition, assume two reforms: enterprise restructuring (laying off excess workers) and creation of a social safety net. Attributes of enterprise restructuring are the number and individual characteristics of the laid-off workers such as age, seniority, family composition, length of residence, sex, type of contract, current wage, and history of employment. The attributes of compensation from the social safety net are rules of eligibility such as length of employment, special circumstances (veteran or not), status of enterprises, rules of benefits such as size and length, types of benefits (monetary or not), technical support of computers, administration, budget, and the like. If some attributes of the two tasks are not matched, laid-off workers may not be compensated appropriately, so they may riot and cause major social, economic, and political disturbances.

Because of the assumption about extreme complementarities, partial reform will never be informative. However, local experiments may be tried. The choice between big bang and gradualism will thus have a purely geographical dimension. Big bang will refer to nationwide experiments with reform, whereas gradualism will refer to strategies where reforms are first experimented with locally. The analysis, however, will focus not only on differences in reform strategies, but also on coordination capacities under the M-form and the U-form.

It is assumed that ex ante a program is well designed in the sense that all the attributes are matched in the blueprint. However, some of the attributes may not suit changing local conditions ex post, and adjusting these attributes may lead to mismatches with the attributes of other tasks, which require further adjustments. Coordination is thus seen as adjustment to unforeseen contingencies called *attribute shocks*. Attributes between reform $1r$ and $2r$ ($r = A, B$) must be matched in order to implement the reform program successfully.

The quality of coordination in attribute matching depends on the quality of the information available to decisionmakers in the organization. Assume a two-tier hierarchy with a top manager and a middle manager. In each period, the middle manager collects information about the attribute shocks and sends a message to the top manager. Each message contains information about all the attributes in one reform. It is assumed that information transmission between any two managers is imperfect so that the probability

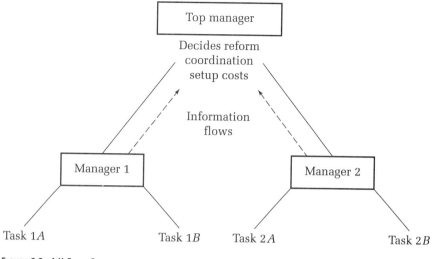

FIGURE 2.2 A U-FORM ORGANIZATION

of each message being correct is λ, where $0 \leq \lambda \leq 1$. Noises in information transmission are assumed to be independent across tasks as well as over time.

The benefits from reform for region A (payoffs for region B are defined symmetrically), when the blueprint is good, are defined as follows: (1) with reform $1A$ but not $2A$ or vice versa, the net present value payoff is $(G + 1)/4$ if the attributes between $1A$ and $2A$ are matched, 0 otherwise; and (2) with change in both reforms $1A$ and $2A$, the net present value payoff is $G/2$ if the attributes between $1A$ and $2A$ are matched, and 0 otherwise. It is assumed that $pG > 1$; that is, the expected gross benefit from change, as compared to the status quo, conditional on good coordination, is positive.

Reform blueprints are assumed to be made available for free, but for each manager there is a setup cost associated with coordinating reforms. For simplicity, it is assumed that only one setup cost is required when only one manager coordinates. In order to implement a reform, the managers need to be trained in how to match attributes of the reform. Because blueprints are free and the setup costs for coordination are not, when a failure occurs in the previous period (because of either a bad program or bad coordination), it is always preferrable to use a new blueprint in the next period rather than to retry the old one.

A U-form organization is set up along "functional lines" (see Figure 2.2). Two middle managers i $(i = 1, 2)$ are responsible for collecting information about shocks in reforms iA and iB. Because the two reforms that need attribute matching are not assigned to the same middle manager, the two middle managers have to report the information to the top manager, who, after receiving information from the two managers, matches attributes between reforms $1r$ and $2r$ $(r = A, B)$.

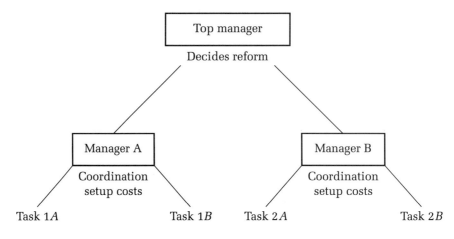

FIGURE 2.3 **AN M-FORM ORGANIZATION**

An M-form organization is set up along "geographical lines" (see Figure 2.3). The middle manager $r(r = 1, 2)$ is responsible for collecting information about shocks in reforms $1r$ and $2r$. Because the two reforms that require attribute matching are assigned to the same manager, and no attribute matching is needed between the tasks across regions, the middle managers can match attributes between $1r$ and $2r$ locally by themselves. The top manager provides a blueprint for reform and decides on the reform strategy.

We first compare the performance of the U-form and the M-form in the case of a big bang reform where the two complementary reforms 1 and 2 are implemented simultaneously in regions A and B.

Under the M-form, every local manager will be responsible for matching the attributes of the two reforms within his region. With perfect local information, attribute matching under the M-form will be performed perfectly. If a program is good, as happens with probability p, the total payoff from the two regions is G. If a program is bad, as happens with probability $1 - p$, the payoff is zero, and a new program will be tried in the next period. Therefore, the expected payoff of reform in an M-form is

$$\pi_{m2} = pG + (1 - p)\delta\pi_{m2} = \frac{pG}{1 - (1 - p)\delta} \qquad (2.31)$$

On the cost side, in the first period, $2C$ is paid because two managers are involved in coordination. With probability p, the reform program is good, so no more costs need to be paid afterward. But with probability $1 - p$ the program is bad, and this fact is discovered after one period of change. Then a new program is tried in the next period. Because the managers need to be retrained for matching attributes, an additional cost of $2C$ is paid in the next period. Therefore, we have

$$c_{m2} = 2C + \delta(1 - p)c_{m2} = \frac{2C}{1 - (1 - p)\delta} \qquad (2.32)$$

Under the U-form, the top manager is responsible for coordinating the two reforms in the two regions because middle managers are specialized in only one reform. He thus receives four messages through noisy communication, each corresponding to one reform in one region. When the program is bad (with probability $1 - p$), the reform fails and a new blueprint will be tried in the next period. If the blueprint is good (with probability p), there are three possibilities: (1) With probability λ^4, coordination is successful for both regions A and B. (2) With probability $(1 - \lambda^2)^2$, coordination fails in both A and B. This possibility will give the same outcome as a bad program. (3) With probability $2\lambda^2(1 - \lambda^2)$, coordination for one of the two regions is successful. In this case, knowing that the blueprint is good, the top manager will use the same blueprint for the region for which the coordination failed and solve only the attribute-matching problem in the next period. Hence, the payoff of reform under the U-form is

$$\pi_{u2} = p[\lambda^4 G + 2\lambda^2(1 - \lambda^2)(\frac{G}{2} + \delta\pi) + (1 - \lambda^2)^2\delta\pi_{u2}] + (1 - p)\delta\pi_{u2} \tag{2.33}$$

where π is the expected payoff of reform for one region for a good program, or

$$\pi = \lambda^2\frac{G}{2} + (1 - \lambda^2)\delta\pi = \frac{\lambda^2 G}{2[1 - (1 - \lambda^2)\delta]} \tag{2.34}$$

Using this recursive formula for π, we obtain

$$\pi_{u2} = \frac{pG\lambda^2[1 - \delta(1 - \lambda^2)^2]}{[1 - \delta(1 - \lambda^2)]\{1 - \delta[p(1 - \lambda^2)^2 + (1 - p)]\}} \tag{2.35}$$

When a reform program is introduced in the first period, a setup cost C is paid (instead of $2C$ in the M-form) because only the top manager does attribute matching. With probability $1 - p$ the program is bad, as discovered after one period. With probability $p(1 - \lambda^2)^2$ the program is good, but coordination fails for both regions. In both cases, a new blueprint is tried in the next period. When the blueprint is good and coordination is successful for at least one of the two regions, the program will be known to be good. In such a case, it is assumed that no new setup cost needs to be paid in the next period. Under this assumption, we have

$$c_{u2} = C + \delta[p(1 - \lambda^2)^2 + (1 - p)]c_{u2} = \frac{C}{1 - \delta[p(1 - \lambda^2)^2 + (1 - p)]} \tag{2.36}$$

Comparing the expected net payoff under the M-form and U-form, respectively, $M_2 = \pi_{m2} - c_{m2}$ and $U_2 = \pi_{u2} - c_{u2}$, one sees that $\pi_{m2} \geq \pi_{u2}$ and $c_{u2} \leq c_{m2}$. The M-form benefits from advantages in coordination due to better use of local information but forgoes economies of scale that give the U-form lower costs in implementing reforms. Relevant parameters in the comparison are λ, the communication quality, and the level of setup costs C. When $\lambda \longrightarrow 1$, $U_2 > M_2$ because $\pi_{m2} - \pi_{u2}$ tends toward 0 and $c_{m2} - c_{u2}$ tends toward $\frac{C}{1 - \delta(1 - p)} > 0$. By continuity, there will thus be a threshold value λ^* above which U_2 will dominate M_2. Similarly, if $C \longrightarrow 0$, M_2 will dominate because of its advantages in coordination. However, for λ not too small, if C is big enough, then U_2 will dominate M_2.

We next compare the trade-off between a big bang and a gradual approach to reforms under the M-form organization. Under the gradual approach, a reform is first tried in one region and later extended to the other region, conditional on the success of its implementation in the first region. If the program is a good one, the first period payoff is $(1 - \delta)(G + 1)/2$. In the second period, the same program is then used in the other region with a payoff of $(1 - \delta)G$ in each period. However, if the program is bad, the experimenting region A will get 0 payoff and the nonexperimenting region B will get $(1 - \delta)/2$. In this case, a new experiment in region A will take place again in the next period. Therefore, the expected payoff of the M-form with experimentation is given by

$$\pi_{m1} = p\left[\frac{G}{2} + \frac{1 - \delta}{2} + \frac{\delta G}{2}\right] + (1 - p)\left[\frac{1 - \delta}{2} + \delta\pi_{m1}\right] = \frac{p(1 + \delta)G + (1 - \delta)}{2[1 - \delta(1 - p)]} \qquad \textbf{(2.37)}$$

The setup cost in the first period is C because only region A's manager does attribute matching. If the program is good, region B will use the same program in the next period, and another cost C will be paid then because region B's manager needs to match attributes according to local conditions. With probability $1 - p$, the program is bad, and a new blueprint must be tried. We are then back to the situation of the first period. Hence we get

$$c_{m1} = C + \delta[pC + (1 - p)c_{m1}] = \frac{C(1 + p\delta)}{1 - \delta(1 - p)} \qquad \textbf{(2.38)}$$

Comparing the net payoffs of gradualism $M_1 = \pi_{m1} - c_{m1}$ and big bang $M_2 = \pi_{m2} - c_{m2}$, one gets a simple expression for $M_1 - M_2$:

$$M_1 - M_2 = \frac{C(1 - p\delta) - (pG - 1)\frac{1 - \delta}{2}}{1 - \delta(1 - p)} \qquad \textbf{(2.39)}$$

The first expression in the numerator, $C(1 - p\delta) > 0$ is the option value of waiting to implement the reform in the second region. The setup cost in the second region will be incurred only once a good blueprint has been found. In contrast to the big bang strategy, under gradualism one economizes on setup costs when a blueprint is bad. This effect is very close to the option value of early reversal of section 2.4. In the latter case, one economized on reversal costs in case of a bad aggregate reform outcome, whereas here one economizes on setup costs. In both cases, one economizes on costs that are sunk under big bang in the event of a bad aggregate outcome.

The second expression in the numerator, $(pG - 1)\frac{1 - \delta}{2} > 0$, is the expected cost of delay in implementing both reforms under gradualism. Depending on which of these expressions dominates, $M_1 \gtreqless M_2$. Note that for $p = 1$, $M_1 - M_2 = \frac{(1 - \delta)}{2}[2C - (G - 1)]$. This expression must be less than zero whenever M_2 is worthwhile undertaking, that is, whenever $M_2 > 1$. Indeed, one checks that with $p = 1$, $M_2 > 1 \iff G - 2C > 1$. Thus, gradualism is always dominated whenever $p = 1$. This result is in essence the same as that in section 2.3 on the dominance of big bang in the absence of aggregate uncertainty. Note also that $\frac{\partial(M_1 - M_2)}{\partial p} < 0$ indicating that the lower the probability that the blueprint is good, the bigger the advantage of M_1 over M_2. Indeed, the less certain the blueprint, the higher the option value of waiting by experimenting with the reform first in only one region, and the lower the expected cost of delay. Note finally that the larger is C, the larger is the advantage of M_1 over M_2.

It is important to note that the U-form does not benefit from the gradual approach. Indeed, the option value of early reversal will be absent because, on one hand, whether one implements partial reform or full reform, the same setup costs will have to be incurred at the center. On the other hand, expected benefits cannot be higher but only lower. In fact, owing to complementarities in reform, attribute matching may be an impossible task. To come back to the example of enterprise reform, it may be impossible to implement layoffs and still preserve social peace without introducing a social safety net.

Combining the comparison of U_2 and M_2 and the comparison of M_2 and M_1, one can see that when λ is close enough to 1, $U_2 > \max\{M_1, M_2\}$. Indeed, in that case, noting that $\pi_{m2} > \pi_{m1}$ and that $c_{m1} < c_{m2}$, we have that $\pi_{m2} - \pi_{u2} \longrightarrow 0$ and $c_{m1} - c_{u2} \longrightarrow \frac{Cp\delta}{1 - \delta(1-p)} > 0$. However, if λ is small and C is large, then M_1 will dominate both M_2 and U_2. Indeed, the larger is C, the larger is the option value of waiting, and thus the advantage of M_1 over M_2. If λ is small, however, then the cost advantage of U_2 will be lower while its benefit will be lower.

Qian, Roland, and Xu (1998) also look at the possibility of parallel experimentation with different reform blueprints under the M-form. The general result is that learning is faster and the benefits from imitation of the successful reforms outweigh the duplication costs of trying different experiments at the same time.

In China's transition from plan to market, the role of regional experimentation was very important. A major feature of the successfully implemented Chinese agricultural reform is its trial-and-error, or experimental, approach. The experiments started in some counties in 1978 when the rest of the Chinese rural areas were operating under the collective farming system. A famous experiment started in Fengyang county of Anhui province where the households in a village began to contract with the local government for delivering a fixed quota of grain in exchange for farming on a household basis. The practice was later imitated by other regions and also promoted by the central government. By 1984 almost all farm households across China had adopted this method.

Another example is that of the Special Economic Zones. In 1980, China formally established four such zones: Shenzhen, Zhuhai, Shantou, and Xiamen. The M-form structure made the local governments in Special Economic Zones capable of coordinating activities across all the industries when the rest of the economy was still under central planning. After a few years, most of the successful practices tested in the Special Economic Zones were adopted nationwide.

Privatization of SOEs in China in the mid-1990s has followed a pattern similar to that of agricultural reform in the late 1970s. Experiments began in some counties, such as Yibin of Sichuan, Shunde of Guangdong, and Zhucheng of Shandong, around 1993. County governments have major responsibilities in coordinating all the related policies, such as changes in corporate governance, ownership structure, dealing with bad debts, and the like. The successful experiments have started to be imitated by other regions.

In recent years, China's state sector began to lay off excess workers. About 10 million workers were laid off by the end of 1996, and an additional 5.6 million workers were laid off in the first half of 1997. The Chinese government again took an experimental approach by delegating responsibilities to municipal governments to coordinate the layoff and reemployment of SOE workers (see Qian, Roland, and Xu, 1998, for a more complete description).

While differences in organizational structures may explain the "spatial" gradualism observed in Chinese reforms, there has also been an important element of "sectoral" gradualism in this country, with radical reform in agriculture preceding reform in industrial sectors. Even if East European economies did not have the option of spatial gradualism, because of their U-form organization, the argument modeled in this section does not preclude the possibility of sectoral gradualism in these economies. However, the model does suggest that even forms of sectoral gradualism would have had to be more comprehensive than in China because of the legacy of the organizational form. For example, it would have been impossible to implement agricultural reform as in China without further reforms in sectors that were involved in the coordination of agriculture.

Under the U-form organization of Soviet agriculture, tractors were provided centrally by the so-called MTS stations. The tasks of providing inputs to the farmers and managing their operations, storage, processing, transport, and road infrastructure were all allocated to separate agencies (van Atta, 1993a). Warehouses and processing plants were likely to be located hundreds of miles away from farms. Farming was subordinate to at least eight different ministries (Butterfield, 1990). The political motives for such a design of economic institutions were to prevent the reemergence of independent, private farms by making farming completely dependent on the specialized organization of production. In contrast to China, local authorities had no control over farming and played mainly a role of expediters, throwing themselves into the search for batteries, belts, and harvester blades, and undoing complex knots in the supply system (van Atta, 1993b). There were serious coordination problems. These coordination problems could not be solved within the U-form despite repeated attempts to improve the situation. For example, in the 1980s a structure called RAPO (*raïonnoe agropromyshlennoe obyedinenie*) was created with the task of locally coordinating activities between the various ministries. Nevertheless, the existing U-form structure was kept in place. This innovation led to a conflict of authority between the functional ministries and the new local coordination structure. The RAPOs did not have power over the resources controlled by the ministries, and they were generally ignored by them. Other attempts at reform, such as the introduction of an overarching ministry Gosagroprom, the introduction of agrofirms at a smaller scale, and even the introduction of leasing contracts (*arenda*), also failed to improve coordination (Butterfield, 1990). When the Soviet system collapsed, the U-form organization had left a difficult legacy for potential private Russian farmers: a high average farm size (60 hectares per household compared to $2/3$ hectare in China), an important dependence on machinery and supplies, outside transport and storage, high capital requirements, and so on.

Note finally that, although each economy in Central and Eastern Europe, with the exception of Yugoslavia, was organized like a U-form, specific reform experiments did take place at the level of countries such as the Yugoslav self-management system introduced in 1965 or the Hungarian reform of 1968. In a sense, country-specific experiments can be seen as similar to the regional experiments in China.

Let us also highlight the benefits from parallel experimentation with reforms in the Central and East European context. These countries in effect used parallel experimentation with different policies of privatization and different policies for financial reform.[14] This approach allows much faster learning on the relative costs and benefits of the various policies. If we imagined a different geographical configuration in which all these countries did not exist but were part of Russia, then learning on the relative value of various reform choices would obviously have been much slower.

[14] *However, contrary to the case of the M-form, parallel experimentation under purely decentralized decision on experimentation leads to the well-known free-riding problem. We will see in Chapter 13 that this was not an important issue because Central European countries were also involved in a "transition tournament" to attract FDI and to obtain faster accession to the EU.*

POLITICAL CONSTRAINTS WITHOUT UNCERTAINTY

In this chapter we discuss the role of political constraints on reform strategies in the absence of uncertainty. Because there is no aggregate uncertainty, this situation corresponds to reforms with sure efficiency gains. The issue of experimentation is then assumed away. There is also no individual uncertainty, so that the dynamics of ex ante and ex post political constraints is absent, as voters know exactly whether they will be winners or losers. Even without uncertainty, however, political constraints remain relevant in the design of reform policies.

3.1 EFFICIENCY AND COMPENSATION OF LOSERS FROM REFORM

The first question that is raised spontaneously by economists in this context is the following: If the efficiency gains from reform are certain, why can't they be used to compensate the losers? If they can be, then political constraints should be irrelevant to the design of reform packages because the efficiency gains accruing to the winners from reform should, by definition, always be large enough to compensate the losers. The distributive impact and the efficiency aspects of reform can then in principle be totally separated. The optimal move is thus to go ahead with the full reform program in order to reach efficiency as quickly as possible and to compensate the losers so as to get their support. Since compensation is always possible by definition, political constraints should have no effect on the speed and sequencing of reforms. Only efficiency considerations should come into play.

In reality, however, we rarely observe efficiency-enhancing reforms where all or most losers are compensated. We also observe resistance to reforms even when they are efficiency enhancing. There are various reasons that may explain these observations.

First, there may be excessively high distortionary costs associated with the collection of the revenues necessary to finance transfers for the compensation of losers. Such costs will be all the more likely to occur in less advanced countries where tax collection powers are weak. They will be still more likely in former socialist economies where there was no separate tax administration given that all productive assets were publicly owned. The sum total of the transfers and the associated distortionary costs may then exceed the efficiency gains.

Second, there may be asymmetric information on the losses incurred by various categories of losers. In that case, the compensating agency may not be able to distinguish individuals suffering important losses from those who suffer lighter losses. The latter can then always pretend to be of the former type and receive informational rents. Informational asymmetry can thus increase the costs of compensation up to a point where they exceed the efficiency gains.

A third reason is related to lack of commitment. If the government cannot commit in a credible way to pay compensating transfers to losers, the latter may fear that the government may in the future renege on its commitments to pay. They will then demand to be paid the net present value of compensating transfers at the time reforms are decided. Even when the financing of the flow of transfers may be feasible, paying their net present value most likely is not.

How do political constraints then affect the speed and design of reforms? We will make an important use of the assumption that the government has agenda-setting powers, and we will see how reform proposals can be shaped by such an agenda setter to satisfy political constraints.

Under the agenda-setting assumption, a reformer makes proposals to a population subject to majority rule. However, the agenda setter has monopoly power over the proposal that is voted upon. Proposals are not subject to amendments proposed by other agents. In contrast, the usual Downsian approach of competitive voting assumes that competing candidates propose a policy with the goal of winning support from a majority of voters. The typical case of agenda setting is a referendum on a policy proposal by a government. The importance of agenda setting has been introduced by Romer and Rosenthal (1979) in a public finance context. In the field of social choice, McKelvey (1976) had shown how dynamic agenda setting can allow governments to exploit Condorcet cycles in the presence of myopic voters. Agenda setting, however, can also be powerful with rational, forward-looking voters, as we will see in this chapter.

In the contexts we will be examining in this chapter, the agenda setter can, for example, be a manager or an external investor making restructuring proposals to the firm's workers where the latter have some institutionalized power. Such was the case in countries like Poland and Hungary where reforms in the direction of Yugoslav self-management had been implemented prior to transition. Alternatively, the agenda setter can be a newly elected reformist government that has to get its reform proposals enacted by parliament, where the various constituencies are represented.

In section 3.2 we will make the extreme assumption that no transfers are possible and see how reform sequencing may make reforms feasible under majority voting. In section 3.3, we explore the impact of asymmetric information. In section 3.4, we look at the impact of the possibility of secession on equilibrium transfers and show that secession or the threat of secession can lead to reductions in transfer payments. These various sets of assumptions all shed light in a different way on the effect of political constraints on the speed and sequencing of reforms, as well as on the design of privatization and restructuring programs. Section 3.5 discusses other models of the political economy of reform. Section 3.6 discusses the existing empirical literature on the political economy of transition, and section 3.7 discusses alternative approaches to the political economy of reforms.

3.2   NO TRANSFERS AND MAJORITY VOTING

In the previous chapter, our analysis of the comparison of big bang and gradualism was made in the context of aggregate uncertainty, where sequencing of reforms can be used to take advantage of the option value of early reversal and thus reduces the costs of experimenting with reforms when there is aggregate uncertainty. In the absence of aggregate uncertainty, gradualism will necessarily imply inefficiencies, since efficiency-enhancing reforms will be delayed. There are, however, conditions under which gradualism may also be optimal when the efficiency gains from reform are certain. The main reason is that reform sequencing can be used to implement divide-and-rule tactics in a context of dynamic agenda setting.

3.2.1   DIVIDE-AND-RULE TACTICS

We first show how an agenda setter can exploit shifting majorities to implement divide-and-rule tactics. We will use a highly simplified version of a model by Wei (1993) that is based on Fernandez and Rodrik (1991).

Consider a reform process that consists of trade liberalization in an economy with two import-competing sectors. Full efficiency requires liberalization (tariff removal) of both sectors. Consumers gain from reform, but producers in import-competing sectors suffer net losses because of output contraction leading to job losses. We do not model the economic part of the model but look instead at reduced-form payoffs to concentrate on the politics. Assume three groups: group 0 being voters not working in sectors 1 and 2, and groups 1 and 2 being workers from the two import-competing sectors. Assume a continuum of voters in each group, and assume for simplicity that each group has a unit mass. Table 3.1 shows the assumptions about net gains from reforms 1 and 2, representing liberalization of sector 1 and sector 2.

Payoffs $g_i > 0 > l_i$, $i = 1, 2$ are purely deterministic and known to all. As in the previous chapter, the discount rate is δ. Workers in an import-competing sector thus lose from liberalization of their sector but gain as consumers from liberalization of the other sector. Nevertheless, overall these two groups suffer a net loss from reform because their losses as producers outweigh their gains as consumers. Otherwise, everybody gains

TABLE 3.1 SEQUENCING A REFORM PACKAGE THAT HURTS A MAJORITY

	Group 0	Group 1	Group 2
Reform 1	g_1	l_1	g_1
Reform 2	g_2	g_2	l_2
Reforms 1 + 2	$g_1 + g_2 > 0$	$l_1 + g_2 < 0$	$g_1 + l_2 < 0$

from liberalization as a consumer. Overall, net efficiency gains are positive: $2g_1 + l_1 > 0$, $2g_2 + l_2 > 0$. Without loss of generality, we assume that reform 2 brings more efficiency gains than reform 1: $2g_2 + l_2 > 2g_1 + l_1$.

Under majority rule, two groups out of three must vote in favor of the government's proposals to have them enacted. The government is assumed to be interested in maximizing efficiency gains subject to political constraints. Assume that there are only two periods and that in each period it can only offer either the status quo, or a single reform, or both reforms. By assumption, it is unable to commit to future proposals, and private agents cannot commit to intertemporal contracts. Transfers are assumed to have such large distortionary costs that they are infeasible. Once a reform has been accepted, it is assumed to be irreversible.

Given that $l_1 + g_2$ and $l_2 + g_1$ are negative, a big bang strategy proposing both reforms at once at $t = 0$, the best from the efficiency point of view, will always be opposed by a majority. A gradualist strategy, however, with reform 1 proposed at $t = 0$ and reform 2 proposed at $t = 1$, will satisfy political constraints and get majority support. Why? Once reform 1 has been adopted, one can easily see that a majority (groups 0 and 1) will vote for reform 2. The question is whether group 2 will vote for reform 1 today, in which case reform 1 will have majority support. If group 2 opposes reform, then it will be blocked. However, in that event, in the second period, the government will credibly propose reform 2 at $t = 1$ and get majority support. Workers from sector 2 are then better off voting for reform 1 in period 1. Indeed, they know that reform 2 will pass at $t = 1$ anyway and they are then better off having a total intertemporal payoff of $g_1 + \delta l_2$ rather than only δl_2.

This is a good example of divide-and-rule tactics where the agenda setter uses different majorities in different periods to get a reform package through that is opposed by a majority. In this case, even though groups 1 and 2 oppose reform, the agenda setter is able to play on their conflicts of interests to divide them. Thus, sector 1 gains from reform 2 and vice versa. The government can therefore make the credible out-of-equilibrium threat of enacting reform 2 at $t = 1$ with the support of groups 0 and 1 in case reform 1 is opposed at $t = 0$, which enables it to get support from group 2 for reform 1 at $t = 0$. Since agents are assumed not to be able to make intertemporal commitments, divide-and-rule tactics are subgame perfect. Voters from group 1 would like to obtain support from group 2 for opposing reforms at $t = 0$ but cannot commit not to vote for reform 2 at $t = 1$. Group 2 voters then have no interest in opposing reform 1 at $t = 0$. If voters from groups 1 and

2 are able to collude, then divide-and-rule tactics won't work. However, it is not clear how they would be able to enforce a collusive agreement among themselves.

The preceding result, however, strongly depends on the finite-horizon structure of the game. Once, we have an infinite horizon for this stationary game, things are different. Indeed, once one reform has been enacted, the second one will go through immediately afterward, since only the workers in that sector will oppose it. Therefore, proposals of reform for a single sector will also fail (provided individual voters do not vote for weakly dominated strategies): workers in the other sector know they will be hurt in the next period!

The divide-and-rule tactics result, however, can be obtained in an even more powerful way in an infinite-horizon framework, as shown by Dewatripont and Roland (1997). Assume that there is an exogenous date at which one of the sectors, say, sector 1, is expected to contract. For example, the coal sector will disappear one day because of depletion of coal reserves. Call that date t_1. At the beginning of period t_1, when sector 1 closes, the government can enlist the support of types 0 and 1 to close sector 2, since workers in sector 1 have just become consumers. Since workers in both sectors expect to lose their job at t_1, each group is ready to vote for closing the other sector at $t_1 - 1$. Partial reform is possible at this point, even though full reform is not. Assume, without loss of generality, that the government would rather close sector 2 first. In that case, given the continuation equilibrium, reform 1 is possible at $t_1 - 2$. Indeed, type 2 workers expect to lose their job at $t_1 - 1$ anyway, and they gain as consumers if reform 1 is adopted at $t_1 - 2$, rather than at t_1. This argument can be repeated, allowing the government to get reform 2 through at $t_1 - 3$, reform 1 at $t_1 - 4$, and so forth. Therefore, the equilibrium involves immediate gradual reform, completed in two periods, with reform 1 enacted in period 1 if t_1 is odd, or reform 2 enacted in period 1 if t_1 is even. This unraveling argument is so powerful as to allow full reform to be completed within two periods, as in the McKelvey (1976) setup with myopic voters, except that here voters are completely forward looking!

Note that sequencing of reforms, though a natural instrument of divide-and-rule tactics, is not a necessary condition for such tactics. The latter can also be used under simultaneous voting and thus also under a big bang strategy with a properly designed voting mechanism. Thus, let us come back to the finite-horizon framework and assume that both reforms are submitted simultaneously to voters and that they must vote separately on each reform. In that case, the only Nash equilibrium involves both reforms being voted by a majority. Indeed, it is a dominant strategy for sector 1 to vote for reform 2. Whether sector 2 voted in favor of or against reform 1, sector 1 always gains from voting for reform 2. The same reasoning applies for sector 2.

The analysis of divide-and-rule tactics not only has general relevance, but also applies in the transition context. It may indeed provide an explanation for the ability shown by a great number of managers to impose major layoffs in firms with significant worker control (Pinto, Belka, and Krajewski, 1993; Estrin, Schaffer, and Singh, 1992; Carlin, Van Reenen, and Wolfe, 1995). While the literature on restructuring explores the incentives of managers of state-owned enterprises to downsize output and employment, the question of how managers of worker-controlled firms are able to overcome resistance to layoffs has so far received little attention.

3.2.2 PACKAGING REFORMS TO GAIN MAJORITY SUPPORT

The preceding example does not imply that gradualism is always politically easier than big bang. Since big bang implies greater economic efficiency, it is quite possible that it commands majority support. It can even be the case that a big bang reform that packages several reforms together commands majority support while sequencing reforms may lead to reform blockage, even in cases where big bang does not necessarily yield a higher joint outcome. The following example, based on Martinelli and Tommasi (1997) shows how.

Modify Table 3.1 by assuming (1) that reform 2 alone hurts a majority (groups 1 and 2) but (2) that the joint outcome of both reforms is favorable to group 2 ($g_1 + l_2 - \Delta > 0$) and thus to a majority. Assume that $\delta = 1$ so that delay is not costly. Assume that gradualism with a sequencing of reform 1 before reform 2 yields a better joint economic outcome and that big bang entails a loss of Δ to each group. For example, big bang may create economic disruption, a case we will analyze in detail in Chapters 7 and 8. Under those assumptions, big bang is nevertheless the only subgame-perfect equilibrium, and gradualism will lead to reform blockage after reform 1.[1] This blockage will be inefficient if the joint outcome of big bang ($2g_1 + g_2 + l_1 + 2l_2 - 3\Delta$) is higher than that of partial reform ($2g_1 + l_1$), that is, if $g_2 + 2l_2 > 3\Delta$ (see Table 3.2).

What big bang does in this case is to package reforms so that a reform like reform 2 that hurts a majority is not proposed in isolation but as part of a package that benefits a majority. A sequencing GR_{12} will get blocked in the middle—that is, after reform 1—because it will be rejected by groups 1 and 2, whereas big bang will be rejected only by group 1. Reversing the sequencing would not help. If reform 2 were proposed first, the best the government could do after its rejection would be to propose reform 1. Unlike the previous case, this proposal would not act as a threat to change the vote of any group. Group 2 is strictly better off having only reform 1 implemented rather than both.

Martinelli and Tommasi illustrate this case with the example of trade and fiscal or public sector reform. They look at a case where it is optimal to first implement fiscal reform and lay off redundant public sector bureaucrats and to implement trade reform later. The reason is that by implementing both reforms simultaneously, higher unemployment is created, whereas with appropriate sequencing, layoffs in government and in the import-competing sector can be smoothed over time. Assuming veto power of interest groups, trade reform would be blocked by the import-competing sector, whereas both reforms can be accepted jointly if the loser from each reform gains from the other reform.

Given the opposite results on the packaging of reforms, as compared to divide-and-rule tactics, it is worthwhile briefly to dwell on the conditions under which the latter or the former is valid. The main difference is that in the divide-and-rule case, there are conflicts of interests between various groups with respect to different reforms. We had an example where one group gained from the first reform and lost from the second and the

[1] Note that this case is similar to the interim status quo bias discussed in Chapter 2.

TABLE 3.2 PACKAGING REFORMS TO GAIN MAJORITY SUPPORT

	Group 0	Group 1	Group 2
Reform 1	g_1	l_1	g_1
Reform 2	g_2	l_2	l_2
Big bang	$g_1 + g_2 - \Delta > 0$	$l_1 + l_2 - \Delta < 0$	$g_1 + l_2 - \Delta > 0$
GR_{12}	$g_1 + g_2 > 0$	$l_1 + l_2 < 0$	$g_1 + l_2 > 0$

second group gained from the second and lost from the first. By packaging both reforms, one unites these two groups who jointly lose from both reforms. On the contrary, by separating the decisions on the reforms, one is able to exploit the conflict of interest and to mobilize the majority that exists in favor of each reform. The case where packaging is optimal is one where it is not possible to find a majority for each reform and where it is necessary to put several reforms together to obtain the support of a majority for the package as a whole.

3.3 TRANSFERS AND ASYMMETRIC INFORMATION

So far in this chapter, reforms have been considered without introducing the possibility of explicit transfers from winners to losers or, equivalently, under the assumption that transfers are prohibitively costly. We can relax this assumption while maintaining a net resource cost of transfers (e.g., because they are financed by distortionary taxation), denoted in percentage terms.

In this section, we show that under asymmetric information over winners and losers, gradualism can be used to reveal information and thus to reduce the amount of transfers, at the cost of delay in reaching allocative efficiency. There will thus be an intertemporal trade-off between the speed of reforms, and thus the speed at which efficiency is reached, and the net present value of compensating transfers.

The issue of speed of reform and costs of compensating transfers can best be highlighted by comparing restructuring policies in East Germany and other transition economies. In the former GDR, restructuring has proceeded very fast with massive layoffs at an early stage of transition. Employment fell by nearly one half between 1989 and 1992 (Sinn and Sinn, 1993)! This policy, however, has been associated with massive transfers from West Germany. Net transfers to East Germany were 128 billion deutsche marks in 1991, 145 billion DM in 1992, and 176 billion DM in 1993. These transfers represent, respectively, 65, 65.5, and 76.5 percent of East German GNP (Gros and Steinherr, 1995)! They have been continuing throughout the 1990s, and in 1998 more than 1 billion DM of transfers had already been paid to East Germany. In contrast, in Central and Eastern Europe, where such massive transfers were not available, layoffs have been more gradual.

TABLE 3.3 REFORMS UNDER ASYMMETRIC INFORMATION

	Group 0	Group 1	Group 2
Net-present-value-payoff	$g > 0$	$\underline{l} < 0$	$\bar{l} < 0$

Within the latter group of countries, "faster" reformers such as Poland, Hungary, and the Czech Republic have been facing higher increases in social security expenditures (unemployment benefits and mainly pensions) because of a higher level of restructuring compared to "slower" reformers that have maintained higher levels of subsidies in ailing industries (Coricelli, 1995).

The following analysis, based on Dewatripont and Roland (1992a, 1992b), allows us to understand the trade-off between increasing the speed of reform and increasing the net present value of transfers.

In order to avoid the divide-and-rule effects of the previous section and to highlight better the effects of asymmetric information, assume that reforms must be unanimously approved to be enacted. In other words, reforms are constrained to be Pareto improving. Consider again a continuum of voters with three types of unit mass each. The net-present-value payoffs of the reform are as shown in Table 3.3.

We assume $\bar{l} < \underline{l}$. We can think of the reform as restructuring of the economy with type 0 workers keeping their job in the part of the economy that is in good health and the other types having to suffer transition costs to move to other new sectors (which are higher for type 2 than for type 1). The benefits of reform to group 0 can be thought of as general equilibrium effects that accrue only after sectoral reallocation has taken place. Workers from groups 1 and 2 thus need to be induced to change sectors for the benefits of reform to materialize. Transfers can then be interpreted as an exit bonus to compensate those groups for the net losses from changing sectors. This framework, however, is abstract enough to apply to many other different kinds of situations. Call $\lambda > 0$ the distortionary cost of transfers.

In a single-period horizon with complete information and minimal targeted transfers to compensate losers, workers from group 1 will receive $-\underline{l}$ and workers from group 2 will receive $-\bar{l}$, the minimum amount of transfers necessary to make them indifferent to accepting or refusing reform. A Pareto-improving reform will then go through if and only if

$$\left(g + \underline{l} + \bar{l}\right) + \lambda\left(\underline{l} + \bar{l}\right) > 0 \tag{3.1}$$

The first expression between parentheses represents the net gains, whereas the second represents the deadweight losses associated with transfers. Even if equation (3.1) is positive, the reform may still face problems of acceptability as a result of asymmetric information. If each individual is assumed to have private information concerning his or her own type, workers can self-select by choosing to keep their job or to take the exit bonus. In any case, it is not possible to discriminate between types 1 and 2 if they both leave: they will always take the highest exit bonus available. Total transfers will thus be $- 2\bar{l}$. Workers with loss of $-\underline{l}$ thus reap an informational rent of $-(\bar{l} - \underline{l})$, and the distortionary costs of transfers are now higher. For the reform to be feasible, we must have

$$\left(g + \underline{l} + \bar{l}\right) + 2\lambda\bar{l} \; > 0 \tag{3.2}$$

which is smaller than expression (3.1). This result could induce the government to go for the alternative of "partial" reform that allows type 2 workers to keep their jobs, so that only type 1 workers suffer transition costs. Workers with lower transition costs can more easily be induced to exit: they only need a compensation of $\bar{l}$. The benefit of such partial reform is that it eliminates the informational rent for workers of group 1. The cost is that it is less efficient. We capture this lower efficiency by assuming that partial reform involves an allocative loss of Δ relative to full reform. The net payoff of partial reform is then

$$\left(g + \underline{l} + \bar{l} - \Delta\right) + \lambda\underline{l} \tag{3.3}$$

Since partial reform is less efficient than full reform, its net payoff must be smaller than that of full reform under perfect information, that is, $(g + \underline{l} + \bar{l} - \Delta) + \lambda\underline{l} < (g + \underline{l} + \bar{l}) + \lambda(\underline{l} + \bar{l})$, which implies that $(\Delta + \lambda\bar{l}) > 0$. Nevertheless, under asymmetric information, since the first best cannot be attained, the trade-off is between higher efficiency under full reform and lower rents under partial reform. Comparing expressions (3.2) and (3.3), one sees that partial reform may dominate full reform if

$$\Delta + \lambda\bar{l} \; < -\lambda\left(\bar{l} - \underline{l}\right) \tag{3.4}$$

where the left-hand side represents the efficiency loss under partial reform relative to the first best and the right-hand side represents the informational rents conceded under full reform relative to the first best. This trade-off between allocative efficiency and rent extraction is well known from the adverse selection literature (see, e.g., Caillaud et al., 1988). It was first applied in the political economy context by Lewis, Feenstra, and Ware (1990), who modeled reform of agricultural policy, an important policy topic in Europe. Because of asymmetric information on the losses of individual farmers when agricultural prices are liberalized, farmers who lose less from reform are able to extract rents because of the necessity of compensating farmers who suffer bigger losses.

The Dewatripont and Roland (1992a, 1992b) model takes the basic setup further by dwelling on an interesting dynamic implication of this trade-off between partial and full reform: whenever inequality (3.4) holds, that is, whenever partial reform dominates full reform in a one-period context, gradualism emerges as the optimal time-consistent reform package.

Indeed, without the ability to commit to partial reform, the government will propose full reform, once partial reform has been implemented and type 1 workers have left. This proposal will always be in the interest of the government because $\Delta + \lambda \bar{l} > 0$, that is, because the cost of compensating group 2 workers is lower than the efficiency gain from full reform. Partial reform is thus not time consistent, and gradual reform will then be the outcome with partial reform today and group 1 leaving and full reform one period later with group 2 leaving. In that case, type 1 workers will not be ready to leave earlier against a compensation of $-\underline{l}$. Indeed, they could choose not to take the exit bonus in period 1 and wait one period, pretend to be a type 2 worker and receive the exit bonus of $-\bar{l}$. In order to be indifferent between leaving today and tomorrow, type 1 workers must receive an exit bonus compensating for their loss if they leave today plus the discounted rent they would receive if they left tomorrow; in other words, they must receive an exit bonus of $-\underline{l} - \delta(\bar{l} - \underline{l}) = -[(1 - \delta)\underline{l} + \delta\bar{l}]$. Gradual reform, with partial reform today and incentive-compatible transfers for group 1, will then give a net payoff of

$$(1 - \delta)(g + \underline{l} + \bar{l} - \Delta) + \delta(g + \underline{l} + \bar{l}) + \lambda[(1 - \delta)\underline{l} + \delta\bar{l}] + \lambda\delta\bar{l} \qquad \textbf{(3.5)}$$

Clearly, expression (3.5) is a convex combination of equations (3.2) and (3.3) (with weights δ and $1 - \delta$), and gradual reform dominates full reform whenever, in a static context, partial reform dominates full reform. Gradualism, while not as good as maintained partial reform, dominates a big bang strategy and is the time-consistent optimum whenever budget considerations are important enough (i.e., λ is high enough).

Hayri (1997) has worked out extensions of the Dewatripont-Roland model under different layoff policies.

3.4   SECESSION AND TRANSFERS

When transfers are too costly to allow reform to go through, it may lead to the temptation of secession, especially if the gains and losses from reform are expected to be unequally distributed geographically. This section illustrates some of the tensions in transition economies created by the different geographical distribution of proreform and antireform interests, contributing to the breakup of Czechoslovakia, Yugoslavia, and the USSR. Even though ethnic conflicts have undoubtedly played an important role in these secessions, conflicts on reform strategies and interregional transfers have also played a prominent role after the introduction of democracy in these countries. The breakup of Czechoslovakia is a clear illustration of such conflicts. In this section, we show not only why differences in local majorities on preferred reform strategies may lead to secession. We also show that the threat of secession itself can be used as an instrument to reduce

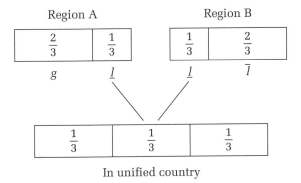

FIGURE 3.1 GEOGRAPHICAL INEQUALITY IN GAINS AND LOSSES FROM REFORM

transfers. In effect, the possibility of secession changes the status quo and can thus be exploited by a reform-minded agenda setter.

We thus adapt the preceding model to introduce differences in the geographical distribution of winners and losers from reform. Assume as before a reform with net distributive gains of g, $\underline{l}$, and $\bar{l}$ each to one-third of the population. In the unified country, a reform-minded agenda setter can get the reform accepted by a majority provided it is paired with transfers of $-\underline{l}$ to losers. We assume as before that there is asymmetric information about the losers so that transfers must be paid not only to the $\underline{l}$ type but also to the $\bar{l}$ type. This assumption is not really necessary here but does not complicate the setup. Under that reform program, the group of winners will thus have to be taxed $-(1+\lambda)2\underline{l}$ to finance these transfers. It is assumed that λ is not too big so that the net gains of winners $g + (1+\lambda)2\underline{l}$ are still positive. The median group is made indifferent between reform and status quo, whereas those losing most, the $\bar{l}$ type, will experience a net loss of $\bar{l} - \underline{l}$ and thus vote against reform.

Against this benchmark of reform in a unified country, assume now that there are two regions of equal size and that the geographical distribution of gains and losses is as follows: all those with payoff g and one-half of those with payoff $\underline{l}$ live in region A, whereas the other half of those with payoff $\underline{l}$ and all those with payoff $\bar{l}$ live in region B. In region A, a majority (including the median voter) gets g, whereas in region B a majority gets $\bar{l}$. This example is illustrated in Figure 3.1. Median voters in each region are thus of different types than the median voter in the unified country.

Assume now that after a reform proposal is voted in the unified country but before that reform is implemented, a referendum on secession is held in each region. After secession, each independent country is free to pursue its own policy of reforms. Call s the cost of secession or, equivalently in this simple setup, the cost associated with implementation of reform in one region only.

What would be the incentive to secede for each region after a decision in the unified country to adopt the reform with transfers of $-\underline{l}$? One sees immediately that a majority in region A may consider the option of seceding in order to adopt a reform involving no transfer payments at all. This would be the case if the cost of secession to the median voter in region A is smaller than the transfers these voters avoid paying by seceding, that is, if

$$s < -(1 + \lambda s)2\underline{l} \qquad \text{(3.6)}$$

However, a majority in region B may also want to secede but for a different motive: in order to have no reform at all. Indeed, after secession, any reform proposal would be rejected in region B because all lose from reform, and thus no group can be taxed to compensate the losers. Secession would take place if the cost of secession to the median voter in region B is smaller than the gain from secession (avoiding the net loss from reform $\bar{l} - \underline{l}$ in the unified country), that is, if

$$s < -(\bar{l} - \underline{l}) \qquad \text{(3.7)}$$

The possibility of secession in a region may of course influence the agenda setter's choice of reform proposal. The equilibrium reform proposal (and also the reform outcome in this deterministic setup) must now not only take the simple political constraint of majority acceptance into account, but it must also take into account the possibility of secession in either region. The reformist agenda setter may indeed want to prevent secession because of the inefficiencies involved. To prevent region A from seceding implies an upper bound on the amount of transfers t paid to the losers such that the costs of secession are always greater than the benefits:

$$t \leq \frac{s}{2(1 + \lambda)} \qquad \text{(3.8)}$$

To prevent region B from seceding, however, compensating transfers must satisfy a lower bound, that is, compensation for the reform losses that would be avoided under secession minus the costs from secession:

$$t \geq -\bar{l} - s \qquad \text{(3.9)}$$

Putting together these two constraints, one gets

$$-\bar{l} - s \leq t \leq \frac{s}{2(1 + \lambda)} \qquad \text{(3.10)}$$

If s is small enough, the set of acceptable t's may be empty, and secession may be unavoidable because of the contradictory requirements of the proreform majority in region A and the antireform majority in region B. If s is higher, the possibility of secession may still alter the initial reform proposal compared to the benchmark case without secession. In particular, a reform-minded agenda setter who wants to minimize transfers, subject to passing the reforms, can set $t = -\bar{l} - s$ and get it accepted by a majority. All those in region A will gain: the amount of transfers paid by the winners will be smaller than those that would make them indifferent between seceding or not. The minority of those who get $\underline{l}$ in region A will gain compared to secession, since they receive some transfers and avoid the costs of secession. However, since t makes those who get $\bar{l}$ indifferent between secession and reform, agents with $\underline{l}$ in region B will even be better off compared to secession. We can see that the possibility of secession permits reducing the amount of transfers paid to the losers from reform because it changes the status quo. Without the possibility of secession, the median voter must get compensation for his losses from reform. With the possibility of secession, a lower level of transfers can be voted. Indeed, in case of rejection of the reform proposal, there will be secession in A, and the $\underline{l}$ in regions A and B will be strictly worse off compared to voting for the proposal, knowing that the latter will not lead to secession.

The redrawing of borders inside Europe after the fall of the Berlin wall has renewed the attention of economists to questions of secession and political integration. Buchanan and Faith (1987) and Berkowitz (1997) show how the taxation power of central government can be strongly reduced by secession threats from regions or states. Treisman (1996) has shown that in the context of Russian transition, higher transfer payments have gone to the more secessionist regions to keep them inside the federation, especially regions like the Tatar and Bashkir republics, where the leaders were politically hostile toward Yeltsin.

Bolton and Roland (1996, 1997) study more generally the effect of differences in income distribution across regions on the incentives to secede. In the spirit of the previous example, it is shown that if the efficiency losses from separation are relatively small, secession may be unavoidable because of contradictory requirements of majorities in the different regions: a majority in a region where pretax income distribution is relatively egalitarian may want to secede to reduce the level of redistributive taxation, whereas a majority in a less egalitarian region may want to secede in order to increase the level of redistribution. Alesina and Spolaore (1997) study the optimal size of nations as resulting from a trade-off between economies of scale in the provision of public goods on the one hand and a composition of public goods that is closer to the preferences of individuals on the other hand (see also Alesina, Spolaore, and Wacziarg, 1997). Casella and Feinstein (1990) and Wei (1991) similarly look at the trade-off between the efficiency advantages of trade in a unified country and the costs of having public goods less close to the preferences of individuals. They analyze how this trade-off evolves with economic development.

The Bolton and Roland model has been extended in several directions. Rivière (1997) explicitly introduces size considerations and economy-of-scale effects in public goods provision. She finds that secession is less likely when regions are of unequal size or when there are many regions. The reason is that a small region relative to the country may have political incentives to secede because of a difference between the regional and the national majority's preferences but that the losses in economies of scale are too big to make secession worthwhile. Alternatively, a big region relative to the country will arithmetically have a majority with preferences close to the majority in the country. Fidrmuc (1998c) has applied the model to the analysis of macroeconomic shocks in a monetary union. The literature on optimal currency areas suggests that fiscal policy should be used to smooth away the effects of asymmetric shocks. Adding politics to the model, however, leads to a more gloomy conclusion, since asymmetric shocks will increase the political divergences between preferences of majorities across regions and increase secessionist tendencies.

While interest in the issues of secession and political integration has strongly revived with transition and the breakup of former communist countries, these issues are to a great extent orthogonal to reforms and are by themselves an important topic of research in their own right. A better understanding of these issues is fundamental for understanding the political architecture of democracy in today's world of globalization and for the stability of the world's economic prosperity itself. The prosperity achieved in the late nineteenth century was brutally halted by World War I, a devastating war between sovereign nations that cost the lives of dozens of millions and led to the advent of barbarian fascist regimes. Can such episodes be avoided in the future, and how? What is the role of international organizations like the United Nations, the World Trade Organization, and so on, and supranational structures like the European Union? How can stable peace and free trade be credibly enforced across sovereign countries? These are burning questions that will be with us for years to come.

3.5   OTHER MODELS ON POLITICAL CONSTRAINTS AND THE SPEED OF TRANSITION

Rodrik (1995) proposes a model to analyze why reform may initially benefit from popular support but may later suffer from backlash and reversal. The framework is one where a reduction in subsidies leads to a reduction in the size of the public sector and to an expansion of the private sector, but at an exogenous lower rate so that unemployment ensues. Subsidies to the public sector are financed by taxes on the private sector. In the beginning of transition, cuts in subsidies can be supported by workers in the public sector because they have a high likelihood of ending up in the private sector. Lower taxes increase both their likelihood of finding a job in the private sector and their income in it. By the same token, the unemployed always favor reform because they can only gain from a reduction in taxes. In the model, the likelihood that a worker in the state sector will end up in the private sector declines as the latter grows. Therefore, it is possible that at some point state sector workers will become opposed to reform because their expected gain from high subsidies in the state sector exceeds their expected gain from lower taxes due to the lower likelihood of getting a private sector job. Rodrik's model delivers an interesting insight, namely, understanding the change in attitude of state sector workers during the reform process. It thus also proposes an explanation of both the wide support for radical reforms in Central Europe early in transition and of the observed backlash against reformers observed later. The model, however, relies on myopic voting behavior. When voting on subsidy reductions at a given moment in time, workers indeed vote without taking into account the effect of future policy reversal on today's votes. Ideally, in the context of transition, one would like to have a dynamic general equilibrium model, incorporating both economic and political decisions of agents in the economy rationally taking into account future expectations regarding economic and political variables. The Fernandez and Rodrik (1991) model does so in fact, but one would like a similar model with intertemporal votes on redistribution policies rather than simply on reform continuation versus reversal. This is far from an easy task.

A model slightly different from the one by Rodrik has been provided by Mehlum (1998). He builds a simple general equilibrium model of consumption and savings with Leontieff production function and CRRA utility function. Taxes on private producers also finance wages in the public sector. The policy variable is the path of reduction of the size of the public sector. Given assumptions on technology and preferences, the capital stock can immediately adjust to a reduction in the size of the state sector. Two policies are compared: a first policy called big bang where the state sector is eliminated in one period and a gradual policy where it is eliminated in two periods. It is assumed that reform is reversed under either policy if the wage level falls below a certain minimum wage. The idea is that there is a rigid floor to wages and that unemployment is created whenever the equilibrium wage falls below that minimum wage. The political assumption is that unemployment always leads to a rejection of reform. Two main results are derived. First of all, a big bang program may be unfeasible compared to a gradual one because the former may require an initial drop in wages that is too large. Second, gradual programs with a strong initial reduction of the state sector may lead to multiplicity of equilibria depending on whether reform is expected to be canceled or not. Expectation of cancellation of reform, whereby future reductions in the size of the state sector are frozen, is self-fulfilling because it leads to an interest rate increase and a wage contraction compared to when reform is not canceled. A fully credible reform path is one where the initial reduction in the size of the state sector is moderate enough so that expectations of cancellation do not lead to cancellation. The model is extremely simple and tractable and incorporates basic general equilibrium considerations. However, even though economic variables fully take into account expectations about the future, the analysis of political constraints is not explicit. Acceptance or rejection of reforms is not explicitly derived from a comparison of expected utilities of different policies. It is simply assumed that reforms get rejected when either unemployment or wage reductions are above a certain threshold.

Dehejia (1995) more rigorously models political constraints within a dynamic general equilibrium model of trade liberalization inspired by Mussa (1978). It is assumed that approval of workers from the import-competing sector, which will face a contraction in size with trade liberalization, is politically necessary. The political constraint is thus that at any point in time, the discounted lifetime value of workers in that sector exceeds that under the status quo, whereby the status quo is defined by the existing tariff at that time period in the import-competing sector. As in the Fernandez and Rodrik (1991) model, workers in the import-competing sector face adjustment (training) costs when moving to the exporting sector. Here gradualism can be politically feasible when big bang is not, mainly because it smooths the adjustment costs for workers.

3.6 SOME EMPIRICAL LITERATURE ON POLITICAL CONSTRAINTS

There is a small but growing empirical literature on political constraints in transition. Much of this literature does not try to verify or discriminate between existing theories. Several papers nevertheless deliver interesting and relevant insights on how political support is endogenously determined.

Fidrmuc (1998a, 1998b) has analyzed the political support for reforms in the Czech Republic (1992 and 1996), Slovakia (1992 and 1994), Poland (1993, 1995, and 1997), and Hungary (1994 and 1998). He makes use of country-level data in these countries to analyze the effects of economic variables resulting from reforms on the votes received by different parties. His main findings, based on estimations using seemingly unrelated regressions, are that the support for right-wing reformist parties is negatively affected by unemployment and the weight of retirees, blue-collar workers, and agricultural workers but is positively affected by the existing size of the private sector, a higher share of white-collar workers, or of people with university education. These findings indeed indicate that there is a regular pattern of perceived winners and losers from reform and that political support for reforms depends on the balance between losers and winners. A dynamic analysis reveals that accountability effects are present and that changes in votes between two elections reveal that swing voters punish incumbents for a bad performance in unemployment or wage growth or reward them for good performance.

The results of Fidrmuc suggest that the stability of the Klaus government as compared to other governments of economies in transition may be related to the lower unemployment rate in the Czech Republic as compared to other transition economies, an issue analyzed in depth by several papers (see, e.g., Ham, Svejnar, and Terrell, 1998; Munich, Svejnar, and Terrell, 1998; and Sorm and Terrell, 1999).

A very interesting empirical analysis has been done by Morduch and Sicular (1999) with respect to the interests of Chinese bureaucrats in the reform process. Contrary to claims about Eastern Europe made by Hellman (1998) that bureaucrats are winners as a result of initial reforms and block further reforms to maintain the high rents they have received from partial reforms, in China rents to bureaucrats increase with the pace of reforms while the benefits of reform are shared with the population at large. The evidence comes from Zouping county. The authors show in a random-effect panel estimate using generalized least squares that the status of village cadre produces higher income (an estimated 18 percent), controlling for location, time, education, and other characteristics. These are thus rents accruing to bureaucrats. Moreover, income for village cadres increases in years where there is an acceleration of reform. The status of village cadre is the most important explanatory variable for higher income of party members (together with location). The source of this higher income of village cadres is mainly a higher wage income in nonagricultural activities, mainly in township and village enterprises (TVEs). Finally, it is shown that income is mainly derived from nonpolitical variables and that increases in income are spread equally among all quintiles except for the effect of party membership, which has a minor impact on overall income, however.

It is worthwhile mentioning here also the case study of Russia by Shleifer and Treisman (2000) looking at the impact of political constraints on reform strategies. As in this chapter, they look at the need for reformers to receive sufficient support for reform proposals. Whereas this chapter and the previous one have emphasized the importance of getting the support of voters, they emphasize the need to get the support of a sufficient number of interest groups in the transition process. They analyze how it was done for privatization and stabilization and how it was not done for tax reform.

Opposition to privatization in Russia could be overcome by designing the privatization program so as to give stakes to managers and workers. This policy was put into effect with the so-called variant 2 of the privatization law, which allowed workers and managers to buy a majority of the shares in their enterprise at a very low price, basically giving them control over the assets. Variant 2 turned out to be the main mode of privatization in Russia. The support of regional governments that had been opposed was bought by giving them control over small-scale privatization. We discuss in more detail in the next chapter the political economy of privatization.

In Russia political opposition to stabilization was extremely important, and attempts by reformers in power to introduce stabilization packages generally failed to satisfy political constraints. It was only in 1995 that the first real stabilization successes could be obtained. Shleifer and Treisman argue that one of the main reasons was that the banking sector's opposition to stabilization could be overcome. The banking sector had been getting huge rents from inflation, mainly because of the negative real interest rates paid to depositors. Easterly and Veiera-da-Cunha (1994) estimate that the financial sector received about 8 percent of GDP in 1992 through arbitrage exploiting the negative real interest rates paid to depositors. Their support for stabilization policies was bought by giving the banks other forms of profit opportunities via the GKOs, short-term government Treasury bills with very high real interest rates. These were a true present to the banks, since access to GKO auctions was restricted to preselected dealers, and both foreign investors and ordinary Russians were prevented from participating. The GKOs made up for the loss of rents from reduced inflation and gave the banks a stake in fighting inflation to keep the GKO returns high.

However, by giving rents to commercial banks to get their support for stabilization, and also through loans for a shares privatization scheme whereby commercial bankers got control over huge industrial assets,[2] the Yeltsin administration helped some of the commercial bankers to build enormous financial and industrial empires, developing into the system of the "oligarchs." The oligarchs then became a major force of opposition to tax reform and effective tax collection.

[2] This privatization involved borrowing by government against the collateral of shares in state enterprises with a substantial premium in case of government default, which was expected to occur. This was extremely controversial not only because of the rents derived but also because some banks were at times both organizers of the auction and participants in the bidding.

3.7 ALTERNATIVE APPROACHES TO THE POLITICAL ECONOMY OF REFORM

The examples developed in this chapter, while highly simplified, show how an agenda setter can use the speed and sequencing of reforms to gain majority support for a reform program. We view these as illustrations of "Machiavellian politics" not in the usual sense of devising political tactics to obtain immoral objectives, but on the contrary as rational methods that can be used by policymakers who care about reform. Agenda-setting models are appropriate tools to analyze economic policy issues taking political constraints into account. The analysis can still deliver policy recommendations, as in usual economic analysis. The only difference is that political constraints are not neglected, as is usually the case in economic policy analysis. Instead, they are directly introduced in the analysis. Agenda-setting models are thus not subject to the often-heard criticism against political economy models that they exclude policy recommendations because the political process is purely endogenous. With agenda-setting models, the political process is only partly endogenous, since one assumes the existence of an exogenous reform-minded policymaker. This kind of analysis can be particularly useful for normative and realistic analysis of the political economy of reform.

However, agenda-setting models can legitimately be criticized on the grounds that they do not fully endogenize the political process. Because of their normative emphasis, they do not go deep enough in the positive analysis of economic policy choices. They do not explain how a reformer comes to power in the first place or the circumstances in which reformers fail to come to power. A deeper analysis requires a fuller picture. It requires the analysis of particular interest groups, their degree of organization and influence, and the effect of this influence on electoral politics. The analysis of the interaction between these interest groups must then be completed by an analysis of the political decisionmaking process and of the interaction between the influence activities of interest groups and the rules of decisionmaking. While rent seeking is constantly mentioned in the policy literature on transition, so far there have not really been attempts to model the transition process using the perspective of rent seeking or interest-group politics using explicit extensive forms games that reflect a given institutional situation. Undoubtedly, this is an interesting topic for future research.

CHAPTER 4

THE POLITICAL ECONOMY OF MASS PRIVATIZATION

In transition economies, political constraints have undoubtedly played an important role in the privatization and restructuring process. At the beginning of the transition process, the fear of the layoffs expected to take place after privatization of state-owned enterprises (SOEs) was an important potential source of political opposition. At the same time, radical policymakers had a sense of urgency in launching and achieving privatization on a large scale. The widespread feeling among them was that, unless privatization programs were launched quickly, and on a historically unprecedented scale, it would be impossible to achieve significant efficiency improvements in the economy. It was even felt, in the typically negative attitude toward managers that prevailed in the beginning of the transition period, that unless privatization was achieved very fast, managers would strip the assets of the firms they were managing. It is in that context that proposals emerged in Poland and Czechoslovakia for *mass privatization*—the massive transfer of ownership from the state into private hands by free distribution or quasi-free distribution.

The first experience of mass privatization began in Czechoslovakia in 1992. For a very low price, Czech citizens received vouchers that they could use to purchase shares in privatized companies. The other spectacular experience of mass privatization was the Russian one that was started in 1994 and that consisted in giving away assets for the most part to managers and workers rather than to citizens. The Czech and the Russian mass privatization programs differed in some important details. First of all, the Czech privatization was targeted on the citizens at large, not on workers. In other words, in the Czech Republic each citizen was to have the ex ante opportunity to receive an equal share of the privatized assets, whereas in Russia workers were to receive shares in their own enterprise. Another important detail is that in the Czech Republic citizens were not allowed to sell for cash shares that were purchased with vouchers for at least a year after the purchase of shares in privatized firms. By contrast, in Russia, shares acquired through mass privatization could be sold for cash.

From the beginning, political motives played a strong role in the design of mass privatization programs. The idea was to use mass privatization as an instrument to create irreversibility in the transition process by giving the domestic population stakes in the success of privatization. This was certainly an important motive in the design of voucher privatization in Czechoslovakia. In Russia the idea was to deprive the government of its wealth so as to weaken a communist government if it came to power and tried to reverse the transition process (Boycko, Shleifer, and Vishny, 1995). In other words, mass privatization was thought of as an instrument to alleviate ex post political constraints. At the same time, it was designed so as to satisfy ex ante political constraints. This motivation is what led to a policy of giveaway to insiders (managers and workers).

In this chapter, we present several models of the political economy of mass privatization. Our reason for doing so is that the previous chapters were relatively general and abstract. The advantage of that generality is that the analysis can apply broadly to a whole set of situations, but the disadvantage is that it is not well suited to analyzing fine differences in the design of reform programs. Given the uniqueness of mass privatization as one of the specific reforms of transition compared to other processes of reform, it is useful to dwell a bit more on the details of such programs and on their economic and political effects. The analysis in this chapter is thus useful in showing how differences in details in the design of mass privatization programs may have strong economic and political effects. The models we present focus mainly on ex post political constraints and how to create irreversibility. In Chapter 10 we will dwell on the economic effects of different privatization policies.

In the first sections we start with the model of political economy of mass privatization put forward by Roland and Verdier (1994). The starting point is that standard privatization policies may lead to renationalization if they create too much unemployment. Mass privatization may be used to shift the balance against renationalization by giving the population stakes in the success of privatization so as to offset potential backlash created by unemployment. In section 4.2 we examine a closely related model by Schmidt (2000) to examine the difference between giveaway privatization to insiders (managers and workers of the firm) and to outsiders. There, it is shown that privatization to outsiders creates more irreversibility because the stakes given to the population are diversified, which is not the case with insider privatization. In section 4.3 we develop a simplified version of a model by Biais and Perotti (1998) that has a richer political structure and examines how a right-wing government can use mass privatization to ensure its reelection. That model can apply to Central and Eastern Europe and explain how Vaclav Klaus used voucher privatization to get reelected, but it also applies to privatization policies as implemented in Western Europe, by the Thatcher government in particular, to show how underpricing of privatized assets can be used for political purposes. In section 4.4 we briefly discuss some empirical literature on the subject. In section 4.5 we discuss some of the economic costs associated with the political benefits of mass privatization programs. Section 4.6 summarizes and concludes the first part of the book.

4.1 MODELING A POSSIBLE PRIVATIZATION REVERSAL

We start with a simplified version of the Roland-Verdier (1994) model. We first show how privatization can create backlash as a result of the ensuing restructuring and layoffs after privatization.

Assume a continuum L of workers in the economy, normalized to 1. For simplicity, there is also a continuum of firms, also normalized to 1. There is thus one worker per firm. Socialist firms are assumed to lose money; that is, their output y_s is lower than the fixed wage w going to workers. Subsidies must be paid to cover the losses $w - y_s$. These subsidies are financed from taxes paid out of wages.

The government's budget constraint is thus

$$tw = w - y_s \qquad (4.1)$$

where t is the tax rate on workers in SOEs.[1]

When a firm is privatized, it is assumed to adopt the following production function:

$$y_p = \min[a_p(n_p), l_p] \qquad (4.2)$$

where y_p is the output of the firm and l_p is the amount of labor in the firm. Again, by normalization, each privatized firm is assumed to have one unit of capital, and $a_p(n_p)$ is the productivity of capital where n_p is the number of privatized firms. Privatized firms choose l_p endogenously to equal $a_p(n_p)$. In this section, we consider a_p to be a constant less than 1 so that when a firm is privatized, it sheds labor in amount $1 - l_p = 1 - a_p$. However, privatization is assumed to make the firm more productive and efficient: $y_p = l_p > w > y_s$. The wage rate is assumed to be downward rigid and remains at level w, independently of privatization.

We first look at a standard privatization policy where private investors take control of firms and incur a fixed cost f to restructure a firm. This is a sunk cost. The timing of the game is as follows. First, all firms in the economy are offered to private investors, and the latter decide independently upon entry and acquisition of firms. We assume a continuum of investors on the interval [0, 1]. After entry has occurred, the government reconsiders its privatization policy and may reverse a given number of privatizations if its preferred amount of privatization is lower than the achieved level of privatization. However, if the government's level of privatization is higher than the realized amount of entry, it cannot force additional investors to enter. At the last stage, production takes place, and effective unemployment occurs.

4.1.1 PRIVATIZATION REVERSAL

We now look at the government's optimization problem. It is assumed to maximize the expected utility of income of the average citizen who faces an unemployment risk. Given the preceding assumptions, the probability of being unemployed and of being deprived

[1] *One may wonder why wages were not set lower so as to avoid taxation of income. This question only reflects the simplification of the model. In reality, socialist firms were heterogeneous, and clearly not all firms were experiencing losses. We come back to the issue of heterogeneity of firms in Chapter 9.*

of income is $n_p(1 - a_p)$ and the probability of keeping a job and getting income $w(1 - t)$ is $1 - n_p(1 - a_p)$. The utility U of income is assumed to be concave, and it is also assumed that $U(0) = 0$. The model can be readily extended to include unemployment benefits, but this complication does not add much to the qualitative results. Employed workers pay a tax to finance subsidies in the nonprivatized firms. The government thus chooses n_p^* to solve

$$\max_{n_p^*} V(n_p) = n_p(1 - a_p)U(0) + [1 - n_p(1 - a_p)]U[w(1 - t)] \tag{4.3}$$

subject to

$$t = \frac{w - y_s}{w} \frac{1 - n_p}{1 - n_p(1 - a_p)}$$

We can easily see that the tax rate decreases with the level of privatization because fewer enterprises must be subsidized:

$$\frac{dt}{dn_p} = \frac{w - y_s}{w} \frac{-a_p}{[1 - n_p(1 - a_p)]^2} < 0 \tag{4.4}$$

Developing the expression for $V'(n_p)$, we get

$$V'(n_p) = -(1 - a_p)U[w(1 - t)] + U'[w(1 - t)](w - y_s)\frac{a_p}{[1 - n_p(1 - a_p)]} \tag{4.5}$$

The trade-off induced by privatization is the following: a higher level of privatization increases the likelihood of losing one's job, the first expression on the right-hand side, but increases the income of employed workers because of a lower tax burden, the second expression on the right-hand side. An interior solution $n_p^* \in (0, 1)$ will equalize these marginal benefits and costs of privatization. Therefore, any amount of privatization n_p in excess of that number n_p^* will be undone. We assume all firms have an equal probability of being renationalized, equal to $\max\left(0, \frac{n_p - n_p^*}{n_p}\right)$.

Investors take into account the possibility of later privatization reversal when deciding entry. Indeed, their entry cost f is assumed to be a sunk cost. As entry is decided independently, investors play Nash with each other. We restrict ourselves to analyzing symmetric equilibria (pure and mixed) where investors choose a probability of entry, given the choice of other investors. Expected net profits $E\pi_p$ depend on the probability of renationalization, which itself depends on the number of entries. We have

$$E\pi_p = (1 - w)a_p \quad \text{for} \quad n_p < n_p^* \tag{4.6}$$

$$= \frac{n_p^*}{n_p}(1 - w)a_p \quad \text{for} \quad n_p \geq n_p^*$$

Using Figure 4.1 and allowing f to vary, we can see that for $f > (1 - w)a_p$ there is a unique equilibrium with no privatization taking place; for $n_p^*(1 - w)a_p > f$ there

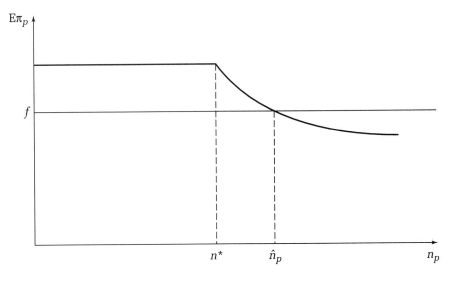

FIGURE 4.1 THE PRIVATIZATION EQUILIBRIUM

is a unique equilibrium with full privatization ($\hat{n}_p = 1$); and for $f \in [n_p^*(1 - w)a_p, (1 - w)a_p]$ there is a unique equilibrium with $\hat{n}_p$ such that $\frac{n_p^*}{\hat{n}_p}(1 - w)a_p = f$. The amount of privatization depends on the entry costs, but there is always a unique equilibrium.

Note that in equilibrium no renationalization takes place, but the real threat of renationalization has a moderating effect on entry. Note also that this moderating effect is welfare enhancing, not welfare reducing. Indeed, without the threat of renationalization, for values of f in the interval $[n_p^*(1 - w)a_p, (1 - w)a_p]$, there would then be full instead of partial privatization. However, in that case, despite the higher efficiency associated with privatization, workers would be exposed to greater risks of unemployment and to a suboptimally low welfare level.

4.1.2   MULTIPLE EQUILIBRIA AND CRITICAL MASS IN PRIVATIZATION

One may question the preceding result of an interior solution for privatization. One can indeed easily argue that the unemployment risks are transitory and that full privatization will eventually lead to full employment with a higher overall efficiency level. This argument does not mean, however, that privatization reversal is not a danger.

To model this question, we assume that there is a positive externality to the size of the private sector. There are various intuitively appealing explanations for such an externality. A first one is related to complementarities already mentioned in previous chapters. To the extent that the profitability inside a firm depends on the quantity, quality,[2] and scope of available inputs, a higher level of privatization may increase the efficiency of each privatized firm. Second, there is a positive network externality related

[2] *Quality includes the reliability of deliveries. Irregularities in deliveries were notorious in the socialist economy owing to pervasive shortages.*

to the existence of a dense network of business relationships, creating a climate of trust based on repeated contracting and social capital (see Roland and Verdier, 1994, for a more exhaustive discussion). This size externality of the private sector is modeled by assuming that above a certain threshold $\tilde{n}$ the production function of private firms becomes

$$y_p = \min[a_p(n_p), l_p] \tag{4.7}$$

with

$$a_p(n_p) = \max\{a_p, a_p + s(n_p - \tilde{n})\}$$

Note that for consistency we assume that $s = \frac{1-a_p}{1-\tilde{n}}$ so that $a_p(1) = 1$; that is, there is full employment under full privatization. Choosing l_p endogenously to equal $a_p(n_p)$ changes the indirect utility function $V(n_p)$, since now, for levels of privatization above $\tilde{n}$, a_p depends on n_p. The optimum level of privatization is now the solution to

$$\max_{n_p^*} V(n_p) = n_p[1 - a_p(n_p)]U(0) + \{1 - n_p[1 - a_p(n_p)]\}U[w(1-t)] \tag{4.8}$$

subject to

$$t = \frac{w - y_s}{w} \frac{1 - n_p}{1 - n_p[1 - a_p(n_p)]}$$

The first-order derivative for $n > \tilde{n}$ is then

$$V'(n_p) = -w\frac{dt}{dn_p}\{1 - n_p[1 - a_p(n_p)]\}U'[w(1-t)] \tag{4.9}$$

$$+ \{n_p a'_p(n_p) - [1 - a_p(n_p)]\}U[w(1-t)]$$

where

$$\frac{dt}{dn_p} = \frac{w - y_s}{w} \frac{-a_p(n_p) - (1 - n_p)[n_p a'_p(n_p)]}{\{1 - n_p[1 - a_p(n_p)]\}^2} < 0 \tag{4.10}$$

Note two things. First of all, the tax rate goes down faster with an increase of privatization, since with the size externality the tax base increases more with the size of the private sector. Second, as before, privatization increases the marginal utility of income, because of higher net wages, but affects the probability of being unemployed. However, the probability of being unemployed does not necessarily increase with privatization. It may actually decrease if n_p is high enough. Indeed, in the second term of the right-hand-side expression of equation (4.9), $U[w(1-t)]$ is multiplied by $\{n_p a'_p(n_p) - [1 - a_p(n_p)]\}$ instead of by $-(1 - a_p)$. Now, $\{n_p a'_p(n_p) - [1 - a_p(n_p)]\}$ can very well be positive. Since $a'_p(n_p) = \frac{1-a_p}{1-\tilde{n}}$, we have

$$n_p a'_p(n_p) - [1 - a_p(n_p)] = n_p\frac{1 - a_p}{1 - \tilde{n}} - 1 + a_p + \frac{1 - a_p}{1 - \tilde{n}}(n_p - \tilde{n})$$

$$= (1 - a_p)\frac{2n_p - 1}{1 - \tilde{n}}$$

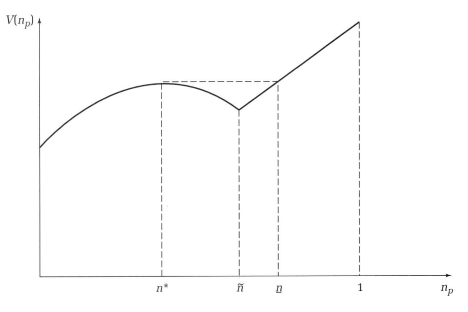

FIGURE 4.2 THE SIZE EXTERNALITY OF THE PRIVATE SECTOR AND THE CRITICAL MASS OF PRIVATIZATION

which can be positive as soon as $n_p > 1/2$. In that case, $V'(n_p)$ will have a positive slope. This will be the case if we assume $\tilde{n} > 1/2$. Figure 4.2 illustrates the effect of the externality on the size of the private sector. Note that there is a "critical mass of privatization"[3] $\underline{n}$ for which $V(\underline{n}) = V(n^*)$. For all $n_p > \underline{n}$, $V(n_p) > V(n^*)$. Any amount of privatization above n^* but below $\underline{n}$ will be undone, but any volume of privatization above $\underline{n}$ will be politically irreversible. Above this critical mass, there will thus be a "virtuous circle" of increased efficiency and creation of jobs, whereas below this critical mass, increased efficiency as a result of more privatization comes at the cost of higher unemployment risks.

The presence of a critical mass of privatization will have an effect on the expected profits of investors. These are given by

$$E\pi_p = (1 - w)a_p \qquad \text{for} \qquad n_p < n^* \qquad\qquad\qquad \textbf{(4.11)}$$

$$= \frac{n^*}{n_p}(1 - w)a_p(n_p) \qquad \text{for} \qquad n^* \leq n_p \leq \underline{n}$$

$$= (1 - w)a_p(n_p) \qquad \text{for} \qquad \underline{n} \leq n_p$$

Figure 4.3 shows the discontinuity in expected profits at $\underline{n}$. This critical-mass effect and the irreversibility it creates generate multiple equilibria. The interesting case is the one with values of f in the range between $\frac{n^*}{\underline{n}}(1 - w)a_p(\underline{n})$ and $(1 - w)a_p$. There will be two Nash equilibria: either full privatization or partial privatization [in an amount n_p such that $\frac{n^*}{n_p}(1 - w)a_p(n_p) = f$].[4] Compared to the case of the previous section, full privatization is added as a Nash equilibrium.

[3] The idea of critical mass was used frequently in the early policy literature on transition reforms to indicate that reform packages had to be comprehensive enough so as to be credible and generate changes in economic behavior.

[4] As can be seen from Figure 4.3, there are also multiple equilibria for values of f up to $(1 - w)a_p(1) = (1 - w)$.

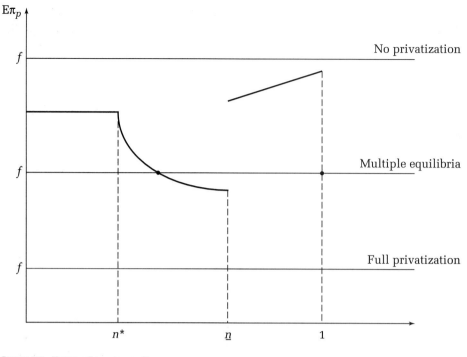

FIGURE 4.3 MULTIPLE EQUILIBRIA IN PRIVATIZATION

The externalities to the size of the private sector make full privatization the first-best outcome from the point of view of welfare. However, this first-best outcome is not necessarily reached because investors are facing a coordination problem. Amounts of investment below the critical mass $\underline{n}$ indeed create the possibility of political backlash and privatization reversal to the local optimum of n^*.

4.1.3 THE POLITICAL EFFECT OF GIVEAWAY PRIVATIZATION

At this point the question arises of whether it is possible to get investors to coordinate on the good equilibrium. One way of helping them to do so is to create political irreversibility by making privatization popular enough with the voters so as to prevent reversal. Such an instrument can be provided by giveaway privatization whereby the population receives ownership rights on the privatized assets.

Assume that a proportion γ of shares in privatized enterprises are freely and equally distributed to the population through a voucher scheme. As a consequence, the average citizen receives dividends in amount $d = \gamma \pi_p n_p$. Dividends thus increase with the size of privatization. The proportion γ, however, is assumed to be bounded above a proportion $\overline{\gamma}$. Indeed, if all shares are distributed to small shareholders, there is no guarantee that restructuring will take place because of the collective-action problems of dispersed ownership. In order not to lose the positive economic effects of privatization, it is necessary to have controlling blockholders who have a genuine incentive to restructure the firm. This factor is what determines the upper bound $\bar{\gamma}$.

Recall that backlash is determined by the trade-off between a higher level of income and a higher probability of unemployment under privatization. Free distribution introduces a counterbalancing force to the negative effect of privatization on unemployment, since an increase in privatization increases the dividend received by citizens, whether they are employed or not. If this counterbalancing effect is strong enough, then expected welfare may increase monotonically with the size of privatization, thereby eliminating any temptation to reverse privatization, and thus leading to full privatization as the only possible equilibrium.

The easiest way to perform the analysis is to concentrate on the range $[0, \tilde{n}]$ below the threshold for which the size externality of the private sector steps in. It is on this range that welfare can decrease with the size of the private sector between n_p^* and $\tilde{n}$. We first look at how the indirect utility function is modified by free distribution. Expected welfare of the average citizen can now be written as $V(\gamma, n_p)$, a function of γ and n_p, since the degree of free distribution affects people's preferences for privatization. Its expression is

$$V(\gamma, n_p) = n_p(1 - a_p)U(\gamma \pi_p n_p) + [1 - n_p(1 - a_p)]U[w(1 - t) + \gamma \pi_p n_p] \tag{4.12}$$

The marginal utility of privatization now becomes

$$\frac{\partial V(\gamma, n_p)}{\partial n_p} = -(1 - a_p)\{U[w(1 - t) + d] - U(d)\} \tag{4.13}$$

$$+ U'[w(1 - t) + d].(w - y_s)\frac{a_p}{[1 - n_p(1 - a_p)]}$$

$$+ \gamma \pi_p\{n_p(1 - a_p)U'(d) + [1 - n_p(1 - a_p)]U'[w(1 - t) + d]\}$$

The first two terms are similar to those in equation (4.5), the first being negative and the second positive, except that with a higher γ both expressions are smaller because of the concavity of U. The third expression is positive and represents the welfare gain from the free distribution of shares. If the latter is big enough, and thus if γ is big enough and U' not too small, so that $\frac{\partial V(\gamma, \tilde{n})}{\partial n_p} > 0$, then $V(\gamma, n_p)$ will be nondecreasing $\forall n_p$.

The political irreversibility achieved through free distribution comes at a cost, however. Indeed, investors must now share the profits from the privatized firms with those who have received free shares. Their net expected gains are now $(1 - \gamma)E\pi_p - f$. This is equivalent to an increase in the entry cost from f to $\frac{f}{1-\gamma}$. Figure 4.4 shows the three possible cases. If $\frac{f}{1-\gamma} < (1 - w)a_p$, then there will be a unique equilibrium with full privatization. If, however, $\frac{f}{1-\gamma} > (1 - w)$, then there will be a unique equilibrium with no privatization. If now $\frac{f}{1-\gamma} \in [(1 - w)a_p, (1 - w)]$, there will still be multiplicity of equilibria because of the externality of private sector size. Mass privatization in this model eliminates backlash and policy reversal but does not eliminate the coordination problem between investors.

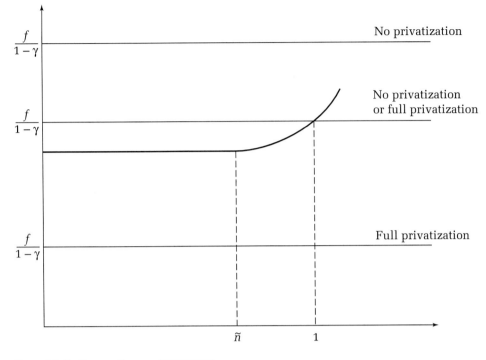

FIGURE 4.4 THE EFFECT OF GIVEAWAY PRIVATIZATION

4.2   GIVEAWAY TO THE POPULATION OR TO INSIDERS

The temptation to renationalize may be affected by the kind of giveaway policy implemented. In the transition experience, one must distinguish between two different kinds of giveaway policies. (In Chapter 10 we will have a comprehensive discussion of all types of privatization policies.) The two types are giveaway to the population at large, as in the Czech privatization program, and giveaway to the firm insiders, managers, and workers, as in Russia. Schmidt (2000) has shown that these two policies differ in the amount of political irreversibility they generate. In particular, giveaway of assets to the population at large leads to more irreversibility. To the extent that voters receive vouchers enabling them to have a diversified portfolio of shares, their stake in the continuation of privatization will be greater than if workers instead receive free shares in their own enterprise, implying more risk.

We now introduce a simplified version of Schmidt's model. We thus modify the previous model in various respects. First of all, we come back to the basic model of section 4.1 without size externalities where privatization is an interior solution. Instead of looking at unemployment as a uniform consequence of privatization across all firms, we assume now that after a core investor has invested restructuring effort f in a privatized firm (where f can be interpreted as effort as in usual incentive models), he faces a probability f of generating a positive profit π_p and a wage $\overline{w}$ for workers, but he also faces a probability $1 - f$ of failure. In that case, no cash flow is generated to pay wages for workers. Income of workers in unsuccessful firms can be supported only by expropriating a proportion $1 - n_p$ of profitable privatized enterprises to give them subsidized jobs at a lower wage rate $\underline{w}$. Alternatively and equivalently in terms of the model, one can assume that the successful enterprises are taxed $1 - n_p$ of their income to cover subsidies $\underline{w}$ for workers from unsuccessful enterprises. The government thus decides on n_p.

As one sees, the public finance assumptions are slightly different than in the model of Roland and Verdier, in which taxes are paid out of all wages to cover subsidies in the state sector. The higher the level of privatization, the lower the tax rate on workers employed. In Schmidt's model, the subsidies to unsuccessful enterprises are independent of the level of expropriation of privatized enterprises. Expropriation only determines the tax rate on successful enterprises. It is assumed that expropriation involves distortionary costs so that only a proportion $\lambda < 1$ of income of expropriated firms is made available as subsidies. Total resources available for subsidization are thus

$$\lambda f (1 - n_p)\pi_p = (1 - f)\underline{w} \tag{4.14}$$

The timing is the same as in the preceding sections. First, the government decides on a mass privatization scheme (to the population or to insiders) and on a proportion γ of shares that are distributed in the mass privatization scheme. Second, the core investors invest f. Then, the expropriation rate $1 - n_p$ is decided by the government, which maximizes the expected welfare of a representative agent. Finally, uncertainty resolution occurs, and payoffs are realized.

We concentrate the analysis on the expropriation decision. We look first, as in the preceding section, at the case where mass privatization gives diversified shares to all agents. In that case, workers of successful and unsuccessful firms all get a dividend of $\gamma f n_p \pi_p$, which increases with γ, the extent of free distribution. Workers in successful firms get income $\overline{x} = \overline{w} + \gamma f n_p \pi_p$, whereas workers in unsuccessful firms get income $\underline{x} = \frac{\lambda f(1-n_p)\pi_p}{1-f} + \gamma f n_p \pi_p$. As one sees, expropriation acts as insurance against the risk of being in an unsuccessful firm. As in the Roland-Verdier model, privatization implies income risks for workers, and privatization reversal acts as an insurance device against this income risk. However, here the probability of ending up with a low income is exogenous and does not depend on the extent of privatization, whereas in the Roland-Verdier model, expropriation reduced the probability of being unemployed and also the income level of employed workers.

When deciding on privatization reversal, the government solves the following problem for the representative agent:

$$\max_{n_p^*} V(n_p) = f U(\overline{w} + \gamma f n_p \pi_p) + (1 - f)U\left[\frac{\lambda f(1 - n_p)\pi_p}{1 - f} + \gamma f n_p \pi_p\right] \tag{4.15}$$

The first-order condition for an interior solution $n_p \in (0, 1)$ yields

$$\frac{U'(\overline{x})}{U'(\underline{x})} = \frac{\lambda - \gamma(1-f)}{f\gamma}$$

A voter will thus optimally trade off the benefits of privatization reversal at the margin, that is, the net marginal benefit from redistribution $(\frac{-\lambda f \pi_p}{1-f} + \gamma f \pi_p)U'(\underline{x})[> 0$ if $\lambda - \gamma(1-f) > 0]$ when in a bad firm, which occurs with probability $(1-f)$ against the marginal cost of expropriation $\gamma f \pi_p U'(\overline{x})$, when in a good firm, which occurs with probability f. Note that the marginal rate of substitution between both states unambiguously declines as γ increases. Indeed, the net marginal income received from expropriation when being in a bad firm is then reduced, whereas the net loss when being in a good firm increases. Increasing the proportion γ of free redistribution can thus reduce the incentives to reverse privatization. Looking at this relationship analytically, the conditions for an increase in γ to reduce the amount of expropriation are

$$\frac{dn_p}{d\gamma} = \frac{-\frac{\partial V'(n_p)}{\partial \gamma}}{V''(n_p)} > 0 \Longleftrightarrow \frac{\partial V'(n_p)}{\partial \gamma} > 0 \qquad (4.16)$$

by concavity of $V(n_p)$, and

$$\frac{\partial V'(n_p)}{\partial \gamma} > 0 \Longleftrightarrow fU'(\overline{x}) + (1-f)U'(\underline{x}) + n_p f \pi_p \{\gamma f U''(\overline{x}) - [\lambda - \gamma(1-f)]U''(\underline{x})\} > 0 \qquad (4.17)$$

The first two expressions on the right are positive and the last expression is positive $\Longleftrightarrow$

$$\frac{U''(\overline{x})}{U''(\underline{x})} < \frac{\lambda - \gamma(1-f)}{f\gamma} = \frac{U'(\overline{x})}{U'(\underline{x})} \Longleftrightarrow -\frac{U''(\overline{x})}{U'(\overline{x})} \le -\frac{U'(\underline{x})}{U'(\underline{x})} \qquad (4.18)$$

that is, if there is nonincreasing absolute risk aversion (NIARA), a reasonable assumption. With NIARA, therefore, a higher share of free distribution will reduce privatization reversal.

Let us now compare the case of insider privatization. In this case, when deciding on privatization reversal, the government solves

$$\max_{n_p^*} V(n_p) = fU(\overline{w} + \gamma n_p \pi_p) + (1-f)U\left[\frac{\lambda f(1 - n_p)\pi_p}{1-f}\right] \qquad (4.19)$$

As compared to the case of diversified mass privatization, note that workers in good firms get $\gamma n_p \pi_p$ instead of $f \gamma n_p \pi_p$, since dividends from their firm are not shared across the population. Moreover, workers in bad firms only get $\frac{\lambda f(1-n_p)\pi_p}{1-f}$, that is, the redistributive subsidies. From the first-order conditions, we get

$$\frac{U'(\overline{x})}{U'(\underline{x})} = \frac{\lambda}{\gamma} \qquad (4.20)$$

The interesting question now is whether there will be more privatization reversal under insider privatization than under diversified privatization. Intuitively, this should be the case, since, under insider privatization, the only income insurance is the one generated from privatization reversal, whereas under diversified privatization, a higher level of privatization increases income across states of nature. Moreover, the risk is higher under insider privatization, since workers in good firms get a higher income and workers in bad firms get a lower income.

To see which privatization method generates less reversal, we take the optimal n_p^* under diversified privatization and plug it in the first derivative with respect to n_p for insider privatization:

$$f\pi_p \left\{ \gamma U'(\overline{w} + \gamma n_p^* \pi_p) - \lambda U' \left[\frac{\lambda f(1 - n_p^*)\pi_p}{1 - f} \right] \right\}$$

Note first that the first-order condition for diversified privatization must be satisfied:

$$\gamma \left\{ f U'(\overline{w} + \gamma f n_p^* \pi_p) + (1 - f)U' \left[\frac{\lambda f(1 - n_p^*)\pi_p}{1 - f} + \gamma f n_p^* \pi_p \right] \right\} \qquad \textbf{(4.21)}$$

$$= \lambda U' \left[\frac{\lambda f(1 - n_p^*)\pi_p}{1 - f} + \gamma f n_p^* \pi_p \right]$$

Note further that by concavity of U

$$-\lambda U' \left[\frac{\lambda f(1 - n_p^*)\pi_p}{1 - f} \right] < -\lambda U' \left[\frac{\lambda f(1 - n_p^*)\pi_p}{1 - f} + \gamma f n_p^* \pi_p \right]$$

Moreover, $U'(\overline{w} + \gamma n_p^* \pi_p) < U'(\overline{w} + \gamma f n_p^* \pi_p)$, which is smaller than $f U'(\overline{w} + \gamma f n_p^* \pi_p) + (1 - f)U' \left[\frac{\lambda f(1 - n_p^*)\pi_p}{1 - f} + \gamma f n_p^* \pi_p \right]$. Therefore, we conclude that $\gamma U'(\overline{w} + \gamma n_p^* \pi_p) - \lambda U' \left[\frac{\lambda f(1 - n_p^*)\pi_p}{1 - f} \right] < 0$ which means, by concavity of U, that the optimal n_p under insider privatization must be lower than n_p^*, the optimal level of privatization under diversified privatization, implying more reversal under insider privatization.

The analysis in this section shows that insider mass privatization (Russia) is less suited than diversified mass privatization (Czech Republic) to satisfy ex post political constraints. This point is reinforced by the fact that in Russia shares obtained via mass privatization could be sold for cash, whereas in the Czech Republic shares were made illiquid for more than a year. The latter measure evidently served to give the population stakes in the success of the privatization program. The reformers wanted to avoid a scenario where part of the population would "cash in" their benefits from mass privatization and later support policy reversals. However, one should not forget ex ante political constraints when comparing forms of mass privatization. The Polish mass privatization program, designed to favor giveaways to the domestic population as in the Czech Republic, was blocked for several years by coalitions of insiders. It is precisely to overcome such potential ex ante political constraints that the Russian mass privatization program was designed to favor giveaways to insiders. Boycko, Shleifer, and Vishny (1995) justify the Russian program by arguing that it was the only politically feasible plan.

The findings of the model of Schmidt may be complemented by those of Polishchuk (1999) related to Russian privatization. The models of Roland and Verdier (1994) and Schmidt (1998) have indeed assumed that mass privatization can be designed to gain political support among voters by spreading wealth broadly among the population. Opposite effects are also possible ex post when mass privatization leads to an extremely unequal distribution of assets among the population. Given the emphasis on getting the support of insiders for fast mass privatization, the distributive aspects of Russian privatization have been neglected. In effect, Russian insider privatization and the subsequent "loan for shares" schemes have created an enormous inequality of wealth. Privatization is seen to be one of the key factors behind the enormous increase in wealth inequality in Russia (Alexeev, 1999). If this higher inequality had been associated with high investment and growth, then the reform would have been supported. However, this was not the case and instead there has been disinvestment and massive capital flight. Polishchuk (1999) builds a model where private investment by capital owners depends on the credibility of security of property rights, which itself depends on the scope for redistribution of wealth given that the latter involves important efficiency costs. When the initial distribution of assets is very unequal, such scope increases. Moreover, the efficiency costs of redistribution are reduced when little investment takes place before the redistribution of assets. There may thus be an inefficient equilibrium with low investment and renationalization of assets and an efficient one where investment takes place and renationalization does in order not to discourage investment. Here, the bad equilibrium can be eliminated by a more equal distribution of assets with privatization. The general lesson is thus the same as in the two previous models, namely, that broad stakes in ownership are important for political support, whereas a very inegalitarian distribution of wealth carries with it the possibility of policy reversal and the negative economic consequences of the expectation of such a reversal.

4.3   THATCHERIAN UNDERPRICING

In contrast to the Roland-Verdier and Schmidt models, the model of Biais and Perotti (1998) focuses less on the insurance aspects of policy reversal than on the direct redistributive aspects. They have a more explicit formulation of the political process with a right-wing and a left-wing party competing for the votes of the median voter. As in many current models in political economy (see, e.g., Alesina, 1988; Besley and Coate, 1997; and others), parties are not able to commit to a platform before the election. In this case, the lack of commitment results in the right-wing party defending the rich and the left-wing party defending the poor. The analysis focuses on how a right-wing party can use underpricing of shares to encourage median income agents to buy enough shares in privatized firms so as to have a stake in voting for the right-wing party rather than the left-wing party. It is a nice example, in the spirit of Aghion and Bolton (1991), of how policy design can endogenously affect the reelection outcome and thereby create irreversibility for privatization. The model not only applies to mass privatization as in Eastern Europe, but also sheds light on privatization policies followed by right-wing governments in Western Europe, in particular the early privatization programs under Margaret Thatcher in the United Kingdom.

Assume three classes of citizens, rich, median, and poor, having in each period an exogenous income, respectively, of w_r, w_m, and 0. The weight of each class is respectively α_r, α_m, and α_p. Average income is thus $\overline{w} = \alpha_r w_r + \alpha_m w_m$, and we assume, as in most real income distributions, that median income is lower than average income: $w_m < \overline{w}$.

There are two periods. In the beginning of period 1, the incumbent government decides on the income tax τ_1 and the level of redistribution g_1. Even when there is no redistribution, some taxation is always necessary to finance the fixed costs s of the state administration. Most importantly, the government decides on a privatization policy. We assume the incumbent government in period 1 is right-wing and, once in power, follows the interests of the rich. Citizens decide, depending on the privatization policy, how many assets they want to buy. After shares have been purchased there are new elections. In period 2, the elected government decides on the income tax τ_2 and the level of redistribution g_2. It may also decide whether to expropriate the privatized assets or not, depriving the owners of the fruits of their investment.

It is assumed that a privatized firm can generate profits π_H provided effort is put in the firm by management. Without effort, the firm generates $\pi_L (= 0)$ which is assumed to be suboptimal because $\pi_H - e > 0$. Management is assumed to provide no effort if it expects expropriation.

Let us first look at the demand for shares of privatized assets by various income groups when there are no elections in period 2 so that the right-wing government is in power for the two periods and no expropriation (taxation of profits) is expected. For an asset price of p, individuals with exogenous per period income w_i and with endogenous privatized assets of q_i are maximizing a two-period intertemporal utility of consumption where we assume for simplicity that the discount rate is equal to 1:

$$\max_{q_i} U[w_i(1 - \tau_1) + g_1 - pq_i] + U[w_i(1 - \tau_2) + g_2 + \pi_H q_i] \tag{4.22}$$

We assume that the utility function takes the usual CARA form: $U(x) = \frac{x^\gamma}{1-\gamma}$ with $\gamma < 1$. It is also assumed for simplicity that no borrowing or lending takes place so that acquiring privatized assets is the only instrument for saving. The first-order condition is

$$pU'[w_i(1 - \tau_1) + g_1 - pq_i] = \pi_H U'[w_i(1 - \tau_2) + g_2 + \pi_H q_i] \tag{4.23}$$

Replacing it by the specific functional form for U and rearranging, we get

$$\left(\frac{p}{\pi_H}\right)^{\frac{1}{1-\gamma}} = \frac{w_i(1 - \tau_1) + g_1 - pq_i}{w_i(1 - \tau_2) + g_2 + \pi_H q_i} \tag{4.24}$$

which, after a few manipulations, gives us the demand for privatized assets

$$q_i = \frac{w_i(1 - \tau_1) + g_1 - [w_i(1 - \tau_2) + g_2]\left(\frac{p}{\pi_H}\right)^{\frac{1}{1-\gamma}}}{\left(\frac{p}{\pi_H}\right)^{\frac{1}{1-\gamma}}\pi_H + p} \tag{4.25}$$

The equilibrium price will be the price p_e for which demand $\alpha_r q_r(p_e) + \alpha_m q_m(p_e)$ equals supply (normalized to 1).

We now look at the optimal choice of policy in period 2. If the right-wing party is reelected and chooses not to expropriate shareholders, it will seek

$$\max_{g_2, \tau_2} U[w_r(1 - \tau_2) + g_2 + q_r\pi_H] \tag{4.26}$$

subject to

$$g_2 + s = \overline{w}\tau_2$$

One sees easily that since $w_r > \overline{w}$, we will have $g_2 = 0$ and $\tau_2 = \frac{s}{\overline{w}}$. Note also that, for the same reason, in period 1, its choice will be $g_1 = 0$ and $\tau_1 = \frac{s}{\overline{w}}$. Note that if the government chose expropriation, the government budget constraint would be $g_2 + s = \overline{w}\tau_2 + \pi_H$, and the tax rate would then be $\tau_2 = \frac{s - \pi_H}{\overline{w}}$.

A left-wing government would always choose the maximal taxation, and it would expropriate because doing so yields net benefits for the poor. The question is what would be the attitude of the median voter. Under a right-wing government, it will get $w_m(1 - \frac{s}{\overline{w}}) + q_m\pi_H$, and under a left-wing government, it will get $\overline{w} + \pi_L - s = \overline{w} - s$. Comparing both, one sees that it will be prepared to reelect the right-wing government only if

$$q_m > q_m^* = \frac{\overline{w} - s}{\pi_H}\frac{\overline{w} - w_m}{\overline{w}} \tag{4.27}$$

This inequality is easily interpretable. One sees that the higher the income inequality ($\frac{\overline{w} - w_m}{\overline{w}}$), the higher must be q_m. The reason is that the higher the inequality, the more the median voters have to gain from redistributive policies implemented by a left-wing government and the higher the level of q_m necessary to persuade them to vote for the right. One also sees that the higher is π_H (which can be interpreted both as the efficiency gains from privatization and as the size of privatization), the lower the q_m necessary to reelect the right-wing government.

Since inequality (4.27) may not be satisfied, the right-wing government will have an incentive to underprice strategically. Indeed, in case $q_m(p_e) < q_m^*$, the government will have to set a price p^* for which $q_m(p^*) = q_m^*$. In that case, the rich will be rationed and allowed to hold only $\overline{q}_r = \frac{1 - \alpha_m q_m^*}{\alpha_r}$. Nevertheless, they are still better off from avoiding a left-wing government in the next period. Note that when the latter occurrence is rationally expected, demand for privatized assets, and thus their price, falls to 0. This outcome will be a self-fulfilling prophecy, and the median voter will gain from voting for the left, since $w_m(1 - \frac{s}{\overline{w}}) < \overline{w} - s$ because $w_m < \overline{w}$.

We thus see that the design of privatization can be used to manipulate the electoral outcome and to create constituencies to continue to support the incumbent government, thereby creating irreversibility for privatization.

4.4 EMPIRICAL EVIDENCE

In the West, underpricing has been frequently observed when shares of public enterprises were put on the stock market (Jones et al., 1997). Moreover, privatizations are at least as underpriced as initial public offerings (IPOs). This fact has posed a challenge for economists. Underpricing in IPOs is traditionally explained by asymmetric information. However, IPOs of public firms tend to be large and well advertised, and both asymmetric information and risk should be substantially smaller than in private IPOs. The Biais and Perotti model suggests that the first-order effect in explaining underpricing in privatization is related to politics.

Additional evidence comes from a study on privatization in forty-nine countries by Bortolotti, Fantini, and Siniscalco (1999). They find generally that right-wing governments tend to privatize more than left-wing governments. However, there are also other determinants of sales: budget deficits and country risk. The latter result brings us back to the effect of uncertainty on attracting investment, discussed in Chapter 2. The latter is also important in explaining revenues from privatization. Revenues from privatization are also higher when there is capital market liquidity and law enforcement. They also find that right-wing governments tend to sell via public offerings rather than via public sales; this finding confirms the idea that privatization serves the purpose of gaining middle-class support for right-wing governments. However, privatization occurs less often through public offerings if a country has a French civil law system where ownership is more concentrated.

The model applies directly to the Czech Republic where the government of Vaclav Klaus was the only one in Central Europe not to be toppled by elections in the aftermath of the first transition years. In Poland and Hungary and in many other countries in Eastern Europe, the initial postcommunist governments did not get reelected and were replaced by coalitions including former communist parties. Klaus was reelected in 1994 shortly after the achievement of voucher privatization, which is widely acknowledged to have contributed to his reelection. The stability of the Czech government during the first years of transition has been noted as an exception for countries experiencing the turmoil of privatization. As noted in Chapter 3, this stability may also in part, or maybe even to a great degree, be due to the lower unemployment rate in the Czech Republic as compared to other Central European countries.

Earle and Gehlbach (1999) provide empirical evidence on the political effects of the Czech privatization program. They use a survey done in January 1996 by the Institute of the Academy of Sciences among a representative sample of 1,459 citizens. They performed ordered probit estimations to analyze the effect of the experience of individuals with the privatization program on the attitudinal responses, controlling for individual characteristics such as gender, age, education, income, and residence. They found that the restitution program that gave property back to families of former owners of businesses and real estate raised the support for reform between 15 and 26 percent and brought about even greater increases in expectations about the economic situation (39 percent) and improvement in living standards (57 percent). They also found that voucher participation had a significant effect on support, but only when individuals retained shares acquired through voucher privatization and did not sell them. In that case, support for reform increased between 18 and 27 percent. Participation in voucher privatization without retention of shares had no effect on support. They also found that those who benefited from restitution and those who kept shares from the privatization program had more free-market attitudes and perceived the new democratic regime as more legitimate than other citizens. The latter responses tend to show that the voucher program increases the perception of fairness of those who benefited from it. The estimates of Earle and Gehlbach, however, may reflect the fact that those who benefited from restitution and retained shares from privatization already had free-market attitudes from their family background. However, the impact of restitution is still significant when one controls for the presence of entrepreneurs in the family. We should note that the latter variable is a relatively imperfect proxy for ideological beliefs, and the results of Earle and Gehlbach must be interpreted with caution.

4.5   THE ECONOMIC COSTS OF MASS PRIVATIZATION PROGRAMS

This chapter has shown that politics plays an important role in the design of privatization policies. Mass privatization plans were designed by reformers such as Vaclav Klaus in the Czech Republic and Anatoli Chubais in Russia to overcome political constraints to transition and create irreversibility. The political aspects of privatization were somewhat neglected in the very early debates on transition, but in reality they proved to be very important. However, the subsequent realization of the political role of privatization led to neglect of the economic cost associated with mass privatization. The preceding models have relied on the assumption that the efficiency of privatization, in terms of restructuring outcomes, is not affected by the free distribution of shares. A core private investor is assumed to restructure the company, while the dispersed small shareholders simply enjoy the rents associated with privatization.

In practice, however, this is not an accurate description of the way mass privatization programs have taken place. In Russia, insiders usually gained full control over the firm, and core investors could not be relied on to restructure the firm. As a result, not only has restructuring been decoupled from privatization, but also insider control can make restructuring more difficult to achieve, as we will see in Chapter 10. In the Czech Republic, mass privatization was designed without having core investors in mind. On the contrary, Czech law prohibited investment funds from holding more than 20 percent of the assets of a privatized firm. In practice, Czech privatization has led to peculiar and very nontransparent corporate governance arrangements. State-owned banks that were to be privatized through voucher privatization set up investment funds that collected the vouchers of Czech citizens and managed them with the promise of a riskless return. These investment funds were thereby able to acquire controlling positions in Czech firms. The result is that the shares of banks were eventually held by the investment funds that had been set up by the banks themselves! The financial sector in the Czech Republic has failed to restructure itself and was in dire straits in the late 1990s.

We do not yet grasp the full economic consequences of the flawed corporate governance arrangements in countries were mass privatization was implemented. These consequences may be very painful and costly in the long term. They were strongly underestimated by most transition experts, even by those critical of the economics of mass privatization. In principle, nothing prevented mass privatization from being associated with the presence of core investors despite the costs of mass privatization for them, analyzed in section 4.1. Associating core investors with mass privatization, however, would certainly have slowed down its pace, remembering that speed was the main objective pursued.

The question is raised of whether these economic costs were worth the political benefits associated with privatization. If anything, bad economic performance after mass privatization undermines the irreversibility it was supposed to create in the first place. However, it would be wrong to judge the privatization performance in transition economies against the standards of economically ideal privatization plans. Political constraints must be taken into account, and a counterfactual analysis must indicate how these constraints could have been satisfied. The Polish experience is probably the closest to such a counterfactual analysis. Because mass privatization was blocked politically, Poland has experienced gradual privatization via sales. Poland was thereby spared the negative, intended or unintended, economic consequences associated with mass privatization. Advocates of mass privatization often claim that the only alternative was status quo and inertia. Such a conclusion is not necessarily warranted. The Polish experience of gradual reform, which can be interpreted along the lines of Chapters 2 and 3, suggests that status quo was not necessarily the only alternative. As seen in those chapters, gradualism can create momentum effects and build constituencies for further reform. Moreover, it can take advantage of divide-and-rule tactics to overcome political resistance. In any case, much research still needs to be done to understand better the economics costs and political benefits of mass privatization in comparison to the costs and benefits of other privatization paths in the light of existing political constraints.

4.6   CONCLUSIONS FOR PART ONE

Let us briefly summarize and comment on the main results from the first part of the book. We have analyzed the effects of political constraints on reform strategies, and in particular on the speed and sequencing of reforms under individual and aggregate uncertainty and in the absence of uncertainty. The analysis of individual uncertainty has put forward the concept of status quo bias. Resolution of individual uncertainty over time generates a difference between ex ante and ex post political constraints. Successful reforms must satisfy both ex ante and ex post constraints, and this necessity is the source of the status quo bias. When uncertainty is only individual, gradualist strategies splitting reform packages can create an interim status quo bias as vested interests created by the first reform may block or undo reforms at the interim stage. Big bang strategies are then generally superior because they can prevent such interim status quo bias by packaging reversible reform packages. When uncertainty is also aggregate, however, gradualism can be a way of overcoming the status quo bias, because it allows for experimentation with reforms and because gradualism has an option value of early reversal that big bang does not have. As a result, voters are more willing ex ante to accept starting a reform process. A crucial condition for this result is that partial reform must achieve partial resolution of uncertainty and thus be informative about broader reform outcomes. Whether this condition of informativeness is present or not may depend on the way reform packages are split. It may also depend on the initial organizational form of central planning. China had better conditions for experimentation with reforms than Eastern Europe or the former Soviet Union because Chinese central planning was organized on a regional basis and not on a functional basis like the Soviet branch ministries. Gradualism was thus tried both more extensively and more successfully in China than in Eastern Europe.

We have also analyzed the sequencing of reforms under complementarities. Correct sequencing can exploit the complementarities to create momentum effects and build constituencies for further reforms. While experimentation under gradualism can make reforms ex ante more acceptable, complementarities make partial reforms unsustainable in the long run and make it necessary either to go ahead with further reforms or to go backward. Sequencing under aggregate uncertainty should thus start with reforms that have a higher likelihood of delivering important gains to a majority rather than starting with reforms that hurt a majority.

In models of political constraints without uncertainty, we have explored the Machiavellian politics an agenda setter can pursue by using divide-and-rule strategies to get reforms accepted. Here, unpackaging reforms may prove useful to play sequential majorities against each other. We have also analyzed the intertemporal trade-off between the efficiency losses from slower reform and the lower intertemporal costs of transfers that result from the partial revelation of information that is possible under a gradual reform.

Finally, we have seen how the details of mass privatization programs, with the objective of giving broad long-term stakes in the success of privatization, can matter in generating sustained political support for reforms or failing to do so.

Which results should be emphasized? In some cases, the efficiency gains from reform are virtually certain in the medium run, and there the theory without uncertainty or only with individual uncertainty should be emphasized. However, especially in the transition context, we think the case of aggregate and individual uncertainty is the most relevant one. The theory takes our own ignorance over the outcomes of complex reform processes into account. In general, many of our models, even when they capture important aspects of reality, are simplistic and ignore many other aspects that can be relevant for real policymaking. One should thus always be cautious when drawing policy recommendations from the results of our models. It is especially damaging for the reputation of the economics profession as a whole, and even more for the populations of the countries concerned, when economists present given reform blueprints as promising sure efficiency gains and then the opposite materializes. This need for caution is especially true in the transition context. Emphasizing unilaterally the irreversibility created by reforms may be misleading and damaging in welfare terms when aggregate uncertainty is important. The theory of reform under aggregate uncertainty thus emphasizes the importance of experimentation, trial and error, and a pragmatic approach open to debate enlightened by good economics. These comments do not mean at all that theory is not useful for policymaking. Often, policymaking decisions are taken on the basis of even less informed judgments. Nevertheless, economists, especially in the transition context, are not yet so knowledgeable that they can present themselves with all the assurance and knowledge that doctors have when treating a sick patient.

Among the many things that have been missing from the analysis of the political economy of reforms, let us highlight mainly the question of the role of particular political institutions in a reform process. Is it easier (or preferable) to pass reforms when the executive branch of government has relative autonomy vis-à-vis the population, or is it better to have the executive closely checked by the legislature? Are presidential regimes or parliamentary regimes better at deciding reforms? Is it better to have coalition governments or on the contrary to have majoritarian governments to pass reforms? Is a large number of veto players a bad thing (blocking good reforms) or a good thing (blocking bad reforms)? This is an important topic for research. Hellman (1998), for example, has emphasized that among democratic transition countries those with more fragmented party systems, coalition governments, and uninsulated executives have had the most progress with reforms, and he hypothesizes that this situation creates better accountability or closeness of politicians to voters and less capture by vested minority interest groups. It is true that often "reformers" are depicted as somewhat special politicians who mainly have in mind the success of efficiency-enhancing reforms they believe in. Insulating them from the pressure of interest groups may be a good thing. However, insulation of politicians from voters also creates the possibility of capture by organized interest groups that represent powerful minority interests and also the possibility of outright abuse of power by opportunistically oriented politicians. However, while more accountability is in general good, mechanisms of checks and balances that create accountability can also create paralysis of decision and attrition. Understanding the properties of various political institutions in generating reforms expected to be efficiency enhancing is clearly an important orientation for future research.

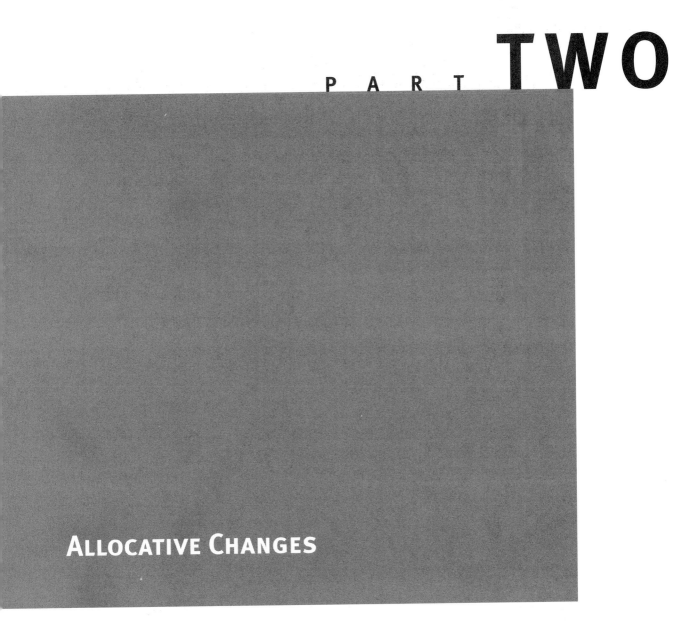

P A R T **TWO**

ALLOCATIVE CHANGES

CHAPTER 5

THE OPTIMAL SPEED OF SECTORAL REALLOCATION

A fundamental component of transition is the important change in the allocation of re-sources that takes place after price liberalization and the replacement of central planning by the market as the system for allocation of resources. If we take the standard (and sim-plified) general equilibrium view of markets illustrated in Figure 5.1, price liberalization, coupled with appropriate incentives for profit maximization and a competitive environ-ment, is meant to bring the economy from point P under central planning to point E after price liberalization. In terms of Figure 5.1, liberalization should induce an allocative shift with an increase in the production of good 2 from x_2^P to x_2^E and a relative decrease in the production of good 1 from x_1^P to x_1^E. Elimination of productive inefficiency should also bring the economy to the Pareto frontier. Liberalization should thus bring about a substantive sectoral reallocation together with an improvement in economic efficiency. As seen in Chapter 1, this change is mostly a reallocation from heavy industry to services and from large firms to smaller firms.

That such a sectoral reallocation should take place after liberalization is standard from elementary economics. The more difficult question is, At what speed should it take place? What is the optimal speed of sectoral reallocation? This question of the optimal speed of sectoral reallocation or economy-wide restructuring has been the object of important debates, especially at the beginning of economic transition in Central and Eastern European economies.

More generally, this question of the optimal speed of transition applies to all situations of sectoral reallocation that involve innovations in capital equipment in some sectors and endogenous capital depreciation in others. Transition can then be defined by the time elapsed before the full replacement of the old equipment. Similar episodes of sectoral reallocation have occurred constantly, albeit at a far less dramatic scale, in the history of capitalism. Among the more striking episodes of recent decades are the closing of coal mines, the shutting down of a large part of steel industry in Europe and

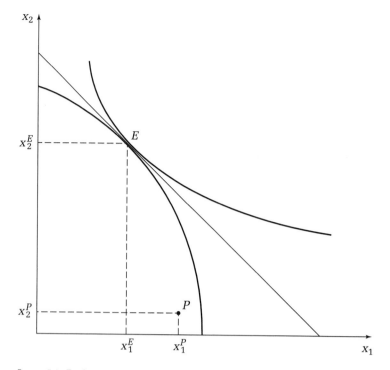

FIGURE 5.1 **THE ALLOCATIVE SHIFT OF LIBERALIZATION**

the United States, the production shifts related to globalization, and the rapid growth of East Asian economies.

In terms of the static general equilibrium approach represented in Figure 5.1, the answer to the question of the optimal speed is that transition should be instantaneous unless there are "frictions" of different kinds. We know from reality that such an important reallocation cannot be instantaneous. The question is then raised of what are the relevant frictions involved and what effect do they have on the optimal speed of sectoral reallocation. Related questions are, Is laissez-faire likely to lead to a process of reallocation that is too slow or too fast? If the instrument to influence the speed of sectoral reallocation is a path of subsidy cuts or enterprise closures, what are the economic effects of closure that is too fast or too slow? What role do political constraints play in this process?

The transition literature differs from the trade liberalization literature (see Mussa, 1978, 1986) in that reallocation is not necessarily between an import-competing and an export-oriented sector. Instead, models of allocative changes under transition consider the case of a closed economy facing internal resource constraints. External borrowing is generally not allowed, mainly because no huge capital flows took place from West to East, but also because many questions related to foreign borrowing have already been studied in the literature on sovereign debt.

In section 5.1 we first explore the role of labor market frictions in determining the optimal speed of transition. In section 5.2 we analyze the role of capital accumulation in sectoral reallocation. A similar message emerges from these two sections: while closure of money-losing enterprises that is too slow has negative effects on the expansion of the new private sector, closure that is too fast can be counterproductive and lead to a slowing of the expansion of the private sector. The mechanisms analyzed are different. In the first case the emphasis is on labor market frictions, while in the second case the emphasis is on the endogenous generation of savings in the economy, a purely neoclassical effect. In section 5.3 we discuss the related theoretical literature, and in section 5.4 the empirical literature. An important empirical literature has developed in particular to analyze labor reallocation in transition. We conclude with a reassessment of the relative importance of the debates on the optimal speed of transition.

5.1 LABOR MARKET FRICTIONS

The model reviewed in this section is the Aghion and Blanchard (1994) model, certainly one of the most cited articles on transition. Sectoral reallocation implies that labor must be transferred from the old, less efficient state sector to the new, more efficient private sector. There are, however, labor market frictions that affect the wage level. Unemployment is then necessary to maintain downward pressure on wages. Lower wages increase labor demand and thus the speed of absorption of labor in the new private sector. An unemployment rate that is too low keeps wages up and reduces the speed of labor reallocation. However, an excessively high unemployment rate cannot be optimal because it implies a fiscal burden in terms of unemployment benefits, assumed to be financed out of labor taxes. In between, there is an optimal rate of unemployment and thus an optimal rhythm of closure of state-owned enterprises (SOEs) that maximizes the speed of labor reallocation.

5.1.1 THE AGHION-BLANCHARD MODEL

We thus start with an economy where the number of workers is normalized to 1. The model is in continuous time. We denote by $N_p(t)$ the number of workers in the private sector at date t, by $N_s(t)$ the number of workers in the state sector at date t, and by $U(t)$ the number of unemployed. We thus have

$$N_p(t) + N_s(t) + U(t) = 1 \tag{5.1}$$

Reductions in the number of state employees $\overset{\bullet}{N_s}(t) = \frac{dN_s(t)}{dt}$ are decided by the government. Increases in private sector employment are decided by market forces according to the following equation:

$$\overset{\bullet}{N_p}(t) = a\{1 - [w(t) + z(t)]\} \tag{5.2}$$

where a is a scale parameter, w is the net private sector wage rate at time t, and z is the tax levied on wages at time t to finance unemployment benefits. Private sector employment is thus a function of the difference between the marginal product of labor in the private sector, normalized to 1, and the wage cost for employers $[w(t) + z(t)]$. The government's budget constraint is

$$bU(t) = [1 - U(t)]z(t) \tag{5.3}$$

where b is the per capita level of unemployment benefits, assumed time-invariant.

Wages are assumed to be set according to efficiency wage considerations. Specifically, call $V_U(t)$ and $V_{N_p}(t)$, respectively, the value of being unemployed and the value of being employed in the private sector. Calling ρ the interest (and also the discount) rate, the equation for $V_U(t)$ is then

$$\rho V_U(t) = b + \frac{\dot{N_p}(t)}{U(t)} \left[V_U(t) - V_{N_p}(t) \right] + \dot{V}_U(t) \tag{5.4}$$

The flow value of being unemployed is thus equal to the level of unemployment benefits plus the probability of being hired by the private sector (assuming for simplicity no job-to-job hires) multiplied by the increase in value from getting a private sector job. To these two expressions, one must add the change in the value from being unemployed. Similarly, we have the equation for $V_{N_p}(t)$:

$$\rho V_{N_p}(t) = w(t) + \dot{V}_{N_p}(t) \tag{5.5}$$

Efficiency wage considerations imply that there must be a wedge c, assumed constant, between the value of being in the private sector and the value of being unemployed, so that

$$V_{N_p}(t) = V_U(t) + c \tag{5.6}$$

This constant difference implies obviously that $\dot{V}_{N_p} = \dot{V}_U$. By taking the difference between equation (5.5) and (5.4), using equation (5.6) and rearranging terms, we have the equation for wage behavior

$$w(t) = b + c \left[\rho + \frac{\dot{N_p}(t)}{U(t)} \right] \tag{5.7}$$

Note that there must always be unemployment in equilibrium; otherwise the wage would go to infinity.

We assume that maximization of the net present value of output is taken as the criterion for determining the optimal speed of reallocation (maximization of intertemporal utility is considered in the next section):

$$\max_{N_s(t)} \int_0^\infty [N_s(t)y_s + N_p(t)y_p]e^{-\rho t} dt \tag{5.8}$$

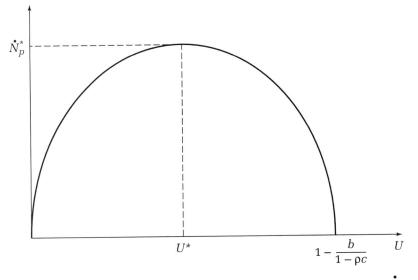

FIGURE 5.2 **THE OPTIMAL LEVEL OF UNEMPLOYMENT** (U^*) **AND THE MAXIMAL SPEED OF TRANSITION** $(\dot{N}_p^*)$

where y_s and y_p denote, respectively, (constant) marginal productivity in the state sector and in the private sector. We have assumed that $y_p = 1$ and assume realistically that $y_s < y_p$. Since private sector marginal productivity is higher than in the state sector, maximizing equation (5.8) is equivalent to maximizing $\dot{N}_p(t)$. Taking equation (5.2) and replacing $w(t)$ and $z(t)$ by their expressions in equations (5.7) and (5.3) and rearranging, we get

$$\dot{N}_p(t) = \frac{aU(t)}{U(t) + ca}\left[1 - \rho c - \frac{b}{1 - U(t)}\right] \tag{5.9}$$

Looking at this expression, we see immediately that $\dot{N}_p(t) = 0$ if $U(t) = 0$, but $\dot{N}_p(t) = 0$ also if the expression between brackets is equal to zero, that is, if $U(t) = 1 - b/(1 - rc)$. In other words, when there is no unemployment, the private sector cannot develop, but when unemployment has reached level $1 - b/(1 - \rho c)$, the private sector cannot develop either. Figure 5.2 shows that the relationship between $U(t)$ and $\dot{N}_p(t)$ represents an inverted U-curve. There is thus an optimal level of unemployment U^* that maximizes $\dot{N}_p(t)$. By setting $\dot{N}_s(t)$ so as to constantly have U^*, one thus maximizes the speed at which the private sector develops, and thus the net present value of output.

The intuition for the optimality of U^* is as follows: If $U(t)$ is below U^*, then the state sector is being closed too slowly and the lower ensuing unemployment puts an upward pressure on wages that in turn reduces labor demand and thus $\dot{N}_p(t)$. This effect is quite straightforward and expected. A less straightforward effect is that excess closures and unemployment above U^* may actually be counterproductive and reduce $\dot{N}_p(t)$.

The mechanism here is the following: Excess unemployment, by reducing net wages, increases the total wage costs because of the fiscal burden of financing unemployment benefits. This higher wage cost in turn has a negative effect on labor demand. The latter effect is important because it implies that an excess rate of closures is likely to be counterproductive. While the model shows that it will be counterproductive for the expansion of the private sector, one sees also that a faster rate of closure can be counterproductive for public finances. Indeed, by closing enterprises too fast in the hope of cutting subsidies, one still has to pay unemployment benefits. In some cases, unemployment benefits may actually be lower than the per worker subsidy of SOEs. Moreover, the model shows that an excess rate of closure tends to reduce the expansion of the tax base out of which unemployment benefits can be financed.

Another way of seeing the effect of excess closure is to see *a contrario* what would happen if we had $b = 0$. Using equation (5.9), it is easy to verify that $\frac{d\dot{N}_p(t)}{dU} > 0 \; \forall U$. Instantaneous closure of the whole private sector then becomes optimal.

The result that excess closures may actually slow down job creation in the private sector is especially interesting. It is also extremely relevant in the context of transition in East Germany. Output in East Germany collapsed virtually overnight after the adoption of the deutsche mark and the insistence of labor unions on introducing West German wage levels in East German firms. In the first few months after unification in 1990, East German industrial output had fallen by nearly 50 percent, and in 1991 it had fallen by two-thirds (Sinn and Sinn, 1993)! In the same period, employment fell from 9.7 million to about 5 million, a fall of nearly 50 percent. This blitzlike destruction of the East German economy did not lead to a faster recovery than in other transition economies. Hoping that an economic miracle would emerge like in 1948, the Germans were bitterly disappointed. That miracle has not materialized so far, and the jury is still out on whether recovery and convergence to West German living standards will take place or whether East Germany will become a new Mezzogiorno kept alive only by massive subsidies from the West. These subsidies weigh considerably on the health of the German economy.

One may question the robustness of the Aghion-Blanchard result on optimal speed. It depends on the specific assumption that unemployment benefits are paid via taxation of labor in the private sector. Ruggerone (1996) has reinterpreted the Aghion-Blanchard model to allow for inflationary finance. Note that any variation on the Aghion-Blanchard model will give the same basic results as long as increases in unemployment must be financed by some form of taxation that has a negative effect on labor demand. Such variations are a popular topic among master's and Ph.D. students.

5.2   ENDOGENOUS CAPITAL ACCUMULATION

If we abstract from labor market frictions, there are also reasons based on capital market or capital accumulation issues explaining why the optimal speed of transition is not instantaneous. We now present a model of the optimal speed of transition focusing on capital accumulation that was developed by Castanheira and Roland (2000). It features ideas similar to those of the Aghion and Blanchard (1994) model, and especially the idea that closing state enterprises too fast may be counterproductive and may slow down the speed of sectoral reallocation. The analysis, however, is based on a general equilibrium approach and is as close as possible to the standard Ramsey model. In particular, the effect of an excessive speed of closure works via the depression of output and savings. For an overly slow speed of closure to have negative effects, however, it is necessary to assume that SOEs have soft budget constraints, a consideration usually absent in other models of the optimal speed of transition.

Introducing dynamic general equilibrium considerations leads to a rejection of the static general equilibrium view according to which the optimal sectoral reallocation should be instantaneous in the absence of frictions. From the dynamic viewpoint, optimality of resource reallocation is not only optimality across sectors but also optimality across *time*, based on the consumption and savings decisions in the economy. It is important to stress that in such an economy, the benchmark result is *not* one of instantaneous transition.

The focus on capital accumulation seems natural, since much of the old capital accumulated under socialism must be scrapped and replaced by new capital, whether in privatized enterprises or in the new private sector. Moreover, from the empirical point of view, there is evidence that the expansion of private activity in Central and Eastern Europe is less impaired by the shortage of labor than by capital shortages (Konings, Lehmann, and Schaffer, 1996; Rutowski and Sinha, 1995). Since capital inflows were very scarce in the beginning of transition, a closed-economy framework seems most appropriate.[1]

The model's features are kept as close as possible to the standard Ramsey model, except that the focus is on the optimal transition path rather than on the steady state. The process of transition starts in a fully state-owned economy and ends when the old socialist capital has been either fully restructured by private owners or replaced by new private capital. There are no installation costs (Tobin, 1969; Hayashi, 1982) or time-to-build considerations (Kydland and Prescott, 1982) or other frictions. The analysis thus concentrates on the basic consumption-savings decision alone.

Even with this benchmark model, macroeconomic effects of the speed of reallocation can be analyzed in a fruitful way by exploiting the general equilibrium features of the model. We first characterize the optimal speed and then discuss the effects of deviations from the optimal speed ("too slow" or "too fast" closure of inefficient SOEs).

As in the Aghion-Blanchard model, transition is modeled as the transformation of a state-owned into a private economy.

Assume that there is one unit of labor per firm and that production functions are of the Leontieff type with $y_p = 1$ and $y_s = A(s)$, $A(s) \in [A_0, A_1]$ with $A_0 < A_1 < 1$. The assumption of Leontieff technology is very reasonable given the limited possibilities for capital-labor technological substitution in the state sector. It makes the steady state

[1] *There are nevertheless interesting international economics issues related to transition. See, e.g., Grafe and Wyplosz (1997).*

more easy to define and simplifies the analysis. Given the assumptions on technology, aggregate output at time t of transition is given by

$$Y(t) = L_p + \int_{A_1}^{L_s(t)} A(s) ds \tag{5.10}$$

where $L_s(t)$ is the index of the least productive SOE in operation at time t. Firms are ranked from the more to the less productive. The latter are optimally closed first when labor is needed in the private sector.

As in the Aghion-Blanchard model, labor is also assumed to be homogeneous and perfectly mobile across firms. There is a fixed inelastic labor supply normalized to 1:

$$L_p(t) + L_s(t) \leq 1, \quad \forall t \tag{5.11}$$

The higher efficiency of a private (or privatized) firm can only be achieved after investment in newly accumulated capital. The representative consumer chooses her consumption level $C(t)$ so as to maximize the following:

$$\max_{C(t)} \int_0^\infty u\left[C(t)\right] e^{-\rho t}\, dt$$

with

$$u\left[C(t)\right] = \frac{C(t)^{1-\sigma}}{1-\sigma}, \quad \forall \sigma > 0, \text{ if } \sigma \neq 1 \tag{5.12}$$
$$= log\left[C(t)\right], \quad \text{if } \sigma = 1$$

where $1/\sigma$ is the intertemporal elasticity of substitution and $\rho > 0$ is the discount factor. Since the analysis is done in a closed-economy framework, capital accumulation is simply determined by savings, the unconsumed part of income, where we assume that one unit of capital is needed per new private firm. Since there is one unit of labor per firm, we thus have

$$\dot{K} = \dot{K_P} = \dot{L_P} \leq S(t) = Y(.) - C(t) \tag{5.13}$$

As capital accumulation drives transition, savings $S(t)$ also determine the *speed of transition*. Perfect mobility of labor implies that wages are always equalized between the two sectors. Given the production technology, equality of wages implies that the return to capital is always lower in the state sector than in the private sector. As a consequence, all investment goes to the new—private—technology.

The steady state of the system (the end point of transition) is of the simplest kind. As there is neither technical progress nor population growth, it involves $C(T) = Y(T)$—no accumulation—and $\partial Y_p(., .)/\partial L_p = \rho$ as in the standard Ramsey model. This steady state can be reached either in a finite length of time or asymptotically, depending on the parameters of the production functions.

5.2.1 THE OPTIMAL SPEED OF TRANSITION

The optimal transition path thus solves the social planner's optimization program:

$$\max_{\substack{K_S(t)),\\ L_S(t),C(t)}} \int_0^\infty \frac{C(t)^{1-\sigma}}{1-\sigma} e^{-\rho t}\, dt \tag{5.14}$$

subject to

$$\dot{K}_p(t) = Y\left(L_s, L_p\right) - C(t)$$

$$L_p(t) + L_s(t) \leq 1$$

The present-value Hamiltonian of this program is

$$H(t) = \left\{ \frac{C(t)^{1-\sigma}}{1-\sigma} + \lambda(t)\ [Y\,(.) - C(t)] + w(t)\left[1 - L_p(t) - L_s(t)\right] \right\} e^{-\rho t} \tag{5.15}$$

where $\lambda(t)$ is the costate variable and $w(t)$ the Lagrange multiplier for labor. In addition to the transversality condition, we have the following first-order conditions:

$$C(t)^{-\sigma} = \lambda(t) \quad (\geq 0) \tag{5.16}$$

$$\frac{\dot{\lambda}(t)}{\lambda(t)} = \rho - \frac{dY(t)}{dL_p(t)} \tag{5.17}$$

Taken together, these first-order conditions imply that

$$\frac{\dot{C}(t)}{C(t)} = \frac{1 - A(L_s) - \rho}{\sigma} \tag{5.18}$$

Note that the social marginal product of capital $dY(t)/dL_p(t)$ is equal to $1 - A(L_s)$. One additional unit of capital yields one more unit of output minus the loss of output in the least productive firm from which labor must be withdrawn. By equation (5.18), the growth rate of consumption is directly linked to the return to capital.

With the accumulation of private capital, employment in the state sector declines continuously, contributing to a decrease in the marginal product of capital and to a continuous shrinking of the state sector. It can be easily shown (see Castanheira and Roland, 1999) that the savings and growth rates also decline along the optimal path. An obvious—though important—implication of optimality is that output never declines along the optimal path. This benchmark model thus cannot be used to characterize as optimal the important output contraction that has taken place in Central and Eastern European economies at the beginning of transition (see Chapter 7).

Figure 5.3 (from Castanheira and Roland, 2000) shows simulations of the transition path. The distribution of technology in the state sector has been chosen to follow $A(s) = 1 - \rho - \varepsilon - a.s$, such that $A(0) < 1 - \rho$. The latter condition implies that all firms are privatized in a finite length of time. All state firms are assumed to have positive value added so that there is no immediate closure of state firms. The simulation has been run with GAMS by discretizing time. For more realism, the capital-labor ratio in the private sector has been chosen equal to 4. Other parameter values are $\rho = 0.03$, $\sigma = 1$,

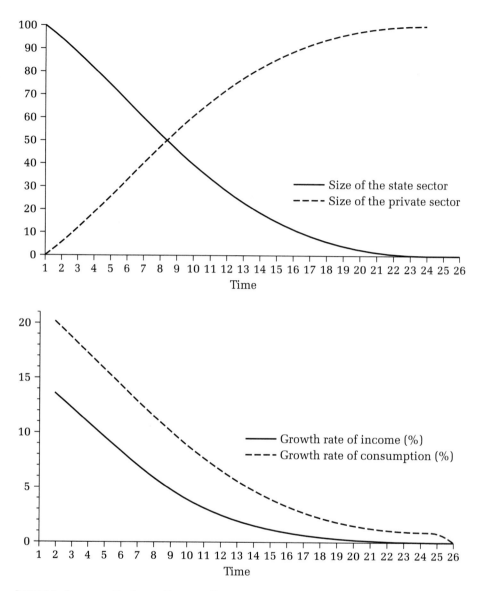

FIGURE 5.3 BENCHMARK: THE OPTIMAL TRANSITION PATH

and $\varepsilon = 0.01$. Given this choice of parameters, total transition lasts 25 periods. Increasing σ substantially lengthens transition (47 periods with $\sigma = 3$ and 111 periods with $\sigma = 10$). Figure 5.3 shows that the speed of transition is hump shaped.

5.2.2   DEVIATIONS FROM THE OPTIMAL SPEED

Let us now look at the economic effects of deviations from the optimal path, the most interesting part of the analysis. In particular, let us see what happens when the govern-

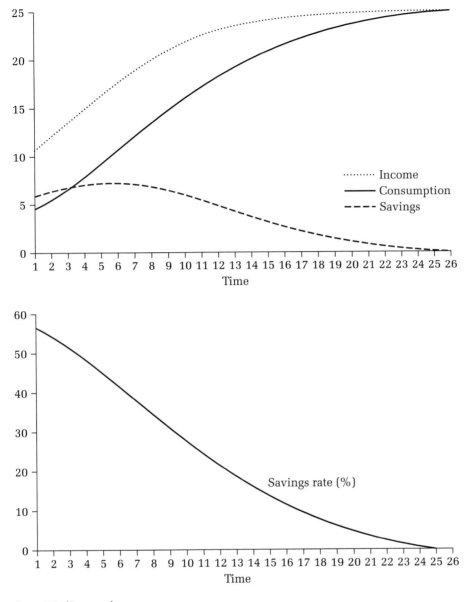

FIGURE 5.3 (CONTINUED)

ment closes down enterprises too fast or too slowly. Such deviations will occur if the government is pursuing an objective different from social welfare. For example, too low a speed of closure may be decided by a conservative government, or too high a speed of closure may be implemented by a radical government.

Let us characterize the effects of exogenous policy actions, where the government acts exogenously on the size of the state sector. It is assumed that the government follows a closure path $\Gamma(t)$, such that

$$L_s(t) \leq \Gamma(t), \quad \forall t \tag{5.19}$$

Note that formula (5.19) is not necessarily an equality. It is possible to have $L_s(t) < \Gamma(t)$ if voluntary exit of workers from the state sector proceeds faster than enterprise closure.

Private agents thus make their consumption-savings decisions by solving

$$\max_{\substack{L_s(t), \\ L_p(t), C(t)}} \int_0^\infty \frac{C(t)^{1-\sigma}}{1-\sigma} e^{-\rho t} \, dt \tag{5.20}$$

subject to

$$\dot{K}_p(t) = Y\left(L_s(t), L_p(t)\right) - C(t)$$
$$L_p(t) + L_s(t) \leq 1$$
$$K_s(t) = L_s(t) \leq \Gamma(t)$$

We then get

$$\frac{\dot{C}(t)}{C(t)} = \frac{1 - w(t) - \rho}{\sigma} \tag{5.21}$$

If the optimal path derived in the preceding section is denoted by $L_s^*(t)$, then excessively slow closure implies $\Gamma(t) \geq L_s^*(t)$ with strict inequality for at least some t, and excessively fast closure implies $\Gamma(t) \leq L_s^*(t)$ with strict inequality for at least some t.

Closure That Is Too Slow

Intuitively, one would think that a speed of closure that is too slow would tend to slow down the process of transition and private capital accumulation. However, this supposition is not generally true unless one assumes some distortion such as soft budget constraints creating a wedge between wages and the marginal product in SOEs. We will say that when SOEs have hard budget constraints (HBC), wage payments cannot exceed the marginal product of labor. Conversely, when they have soft budget constraints (SBC), wage payments will be higher than the marginal product of labor. Note that these do not constitute definitions of hard versus soft budget constraints but rather their consequences. In Chapter 9 we will analyze rigorous microeconomic foundations and explanations for why firms have hard versus soft budget constraints.

When SOEs have hard budget constraints, then the wage rate cannot exceed output in the least productive state firm at any moment in time. Therefore, $w(t) \leq A(L_s)$. In that case, we make the interesting observation that excessively slow closure does not have any adverse effects on the speed of transition. Indeed, the private sector will always compete for labor in the state sector and bid up to $A(L_s)$ to hire away labor in the least productive firm at each moment in time. Since SOEs have hard budget constraints, the SOE can

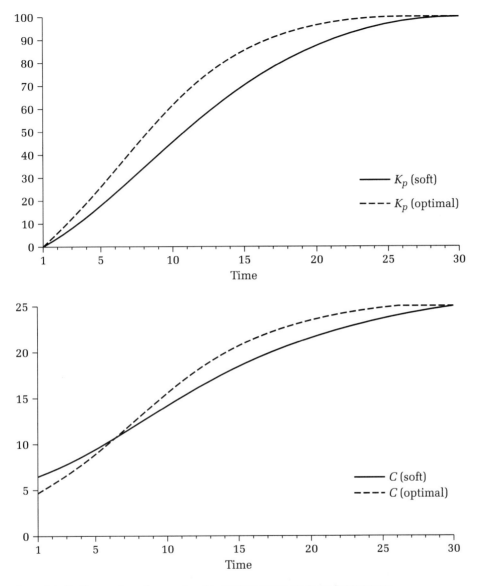

FIGURE 5.4 THE SLOWING DOWN EFFECT OF SOFT BUDGET CONSTRAINTS AND CROSS-SUBSIDIZATION

bid up the wage rate up to $A(L_s)$ but not further. Therefore, the optimality conditions remain fulfilled. Basically, closure that is too slow represents no constraint at all, since the private sector will bid away labor in SOEs before the firms are closed. Therefore, when SOEs have hard budget constraints, an overly slow rate of closure does not prevent the economy from following the optimal speed of transition.

However, if there are soft budget constraints and $w(t) > A(L_s)$, then the transition process will be slowed down because the higher wages will discourage investment in the private sector. Figure 5.4 displays the transition path when the government exhausts all

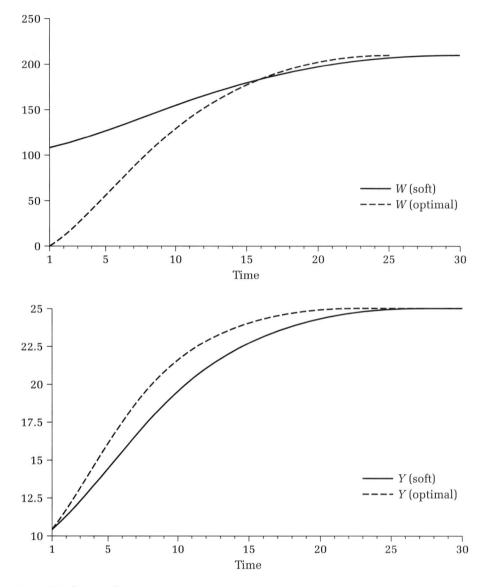

FIGURE 5.4 (CONTINUED)

possibilities of softening the budget constraints of state firms through cross-subsidization. The slowing down effect on savings early in transition is quite clear.

Even with very unproductive state firms, hardening budget constraints is enough to ensure the optimal path of transition under laissez-faire conditions. The usefulness of hardening of budget constraints in the state sector has been increasingly acknowledged in the transition literature since the empirical work of Belka, Krajewski, and Pinto (1993). However, the model of this section says nothing about whether budget constraints will in effect be hard or not, a subject that we will come back to in Part Three.

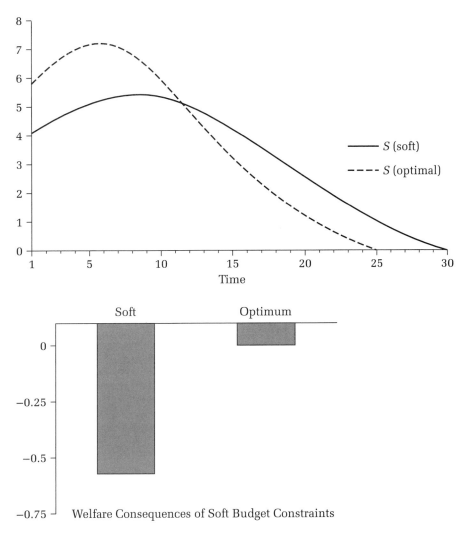

Welfare Consequences of Soft Budget Constraints

FIGURE 5.4 (CONTINUED)

Closure That Is Too Fast

What happens when there is excessively fast closure? There are reasons to expect a systematically faster transition with accelerated closure. Indeed, in contrast to the Aghion and Blanchard model, there are no costs to closure in terms of taxes or unemployment benefits in this model. Fast closure drives down wages and thus increases the return to investment. This *substitution effect* increases the accumulation *rate*. However, it is here that the general equilibrium framework plays a useful role. Indeed, there is also an *income effect* of excess closure, that is, the loss of output from closed firms. This income effect would tend to depress savings and thus to have an effect opposite to that of slowing down transition. We must also consider a third effect, namely, a consumption-smoothing effect. A future expected shock associated with enterprise closure induces consumers to

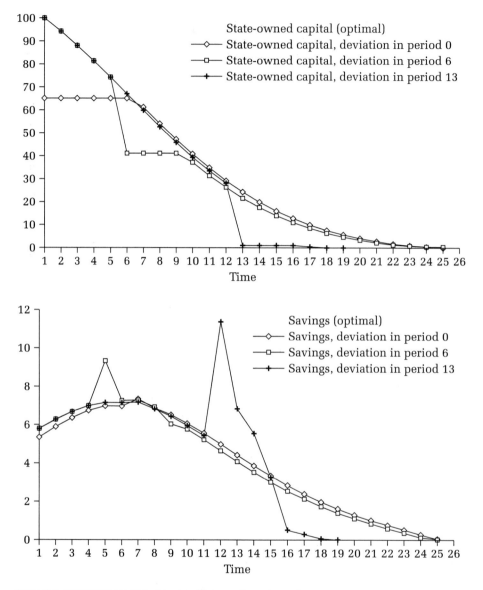

FIGURE 5.5 TIME EFFECT OF A GIVEN DEVIATION (CONSTANT FALL IN INCOME)

smooth the evolution of the savings rate across time. For the sake of clarity, and in order to isolate the first two effects, we concentrate the analysis on the case of "unexpected" excess closure compared to the optimal path where this third effect is not present.

Figure 5.5 illustrates the effects of an excess closure of identical size but implemented at different points in time. Each graph plots four paths of transition: the optimal path and paths with excess closure in periods 0, 6, and 13. Each deviation generates an

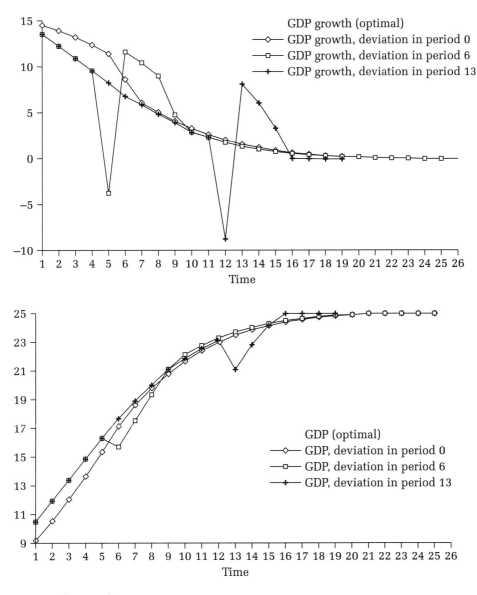

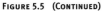

FIGURE 5.5 (CONTINUED)

output fall of equal size as measured at time 0. One sees that the early deviation generates a slower transition (the length of the transition increases by one period) and a higher welfare loss compared to later deviations, despite a lower variability of consumption. Early excess closure leads to higher measured GDP growth early in transition. This higher growth, resulting from the initial depression in income, should not hide the systematic welfare loss and, sometimes, the overall slowdown of transition.

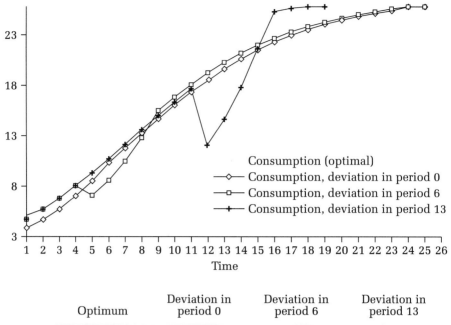

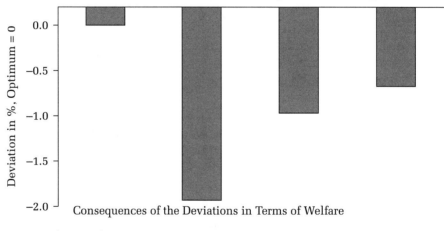

FIGURE 5.5 (CONTINUED)

The preceding model also relates directly to the new literature on transitional dynamics. King and Rebelo (1993) have studied how transitional dynamics can explain economic growth. The Castanheira and Roland (2000) model produces transitional paths for real variables (capital or savings) that are close to the ones of King and Rebelo but do not feature interest rates as unrealistically high as theirs, mainly because accumulation is considered here jointly with the process of reallocation and because of the different aggregate production function. Also, in the preceding model, the savings rate must necessarily decline along the optimal transition path, which is not the case with King and Rebelo (1993). In their simulations, they obtain a growing savings rate when the elasticity of substitution is sufficiently low, which might create an acceleration in the growth rate of the economy. This result occurs because the steady-state savings rate is strictly positive in their model, whereas it is zero in the Castanheira and Roland model.

5.3   RELATED THEORETICAL LITERATURE

There are other papers that look at the problem of sectoral reallocation of resources from the point of view of the speed of transition. Atkeson and Kehoe (1996), like Aghion and Blanchard (1994), analyze the role of search frictions on the labor market but in a general equilibrium framework with social insurance. All workers start off in the state sector and search for a job in the private sector where they have a probability of finding a good match with high productivity and a probability of finding a bad match with lower productivity. They then compare the case where agents do not benefit from social insurance when searching and the case where they are insured. Their main result is that social insurance, though increasing welfare, reduces the speed of sectoral reallocation, because of the general equilibrium effects of the model. Even though social insurance increases the willingness of an individual agent to search, in general equilibrium consumption-smoothing demands of agents can only be satisfied from the income produced by agents who do not search, that is, by a lower speed of transition.

Chadha and Coricelli (1994) model the greater strains on the government budget when the speed of reallocation is faster. Gavin (1993) develops a model that emphasizes the role of congestion externalities in the labor market if sectoral reallocation is too fast.

5.4   THE EMPIRICAL LITERATURE ON SECTORAL
AND LABOR REALLOCATION

Apart from East Germany, which fits quite well the effects of excess rates of closure shown in the models in this chapter, in other transition economies the dangers of excess closures have not materialized. There has not been a big wave of enterprise closures either at the beginning of transition or at a later stage. Even though there have been few enterprise closures, there has been a wave of layoffs in SOEs, but these followed the output fall by more than a year in most countries. The output fall has not been associated with important intersectoral shifts, as documented by Fingleton and colleagues (1996), Jackson and Repkine (1997), or Grosfeld and Nivet (1997b). Sectoral shares in industrial output across transition economies have in general remained much more stable than expected.

An important empirical literature has developed on labor reallocation in transition countries which yields many important and interesting findings that were not predicted at the beginning of transition. Aggregate labor statistics show a reduction in state sector jobs and an increase in private employment and unemployment. These findings are in line with the Aghion-Blanchard model. However, a detailed look at the data reveals some striking facts reported in Boeri (1999, in press).

First of all, a substantial part of outflows from the state sector was due to job leavers, not to job losers. The bulk of flows from employment to unemployment in Central Europe was a result of quits. Moreover, outflows from employment out of the labor force tended to be higher than outflows from employment to unemployment. For example, in Poland in 1992 and 1993, the former were twice as important as the latter.

Second, the monthly inflow rates into unemployment (unemployment inflows as a percentage of the working-age population) were at most half a percentage point in most transition countries, compared to more than 1 percent in Europe and 2–3 percent in North America (Boeri, 1999). The large increase in unemployment observed in most transition countries was thus not due to high rates of layoff in SOEs but mostly to very low rates of flow out of the unemployment pool: at most 5 percent of job seekers were leaving unemployment every month because they had found a job. Compared to other countries, the Czech Republic has maintained a lower unemployment rate (see Ham, Svejnar, and Terrell, 1998; Svejnar, Munich, and Terrell, 1997).

Third, job-to-job flows tended to be more important than flows by way of unemployment (see, e.g., Sorm and Terrell, 1999).

Fourth, overall worker mobility in transition economies has in fact turned out to be very low. Different measures of worker mobility show that it tends to be lower than in countries with sclerotic labor markets like Italy. Worker mobility is lower than measures of structural change. Here also, it is worthwhile reporting significant differences across countries. For example, the standard deviation of employment growth rates across sectors in Russia has been between one-half and two-thirds of the level observed in Visegrad countries (Poland, Hungary, the Czech Republic, and Slovakia) while Romania and Bulgaria are somewhere in between. Moreover, the employment-to-output elasticity, measuring the responsiveness of employment to output changes, has also been markedly different across countries: 0.8 for Visegrad countries in 1989–92 compared to 0.17 for Russia in 1991–94, periods when the output fall was the steepest (Boeri, 1999). In Chapter 9 we will see that these low elasticities are interpreted in some of the literature as indications of soft budget constraints.

Voluntary quits and job-to-job flows do tend to show that it is not the rate of layoffs that has in practice determined the dynamics of labor reallocation but voluntary mobility decisions of workers, tending to show, in line with the Castanheira-Roland model, that the rate of closures and layoffs was too slow rather than too fast. The more worrying news is the stagnancy of the unemployment pool. Boeri (1999) argues that unemployment benefits were too generous at the beginning of transition and tended to lead de facto to the withdrawal of low-skilled workers from the labor force.

Faggio and Konings (1999) analyze job flows in five transition countries: Poland, Estonia, Slovenia, Bulgaria, and Romania between 1993 and 1997. They find that most of the job reallocation occurs within sectors and regions rather than across sectors and regions. Higher job growth takes place in foreign-owned firms, whereas small businesses have the highest turnover. At the macrolevel, job destruction dominates job creation early on but job creation picks up and equals job destruction as transition progresses.

The lower labor mobility in Russia has been compounded by a very low mobility of labor across regions. Friebel and Guriev (1998) explain this low mobility by the increasing share of in-kind payments to workers that have the effect of "attaching" workers to their factory, reducing their outside options, and facilitating holdup of workers by enterprise managers and owners.

5.5 HOW RELEVANT WAS THE OPTIMAL SPEED DEBATE?

The models in this chapter have mainly emphasized the effects of excessively slow and excessively fast closure of SOEs on the speed of sectoral reallocation. The lessons from this chapter have undoubtedly a general appeal as they can apply to all sorts of episodes of sectoral reallocation.

The excessive speed of closure of SOEs exhibited by the models in this chapter applies directly to the East German experience, where it most likely had an adverse effect on the speed of reallocation. In line with the Aghion and Blanchard model, the rapid closure of East German industry has contributed to an increase in the burden of taxation in Germany that has a negative effect on labor demand in the economy. In line with the Castanheira and Roland model, it had led to a serious depression in the East German economy. Beyond the East German experience, the question is raised of the extent to which the models in this chapter provide an explanation for the important output fall observed at the beginning of transition.

As seen in the previous section, reality has been quite different. There has not been excess labor shedding in other transition economies, and sectoral shares of output have moved less than expected. These models can thus not be mobilized to explain the important output fall that took place early in transition and that we will analyze in Chapter 7. Rather, the models in this chapter reflect debates that took place early on in the transition period on the costs and benefits of speed in enterprise closure. There was a widespread feeling then in policy circles that radical closure of SOEs would mostly bring only economic benefits despite the social costs and would be economically desirable if politically feasible. The models in this chapter show that there may be substantial economic costs associated with excessive speed of closure in terms of a lower speed of sectoral reallocation. These results remain true even if excess labor shedding has only been observed in East Germany.

CHAPTER 6

SPEED AND METHODS OF PRICE LIBERALIZATION

Price liberalization is a key element of transition, because it is a necessary condition for the introduction of the market mechanism. Since the objective of liberalization is to bring about a dramatic improvement in the allocation of resources, there is an important efficiency dimension to price liberalization. However, there is also an important redistributive dimension that may have political economy implications, since price liberalization will in the short run create winners and losers. Both dimensions, efficiency and redistribution, play a very important role.

Lipton and Sachs (1990a) and Boycko (1992) have mostly emphasized the efficiency dimension by putting forward the proposition that price liberalization is welfare improving. A very schematic presentation of that idea, as presented by Lipton and Sachs, is the following. Assume that supply is inelastic at a level Q. Assume that there is an average cost of queuing s so that when the price level for a good is below the market-clearing price, the expected welfare for the representative agent is $Q - s$. After price liberalization, the price may be higher, but there is no queuing anymore and supply is still at level Q. Therefore, welfare is raised to level Q. The idea can be presented in a more sophisticated way within a general equilibrium model, but the basic idea will be the same as long as one reasons within a representative agent framework.

In reality, individual heterogeneity with differences in taste and mostly in income is a key fact of life. Assuming inelastic supply, rationing by the price mechanism will favor individuals with the highest willingness to pay. In practice, differences in income will favor individuals with higher income who have the highest ability to pay. When there is quantity rationing, poor individuals who get served at a lower price may get important consumer surpluses despite the aggregate inefficiency of queuing, possibly making this form of rationing preferred by a majority (see, e.g., Sah, 1987). If we think a bit about this issue, we realize that central planning could have perfectly coexisted with flexible prices for consumers. Since supply to consumers would have been totally inelastic to market prices because supply was determined by the central planning system, this system would have been equivalent to rationing by prices. This form of rationing would have had no effect on allocative decisions within the state sector and thus would not have led to a loss of control of central planners over resources. The only important effects would have been on the redistribution of consumer goods across income categories. One may then wonder why under socialism rationing by quantities and queuing was chosen over rationing by prices. A quite likely answer is that this form of rationing was preferred by a majority over rationing by prices. If not, communist leaders could easily have made themselves more popular by introducing flexible prices, while maintaining the central planning system intact.

These few thoughts about rationing by prices serve only to show the importance of the redistributive dimension in price liberalization, next to the efficiency dimension. When the redistributive dimension is important enough, political constraints will appear and will have to be dealt with. These political constraints are reinforced when we take into account the fact that bureaucrats and regulators may benefit directly from the persistence of price controls because the latter represent opportunities for soliciting bribes from consumers with a high willingness to pay (see the model of Shleifer and Vishny, 1992).[1]

Data on the degree of price liberalization in selected transition economies can be seen in Table 6.1. Unfortunately, we lack data for Russia and Ukraine. The general pattern is one of important though not full liberalization early on in transition. Note, however, the important reversal of price liberalization in Bulgaria between 1994 and 1996, indicating that political constraints have been at play. In many countries of the former Soviet Union, prices remained under central control for a longer period indicating possible political constraints. In Latvia there was quick price liberalization in 1992, but since 1994 there has been an increase in price controls.

Usually, economists argue against partial price liberalization as a way to get around political constraints of price liberalization because of the economic distortions created. In section 6.1, drawing on Murphy, Shleifer, and Vishny (1992), we show that partial price liberalization may lead to substantial diversion of resources that may reduce allocative efficiency even compared to central planning. Since partial price liberalization is distortionary and results in efficiency losses, a natural way to deal with political constraints is to fully liberalize prices and to compensate the losers. We know, however, from Chapter 3 that there are cases where this approach may not be feasible because of the distortionary costs of raising funds to compensate losers. In the experience of the Chinese transition, a new method has been found both to achieve efficiency and to avoid creating losers. This is the so-called dual-track liberalization whereby planned deliveries between firms are frozen at a certain level and contracted at planned prices while all residual output produced by firms can be freely sold at market prices and all profits from this residual output accrue to firms. Dual-track liberalization is an original method found to overcome the political constraints associated with price liberalization while avoiding the pitfalls of partial liberalization. The Chinese dual track thus represents a clever form of gradualism in price liberalization in the sense that the plan track is gradually phased

[1] *Berkowitz (1996), however, shows that local government officials who wish to be reelected will not support price controls when the size of the private sector is big enough.*

TABLE 6.1 SHARE OF ADMINISTERED PRICES IN THE CONSUMER PRICE INDEX (PERCENT)

	1990	1991	1992	1993	1994	1995	1996	1997	1998
Poland	11	11	11	10.6	12	12	11.6	10.6	10.6
Hungary	16	11	10.9	10.8	11.8	12.9	12.8	15.9	
Czech Republic		27.9	18.3	17.9	18.1	17.4	17.4	13.3	13.3
Slovenia			23.7	19.8	18.4	22.5	22.4	20.4	17
Slovakia				21.8	21.8	21.8	21.8	14.9	14.9
Bulgaria	70	24	16	26	43	46	52	14.4	15.8
Romania	85	47	29	20	18	18	18	7	
Armenia				8.9	12.8	6.2	7.7	7	6.9
Azerbaijan					77	77	8	6	6
Belarus		90	80	70	60	45	30	27	
Estonia					21.1	18	24	24	24
Georgia					13.4	13	13	8.3	
Latvia			6.1	6.1	16.6	16.6	17.8	19.6	20.4

Source: *European Bank for Reconstruction and Development*, Transition Report *(London: EBRD, 1999).*

out so that eventually the whole economy is fully liberalized. The speed of the phasing out, and thus the speed of liberalization, can thus be adjusted as a function of the political constraints. The system of dual-price liberalization will be examined in section 6.2. In section 6.3 we present some evidence on resistance to price liberalization illustrating the importance of its distributive effects, and in section 6.4 we present some empirical evidence on the allocative effects of dual-track liberalization.

6.1 PITFALLS OF PARTIAL LIBERALIZATION

Economists know well from price theory that if not all prices are liberalized there will be allocative distortions. Murphy, Shleifer, and Vishny (1992) have emphasized the devastating effects of price liberalization when the same goods can be exchanged freely by some agents in some locations and not by other agents in other locations. For example, assume the equilibrium price for Washington apples is at 15. If the price is artificially set at 10 by a central planner, there will be excess demand and shortages. If, however, the price of 10 is fixed in only thirty U.S. states and not in the remaining states, then apples can be sold in the latter in large quantities at a price of $10 + \varepsilon$, thereby diverting

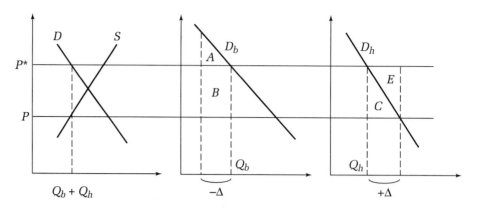

FIGURE 6.1 INPUT DIVERSION UNDER EFFICIENT INITIAL RATIONING

supply away from the states where prices are fixed. This diversion will have the effect of strongly increasing the observed shortage.

Coming back to the theme of complementarities in reform discussed in Chapter 2, the Murphy, Shleifer, and Vishny model is a good illustration of the disruptions that can be caused by partial reform. Their analysis was produced to explain the input diversion that took place in the state sector in the Soviet Union during the Gorbachev period when a small private sector was allowed to develop (under the name of "cooperatives" given the ideological taboo that existed against private ownership).

The analysis can be illustrated graphically in an easy way. Assume that there is one input, timber, that can be used to produce houses (sector h) or boxcars (sector b). House production is assumed to become private, but boxcar production is assumed to remain state controlled. The price of timber P is assumed to be below the market-clearing level. It is also the price really paid by both sectors. In other words, it is assumed that there are no bribes to pay for inputs. Producers are assumed to be on the market supply curve, and initial efficient rationing is assumed so that both sectors are allocated quantities Q_h and Q_b for which they both have the same willingness to pay P^*. After partial reform, timber can be sold freely, but the boxcar sector is forced to buy at price P, whereas the house sector is free to buy at any market price.

Figure 6.1 illustrates the setup and shows the effect of partial price liberalization. Since h can buy timber at any price above P, it can obtain timber at price $P + \varepsilon$ and obtain an additional quantity Δ so that its total demand $Q_h + \Delta$ at price $P + \varepsilon$ is satisfied. As total supply at price P is equal to $Q_h + Q_b$, sector b will receive $Q_b - \Delta$ instead of Q_b as previously. The welfare effects are easily found. Sector h gains area C under its demand curve, which is the increase in consumer surplus, whereas sector h loses areas A and B. Noting that area B is equal to the sum of areas C and E, there are clear welfare losses equal to $A + E$. The higher the elasticity of demand for timber by h, the higher the diversion Δ. The lower the elasticity of demand for timber by b, the larger the welfare loss A.

It is easy to see that with efficient initial rationing, there will always be an overall welfare loss. Indeed, the gain by h is always smaller than $\Delta(P^* - P)$ as long as D_h is

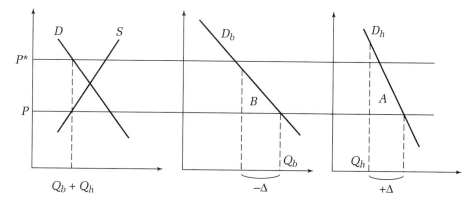

FIGURE 6.2 INPUT DIVERSION UNDER INEFFICIENT INITIAL RATIONING

negatively sloped, whereas the loss to b is always higher than $\Delta(P^* - P)$ under efficient rationing, since P^* is the willingness to pay at the margin for quantity Q_b.

When the assumption of initial efficient rationing is dropped, the welfare loss from liberalization is less clear-cut and will depend on the degree of inefficiency in initial rationing and on demand elasticities. Figure 6.2 illustrates a case with initial inefficient rationing where the willingness to pay of h for quantity Q_h is much higher than the willingness to pay of b for quantity Q_b. Call A the gain of sector h and B the loss of sector b. In this case, it is easily seen in Figure 6.2 that diversion improves welfare. Diversion, by reducing the willingness to pay of h and increasing that of b can thus actually decrease the divergence between the willingness to pay of both and reduce the inefficiencies from central planning. The welfare effects of partial price liberalization will thus depend on the initial inefficiency in rationing and on the elasticities of demand in h and in b as discussed earlier.

Note that diversion is made possible here because the delivery plan Q_b cannot be enforced. If it is enforced, then the allocation remains the same as under central planning, and there is no improvement in efficiency unless additional reforms are introduced. The possibility of enforcing delivery plans allows for a very original policy of liberalization as introduced in China. The Chinese dual-track system both provides the efficiency effects of price liberalization and protects individual agents from welfare losses because it is designed to be Pareto improving. Moreover, it can be efficient under the same general conditions as in models of full price liberalization.

6.2   DUAL-TRACK PRICE LIBERALIZATION

The dual-track approach to price liberalization means that (1) in the plan track, production and prices are frozen at a defined preexisting level, usually last period's output level, and (2) in the market track, liberalization is carried out at the margin so that fully free market transactions can take place outside the plan track. Moreover, producers are fully residual claimants of profits on the market track. All prices are thus liberalized at the margin, but preexisting planned deliveries continue to be enforced at planned prices.

The agricultural reform undertaken in China in 1979, with the introduction of the contract responsibility system, may be regarded as the first successful application of the dual-track approach in the context of transition (for a comprehensive overview of the dual-track reforms in China, see Byrd, 1991, and Naughton, 1995). The commune was assigned the responsibility to sell a fixed quantity of grain (or other) output to the state procurement agency as previously mandated under the plan at predetermined plan prices. The commune was supposed to pay a fixed amount of taxes to the state as well. At the same time, it had the right to receive a fixed quantity of inputs, principally chemical fertilizers, from state-owned suppliers, again at predetermined plan prices. Subject to fulfilling these conditions, the commune was free to do whatever it wished—for example, produce whatever it considered more profitable, sell any excess output on the free market, and retain any profit. The commune reassigned the collective responsibilities (and rights) to the individual farm households, allocating to them their shares of the commune's land and capital (and chemical fertilizers), and making them individually and directly responsible for the fulfillment of their shares of the delivery quota and taxes.

The dual-track system was later implemented in industry, first in the oil sector in 1981 and then in all industry in 1984. The industrial reform represented, in part, an attempt to extend the contract responsibility system to the industrial sector, based on the successful experience of the agricultural reform. Mandatory delivery quotas as well as the quantities of plan-allocated inputs for each enterprise were frozen at existing levels, and the enterprises were free to produce whatever they deemed profitable, sell their output on the free market, and retain any profit as long as they fulfilled their delivery quota. At the same time, parallel free markets for the above-quota outputs of enterprises were introduced, while the within-quota outputs continued to be sold at the generally lower plan prices to authorized purchasers.

Prior to the economic reforms of 1979, many essential consumer goods and services, such as grain, cooking oil, meat, electricity, housing, and monthly passes for mass transit were rationed by means of coupons in the urban areas at lower than what would have been free-market prices. With the introduction of the free markets and the two-tier price system, urban residents continued to be able to purchase grain, meat, and electricity (lifeline rates), and pay housing rents (for those who had housing) at the same prereform prices within the limits of the prereform rationed quantities. The coupon system remained in place until 1993. At the same time, consumers were able to purchase freely any quantity of any good at free-market prices. They were thus not made worse off than before. The state was also no worse off because the quantities of goods that it would have to supply at the plan prices remained the same.

The dual-track system is a concrete mechanism to implement price liberalization in a Pareto-improving way. If the entire economy is liberalized following the big bang approach, transition is unlikely to be Pareto improving unless explicit compensation schemes can be adopted, which, as stated in Chapter 3, may be too costly and lack credibility. The advantage of the dual-track approach is that it builds on preexisting institutions of the plan to maintain the preexisting rents of economic agents. It provides implicit lump-sum transfers to compensate potential losers of the reform by maintaining the status quo for part of the economy, and makes potential winners strictly better off through liberalization at the margin. As these transfers are only implicit, they do not require explicit (distortionary) taxation to be implemented. As they are lump sum, they are not distortionary either. The dual-track approach is thus an original and important method to deal with political constraints to transition without necessitating explicit compensation schemes. The dual-track strategy also utilizes the existing information contained in the original plan. Moreover, the original plan is enforced through existing institutions without requiring the setting up of new institutions.

Byrd (1987, 1989) has shown the conditions under which dual-track pricing is efficient when there is physical enforcement of plan quotas. Sicular's (1988) model of the dual-track system in early agricultural reforms had already shown that it operated as a system of lump-sum transfers and proved its efficiency. Lau, Qian, and Roland (1997) provide a general equilibrium analysis of the efficiency and Pareto-improving character of dual-track price liberalization. It is shown that when enforcement of the plan is not in physical terms, but in terms of the income streams it generates, then the conditions for efficiency are exactly the same as in standard general equilibrium theory because secondary markets can be created exchanging the rights and obligations of the plan track.

Here, we follow the partial equilibrium analysis of Lau, Qian, and Roland (2000), which is useful to illustrate the Pareto-improving character and efficiency characteristics of dual-track liberalization as well as the distribution of rents generated by the dual-track system, depending on the initial conditions of supply and demand.

6.2.1   Efficient Supply and Rationing

We first take the case of efficient supply and rationing under the plan, as in section 6.1. This is the most obvious case to analyze, but we will emphasize that it rests on special assumptions with regard to the initial situation. It is also assumed that the equilibrium market quantity Q^E exceeds the planned quantity Q^P. This is the most realistic case for most markets. The existence of subsidies and money-losing activities in most sectors may give the superficially opposite impression that output was above the efficient aggregate quantity. There are, however, good reasons to believe that in many cases supply and rationing were organized inefficiently and that there were all sorts of sources of slack in the economy. Owing to the very poor incentives of economic agents in the planned economy, the production was thus often organized deep inside the production possibility frontier. Even if the plan seemed taut and shortages were observed, once incentives are provided, new resources can be released for production, and the scope for expansion of production can be substantial. Nevertheless, we also discuss further in this section the case where Q^P exceeds the equilibrium market quantity Q^E.

Efficient planned supply means that total planned supplies Q^P are delivered by the producers with the lowest marginal costs. In other words, any additional supply above the planned quantity is produced at a higher marginal cost than planned supplies.

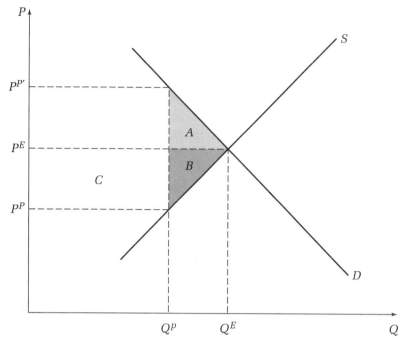

FIGURE 6.3 THE DUAL TRACK UNDER EFFICIENT SUPPLY AND RATIONING

Similarly, efficient rationing means that Q^P is delivered to buyers with the highest willingness to pay. Any above-plan purchases originate then from agents with a lower willingness to pay than $D(Q^P)$ where D is the demand curve. The whole analysis can be made with the help of Figure 6.3.

Let us start first with the case where the planned price P^P is below the market equilibrium price P^E. Dual-track price liberalization means that Q^P continues to be delivered at price P^P but that any additional quantity can be purchased freely at a market price with producers being full residual claimants of profits from market sales. This is thus price liberalization at the margin. Since $Q^P < Q^E$, it follows immediately that the market track will provide an additional $Q^E - Q^P$ at price P^E. The allocative outcome under dual-track liberalization will thus be the same as under big bang price liberalization where the plan track is fully abolished and price P^E applies to all quantities traded. The only difference is the distributional outcome. Under big bang liberalization, consumers gain shaded triangle A but lose rectangle C equivalent to $Q^P(P^E - P^P)$. In Figure 6.3, we have an example where $C > A$, showing that consumers can be made worse off from big bang price liberalization because of the loss of rents from the price increase. The area C is captured by producers who also gain triangle B. In our example, in order to make everybody better off under big bang liberalization, consumers would have to be compensated through government transfers. The dual track, however, by construction, achieves Pareto improvement without requiring any explicit transfers. Indeed, consumer rents C are maintained by the plan track, while consumers gain A and producers gain B.

Note that when the planned price is above the market-clearing price ($P^{P\prime}$ in Figure 6.3), the analysis remains essentially the same. In this case, the dual track protects producer rents. Neither the allocative outcome nor the additional rents that producers and buyers get from the market track are affected if the planned price is $P^{P\prime}$ instead of P^P.

In this simple case with efficient rationing and supply, the market track simply emerges besides the plan track to achieve efficiency-enhancing production increase while making both buyers and sellers better off. The market track can be filled either by new emerging firms appearing at the fringe or by existing SOEs that gain from supplying the market. Note that if producers are fully residual claimants of profits on the market track, they have full incentives to maximize profits and produce under efficient conditions. Even if incentives for the plan track are ill-designed, they become irrelevant because of the incentives provided by the market track. Indeed, any efficiency gain that can be achieved on the plan track will result in gains on the market track for which producers are full residual claimants. Thus when producers are given first-best incentives at the margin, they will behave in a profit-maximizing way. Just as much as liberalization at the margin is all that is needed for efficient allocative decisions, first-best incentives at the margin are all that is needed to achieve productive efficiency.

That said, it is necessary to emphasize that the preceding reasoning relies strongly on the assumption of efficient rationing and supply. In general, however, there is no reason to believe that supply and rationing were organized efficiently under socialism. Suppliers with high and low marginal costs coexisted. Slack in production capacity coexisted along with shortages (Kornai, 1980). Kornai therefore always warned against a too rapid use of the concepts of excess supply and demand in the socialist economy. Since there is no reason to assume that the organization of rationing and supply was efficient, it is difficult to grasp the initial conditions under the planning system, in terms of usual market analysis. Lau, Qian, and Roland (in press) demonstrate that, irrespective of the initial situation of supply and rationing, dual-track price liberalization is always Pareto improving. Moreover, efficiency can be achieved under exactly the same conditions as big bang price liberalization provided enforcement of the plan track is in terms of the rents it generates rather than in terms of physical quantities. In the latter case, secondary markets can emerge so that inefficient producers can subcontract the production of their delivery quotas to efficient producers at market prices and beneficiaries from planned deliveries can resell their delivery rights at market prices to buyers with a higher willingness to pay.

6.2.2 INEFFICIENT SUPPLY AND RATIONING

We first show how the dual track works when either supply or demand is organized inefficiently. We compare two cases each time. The first case is one of limited liberalization where secondary markets for plan-allocated quotas are not allowed and thus physical enforcement of plan quotas is required. The second case is one of full liberalization at the margin where market resales and market purchases for redelivery are all allowed

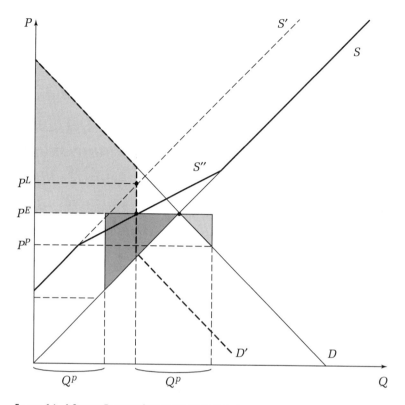

FIGURE 6.4 A CASE OF EFFICIENT SUPPLY AND INEFFICIENT RATIONING

by planned suppliers or rationed users, as long as its obligations under the plan are all fulfilled.

Figure 6.4 shows the case of efficient supply but inefficient rationing. Even though this case is just an example, it gives some interesting insights in comparison to the previous case of efficient supply and rationing.

We assume that the planning system delivers Q^P (produced by the most efficient suppliers) to agents whose willingness to pay is not the highest, and even to agents whose willingness to pay is lower than the market equilibrium price P^E. We start again from a situation where $P^P < P^E$. An important distinction that now emerges is whether resale of rationed goods is allowed or not.

Assume first that resale of goods allocated under the plan is not permitted. The market supply curve on the market track will then be represented by S', since the most efficient portion of the supply curve is taken by production for the planned quantity Q^P. Similarly, market demand is represented by D' (broken line in Figure 6.4) to take into account the fact that a portion Q^P with rather average willingness to pay is served by the plan to take into account the inefficiency in initial rationing. Therefore, we have the vertical kink in D' and the downward vertical shift of the lower portion of the demand curve. Under limited market liberalization, the market equilibrium price is then $P^L > P^E$. By construction again, the result will be Pareto improving, since Q^P will continue to be traded at price P^P and additional quantities will be exchanged at price P^L. Note, however, that the outcome will not be efficient because there are agents who are not served by the market, namely, those who have a willingness to pay lower than P^L but higher than the willingness to pay of those agents served by planned deliveries. The latter then crowd out the former, creating an obvious inefficiency.

Efficiency can however be achieved on the particular market we are considering, while maintaining Pareto improvement, if resale of planned deliveries is allowed. In that case, agents served by the plan at price P^P can resell at the market price. When resale is allowed, the supply curve then becomes S'' (in bold in Figure 6.4) taking into account supply and resales of planned deliveries for various price levels. Slightly above P^P, the supply curve coincides with S' because no agents served under the plan are willing to resell at those prices. However, when the price increases, more and more agents are willing to resell up to the point where all agents served by the plan prefer to resell all the quantities allocated to them, in which case the supply curve coincides with S. The equilibrium price will then be P^E, and efficiency will be achieved as agents with willingness to pay below P^E will resell and agents with willingness to pay higher or equal to P^E will be served by the market. By allowing for the resale of planned goods, one thus can reach efficiency, whereas by insisting on physical enforcement of the plan with prohibition of resale, one will typically not reach an efficient outcome.

The shaded areas show the additional rents created by the dual track with resale. The interesting feature to note here is that resale creates additional rents for inefficient agents served by the rationing system of the plan (the shaded triangle above D below P^E). Indeed, agents whose willingness to pay is lower than P^E derive a rent because of their right to buy inputs at price P^P and because of the possibility created to resell those inputs at price P^E. These additional rents, however, are associated with efficiency-enhancing trades and with increased consumer surplus associated with the fall in equilibrium price $(P^L - P^E)$ when resale is allowed.

Early criticisms of dual-track pricing in China mentioned the arbitraging profits agents could make from resale of planned deliveries. This criticism is related to the additional rents these agents can capture under dual-track pricing. The analysis here shows clearly that these additional rents, which can be criticized on equity grounds, should be weighed against the efficiency increase from resale and from the Pareto-improving property of dual-track pricing. Indeed, under big bang liberalization, no such additional rents are created, but pains are inflicted on losers from price liberalization, and the property of Pareto improvement is lost.

What happens if the planned price is above P^E at a price $P^{P\prime}$ (not shown in Figure 6.4) instead of P^P? Again, very little is changed in the analysis, which we leave for the reader. The only difference is that, under the initial planning conditions, the inefficient buyers (with low willingness to pay) must receive subsidies in order to agree to purchase planned deliveries Q^P at price $P^{P\prime}$. For the rest, the analysis will remain essentially the same. The plan track will now protect the interests of producers, but both the allocative outcome and the additional rents created by the dual track will be exactly the same. An example of a planned price above the equilibrium price could be that of wages in the state sector exceeding the market wage. Under the dual-track approach, an enterprise whose marginal product of labor is below P^E will still pay the planned wage, but will "resell" its labor on the market for P^E, thereby reducing its loss to the difference between $P^{P\prime}$ and P^E rather than to the difference between $P^{P\prime}$ and the marginal product of labor. In China this practice corresponds roughly to the common practice of "labor reallocation" with compensation such as housing. Reallocated workers preserve their preexisting rents because they continue to receive the planned rather than the market wage rate.[2] Under this scheme, workers should have an incentive to leave their enterprise and accept the lower market wage rate while simultaneously not being hurt.

Sachs and Woo (1992) have argued that in order to achieve an efficient labor reallocation in Eastern Europe and the former Soviet Union, it is necessary to fully cut subsidies and close down money-losing state enterprises because a subsidized wage rate that is too high prevents employees of SOEs from moving to the more efficient non-SOEs that pay the lower market rate of total compensation. This is exactly a situation of inefficient rationing in the labor market with the plan wage rate above the fully liberalized market equilibrium wage. Contrary to Sachs and Woo's assertion that only an immediate and full cut in subsidies can achieve efficient labor reallocation, the analysis makes clear that the dual-track approach with full liberalization can provide a mechanism for achieving an efficient labor reallocation in a Pareto-improving way, without hurting workers.

Assume now a case of efficient rationing but inefficient supply. Those who produce the planned supplies have higher marginal costs than other producers, whether SOEs or private enterprises. Here, also, whether secondary markets are allowed or not will play an important role in determining the efficiency of the outcome. In particular, we will see whether or not inefficient producers are allowed to subcontract their planned obligations. The analysis is done with the help of Figure 6.5.

Assume first that the planned price is P^P and that there is no subcontracting. At price P^P, inefficient producers must be paid a subsidy s (assuming asymmetric information) in order to produce without making losses. Since buyers with the highest willingness to pay are matched with inefficient sellers, demand under the market track is represented by D', which represents a leftward horizontal shift of D by the amount Q^P. Market supply is represented by S' with the vertical kink to take into account that a portion of the supply curve is taken up by initial planned supply coming from inefficient producers. Under limited market liberalization, the equilibrium price is then $P^L < P^E$. Again, Pareto improvement is achieved by construction, but the outcome is inefficient because more efficient suppliers, with marginal costs above P^L but below P^E (the efficient equilibrium level), are crowded out of production by less efficient producers working for the plan.

Efficiency in the market, however, can be achieved in a Pareto-improving way by allowing inefficient producers to subcontract their production while keeping their subsidy. In that case, they gain by abstaining from production, purchasing Q^P on the

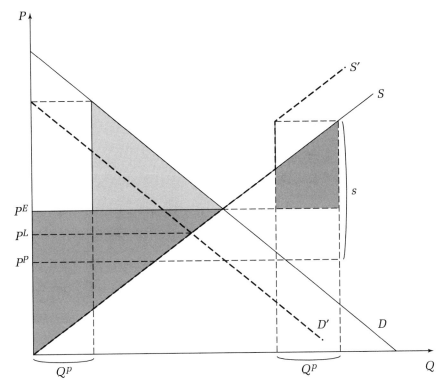

FIGURE 6.5 A CASE OF EFFICIENT RATIONING BUT INEFFICIENT SUPPLY

market at the equilibrium price and reselling it at price P^P to the customers assigned by the plan. Because of subcontracting, demand shifts from D' to D. The equilibrium price then becomes P^E, and market efficiency is achieved.

The shaded areas in Figure 6.5 indicate the additional rents created by dual track with subcontracting. Note again that the inefficient agents (here the suppliers) can use their position under the plan to get additional rents. Here, subcontracting generates rents below S and above P^E. Indeed, since producers have marginal costs above P^E, they gain from purchasing goods at that price rather than producing it themselves, and thus reduce their losses. These additional rents enjoyed by the inefficient producers, however, are associated with a higher level of efficiency and also with higher rents for other more efficient producers because the latter supply the market. They also benefit from a higher equilibrium price than in the absence of subcontracting (at equilibrium price P^L).

If the planned price is above P^E then, as in the preceding case, the analysis remains unchanged except for the subsidy to inefficient producers that becomes much lower. The rents and allocative outcome remain exactly the same.

The preceding cases were of course only stylized examples. We now consider the more general case in which Q^P is not necessarily allocated to users with the highest willingness to pay and some of the planned suppliers may have higher marginal costs than other potential suppliers. We first look at the case of limited liberalization where no secondary markets are allowed. What can we say in general about the equilibrium price and quantity in those cases?

We first show that under limited liberalization, the combined production of the plan and the market track always exceed the equilibrium market production. If the equilibrium price under limited liberalization P^L is lower than P^E, then every potential user with a willingness to pay greater than or equal to P^E will be an actual user. Moreover, since rationing is not necessarily efficient, there may also be actual users of planned supplies whose willingness to pay is below P^E. Thus, total actual demand, $Q^P + Q^L$, must be greater than or equal to Q^E. If, on the other hand, $P^L \geq P^E$, then every potential supplier with a marginal cost less than or equal to P^E will be an actual supplier. Moreover, since planning of supply is not necessarily efficient, there may also be one or more actual suppliers whose marginal costs are above P^E. Thus, total actual supply, $Q^P + Q^L$, must also be greater than or equal to Q^E. Thus, under limited liberalization, $Q^P + Q^L \geq Q^E$.

We now examine the case of full liberalization of the market track. Rationed users are now allowed to resell rationed goods in the market. Similarly, planned suppliers are allowed to purchase the goods on the market to fulfill their delivery obligations instead of producing the goods themselves. It is easy to see that the equilibrium price must be P^E and the equilibrium total quantity must be Q^E. If the equilibrium price under full liberalization were $P^F \leq P^E$, then total demand must be $Q^F \geq Q^E$. In equilibrium, total supply must then also be equal to Q^F. If all subcontracting opportunities are exploited, therefore, then no producer with marginal costs below $S(Q^F)$ remains idle, and there is no supply at marginal costs higher than $S(Q^F)$. But then the equilibrium price must be at $S(Q^F) > P^E$. Therefore, it cannot be that $P^F \leq P^E$. Similarly, if the equilibrium price were $P^F \geq P^E$, then total supply must be $Q^F \geq Q^E$. In equilibrium, demand must then also be equal to Q^F. If all resale opportunities have been used, then all buyers with willingness to buy above $D(Q^F)$ are served and all those with willingness to buy below $D(Q^F)$ have resold. But then the equilibrium price must be $D(Q^F) < P^E$. Therefore, it cannot be that $P^F \geq P^E$.

The basic idea is that under full liberalization any producer with a marginal cost below the willingness to buy of a potential buyer will find a profitable exchange, and all exchange opportunities are exhausted at the equilibrium price P^E. This will be the case because any producer with marginal costs above the equilibrium price will benefit from subcontracting and any buyer with willingness to buy below the equilibrium price will benefit from reselling.

We thus see that Pareto improvement is achieved under the dual-track system, either under limited or full liberalization, but that market efficiency is achieved under full liberalization when secondary markets are allowed.

This discussion also helps us to see what would happen if the market were liberalized sequentially, that is, if limited market liberalization were implemented in a first stage, and then one went to full market liberalization in a second stage. Since limited liberalization always leads to inefficient overproduction relative to the market equilibrium,

Pareto improvement is still attained, by construction, for agents within the plan track, but not necessarily for agents in the market track. If the equilibrium price P^L under limited liberalization is higher than P^E, then when full liberalization occurs in a later stage, new private producers will be hurt. They will lose producer rents because they will face the competition from agents reselling their planned deliveries. Similarly, if the equilibrium price under limited liberalization is lower than P^E, one can see that new buyers under limited liberalization would get hurt by full liberalization, since many producers would "buy" their planned deliveries on the market rather than produce it themselves, thereby pushing up the market price and reducing consumer surplus for those buyers.

This is thus a case where gradual liberalization—in the sense of achieving first limited market liberalization with no secondary markets allowed, followed later by a liberalization of secondary markets—will hurt agents who get rents from the initial reforms. To the extent that those agents have the power to block reforms, this case would be an illustration of the models in Chapters 2 and 3 that show how some forms of gradualism can block reforms.

6.2.3 THE PLAN QUANTITY GREATER THAN THE MARKET QUANTITY

In order to complete the analysis, it is useful to look at the case where the market equilibrium quantity is always lower than the planned quantity. This case may apply to the overproduction of tanks and other low-quality unwanted goods or possibly to the overemployment of labor.

Under limited market liberalization, the plan track and the market track are completely segregated. By assumption, $Q^P \geq Q^E$. Generically there can still be positive demand and supply in the market track, because among the residual users and suppliers there are still those with high willingness to pay and low marginal costs. Clearly, the dual-track approach is Pareto improving, but physical fulfillment of the plan production target is incompatible with efficiency because the planned quantity is greater than the efficient market quantity.

However, Pareto improvement and efficiency can be achieved if we assume again that the enforcement of the plan is in terms of the rents that it generates rather than in terms of physical output targets. With $P^P < P^E$, a planned supplier can buy back from the market, in equilibrium, at $P^E - P^P$, delivery obligations (which may be interpreted as "call options" exercisable at P^P, held by the rationed users) in the good that is supposed to be delivered under the plan, thus reducing or even eliminating the necessity of making physical deliveries (and actual production). A rationed user should be indifferent between accepting physical delivery or selling his delivery rights ("call options"), at a price $P^E - P^P$, since it is always possible to buy at the market price P^E. Profitable market exchanges of rights and obligations are possible because of the inefficiencies caused by the plan. Under this scenario, the net output of the good will be equal to Q^E, and yet there will be no complaints about the nonfulfillment of plan obligations from anyone. Indeed, the planned suppliers and rationed users will have all given or received value for their rights and obligations under the plan and are in fact at their optimized levels of profits and utilities.

The case of $P^P > P^E$ can be similarly analyzed. A rationed user can buy back from the market acceptance obligations (which may be interpreted as "put options" exercisable at P^P, held by the planned suppliers) at price $P^P - P^E$ in the good that it is supposed to receive under the plan. To take the example of the labor market, under full market liberalization, enterprises allocated labor under the plan will "resell" labor at a loss of $P^P - P^E$ per unit if its marginal product falls below P^E. This practice is equivalent to a subsidy scheme at the rate of $P^P - P^E$ provided by the enterprise. Workers within the plan whose reservation wage is higher than P^E accept the subsidy and quit the job. Thus, all enterprises will actually employ labor up to the point at which the value of the marginal product is equal to P^E. Any worker with a reservation wage below or equal to P^E will be actually employed. Efficiency in the labor market is thus achieved. Moreover, by construction again, the allocation is Pareto improving because nobody is made worse off, including the workers who leave the labor market, workers who stay, and the enterprises employing workers. Workers and enterprises outside the plan are also clearly better off because of the new opportunities offered by the market track.

6.2.4 EFFICIENCY AND PARETO IMPROVEMENT UNDER THE DUAL TRACK

We should emphasize here that there is a difference between the efficiency and Pareto-improvement properties of dual-track liberalization. Pareto improvement is obtained by construction and will hold independently of whether conditions for efficiency are present in reality or not. Thus the political economy advantages of the dual track induced by this Pareto improvement should be seen as robust to differences in market conditions. The efficiency properties are more theoretical. The point made is that theoretical conditions for market efficiency are the same under dual-track liberalization as under full liberalization. In reality, conditions for market efficiency are likely not to be present in either case, because of imperfect competition (see W. Li (1999) for an analysis of the dual-track system under a monopoly) or to transaction costs when markets do not preexist (see Chapter 7).

6.2.5 ENFORCEMENT OF THE DUAL TRACK

A crucial difference between the setup in this section and the Murphy, Shleifer, and Vishny (1992) model is the role of enforcement of planned obligations. In their model, there can be no assurance that the partial reform is Pareto improving, since suppliers are free from any delivery obligations. This is the reason why diversion of inputs can take place. Moreover, inefficiency of the plan (e.g., inefficient planned supply) may persist under partial reform because not all firms are allowed to participate in market transactions at the margin.

The idea that enforcement of the plan track is possible under transition is not unreasonable—and it was enforced in practice in China—but it is useful to discuss conditions that may or may not make enforcement possible.

First, even if incentives to evade quotas may be stronger under reform than under central planning, these incentives would be the same in regard to the fulfillment of ex post unprofitable contracts in a conventional market economy. In either case, the government has the responsibility for contract enforcement. Moreover, in a previously centrally planned economy such enforcement can be implemented by utilizing the existing institutions. Assuming that plan enforcement is impossible amounts to assuming that normal market contracts cannot be enforced in a transition economy, a worrying assumption if there is one! As we will see in Chapter 8, the dual-track system itself can provide resources that make law and contract enforcement endogenous.

Second, enforcing the preexisting plan is informationally much less demanding for the government than drawing up a new plan. Under central planning, the information requirement for drawing up a plan was huge because the market was not used. Enforcing a preexisting plan based on past output is different. In fact, the dual-track approach uses minimal additional information as compared with other possible compensation schemes.

Third, under the dual track, the focus of plan enforcement shifts to deliveries as opposed to production: an enterprise can fulfill its production target and yet at the same time fail to make any planned deliveries by selling the entire production on the market track. Therefore, the focus of enforcement shifts naturally from physical production to deliveries. Typically, enforcement action is undertaken only in response to complaints from the plan-mandated recipients of the planned output deliveries.

Fourth, the rents of the economic agents under the preexisting plan can be protected without the enforcement of (generically inefficient) physical deliveries. Physical deliveries are also difficult to enforce, unless the state actively monitors the individual interenterprise material flows of the plan. Under the dual track, the state needs only to react when delivery disputes arise, taking into account that there will be cases when it is in the joint interests of the planned suppliers and the rationed users to evade the plan. Under full liberalization at the margin, the enforcement of the rights and obligations under the plan by the government is in terms of the rents generated. The plan-allocated delivery quotas can be viewed as the combination of a put option on the part of the planned suppliers to sell at price P^P to the rationed users, and of a call option on the part of the rationed users to buy from the planned suppliers also at price P^P. The enforcement of the rights and obligations under the plan amounts to enforcement of these options.

There are also reasons that may make enforcement of the plan track difficult.

First, it is difficult, if not impossible, to enforce the allocation of consumer goods, especially when the planned price is above the market price. For example, low-quality consumer goods may become unwanted once the market is open to nonplanned suppliers. According to the logic of the dual-track approach, the rationed users who no longer purchase planned quantities at the plan price must compensate the planned suppliers to maintain the latter's rents. This requirement is clearly more difficult to enforce if the rationed users are consumers rather than producers.

Second, compliance with the plan by economic agents depends on their expectations of the credibility of government enforcement. If government enforcement is not credible, then the economic agents will have no incentive to fulfill their plan obligations. If anyone thinks that the plan-mandated deliveries at plan prices are not going to be received by him or her, he or she will not make the plan-mandated sales at the fixed plan prices either. In general, multiple (self-fulfilling) equilibria (outcomes) may be possible under a dual-track approach, depending on the expectations of the credibility of state enforcement. Chapter 8 discusses mechanisms under which the bad equilibrium can be eliminated under the dual track.

Third, the government must not only be able to enforce the existing plan track. It must also be able to commit not to extend it. If the government lacks commitment to maintain the plan at its preexisting level, it may be tempted to use the information revealed on the market track about firms' capacity in order to ratchet up enterprise plans. This action may then lead enterprises not to engage on the market track or to engage only in a rather lukewarm way. This is the so-called ratchet effect, which was an important incentive problem under socialism and which we will discuss in Chapter 9. The ratchet effect seems to be an important reason explaining why attempts to introduce forms of dual track like the Goszakaz system in the Soviet Union under Gorbachev did not produce results. In China the ratchet effect did not appear. Not only was the plan track enforced, but there has been a tendency toward either gradual phasing out of the plan track or toward "growing out of the plan," with the plan track becoming an always smaller relative share of production (see Lau, Qian, and Roland, 2000, for evidence).

In the former Soviet Union after the collapse of communism, it can be argued that the dual-track system could not be enforced because of the collapse of government. In part, one of the tragedies of transition in Russia is perhaps that there was an abrupt shift from a situation where the dual track would not have been effective because of the ratchet effect resulting from lack of commitment with a "too strong" government to a situation where it could not be enforced as a result of government collapse with a "too weak" government. We will discuss in Chapter 8 possible causes and consequences of government collapse in the transition process.

6.2.6 THE DUAL TRACK AND CORRUPTION

An important criticism of the dual-track system is that it fosters corruption. Indeed, corruption was one of the major slogans of students demonstrating in Tiananmen square in 1989. Protests against corruption were mainly directed against *guandao,* the diversion of goods by officials from the plan track to the market track. It is useful to distinguish between two types of diversion.

A first type of diversion is the one analyzed in Figure 6.4. There we compared the dual-track mechanism when secondary markets are allowed or not allowed. An intermediary case is one where secondary markets are not allowed but they nevertheless take place. Whether secondary markets are allowed or not, we have shown that the dual track can give additional rents to input buyers. Buyers who have the right to purchase inputs at the planned price P^P but who have a willingness to pay lower than the market price P^E will benefit from reselling the goods on the market and cash in a net rent of $(P^E - P^P)$ minus their willingness to pay. As discussed before, even though the dual track is Pareto-improving, these additional rents going to agents who already benefit from privileges under the planning system can seem shocking in the light of usual perceptions of fairness.

A second type of diversion documented by W. Li (1999) is that by officials in the planning system who divert part of the production under the plan quotas and resell them on the market. Data from China indeed reveal a discrepancy between market *purchases* reported by enterprises and market *sales* reported. For example, in 1987 total purchases of steel at market prices were about 37.56 million metric tons, whereas total sales reported were only 12.38 million metric tons and imports were only 12.02 million metric tons. Even if all imports had been sold at market prices, total purchases would still leave 13.16 million metric tons of purchases unexplained. Using data from 769 SOEs, Li finds that proceeds from this kind of diversion ranged from 8 percent of GNP in 1980 to 11 percent in 1988. His data also reveal that such diversion was already taking place in the beginning of the 1980s, before the introduction of the dual track. This finding suggests that it is not the dual track per se that was a source of corruption but the central planning system itself (as in the analysis of Shleifer and Vishny, 1992). Diversion is also found to be a positive function of the difference between the market price and the plan price, the latter acting like a marginal cost for a plan official. Nevertheless, the dual track reduced the transaction costs of selling diverted goods and contributed to increased diversion by officials. The dual track may thus have generated support for reforms among those officials but at the cost of uproar among the population.

While the first kind of diversion is directly related to the dual-track system, the second type is less. Diversion of government-owned goods by government officials is present in many countries. Nevertheless, it remains a fact that perception of corruption in Chinese public opinion was associated with the dual-track system.

This negative perception of the dual track in Chinese public opinion points to a weakness of the Pareto criterion both in terms of ethical judgments and in terms of political constraints. The Pareto criterion can be seen as the ethical criterion that is the closest to the economist's view of rationality. However, it does not account for notions of fairness based, for example, on envy. This ethical limitation also implies a limitation in terms of political attractiveness because satisfying the Pareto criterion does not prevent popular uproar against reforms generating outcomes that are seen as unfair and illegitimate even though no losers are generated from those reforms. One must thus exercise caution when looking at the advantages of the dual track, since the new rents it may generate (legally or illegally) can be a source of popular discontent, as they were in China. This conclusion will be all the more true if one views popular support for reforms as a condition for their sustainability.

If, however, one emphasizes the need to get the support of bureaucrats for reform, then the rents given to the latter under the dual-track system should be seen as an instrument going in the right direction. One can also make a more subtle argument combining ideas from Chapters 2 and 3. To the extent that the dual-track system allows bureaucrats and SOE managers to experiment with entrepreneurial activity and discover profitable opportunities, popular discontent can be used productively to get rid of the plan track later. Indeed, since the plan track gives extra rents, SOE managers and bureaucrats who benefit from them will want to lobby to maintain the rents created by the dual track. Popular pressure against the dual track, however, will push either in favor of reform reversal or in favor of reform continuation with phasing out of the dual track. If sufficient profitable opportunities have been discovered by means of the market track, a majority of SOE managers and bureaucrats will prefer phasing out rather than reform reversal. Such an explanation is consistent with the observation of gradual phasing out of the dual track in China (Lau, Qian, and Roland, 2000).

6.2.7 THE DUAL TRACK BEYOND TRANSITION

Although dual-track liberalization is an original institution that has emerged in the context of Chinese transition with the original characteristics of being both efficiency enhancing and Pareto improving, the principles from the dual track can apply to other kinds of reform in other countries: labor market reform, pension reform, and so on. It is particularly appealing to the extent that it makes it possible to compensate losers from reform by using the existing "old" institutions to preserve the rents of those who are to lose from reform. At the same time, the Pareto-improving character of reform must not necessarily imply concessions to efficiency.

Rodrik (1999) reports on the case of the successful reforms of Mauritius. We present a whole excerpt from the paper because it illustrates nicely not only the benefits of the dual track but also the political economy of reforms emphasized in Part I:

> Mauritius' superior economic performance has been built on a peculiar combination of orthodox and heterodox strategies. To an important extent, the economy's success was based on the creation of an export processing zone (EPZ) operating under free-trade principles, which enabled an export boom in garments to European markets and an accompanying investment boom at home. Yet the island's economy has combined the EPZ with a domestic sector that was highly protected until the mid-1980s. Mauritius is essentially an example of an economy that has followed a two-track strategy not too dissimilar to that of China.
>
> This economic strategy was in turn underpinned by social and political arrangements that encouraged participation, representation and coalition-building. Rather than discouraging social organization, governments have encouraged it. . . .
>
> The circumstances under which the Mauritian EPZ was set up in 1970 are instructive, and highlight the manner in which participatory political systems help design creative strategies for building locally adapted institutions. Given the small size of the home market, it was evident that Mauritius would benefit from an outward-oriented strategy. But as in other developing countries, policy makers had to contend with the import-substituting industrialists who had been propped up by the restrictive commercial policies of the early 1960s prior to independence. These industrialists were naturally opposed to relaxing the trade regime.
>
> A Washington economist would have advocated across-the-board liberalization, without regard to what that might do to the precarious political and social balance of the island. Instead, the Mauritian authorities chose the two-track strategy. The EPZ scheme in fact provided a neat way around the political difficulties. The creation of the EPZ generated new opportunities of trade and of employment, without taking protection away from the import-substituting groups and from the male workers who domi-

nated the established industries. The segmentation of labor markets early on between male and female workers—with the latter predominantly employed in the EPZ—was particularly crucial, as it prevented the expansion of the EPZ from driving wages up in the rest of the economy, thereby disadvantaging import-substituting industries.

New profit opportunities were created at the margin, while leaving old opportunities undisturbed. There were no identifiable losers. This in turn paved the way for the more substantial liberalizations that took place in the mid-1980s and in the 1990s. (pp. 20–21)

6.3 EVIDENCE ON THE RESISTANCE TO PRICE LIBERALIZATION

There is evidence from Russia that price liberalization has led to the erection of effective trade borders between regions. The "red belt" regions in Russia, where communist control is still prevalent, have witnessed a return to price controls. Red belt regions are regional entities (republics, oblasts, districts) that voted against the reformers and in favor of the communists during the 1996 elections. Berkowitz and DeJong (1999), applying the methodology of Engel and Rogers (1996), have shown that, together with these price controls, internal trade barriers have been erected to prevent diversion of goods with lower-than-market-equilibrium prices. These borders are a significant factor in explaining differences in price dispersion across regions. Such facts are in line with the diversion analysis of section 6.1. They are a natural consequence of the political opposition generated by the redistributive effects of price liberalization. The erection of such trade borders has obvious effects of economic disintegration within Russia.

6.4 EVIDENCE ON THE ALLOCATIVE EFFECTS OF DUAL-TRACK LIBERALIZATION

W. Li (1997) has done an empirical analysis of the changes in allocative efficiency induced by reforms in China, in particular the effects of dual-track liberalization. He uses data from 769 Chinese SOEs between 1980 and 1989. He finds a marked improvement in the marginal productivity of factors, mostly of labor and of material inputs. These improvements, especially for labor inputs, are suggestive of the allocative improvements induced by dual-track liberalization. He also found an important increase in the growth of total factor productivity (TFP). During the period analyzed, TFP growth averaged 4.68 percent a year while real output growth for the sample was on average 6.4 percent per year. While improved incentives in SOEs contributed to TFP growth (more on this topic in Chapter 9), improved factor allocation and increased market competition also contributed significantly to TFP growth. Improved factor allocation is measured by the correlation between measured marginal productivity and changes in factor allocation.

Increased competition is measured by a decline in the markup ratio of price over marginal cost. This ratio declined by 15 percent between 1980 and 1989. Increased market competition is also an effect of the dual-track system as free entry on markets is encouraged at the margin. Overall, this evidence suggests that the dual-track liberalization in China introduced in the early 1980s, together with other reforms aiming at better allocation of resources and increased competition, led to substantial improvement of enterprise performance.

6.5   CONCLUSION

We have seen in this chapter, when discussing the speed of price liberalization, that, while gradual liberalization of prices may introduce distortions and reduce welfare, as shown by the analysis of Murphy, Shleifer, and Vishny, the dual-track approach to liberalization followed in China represents a very original innovation for the transition process from capitalism to socialism. We have emphasized mostly the political economy advantage of the dual track, due to its Pareto-improving feature, a nonnegligible element in the transition context.

From the political economy point of view, we have also seen that it is better to fully liberalize all markets at the margin under the dual track than to implement limited market liberalization first and only later to allow for secondary markets for resale and repurchase of planned goods. Indeed, limited liberalization with physical enforcement of quotas leads to equilibrium prices that diverge from the full liberalization equilibrium prices and may thereby create rents for economic agents that get lost once secondary markets are allowed. Such effects can have very negative consequences for the political momentum of reforms if agents who are given rents under limited liberalization also have enough political power to block further reforms. A general lesson from this analysis is that partial reforms that provide market rents (due to market power or other sources of rents) to agents who also have political power can be a recipe for blocking reforms. This conclusion reinforces some arguments on sequencing made in Part One—namely, the importance of introducing competition sufficiently early in the reform process. Among those arguments, recall the idea that privatizing firms before introducing genuine competition policy would be another example of a wrong sequencing that could block reform momentum because of the rents created by privatization and that threaten to get lost with the introduction of competition policy.

We have also discussed the conditions under which market efficiency is obtained under the dual track, compared to big bang market liberalization. In doing this efficiency comparison, we have based ourselves not on reality but on price theory, making the usual assumptions that yield competitive market equilibria. This approach assumes that markets form immediately under transition, as soon as prices are liberalized. In reality, however, big bang price liberalization has been associated with substantial output falls, the subject of the next chapter. In that context, the dual-track approach may have another virtue, namely, that of preventing such a serious output fall.

CHAPTER 7

LIBERALIZATION AND THE OUTPUT FALL

7.1 THE OUTPUT FALL IN CENTRAL AND EASTERN EUROPE

One of the most striking stylized facts about transition in Central and Eastern Europe is the major output fall that took place at the beginning of transition. No country in Central and Eastern Europe seems to have been able to avoid experiencing such a serious fall in output. There are important disagreements on the exact numbers involved[1] but few disagree that this fall has been large. Early figures based on industrial production showed output falls in the 30 percent range. Such statistics gave an exaggerated view of the output fall, in part because industrial production was overdeveloped relative to services. It is thus normal to expect a contraction of industrial output during transition. Such a fall should be accompanied by an increase in welfare because distortions in the composition of national output are being corrected. A better measure of the output fall is provided by the evolution of consumption and investment, that is, by final expenditures as measured by GDP.

Table 7.1 gives us an idea of the magnitude of the figures. These figures are not in the 30 percent range, but they are still impressive. The cumulative fall in GDP does not reach the 30 percent level of the Great Depression in Poland, Hungary, the Czech Republic, and Slovakia but largely exceeds it in Russia and Ukraine.

When looking at Table 7.1, it is interesting to note that the greatest output fall in the various countries coincides in general with the timing of price liberalization. Even though most countries experienced a decline in output for several years in a row, the biggest decline usually took place the year a country experienced liberalization. This is clearly the case for countries that chose big bang price liberalization: Poland in 1990, Czechoslovakia in 1991, Russia in 1992, and Ukraine in 1994. Hungary had gradual price liberalization, but the year of the biggest output fall is 1991, the year of the CMEA

[1] Some authors argue that an important part of the output fall is mainly a statistical exaggeration that is due either to underreporting of the private sector (Berg and Sachs, 1992) or to overreporting of the state sector under socialism (Winiecki, 1991; Åslund, 1994). The latter explanation cannot be valid for countries like Poland and Hungary where mandatory planning (with its incentive system based on output targets) had been abolished many years earlier. The former explanation has validity mostly in countries of the former Soviet Union that have experienced a continuous output fall since the beginning of transition. We will discuss that case in the next chapter. In Central Europe, however, there has not been an increase in the size of the unofficial economy, and there was nevertheless a substantial output fall in the beginning of transition followed later by a recovery trend.

TABLE 7.1 REAL GDP GROWTH IN CENTRAL AND EASTERN EUROPE (PERCENT CHANGE)

	1989	1990	1991	1992	1993	1994
Poland	0.2	−11.6	−7.6	2.6	3.8	5.0
Hungary	0.7	−3.5	−11.9	−3.0	−0.9	2
Czech Republic	1.4	−0.4	−14.2	−6.4	−0.9	2.6
Slovakia	1.4	−0.4	−14.5	−7.0	−4.1	4.8
Russia	n.a.	n.a.	−13	−19	−12	−15
Ukraine	4	−3	−12	−17	−17	−23

Source: *European Bank for Reconstruction and Development,* Transition Reports.

breakdown. That episode can be considered as price liberalization at the level of the whole region, since from 1991 onward, all foreign trade between former countries of the Soviet bloc started to take place at world prices and in dollars. Rodrik (1994) estimated that most of the output fall in Hungary can be attributable to the CMEA breakdown, whereas in the case of Poland and Czechoslovakia, a substantial part of the output fall cannot be explained by the impact of the CMEA breakdown. Another interesting thing to notice is that, for the years prior to liberalization, a substantial output fall can already be observed, certainly in Russia and Ukraine.

7.2 EXPLANATIONS FOR THE OUTPUT FALL

Early debates on the causes of the output fall were most often couched in pure macroeconomic terms of aggregate supply and demand. Various explanations have focused on the role of excess falls in aggregate demand (Bhaduri, Laski, and Levcik, 1993; Berg and Blanchard, 1994; Rosati, 1994), associated with stabilization policies, especially in Poland. Blaming stabilization policies alone cannot provide a satisfactory explanation. Indeed, the experience of developing and developed countries shows that stabilization policies do not lead to such important output falls and may in some cases lead to increases in output (Kiguel and Liviatan, 1992). Moreover, it is difficult to claim that Russia experienced excess stabilization in 1992, the year of its biggest output decline.

Turning to aggregate supply explanations, one does not get very far in understanding the output fall by simply postulating a fall in aggregate supply. It is important to have microfoundations for such a fall. Because of the coincidence of a sharp output fall with liberalization, when searching for microeconomic foundations of the explanation for the output fall, one must ask, Why may a sharp output fall be associated with or even generated by liberalization? An associated question is whether the speed of liberalization has an effect on output dynamics in transition.

Gomulka (1992) and Kornai (1993) have provided informal explanations of the output fall as related to price liberalization. The main idea is that the output contraction in sectors experiencing a decline in relative prices is not compensated by an output increase—which takes more time—in sectors where relative prices go up. In terms of the analysis of Chapter 5, this idea can be translated by stating that the speed of closure in the shrinking sector has been excessive. Even if this were the case, then, as pointed out by Rosati (1994), one would expect a contraction in shrinking sectors, and, at best, no growth—but also no output fall—in the sectors experiencing an increase in their relative price level. However, an output fall has been observed in all sectors.

Among formal models, a first explanation is the credit crunch hypothesis put forward by Calvo and Coricelli (1992). When stabilization policies were put in place in Poland in 1990 and high real interest rates were imposed on enterprises together with the announcement of hard budget constraints, enterprises strongly reduced their demand for credit, thereby reducing their output levels. Even though this explanation seems important (in Poland bank credits became very expensive in early 1990), it cannot be the whole story. One has indeed also seen simultaneously an increase of interentreprise arrears: when enterprises could not get credit from banks, then they would extend credit to their clients, in the expectation that they would be repaid. The ease with which enterprises were ready to extend credit was directly related to their expectations about bailouts and soft budget constraints. The softer the budget constraints, the more ready enterprises were to extend easy credit to their clients. Indeed, the chains of interenterprise arrears thus created tended to reduce the credibility of a no-bailout policy and to soften budget constraints, as shown by Perotti (1998), whose model we will discuss in Chapter 12. Evidence from Central Europe also seems to indicate that budget constraints did not harden instantaneously but were hardening only gradually over time (see Chapters 10 and 12). Also, more recent evidence on financial intermediation that we will discuss in Chapter 12 tends to show that there was not a generalized credit squeeze for firms in most transition economies. Moreover, again in the case of Russia, price liberalization has not been associated with any strong stabilization policy, and budget constraints remained soft in general. Measures to harden budget constraints generally lacked credibility and had little effect on agents' behavior (Litwack, 1993). It is thus a bit difficult to believe in a general explanation of the output fall based on a strong credit crunch in the early liberalization phase.

Other explanations are based on models with labor market frictions that result from sectoral shifts, such as the Atkeson and Kehoe (1996) model discussed in Chapter 5. Such sectoral shifts, however, take place in other economies and do not usually lead to such strong output falls. Moreover, as stated in Chapter 5, the evidence does not point toward particularly strong sectoral shifts taking place directly after liberalization.

Sussman and Zeira (1994) emphasize the role of network externalities in explaining the output fall in a model where a new technology (or language) must replace the old one. Because of network externalities associated with a "language," complete adoption of the new language may be associated with a transitory fall of output in the economy. While this model is interesting and may play a role in explaining more long-term phenomena, it is difficult to have a concrete interpretation of what the adoption of a new language precisely means in the context of transition economies and why output fall should be contemporaneous to liberalization.

Another possible explanation for the output fall is based on monopoly behavior by enterprises after liberalization. W. Li (1999) and Blanchard (1997) have put forward a double marginalization argument: the central planners behaved like a single verti-cally integrated monopoly, whereas liberalization led to multiple monopolies charging monopoly prices to downstream monopolies. This argument did not appear extremely convincing early in the transition. While it is valid in a closed economy, the objection to it is that trade liberalization creates import competition, thereby eliminating monopoly effects. Also, empirical evidence has been put forward suggesting that industrial concen-tration in Russia was less strong than initially thought (see Brown, Ickes, and Ryterman, 1994; Joskow, Schmalensee, and Tsukanova, 1994). The evidence by Berkowitz and DeJong (1999) cited in Chapter 6, however, should lead us to be cautious before re-jecting the monopoly argument. Indeed, low concentration levels for Russia may be compatible with regional monopolies. Also, standard concentration indices based on a minimum level of aggregation may miss the strong level of specialization created by central planning. Firms must invest in order to change their technology to favor substi-tutable products that allow them to compete with other firms on less narrow markets. In the very short run, after liberalization, firms do not have the opportunity to make such investments, and a monopoly situation may persist in the aftermath of liberalization. The analysis of the M-form and U-form organization of central planning in China versus Eastern Europe would tend to suggest that the monopoly effect of liberalization should be stronger in the latter region, especially in the former Soviet Union where competition from imports is less likely to play an important role because of the important distance from Western markets.

The most interesting type of explanation for the output fall is, in my view, related to the disorganization effects of liberalization on existing production links. In the next two sections we present two models of the disorganization effects of price liberalization. These models are interesting to the extent that they do not assume that markets already exist at the time of liberalization or that they are created instantaneously.

The analysis is led at a more inframarginal level than at the level of markets, looking at the decision problems of individual firms or producers in the spirit of modern microeconomics. This kind of analysis is relevant to all contexts of liberalization where some markets are not yet created. The inframarginal level of analysis allows us to understand not only the dynamics of emergence of new markets but also the disruptive effects of liberalization when these new markets are not yet in place. For traditional economic analysis, whether markets are already present or not would be irrelevant, since the existence of markets with their institutional underpinnings, communication channels, and information networks is a priori *assumed*. Traditional analysis is very misguided in this particular context of transition because it cannot lead to predicting the output fall associated to price liberalization. In effect, the output fall was not predicted by economists advising transition countries because their thinking was based on traditional market analysis and on the neglect of the initial institutional conditions of liberalization in transition economies.

In section 7.3 we put forward a model where liberalization induces disorganization of existing production links as a result of inefficient bargaining when legal contracting institutions are absent. In section 7.4 we develop a model of disorganization that results from search frictions and investment specificities. The absence of preexisting markets makes search more costly, and as a result of investment specificity, agents will only invest once they have found long-term business partners. Both search frictions and investment specificity may generate a serious output fall at the time of liberalization. We show also how dual-track liberalization as implemented in China but not in Eastern Europe may prevent such an output fall. Section 7.5 discusses related literature. Section 7.6 presents the empirical evidence on disorganization models. As explained in the conclusion of the chapter, the models in this chapter explain the initial output falls associated with liberalization. They do not explain the continuous output fall observed in Russia and other countries of the former Soviet Union but not observed in Central Europe, a topic that will be dealt with in Chapter 8.

7.3 DISRUPTION AND BARGAINING INEFFICIENCY

The first model we review is that by Blanchard and Kremer (1997). In this model, the output fall is the result of disruptions in production chains when there are bargaining inefficiencies between firms as a result of asymmetric information.

Consider the problem of a state-owned enterprise (SOE) that needs n inputs to produce n outputs. Production technology exhibits strong complementarities, so that if one input is missing, output is equal to zero.

Each input is provided by one supplier having an alternative use of it that yields a net benefit of h for the supplier. It is assumed that h is distributed uniformly on the support $[0, \bar{h}]$ with cumulative density function F such that $F(0) = 0$ and $F(\bar{h}) = 1$. A crucial assumption is that h is private information for the supplier. The SOE is assumed to make a take-it-or-leave-it offer of a price p to each supplier for its input. Since all suppliers are ex ante identical, there is no reason to make different offers to different suppliers. If $p > h$ for the n suppliers, then production takes place. Otherwise, if $p < h$ for at least one supplier, then output is disrupted, and all suppliers turn to their alternative use.

Consider first what the offer must be in order to make sure that production takes place. Given asymmetric information, the SOE must offer $\bar{h}$ to all suppliers in order to assure incentive compatibility. This solution gives rents of $\bar{h} - h$ to suppliers. Moreover, it may even make production unprofitable if $\bar{h} > 1$, because then net profits would be $n(1 - \bar{h}) < 0$.

The SOE may thus prefer to trade off a positive probability of disruption against a lower offer of p. The choice of p is then made by maximizing the expected profits of the SOE

$$\max_{p} E\pi = F(p)^n(1-p)n \tag{7.1}$$

where $F(p)^n$ is the probability that production takes place in the SOE and $(1-p)n$ is the profit made when producing. The first-order condition gives us

$$\frac{F(p)}{f(p)} = (1-p)n$$

which, given the assumption of the uniform distribution, and recalling that it is never optimal to set p above $\bar{h}$, yields

$$p = \min\left\{\frac{n}{n+1}, \bar{h}\right\} \tag{7.2}$$

Assuming that there is a continuum of SOEs in the economy on the interval $[0, 1]$, by the law of large numbers, production in the state sector and the private sector can be measured by expected output in both sectors, respectively, Y_s and Y_p, which are given by

$$Y_s = n\left(\frac{p}{\bar{h}}\right)^n \tag{7.3}$$

$$Y_p = \int_0^{\bar{h}} \cdots \int_0^{\bar{h}} (h_1 + \cdots + h_n)f(h_1)\ldots f(h_n)dh_1\ldots dh_n$$

$$- \int_0^p \cdots \int_0^p (h_1 + \cdots + h_n)f(h_1)\ldots f(h_n)dh_1\ldots dh_n = \left[1 - \left(\frac{p}{\bar{h}}\right)^{n+1}\right]n\frac{\bar{h}}{2} \tag{7.4}$$

where Y_p is the expected outside opportunity conditional on at least one private opportunity being greater than p.

Figure 7.1 shows us how total output $Y_s + Y_p$ behaves as a function of $\bar{h}$. Note that Figure 7.1. is not a representation of output dynamics but of the comparative statics of output depending on $\bar{h}$. The striking result is that an output fall is possible for intermediate values of $\bar{h}$ but not for either low or high values of $\bar{h}$. Indeed, when $\bar{h}$ is very low, then it will always be possible (and optimal) to pay the suppliers $\bar{h}$ in order to keep them as suppliers. However, as $\bar{h}$ increases, suppliers get more and more rents, and it becomes optimal to reduce the probability of production in order to reduce p. Simultaneously, the higher the $\bar{h}$, the higher the expected private sector output and the higher the net gain from disrupting existing SOE output. For intermediate values of $\bar{h}$, the output loss in the state sector is not compensated by the output gain in the private sector.

This loss is due to inefficient bargaining. If there were efficient bargaining, all suppliers and the SOE could in principle jointly pay the suppliers who have drawn $h > p$ in order to prevent them from stopping to supply goods for the SOE. Indeed, their joint surplus from doing so is higher than their surplus under the output fall.

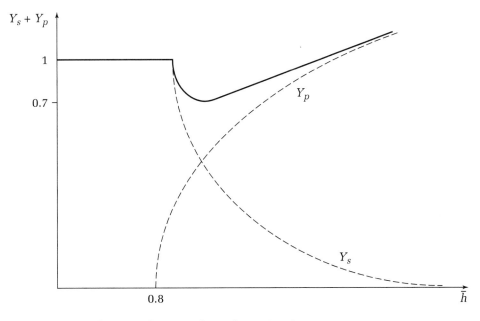

FIGURE 7.1 EXPECTED OUTPUT AS A FUNCTION OF OUTSIDE OPTIONS ($n = 4$)

Note also that when n increases, the output fall becomes more pronounced. The higher n, the higher the equilibrium price, and thus the higher the value of $\bar{h}$ required to have a positive probability of collapse of output in the state sector (thus with $\bar{h} > p$) but also the smaller the probability that state production takes place, for p given smaller than $\bar{h}$, and thus the greater the initial collapse as $\bar{h}$ increases. Indeed, when n goes to ∞, $p \longrightarrow 1$, and thus as soon as $\bar{h}$ exceeds 1, the probability of an output collapse switches from 0 to 1, leading to an expected output $Y_p + Y_s$ of $n\bar{h}/2$ for $\bar{h}$ slightly above 1, compared to n for $\bar{h} = p < 1$, which can mean an output fall of 50 percent!

We can interpret n as a measure of complexity of production. The greater the complexity of production, the bigger the output fall. This interpretation suggests that economies with more complex production links should experience a higher output collapse than less developed countries. This may be seen as a partial explanation for why China did not experience an output fall. There are other reasons, however, as we will see in the next section.

Note that two important assumptions play an important role in explaining the output fall: asymmetric information (and inefficient bargaining) and technological complementarities. The former assumption may be questioned more than the latter. For example, the SOE could offer a contract to pay the outside option, upon verifying it, plus an extra sum. If this is presented as a take-it-or-leave-it offer, then it is in the interest of suppliers to accept the offer. However, if the outside option is not verifiable, a reasonable assumption especially if the legal system is not well developed, then the take-it-or-leave-it price offer analyzed in the model may be the only solution. There are thus reasons both to doubt and to believe the assumption of inefficient bargaining. However, in the context of transition where legal institutions of contracting and traditions of contract enforcement were not yet present at the time of liberalization, there are certainly more reasons to believe that assumption. However, as we see in the next section, the assumption of inefficient bargaining is not necessary in order to generate an output fall.

7.4 SEARCH FRICTIONS AND SPECIFIC INVESTMENT

In this section we develop the model of Roland and Verdier (1999a) where the output fall is also explained by disruption of output following liberalization. Here, the explanation does not rely on inefficiencies in bargaining but rather on search frictions and investment specificity.

As before, liberalization means the freedom for enterprises to search for new clients and suppliers. More efficient opportunities become available to all enterprises, but the search process generated involves externalities: search by many bad clients may reduce the quality of the overall matches. Unlike in job search models, when enterprises are searching, they can maintain their existing production links with suppliers and clients, as long as the latter have not found new matches. However, the important assumption is that there are relation-specific (in the Williamsonian sense) investments that take place only after a new long-term partner is found. If many enterprises prefer to keep on searching at least one more period, they will not invest while searching. Aggregate output may thus fall after liberalization because of the failure of enterprises to replace obsolete capital and because of a fall in investment demand. The explanation does not require capital market imperfections à la Calvo-Coricelli even though such imperfections may reinforce the effects of the model. It does not require inefficiencies in bargaining either. Moreover, the outside options of producers are endogenized, since this is a model of two-sided matching.

Assume an economy with two sectors, a consumption goods sector and an investment goods sector. In the consumption goods sector, output depends on the quality of the match between producers. This match can be seen as a supplier-client relationship or as any form of joint relationship in production.[2] The net present value of a match is given by $V_{ij} = h_i h_j$ where h_i and h_j are a measure of the productivity of partners i and j. Each partner can be one of two types H (high productivity) or L (low productivity). We assume $h_L = 1$ and $h_H = h > 1$. Given this technology, it is more efficient to have H types match with other H types and L with L types rather than have H match with L types.

Denote by m_1^H and m_1^L the proportion of H and L among all consumption good producers at time 1 so that $m_1^H + m_1^L = 1$. The number of producers is normalized to 1.

[2] Kremer and Maskin (1996) use a similar model in their explanation of the growth in wage inequality in recent years in industrialized countries.

7.4.1 THE INITIAL SITUATION UNDER SOCIALISM

It is assumed that socialism was characterized by inefficient matches because of distorted prices. Specifically, under the socialist economy the sector was characterized by m_1^H

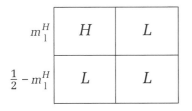

FIGURE 7.2 INEFFICIENT MATCHES UNDER SOCIALISM

HL pairs and thus $1/2 - m_1^H$ LL pairs. Figure 7.2 shows the matches that existed under socialism.

The efficiency gain to be made from sorting to match the H together and the L together is given by

$$\tfrac{1}{2} m_1^H h^2 + \tfrac{1}{2}(1 - m_1^H) - (m_1^H + \tfrac{1}{2} - m_1^H) = \tfrac{1}{2} m_1^H (h - 1)^2$$

The output flow of a match during period t is assumed to be $\theta_t \frac{1-\delta}{1-\delta^T} h_i h_j$ where $\theta_t = 1$ for $t = 1, \ldots, T$ and $\theta_t = 0$ for $t > T$. Parameter θ_t is capturing a simple assumption on obsolescence, namely, that capital in a match lasts exactly T periods, and does not depreciate until then. Under socialism, $1/T$ of capital is thus replaced every period. Call p the unit investment cost per pair. Total annual investment outlays are thus equal to $p/2T$. There is no "time-to-build" lag, so that aggregate output of the consumption goods sector is equal to the output flow of each pair.

Adding output in the consumption and investment goods sector, total aggregate GNP under socialism is

$$\frac{1-\delta}{1-\delta^T}(m_1^H + \tfrac{1}{2} - m_1^H) + \frac{p}{2T} \tag{7.5}$$

After liberalization, search for new and more efficient partners sets in. The following two assumptions play an important role in what follows.

First, it is assumed that the probability of finding a type H in period t is equal to the proportion of type H who are searching in period t. This assumption of random matching reflects the fact that markets and their informational networks do not yet exist at the time of liberalization. It thus takes time for producers to find appropriate matches. Otherwise, efficient matches are reached within one period, and no output fall is possible.

The second important assumption is that investments are relation-specific in the Williamsonian sense, so that an investment valid for an existing match loses its value if taken into a new match. For this assumption to "bite," it is assumed that an investment is not profitable if it lasts only one period; that is, the output flow of the most productive type of pair (the HH pairs) is lower than the investment cost p. Moreover, investment is assumed to be profitable in all pairs, including the least productive LL pairs. We thus have the two following inequalities:

$$\frac{1-\delta}{1-\delta^T} h^2 < p < 1 \tag{7.6}$$

To make things simple, the analysis is done within a two-period model.[3] There are typically many equilibria in these kinds of search models, since this is a coordination game. The analysis therefore concentrates on checking for the existence of "all search equilibria," that is, equilibria where all agents search in period 1 and all agents search in period 2 except the H who have found an H in period 1.

7.4.2   CONDITIONS FOR AN "ALL-SEARCH" EQUILIBRIUM

First, an all-search equilibrium may not exist if an L type can give a transfer to an H type that is high enough to dissuade the latter from searching in period 2 but not so high that the L type would prefer not to search himself in period 2. In other words, an all-search equilibrium will not exist if one can find a transfer t such that

$$\delta V_2^H \le t \le (h - p) - \delta V_2^L \tag{7.7}$$

where V_2^H and V_2^L represent the value of searching in period 2 for the H and the L type, respectively, and where δ is the discount rate. The right-hand inequality reflects the incentive compatibility constraint for the L type. The latter implies that the total net value of the match $(h - p)$ minus the transfer t to the H type cannot exceed δV_2^L, the value of searching in period 2 for the L type.

Assuming without loss of generality that, when searching in period 2, the surplus is shared 50–50 between the partners, and denoting by q_2^H the probability of finding an H type in period 2, V_2^H and V_2^L are then given by

$$V_2^H = q_2^H \frac{h^2 - p}{2} + (1 - q_2^H) \frac{h - p}{2}$$

$$V_2^L = q_2^H \frac{h - p}{2} + (1 - q_2^H) \frac{1 - p}{2} \tag{7.8}$$

For an all-search equilibrium to exist, following formula (7.7), it must be that $\delta V_2^H > (h - p) - \delta V_2^L$. In the appendix to this chapter, we show that this inequality is a sufficient condition for the existence of an all-search equilibrium and that it is verified when the following condition is satisfied:

$$m_1^H \ge m_h^o(h) = \frac{A(h) - 1}{h - A(h)} \tag{7.9}$$

where

$$A(h) = \frac{2}{h + 1} \frac{h - p(1 - \delta)}{\delta}$$

What is the intuition behind the condition for the existence of an all-search equilibrium? There are costs and benefits to searching. The benefit is the probability of finding a better partner in period 2, the last period of search. The cost is that one delays investment and production because investment is only profitable once one has found a long-term partner.[4] In order to want to search, the marginal benefit h of finding an H type and the probability m_1^H of finding one must be high enough. In other words, the outside opportunities from search must be important enough. This relationship is what is reflected in the condition $m_1^H \ge m_h^o(h)$.

[3] See Roland and Verdier (1999a) for an endogenous search length in an infinite-horizon framework. Search stops endogenously because, as there are fewer and fewer H types unmatched with an H type, the probability for an H type to find another H type declines, and so does the expected net benefit from searching.

[4] Otherwise, search would have only benefits and no costs.

Comparative statics shows that the threshold for existence of an all-search equilibrium decreases with δ and with p, the cost of investment.

$$\frac{\partial m_h^o}{\partial \delta} = \frac{2(h-1)(p-h)}{(1+h)\{\delta[h-A(h)]\}^2} < 0, \quad \frac{\partial m_h^o}{\partial p} = \frac{-(1-\delta)2(h-1)}{\delta(1+h)\{[h-A(h)]\}^2} < 0$$

The intuition is straightforward. An increase in δ increases the marginal benefit from searching and thus relaxes the equilibrium condition. Similarly, an increase in p reduces the cost of searching, since it reduces the benefit from investing today.

7.4.3 OUTPUT DYNAMICS

Let us now look at the output dynamics under an all-search equilibrium in period 1. Output in the consumption goods sector will be generated by the new HH pairs that were matched in period 1 directly. There will also be production by the remaining HL and LL pairs whose capital has not become obsolete. It is assumed that α is the proportion of HL pairs with $\theta = 1$ and β the proportion of LL pairs with $\theta = 1$. Recall that under an all-search equilibrium, it is not worthwhile to undertake an investment that lasts only one period. Therefore, under an all-search equilibrium, investment replacement will not take place in period 1, and this lack of investment will be an important source of output fall. The only new investments that will take place are those for successful matches, that is, the new HH pairs. Denoting m_1^H by m, the variation of output in the consumption goods sector is then given by

$$\Delta Q = \frac{1-\delta}{1-\delta^T} \left\{ \left[\frac{m^2}{2} h^2 + m(1-m)\alpha h + (\tfrac{1}{2} - m)\beta \right] - (mh + \tfrac{1}{2} - m) \right\}$$

Period 1 output is given by the first expression in brackets. Out of $m\,H$ types, m^2 have found an H type. There are thus $\frac{m^2}{2}$ successful HH pairs producing h^2. Since all other agents decide to search, there are $m^2\,L$ type agents without a partner. There are then $m(1-m)\,HL$ pairs, of which α have $\theta = 1$, and $(\tfrac{1}{2} - m)\,LL$ pairs, of which β have $\theta = 1$. This expression can be rewritten to see the output dynamics better:

$$\Delta Q = \frac{1-\delta}{1-\delta^T} \left\{ \frac{m^2}{2}(h^2 - h) - \frac{m^2}{2}h - [m(1-m)(1-\alpha)h + (\tfrac{1}{2} - m)(1-\beta)] \right\} \qquad \textbf{(7.10)}$$

From equation (7.10), we can identify three effects:

1. The first expression between parentheses is the *efficiency gain* from the new HH pairs that have been formed.

2. The second term is the *disruption effect* for the $m^2\,L$ types who have lost their H partner.

3. The third expression is the *capital depreciation effect* for the remaining HL and LL pairs that results from the fact that agents do not undertake any replacement investment if they intend to search in the next period.

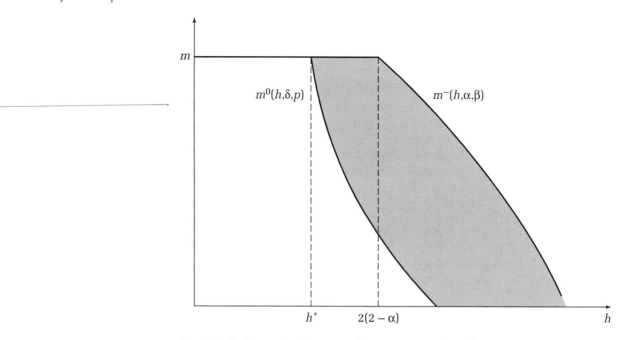

FIGURE 7.3   THE SPACE OF (m, h) **PARAMETERS CONSISTENT WITH AN OUTPUT FALL**

The whole expression must be negative in order to have an output fall in the consumption goods sector. This will not necessarily be the case for all values of parameters $m, h, \alpha,$ and β. For example, if there were no capital depreciation and $\alpha = \beta = 1$, there will be an output fall only if $h < 2$. However, one can verify that h must be > 2 to have an all-search equilibrium.

The condition for an output fall in the consumption goods sector is defined by the following function $m^-(h, \alpha, \beta)$. For an output fall to occur, m and h must be big enough so as to generate an all-search equilibrium. However, m and h cannot be too big. Otherwise, no output fall will be generated. Indeed, a high m and a high h will generate a high efficiency gain from the successful matches, and this may more than compensate the output fall that results from the absence of capital replacement and the disorganization of the HL matches that have dissolved. The higher the h, the lower the m consistent with an output fall. The space of (m, h) parameters consistent with an output fall is the shaded area in Figure 7.3.

As we can see, the logic behind the output fall in Figure 7.3 is quite similar to that in the Blanchard-Kremer model. The general idea is the same: outside opportunities must be great enough so as to disrupt existing production relations but not so great that they do not offset the negative effects of the disorganization created by them. Inefficient disruption will take place because of externalities in the liberalization process: inefficient bargaining in the Blanchard-Kremer model and search externalities under investment specificity here. The externality comes from the fact that, in the all-search equilibrium,

TABLE 7.2 SIMULATIONS ($P = 0.99$, $\delta = 0.97$)

α	0.500	0.75	0.85	0.500	0.75	0.85
β	0.500	0.75	0.85	0.500	0.75	0.85
m	0.300	0.3	0.3	0.500	0.5	0.5
h	3.700	3.7	3.7	3.700	3.7	3.7
T	2	4	6.67	2	4	6.67
GNP growth (%)	−33.7	−14.8	−2.6	3.4	23.9	41.2
Efficiency gain (%)	25.0	25.2	25.5	53.4	53.8	54.2
Disruption effect (%)	−9.3	−9.3	−9.4	−19.8	−19.9	−20.1
Depreciation effect (%)	−27.2	−13.7	−8.3	−19.8	−10.0	−6.0
Investment fall effect (%)	−22.2	−17.0	−10.3	−10.4	0.0	13.2

everybody is individually better off from trying to pair with an H type than with an L type.

Note that without investment specificity, no output fall would ever be possible in this model. Indeed, assume that investment is not necessary to sustain production for a specific pair. This will be the case, for example, if partners are only trading partners on the market. In that case, as soon as $h > 1$, agents will always want to search. At the same time, output can never fall. Indeed, it is always possible to produce with the match of the current period without committing to any long-term relation with that match. Searching thus has no cost, in terms of current output.

Turning to the variation of investment under an all-search equilibrium, it is given by the following expression:

$$\Delta I = \frac{p}{2} \left(m_1^{H2} - \frac{1}{T} \right) \tag{7.11}$$

There will thus be a fall in investment if $m_1^H < \sqrt{\frac{1}{T}}$. The total output fall is given by output variation in the consumption goods and investment sector.

Table 7.2 shows results of simulations with different parameters for m, h, α, β, δ, and p. The first three columns of figures show that capital depreciation potentially has a large effect on the output fall through the depreciation effect in the consumption goods sector and the investment fall effect. The investment fall is the main determinant of the output fall. This observation leads to predicting strong falls in investment rates associated with the output fall. Also the magnitude of m_1^H plays an important role, as can be seen from Table 7.2. The three right-hand columns show that the sign of output variation can be reversed if the proportion of H types goes up to $\frac{1}{2}$.

More realistic calibrations could be obtained by introducing multiplier effects of the fall in aggregate demand on the consumption goods sector. The disruption effect would also be much stronger if, instead of assuming production pairs, one had production teams with n partners instead of two partners as in the current model. The formal analysis of such a case, however, would also be more complex, especially the derivation of the conditions for an all-search equilibrium.

Another situation that would also increase the likelihood of instantaneous output fall for given structural parameters is the situation where domestic agents expect some foreign investment liberalization in the future. To see that point, suppose, as seems natural, that foreign investors are of the H type and that they are expected to enter into the domestic economy in period 2. Assume also that their expected number in this period is X. Then one sees quite immediately that the conditions for an all-search equilibrium are more likely to be satisfied, the greater is X. However, X does not affect the condition for an output fall in the first period. Hence an output fall becomes more likely the larger is X. The intuition is quite clear: if domestic agents anticipate that they may be able to make a good match with foreigners in the next period, their option value to wait increases, and they are more ready to reject a first-period bad match and to delay investment.

7.4.4 OUTPUT DYNAMICS UNDER DUAL-TRACK LIBERALIZATION

In the previous chapter we showed that dual-track liberalization has great political advantages, since it allows the implementation of Pareto-improving reforms. Here we emphasize that dual-track gradual liberalization has the effect of eliminating the initial output fall after liberalization.

In the dual-track system, existing output links and output obligations must be maintained. On one hand, the output flow from "socialist" matches is maintained. On the other hand, liberalization at the margin allows producers to search for new partners for additional activities under the same conditions as in the previous sections. To take into account possible resource constraints (which we do not model explicitly but which are not necessarily present if, as seen in Chapter 6, secondary markets are allowed), we assume that only γp can be invested in a new match, $0 \leq \gamma \leq 1$, yielding a value $\gamma h_i h_j$.

It is easy to see that the conditions for an all-search equilibrium are the same under dual-track liberalization as under full liberalization. Indeed, the condition for search is still

$$\delta V_2^H > (h - p) - \delta V_2^L$$

and the period-2 search values become

$$V_2^H = q_2^H \gamma \frac{h^2 - p}{2} + (1 - q_2^H) \gamma \frac{h - p}{2}$$

$$V_2^L = q_2^H \gamma \frac{h - p}{2} + (1 - q_2^H) \gamma \frac{1 - p}{2}$$

(7.12)

It is easy to see that the conditions for an all-search equilibrium are independent of γ. Under dual-track liberalization, the same coordination problem arises as under full liberalization, and the same search externalities are present. The conditions for an all-search equilibrium are the same because the costs and benefits of searching are both multiplied by the factor γ. This fact reflects the constant returns to scale for similar matches.

Moreover, and this is the important point, output never falls under the dual track. Indeed, the output fall is prevented, by construction, since disruption is prohibited. Previous plan quotas must continue to be enforced for this outcome to be possible. A possible cost of the dual track is that inefficient allocation of resources may be maintained in the plan track. As seen in Chapter 6, however, full efficiency can be obtained if the plan track must be enforced not in physical quotas but in terms of the income streams that it generates, and if "secondary markets" are allowed so that rights to buy planned supplies can be resold and obligations to produce plan quotas can be subcontracted.

7.5   RELATED LITERATURE

Atkeson and Kehoe (1997) model a costly process of starting new private enterprises. This process involves not only physical capital but also organizational capital. The latter only develops over time through learning. It is mainly because of this "time-to-build" aspect that output may initially fall in their model. The model also predicts a fall in the rate of physical investment because early on in transition there is mainly investment in organizational capital.

Marin and Schnitzer (1999) consider a holdup story in a production chain with n firms. Buyers must make relation-specific investments and are credit constrained. Sellers can lend to buyers by letting the latter accumulate payment arrears but face possible costs in enforcing repayment of these credits. Buyers can use their credit constraint in the bargaining to prevent being held up by the input supplier. However, if the financial constraint becomes too large, the seller may not be willing to deliver the input good. In this case, barter deals may serve as a "hostage" to alleviate the credit problem, thereby helping to deal with the holdup problem. Barter deals may thus act as collateral, allowing reduction of the costs of enforcing repayment of credits to the buyers. This reduction in enforcement costs may make sellers willing to lend. However, compared to a situation without financial constraints of buyers, the relatively low collateral value of barter goods reduces the incentives of sellers to hold up buyers who make relation-specific investments. Barter may thus altogether act as an instrument to alleviate disorganization of existing production links. Using data from Ukrainian firms, Marin and Schnitzer find that there is an inverted-U-shape relation between financial arrears and barter on one hand and enterprise performance on the other hand. The larger the arrears, reflecting the financial constraint, the more the buyer is able to prevent being held up, and thus the larger the level of production. But if arrears are too high, the input supplier refuses to participate in the deal, and no production takes place at all. Similarly, barter contributes to maintaining the level of production by relaxing the financial constraint. However, when the barter exposure becomes too large, it prevents the input purchaser from fighting holdup by the supplier.

The increase of barter relations in the former Soviet Union is indeed one of the striking phenomena of the late 1990s. In 1997 barter accounted for about 45 percent of economic activity in Russia.[5] The causes and consequences of this unique phenomenon of a sharp increase in barter are an interesting topic for research (see, e.g., Commander and Mumssen, 1999; Commander and Dolinskaya, 1999; Gaddy and Ickes, 1998). While barter may serve to alleviate the short-term negative disruptive effects of liberalization, its negative effects must also be emphasized. The explosion of barter in Russia and the former Soviet Union works as a rampant "bottom-up" return to central planning that eliminates the forces of free prices and competition. It locks good and bad firms in relationships where the latter receive implicit cross-subsidization from the former. As we will see in Chapter 12, this kind of lock-in effect tends to perpetuate a vicious circle of soft budget constraints in the economy because of the spillover effects that financial toughness toward bad firms would have on the good firms. These spillover effects create a vicious circle of payment arrears, barter, and soft budget constraints, preventing effective restructuring.

7.6   EMPIRICAL ANALYSIS

While there is a huge literature looking at the impact of economic policies such as stabilization on output performance across countries, there is relatively little empirical analysis directly testing theories of the output fall. Blanchard and Kremer (1997) used Russian input-output data to construct a measure of the complexity of production, their parameter n, and found that it had a significant negative impact on output growth.

Konings and Walsh (1999) have used Ukrainian data to test both models presented in this chapter. Their data provide indirect evidence but are worthwhile reporting. They use a data set of 300 Ukrainian firms sampled during the autumn of 1997. It includes firms that existed under central planning as well as newly established, so-called *de novo* firms. The presence of the latter is interesting and allows testing for disorganization effects. Price liberalization occurred in 1994, so data from three years later are not ideal. Nevertheless, the data are not too far away in time from the year of price liberalization. Firms are all from markets that are expected to grow, so they were not facing market demand problems. Evidence to support the Blanchard and Kremer model is found. A measure of complexity (the number of major products produced by firms) had a negative impact on employment growth in traditional firms but not in de novo firms. The Roland and Verdier model is tested by looking at whether firms made investments in 1996, taking into account whether their equipment was old (more than nine years) or not. New investment made a big difference in employment and productivity growth for traditional firms, especially if their existing equipment was old, whereas it made a smaller difference on productivity growth (and even an insignificant effect on employment growth) for de

[5] Russian Economic Barometer. *This figure is exaggerated, however, because the Russian definition of barter is broader than the usual concept and includes, among other things, exchange against promissory notes.*

novo firms. The latter evidence is only indirect to the extent that it does not explain disorganization, but it does suggest the importance of new investment in traditional firms and thus the effects of a lack of investment in traditional firms. The results are encouraging given the difference with respect to the de novo firms, after controlling for other variables like size of firms and their competitive environment.

Repkin and Walsh (1999) have looked at data for Bulgaria, Hungary, Poland, and Romania, all of which have experienced a U-shaped path of output following liberalization. They confirm the finding already reported in Chapter 5 that there was no substantial sectoral reallocation of output along the observed macroeconomic output path. However, they show an important difference in the output dynamics of firms working for export to the EU and firms working for export to the former CMEA block. Within sectors, exports to the EU have been growing continuously since the beginning of transition, whereas exports to the former CMEA block are found to have declined constantly. The recovery of output is mainly driven by the increasing share of exports to the EU. Moreover, the dynamics of exports to the EU has been positively influenced by foreign direct investment. This empirical evidence provides an alternative explanation to the U-shaped path of output. Further research should try to separate the effects of disorganization analyzed in this chapter from those related to varying demand in the EU market, the domestic market, and the export market to the former CMEA block.

7.7   CONCLUSION

At the beginning of transition in Eastern Europe, nobody expected an output fall as large as the double-digit fall observed in all Central and Eastern European countries. Most economists expected at least a moderately positive supply response from liberalization, because it was taken for granted that markets would form almost immediately. Markets did emerge quickly, and there was a supply response through entry by small private businesses. However, the disruption effects of liberalization on existing production links were largely underestimated. It took several years before economists came up with models that even started to give a convincing explanation for the output fall.

One important difference between the Blanchard-Kremer and Roland-Verdier models should be highlighted. The former is not really a dynamic model, and the output fall can be understood in terms of a comparative statics exercise. It can however be interpreted dynamically as leading to a permanent output fall. The Roland-Verdier model features only an *initial* output fall followed by a higher level of output than under socialism. In reality, even though all Central and Eastern European countries experienced an initial output fall, there is a striking difference between the performance, for example, of Poland, which has recovered from the output fall, and Russia, where there seems to be a permanent negative output shock. The models in this chapter have emphasized the impact of liberalization in a socialist economy with no (or hardly any) preexisting markets. These models mostly give an answer to the question of the initial output fall, but cannot explain this longer term difference between Poland and Russia. This topic will be tackled in the next chapter.

7.8 APPENDIX

Replacing V_2^H and V_2^L by their expressions, we get

$$\delta \left[q_2^H \frac{h^2 - p}{2} + (1 - q_2^H) \frac{h - p}{2} \right] > (h - p) - \delta \left[q_2^H \frac{h - p}{2} + (1 - q_2^H) \frac{1 - p}{2} \right]$$

By rearranging, we get

$$\delta \frac{h + 1}{2} \left[q_2^H (h - 1) + 1 \right] > h - p(1 - \delta) \tag{7.A1}$$

We check also that an L type who is with an L type with $\theta = 0$ prefers to search. This preference implies

$$\left[q_2^H \frac{h - p}{2} + (1 - q_2^H) \frac{1 - p}{2} \right] > 1 - p$$

By rearranging, we get

$$\delta \left[q_2^H (h - 1) + 1 \right] > 1 - p(1 - \delta) \tag{7.A2}$$

One checks easily that if formula (7.A1) is satisfied, then formula (7.A2) also is. Given that agents with $\theta = 0$ have more incentives to search than agents with $\theta = 1$, everything else equal, then as long as formula (7.A1) is satisfied, an all-search equilibrium will exist. By definition,

$$q_2^H = \frac{m_2^H}{m_2^H + m_2^L} = \frac{m_1^H (1 - m_1^H)}{m_1^H (1 - m_1^H) + (1 - m_1^H)} = \frac{m_1^H}{m_1^H + 1}$$

Formula (7.A1) after replacement and rearrangement, thus becomes

$$m_1^H h + 1 > \frac{2}{h + 1} \frac{h - p(1 - \delta)}{\delta} (m_1^H + 1)$$

Defining $A(h) \equiv \frac{2}{h+1} \frac{h - p(1 - \delta)}{\delta}$, we get

$$m_1^H \geq m_h^o(h) = \frac{A(h) - 1}{h - A(h)}$$

In order to be consistent with the model, m_h^o must be smaller than $\frac{1}{2}$ because there are more L types than H types. Now, $\frac{A(h)-1}{h-A(h)} < \frac{1}{2} \iff A(h) < \frac{h}{3} + \frac{2}{3}$. Taking into account that $A(h)$ is a concave function $\{A' = \frac{2}{\delta} \frac{[1+p(1-\delta)]}{(h+1)^2} > 0, A'' = \frac{-4[1+p(1-\delta)]}{\delta^2 (h+1)^3} < 0\}$, the former inequality defines a threshold value h^* defined in such a way that $A(h^*) = \frac{h^*}{3} + \frac{2}{3}$ so that $m_h^o < \frac{1}{2} \iff h \geq h^*$.

CHAPTER 8

GOVERNMENT COLLAPSE AND ECONOMIC PERFORMANCE

8.1   INTRODUCTION

In the previous chapter, the analysis of the output fall helped us to understand how disorganization following big bang liberalization could explain the initial, and sometimes quite significant, output fall that occurred in most transition economies. However, while some countries like Poland and most Central and Eastern European countries have recovered growth after that initial output fall, other countries like Russia and other economies from the former Soviet Union have witnessed a continued output decline with few if any signs of recovery. In those countries, it seems that a more permanent income shock can be observed. How can we explain such differences?

A paradox is that differences in reform strategies are not so huge between those countries despite the divergence in output trajectories. If we compare Russia with, say, Poland and the Czech Republic, we do not see any major difference in reform strategies. All countries have liberalized early on. While Russia and the Czech Republic have had policies of mass privatization, Poland did not. Although economic developments in the Czech Republic have been less brilliant than in Poland in the late 1990s, the difference between the GDP paths in those countries is smaller than the differences between Russia and other countries (see Chapter 1). One important difference is that stabilization policy succeeded much better in Poland than in Russia, where political constraints were quite important. However, there was no major difference between the stabilization *strategy* of reformers in Russia and strategies in other countries. Moreover, inflation has slowed down in Russia, starting in 1995. How therefore can we explain such a big difference in output trajectories?

In this chapter we look at the role of government collapse and the role of government institutions in securing private contracts. We put a special emphasis on the role of law enforcement. The vision put forward by many transition experts that markets evolve spontaneously with liberalization neglects another spontaneous emergence, namely, that of criminal activity preying on private producers. The impressive emergence of organized crime in Russia in particular reminds us of the importance of law enforcement to protect private economic activity from predatory behavior. This dimension has played a critical role in the takeoff of industrialization in economic history (North, 1990) and is likely to play an important role in determining economic success and failure in transition economies.

Focusing on the dimension of law enforcement, we see immediately that it is a major problem in Russia with the rise of the Mafia phenomenon and the general increase in criminality. It is less of a problem in Poland and other countries. For example, Johnson, Kaufmann, McMillan, and Woodruff (1999) using surveys in manufacturing firms found that in Russia and Ukraine around 90 percent of managers say firms pay "Mafia protection," while the corresponding figure in Poland is only 8 percent (15 percent in Slovakia and 1 percent in Romania).[1] Similar results were reported by Frye and Shleifer (1997) in surveys of Russian and Polish retail stores. In Russia, 76 percent of surveyed shopkeepers said that one cannot operate a store without paying for private protection, and 39 percent had been contacted by the Mafia in the previous six months. The corresponding figures in Poland were 8 percent and 6 percent. Pissarides, Singer, and Svejnar (1996) in a comparative survey of small and medium enterprises in Russia and Bulgaria found that Russian firms had a greater mistrust of external organizations providing security and insurance. Only 44 percent of Russian firms surveyed employed a security company or external individuals for protecting their premises compared to two-thirds of Bulgarian firms. Russian firms showed a much greater preference for in-house protection. Moreover, only 25 percent of Russian small and medium-sized enterprises (SMEs) surveyed reported having fire and burglary insurance as opposed to 65 percent of Bulgarian SMEs.

The lack of the rule of law in countries like Russia has led to an increase in predatory activities that are likely to have adverse effects on productive activity and in particular to slow down the emergence of the new private sector. The question then is, Why is there law enforcement in some countries and less (or hardly any) in other countries? (This question is also relevant beyond the realm of transition economies.) Since the rule of law is enforced by government, the question is, Why are some governments too weak to enforce the law and others are not?

One sees immediately that there is an important coordination problem to be solved in law enforcement. This coordination problem has at least two dimensions.

First of all, coordination is necessary to provide the public good of crime-control technology and law enforcement. This coordination is usually solved through tax collection, but tax collection itself is likely to be endogenously weak in countries where law enforcement is weak. Figure 8.1, drawn from Schaffer and Turley (1999), gives a rough idea of differences in tax collection abilities of tax administrations in various transition countries. They normalize value-added tax rates to 20 percent to correct for differences in rates across countries and on that basis compute VAT revenues as a percentage of GDP, the

[1] *Johnson and colleagues also found significant differences in government corruption, trust in courts, tax rates, and the size of the unofficial economy between the two groups of countries.*

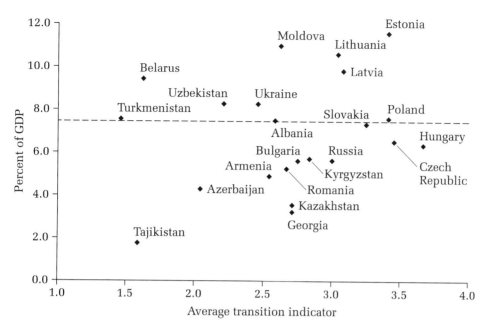

FIGURE 8.1 VAT IN PERCENT OF GDP NORMALIZED TO 20 PERCENT RATE, 1997, VERSUS EU AVERAGE

Source: Schaffer and Turley (1999)

broken line representing the EU average. One sees a clear positive correlation between progress in transition, measured by the EBRD transition indicator, and tax collection ability. Moreover, although one does observe countries with high tax collection and low transition progress, such as Belarus and Turkmenistan, there are no countries that are advanced in the transition progress but that have low tax collection ability. Strong tax collection powers are thus certainly not a sufficient condition for success in transition, but they appear to be a necessary condition.

Second, there is a coordination problem in compliance with law. For given expenditures on repression, strong compliance by all citizens ensures effective control, whereas weak compliance decreases the expectation of getting caught and thus the disincentive to break the law. These coordination problems in law enforcement typically lead to a prediction of a multiplicity of equilibria. Such a multiplicity may serve as a point of departure to explain why countries with similar reform strategies may have such different outcomes in law enforcement. However, multiplicity of equilibria does not provide us with great predictive power because we do not have well-accepted theories to explain why some equilibria are selected and not others. Can we explain why there is law enforcement in some countries and not in others? In order to answer that question, we would like to know whether there are institutional mechanisms for eliminating the "bad" stable equilibrium.

In section 8.2 we present simple models of law enforcement to explain the rise of the unofficial economy and of organized crime. In sections 8.3 and 8.4 we analyze institutional mechanisms that serve to eliminate the bad equilibria with weak law enforcement. In section 8.5 we review the empirical literature on issues related to government collapse. In particular, we discuss the transition-related empirical literature on the causes of the expansion of the unofficial sector, the literature on the causes of government corruption, and the literature on contract enforcement in transition.

8.2 GOVERNMENT COLLAPSE OR LAW ENFORCEMENT

The first model of multiple equilibria related to the question of law enforcement in transition is by Johnson, Kaufmann, and Shleifer (1998). They present a very simple model of competing public good provision by government and by private protection agencies.

8.2.1 MAFIA AND GOVERNMENT PROTECTION

Assume a one-period model. Take a transition economy where the population size is normalized to 1. Individuals are atomistic and choose to maximize utility as follows:

$$\max_{\alpha} \alpha U_I + (1 - \alpha) U_P \tag{8.1}$$

given the choices of others, where α is the probability of being in the unofficial sector and getting utility U_I, and $(1 - \alpha)$ is the probability of producing in the official sector and getting utility U_P. Individuals are assumed to be risk neutral. The analysis is restricted to symmetric Nash equilibria where individuals choose α optimally given that α is chosen by others.

Utility is assumed to be equal to income. Individuals choosing to produce in the official sector pay a tax rate τ_P and then have access to a technology expressed by the concave production function $Q_P(T) = T^\beta$ where T represents tax revenues with $\beta \in (0, 1)$. This "technology" should best be thought of as representing the beneficial effects of law enforcement. Not all tax revenues need to be spent on public goods. All that matters is that a share of any increase in tax revenues is allocated to public good provision. Public good provision is seen mainly as law and order. Only firms in the official sector that pay their taxes are assumed to have access to the public good: police protection, courts, and the like. Tax revenues are $T = \tau_P(1 - \alpha)Q_P$. We thus have

$$T = \tau_P(1 - \alpha)T^\beta \qquad \text{or} \qquad T = [\tau_P(1 - \alpha)]^{\frac{1}{1-\beta}} \tag{8.2}$$

and

$$Q_P = [\tau_P(1 - \alpha)]^{\frac{\beta}{1-\beta}} \tag{8.3}$$

Similarly, in the unofficial sector, firms are assumed to seek private protection from the Mafia, pay a tax τ_I, and have access to a production technology $Q_I = R^\varepsilon$ where R represents racket revenues with $\varepsilon < \beta$. Technology in the unofficial sector is thus assumed to be less efficient than in the official sector. Nevertheless, it may still be possible for the official sector to collapse because of size externalities. The utilities of agents in the public and unofficial sectors, respectively, are

$$U_P = (1 - \tau_P)Q_P = (1 - \tau_P)[\tau_P(1 - \alpha)]^{\frac{\beta}{1-\beta}} \tag{8.4}$$

$$U_I = (1 - \tau_I)Q_I = (1 - \tau_I)[\tau_I \alpha]^{\frac{\varepsilon}{1-\varepsilon}} \tag{8.5}$$

Note that the optimal tax rate τ_P is equal to $\frac{\beta}{\beta+(1-\alpha)(1-\beta)}$ and is increasing in α. It is equal to β when $\alpha = 0$ and equal to 1 when $\alpha = 1$. It is not necessary to assume that the tax rate is set optimally; however, it is interesting to note that the optimal tax rate increases when α increases, that is, when the tax base decreases.

We see immediately that there are two corner equilibria with $\alpha = 0$ (no unofficial economy) and $\alpha = 1$ (no official economy). These equilibria are stable. Indeed, around $\alpha = 0$, U_I is close to 0 while U_P is close to $(1 - \tau_P)\tau_P^{\frac{\beta}{1-\beta}}$. It is in nobody's interest to deviate, and a similar reasoning can be made around $\alpha = 1$. These equilibria are also robust to changes in τ_P and τ_I. There is also an unstable equilibrium α^* for which $(1 - \tau_P)[\tau_P(1 - \alpha^*)]^{\frac{\beta}{1-\beta}} = (1 - \tau_I)[\tau_I \alpha^*]^{\frac{\varepsilon}{1-\varepsilon}}$. There is thus multiplicity of equilibria with an efficient equilibrium in which all citizens are law abiding and there is no unofficial sector. There is also an inefficient equilibrium with lower aggregate output and government collapse where all economic agents hide in the unofficial sector.

An important assumption of this model is that government revenues are not used either to combat the Mafia or to prevent economic agents from entering the unofficial sector.

8.2.2 CRIME AND PUNISHMENT . . . AND TAXES

We now look at a model due to Roland and Verdier (1999b) where government revenues are used to punish criminals and where citizens choose between being honest producers and predators. We assume that, when entering the underground economy, agents join the Mafia and become predators who rob honest producers. Call U^R the utility of a robber and, as before, U^P the utility of an honest producer.

In their economic activity, agents are assumed to meet another agent within the period according to a random matching process. Therefore, α is the probability of meeting a predator, and $(1 - \alpha)$ is the probability of meeting a producer. When a producer meets a predator, he is robbed with probability 1 of his income. Otherwise, his income remains unaffected. When a predator meets another predator, it is assumed that their income remains likewise unaffected because they have nothing to steal from each other.

Income generated by private production is AK_p with a marginal productivity $A > 1$ and with K_p denoting private capital. The total capital stock in the economy is equal to K. Capital managed by the government $K - K_p$ is assumed to be used inefficiently and yields a marginal productivity of 1. Call q the probability that a predator is caught, in which case he gets 0.[2] When a producer is robbed, his income is also 0, but when he is not robbed, his income is taxed by the government at rate τ in order to finance law enforcement. Taking into account these payoffs and the random matching, expected payoffs from being a predator and a producer, respectively, are given by

$$U^R = (1 - \alpha)AK_p(1 - q) \tag{8.6}$$

$$U^P = (1 - \alpha)AK_p(1 - \tau) \tag{8.7}$$

As can be seen, both U^P and U^R increase with K_p and decrease with α. The latter effect is related to the matching assumption. Private production is discouraged when there is a lot of predatory activity, but so is the predation because there are fewer producers to rob. The main difference between both payoffs is the relative difference between q and τ.

Expenditures G on crime-control technology affect the probability of being caught q for which the following functional form is assumed:

$$q(\max\{0, -S - \gamma\alpha + G\}) \quad \text{with} \quad \gamma > 0, \quad q(0) = 0, \quad \frac{\partial q}{\partial G} > 0, \quad \frac{\partial^2 q}{\partial^2 G} < 0 \tag{8.8}$$

When looking at formula (8.8), the first thing to note is that there is a fixed cost S that must be borne before repression technology can be made effective. Without such a fixed cost, infinitesimal amounts of government expenditures on repression would still have some positive effect. Another important assumption is that q decreases with α. The more predators there are, the less easy it is to catch any single one of them. This is the *law-compliance externality*. By deciding whether or not to abide by law, citizens affect the probability of punishment of predators.

Given the preceding assumptions, for a given G, $U^P > U^R$ and $\alpha = 0 \Longleftrightarrow q > \tau$. In effect, in order to decide to be honest producers, individuals must face a higher expected disutility from being a predator relative to the disutility from taxation when being honest.

We first look at the case of an economy where all the capital stock has been privatized: $K_p = K$. We can think of such an economy as a transition economy that has undergone mass privatization. The government then relies on the taxation of private income to finance repression technology. We thus have

$$G = \tau(1 - \alpha)AK \tag{8.9}$$

There are two coordination problems one is facing here. A first is related to the law-compliance externality. The higher is α, the lower is q because of the law-compliance externality and thus the higher is the incentive to become a predator. The second is the fiscal externality as in the model of section 8.2.1: the higher the α, the narrower the tax base and the higher the tax rate necessary to sustain a given level of government revenues.

As before, we have two stable equilibria: a law enforcement equilibrium with $\alpha = 0$ and a government collapse equilibrium where $\alpha = 1$. If all agents decide to be honest, then even a very low tax rate may suffice to finance sufficient repression technology to deter

[2] *This assumption can be interpreted in two ways: either the police recover the goods stolen by the predator, or the punishment inflicted on him is severe enough so as to offset his illegal gains.*

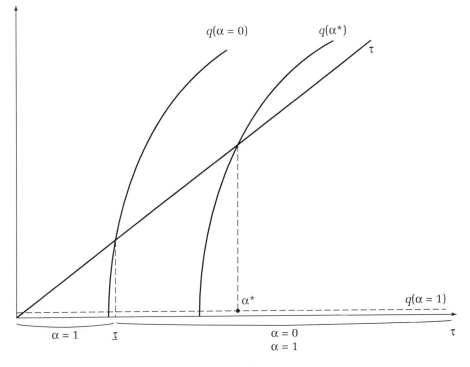

$q(\alpha = 0)$ $q(\alpha^*)$ τ

α^* $q(\alpha = 1)$

$\alpha = 1$ $\underline{\tau}$ $\alpha = 0$ τ
$\alpha = 1$

FIGURE 8.2 LAW ENFORCEMENT AND GOVERNMENT COLLAPSE EQUILIBRIA

predators. This is the "good" enforcement equilibrium. The minimum tax rate necessary to sustain that equilibrium is $\underline{\tau}$ such that $\underline{\tau} = q(-S + \underline{\tau}AK)$.

However, if many agents decide to become predators, they will each face a lower probability of being caught, increasing the incentive to become a predator. Also, in order to deter predators, producers will be faced with a higher tax rate, because of the smaller number of honest producers, thereby encouraging them to be predators. We then have the "bad" equilibrium with no law enforcement. As before, there is also an unstable equilibrium with α^* such that $U_P = U_R$.

Figure 8.2 illustrates the multiplicity of equilibria. Note that as in the preceding model, apart from the interior (unstable) equilibrium, τ can be indeterminate. It can be chosen arbitrarily in the equilibrium with $\alpha = 0$ as long as it is larger than $\underline{\tau}$, and it is irrelevant in the case with $\alpha = 1$. In the former case, with $\alpha = 0$, all that is needed is to prevent any producer from deviating. The latter case, $\alpha = 1$, is reminiscent of the Russian situation where tax rates are considered to be high but are irrelevant because tax collection is low (see Berkowitz and Li, in press). It seems reasonable that the tax rate is not determinate. Indeed, countries where one observes law enforcement are not necessarily countries with a large size of government, as we will see in section 8.5 when discussing empirical evidence.

From the point of view of welfare analysis, in the framework of the model it is best to set τ as small as possible, subject to being compatible with the law enforcement equilibrium. Note that when $\alpha = 0$, a predatory government that would divert tax revenues for the private benefits of its members would tend to increase τ above the minimum necessary but would always want to keep it below q in order not to lose its tax base. If taxation is decided independently by independent predatory government agencies, then an additional coordination problem would arise within government, leading to excess taxation. This lack of coordination among predatory government agencies would then be another cause of multiplicity of equilibria.

It should be noted that law compliance and the fiscal externality are not sufficient conditions to generate multiplicity. The $\alpha = 1$ equilibrium can be eliminated if one assumes different functional forms and changes the setup. One can, for example, introduce Inada conditions in private output and formulate an assumption other than random matching so that one has a strict incentive to deviate from $\alpha = 1$ (see, e.g., Savvateev, 1998). In the current framework the marginal product remains bounded at A, and nobody has an incentive to become a producer if surrounded by predators. Similarly, with other assumptions on predation, the $\alpha = 0$ equilibrium can be eliminated if the marginal benefit from predation becomes very large around $\alpha = 0$.

The multiplicity of equilibria should nevertheless be seen as relevant to understanding transition. Indeed, the massive societal change creates a huge coordination problem, and coordination in law enforcement is one of the important coordination problems. Russia can be seen as an example of the bad equilibrium where there is little law enforcement and where predatory activities have an adverse effect on productive activity. Poland and Central European countries that are candidates for accession to the European Union can be seen as examples of the good equilibrium.

We should note that the stability of the bad equilibrium can also be seen in a broader sense with a more detailed model. For example, Sonin (1999) looks at a model where rich agents like the Russian oligarchs have advantages in rent seeking in a situation of low security of property rights. Since they benefit from such low security, they can capture government decisionmaking to prevent reforms that would enhance security of property rights.

Although multiplicity of equilibria may allow us to understand the divergence in output trajectories across transition economies, this approach is not very predictive. Can we learn something about the selection of equilibria? Are there transition strategies that eliminate the multiplicity of equilibria? We focus on that question in the rest of the chapter.

8.3   LAW ENFORCEMENT AND DUALISM

The massive transfer of ownership into private hands gives the government access to an efficient repression technology only if it is able to collect sufficient tax revenues. This massive transfer may be the deliberate effect of policies of mass privatization to "get the state out of the economy" or of simple state collapse and private rent grabbing. The outcome is the same. The bad equilibrium can therefore in general not be excluded, since the government cannot levy taxes when private agents choose to be predators. One possible way of eliminating the bad equilibrium, or more precisely of making it unstable, is for the state to keep direct control over enough resources so as to maintain a sufficiently effective crime-control apparatus. In the spirit of incomplete contract theory, one can argue that state ownership gives the state administration direct control over resources rather than indirect control relying on effective collection of tax revenues. Even though a policy of keeping direct control over resources by the state may be costly in terms of economic efficiency, it may be an important instrument for overcoming the coordination problem in the transition context.

Assume in the model of section 8.2.2 that $K - K_p > S + \gamma$ is left under state control and used to finance G. In that case, $q(-S - \gamma + K - K_p) > 0$, and it is always possible to set $\tau < q$, in which case any $\alpha \in (0, 1)$ cannot be an equilibrium since $U^R < U^P$. Also, any slight deviation of α below $\alpha = 1$ would directly lead to $\alpha = 0$. In other words, the equilibrium at $\alpha = 1$ is now unstable. The only stable equilibrium is thus $\alpha = 0$. Note that U^P is maximized at $\tau = 0$. Thus, as long as $K - K_p = S + \gamma + \varepsilon > 0$ for any $\varepsilon > 0$, the good equilibrium can be sustained and the stability of the bad equilibrium eliminated.

In terms of welfare, compared to the case of full privatization, implementing $q(-S - \gamma + K - K_p)$ involves a trade-off between efficiency losses and economies in tax distortions. Welfare is equal to $A(K - S - \gamma - \varepsilon)$ compared to $(1 - \underline{\tau})AK$. The latter expression represents welfare under the good equilibrium with $\alpha = 0$ under full privatization where $\underline{\tau} = q(-S - \varepsilon + \underline{\tau}AK)$, the minimum tax rate compatible with the good equilibrium and full privatization. We thus have $\underline{\tau} = \frac{q^{-1}(\tau) + S + \varepsilon}{AK}$. Note that $\frac{q^{-1}(\tau)}{AK}$ is a measure of the tax distortion. With no tax distortion under full privatization, the welfare loss is only of S, which is unambiguously smaller than $A(S + \gamma + \varepsilon)$, the welfare loss under partial privatization. The expression $(A - 1)(S + \varepsilon)$ is in that case the efficiency cost of the public sector, while $A\gamma$ is the cost paid to eliminate the coordination problem due to the law abidance externality. Because of the tax distortion, $(1 - \underline{\tau})AK$ is strictly smaller than $(1 - \frac{S+\varepsilon}{AK})AK$, the welfare level without tax distortion. If the tax distortion is small enough, welfare is higher under full privatization; otherwise, it may be smaller. This trade-off between lower efficiency of state control but less tax distortions has been modeled by Gordon, Bai, and Li (1999).

With the existence of a public sector, welfare is maximized at $\tau = 0$ not because private taxation would be less efficient as a means of financing crime-control technology. It is more efficient in the model. The reason τ is equal to zero is that this is the cheapest way, in terms of welfare, of deterring individuals from becoming predators rather than producers. If $\tau > 0$, then it is necessary to increase q purely for incentive purposes, requiring in turn that τ be set high enough. Note incidentally that in equilibrium (with $\alpha = 0$), q is strictly greater than τ and U^P is strictly greater than U^R.

At least two important ingredients of these results have a clear flavor of the Chinese transition experience: (1) the state keeps direct control over resources;[3] (2) taxation of the nonstate sector is kept at a minimum level. This dualistic feature is quite typical of

[3] *This direct control is obviously associated with huge disadvantages not modeled here, Tienanmen repression being one example. However, maintaining direct control over state resources does not necessarily have to be associated with political dictatorship as it is in China.*

Chinese transition. In China taxation is very low. In 1996 budgetary revenues in China amounted to only 11 percent of GDP, less than Russia! However, government-controlled output has remained important and is still roughly one-third of GDP (Bai et al., 1999). Thus, the Chinese government has been less dependent on tax collection to finance government activities because of this dualism, in contrast to other transition economies where government has lost most of its direct control over resources.

In Chapter 6 we analyzed the efficiency and political economy aspects of dual-track liberalization. In Chapter 7 we analyzed how the dual track, by design, prevents the output fall. Here, we see the law enforcement benefits of dualism. Interestingly, a key assumption necessary for dual-track liberalization to work, as seen in Chapter 6, is the state's enforcement capacity. *Here, we have shown that dualism is a mechanism to maintain law enforcement and eliminate the government collapse equilibrium.* The analysis in this chapter thus nicely complements that of Chapter 6.

Caveats are nevertheless in order. We saw in Chapter 6 that the dual track has been perceived as associated with corruption. Corruption within government structures is likely to reduce the overall efficiency of public good provision. Nothing in the model guarantees that state resources will be used for crime-control technology. State resources may very well be diverted, and control over state resources may be used for abuse of power. Since these questions are outside the model, we do not want to dwell too much on them. The model only shows some conditions necessary to obtain coordination in law enforcement. As stated earlier, it is nevertheless in the interest of a predatory government to prevent predatory private behavior. Institutional guarantees for adequate use of resources would imply, for example, separation of powers with the judiciary arm of government having sufficient power to restrain the executive from deviating from policy announcements, together with mechanisms for adequate selection of policies like electoral accountability (see, e.g., Persson, Roland, and Tabellini, 1997, in press).

8.4   THE EU ACCESSION EFFECT

If A is very high, then the preceding strategy becomes very costly as a way to obtain law enforcement. It may then be better to borrow abroad to pay the cost of credible enforcement and to relinquish state control over assets immediately at the beginning of transition and thus to set $K_{pt} = K$ $\forall t$.

Such a strategy of borrowing will presumably be easier in the case of smaller countries. However, the burden of debt servicing is an important cost associated with such a strategy. As we will see, an even better solution to obtain law enforcement is related to accession to the European Union. The prospect of accession itself may act to eliminate the bad equilibrium. The analysis follows Roland and Verdier (1999b).

We must now introduce a dynamic model to analyze the problem of loan servicing and the effects of the prospect of accession. The most simple, and at the same time most reasonable, modification of the model is to assume that expenditures on crime-control technology can partly be seen as an investment. Many aspects of crime-control technology can be seen as investments that must be borne initially but carry benefits into the future. Immediate examples that come to mind are the training of specialized police forces or the establishment of information networks on criminal activity. Another example is the establishment of a reputation for efficiency and incorruptibility, which can be initially very costly to achieve but nevertheless can serve as an effective means of deterring criminal activity. In order to take into account this investment aspect of crime-control technology and taking into account the assumption that $K_{pt} = K$ $\forall t$, expenditures are then modeled in the following way:

$$G_t = \tau_t AK(1 - N_t) + (1 - \mu)G_{t-1} \tag{8.10}$$

where the tax rates τ_t are decision variables in period t, and N_t represents the number of predators in period t.

The new element is the last term on the right-hand side showing that past expenditures have persistence. The higher the μ, the lower the persistence.

It is also assumed that a choice to be a predator in period 1 cannot be reversed in period 2 but that a choice to be a producer always can. This assumption will play an important role in the rest of the analysis. There will thus always be at least $N_1 = \alpha_1$ predators in period 2. Call α_2 the choice variable of an individual who was a producer in period 1. The number of predators in period 2 is thus $N_2 = \alpha_1 + (1 - \alpha_1)\alpha_2 < 1$.

An amount B is borrowed in period 1 and reimbursed in period 2 at interest rate ρ. It is assumed that a sovereign loan is reimbursed as long as tax revenues are sufficient for that purpose. There is thus no strategic default. Consider the following timing: in period 1 the government commits to a certain policy schedule (B, τ_1, τ_2); then agents choose between being predators or producers in period 1 and in period 2; finally the government, whenever it can, reimburses the debt.

What are the conditions under this scenario to have $\alpha_1 = \alpha_2 = 0$ as a unique stable equilibrium? The borrowing constraint already changes the nature of the equilibrium, since in period 2 the loan must be paid back out of tax revenues from law-abiding citizens:

$$B(1 + \rho) < \tau_2 AK \tag{8.11}$$

Constraint (8.11) sets a lower bound on τ_2. Moreover, in the second period, in order to have $\alpha_2 = 0$ in equilibrium, one must have

$$q_2\{-S - \gamma\alpha_2 - B(1 + \rho) + \tau_2 AK(1 - \alpha_2)(1 - \alpha_1) + (1 - \mu)[B + \tau_1 AK(1 - \alpha_1)]\} \geq \tau_2 \; \forall \alpha_2 \tag{8.12}$$

In particular, this condition must hold against any deviation, including the deviation $\alpha_2 = 1$. Finally, in order to choose in period 1 to be a producer rather than a predator, for any α_1, and given that $\alpha_2 = 0$, we must have

$$(1 - \alpha_1)[AK(1 - \tau_1) + AK(1 - \tau_2)] > (1 - \alpha_1)\{AK[1 - q_1(-S - \alpha_1\gamma + G_1)] \tag{8.13}$$
$$+ AK[1 - q_2(-S - \alpha_1\gamma + G_2)]\}\forall \alpha_1$$

with

$$G_1 = B + \tau_1 AK(1 - \alpha_1)$$

and

$$G_2 = \tau_2 AK(1 - \alpha_1) + (1 - \mu)[B + \tau_1 AK(1 - \alpha_1)] - B(1 + \rho)$$

Roland and Verdier (1999b) show that the conditions for a borrowing equilibrium to be sustainable can be rather stringent. We skip here the analysis of those conditions but the intuition is the following. The value B must be high enough so as to convince agents in period 1 to become producers rather than predators. The higher is B, the higher is the amount that must be reimbursed in period 2. Such an increase has two effects: first, it increases τ_2 because of the reimbursement constraint (8.11), but second, it increases τ_1 required to invest in crime-control technology in period 1 so as to maintain incentives not to become predators in period 2 [condition (8.12)]. Since B increases both τ_1 and τ_2, the necessary amount of foreign borrowing necessary to deter predators in period 1 may make it impossible to raise enough taxes in that period to deter predators in period 2 also. In other words, the required τ_1 may be greater than 1. This will be the case if AK is small enough or if μ is close enough to 1, conditions that are likely to hold in transition economies, as well as in many other economies. Another way of putting it is that even if external borrowing can solve the coordination problem in the first period to eliminate the bad equilibrium, it may then not be in a position to do so in the second period because of the conflicting objectives of reimbursing the foreign debt and of investing enough in crime-control technology.

We now assume that the transition country borrowing in the first period has the possibility of accession to the European Union in the second period. This case mirrors closely that of Central European countries like Poland, the Czech Republic, Hungary, Slovenia, and Estonia that are the "first-round" accession countries.

It is assumed that, after accession, the repression technology is jointly financed by the Union. Even though this assumption does not reflect the current institutional reality of public finances in the European Union, it is not unlikely that such repression technology will, at least partly, be financed in common. Moreover, public finances are fungible, and accession to the European Union is likely to give those countries access to structural funds from the European Union that can contribute to a substantial part of those countries' budget.

Denote by $K\beta$ the capital per capita in the union after accession. Call $\theta = \frac{1}{\beta}$ the share of the initial transition country, and call G_0 the initial repression budget in the European Union. In order to keep things simple, all relevant variables are expressed in per capita terms. It is assumed that no income redistribution takes place, so that the per capita income of accession country members remains AK.

The second period constraint to induce $\alpha_2 = 0$, which will also be the constraint for the Union, will be

$$q_2(-S - \gamma\alpha_2 + G_2) \geq \tau_2 \ \forall\alpha_2 \tag{8.14}$$

$$G_2 = \tau_2 AK\beta(1 - \alpha_2)(1 - \alpha_1) + (1 - \mu)\left\{[B + \tau_1 AK(1 - \alpha_1)]\frac{1}{\beta} + G_0\frac{\beta - 1}{\beta}\right\}$$

As one can see, reimbursement of the debt is canceled out, since repression technology is financed out of a common budget. Also, if G_0 and β are high enough, the equilibrium with $\alpha_2 = 0$ can easily be sustained. Provided the accession country is small enough relative to the EU, accession is not likely to have a negative impact on law enforcement in the EU.

Let us now assume that accession is paired with conditionality. It is assumed that under conditionality, accession can only take place after the observation of $\alpha_1 = 0$ in period 1. When looking at period 1 choices of individuals, we must therefore look at the consequences of not meeting conditionality. We use the superscripts a for accession ($\alpha_1 = 0$) and na to indicate no accession ($\alpha_1 > 0$). We assume that the domestic government precommits to a certain policy schedule $(B, \tau_1, \tau_2^{na}, \tau_2^a)$ before agents choose to be predators or producers in periods 1 and 2.

Conditional on $\alpha_1 = 0$, a producer who chooses to be a producer in period 2 gets $AK(1 - \tau_1) + (1 - \alpha_2^a)AK(1 - \tau_2^a)$, whereas if he chooses to be a predator in period 2, he gets $AK(1 - \tau_1) + (1 - \alpha_2^a)AK(1 - q_2^a)$. When condition (8.14) is met, the payoff of the former is higher than of the latter. However, if $\alpha_1 > 0$, conditionality implies that accession will not take place. In that case, someone who chooses to be a producer in period 1 gets $(1 - \alpha_1)[AK(1 - \tau_1) + (1 - \alpha_2^{na})AK(1 - \tau_2^{na})]$ if he chooses to be a producer in period 2 and $(1 - \alpha_1)[AK(1 - \tau_1) + (1 - \alpha_2^{na})AK(1 - q_2^{na})]$ if he chooses to be a predator in period 2. The important thing to see here is that, when deciding in period 1 whether to become a producer or a predator, individuals must take into account the possible choice of others to become predators, which implies no accession and thus the possibility of multiple equilibria! The second period will thus play less of a role in motivating agents' choice in period 1. Borrowing will still be necessary to induce honest behavior in period 1 (see Roland and Verdier, 1999b, for the analysis).

Let us now look at what happens without conditionality. In this case, the choice in period 1 of being a producer rather than a predator implies that to have $\alpha_1 = 0$, one must have

$$(1 - \alpha_1)[AK(1 - \tau_1) + AK(1 - \tau_2^a)] > (1 - \alpha_1)[AK(1 - q_1) + AK(1 - q_2^a)]$$

which implies $q_1 > \tau_1 - (q_2^a - \tau_2^a)$. Since in equilibrium, $q_2^a > \tau_2^a$ (remember that this condition is necessary to prevent any deviation in period 2), stability of the enforcement equilibrium can be achieved with $B = 0$ and thus $q_1 = 0$ with $\tau_1 = 0$. With unconditional accession, one can afford to have $\tau_1 = 0$ and thus not borrow at all to sustain the good equilibrium, since in equilibrium $q_2 > \tau_2$, with or without conditionality. Therefore, as long as $\tau_1 = 0$, $q_1 = 0$ is sufficient as an incentive for all agents to become producers.

In other words, the better prospects for producers than for predators after accession are sufficient to deter would-be predators. The absence of conditionality maintains this incentive, even if some agents considered deviating.

Conditionality is not efficient here because the accessing economy must, in order to have access to superior crime-control technology in period 2, prove that it is able in period 1 to achieve the law enforcement equilibrium. By contrast, without conditionality, zero borrowing can achieve the law enforcement equilibrium in the first period. With conditionality, accession is conditional on what others do. Without conditionality, this is no more the case. The prospect of accession itself is what gives incentives. In a way, conditionality reduces the expected benefit from accession because of the coordination problem individuals are facing in the light of accession. *Conditionality creates a coordination problem that is absent without conditionality.* This insight shows that conditionality can be counterproductive when coordination is necessary to achieve the conditions for accession. Standard thinking on conditionality is based on traditional principal-agent and moral hazard models where the country receiving the loan is viewed as a single agent.[4] Whereas in many cases this approximation may be valid, in other cases it may lack the important dimension of coordination. Coordination is an issue, for example, in case of collective debt rescheduling of sovereign debt based on conditionality (the foreign debt of the former Soviet Union or the foreign debt of Latin American countries in the 1980s).

The accession effects may thus explain part of the difference between the different trajectories in Russia and in Central European countries like Poland. More generally, the accession effects on the success of reforms in Central European countries have been neglected in the transition literature where reform trajectories are analyzed independently of their international context. This is an issue to which we will come back in the concluding chapter. Indeed, in the case of Central Europe, the geopolitical aspects of breaking away from Russian domination to join the Western European club have strongly affected the perception of the costs and benefits of reform in Central Europe compared to Russia.

An implication of this idea is that the comparison between Polish and Russian transition cannot be done solely in terms of the strategies chosen. Another implication is that Russia, which lacks anything like the prospect of accession, should be compared with other countries that must find alone their path to success in transition. This points to the relevance of the Chinese transition experience for Russia and to the relevance of dualism in transition.

8.5 THE EMPIRICAL LITERATURE

There is a rather important empirical literature on issues related to government collapse in transition. We review the three most important issues raised in this empirical literature: (1) the rise of the unofficial economy in some countries; (2) corruption; and (3) private contracting under conditions of weak law enforcement.

[4] *See Berglöf and Roland (1997) for a policy analysis of accession along those lines.*

TABLE 8.1 THE EVOLUTION OF THE UNOFFICIAL ECONOMY AS A PERCENTAGE OF GDP IN SELECTED TRANSITION COUNTRIES

Country	1989	1995
Hungary	27	29
Poland	15.7	12.6
Czech Republic	6	11.3
Slovakia	6	5.8
Estonia	12	11.8
Russia	12	41.6
Ukraine	12	44.2
Georgia	12	62.6

Source: *Johnson, Kaufmann, and Shleifer (1998).*

8.5.1 THE UNOFFICIAL ECONOMY

A first striking fact is that estimates of the unofficial economy have varied widely since the beginning of transition, as shown in Table 8.1. Estimates of the size of the unofficial economy are based on energy consumption data and estimates of output–energy elasticities. Accordingly, these figures should be taken with great caution, a usual caveat applying to estimates of the size of the unofficial economy.

What is nevertheless striking when looking at Table 8.1 is that countries like Hungary and Poland that started reforms earlier had a relatively larger unofficial sectors compared to Czechoslovakia and the former Soviet Union. One must recall that this was a time when the private sector was tolerated only as part of the unofficial economy and the countries with more progress in reforms like Hungary and Poland had a greater tolerance for the unofficial economy. The size of the unofficial sector in 1989 thus reflects progress in reform before the collapse of the communist regimes, Czechoslovakia being the most unreformed economy at that time. Interestingly, apart from the Czech Republic, accession countries and Slovakia have not experienced a significant increase in the size of the unofficial sector, whereas in Russia and the Ukraine, it has reached 40 percent of GDP and in Georgia nearly two-thirds of GDP. Johnson, Kaufmann, and Shleifer (1998) found that the size of the unofficial economy (and economic growth) was affected negatively (and positively) by measures of liberalization, privatization, tax fairness, less crime, and measures of the rule of law. Nevertheless, a "former Soviet Union" dummy remains an important variable that affects the size of the unofficial economy positively and the growth performance of countries negatively.

Johnson, Kaufmann, McMillan, and Woodruff (1999) have had a more detailed look at the determinants of unofficial activity in Poland, Slovakia, Romania, Russia, and Ukraine. Russian and Ukrainian firms report that they pay higher taxes, more bribes to

TABLE 8.2 TAXATION, REGULATION, CORRUPTION, THE LEGAL SYSTEM, AND THE SIZE OF THE UNOFFICIAL SECTOR

	Poland	Slovakia	Romania	Russia	Ukraine
Percentage of sales not reported	5.4	7.4	5.7	28.9	41.2
Taxes as percent of sales	15.5	16.4	17.2	23.9	24.2
Percent who think firms make extralegal payments for government services	20	38	20	91	87
Percent of firms saying that firms pay for mafia protection	8	14.9	0.6	92.9	88.8
Percent of firms saying courts can be used to enforce an agreement	72.9	67.9	86.9	58.4	54.7

Source: *Johnson, Kaufmann, McMillan, and Woodruff (1999).*

government officials, and more payments to Mafia. At the same time, the benefits of being in the official sector (access to courts and credit) appear smaller in those two countries. Table 8.2 provides some key summary statistics of their research. Regressions on Poland, Slovakia, and Romania tend to show, on one hand, that in these countries the main reason for hiding output is to evade government extortion. On the other hand, these are also the countries where the unofficial sector has not expanded, in contrast to Russia and Ukraine.

Friedman and colleagues (1999) look at the determinants of unofficial activity in sixty-nine countries around the world and find that higher tax rates are associated with less unofficial activity. Higher government revenues and a lower unofficial sector are associated with less corruption, less regulation, and a better legal environment. Their research suggests that weak government institutions lead to weak tax collection, bad government services, and a high share of the unofficial economy. Schneider and Enste (1998) provide a comprehensive survey of what is known about the shadow economy in the world.

Campos (2000) remarks that there is an important difference between the unofficial sectors of transition economies and those of developing economies. In the latter, the shadow economy is characterized by a low capital intensity and small size of operations, whereas in the former, unofficial production is done mainly in big enterprises with a high capital intensity, such as oil refining. Output hiding in transition economies is typically in the manufacturing sector. This fact casts doubt on the view that the cause of the unofficial economy is excessive government intervention and extortion. The ability of large firms to hide output is more convincingly explained by the political power of large firms in a situation of government collapse and institutional vacuum.

Campos emphasizes that the policy consequences of the explanation of the size of the shadow economy based on either excessive government interference or institutional collapse are quite different. In the former case, tax cuts and regulations limiting government intervention should suffice to solve the problem. With the latter explanation, the unofficial sector appears to be deeply entrenched and its negative effects on aggregate performance are likely to be felt over a longer period of time. Only deep and credible institutional reforms are likely to solve the problem, and it is not clear how and when these can be implemented.

Campos provides tests of these two alternative hypotheses by performing Granger causality tests. He finds that for the countries of the former Soviet Union macroeconomic instability (inflation), a variable associated with institutional collapse, is the main cause of the increase in the size of the shadow economy, and he does not find robust evidence that higher government expenditures (a proxy for excessive government intervention) cause the increase in the size of the shadow economy. For all transition economies, he finds that higher inflation, lower investment, and a higher exchange rate Granger-cause the shadow economy to be larger. This finding tends to suggest that the explanation based on government collapse makes more sense than the one based on excessive government intervention. However, one needs much better measures of institutional variables to have really convincing evidence. It is also not clear to what extent the two hypotheses are mutually exclusive. On the one hand, in a situation of government collapse, individual bureaucrats will abuse their power by preying on private agents. On the other hand, if the unofficial economy is mostly biased toward big firms (a point that remains to be established even if capital intensity is certainly higher than in developing economies), then it does seem reasonable to think that the latter do not really "hide," but simply ignore any obligations imposed by a weak government because they have enough power to ignore such obligations.

8.5.2 Corruption

Corruption is an important phenomenon observed in transition economies. Empirical work on corruption has started to develop in recent years based on international compilations of surveys by Transparency International. Empirical analysis based on perceptions of corruption has both strengths and weaknesses. Objective measures of corruption are likely to follow an inverse-U-shaped pattern: a low number of corruption trials or investigations should be observed in noncorrupt countries or in very corrupt countries where the police and courts are completely captured. Subjective measures do not share this drawback. However, perceptions may be biased by the media, prejudice, and all sorts of informational externalities. Such biases can be controlled, to a certain extent at least, by comparing surveys among, say, the domestic population and foreign businessmen.

Mauro (1995) has shown that corruption has a negative impact on investment and growth. Wei (1997) has shown that corruption has a negative impact on foreign investment, and Wei (1998) shows that corruption does not reduce but increases the transaction costs of doing business.

Treisman (1999a) has done a cross-country study of the determinants of corruption. The following variables are found to reduce perceptions of corruption: (1) a Protestant tradition or a history of British rule, (2) a higher level of development as measured by GDP per capita, (3) a higher openness to trade as measured by the share of imports in GDP, (4) a unitary state, and (5) long exposure to democracy.

The fact that former British colonies tend to be less corrupt could be attributed to the existence of the Anglo-Saxon common law system (as in La Porta et al., 1999), but controlling for British colonial heritage, existence of a common law system tends to increase perceptions of corruption. Another possible explanation may be (1) that of a distinct legal culture that existed in British colonies emphasizing a procedural notion of justice rather than a substantive notion of justice and also (2) a superior administration of justice.

The role of Protestantism seems less related to the traditional work ethic emphasized by Weber but more to stronger values of individualism and self-reliance as opposed to higher "family values" in other cultures that may encourage nepotism and corruption (Lipset and Lenz, 1999).

The level of development is itself likely to be influenced by corruption. However, instrumenting by distance to the equator shows a significant effect of development on corruption.

The effect of federal structures seems robust, controlling for ethnic diversity, size of the country, level of development, and other variables. It is not clear a priori why this may be the case. Preliminary evidence in Treisman (1999b) suggests that the existence of separate police forces in federal states is an important determinant of a higher level of corruption. However, it is not clear at this stage what mechanisms are at play that yield a higher corruption level in federal states.

Democracy has only a small impact, but countries with a long democratic experience are perceived to be less corrupt. There may be an endogeneity bias here to the extent that corrupt officials may stifle democracy. A similar endogeneity problem may be present with openness to trade. In any case, the quantitative estimate of democracy and openness to trade appears to be very small.

It is also interesting to note which variables do not influence corruption. Thus variables of ethnolinguistic fragmentation do not appear significant, once one controls for the level of economic development. The same is true for dependence on raw material exports. Similarly, higher wages for government officials do not appear significant in reducing corruption. The data thus do not confirm an efficiency wage theory of corruption. Similarly, smaller state intervention and political instability do not appear to have an effect on corruption perception.

How do these results apply to transition economies? In the Transparency International Index, Poland, the Czech Republic, and Hungary are in the middle range together with Greece, South Korea, Malaysia, South Africa, and Jordan. They do better than Spain or Italy. Russia and China come much lower and are together with India, Bangladesh,

Venezuela, Cameroon, and Indonesia. Russia's index substantially worsened between 1996 and 1998, causing it to be perceived as more corrupt than Pakistan, whereas China's index has constantly improved, moving it closer to Turkey and Mexico. The lack of experience with democracy seems to be the main factor explaining corruption perception in those countries, controlling for level of development and openness. In Russia, the federal structure and lower openness to trade are compounding factors. The analysis suggests an important element of inertia in perceptions of corruption. Bringing corruption down in individual countries is certainly a long-lasting task.

8.5.3 PRIVATE CONTRACTING UNDER WEAK LAW ENFORCEMENT

So far in this chapter, we have emphasized the main inefficiencies associated with government collapse, namely, the rise of the shadow economy and of predatory activity by organized crime. Obviously, the absence or the weakness of law enforcement has an effect on contract enforcement between private parties. In particular, all sorts of substitutes for legal contract enforcement appear. The concept of relational contracting (Macaulay, 1963) refers to various enforcement mechanisms that supplement the law or act in place of the law.

Reputational concerns play a fundamental role in relational contracting. In order to sustain bilateral contracting and to reduce incentives for opportunistic behavior in private contracting, it is necessary to create a situation of lock-in between partners and to invest in specific long-term relationships that can sustain cooperation between parties. By doing so, one reduces one's outside options and makes credible the threat of sanctions from the other party. Sanctions can also be multilateral and operate on the basis of social exclusion of cheaters. Trade associations can act as repository of information on reputations and publicize cheating by traders and producers or enforce sanctions of exclusion. Wholesalers and intermediaries play a similar role. Moreover, they have a self-interest in dealing only with reliable partners. They play an important role in reducing the asymmetric information on the quality of business partners and their products.

Private methods for contract enforcement may be substitutes or complements to legal contract enforcement. When they act as substitutes, they are never perfect, and inefficiencies are associated with private methods of contract enforcement. Lock-in involves the loss of competitive outside business opportunities. Closed networks that are good at imposing sanctions also limit business opportunities. These inefficiencies reduce competition and increase the likelihood of collusive behavior. The use of private protection undermines the rule of law and creates opportunities for organized crime to hold up business firms.

McMillan and Woodruff (1999a, 1999b) have analyzed these questions of private contract enforcement empirically using data on Vietnam. Johnson, McMillan, and Woodruff (1999a, 1999b, 1999c) have performed similar and more extensive analysis using data on Poland, Slovakia, Romania, Russia, and Ukraine.

In Vietnam courts are very ineffective. Only 9 percent of managers interviewed said courts or government agencies can be of help in enforcing agreements with customers or suppliers, and only 2 percent said they would appeal to courts or local authorities over

TABLE 8.3   TRUST AND RELATIONAL CONTRACTING

	Poland	Slovakia	Romania	Russia	Ukraine	Vietnam
Percentage participating in trade associations providing information on suppliers and customers	20.8	23.4	44.2	60	64.1	26
Percentage of bill paid after delivery	83.5	69.7	48.1	11.8	37.5	38
Percentage having customer managed by family or friend	6.4	13.4	30.5	22.2	18.7	14.6
Percentage that would buy from new supplier at price 10 percent lower than current supplier	42.5	48.4	62.5	1.4	7.9	29

Source: *McMillan and Woodruff (1999a); Johnson, McMillan, and Woodruff (1999a).*

conflicts related to the quality of goods. As we saw in Table 8.2, firms in Eastern Europe trust the ability of courts much more, and even those in Russia and Ukraine, where courts are less trusted than in Poland, Slovakia, and Romania, fare better than Vietnam.

Table 8.3 gives some summary data that are useful in comparing mechanisms of trust and contract enforcement in the various countries. Participation in trade associations that provide information about customers and suppliers is very high in Russia and Ukraine and lower in the other countries. The second row shows the average percentage of a bill paid after delivery. This is interpreted as a measure of trust. Seen this way, the figures are the highest in Poland and Slovakia and the lowest in Russia. One must, however, be careful because these figures may measure not only trust but also the degree of softness of budget constraints. This may be what is reflected in the higher average payment after delivery for Ukraine, and possibly for Vietnam, as compared to Russia.

The percentage of firms having family or friends as customers reflects the fact that relational contracting may be better enforced when there are social or community sanctions to opportunistic behavior. At the same time, the absence of good legal systems restricts the number of potential partners one may do business with. This percentage is highest in Romania and lowest in Poland.

As said previously, an obvious cost of a bad law enforcement mechanism is the degree of lock-in and reduction of competition. Firm managers were asked whether they would buy from a new supplier if he proposed to sell inputs at a 10 percent lower price. This figure is relatively low overall for all countries, except for Romania. It is below 10 percent in the Ukraine and virtually zero in Russia. These figures clearly show the inefficiencies associated with the absence of well-functioning legal systems.

Econometric analysis gives a more accurate description of relational contracting. Thus in Vietnam, when a firm has a competitor nearby, its propensity to provide trade credit to customers is reduced by 13 percent, and each additional nearby competitor reduces it further by 4 percent. The length of the relationship also matters. After two years of doing business, a customer receives on average 14 percent more trade credit than a new customer.[5] When information on customers comes from business networks, the propensity to provide trade credit is substantially higher: on average 20 percent more of a bill can be paid after delivery. Interestingly, when the information comes by way of family or social networks, it has no significant effect on trade credit.

In Eastern Europe both the courts and trade associations have a significant effect on building trust. A firm that belongs to a trade association is 6 percent more likely to provide trade credit, and a firm that trusts the effectiveness of the courts is 8 percent more likely to provide trade credit. Lock-in and reduced competition also help. Having one fewer competitor located nearby raises the probability of offering credit by 2 percent. Three years after the start of a relationship, the probability of credit increases by 21 percent. Customers identified through business networks are 12 percent more likely to be granted credit, whereas customers identified via social networks are 14 percent more likely to receive credit. Managers who trust courts are more likely to use business networks and less likely to use social networks, suggesting that business networks act as complements to courts, whereas social networks appear as substitutes. Manufacturers who trust courts are also less likely to gather ex ante information on their customers.

Table 8.4 shows the relationship between security of property rights and measures of the development of market infrastructure. Johnson, McMillan, and Woodruff (1999b) asked managers whether they were ready to invest $100 today to receive $200 in two years. The figure is around 20 percent in Poland, Slovakia, and Romania but around 100 percent in Russia and Ukraine. This variable correlates rather well with more direct measures of security of property rights. Insecurity of property rights makes firms reluctant to reinvest profits even when they are relatively high because they fear the predatory environment in their economy. Insecurity of property rights is a first-order effect in determining the level of investment in a country. Financial reforms destined to enhance the intermediation of funds and the supply of credit cannot be effective if demand for credit is relatively low because of insecurity of property rights.

The other rows in Table 8.4 show measures of development of market infrastructure taken from Johnson, McMillan, and Woodruff (1999c). Use of wholesalers in business is more developed in Poland and Slovakia than in Romania, Russia, and Ukraine. Similarly, firms in Poland, Slovakia, and Romania sell up to twice more outside their own city. They also sell more to other private firms and less to SOEs and spinoffs. When discussing the

[5] Note that the investment in trust between business partners is an example of a relation-specific investment, which played an important role in the Roland-Verdier (1999a) model to explain the output fall.

TABLE 8.4 DEVELOPMENT OF PROPERTY RIGHTS AND MARKET INFRASTRUCTURE

	Poland	Slovakia	Romania	Russia	Ukraine
Percentage of managers who would not invest $100 now to receive $200 in two years	22.1	24.6	16.2	98.9	99.3
Percentage of a firm's sales going through a wholesaler	26	19	7	5	4
Percentage of firm's sales going to different cities or countries	64.7	67.6	53.8	23.3	30.5
Percentage of sales not to SOEs or spinoffs	61.3	55.5	67.7	38.1	36.3

Source: *Johnson, McMillan, and Woodruff (1999b, 1999c).*

effects of price liberalization in the absence of market infrastructure in Chapter 7, we did not take into account the importance of security of property rights in encouraging the development of market infrastructure. Cross-country variation in the security of property rights related to government collapse seems to be a first-order effect in explaining why some countries have undergone output recovery after an initial output fall and others have experienced a continuous decline.

8.6   CONCLUSION FOR PART TWO

In this second part of the book, we have analyzed the general equilibrium and macroeconomic effects of the allocative changes that take place in transition economies in relation with the closure of money-losing SOEs and of price liberalization.

We have first analyzed models of the optimal speed of sectoral reallocation. Here a common theme was that, while a closure of SOEs that is too slow would slow down sectoral reallocation because of labor market tensions or soft budget constraints, a closure of SOEs that is too fast could also slow down the rhythm of sectoral reallocation either because of the fiscal burden it imposes on the new private sector or because of the reduction in savings and investment induced by an overly strong output contraction. The latter result is especially valid for East Germany, the former GDR.

We have analyzed the speed and methods of price liberalization. While partial price liberalization can create distortions and important diversion of goods, price liberalization has important redistributive effects and may hurt many groups in the population despite its efficiency effects. An original method that both yields the efficiency effects of price liberalization and has the property of being Pareto improving is the method of dual-track price liberalization developed in China. Despite being Pareto improving, dual-track liberalization tends to give rents to agents who already had a privileged position in the centrally planned economy. Although it can be seen as a method to gain the support of bureaucrats for reform, it can also create resentment among the population.

The dual track is also useful in preventing a macroeconomic output fall following price liberalization because maintaining the plan track at a frozen level of production prevents disorganization of existing output links. Such an output fall has been observed in all Central and Eastern European countries after price liberalization. The magnitude of this output fall came totally unexpectedly, mainly because economic advisers to governments of countries in transition had traditional price theory in mind when thinking about the effects of price liberalization. Traditional price theory assumes the preexistence of markets and market networks. This is not a problem in advanced market economies but was a problem in former socialist economies where there were no preexisting markets. Models explaining the output fall go beyond traditional market analysis to focus on individual contracts and the environment of contracting. These models show that price liberalization may generate a substantial output fall as a result of disorganization of production links. Such falls occur because of inefficiencies in bargaining in environments with deficient legal systems or because of a combination of search frictions and relation-specificity in enterprise investment. In the latter case, liberalization will induce immediate disorganization and a fall in investment, and the establishment of new and more efficient business links will inevitably take more time.

While the output fall has led to recovery in Central European countries, continuous and stronger output decline has been observed in most countries of the former Soviet Union. We have analyzed models of government collapse in transition leading to a rise in the shadow economy and in organized crime.

What comes out of this part of the book most strongly is how the transition experience confirms the importance of institutions underpinning a successful market economy. The absence of a minimally strong government with legal institutions securing property rights and law enforcement leads more quickly to chaos than to successful markets and substantially deters entry of new entrepreneurs. This is a first-order effect in transition that explains the economic trauma of transition in countries like Russia. A large consensus is forming in the community of researchers working on transition on this first-order effect of the security of property rights. In the same spirit, price liberalization without preexisting market institutions does not yield a positive supply response but can generate a substantial output fall. The conclusions coming out of this part of the book are consistent with those from Part I, where the analysis of the political economy of sequencing of reforms showed the political economy advantages of implementing institutional reforms early in the transition process.

This emphasis on the importance of institutions in transition, however, does not necessarily mean that the institutions from the successful market economies should simply have been copied overnight in transition countries. Such a conclusion would be much too simplistic. The transition experience shows that specific transitional institutions can be created that fit the initial conditions of transition and that will support market reforms, while building political support and preventing a macroeconomic output fall. The dual-track system is the archetype of such a transitional institution. Indeed, it builds on the preexisting institutions that are retained in order to preserve existing rents and to prevent disorganization while at the same time letting markets develop. Transition via the dual track is clearly at odds with the radical reformist strategy that was popular in Eastern Europe in the beginning of transition and that consists in advocating a rapid and thorough destruction of all the previously existing institutions and letting markets develop on the ashes of the communist state. The theory analyzed in Chapter 8 has shown that multiplicity of equilibria typically result from such a strategy, government collapse being one of them.

While the transitional institution of the dual track implemented in China has played a positive role in letting markets develop, building support for reforms, and preventing the output fall, many questions remain unsolved as to how the dual-track system can be credibly phased out in a gradual way, what influence it has on the creation of specific business practices on the market track, and whether it locks in future institutional developments in a positive or negative way. This is certainly an important area for future research.

More research also needs to be done on law enforcement and on the fight against organized crime and corruption. So far, the empirical literature has focused more on the determinants of the unofficial economy and on private contract enforcement than on law enforcement. Research also needs to be done to test for potential accession effects in understanding differences between outcomes of institutional building in Russia and the former Soviet Union on one hand and Central Europe on the other hand.

PART THREE

GOVERNANCE CHANGES

CHAPTER 9

SOLVING THE INCENTIVE PROBLEMS INHERITED FROM SOCIALISM

In Part III, we analyze governance and incentive changes under transition. This is a large topic that can only be covered partially in this book.

Since we want to focus on the specificities of transition, in this chapter we will focus on the most important microeconomic relationship of socialism, the *government-firm relationship*. Understanding that relationship is important in order to improve our understanding of the difference between privately and publicly owned firms.

We will contrast two views of the government-firm relationship. A first view emphasizes the difference in objectives between government and private agents. According to this view, politicians are pursuing different goals from economic efficiency. They then intervene in firms in order to achieve these objectives. A second view emphasizes the commitment problem that government is facing in its relation to firms and analyzes the effects of that commitment problem. The lack of government commitment is seen as the source of inefficiencies.

According to the first view, inefficiencies in government-firm relations result necessarily from government interventions. In other words, managers would tend to pursue efficiency objectives but are prevented from doing so by government intervention that forces them to deviate from efficiency. According to the second view, lack of commitment itself may be a source of inefficient intervention *even if* government pursues efficiency objectives. This will be the case with the ratchet effect that we will discuss in section 9.2. Moreover, the lack of commitment of government can be exploited by rational self-interested private agents to obtain economic rents. This will be the case with the soft-budget-constraint problem discussed in section 9.3.

These two views are not necessarily contradictory. They can and should be seen as complementary focuses of analysis, to the extent that both problems (differences in objectives and commitment) are simultaneously present in reality. Moreover, both views raise in a nontrivial way the question of why privately owned and publicly owned firms behave differently.

Indeed, if government intervention is the source of inefficiency, why should government intervene more in public firms than in private firms? Ultimately, differences in ownership mean differences in government power over public and private firms, and they will make a difference, as we will see in section 9.1. However, government can still intervene in many different ways in private firms, namely, by taxation and regulation. It is thus important to specify the differences in government power over private versus public firms and show how these differences result in differences in performance.

Similarly, the lack of commitment power of government exists as much for private as for public firms. The government cannot, for example, commit not to change legislation or taxation in private firms. So, when thinking of differences in behavior across types of ownership, it is important to see to what extent and how the commitment problem is solved in a particular institutional context.

Both views also emphasize government power as the source of inefficiency. According to the first view, it is the power to intervene that is a direct source of inefficiency. According to the second view, lack of commitment comes from the absence of a third party to enforce commitment. The government is usually the third party for private contracts. However, there is a priori no credible third party to government-firm relations because government has the monopoly power over violence, especially under forms of government, like the communist regime, where government is not accountable to voters and where there is no system of checks and balances and separation of powers that can curtail the power of individual government agencies and impose the rule of law to control government discretion and arbitrariness.

9.1 GOVERNMENT INTERVENTION IN FIRMS

The first view discussed in the preceding paragraphs can be represented by the analysis of Shleifer and Vishny (1994). Their main idea is that private firms are more efficient because when control rights are in private hands, it is more costly for government to intervene in a private firm to force it to deviate from efficient decisions.

In their model, there are three players: the treasury, playing a passive role; the politician; and the manager of a firm, public or private. We present the main aspects of their model in this section.

Define L as the excess level of employment in the firm,[1] w as the level of wages for excess labor, and $B(L)$ as the benefit of excess labor to the politician, assumed to be concave. Politicians may, for example, derive political benefits by providing jobs to the unemployed. When there is no excess labor, the level of profits inside the firm is π. Denote by α the fraction of the firm's cash flow owned by the manager and by $1 - \alpha$ the fraction of cash flow owned by the treasury. If the firm is entirely state owned, $\alpha = 0$. If it is entirely privately owned, $\alpha = 1$. Differences in ownership, however, are not only amenable to differences in *cash flow rights*. Borrowing from Grossman and Hart (1986) and Hart and Moore (1990), ownership implies differences in *control rights*. Introducing these two dimensions (cash flow rights and control rights)[2] allows us to have a finer typology

---

[1] *By normalization, $L = 0$ is defined as the efficient level of labor in the firm. There is no explicit definition of efficiency, but it is assumed that this efficient level is achieved in the absence of government intervention.*

[2] *Note that in the Grossman-Hart-Moore framework, control rights are what matters most to define ownership.*

than the usual public-private dichotomy. Thus, under public ownership, government may have substantial cash flow rights but relinquish control rights to management. This system is called "commercialization" and reflects the autonomy that SOEs received under reform socialism. Similarly, a private firm may have all the cash flow rights while government has substantial control rights over the firm. This is the case of a regulated firm.

Since the politician derives benefits from excess labor, he must persuade the manager to hire L and pay him a transfer t for that purpose. Since a portion $(1 - \alpha)$ of the firm's cash flow $(t - wL)$ goes back to the treasury, the net transfer is then

$$T = t - (1 - \alpha)(t - wL) = \alpha t + (1 - \alpha)wL \tag{9.1}$$

If the state has all the cash flow rights ($\alpha = 0$), then the net transfer is wL, whereas if management has all the cash flow rights ($\alpha = 1$), then the net transfer is t.

It is assumed that there is a convex cost $C(T)$ of raising funds for the politician. The easiest example to think of is the political costs associated with tax increases to finance L, but alternative interpretations are possible. It is assumed that $C(T) < T$ on $[0, \overline{T}]$, which will be the relevant range we will look at. The reason for this assumption is that the money does not come directly from the politician's pockets.

The politician's utility is

$$U_p = B(L) - C(T)$$

The manager's utility is

$$U_m = \alpha \pi + T - wL$$

9.1.1   Government Control over Firms

In this context, ownership will affect the reservation utility of the manager. When the government has control rights over the firm, it has power over the manager. Consequently, the latter can be brought down to his reservation utility, assumed to be zero. The government's problem is then to choose L and T in order to maximize the following:

$$\max B(L) - C(T) \tag{9.2}$$

subject to

$$\alpha \pi + T - wL \geq 0$$

We get the following first-order conditions:

$$B'(L) = wC'(T) \tag{9.3}$$
$$T = wL - \alpha \pi$$

Assuming, without loss of generality for the results we are interested in, that the politician has all the bargaining power, the results can be analyzed as in Figure 9.1.

The curve $B'(L) = wC'(T)$ is a downward sloping function of L.[3] Decreasing the level of L increases $B'(L)$ and thus $C'(T)$, and therefore T must be increasing. The

[3] Note that this is not an indifference curve for the politician. The further one goes down that curve, the higher the utility of the politician, since L increases and T decreases.

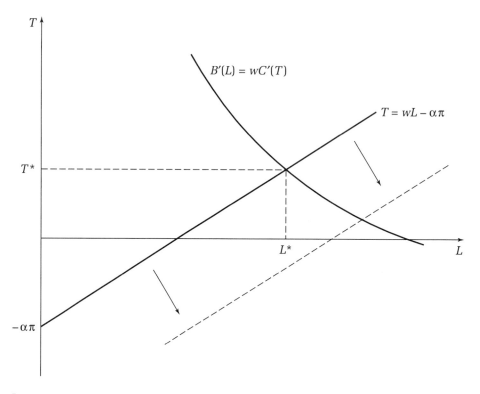

FIGURE 9.1 EXCESS EMPLOYMENT AND TRANSFERS UNDER PUBLIC OWNERSHIP

solution is (L^*, T^*) at the intersection between the upward sloping individual rationality constraint of the manager and the curve $B'(L) = wC'(T)$.

What is the effect of giving more cash flow rights to management? As one can see from Figure 9.1, such an action will have the effect of shifting the individual rationality constraint of the manager downward, thus leading to an increase in L and a decrease in T. Thus regulated private firms will have more excess employment than conventional SOEs. The idea is that the government can use its power over the firm to force the latter to pay for the excess employment using the transfer it receives from the government.

9.1.2 PRIVATIZATION

What happens now after privatization when the government loses control rights over the firm? In this case, the reservation utility of the manager will be different. Without government intervention, management can get $\alpha\pi$. Thus, after transfers, the net utility of the manager must be at least equal to $\alpha\pi$. The government's problem then becomes

$$\max B(L) - C(T) \tag{9.4}$$

subject to

$$T - wL \geq 0$$

As we will see in Figure 9.2, the reservation utility of the manager is shifted upward and is independent of α. The effect is to reduce the level of excess employment and to increase the amount of net transfers. In other words, it becomes more costly to pay the manager to convince him to hire excess labor and make inefficient decisions. Thus, while government intervention is possible in private firms, it is more costly and thus should be seen less often than in government-controlled firms.

Note also that allocation of cash flow rights (variations in α) do not influence the solution when control rights over the firm belong to the manager. This result suggests that transfer of control rights is what counts most. It also suggests, however, that commercialization should be equivalent to full privatization, a somewhat counterintuitive result given that increases in enterprise autonomy under reform socialism have led to enterprise behavior that substantially deviates from that of private firms (see, e.g., Brus and Laski, 1989). We will see later in this chapter that, when integrating the soft-budget-constraint phenomenon, one can account for a difference in behavior between commercialized and private firms.

Shleifer and Vishny generate a difference in behavior between commercialized and private firms by assuming that there is a "decency constraint" whereby net transfers to the firm cannot give the manager a higher utility than K:

$$\alpha\pi + T - wL < K$$

We then get

$$T = \max\{0, K + wL - \alpha\pi\}$$

In that case, the solution will be $L = 0 = T$ as soon as $\alpha\pi > K$. Indeed, the "decency constraint" will not allow for any $L, T > 0$ without getting below the individual rationality constraint of the manager. The idea of a decency constraint, however, is a bit ad hoc even though it certainly reflects a deeper political economy mechanism that we do not yet really understand.

A last remark to be made is on the effects of changes in $C(T)$. Assuming that a strengthening of the power of the finance ministry (or a tightening of monetary policy or increased accountability to voters) makes it more costly for politicians to raise funds, then this will imply an increase in $C(T)$. This will shift the curve $B'(L) = wC'(T)$ downward. The combined effects of privatization and of an increase in $C(T)$ can thus decrease both L and T as can be seen in Figure 9.2.

Note that these results on the difference between private and public ownership disappear once one allows for bribes between the politician and the manager. In that case, the level of L and T will be the same under public and private ownership. Only the level of bribes will change. This is a direct consequence of the Coase theorem. The proposition that the public or private nature of ownership is irrelevant under conditions of the Coase theorem has also been expressed by Williamson (1985), Sappington and Stiglitz (1987), and Shapiro and Willig (1990).

Empirically, estimates of the amount of excess labor in firms have been provided within the self-management literature (see, e.g., Prasnikar et al., 1994). The idea is that if

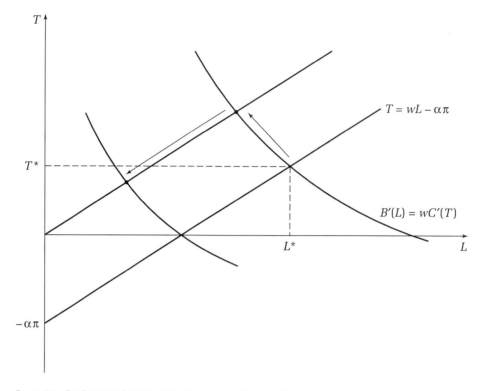

FIGURE 9.2 THE COMBINED EFFECTS OF PRIVATIZATION AND MONETARY TIGHTENING

the firm deviates from pure profit maximization and places a weight on the objective of employment, then estimates of excess labor can be derived from a labor demand equation augmented with the reservation wage of workers. The coefficient on the latter variable can then be used to infer whether the firm is holding excess labor or not.

A problem with the Shleifer-Vishny model is that it cannot account for why privatization would take place, since it goes against the interest of a politician who always prefers to keep control over firms rather than give them away. The view it gives of politician behavior is too homogeneous and does not take into account feedback between voters and other interest groups and politicians. The view that politicians do not care per se about efficiency but have other objectives in mind is difficult to dispute, unless one has a very naive view about politics. However, elections and other mechanisms such as separation of powers are ways of making politicians accountable to voters in a democracy even though rents to politicians can hardly be avoided (see, e.g., Persson, Roland, and Tabellini, 1997). These are forces that reduce the inefficiencies associated with government power in democracies. Moreover, there are heterogeneous interests in society, and shifts in electoral patterns bring to power different coalitions representing different interest groups in society that have different stakes in different policies. Depending on the circumstances, the interests of some interest groups and coalitions can be partly congruent with efficiency, and thus governments representing those forces, while serving only particularistic interests, may make decisions that are efficiency enhancing.

A final remark about the Shleifer and Vishny model is that the model could easily be reinterpreted in a diametrically opposed way. One could take the view that $L = 0$ is an inefficient level of employment that generates unemployment, but that managers do not internalize the social costs generated by unemployment. In that case, the government could be a benevolent one trying to achieve a more efficient level of employment. This possibility of a dual interpretation suggests the need to come up with finer models with a well-defined criterion of efficiency that can be used to compare private and public ownership.

9.1.3 TRADE-OFFS IN PUBLIC AND PRIVATE PROVISION OF PUBLIC GOODS

In the same spirit of the incomplete contract approach, Hart, Shleifer, and Vishny (1997) analyze the difference between public good provision (prisons, police, schools, health care, foreign policy) by a private or by a public firm. The manager of a firm can implement *cost reductions* and *quality innovations*. It costs him time or effort e to come up with a cost innovation yielding a public cost reduction of $c(e)$. It costs him time or effort i to come up with a quality innovation yielding a public benefit of $\beta(i)$. The cost reduction, however, may lead to a reduction in quality of the public good $-b(e)$. It is assumed that $c(e)$ and $b(e)$ are positive convex functions of e, but $c(e) - b(e)$ is positively sloped and concave, and so is $\beta(i)$.

The first best is the solution to joint welfare maximization:

$$\max_{e,i} -b(e) + \beta(i) + c(e) - e - i$$

The solution (e^*, i^*) satisfies the following first-order conditions:

$$-b'(e^*) + c'(e^*) = 1 \tag{9.5}$$
$$\beta'(i^*) = 1$$

What is the effect of contractual incompleteness and ownership? It is assumed that both i and e are observable but not verifiable. Variations in costs and quality do not constitute breaches of contract. There is, however, the possibility of ex post renegotiation once e and i have been invested. The surplus is assumed to be split 50–50 according to Nash bargaining. Under private ownership, the manager is fully residual claimant on reductions in costs. However, it is in his interest to renegotiate with the government over the quality innovation because the latter is not part of the initial contract. The manager's choice (e^P, i^P) will thus be the solution to

$$\max_{e,i} \tfrac{1}{2}\beta(i) + c(e) - e - i$$

yielding first-order conditions

$$c'(e^P) = 1 \tag{9.6}$$
$$\tfrac{1}{2}\beta'(i^P) = 1$$

Under public ownership, the manager needs approval of government to implement both innovations. Moreover, the government can replace the manager and appropriate a fraction λ of the returns on his ideas. The manager's share of the surplus will then be $\frac{1-\lambda}{2}[\beta(i) + c(e) - b(e)]$. He will then choose (e^G, i^G) to solve

$$\max_{e,i} \frac{1-\lambda}{2}[\beta(i) + c(e) - b(e)] - e - i$$

yielding first-order conditions

$$\frac{1-\lambda}{2}[c'(e^G) - b'(e^G)] = 1 \tag{9.7}$$
$$\frac{1-\lambda}{2}\beta'(i^G) = 1$$

A comparison of equations (9.5), (9.6), and (9.7) immediately yields the following results:

$$e^G < e^* < e^P$$
$$i^G < i^P < i^*$$

Thus private provision will tend to overreduce costs, at the expense of quality, and to underinvest in quality innovation. This distortion is related to the quality reduction spillover from cost reductions. Public provision will lead to underinvestment in both cost reduction and quality innovation because of blunted incentives. In some cases, the quality spillover is strong enough so that public provision is preferable. This seems to be the case for prisons. In other cases, this spillover is not strong, and private provision is better, a finding that conforms to our intuition of public procurements. In other cases, like schools and health care, conclusions are less obvious though the indicated trade-off seems clearly present.

9.1.4 Control Rights and Information

The incomplete contract approach emphasizes the differences in control rights of government in public and privatized firms (see also Perotti, 1995). Another approach developed by Shapiro and Willig (1990), Schmidt (1995), and Laffont and Tirole (1993) emphasizes the difference in information that government has about private and public firms. The idea is that government is less informed about private than public firms. This is justified by the fact that ownership over the latter gives privileged access to the accounts of the firm. Because of this difference in information, privatization lowers the government's ability to extract rents from firms. In Shapiro and Willig (1990) the benefit of privatization is that reduced information acts as a constraint on a malevolent government agency that pursues objectives different from efficiency. In Schmidt (1995) the government is benevolent but suffers from a lack of precommitment. This lack of commitment dulls the incentives of the manager to reduce costs. Indeed, having information about the cost structure, in a state-owned firm, the government will always subsidize costs to implement ex post efficient production levels. If the firm is privatized, the optimal regulation scheme will distort allocative efficiency by inducing an inefficiently low production level if costs are high, but such a result will improve the managers' ex ante incentives to invest in cost-cutting technology. Laffont and Tirole (1993) compare a publicly owned firm with a regulated private firm. As in Schmidt, the former dulls profit incentives because of a lack of ex post commitment. A private regulated firm, in contrast, is better protected from ex post expropriation of profits, but it has two principals, the shareholders and the regulator. This fact dilutes ex ante incentives because of conflicting objective from the two principals.

9.2 THE RATCHET EFFECT

In the Shleifer-Vishny (1994) model, inefficiencies in SOEs were derived directly from government preferences that were at odds with efficiency. Assuming, however, that government would care about efficiency, would it suffice to give SOEs correct incentives to remove the inefficiencies associated with socialism? Not necessarily. We already mentioned the problem of the absence of commitment power from government when discussing Schmidt's analysis of privatization. We dwell on that fundamental problem in the government-firm relationship in the rest of this chapter.

We look at the government-firm relationship as a simple principal-agent relationship. We assume that the government does care about efficiency and tries to give firms incentives to act efficiently but lacks commitment because of the absence of a third party. The assumption that government pursues efficiency objectives can easily be criticized for its lack of realism. Its main purpose, however, is analytical. It serves to analyze the effect of the lack of commitment on the part of government, and in particular the welfare effects of the lack of commitment, and to try to understand how this commitment problem can be dealt with endogenously.

We focus first on the *ratchet effect,* a term coined by Berliner (1952) in his analysis of management behavior in Soviet-type firms. Under central planning, managers were given strong incentives to fulfill their production plan. However, they were also given incentives to overfulfill the plan, and each additional percent of overfulfillment would be rewarded by additional bonuses. Nevertheless, managers tended not to take the opportunity to earn additional bonuses and were very conservative in their plan overfulfillment, rarely exceeding 2 percent. The reason is that they were afraid that next year's plan would be ratcheted up if they used all their capacity. By producing at 110 percent instead of 102 percent, they would get more bonuses today but would receive tauter plans in the future. Models of the ratchet effect in the context of Soviet planning include Weitzman (1980), Keren, Miller, and Thornton (1983), Bain and colleagues (1987), and Roland and Szafarz (1990).

The ratchet effect, however, is a more general incentive problem than under central planning. Obvious examples would include divisions within organizations spending all their budget at the end of the year, even on useless items, in order to avoid suffering from budget cuts in the future; competent secretaries or workers slowing down their work pace in order to avoid receiving a higher workload, and so on. In contract theory, the ratchet effect has been modeled as a dynamic commitment problem in a repeated principal-agent relationship by Freixas, Guesnerie, and Tirole (1985), Laffont and Tirole (1988, 1993), and Litwack (1993).

Here we present a simple model of the ratchet effect based on Roland and Sekkat (in press). There are N managers in the economy, with one manager per firm, and N is normalized to 1. Each manager may be either a high-productivity type ("good manager") characterized by the parameter $\bar{\theta}$ or a low-productivity type ("bad manager") characterized by the parameter $\underline{\theta}$, with $\underline{\theta} < \bar{\theta}$. Good managers are present in proportion p and bad managers in proportion $(1 - p)$. These proportions are known to the government, but individual type is private information. Managers can choose between two unobservable effort levels in their enterprise: high effort $\bar{e}$, yielding disutility $\bar{e}$, and low effort $\underline{e}$, yielding disutility $\underline{e}$, with $\underline{e} < \bar{e}$.

The government can only observe the output y of a given firm, which is a function of type and effort: $y = y(\theta, e)$. Output is defined here as value added after wage payments, depreciation, and the like. It is equal to profits plus managerial salaries. The following assumptions are made on output:

$$y(\bar{\theta}, \bar{e}) > y(\bar{\theta}, \underline{e}) = y(\underline{\theta}, \bar{e}) > \bar{e} > \underline{e} > y(\underline{\theta}, \underline{e}) \tag{9.8}$$

There are thus three possible output levels. The highest, which we denote $y_1 \equiv y(\bar{\theta}, \bar{e})$, can only be achieved by the good manager after high effort. The intermediate level, $y_2 \equiv y(\bar{\theta}, \underline{e}) = y(\underline{\theta}, \bar{e})$, can be achieved by both types but under different conditions of effort. The lowest level, $y_3 \equiv y(\underline{\theta}, \underline{e})$, occurs when the bad manager exerts low effort. As shown by the right-hand inequalities, it is assumed that high effort from the bad manager is socially profitable while low effort is not.

When y_1 or y_3 is observed, the government can immediately infer the agent's type, whereas when y_2 is observed, the government may not be able to tell whether the manager is good or bad. Hence, even though y_3 is unprofitable, this output level may yield intertemporal benefits because it provides a way to separate the good managers from the bad ones.

In a one-period framework under asymmetric information, an incentive scheme, or wage schedule, devised by the government is a triplet $\mathbf{w} = \{w_1 = w(y_1), w_2 = w(y_2), w_3 = w(y_3)\}$.

The individual agents' choice of effort is the solution to

$$\max_e w(y) - e \tag{9.9}$$

subject to

$$w(y) - e \geq 0$$

The government's choice of an incentive scheme is determined by the maximization of expected output, net of payments to managers, taking into account managers' choice of effort level:

$$\max \pi = p\{y(\bar{\theta}, \mathbf{w}) - w[y(\bar{\theta}, \mathbf{w})]\} + (1 - p)\{y(\underline{\theta}, \mathbf{w}) - w[y(\underline{\theta}, \mathbf{w})]\} \tag{9.10}$$

where $y(\bar{\theta}, \mathbf{w})$ and $y(\underline{\theta}, \mathbf{w})$ are the output levels chosen by each type depending on the incentive scheme. Note that the government is treated here only as a principal and not as a welfare maximizer. This assumption is not crucial for the results but simplifies the analysis. It is also assumed that the government is subject to a full employment constraint and is not willing, for political reasons, to cease operation of money-losing firms or to encourage bad managers to exit. This assumption seems natural under a socialist economy. It is also assumed that

$$y_i - y_{i+1} > \Delta e = \bar{e} - \underline{e} \tag{9.11}$$

We first look at the asymmetric information case in a one-period framework. Because of equation (9.11), the central planner is better off proposing the following scheme:

$$\mathbf{w}_A = \{w_1 = \bar{e} + \Delta e, w_2 = \bar{e}, w_3 = \underline{e}\}$$

The $\bar{\theta}$ type get a rent of Δe, but the additional output is higher than the additional wage Δe for producing y_1 instead of y_2. Total profits will thus be

$$\pi_A = \pi_F - p\Delta e$$

where $\pi_F = py_1 + (1 - p)y_2 - \bar{e}$ is the government payoff under the full-information optimal incentive scheme. Given formulas (9.8) and (9.11), the latter consists in having both types exert high effort and get exactly compensated for their effort.

9.2.1 THE RATCHET EFFECT UNDER SOCIALISM

We assume no discounting. We know then that the two-period model with commitment is the same as the one-period model repeated twice. What happens if there is a lack of commitment? Incentive scheme $\mathbf{w}_A$ repeated twice cannot be an equilibrium. Indeed, after the first period the government has learned the type of each agent. It will then have an incentive to apply the full-information incentive scheme whereby agents get no rents. By choosing $\bar{e}$ in the first period, agents of type $\bar{\theta}$ only get rents of Δe over the two periods. They are better off choosing $\underline{e}$ in the first period because then they pool with the agents of type $\underline{\theta}$. In that case the government does not learn their type, and scheme $\mathbf{w}_A$ can be applied in the next period. They then get a rent of $2\Delta e$, which is strictly better. In order to get the type $\bar{\theta}$ to produce y_1 in the first period the government must thus concede a rent of $2\Delta e$ in the first period. The first-period incentive scheme will then be $\{w_1 = \bar{e} + 2\Delta e, w_2 = \bar{e}, w_3 = \underline{e}\}$ followed by the second-period, full-information incentive scheme. Under this separating equilibrium, the two-period payoff for the government is

$$\pi_S = p[y_1 - (\bar{e} + 2\Delta e)] + (1 - p)(y_2 - \bar{e}) + \pi_F \tag{9.12}$$

With a pooling outcome, the payoff of the central planner will be

$$\pi_P = y_2 - \overline{e} + \pi_A \qquad\qquad (9.13)$$

One sees immediately that

$$\pi_S > \pi_P \Longleftrightarrow y_1 - y_2 > \Delta e$$

which is the case because of assumption (9.11).

Here also one has the usual ratchet result that, in the absence of government precommitment, a higher first-period cost, compared to the commitment solution, is necessary to obtain separation. Separation in this model is always preferable to pooling if there are no extra costs associated with the higher first-period incentive payments. Nevertheless, managerial incentive bonuses must be paid out of the net product. If we assume no external borrowing,[4] then it may be the case that separation is infeasible if the first-period surplus under separation is negative, that is, if $\pi_F - 2p\Delta e < 0$, which will be the case if

$$p > \underline{p} = \frac{y_2 - \overline{e}}{2\Delta e - (y_1 - y_2)}$$

In that case, the outcome will be the pooling equilibrium, unless there is a better "cheaper" separation scheme where the bad managers are induced to provide low effort in the first period. Another separating scheme is one where $\{w_1 = \overline{e}, w_2 = \underline{e}, w_3 = \underline{e}\}$ is offered in the first period and the full-information incentive scheme is applied in the second period. The $\underline{\theta}$ type produce y_3 in the first period, which brings a loss of $\underline{e} - y_3$, but this has the advantage of eliminating any informational rents in the second period. Once the $\underline{\theta}$ type produce y_3, then the $\overline{\theta}$ cannot pool with them anymore. The payoff is then

$$\pi_{S'} = p(y_1 - \overline{e}) + (1 - p)(y_3 - \underline{e}) + \pi_F$$

One sees that

$$\pi_P > \pi_{S'} \Longleftrightarrow p < \overline{p} = \frac{y_2 - y_3 - \Delta e}{y_1 - y_3}$$

If $\frac{y_2 - \overline{e}}{2\Delta e - (y_1 - y_2)} < \frac{y_2 - y_3 - \Delta e}{y_1 - y_3}$, then the pooling equilibrium is optimal for the government on $[\underline{p}, \overline{p}]$.

The intuition is the following. If p is large enough, then it is optimal to apply the "cheap" separation scheme in the first period. Indeed, the first-period costs of the losses from producing y_3 tend toward 0 when $p \longrightarrow 1$, and the full-information incentive scheme can be applied in the second period. However, if p is small enough, then the more "expensive" efficient separation scheme will tend to yield a positive surplus in the first period because the total first-period rents given to the $\overline{\theta}$ for producing y_1 become smaller when p becomes smaller. That scheme will then become feasible and will not violate the borrowing constraint.

[4] One can also assume costly borrowing. The analysis is then a bit longer. See Roland and Sekkat (in press).

Focusing on the pooling equilibrium in the socialist economy before transition seems reasonable, as pooling can be seen as a plausible characterization of managers in an economy where the ratchet effect is a pervasive phenomenon, leading to managerial slack as described in the work of Berliner and others.

The preceding result, however, goes further. It says something about the efficiency limits of profit-oriented government activity under market socialism. In the early years of central planning, the objective of efficiency was generally sacrificed in order to reach the ambitious quantity targets of the plan. In subsequent periods, the drive toward efficiency led to proposals for economic reform. The most radical idea of reform was that of market socialism, consisting in maintaining the public ownership of the means of production but allowing the market to allocate resources (see Bardhan and Roemer, 1992). The preceding result tells us that when the state is the sole employer of managers and when it cannot credibly precommit to fixed incentive schemes, then there are conditions under which it will not be possible to eliminate managerial slack, even when profit maximization is the objective. The fact that managerial careers are limited to one choice, in the public sector in this case, is crucial for that result. Indeed, it allows the state to exercise a holdup power on managers.

Compared to other ratchet models from the literature (e.g., Hart and Tirole, 1988; Laffont and Tirole, 1993), this model not only has the advantage of simplicity, because of the discrete effort levels, but also has the pooling equilibrium result from simple general equilibrium considerations that are absent in the ratchet literature. Such general equilibrium considerations are important, however, when analyzing incentives problems of socialism and transition.

9.2.2 THE RATCHET EFFECT AND THE MANAGERIAL LABOR MARKET

The ratchet effect was an important incentive problem under socialism and was much discussed in the context of central planning. However, there is hardly any reference to the ratchet effect in the transition literature. Many researchers working on transition probably do not even know about the concept. This fact suggests that the ratchet effect has ceased to be a problem rather early in the transition process. How could that be the case?

The main difference between socialism and transition is the existence of a private sector under the latter. This can affect managerial incentives in two different ways. First, managers have the option, which they did not have before, of leaving the state sector and going to work for a private firm. Second, managers can leave the state sector without leaving their enterprise if the latter is privatized. The prospect of being hired by a private firm or of remaining as manager of their firm when it is privatized gives incentives to managers to restructure in the first period. In what follows, we will identify high effort with restructuring. An implication of the introduction of the private sector is that competition for managers will give incentives for government to commit to its incentive schemes.

Assume now that, after period 1, managers have the opportunity of working in the private sector. Private sector variables are indicated by an asterisk (*).

The following assumptions are made on the private sector. The technology is nonsubstitutable. One and only one manager is needed per new firm. All firms are identical, and production is a function $f(\theta, e)$ of talent and effort. The production function satisfies the following conditions:

$$f(\bar{\theta}, \bar{e}) \equiv y_1^* > f(\bar{\theta}, \underline{e}) \equiv y_2^* \geq f(\underline{\theta}, \bar{e}) \equiv y_3^* > \bar{e} > \underline{e} > f(\underline{\theta}, \underline{e}) \equiv y_4^* \qquad (9.14)$$

$$y_1^* - y_2^* \geq y_1 - y_2$$

The first set of conditions in formula (9.14), more particularly $y_2^* \geq y_3^*$, implies that, compared to the public sector, private sector technology is relatively more sensitive to talent than to effort. The second set of conditions implies that for good managers, a higher effort yields a higher increment in output than in the public sector.

Since managerial type is private information, private investors have to decide on a wage offer. First, investors decide whether or not to make an offer to a manager, on the basis of expected profits when hiring him. Wage contracts are made contingent on output performance. However, hiring a manager involves a cost K that must be sunk at the time of the hiring, which takes place before output performance can be observed. Government incentive schemes for the second period are announced at the same time as wage offers in the private sector. Technology in both sectors is common knowledge. On the basis of wage offers in the private and public sectors, managers decide whether or not to leave for the private sector.

Call $w^*(y_j^*, y_{it1})$ the private sector wage offer for producing y_j^* in the private sector after having produced y_{it1} in the state sector in period 1. Similarly, define the analogous wage offer by the state as $w(y_j, y_{it1})$.

Let us now look at the intertemporal incentive compatibility constraints to choose y_1 and y_2 in period 1 for the $\bar{\theta}$ and the $\underline{\theta}$ types, respectively:

$$w(y_1) - \bar{e} + \max\{w^*(y_1^*, y_{1t1}), w(y_1, y_{1t1})\} - \bar{e} \qquad (9.15)$$

$$\geq w(y_2) - \underline{e} + \max\{w^*(y_1^*, y_{2t1}), w(y_1, y_{2t1})\} - \bar{e}$$

$$w(y_2) - \bar{e} + \max\{w^*(y_3^*, y_{2t1}), w(y_2, y_{2t1})\} - \bar{e}$$

$$\geq w(y_3) - \underline{e} + \max\{w^*(y_3^*, y_{3t1}), w(y_2, y_{3t1})\} - \bar{e}$$

These intertemporal incentive compatibility constraints represent conditions under which managers are induced to choose $\bar{e}$ in period 1, given that they will be induced to choose $\bar{e}$ in the second period, whether they will be in the public or in the private sector. The first constraint is the incentive compatibility constraint for the $\bar{\theta}$ to produce y_1 in period 1 instead of y_2, and the second one is the incentive compatibility constraint for the $\underline{\theta}$ to produce y_2 in period 1 instead of y_3. Given conditions (9.11) and (9.14), if the private (or public) sector is able to attract (or to keep) a manager, it will prefer that he provide high effort.

When the government was a monopsonist, under socialism, it could take advantage of the information acquired in the first period to drive managerial rents to zero in the second period, thereby increasing the incentive compatible $w(y_1)$. Competition for managers in the second period, however, will tend to give managers rents that *reduce* the incentive compatible $w(y_1)$.

It is useful to distinguish here between two cases, one in which private firms are prepared to hire both good and bad managers and one in which they are only prepared to hire good managers. Let us first look at the former case.

The private sector is ready to bid up to $y_1^* - K$ to get a good manager to produce y_1^*. Similarly, the public sector is ready to bid the wage up to y_1. In this case, one sees that the wage offers are independent of past performance because only good managers can produce y_1^* and y_1. This fact strongly simplifies the intertemporal incentive compatibility constraints (9.15) because the wage offers on both sides of the inequalities are the same. It is then easy to see that $w(y_1) = \bar{e} + \Delta e$, $w(y_2) = \bar{e}$. Given equation (9.11), one can verify that the first-period wages will be optimal from the government's perspective.

As one sees, first-period wages are exactly those that would obtain if the government could commit to long-term incentive schemes. The commitment solution is thus obtained through competition on the managerial labor market. The reason is that competition for managers gives them rents in the second period. If $y_1 < y_1^* - K$, then good managers will leave for the private sector. Otherwise, they will stay in the public sector. In both cases, however, restructuring takes place in the first period.

What happens if the private sector is only willing to hire good managers? For this to be the case, a necessary condition is that expected profits be negative if the identity of the manager is not sure:

$$p[y_1^* - w^*(y_1^*, y_{2t1})] + (1 - p)[y_3^* - w^*(y_3^*, y_{2t1})] < K \tag{9.16}$$

remembering that y_3^* is the highest output level that the type-$\underline{\theta}$ manager is able to produce in the private sector when exerting high effort. As $w^*(y_1^*, y_{2t1})$ and $w^*(y_3^*, y_{2t1})$ must be higher than $\bar{e}$, inequality (9.16) is always fulfilled if $K > p(y_1^* - y_3^*) + y_3^* - \bar{e}$.

To see what is changed when the private sector only wants to hire type-$\bar{\theta}$ managers, let us go back to the intertemporal incentive compatibility constraints (9.15). As the private sector is not ready to make a wage offer to managers who produced y_{2t1}, the best wage a good manager can expect to get in the second period after having produced y_{2t1} is a public sector wage $w(y_1, y_{2t1}) = \bar{e} + \Delta e$ for producing y_1. However, if y_1 was already produced in period 1, the manager can expect an offer of $\min\{y_1, y_1^* - K\}$. One can then easily derive the first period wage for y_1: $w(y_1) = 2(\bar{e} + \Delta e) - y_1$ when the manager goes to the private sector and $w(y_1) = 2(\bar{e} + \Delta e) - (y_1^* - K)$ when he stays in the public sector. Compared to the preceding case where both good and bad managers could be hired in the private sector, $w(y_1)$ is lower by $(\bar{e} + \Delta e) - \min\{y_1, y_1^* - K\}$. This difference reflects simply the higher wage good managers can get in the second period in the preceding case: $\min\{y_1, y_1^* - K\}$ instead of $\bar{e} + \Delta e$.

The discussion so far leads to the result that good managers will always be induced to put up high effort in period 1. This result is quite robust and does not depend on specific parameter values. Moreover, when the private sector can outbid the public sector, $w(y_1)$ is always unambiguously lower than under the commitment solution. Using conditions (9.8) and (9.11), one sees easily that $2(\overline{e} + \Delta e) - y_1 < \overline{e} + \Delta e$. The reason is that the incentive compatibility constraint (9.15) for producing y_1 in period 1 is relaxed because, when producing y_2, a good manager loses a wage offer from the private sector. He thus has less incentive to hide his type in period 1.

Note that in a situation when the private sector wants to hire only good managers, even though only bad managers stay in the state sector, the latter will still be given incentives for high effort and an output of y_2 will be achieved. An implication of this result is that prospects of future privatization of a firm may encourage restructuring. If future privatization results in a better wage for the manager in the privatized firm, he will be encouraged to restructure earlier on, especially if private investors are only interested in hiring good managers.

The results of this section on the ratchet effect and the managerial labor market can be reinterpreted to apply to a more general context than that of transition. One interpretation is that of competition for managers between firms having different technologies. The model tells us that the ratchet effect will be absent once there is a managerial labor market. Imperfect information on managerial types may even lead to lower first-period wages compared to the commitment solution. The latter result is reminiscent of Holmström (1982), though the logic is different here.

The model also tells us that public sector efficiency can be enhanced if managers have the possibility, during their careers, to switch to the private sector. The industrial organization literature has usually emphasized the disadvantages of such "revolving door" arrangements, which exist in the United States and Japan (or *pantouflage* in France) because a regulator may collude with the private sector in order to receive a job later in his career. However, the efficiency advantages of such arrangements, giving outside options to state managers and thus breaking the quasi-monopsony of government, have not been much emphasized so far.

The model shows why the ratchet effect may have disappeared very early on in the transition period. Indeed, as soon as a private sector started to develop sufficiently fast, government's monopsony power over managers disappeared, thereby solving the commitment problem at the heart of the ratchet effect.

This result also sheds light on an important and unexpected observation of transition economies, namely, early restructuring in many SOEs before privatization. In the initial phase of transition, a predominant view among analysts was that quick privatization was of utmost importance in order to avoid decapitalization of assets by entreprise managers facing an endgame situation. The implicit assumption was that managers would lose their jobs and that it was a top priority to deprive them of their control over enterprises. In practice, this assumption has proved wrong. First of all, privatization has proved to be much slower than expected, at least in Poland. More surprisingly, the assumption of decapitalization and squandering of state assets has been rejected by empirical evidence. Studies by Pinto, Belka, and Krajewski (1993), Estrin, Schaffer, and Singh (1992), Basu, Estrin, and Svejnar (1994), and Carlin, Van Reenen, and Wolfe (1995) show on the contrary that managers of state-owned entreprises are actively restructuring and that labor shedding is occurring. Econometric evidence on Poland (Pinto and van

Wijnbergen, 1995) points to changes in entreprise behavior: since 1992 there has been a positive correlation between profits and investment, as opposed to a negative correlation previously.

The model can provide an explanation for the observation of early restructuring. If preprivatization performance is observed by private investors, it will influence their willingness to acquire a firm and offer an incentive contract to managers. The possibility of privatization may thus elicit preprivatization restructuring by managers, thereby enhancing the likelihood of being privatized.

Aghion, Blanchard, and Burgess (1994) have also pointed to career concerns as a potential explanation for restructuring in SOEs. However, they did not analyze a dynamic adverse selection problem as here. They model the costs and benefits of delaying restructuring for managers who face a positive exogenous probability of losing their job when their firm is privatized. This approach yields in their model a negative correlation between restructuring and prospects for privatization, which can, however, be mitigated by exogenous career concern effects. In contrast, the Roland-Sekkat model leads to a prediction of a positive correlation between restructuring and prospects for privatization, in line with the findings of Estrin, Schaffer, and Singh (1992). Here, parameters such as the probability of being privatized and rewards for good managers are not exogenously given, but are derived endogenously. The Aghion, Blanchard, and Burgess (1994) model also begs the question of why firms have not restructured earlier under socialism when privatization was not an option. The model of this section explains why restructuring did not occur under socialism.

9.3   THE SOFT BUDGET CONSTRAINT

Soft budget constraints were one of the most important incentive problems in socialist economies. The soft-budget-constraint problem, associated with the name of Kornai (1980), relates to a well-known situation under socialism where the planner could not commit not to bail out money-losing firms. Soft budget constraints were a key characteristic of socialist economies. J. Kornai (1980, 1992) not only coined the concept but showed the role of soft budget constraints in explaining the emergence and reproduction of shortages, the weakening of price responsiveness of firms, and various other inefficiencies in the socialist economy. He also emphasized their existence and relevance in capitalist economies in the banking sector, the public sector, and other spheres of the economy. Twenty years later, the concept of soft budget constraints has become part of the vocabulary of economics. Its importance and relevance are acknowledged beyond socialist economies. There are well-known examples of soft budget constraints in large corporations (Chrysler) or in the banking sector (bailout of the S&Ls). Soft budget constraints in the banking sectors of East Asian economies are believed to have played an important role in the major East Asian crisis of the late 1990s.

Soft budget constraints have been an important concern in transition economies. Just to give a few examples:

- Continued soft budget constraints may prevent unprofitable enterprises from restructuring because they lack the negative incentives related to the threat of bankruptcy.

- Soft budget constraints may be an obstacle to the process of sectoral reallocation as continued subsidies to money-losing firms may prevent private firms from bidding efficiently for workers employed in inefficient SOEs (see Chapter 5).

- Macroeconomic stability may be jeopardized because continued soft budget constraints in SOEs make it difficult to keep government expenditures under control, as illustrated by the case of Russia in its first years of transition (Litwack, 1993).

The necessity of hardening budget constraints of enterprises in economies in transition has clearly been recognized in the now extensive literature on transition. How to effectively and credibly harden budget constraints, however, has been less the object of detailed analysis.

The early literature on transition, dominated by debates over macroeconomic stabilization, was also characterized by the relative neglect of institutions. "Hardening budget constraints" was most often seen as a pure policy variable or as a direct choice of action on an exogenous policy variable. In other words, it is as if, when policymakers decide to harden budget constraints and make such announcements, hard budget constraints will follow. The question of the credibility of such announcements and decisions has been given little attention. One reason for this lack of attention is that, in an important part of the literature on transition, soft budget constraints are identified with subsidies. For example, Aghion, Blanchard, and Burgess (1994, p. 1331) talk of "subsidies, a plausible characterization of a soft budget constraint." Boycko, Shleifer, and Vishny (1995, p. 314) write of "subsidies from the Treasury to firms, also known as soft budget constraints." Seen in that perspective, hardening budget constraints is then nothing else but a decision to cut subsidies. It is thus not astonishing to see the hardening of budget constraints as an exogenous policy variable. Also, a fundamental problem with the discussion of soft budget constraints in the context of centrally planned or transition economies has been the lack of formalization of the concept.

A fundamental contribution to the understanding of the mechanism of soft budget constraints has been provided by Dewatripont and Maskin (1995), who view soft budget constraints as endogenous to specific institutions. Soft budget constraints are seen as a dynamic incentive problem where a funding source (be it a government or a bank) cannot commit to hold an enterprise to a fixed initial budget and is led to bail it out ex post. Their key insight is that an agent may have a soft budget constraint because it is ex post optimal for the investor to bail him out instead of liquidating his activity, since any prior funds invested in the firm are sunk costs. Seen in that perspective, soft budget constraints represent an inefficiency: the funding source would like to commit ex ante not to bail out firms, but if it cannot make such a commitment, it may be tempted to refinance the firm ex post because the initial injection of funds is sunk.

More broadly, the Dewatripont-Maskin model helps us understand soft budget constraints as a more general dynamic commitment problem where an agent can fail to take an efficient action, or undertake an inefficient action, because he knows he will receive additional finance. Hardening of budget constraints thus means creating conditions for a credible commitment not to refinance an agent. Here, the interesting question is not whether soft budget constraints are desired or not but what are the institutional conditions under which one has hard or soft budget constraints. Hardening budget constraints is thus not simply a matter of direct policy choice, but rather the result of institutional design.

This distinction is important for transition. Indeed, if soft budget constraints are the result of a dynamic commitment problem, then decisions to harden budget constraints cannot be credible unless institutions are in place that make a commitment to hard budget constraints credible. Kornai (1995) himself insists very much on this point in the context of transition:

> There are a great many influences on the government tempting it to loosen the financial discipline and soften the budget constraint. . . . Since the period of tougher financial discipline began, exceptional procedures have been followed in several cases, in many of which the bargaining led to agreement. The remnants of the soft budget constraint are clearly visible. There is a danger that the frequency of the exceptions will undermine the credibility of the government's pledges concerning the tough financial discipline. (p. 150)

Kornai's seminal work has focused mainly on the consequences of the soft budget constraint, namely, the emergence of pervasive shortages under socialism. Among the various causes he has put forward to explain the existence of soft budget constraints, his primary explanation is related to political constraints, that is, to the desire of "paternalistic" governments to avoid socially and politically costly layoffs. In his own formalization (Kornai and Weibull, 1983) the government simply bails out unprofitable firms and thus undermines ex ante incentives. Understanding the phenomenon of paternalism, in particular its underpinnings in political economy, is worthwhile in its own right, but Dewatripont and Maskin's (1995) analysis of the soft budget constraint has shown that paternalism is neither a necessary nor a sufficient condition for soft budget constraints. It instead stresses dynamic commitment problems in the presence of irreversible investment.[5] This argument does not at all mean that paternalism is not relevant in our empirical understanding of soft budget constraints. The Dewatripont-Maskin framework, however, provides the tools to understand soft budget constraints beyond the issue of paternalism, and thereby to understand the causes of soft budget constraints beyond socialism and transition.

[5] *Schaffer (1989) also models the lack of commitment of government not to rescue a money-losing firm.*

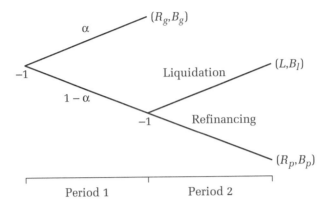

FIGURE 9.3 THE TIMING AND STRUCTURE OF DECISIONS LEADING TO SOFT BUDGET CONSTRAINTS

9.3.1 THE BASIC MODEL OF SOFT BUDGET CONSTRAINTS

We start with an adaptation of the Dewatripont-Maskin model to the context of socialism. We look at a government-firm relation in a two-period setting. In the beginning of period 1, firms draw n projects (normalized to 1 without loss of generality) and decide whether or not to submit them to the government. Projects are of two types, either good in proportion α or poor in proportion $(1 - \alpha)$. Project types are unknown to the government ex ante, and all have a start-up cost of 1 monetary unit. At the end of period 1, good projects yield a gross monetary and taxable return of R_g and deliver private benefits $B_g > 0$ to the firm's management. Poor projects yield zero return after one period. The government can then choose to liquidate the firm's assets, in which case it gets a liquidation value L while the manager gets a net private benefit of $B_l < 0$ representing the disutility to the manager of liquidation. The government can also refinance the loan, injecting an additional monetary unit to get, at the end of period 2, a gross return R_p, while the firm gets a private benefit of $B_p > 0$. For simplicity, we assume no discounting.

The timing and structure of the game are depicted in Figure 9.3. We assume that the government maximizes the net returns to investment plus the private benefits of firms. This assumption incorporates the idea that the government may care about the loss of jobs for political reasons. This attitude can be interpreted as "paternalism." All monetary returns are assumed to go back to the government as repayment for the initial loan. Firm managers are thus solely interested in maximizing their total net private benefits.

The firm is said to have a soft budget constraint if it gets refinanced. If the prospect of refinancing causes the firm to submit poor projects when the prospect of liquidation would induce it not to submit those projects, there is an incentive problem.

The analysis is very easy but extremely insightful. Since $B_p > 0$ and $B_l < 0$, a firm drawing a poor project will always prefer to submit it if it knows the project will be refinanced. It will prefer not to submit a poor project if it expects the project to be liquidated. However, if $R_p + B_p - 1 > L + B_l$, the government will always prefer to refinance poor projects. Such refinancing will be inefficient as soon as $R_p + B_p < 2$.

Indeed, in that case, from the ex ante point of view, a poor project will bring a total negative return. This inefficiency reduces the total ex ante expected return on lending given the asymmetric information. Projects will be financed if

$$\alpha(R_g + B_g - 1) + (1 - \alpha)(R_p + B_p - 2) > 0$$

that is, if

$$\alpha > \alpha^S = \frac{2 - R_p - B_p}{R_g + B_g - R_p - B_p + 1} \tag{9.17}$$

Thus, if $L + B_l + 1 < 2$ and $\alpha > \alpha^S$, the only subgame-perfect equilibrium will be one where poor projects are submitted, all projects are financed, and poor projects are refinanced. In other words, firms have soft budget constraints. It is the inability of the government to commit not to refinance that causes firms designing poor projects to submit them. The inability to commit is what causes soft budget constraints because the initial investment is a sunk cost. Therefore, it can be ex post optimal to refinance a project that is losing money from the ex ante point of view (the usual accounting view of taking losses). If the government were able to commit to liquidating, it would be better off because this commitment would act as a credible threat having the effect of disciplining firms.

9.3.2 THE SOFT BUDGET CONSTRAINT AND THE RATCHET EFFECT

Both the ratchet effect and the soft budget constraint syndrome are general incentive problems that apply beyond the socialist system, but they were particularly present under socialism given the close relationship between firms and the government. Both problems are intuitively related: the temptation to extract resources from good firms (the ratchet effect) is particularly high when there is an incentive to refinance bad firms (because of the soft budget constraint). Moreover, bad firms have few incentives to respect financial discipline if they know they can rely on cross-subsidization to bail them out. There is thus a complementarity between these two incentive problems, leading to lower efficiency in both good and bad firms.

Following Dewatripont and Roland (1997), take the same setup as in the previous subsection and assume that good projects can also be refinanced in period 2, but assume that second-period finance for good and poor projects can come solely from the first-period returns. Assume that, by exerting "effort" in period 1 at cost e, managers with good projects can, with an additional unit of funds at the beginning of period 2, generate a gross return $\hat{R}_g \geq R_g > 1$ with a positive private benefit $\hat{B}_g$ in period 2. Without effort, returns are R_g and B_g. Figure 9.4 shows the structure of the game.

It is assumed that exerting effort is optimal for the manager, that is, that

$$\hat{B}_g - B_g > e$$

It is, therefore, also socially optimal. Assume, however, that $R_p + B_p > \hat{R}_g + \hat{B}_g$. In this case, refinancing poor projects will be an ex post priority for government that will

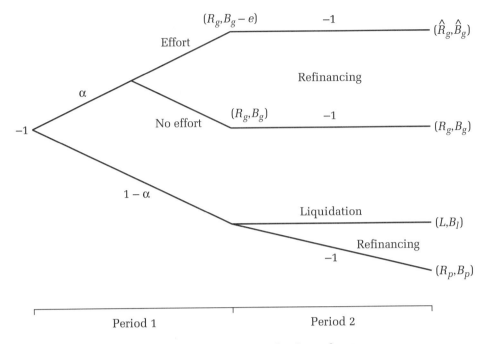

FIGURE 9.4 THE CONNECTION BETWEEN THE RATCHET EFFECT AND THE SOFT BUDGET CONSTRAINT

crowd out the refinancing of good projects. In a soft-budget-constraint equilibrium (with conditions as before), the total returns from first period are αR_g, as opposed to R_g under a hard-budget-constraint equilibrium. Under a soft-budget-constraint equilibrium, good projects only receive $\alpha R_g - (1 - \alpha)$, whereas in a hard-budget-constraint equilibrium, they would all be refinanced. If $\alpha < \frac{1}{R_g}$, there is thus only a probability $\frac{\alpha R_g - (1 - \alpha)}{\alpha} < 1$ that a good project gets refinanced under a soft-budget-constraint equilibrium. Assuming risk neutrality, if

$$\frac{\alpha R_g - (1 - \alpha)}{\alpha} (\hat{B}_g - B_g) < e$$

then agents with good projects will be discouraged from putting up effort. The effect is similar to the ratchet effect, though not identical because information revelation plays no role here. This very stylized presentation of the interaction between ratchet effect and soft budget constraint nevertheless gives a flavor of the cross-subsidization that took place under socialism.

9.3.3   THE LACK OF INNOVATION UNDER SOCIALISM

Qian and Xu (1998) have pointed to the link between the soft budget constraints and the lack of innovation in centrally planned economies. Because of soft budget constraints, the centrally planned economy lacked the capacity to screen innovation projects ex post as is the case in the market economy through the mechanisms that we will analyze later in this chapter as well as in Chapters 11 and 12. Therefore, it had to rely on ex ante screening.

Assume, therefore, that by incurring a cost σ the planner can screen the unit mass of projects received. In that case, he receives a signal θ_g (good project) or θ_p (poor project). There is a probability $\gamma \in (\underline{\gamma}, 1]$ that the signal is correct, that is, that the project is good if the signal is θ_g or poor if the signal is θ_p. There is thus a probability $1 - \gamma$ that the signal is incorrect. It is assumed that $\underline{\gamma}$ is such that when prescreening is used, a project for which a signal θ_g was received will optimally be accepted and a project for which a signal θ_p was received will optimally be rejected. The expected return from screening will then be the following:

$$\alpha\gamma(R_g + B_g - 1) + (1 - \alpha)(1 - \gamma)(R_p + B_p - 2) - \sigma \tag{9.18}$$

Apart from the cost σ, a cost from screening is that there will be Type I errors; that is, good projects will be screened out. The main benefit is that there will be fewer Type II errors—poor projects that are not screened out. If γ tends toward 1, then both Type I and Type II errors will be minimized. However, γ may be sufficiently low that it is not worthwhile to prescreen. Prescreening can thus work relatively well when there is relatively good prior knowledge about the quality of projects (high γ) but works poorly when prior knowledge is bad (low γ). This relationship may explain why space industry was relatively well advanced in the socialist economy but socialist computer industry lagged hopelessly behind capitalism. In the former the relevant principles from physics were relatively well understood from the outset, whereas in the latter the principles of computer industry and solid-state physics were developed together or even after the development of computer industry.

Taking hard budget constraints as a benchmark, note that a high level of prior knowledge does not make prescreening equivalent to the enforcement of hard budget constraints. If there are hard budget constraints (achieved through mechanisms which we will analyze later), poor projects will not be submitted ex ante because $B_l < 0$. The expected net return to projects is thus $(R_g + B_g - 1)$ compared to $\alpha(R_g + B_g - 1) - \sigma$ under perfect prescreening, that is, when $\gamma = 1$. Perfect prescreening is thus not a perfect substitute for hard budget constraints because fewer good projects still get submitted. Indeed, since one lacks the incentive effects of hard budget constraints, bad projects still get submitted and tend to clog the prescreening process. Therefore, only a proportion α of good projects get funded.

9.3.4 SOFT BUDGET CONSTRAINTS AND SHORTAGE

In Kornai (1980) the soft budget constraint is the main cause of widespread shortages because soft budget constraints lead to increased demand for inputs. Among formal models examining the effect of soft budget constraints on shortages, see Goldfeld and Quandt (1988, 1990) and Hillman, Katz, and Rosenberg (1987). Qian (1994) has offered an alternative explanation of how soft budget constraints could lead to shortages in the socialist economy, based on the Dewatripont-Maskin model. The idea is that shortage may be a mechanism to partially curb soft budget constraints in firms because shortages of inputs may reduce the benefits that firms with soft budget constraints get from refinancing.

Assume thus that in the second period the inputs needed for poor projects can also be purchased by consumers. Assume that these inputs are given in quantity $\bar{x}$ with inelastic supply. Without soft budget constraints, and thus with no refinancing of poor projects, if consumers' inverse demand function is $v(x)$, they will thus pay a market-clearing price $p = v(\bar{x})$. When poor projects are refinanced, however, consumer demand can be crowded out by the demand for inputs for poor projects. Assume that one unit of input is needed for each poor project. The market-clearing price will thus be $p^* = v[\bar{x} - (1 - \alpha)] > p$. Compared to the preceding analysis, refinancing will now have a cost of p^*. As long as $R_p + B_p - p^* > L + B_l$, there will still be soft budget constraints.

Soft budget constraints in the enterprise sector thus inflict a double loss on consumers through crowding out and higher prices when prices are flexible. In Chapter 6 we argued that central planners probably shied away from flexible prices for consumers in the socialist economy because of the redistributive effects from the poor to the rich and that poorer consumers benefited from rationing despite its overall inefficiency effects. Qian has pointed to the potential crowding-out effect of flexible prices on consumers (who face hard budget constraints) by enterprises that face soft budget constraints. He shows that rationing, and thus the introduction of shortage, may serve as a way to mitigate hard budget constraints. Assume that instead of flexible prices, goods are rationed between consumers and enterprises. Assume that enterprises can receive q units of goods and consumers receive $\bar{x} - q$. Assume without loss of generality that the price is set to $p \in (1, p^*)$. Since there are $(1 - \alpha)$ units of inputs needed to refinance all poor projects and assuming that all face an equal probability of being served under rationing, then each poor project faces a probability $\frac{q}{1-\alpha}$ of receiving the input. When submitting a poor project, the expected private benefit of a manager is then $\frac{q}{1-\alpha} B_p + (1 - \frac{q}{1-\alpha}) B_l$. This expected benefit will be negative as soon as $q < (1 - \alpha) \frac{-B_l}{B_p - B_l}$. In that case, he will be deterred from submitting a bad project. The conclusion of the analysis is that, to the extent that state ownership leads to soft budget constraints, it also leads to choose rationing by central planning because the market mechanism under state ownership leads to crowding out of consumers that face hard budget constraints by enterprises who face soft budget constraints. In section 9.2 we pointed to the fact that under market socialism the ratchet effect could thwart profit incentives. Qian's analysis points to potential adverse effects of the market mechanism under state ownership when soft budget constraints are prevalent.

An immediate implication of Qian's analysis is that price liberalization in transition economies can actually worsen the soft budget constraint problem. This is an implication that has been completely neglected by most early analysts of transition, who assumed implicitly that price liberalization would take place in a context of hard budget constraints. In China, for example, the number of unprofitable enterprises increased from less than 10 percent in 1985 to more than one-third in the 1990s. In Central and Eastern Europe, a similar deterioration of enterprise performance seems to have been observed early in transition. One must of course be careful before drawing inferences from raw data. For one thing, price liberalization itself by correcting relative prices reveals losses that were not measured when planned prices were used. Also, competition from the new private sector can contribute to the deterioration of SOE performance. Other causes of SOE deterioration can also be thought of. Nevertheless, it is a worthwhile research topic to take a serious look at the relation between price liberalization and the softening of budget constraints.

A simple example, slightly different from Qian's model but in the same spirit, can illustrate this point. In countries where partial reforms were introduced, wages were partially liberalized. Prior to reforms, there was strong central control over wages, one of the main instruments to keep macroeconomic balance in centrally planned economies. Partial or de facto liberalization of wages occurred as a consequence of relaxation of such controls in countries like Yugoslavia under self-management after 1965, Poland, Hungary, and the Soviet Union after 1987. As enterprises had soft budget constraints, this kind of liberalization very quickly led to wage inflation, which contributed to an increase of shortage for consumer goods, when the latter were still rationed as was the case in the Soviet Union, and to increases in aggregate excess demand that led to a deterioration of enterprise performance as well as to strong inflationary pressures.

9.3.5 SOFT BUDGET CONSTRAINTS AND ENTERPRISE AUTONOMY

In a similar vein, one can argue that increased enterprise autonomy under reformed socialism can lead to a worsening of the soft-budget-constraint problem. The argument is slightly different from the preceding one. It states that loss of government control over firms, by reducing monitoring activities, can worsen soft budget constraints.

To see this point, modify the basic Dewatripont-Maskin model by assuming as in Qian and Roland (1998) that moral hazard takes the more traditional form of effort provision rather than project submission. Assume that when managers exert effort, poor projects can deliver a verifiable return of R_g and a private benefit, net of effort, of B_g. Figure 9.5 shows the structure of the game. One can verify that the conditions for the government to refinance a poor project are exactly the same as in the basic Dewatripont-Maskin model. Note, however, that in this version of the soft-budget-constraint model, for soft budget constraints to occur, the manager must prefer to exert low effort rather than high effort even when his project is refinanced. We must thus have $B_p > B_g > 0$. It is not necessary anymore to assume $B_l < 0$, and we can for simplicity assume $B_l = 0$.

Assume that the government monitors enterprises with probability p, in which case it forces them to choose high effort. The outcome in those enterprises is then (R_g, B_g). They thus behave as if they had good projects. Stronger monitoring will then reduce soft budget constraints, and now only a proportion $(1 - p)(1 - \alpha)$ will be subject to bailouts. Loss of government control then leads to a reduction in p and thus to an increase in overall bailouts.

It is interesting to contrast this result with the Shleifer-Vishny model where transfer of control from the government to the manager leads to an increase in efficiency. In

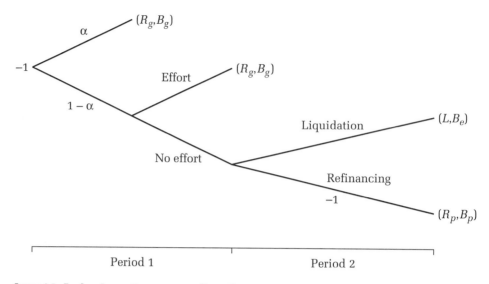

FIGURE 9.5 THE SOFT BUDGET CONSTRAINT WITH MORAL HAZARD

the years of reform socialism, it was generally believed that by giving more autonomy in decisionmaking to managers, better decisions would be made because managers have better information about local conditions. This conclusion seemed obvious because the rigid rules imposed from above had often led to blatant inefficiencies at the micro level. Under socialism, only conservative central planners advocated maintaining centralized government control over firms. However, by now it has become a consensus view that increased enterprise autonomy under socialism led to a softening of budget constraints, be it in Yugoslavia, Hungary, Poland, or Russia. How do we explain the difference between this insight and the result of the Shleifer-Vishny model? Here, enterprise autonomy leads to softer budget constraints because the enterprise manager is able to exploit this autonomy to extract ex post refinancing from the government. This softening of budget constraints related to loss of control is absent in the Shleifer-Vishny model. In the Shleifer-Vishny model, the source of inefficiency is government intervention, and there is no managerial opportunism. Loss of control makes it more costly to intervene and thereby increases efficiency.

However, in this model one can see that loss of control may also allow the manager to appropriate higher returns. Assume that loss of government control also leads to a reduction in the verifiable returns when high effort is provided. These returns thus become $R'_g = R_g - \pi$. In that case, the manager can appropriate $B_g + \pi$ instead of B_g. If $\pi > B_p - B_g$, then it pays the manager to choose high effort rather than low effort. In that case, soft budget constraints will disappear because loss of government control increases the returns to effort that the manager can obtain. He will be more interested in maximizing profits than in obtaining subsidies from the government. Loss of control of government

TABLE 9.1 ESTIMATES OF THE SHORT-TERM ELASTICITIES
OF LABOR DEMAND TO OUTPUT

	1990–91	1991–92
Czech Republic	.119	.591
	(.030)	(.944)
Slovakia	.063	.328
	(.035)	(.027)
Poland	.226[a]	.397[b]
	(.025)	(.009)
Hungary	.236[a]	.459
	(.129)	(.097)
Russia		.038[c]
		(.050)

Source: *Basu, Estrin, and Svejnar (1994).*

Standard errors are in parentheses.

[a] *1989–90.*

[b] *1990–91.*

[c] *1993–94.*

of labor demand have increased over time in most countries, as can be seen in Table 9.1. In Russia in 1993–94, the elasticity was not significantly different from 0. Grosfeld and Nivet (1997a, 1997b) also find increasing elasticities for a large panel of large Polish industrial enterprises between 1989 and 1994. Grosfeld and Nivet also find a reduction in cross-subsidization between firms as measured by an increase in the elasticity of net profit to gross profit.

CHAPTER 10

COMPARING POLICIES OF PRIVATIZATION AND RESTRUCTURING

The discussion in the previous chapter focused on how privatization, as compared to state ownership, helps to solve the ratchet effect and the soft budget constraint. Another important debate that has taken place, especially in the early phases of transition, concerns the comparison between various *methods* of privatization. Given the size of the total assets to be privatized and the absence of preexisting private wealth in transition economies, the need arose to introduce new privatization methods. The policy debate has mostly opposed partisans of massive giveaways emphasizing speed (Blanchard et al., 1991; Lipton and Sachs, 1990b; Frydman and Rapaczynski, 1994; Boycko, Shleifer, and Vishny, 1995) to partisans of economic efficiency and revenue maximization through gradual sales (Kornai, 1990) or sales against noncash bids (Maskin, 1991; Aghion and Burgess, 1993; Bolton and Roland, 1992; Demougin and Sinn, 1992; Sinn and Sinn, 1993).

The transition experience has shown that the debate on privatization methods goes far beyond the simple comparison of various techniques of transfer of ownership. Many things are at stake. Not only do the privatization methods have a direct impact on the corporate governance of the privatized firms and on the restructuring outcomes. Privatization policies also have an impact on the macroeconomic situation, on public finances, on the development of the financial sector, and more broadly on political and institutional stability.

In the beginning of transition, one could have invoked the Coase theorem, and many economists have done so, to claim that specific privatization methods were not very important or were even irrelevant. Inefficient transfer of ownership, in particular the famous Russian insider privatization, would, according to the Coase theorem, be corrected because more efficient buyers would end up purchasing assets from less competent initial owners given the gains to be made from trade. In practice, this result has not occurred, and there has been a lock-in of the initial transfer of ownership, especially in the case of mass privatization.

The experience with privatization even suggests that the choice of a privatization policy may lock a country into a specific path of economic development or underdevelopment. How privatization is dealt with can thus have lasting effects not only on the microeconomic performance of enterprises and on economy-wide performance but also on wealth distribution, the evolution of social cohesion and social norms, and the evolution of laws and political institutions.

In order to be able to compare different privatization and restructuring policies and their broad effects, a comprehensive analysis is needed. There are many dimensions involved in privatization and restructuring, and a truly comparative analysis should try to take all relevant dimensions into account. So far we do not have anything approaching an all-encompassing theory allowing us to make such a comprehensive analysis. Despite the shortcomings of theory, however, there is a rapidly accumulating literature on privatization and restructuring. While the evidence it provides does not yet enable us to draw full conclusions in comparing privatization and restructuring policies, it does yield interesting insights that will spawn further theoretical and empirical work.

Given the fragmentary theoretical and empirical results we have, we will try in a first section to provide a broad framework to try to understand and evaluate the different privatization policies. We put a special emphasis on the effect of privatization policies on enterprise restructuring but at the same time integrate other dimensions such as public finance, macroeconomic equilibrium, and political economy. This first section of this chapter is different in style from the rest of the book because it does not rely on formal models. We felt nevertheless that it was necessary to include this verbal analysis to give a comprehensive enough overview of the effect of different privatization policies on corporate governance and restructuring.

In a second section we review models related to privatization and restructuring. We show how insider privatization may create entrenchment and prevent the efficient resale of assets to outsiders. We also show the conditions under which insider privatization may be beneficial compared to state ownership and the conditions under which it may lead to diversion of funds, asset stripping, and soft budget constraints. Finally, we analyze ways to optimally design mechanisms of sales of assets when buyers are cash constrained and there is the possibility of asset stripping.

In a third section we review the empirical literature. Many of the findings from that literature shed light on the issues put forward in the first section of this chapter, namely, the relative importance of incentives versus selection of owners in privatization and the effects of various privatization policies on measures of enterprise restructuring and performance.

10.1   THE DIFFERENT APPROACHES TO PRIVATIZATION

The process of large-scale privatization in former socialist economies is a historically unprecedented experience for which no ready recipes existed. Most economies in tran-

TABLE 10.1 DIFFERENT METHODS OF PRIVATIZATION

	Top-Down	Bottom-Up
Giveaway:		
To insiders	Russia	
To outsiders	Czech Republic	
Sales:		
To insiders		Poland (noncash)
		Hungary (noncash)
To outsiders	East Germany	

sition started privatization more or less with the same policy based on the experience of the United Kingdom. It involved a reassertion of the state's property rights over enterprises (called in general commercialization)[1] and a centralized policy of sales after a process of valuation of the enterprises picked out by government for privatization. This policy has quickly been abandoned in all countries. A bit later in the transition process, one would have thought that all countries would converge to a policy of mass privatization by giveaway through vouchers. This has not been the case either. Each economy in transition developed its own privatization policy with different combinations of direct sales, managerial buyout, and vouchers. Hungary, for example, has consistently been avoiding mass privatization. Actual practice of privatization differs even more as some policies appeared politically feasible in some countries but not in others where political constraints had to lead to changes in privatization policies.

It is useful to define the major distinctions defining privatization methods. A first and obvious distinction is whether firms are sold or given away. Among sales, one should distinguish again between cash and noncash sales. Forms of noncash sales pioneered in Hungary include payments against installments, payment against credit, partial acquisition of shares with plans for future share acquisitions, leasing contracts, and others. A second distinction is whether assets are transferred to outsiders or to insiders, the latter being managers and possibly workers, the former being outside investors, domestic or foreign. A third distinction is between top-down and bottom-up privatization. Top-down privatization means that the government takes the initiative in privatizing a firm, and bottom-up privatization means that the initiative to privatize comes from outside investors or from the manager of the firm. Table 10.1 provides a rough classification of the main policies followed in some of the main transition countries that started privatization early in the transition process.

Before proceeding further, it is useful to give some further data. Table 10.2 gives a rough estimate of the evolution of the share of the private sector in GDP for selected transition economies from Central and Eastern Europe. Not only the effects of privatization are demonstrated, but also the progress made by new start-ups and their dynamism. One sees that countries that implemented fast giveaways, like the Czech Republic and Russia, had very fast growth in the size of the private sector: from 30 to 65 percent between 1992

[1] *In Russia commercialization meant enterprise autonomy vis-à-vis the branch ministries and thus represented the opposite of reassertion of state ownership.*

TABLE 10.2 PRIVATE SECTOR SHARE IN GDP

	1990	1991	1992	1993	1994	1995	1996	1997	1998
Poland	30	40	45	50	55	60	60	65	65
Hungary	25	30	40	50	55	60	70	75	85
Czech Republic	10	15	30	45	65	70	75	75	75
Slovenia	15	15	20	25	30	45	45	50	50
Slovakia	10	15	30	45	55	60	70	75	75
Bulgaria	10	15	25	35	40	45	45	50	65
Romania	15	25	25	30	35	40	60	60	60
Russia	5	5	25	40	50	55	60	70	70
Ukraine	10	10	10	15	40	45	50	55	55

Source: *EBRD Transition Report (1999)*.

and 1994 in the Czech Republic and from 25 to 50 percent between 1992 and 1994 in Russia. Countries like Ukraine or Slovenia that did not have very active privatization policies had the slowest growth of the private sector. Note, however, that Hungary, despite its gradual privatization policy, had the biggest share of the private sector in 1998 with 85 percent.

Table 10.3 shows the evolution in revenues from privatization. Hungary and Slovakia, which adopted a policy of sales, generated cumulative revenues of about 12 to 13 percent, whereas Russia and the Czech Republic had negligible revenues. The revenues from privatization in Hungary and Slovakia can nevertheless be considered relatively low. Later we will discuss the reason why privatization revenues tend to be low in transition economies.

10.1.1   THE OBJECTIVES OF PRIVATIZATION

Definite criteria are needed to assess privatization policies. Therefore, one needs to understand the objectives and constraints of privatization. The obvious objective is greater efficiency.

10.1.1.1   Greater Efficiency

The greater efficiency that can be reached through transfer of ownership and corporate governance under private ownership depends on the degree to which it achieves (1) better matching between managerial talent and productive assets and (2) better incentives for management.

TABLE 10.3 CUMULATIVE PRIVATIZATION REVENUES (AS A PERCENT OF GDP)

	1990	1991	1992	1993	1994	1995	1996	1997	1998
Poland		0.2	0.6	1.1	1.9	2.8	3.8	5.3	6.7
Hungary		0.1	1.2	1.8	2.7	5.9	9.6	12.6	13
Czech Republic					1.6	2.6	2.8	3.3	
Slovenia						0.4	0.8	1.3	1.8
Slovakia			3.7	4.8	6.9	9.4	11.4	11.9	12.3
Bulgaria				0.4	1.5	0.9	2.9	5.6	5.3
Romania				0.1	0.4	1.2	2.2	4.1	6.1
Russia			0.8	1.1	1.3	1.5	1.7	1.7	2.3
Ukraine				0.1	0.3	0.4	0.7	0.8	1.3

Source: *EBRD Transition Report (1999).*

Better Managers   In the previously centrally planned economies the allocation of managers to firms was not necessarily done on the basis of productive efficiency. The incumbent managers' ability to obtain subsidies and negotiate favorable production plans with the ministries is no longer a relevant skill in the market economy, whereas marketing, accounting, capital budgeting, fund-raising skills, and a good knowledge of markets are important. Since many of the skills required under the centrally planned economy became obsolete and because of the lack of experience of management in a market environment, appropriate managerial skills are a scarce resource, thereby potentially increasing the importance of correct matching.

In a developed market economy, correct matching of managers and assets is achieved through the managerial labor market and the capital market. In economies in transition, those markets, especially the capital market, did not preexist, and privatization could be designed so as to allocate managers to assets efficiently. However, there is also scope for mistakes, as transfers of assets to "wrong owners" may not be corrected easily.

Better Incentives   Privatization in principle provides incentives for high effort. In a world of manager-owners, private ownership confers full marginal return to effort through the residual rights to income. In reality, however, things are not so simple. First, ownership of assets is often joint ownership, and returns must be shared between owners. Second, there is the problem of separation of ownership and control, which creates a problem of managerial incentives because managers are generally not the owners of the assets they run. The incentive problem of managers can be and has been mitigated in most market economies through the discipline of competition in the product market

(Hart, 1983), the market for managers (Fama, 1980; Holmström, 1982), and the capital market, either through takeovers (Manne, 1966; Grossman and Hart, 1980; Scharfstein, 1988) or through bank monitoring (Mayer, 1988; Hellwig, 1991). The recent literature in corporate finance has also stressed the important role of debt in providing incentives to managers (Grossman and Hart, 1982; Jensen, 1986; Aghion and Bolton, 1992; Hart and Moore, 1998).

10.1.1.2   Efficiency and Restructuring

While greater efficiency is the objective of privatization, the actions taken by the new or incumbent management to achieve greater efficiency in the firm are generally referred to as restructuring. The notion of enterprise restructuring is initially a rather vague notion with fuzzy content. A useful distinction introduced by Grosfeld and Roland (1997), which has been used widely in the transition literature, including various EBRD reports, is that between defensive and strategic restructuring.

Defensive restructuring means taking measures to reduce costs and scale down unprofitable enterprise activity: cutting the obsolete production lines, shedding labor, getting rid of nonproductive assets, and the like. These measures are "defensive" in the sense that their primary goal is the immediate survival of the enterprise. Defensive restructuring does not as such necessarily imply the existence of a strategy for reorienting the enterprise's activity under the new economic conditions. It may be done as a result of survival-oriented behavior of managers and workers. However, it may also constitute the painful but necessary initial ingredient of a long-term strategic plan aiming at maximizing the enterprise's value.

Strategic restructuring refers to the objective of innovation and investment necessary to enhance enterprise performance. It is based on a thoughtful business strategy responding to the necessity of a profound redeployment of assets. It implies the introduction of new product lines and new processes, new technologies and new investments. It necessitates a great deal of entrepreneurial skill and imagination, good judgment about investment opportunities, and adequate incentives. It also requires sources of finance for the new projects. New investments can be financed from the firm's retained earnings or by way of financial markets through bank credit or issuing of equity and debt on the market. Managers with good investment projects should have opportunities to get adequate finance, and investors must have adequate incentives to select and monitor the implementation of the projects. The issue of access to outside finance is thus fundamental for strategic restructuring. Since strategic restructuring requires investment, it cannot succeed in firms with no retained earnings when outside finance is not available or cannot be made available. The degree to which privatization contributes to solving the issue of outside finance is thus important in determining the success of strategic restructuring.

Defensive restructuring does not necessarily have to precede strategic restructuring. Both parts can (and ideally should) be done more or less simultaneously. The conceptual distinction between these two types of restructuring is useful, however, because they both address different problems, and they do not require the same instruments and skills to be conducted successfully.

Bad managers expect that if their enterprise undergoes the process of strategic restructuring, they will lose their current jobs because of their lack of competence and will receive lower incomes in alternative employments. They are therefore unwilling, or maybe even unable, to engage in defensive restructuring. It is in their interest to oppose privatization of their enterprise to outside owners and to engage in asset dissipation, because they are facing an "endgame" situation (Akerlof et al. 1991; Lawrence and Lawrence, 1985) where they have nothing to lose. Privatization in that case is an important instrument to replace those managers. The objective of matching managers and assets is fundamental here. It is a misplaced effort to try to give incentives to these managers to restructure. It is indeed not in their interest to restructure because they do not have the adequate skills to keep their jobs in a market environment and are not able to acquire them. Management is also a key element in determining resistance to layoffs. Even if the labor force is relatively skilled and not very many layoffs should be expected, management tends to have superior information about the potential future of the firm and is able to mobilize workers against the "dangers" of privatization.

Good managers expect to gain from strategic restructuring. They expect not only to keep their jobs, but also to earn higher incomes after modernization of their enterprise. Even though they may lack given skills in modern management techniques, they have at least the skills of learning fast and adapting quickly and in a profitable way to changes in their environment. They may, however, face substantial and variable costs of effort in dealing with defensive restructuring. Good managers with high variable costs of defensive restructuring thus face purely an incentive problem.

One immediately sees that *heterogeneity* in managerial skills may be a key factor in explaining differences in attitudes toward preprivatization restructuring. Bad managers should be expected to show a behavior of inertia and thus oppose privatization to outside owners for strategic reasons, whereas good managers who face sufficiently small costs of defensive restructuring can be expected to take active measures in that direction and will even want strategic restructuring of their enterprise to be accelerated. Things are not so simple, however. If the costs of engaging in defensive restructuring are sufficiently high, good managers may also show inertial behavior, not because they need to be replaced but because they lack incentives. They would, however, be undistinguishable from bad managers.

This heterogeneity in managerial skills can be seen from the diversity in behavior of managers of SOEs witnessed at the beginning of transition. Although initial expectations of many analysts were extremely pessimistic, predicting large-scale asset stripping unless assets were not privatized as quickly as possible, one has observed surprisingly frequent cases of restructuring in SOEs. As documented by the now relatively large empirical literature on enterprise restructuring (see, e.g., Pinto, Belka, and Krajewski, 1993; Estrin, Schaffer, and Singh, 1992, 1993; Bouin and Grosfeld, 1995), restructuring in SOEs is generally initiated by managers of the firms themselves. We have seen in Chapter 9 how career concerns of managers can motivate such restructuring behavior. However, such active restructuring was not the rule either. One of the main conclusions of Carlin and colleagues (1995), who surveyed all the existing studies on enterprise restructuring in Central and Eastern European Countries between 1990 and 1993, is that managerial behavior in CEECs is indeed very diverse, with evidence both of restructuring before privatization and of inertia and resistance to privatization and restructuring, including active rent-seeking behavior, in order to insulate firms from competitive pressures.

10.1.2 THE CONSTRAINTS FACING PRIVATIZATION POLICIES

In assessing various privatization policies, one must take into account the various constraints such policies face. The size of the privatization effort in transition economies means that one must pay careful attention to the macroeconomic and public finance effects of the change in ownership of such a large fraction of assets. These effects were smaller in the case of privatization in more advanced industrial economies like the United Kingdom and France. Nor can one ignore the informational and administrative constraints. Last and not least, the political constraints, which were discussed at length in Part I, play a very important role.

10.1.2.1 The Stock-Flow Constraint

The main macroeconomic constraint faced by the Eastern European countries is a stock-flow constraint, as emphasized by Sinn and Sinn (1993), Demougin and Sinn (1992), and Bolton and Roland (1992). Given the absence of preexisting private wealth in socialist economies, at the beginning of the transition process the stock of state assets could at best be sold against the flow of annual savings of the population plus the—small—stock of existing savings. The stock-flow constraint could partly be relaxed through import of capital but could not be eliminated because of international capital market imperfections, exchange rate risks, lack of information, and the huge aggregate uncertainty surrounding institutions of transition economies. In practice, international flows of capital to the East were rather meager at the beginning of transition.

The stock-flow constraint can be dealt with by delaying privatization of assets to generate more government revenues, but this is an inefficient solution. It can also be dealt with by mass privatization whereby assets are given away or sold nearly for free to the population. However, by taking this approach one runs into the fiscal constraint.

10.1.2.2 The Fiscal Constraint

As the state system had to be completely reformed in the aftermath of communism, tax systems had to be established. Indeed, under central planning, tax systems were not really needed, as the government had direct control over productive resources. With privatization, the government must rely mainly on tax collection to finance public goods. Tax administrations must be set up, accumulate experience, and gain credibility in implementing tax laws by cracking down on tax fraud and evasion in the private sector. As we saw in Chapter 8, this is far from being an obvious task, and one may have bad equilibria where taxes are not collected and government is too weak to enforce law and collect taxes. Privatization revenues are thus potentially an important tool to fill the gap created by the deficiencies of a new tax administration.

Government revenues are an issue because there is an irrepressible level of government expenditures that cannot be compressed. First of all, unemployment benefits have to be paid to workers laid off in enterprises that have closed. Laying off workers is more efficient when the subsidy per worker from keeping the enterprise operating is higher than the level of unemployment benefits. It is, therefore, also more efficient not to close those enterprises for which the unemployment benefit would be higher than the subsidy per worker necessary to allow the enterprise to break even. This point has been made by Akerlof and colleagues (1991) and by Begg and Portes (1993) in the case of East Germany where the double shock of monetary unification and of wage increases put most East German enterprises into the red. One can be even more precise. From a dynamic point of view, under the optimal speed of sectoral reallocation discussed in Chapter 5, there is a dynamic optimal path of enterprise destruction and creation that leads to an optimal path of subsidies and unemployment benefits. However, even the mix of subsidies and unemployment benefits that would minimize public expenditures still represents a level of irrepressible public expenditures. Once this minimum level is attained, it is illusory to try to obtain further cuts in expenditures. Any further closure of enterprises with the aim to cut on subsidies would lead to proportionally higher expenditures on unemployment benefits, and thus to a higher overall level of public expenditures. The public finance problem in transition cannot be assumed away by putting forward policies involving unrealistically low levels of government expenditures. Moreover, infrastructure investment also has to be undertaken after privatization to introduce modern systems of telecommunications, new roads, and so on.

Despite expected efficiency gains from privatization, there is an obvious danger of macroeconomic disequilibrium in the transition period related to the potential breakdown of government revenues and irrepressible government expenditures. The budgetary impact of privatization policies is thus not without importance.

10.1.2.3 Political Constraints

Political constraints were discussed at length in Part One. Let us only repeat that ex ante political constraints may lead governments to choose privatization policies that are less efficient from the microeconomic viewpoint and that may carry important costs from the point of view of macroeconomic stability. Governments may also want to exploit a window of opportunity if ex ante constraints are favorable in order to relax ex post political constraints by increasing the costs of reversing privatization policies.

From the point of view of political constraints with respect to restructuring, the ultimate goal of privatization, heterogeneity in managerial skills, means that there must be resistance from bad managers to privatization policies that threaten their job. It also implies that support from good managers can be won for privatization policies, especially if they are to gain from it. Good managers in very profitable enterprises who have empire-building motives, however, will also tend to resist privatization policies that give control to outsiders. Resistance to given privatization policies may thus come from different angles as a result of different managerial motivations. Application of the theory of political economy of reform discussed in Part One may thus lead to the devising of privatization policies that gradually build constituencies or that use divide-and-rule tactics playing one group against the other.

We would also like to add here a political economy dimension that is important from the positive point of view, that of rent seeking. Rent seeking plays an important role, especially when governments are weak and do not have the necessary powers to control the setting of the political agenda. Privatization involves dividing the spoils of the communist state. The transfer of the bulk of government wealth to private hands is a unique historical opportunity for rent seeking. Accordingly, there is a lot of scope for large-scale rent-seeking activities in the context of privatization in Eastern Europe. Political decisions on how to privatize must be made. Clearly, it pays for various groups to engage in active lobbying in order to try to obtain, for free if possible, as big a share as possible of the assets. Competition between various groups in this huge rent-seeking process tends to lead to wasteful rent dissipation. Workers favor the transfer of ownership to them or oppose the privatization of their firm. Such an outcome, of course, is opposed by yet other interest groups who will lobby for other solutions. Even if there is some broad agreement on a few basic principles of free distribution, quantitative differences between different programs can make a big difference in terms of the rents given to different groups. Some of the most well known mass privatization programs put forward (Svejnar, 1989; Blanchard and Layard, 1990; Åslund, 1991; Lipton and Sachs, 1990b and others) differed in the proportion of firms going in the mass privatization program or in the proportion of free shares going to workers and managers and to the population. To give an example, giving either 20 or 25 percent of shares to workers for free makes a big difference to them, even though no objective criterion would allow a determination in favor of one percentage or the other. The more there is to distribute, the higher the stakes and the more it pays to engage in rent seeking. In a country like Russia, which has the largest world reserves in valuable natural resources, rent seeking could have been predicted to reach extraordinary heights.

At the beginning of transition, the view was expressed that the most important thing was to get the state out of the economy. Fast privatization was viewed as the instrument to achieve this objective. If we take the rent-seeking perspective seriously, we know that privatization does not prevent lobbies from intervening and constantly trying to influence decisions of a weak government both before and after privatization.

One should emphasize that the option for free distribution of assets rather than sales has negative effects in terms of rent seeking. Once governments opt for free distribution, they open the gates for a big rent-seeking game. Conversely, policies of competitive sales would minimize rent dissipation in the privatization process. However, it is not clear that weak governments in Eastern Europe were and are really able to resist the lobbying activities of those who favor free distribution. If their resistance to lobbying from various pressure groups is particularly weak, it is not clear why they should be able, in the domain of privatization more than in others, to resist rent-seeking pressures. Seen from the rent-seeking perspective, mass privatization is less the response of an agenda-setting government to political constraints than the outcome of rent-seeking pressures to redistribute wealth.

Rent-seeking works in the direction opposite to privatization. Privatization tends to clarify property rights. Rent-seeking creates confusion over property rights by constantly trying to change the distribution of property rights through political means, implying the constant redefinition of the boundaries of existing laws.

10.1.2.4 Informational Constraints

Since the goal of privatization is to enhance efficiency, a privatization agency must deal with the problem of how best to allocate state assets to private owners and owner-managers. It cannot avoid the question of determining who is the buyer with the best use of the asset. The privatization agency thus faces at least the same informational constraints as a conglomerate contemplating the sale of a subsidiary. This problem is all the more relevant in the absence of well-functioning mechanisms like takeovers or other market mechanisms, so that the initial allocation of ownership and control is likely to remain more or less unchanged for many years to come. Informational constraints are even more important in the emerging markets of former socialist countries.

10.1.2.5 Administrative Constraints

Given the scarcity of good administrative skills with respect to privatization and the fiscal cost of such administration, the administrative constraint is an important concern. Defining ownership titles on state assets and registering the transfer of these assets to private individuals, let alone valuing the assets to be privatized and finding potential buyers, constitute a very time-consuming process. If one adds on top of that informational asymmetries and the need to give correct incentives to the bureaucrats in charge of privatization (see Friebel, 2000), then one understands fully the importance of the administrative constraint. Now, the demands on administration vary with the different privatization policies. Top-down sales are the most demanding on administration, while bottom-up initiatives are less demanding.

10.1.3 SUMMARIZING THE OBJECTIVES AND CONSTRAINTS

The results of the whole discussion so far can be summarized in Figure 10.1. The horizontal axis measures managerial skills in a given sector, with more talented managers being more to the right. In order to simplify the discussion, we assume that current profitability is positively correlated with managerial skills. If we abstract from product market competition aspects, then we may think that good managers are more able than bad managers to achieve better productive efficiency, even weakly, and thus to better maintain the quality of the assets. Such an assumption obviously cannot hold across sectors, but for a given market, assuming even a weakly positive correlation between managerial skills and profitability seems reasonable. Figure 10.1 thus represents the

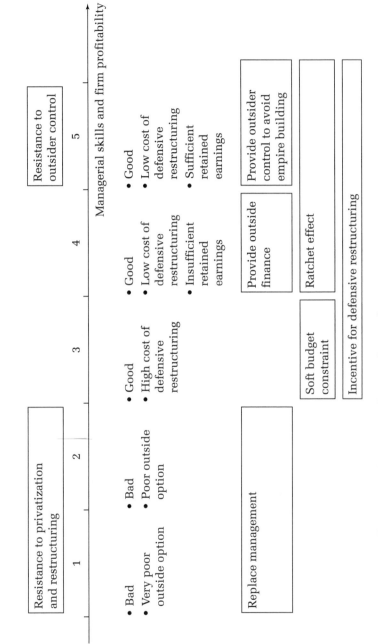

FIGURE 10.1 **MANAGERIAL HETEROGENEITY, RESTRUCTURING TASKS, AND POLITICAL CONSTRAINTS**

variety of restructuring problems inside a given sector. We identify five different types of managers:

- Type 1 managers are bad and thus need to be replaced; moreover, they have a very poor outside option when losing their current job, meaning that they would need to be compensated in order to remain indifferent to the status quo.

- Type 2 managers need also to be replaced but have a somewhat better outside option, meaning that they would need less compensation.

- Type 3 managers are good and expect to gain from strategic restructuring, but face high costs of defensive restructuring.

- Type 4 managers are good but face lower costs of restructuring; moreover, they have insufficient retained earnings to finance strategic restructuring.

- Type 5 managers are good, face a low cost of restructuring, and have sufficient retained earnings.

Below the axis, we show the economic problems to be solved in the restructuring process for these different categories of managers. Types 1 and 2 need to be replaced, whereas Types 3, 4, and 5 need to be given incentives to engage in defensive restructuring. Type 3 managers face a soft-budget-constraint problem because their enterprise is losing money and can only achieve profitability after incurring the high costs of defensive restructuring. In contrast, Types 4 and 5 are currently profitable and would rather face an initial ratchet-effect problem. Type 4 faces the problem of finding outside finance, whereas Type 5 has a potential moral-hazard problem of "empire building."

Above the axis, we show that the sources of resistance to privatization come from Types 1 and 2, who expect to be laid off, whereas Type 5 resists outsider control.

Figure 10.1 allows us to apprehend the heterogeneity in problems to be solved through restructuring, and thus the necessary heterogeneity in responses. In itself, however, it only represents a typology of problems to be solved depending on managerial skills, need for external finance, and degree of dependence of firms on government. The design of solutions does not follow immediately from this typology. Given the informational constraint, managers of different types are ex ante not distinguishable. Restructuring and privatization policies must thus be designed in such a way as to screen these different types of managers.

This typology provides, to our knowledge, the most comprehensive framework existing so far to start thinking about the effects of various privatization policies.

Before using this framework to evaluate different privatization policies, it is important to consider the difference in initial conditions in different countries. Privatization policies appear as packages, and thus pursue various goals simultaneously. In order to analyze how various privatization policies achieve these goals, it is important to ask how differences in initial conditions may matter.

In terms of the present framework, countries may differ in the proportions of the different types. In some countries, managers of Types 4 and 5 may be more frequent, whereas in other countries, there may be more managers of Types 1 and 2. Even if the efficiency problems of these different types can in principle be solved by the establishment of financial markets, the political constraints to restructuring will be stronger when a greater proportion of managers need to be replaced. There are, however, different variables that are important in determining initial country conditions. One important variable is the degree of insider control. According to the preceding discussion, the soft-budget-constraint problem is likely to be more important in countries where there was initially a higher degree of insider control. Similarly, the difference in initial macroeconomic conditions would reflect similar trends. Countries having past experience of reform have seen a higher degree of insider control, and also a more unbalanced macroeconomic situation. In terms of our framework, therefore, the proportion of Type 3 is likely to be more important. A last difference to mention that is of practical importance is the difference in the degree of political constraints. This not only refers to the differences in relative strengths of various pressure groups and coalitions, but also to differences in the relative support that governments need to adopt and implement policies. Stronger governments in practice often need weaker majorities, whereas weaker governments generally face more stringent majority rules and tend to govern more by consensus, and as a result there is often more paralysis of decisionmaking.

10.1.4   EVALUATING DIFFERENT PRIVATIZATION POLICIES

We can compare various privatization policies in terms of the preceding discussion. We will compare the following policies: (1) fast giveaway, most commonly called mass privatization, to outsiders, the policy mainly applied in the Czech Republic, (2) mass privatization to insiders, the policy mainly applied in Russia, (3) bottom-down sales to outsiders, the policy mainly applied in East Germany, and (4) gradual sales to outsiders, the policy mainly applied in Hungary and Poland.

10.1.4.1   Mass Privatization to Outsiders

Let us first look at the effects of fast giveaway to outsiders, under dispersed ownership. In essence this is the policy objective pursued in Czechoslovakia by Vaclav Klaus, even though in practice things turned out differently, as we will see.

Privatization to outsiders is in principle a better method than privatization to insiders to achieve efficient matching and to replace incompetent managers. However, this generalization will not be true if privatization results in dispersed outside ownership, because of the well-known free-rider problem associated with dispersed ownership: small shareholders do not have enough incentives to bear the costs of collective action but benefit from its results. Dispersed ownership thus leads to insufficient monitoring of incumbent managers. The Czech privatization program was initially designed in a way that would lead to dispersed ownership. For a flat fee of 1,000 koruny any citizen over eighteen could purchase a booklet of vouchers worth 1,000 points with which to bid for shares of firms being privatized. The book value of the counterpart of a booklet of vouchers has been evaluated at over 80,000 koruny. Moreover, the law prevented investment funds from holding more than 20 percent of shares in a firm. This legal provision plus the purchase of shares by a large number of shareholders, each having few voucher points, were expected to lead to dispersed ownership. Czech managers understood well the effects of dispersed ownership. Before the first wave of mass privatization, privatization projects for each firm were to be submitted by managers and potential investors. Incumbent managers tended to favor privatization of their firm through the voucher program, expecting that the ensuing dispersed ownership would leave them in control. Among the enterprises participating in the first wave of the voucher scheme, 85 percent of the privatization projects approved by the Ministry of Privatization were submitted by managers (Bouin and Grosfeld, 1995).

The objective of giving managers an incentive to engage in defensive restructuring, however, is partly achieved with this privatization method. Managers who have low costs of defensive restructuring benefit from signaling themselves to potential investors who may be more prone to bring fresh capital into firms where managers have already started actively to restructure. However, because privatization is in the form of giveaway to liquidity-constrained agents, the problems of transfer of ownership and of financing strategic restructuring are decoupled, and the problem of finding outside finance for firms must still be solved after privatization. Incentive problems, however, may be only partly solved, and the soft-budget-constraint problem may continue to prevail in firms where managers are either incompetent or have a high cost of defensive restructuring. As we will see in section 10.2, they may still take the state hostage and use threats of layoffs in order to get bailed out.

The stock-flow constraint is not satisfied, but the problem is eliminated under giveaway privatization, since revenues are not seen as an objective. However, the fiscal constraint may be violated, and this fact may undermine public good provision or macroeconomic stability. The administrative constraint is likely to be met because, despite the top-down approach to privatization, the administrative requirements in case of giveaway privatization are much less important than for any other top-down privatization scheme.

Mass privatization policy addresses political constraints related to restructuring. Ex ante acceptability is enhanced because incompetent managers are less afraid to lose their job when they face dispersed owners. For the same reason, managers with empire-building motives in profitable firms do not have to fear outsider control. As we saw in Chapter 4, giveaway privatization relaxes ex post political constraints.

One may argue that the problem of dispersed ownership is likely to become less acute over time if small shareholders are allowed to sell their shares. Faced with liquidity constraints, the latter are tempted to sell their shares quickly. However, this possibility has a political cost, discussed in Chapter 4. It reduces irreversibility of privatization, since agents who sell their shares in private firms no longer have stakes in the political success of privatization. In the Czech privatization scheme, it was for this reason that individuals were not allowed to sell their shares for cash for a year after privatization. Moreover, given the importance of wealth constraints in transition economies, it is not clear that those having the greatest ability to pay for shares also have the greatest willingness to pay. In that case, transfer of ownership will not meet the criterion of allocative efficiency.

The negative effects of dispersed ownership with a policy of mass privatization to outsiders can be mitigated when financial intermediaries act as instruments of outsider control inside the firms. Financial intermediaries may be mutual funds holding shares in enterprises and owned by small shareholders, as in the design of the initial Polish Mass Privatization Program, or they may be universal banks holding shares and debt claims on firms, and collecting accounts of small depositors. If we assume that financial intermediaries will take an active role in the restructuring of firms and act on behalf of the interest of the small shareholders or depositors, then indeed, as outside owners they should play an active role in replacing incompetent management when necessary. Their profit incentive will also lead them to engage in defensive restructuring, removing the initiative from the manager. As intermediaries, they will channel funds to their optimal uses and provide control over the use of funds. They will also have an incentive to directly harden the budget of firms under their control, provided they find it more profitable to take that approach rather than to lobby the government for subsidies to bail out firms.

Such behavior is by no means guaranteed. Indeed, even if financial intermediaries have concentrated stakes in firms, the free-rider problem of monitoring identified earlier will reproduce here at the level of intermediaries, as small shareholders and depositors will have no incentive to monitor the management of financial intermediaries. In Western economies, the function of monitoring of intermediaries is usually done by the adequate regulatory bodies (see, e.g., Dewatripont and Tirole, 1994a). Having an adequate legal and regulatory framework is thus a crucial condition for the success of mass privatization to intermediaries. Curiously, the Klaus government in the Czech Republic, which was the first to implement mass privatization, did not consider that the legal and regulatory framework was very important (Anderson and Kegels, 1997).

Note, however, that if intermediaries turn out to be effective, this privatization policy is less likely to address the political economy constraints of restructuring at the enterprise level, and may thus face problems of ex ante acceptability. The Polish Mass Privatization Program, designed as early as 1990 and advertised as the fastest and most efficient method of privatization, has failed to be accepted and implemented, and has remained in limbo for more than four years because it was systematically blocked in parliament by coalitions representing firm insiders (managers and workers). Ironically, the Czech privatization program, initially designed to yield a structure of dispersed ownership, turned out, rather unexpectedly, to be close to the Polish plan, as investment funds were spontaneously created, mostly by existing banks, to collect vouchers of the population, in return for promises to pay back at least ten times the purchase value of vouchers. It was only when investment funds appeared that citizens started showing some enthusiasm for the voucher program. By January 1992 only 2 million voucher booklets had been purchased, but after the campaign advertising investment funds, there were eventually 8.56 million voucher holders, nearly three-quarters of all eligible citizens. More than half of the voucher points ended up eventually in the hands of the thirteen largest investment funds (Kotrba and Svejnar, 1994).

It is interesting to ask why the Czech program gained political acceptance but not the Polish program. Initial country conditions play an important role. Czechoslovakia had no past record of economic reforms, and thus no worker councils. State control over firms had not weakened, and the more or less initially balanced macroeconomic situation shows that the soft-budget-constraint problem was less massively prevalent than in Poland. Also, in a rent-seeking perspective, the stronger power of workers in Poland can explain why the latter blocked mass privatization to outsiders. These considerations are important because they point to the importance of the initial conditions in the Czech privatization experience. Designers of the Russian mass privatization program learned the lesson of the Polish failure and chose a privatization policy based on giveaway to insiders.

The Czech privatization program has successfully met ex post political constraints, as the population received stakes in its success through the voucher program. The timing of the first wave of privatization was also orchestrated so as to ensure Vaclav Klaus an electoral success that strengthened his political position (see Chapter 4).

One should emphasize, however, that there is no foolproof method to obtain irreversibility, only ways to make it more costly. The Slovak example shows that after the first wave of privatization in Czechoslovakia, the results of the first wave were not undone by the Slovak government, but the momentum was clearly lost, as privatization halted.

With the benefit of experience, the Czech program has turned out to be disappointing. The corporate governance structure that came out of mass privatization was very incestuous. Most investment funds were set up by banks that were to be privatized through vouchers. As a result, banks were privatized to investment funds that belonged to banks! This practice resulted in full insider control. Moreover, because of the inadequacies in the legal and regulatory framework, all sorts of forms of asset stripping of privatized assets became possible, leading to the illegitimate enrichment of fund managers and to great disillusionment among the public (Ellerman, 1998). Asset stripping is always possible under policies of mass privatization when there is no efficient matching. Those who end up controlling the assets for free or for a crumb of bread may prefer to engage in asset stripping, even when the latter would be a less profitable option than privatizing the assets to a more efficient owner.

10.1.4.2   Mass Privatization to Insiders

The effects of giveaway to outsiders under dispersed ownership are roughly equivalent to a policy of giveaway to insiders, which is the policy followed in Russia. This comparison is interesting because the initial Czech plan of mass privatization was one designed to induce dispersed ownership. Neither of those policies provides a mechanism for replacing incompetent management because, in one case, the latter receive ownership of the assets, and in the other case, no strong outsider control is provided. For that same reason, both tend to favor insider entrenchment for managers of profitable firms with empire-building motives. Both also tend to provide insufficient outside finance for strategic restructuring. Both types of policies give incentives for defensive restructuring because insider control yields de facto residual rights of control to incumbent managers. They both contribute to harden budget constraints only to the extent that giveaway increases the cost of public funds. They both address ex ante political constraints of restructuring. However, as stated previously, since the fiscal constraint is likely to be violated, the ensuing loss of governmental wealth may have disastrous consequences for macroeconomic stability. Bolton and Roland (1992) warned against the macroeconomic consequences of giveaway privatization because of the danger of a fiscal breakdown not compensated by privatization revenues. Unfortunately, this dire prediction came true in the case of Russia. Mass privatization deprived government of most of its wealth, and the inability to create (or slowness in creating) a credible tax administration led to a dangerous breakdown in tax collection from which the Russian economy has still not recovered. As seen in Chapter 8, the government collapse has led to a situation of general insecurity of property rights. It is very difficult to make such a situation reversible because the combination of a weak government and powerful industrial groups controlled by insiders allows the latter to use their political clout to block any attempt to reform taxation.

10.1.4.3 Top-Bottom Sales to Outsiders

Top-bottom sales are the policy followed mostly in East Germany. From the point of view of allocative efficiency, the more competitive the process, the less important the role of the informational constraints. Concretely, sales through competitive auctions are more likely to allocate assets efficiently than bilateral sales. Under the latter, the seller is neither sure he is facing the most efficient buyer (with the greatest willingness to pay) nor sure about the willingness to pay of the buyer he is facing. Competitive auctions reduce informational rents of buyers and increase the likelihood of selling assets to the more efficient buyers. Sales give correct incentives, again assuming away the problem of dispersed ownership. They also lead more naturally to strategic restructuring, since buyers are willing and able to put up the funds necessary for new investments. They therefore do not have the feature of "decoupling" between transfer of ownership and provision of outside funds that is present in giveaway schemes.

Privatization through sales, however, does face the stock-flow constraint. This may create an incentive to reduce the speed of privatization in order to increase revenues. Indeed, since under the stock-flow constraint revenues from privatization of a stock of assets in any given year are constrained by the flow of savings of that year, the privatization agency faces a dilemma between fast sales and low revenues on one hand and slower sales with higher revenues on the other hand. It is the former choice that was taken in East Germany. This approach poses problems in terms of the fiscal constraint. Even the powerful West German economy suffered a terrible fiscal strain from the transition in East Germany. Part of this strain was due to the strong wage increases after unification, which dramatically reduced the value of East German enterprises, and to the major social expenditures intended to buffer the shock of transition in East Germany. (Recall also the trade-off in Chapter 3 between the speed of reform and its intertemporal budgetary costs to compensate losers.) However, because of the stock-flow constraint, prices were lower than they could have been despite the factors mentioned previously (see Sinn and Sinn, 1993, for a detailed analysis).

Political constraints to restructuring are likely to be important here because of resistance of managers and workers, and it is not a coincidence that East Germany is the only country where a very fast policy of sales could take place given the context of unification, where this resistance was less likely to feed through the political process owing to the dominance of the West German population in German politics.

Administrative constraints are also very important with this kind of policy. In Germany, there was a staff of 3,000 employees at the Treuhandanstalt alone. The Polish, Hungarian, and Czechoslovak administrative privatization efforts were much smaller in comparison; Poland's Ministry for Ownership Changes only had 200 employees, Hungary's SPA only 140. Worse, Hungary's SPA did not have the financial means to pay consultants for auditing the first twenty enterprises to be privatized (Okoliczanyi, 1991). The Czech Republic's Ministry of Privatization had only sixty employees, and the whole government machinery had to be involved in the administration of the privatization program.

10.1.4.4 Gradual Bottom-Up Sales to Outsiders

Finally, we look at the effects of a policy of gradual sales, the policy that was de facto implemented in Poland and Hungary. In order to avoid any confusion, let us immediately state our definition of gradual sales. We do not mean that enterprises are put on sale in a gradual way. When looking at privatizations in Poland and Hungary, the method of top-down sale has in general proved to be very slow and cumbersome. The most frequent form of privatization has been the bottom-up approach whereby one or several potential buyers, insiders or outsiders, signal their interest in purchasing a firm. In the bottom-up approach, a gradual process of sales is not the result of a limit in the supply of assets, but of a limit in the demand for privatizable assets.

In the cases under consideration, the limited demand for assets is not really related to the limited private domestic wealth because sales to domestic buyers take mostly the form of sales against noncash bids, such as leasing, partial purchases, installment payments, purchase against future payments associated with debt contracts, and so on. Noncash bids have been advocated by several economists (among others Sinn and Sinn, 1993; Bolton and Roland, 1992; Demougin and Sinn, 1992) as a way to accelerate the transfer of the stock of wealth into private hands, because of the limitations in existing private wealth in CEECs.

A limited demand for assets is more likely to be related, among other things, to asymmetric information about the quality of the firm's assets, and probably more importantly about the quality of incumbent management. Private investors, usually foreign investors, are more keen to acquire first those firms where the quality of assets and management yields the more promising expected returns. Preprivatization restructuring can serve here as a useful screening device. As we saw earlier in this chapter, bad managers have no incentive to accelerate the privatization of their firm and lack the necessary skills to engage in defensive restructuring. However, in line with the analysis of Chapter 9, good managers expect to gain from strategic restructuring and have all interest in attracting the attention of private investors by being active in defensive restructuring, provided the costs are not too high.

According to the previous reasoning, gradual sales in the future delay the problem of replacing incompetent managers, since private investors tend to shy away from firms where no preprivatization restructuring has taken place. However, they solve the problem of finding outside finance and control in a double sense. First of all, good managers in general gain access to external finance for strategic restructuring when their firm is privatized, since investors who bear the costs of purchasing the firm generally have a business project for the future. The available evidence (Carlin, Van Reenen, and Wolfe, 1995; EBRD *Transition Report,* 1995) shows that external finance for the purpose of strategic restructuring is provided mostly in firms privatized to foreign investors. Second, managers of firms able to self-finance their activities from their retained earnings but with empire-building motives will get better incentives. If these firms are sold to their managers against noncash bids, as proposed by Bolton and Roland (1992), rather than given away, they are likely to have a higher debt-equity ratio because part of the acquired shares will be purchased through loans. Recent theory in corporate governance (Jensen, 1986; Dewatripont and Tirole, 1994b) shows that a debt-equity ratio that is too low may, through weaker contingent control by creditors, reduce the incentives of managers and entrepreneurs. Sales of good firms against noncash bids may thus enhance incentives compared to giveaway.

Under gradual privatization, the best firms tend naturally to be privatized first because they are the most likely to find a buyer. From the political economy point of view of ex ante political constraints outlined in Chapter 2, this is also the correct sequencing. When the best firms get privatized first, the likelihood of large redundancies in these firms is smaller, and the likelihood of successful economic performance is higher. Initial economic successes for privatized firms enhance support for privatization and build constituencies for further reforms. Note also that when the best firms are privatized first, they have hard budget constraints from the beginning because the smaller likelihood of redundancies is less likely to violate the economy-wide political constraint to restructuring. The government can thus credibly commit in bad states not to intervene in those firms.

Administrative constraints are also much less important, since if proposals are generated from below, the burden of providing the information is not concentrated in the privatization agency but is shared more broadly.

10.1.4.5   Summary

In terms of restructuring outcomes, the policies we have been discussing are much less far apart than in terms of transfer of ownership. A policy of fast giveaway may

TABLE 10.4 EFFECTS OF PRIVATIZATION POLICIES

	Mass Privatization to Outsiders	Mass Privatization to Insiders	Top-Down Sales to Outsiders	Gradual Bottom-Up Sales to Outsiders
Objectives:				
Efficient matching	Yes	No	Yes	Yes
Profit incentives	Yes[a]	Yes[a]	Yes	Yes
Defensive restructuring	Yes	Partial	Yes	Gradual
Strategic restructuring	No	No	Yes	Gradual
Constraints:				
Stock flow	No	No	No	Yes
Fiscal	No	No	Yes	Yes
Informational	Yes	No	No	Yes[d]
Administrative	Yes	Yes	No	Yes
Political	Yes[b,c]	Yes[c]	No	Yes

[a] Possibility of asset looting

[b] Ex ante: depending on initial country conditions.

[c] Ex post: depending on dynamics of concentration of ownership and wealth.

[d] If competitive bidding.

encompass all (or a majority of) SOEs, whereas a policy of gradual sales will only concern the better firms. However, quick defensive restructuring outcomes will tend to be observed only in the better firms under both policies. Moreover, the problem of access to outside funds for strategic restructuring is not solved by mass privatization. This analytical prediction reflects partly the comment often heard that giveaway privatization does not yield restructuring whereas "genuine" sales do. The preceding reasoning shows more precisely that fast-giveaway privatization does not yield "faster" restructuring than gradual sales. Table 10.4 summarizes the different effects of the policies discussed.

Apart from the effects on enterprise restructuring, policies of mass privatization may contribute to a deterioration of the public finance problem in transition economies and jeopardize macroeconomic equilibrium. The actual experience of mass privatization in the Czech Republic and in Russia suggests that one must think deeper about the possible inefficient institutional lock-ins created by mass privatization whereby the powerful interest groups created by mass privatization are able to capture the state and block reforms aimed toward more enforcement of tax collection, more transparent financial and prudential regulations, effective implementation of bankruptcy rules, and so forth. These lock-ins can also be the source of major political instability in the future.

10.2   MODELS OF PRIVATIZATION

In this section we review models touching on partial aspects of privatization policies. All the models reviewed in this section depart from the common simplistic view that once the firm has new owners, they will necessarily have incentives to maximize profits and the value of the firm. The first two models deal with insider privatization. The first model, due to Aghion and Blanchard, is directly related to the preceding discussion. It shows how insider privatization can lead to inefficient entrenchment and prevent the efficient sale of the enterprise assets to outsiders. The second model, due to Debande and Friebel, shows that insider privatization may induce a trade-off between better incentives and soft budget constraints. The reason is that, in the environment of transition economies, the greater autonomy given to enterprises increases both the incentives to maximize profits on the market *and* the rent-seeking incentives to extract refinancing from government, and that the former incentives may be weaker than the latter. At the same time, it is probably the first model to have shown incentives for asset stripping under insider privatization.

The third model, due to Bolton, Pivetta, and Roland, is more normative. It asks what the optimal privatization contracts are in the presence of noncash bids. As seen earlier, wealth constraints are a fundamental component of the privatization landscape in transition economies, and noncash bids are a way of dealing with these constraints. The dimension of moral hazard is integrated to allow for the possibility of suboptimal effort or even outright asset stripping by the new owners, since in various countries asset stripping continues after privatization. The analysis shows that noncash bids can be optimal even in the absence of wealth constraints.

10.2.1   The Vested Interests of Insider Privatization

Aghion and Blanchard (1998) look at inefficiencies stemming from insider privatization. In particular, they show how, abstracting from soft budget constraints and rent-seeking activities, insider privatization may lead to entrenchment. Their model refutes the idea that insider privatization should not be a major concern because outside owners who are able to run the assets more efficiently will buy off the assets and thus efficient allocation of assets will eventually be achieved. They show that this is not necessarily the case and that insider privatization may prevent such efficient takeovers, thus confirming the argument made earlier that it is important for efficiency reasons to use privatization, in particular outsider privatization, to achieve efficient matching between assets and managers.

Assume a representative firm employing a unit mass of workers. Without restructuring under insider ownership, the output per worker is R_i, which is low but nevertheless sufficient to keep the firm alive. If the firm is sold to an outside owner who can restructure it, restructuring enables the firm to produce $R_o > R_i$ where R_o is net of the costs of restructuring. At the same time, restructuring requires that a proportion λ of the workers be replaced. Agents are assumed to be risk neutral. Workers newly hired receive a wage w, whereas laid-off workers get unemployment benefits b. Implicitly assuming efficiency wages (as in the Aghion-Blanchard labor reallocation model of Chapter 5), there is a wedge c between the wage rate and unemployment benefits: $w = b + c$.

We assume a one-period model so that the value of the firm and its profit are identical. The maximum price v^b an outside buyer is ready to pay for acquiring control over the firm is its product after restructuring net of wage costs:

$$v^b = R_o - w \tag{10.1}$$

What is the minimum price v^s at which insiders will agree to sell? Collectively, they may decide not to restructure the firm in order to avoid layoffs. However, if they sell, their expected income is the unemployment benefits for the proportion λ of workers and the wage w for the workers who are not laid off: $\lambda b + (1 - \lambda)w = w - \lambda c$. We thus have

$$v^s = R_i - w + \lambda c \tag{10.2}$$

Resale to outsiders will thus take place if and only if $v^b > v^s \Longleftrightarrow R_o > R_i + \lambda c$. As we see, for resale to outsiders to take place, it is not only necessary to have an increase in efficiency $R_o - R_i$. This increase in efficiency must also be big enough to compensate workers for λc, the losses to insiders from restructuring. The higher λ and c, the higher the wedge necessary to convince insiders to sell. This fact creates a social inefficiency because efficiency-enhancing restructuring by outsiders will be blocked by insider entrenchment.

This inefficiency could be eliminated if there were a way to use the efficiency gains (from the higher value of the firm plus the higher income for the workers hired to replace the λ insiders) to compensate the losers. The ownership rights given to insiders with privatization give them a right to veto outside privatization that puts them in a position to demand full compensation for their loss from restructuring. The more difficult it is to finance such compensation, the more the insiders are able to block efficient restructuring.

We have assumed so far that workers decide collectively whether or not to sell to outsiders. If each worker has the right to sell his individual share in his firm, things will be different. In that case, a worker's decision to sell or not will be the same as that of a minority shareholder. He will want to sell only if he can extract the surplus from restructuring. In that case, we have $v^s = R_o - w$, which from equation (10.1) is equal to v^b. Indeed, an individual worker expects restructuring to take place whether he keeps his share or not. In both cases, he loses λc. In the beginning of the Russian mass privatization process, reformers hoped that insiders would sell their shares in this way, thereby paving the way for outsiders to take over and restructure firms. This plan did not work because workers and management colluded to prevent individual resale of shares. The way it often happened was that the manager acted as a "custodian" of the shares of workers so that workers who wanted to sell had to go explicitly to the management of the firm to ask for their share (Frydman and Rapaczynski, 1994).

A straightforward extension of the model shows that higher unemployment with a more depressed macroeconomic situation is a further obstacle to takeover of insider-privatized firms. Assume that restructuring is uncertain and that a profit of $R_o - w$ is achieved with probability $\frac{1}{2}$ but that with probability $\frac{1}{2}$ no profit can be achieved. In that case, the maximum price for an outside buyer is $\frac{1}{2}(R_o - w)$, and the condition for resale becomes $v^b > v^s \iff \frac{1}{2}R_o > R_i - \frac{b}{2} - (\frac{1}{2} - \lambda)c$. Assuming that a higher unemployment rate will imply a lower b, we see that the condition for resale to outsiders is more stringent when b decreases. The reason is simple: a reduction in b reduces v^b less than v^s because of the uncertain outcome of restructuring.

10.2.2 BETTER INCENTIVES VERSUS SOFTER BUDGET CONSTRAINTS AND ASSET STRIPPING

Although the models in the previous chapter highlighted the incentive problems of SOEs under socialism, in these models privatization always represents a strict improvement over state ownership. In the following model, due to Debande and Friebel (1995), while privatization unambiguously increases managerial incentives, it may nevertheless lead to an increase in the soft-budget-constraint problem and a worsening in subsidy payments by government to firms. Moreover, it may lead to asset stripping. The Debande-Friebel model combines the Shleifer-Vishny and Dewatripont-Maskin models.

They look at the restructuring decisions of SOEs and firms privatized to insiders. Restructuring requires both managerial effort and funds, the latter normalized to 1. Effort has a cost $e \in [0, \bar{e}]$ to the manager that is known only to him and not to the government. The cost of effort is assumed to be uniformly distributed on the support $[0, \bar{e}]$. The number of managers and firms is normalized to 1. The unit of funds is assumed in both cases to come only from the government, an assumption which reflects the fact that insiders are not in a good position to secure funds from private investors unless they relinquish sufficient control rights. This assumption also approximates well the situation of many insider privatizations where the assets were given away to insiders who were able to secure loans from state-owned banks that were not yet privatized.

After initial injection of funds, three situations are possible:

1. The manager keeps the status quo, sheds no labor, and does not exert effort, yielding $R(L)$ where L denotes the excess labor in the firm.

2. The manager exerts no effort but sheds labor to cut losses, yielding a return of $R(0)$.

3. The manager exerts effort and completely restructures the firm. In that case, the excess workers of the firm L can be used productively, yielding a return of $R_e(L)$ where the subscript indicates the effort level.

TABLE 10.5 PAYOFFS IN STATE-OWNED ENTERPRISES

	Government	Management
Complete restructuring	$R_e(L) + B_G - 1$	$B_M - e$
No effort, no layoffs	$R(L) + B_G - 1$	B_M
No effort, layoffs ($L = 0$)	$R(0) - 1$	0

As we see, situations 2 and 3 are close to the ideas of defensive and strategic restructuring except that $R_e(L)$ is achieved through effort, not through additional outside funds.

It is assumed that under the status quo, the firm is losing money: $-1 \leq R(L) \leq 0$, and that shedding labor helps to restore profitability: $1 \leq R(0) \leq 2$. However, full restructuring exerting effort is efficient and it is assumed that $R_e(L) \geq R(0) + 1$.

In a first stage under state ownership, the government has control rights and cash-flow rights over the firm, but it relinquishes both under privatization.

Regarding preferences, it is assumed that the government cares about returns but also derives a private benefit B_G from excess employment where $1 \leq B_G \leq 2$. This assumption means that the government would be willing to pay at least 1 to maintain high employment but would find it wasteful to spend more than 2 on that objective. Thus, the government cares about both efficiency *and* excess employment. Contrary to the Shleifer and Vishny model, it is assumed that managers also derive rents from excess employment in the amount $B_M \in [0, 2]$. There are several reasons why managers may enjoy such rents. A first reason is the empire-building motive à la Jensen (1986) that was emphasized in section 10.1. Another reason may be the reluctance to shed labor and face the psychological stress of a labor conflict. Management may also partially be captured by workers who are often majority shareholders in insider-privatized firms. The size of firms is also a factor that may affect positively the political influence of managers, and thus their participation in all sorts of rent-seeking ventures. This effect is especially likely in the case of transition economies like Russia.

In the SOE in the absence of privatization, therefore, the timing of moves is the following: after learning his cost of effort, the manager decides how much effort to invest, and the government injects funds for restructuring and controls the use of those funds. Even though effort cannot be controlled by government, it can use its ownership right over the firm to ensure that the funds are not diverted by management. In a second stage, after having observed the extent of restructuring, the government decides whether or not to reduce the level of employment. Table 10.5 shows the payoffs to the government and management.

In a privatized firm, government loses control over the use of funds, and management is residual claimant on profits. The latter, however, must pay back its loan on the verifiable profits it makes. Because government loses control of the firm, management is

TABLE 10.6 PAYOFFS IN AN INSIDER-PRIVATIZED FIRM

	Government	Management
Complete restructuring	B_G	$R_e(L) + B_M - e - 1$
Liquidation	-1	$+1$
No effort, no layoffs	$B_G - 2$	$R(L) + B_M + 1$
No effort, layoffs $(L = 0)$	$R(0) - 2$	$+1$

able to divert loaned funds for its own private consumption. This diversion of funds corresponds to the widely observed behavior of asset stripping by insiders who have gained control over the assets of the firm. As before, the insider manager can also decide on his level of effort when using the funds to restructure. Government cannot verify whether the manager has diverted funds. The government then faces the choice of either accepting the liquidation of the firm, and thus layoffs, or injecting an additional unit of funds used for restructuring, but then preventing the funds from being diverted. There is thus a potential soft-budget-constraint problem that results from sequential lending. When management is refinanced, it can either use the funds to retain excess workers [recall that $R(L) \leq 0$] or lay them off and remit the profits from restructuring to government as partial payback for the loan. It is assumed that L cannot be contracted upon ex post.

Thus, when the firm restructures completely, it receives all profits after paying back the loan to government and paying the cost of effort. When refinancing the firm, the government gets either the profits from layoffs [$R(0) < 2$] or the private benefits from keeping excess employment ($B_G < 2$). Table 10.6 shows the payoffs for the case of an insider-privatized firm.

Let us now derive the main results of the model. First look at the incentives of government. Under state ownership, absent complete restructuring, the government prefers to maintain excess employment if $B_G > R(0) - R(L)$ (an "employment-maximizing" government) and prefers layoffs if $B_G < R(0) - R(L)$ (a "budget-stabilizing" government). Under privatization, the government will always be willing to refinance a firm asking for an additional loan. Indeed, since B_G and $R(0)$ are both greater than 1, the continuation value is higher under refinancing than under liquidation. Nevertheless, there is still the inefficiency of the soft-budget-constraint problem, since B_G and $R(0)$ are both ≤ 2.

For the manager under state ownership in the case of an "employment-maximizing" government, his optimal effort will always be zero, whereas if he faces a "budget-stabilizing" government, the cut-off level of effort will be $e = B_M$. Managers with a cost of effort above B_M will then exert no effort, whereas managers with a cost of effort below B_M will exert effort. Under privatization, the manager will always at least weakly prefer to ask for refinance if he chooses to divert funds. He will strictly prefer so and will also maintain excess employment if $R(L) + B_M > 0$. Call this a "rent-seeking" manager. On the contrary, call the manager a "profit-oriented" manager if $R(L) + B_M < 0$. However, private ownership also gives positive incentives because the manager is residual claimant of profits. There will always be full restructuring if

$$R_e(L) + B_M - e - 1 > \max\{R(L) + B_M, 0\} + 1$$

implying a cut-off level of effort of

$$e = R_e(L) - 2 + B_M - \max\{R(L) + B_M, 0\}$$

A first result that can be immediately derived is that if the government is "employment maximizing" and the manager is "profit oriented," then privatization will imply better incentives than under state ownership. Indeed, the cut-off level for effort e_p^p, where the superscript stands for private and the subscript for profit-oriented, is $e_p^p = R_e(L) - 2 + B_M > B_M$, since $R_e(L) \geq R(0) + 1$ and $R(0) \geq 1$, implying that $R_e(L) \geq 2$. This is the standard result of the positive effects of privatization.

Moreover, the model helps us to understand why the government wishes to privatize, which was not the case in the model of Shleifer and Vishny. Indeed, under state ownership, the government gets a payoff of $R(L) + B_G - 1 < B_G$ where B_G is the benefit the government derives from full restructuring after privatization. It is easy to see that if $R_e(L)$ is sufficiently high, then e_p^p will be close enough to $\bar{e}$, the maximum cost of effort. In that case, privatization will give incentives to provide effort for most managers, and the government will thus derive a higher payoff from privatization. In other words, the interests of government and managers may be aligned in privatization, since profit incentives are large enough so as to create jobs without requiring inefficient government intervention for that purpose.

In contrast to the preceding result, privatization may worsen incentives. If the government is of the "budget-stabilizing" type, the cut-off level of effort under state ownership is equal to B_M, whereas under privatization, if managers are of the "rent-seeking" type, it is $e_r^p = R_e(L) - R(L) - 2$, which can be $< B_M$. In that case, despite the fact that privatization gives the manager residual claims on profit, the expected profits under full restructuring are weak relative to the benefits of asset stripping and rent seeking to extract subsidies from government.

The loss of government control from privatization can also result in an increase in subsidies to insider-privatized firms compared to subsidies to SOEs even when incentives are improved. Indeed, consider the case where the government is employment maximizing and the manager is of the rent-seeking type. In that case, total subsidies to the SOE are $1 - R(L)$, whereas total subsidies under privatization are $2(1 - \alpha_r^p)$ where $\alpha_r^p = \frac{e_r^p}{\bar{e}}$. Under privatization, the higher incentives lead to a remittance of α_r^p out of the initial investment, but the loss of control also leads to refinance $(1 - \alpha_r^p)$, which was not the case under state ownership. If the latter effect is sufficiently important, then privatization may lead to an increase in subsidies because the privatized firm can better extract rents from an employment-maximizing government. Specifically, subsidies under privatization are higher if $R_e(L) < R(L) + 2 + \frac{1+R(L)}{2}$.

The results of the Debande and Friebel model deliver a richer set of insights than do simplistic views on privatization. In particular, it allows us to understand potential pitfalls from insider privatization such as asset stripping and soft budget constraints. In the next two chapters, we will go further in detail into the institutional conditions that yield soft versus hard budget constraints in relation with other variables of the transition environment.

10.2.3 PRIVATIZATION WITH NONCASH BIDS AND EX POST MORAL HAZARD

The sale of assets against noncash payments creates an ex post moral-hazard problem: the buyer will have fewer incentives to maximize the value of the assets if he must share the benefits of his effort. This moral hazard may even take extreme forms such as asset stripping or failure to honor promised payments. In the absence of wealth constraints, it therefore seems optimal to avoid noncash payments in order to circumvent this ex post moral-hazard problem.

This intuition does not carry through, however, when the seller faces asymmetric information about the buyer's ability. When there is asymmetric information on management ability, the use of noncash payments is optimal even when there are no wealth constraints, despite the distortion created by the ex post moral hazard. Low-ability types serve as a useful screening device to extract rents from high-ability types. Wealth constraints are thus not a necessary condition for the optimality of noncash payments.

This result on the optimality of noncash payments in asset sales is an application of the general principle that optimal contracts with adverse selection and moral hazard optimally trade off distortion of incentives of low types against extraction of rents from high types. It carries through to the case of auction of assets and to the analysis of sales and auctions with asymmetric information both on ability and on wealth.

In the Bolton, Pivetta, and Roland (1997) model, consider the sale of an asset with uncertain output $q \in \{0, \overline{q}\}$. Potential buyers differ in their ability $\beta_i \in \{\beta_L, \beta_H\}$, $\beta_L < \beta_H$. The buyer is a high-ability type β_H with probability α and a low-ability type β_L with probability $(1 - \alpha)$. Ability interacts multiplicatively with effort to determine the probability $\beta_i e$ of producing $\overline{q}$. Effort e is a continuous variable $\in R^+$. The cost of effort is a convex function of effort $g(e) \equiv \frac{e^2}{2}$. Expected output for type i is thus $\beta_i e \overline{q}$.

A privatization contract for type i is a pair (m_i, X_i) where m_i is a cash payment and $X_i \geq 0$ is a noncash payment paid out of future output.

The buyer's utility $U(\beta_i)$ is defined as follows:

$$U(\beta_i) = \beta_i e(\overline{q} - X_i) - m_i - \frac{e^2}{2} \tag{10.3}$$

For a given sales contract, the optimal choice of effort is then

$$e_i^* \equiv Arg \max U(\beta_i) = \beta_i(\overline{q} - X_i) \tag{10.4}$$

The buyer's optimal choice of effort is independent of m_i but is a decreasing function of X_i. Noncash payments thus clearly distort the choice of ex post effort.

The government is assumed to design sales contracts in order to maximize revenues. Start with the case where the ability of buyers is observable. Assume that the wealth of buyers is observable and is equal to M for both types. The problem is thus one of pure moral hazard that is the solution to

$$\max_{m_i, X_i} \alpha(\beta_H e_H^* X_H + m_H) + (1 - \alpha)(\beta_L e_L^* X_L + m_L) \tag{10.5}$$

subject to

$$m_H \le M$$
$$m_L \le M$$
$$\beta_i e(\overline{q} - X_i) - m_i - \frac{e^2}{2} \ge 0, \qquad i = L, H$$

where the first two constraints are the wealth constraints and the next ones are the individual rationality or participation constraints for each type.

Given that ability is observable, the seller can nail down each buyer type to his individual rationality constraint. Note that if M is large enough so that only the individual rationality constraints bind, the first-order conditions for X_H, X_L, m_H, and m_L are

$$\alpha\beta_H^2(\overline{q} - 2X_H) - \lambda_H\beta_H^2(\overline{q} - X_H) = 0 \tag{10.6}$$
$$(1 - \alpha)\beta_L^2(\overline{q}X_L - 2X_L) - \lambda_L\beta_L^2(\overline{q} - X_L) = 0$$
$$\alpha = \lambda_H$$
$$(1 - \alpha) = \lambda_L$$

where λ_H and λ_L, respectively, are the Lagrange multipliers for the individual rationality constraints of the high and the low type.

These equations imply $X_H = X_L = 0$. The individual rationality constraints then yield $m_i = \frac{1}{2}\beta_i^2\overline{q}^2$.

We thus get the expected result that when wealth constraints are not binding, it is never optimal to have noncash payments. Optimal sales contracts are pure cash payments. Noncash payments are not optimal because they distort incentives. With pure moral hazard, noncash payments serve a purpose only when agents are wealth constrained.

We now introduce asymmetric information on ability. The seller's problem is now as follows:

$$\max_{m_i, X_i} \alpha(\beta_H e_H^* X_H + m_H) + (1 - \alpha)(\beta_L e_L^* X_L + m_L) \tag{10.7}$$

subject to

$$m_H \leq M$$
$$m_L \leq M$$

$$\beta_i e_i^* (\overline{q} - X_i) - m_i - \frac{e_i^{*2}}{2} \geq 0, \qquad i = H, L$$

$$\beta_H e_{H|H}^* (\overline{q} - X_H) - m_H - \frac{e_{H|H}^{*2}}{2} \geq \beta_H e_{L|H}^* (\overline{q} - X_L) - m_L - \frac{e_{L|H}^{*2}}{2}$$

$$\beta_L e_{L|L}^* (\overline{q} - X_L) - m_L - \frac{e_{L|L}^{*2}}{2a} \geq \beta_L e_{H|L}^* (\overline{q} - X_H) - m_L - \frac{e_{H|L}^{*2}}{2a}$$

where the last two constraints are the incentive compatibility constraints and where $e_{i|j}^* \equiv \beta_j(\overline{q} - X_i)$ is the optimal effort chosen by type j pretending to be type i when cash payments are X_i.

We first look at the case where contracts are restricted to pure cash payments where $X_i = 0$. Replacing $e_{i|j}^*$, the incentive compatibility constraints become

$$\frac{1}{2}\beta_H^2 \overline{q}^2 - m_H \geq \frac{1}{2}\beta_H^2 \overline{q}^2 - m_L \qquad (10.8)$$
$$\frac{1}{2}\beta_L^2 \overline{q}^2 - m_L \geq \frac{1}{2}\beta_L^2 \overline{q}^2 - m_H$$

Inspection of these constraints shows immediately that m_H must be equal to m_L. We thus see that pure cash payments do not allow the screening of types in this model. Indeed, by having $X_i = 0$, buyers have full incentives because they are full residual claimants on the asset. However, cash payments alone do not allow for screening, independently of the level of wealth.

We now turn to the analysis of optimal contracts with cash and noncash payments. Call λ_H, λ_L, μ_H, μ_L, θ_H, and θ_L the Lagrange multipliers for the high and low types, respectively, for the individual-rationality, wealth, and incentive-compatibility constraints.

Note first that when M is very small so that the budget constraints are binding but none of the individual-rationality constraints binds, unconstrained optimization of condition (10.7) yields $X_H = X_L = \frac{\overline{q}}{2}$. It is easy to see that the incentive-compatibility constraints are then automatically satisfied.

If M is very large so that the wealth constraints are not binding, the first-order conditions yield

$$\frac{\partial L}{\partial X_H} = 0 \Longrightarrow \alpha \beta_H^2 (\overline{q} - 2X_H) = \theta_H \beta_H^2 (\overline{q} - X_H)$$

$$\frac{\partial L}{\partial m_H} = 0 \Longrightarrow \rho = \theta_H \Longrightarrow X_H = 0$$

$$\frac{\partial L}{\partial X_L} = 0 \Longrightarrow (1 - \alpha)\beta_L^2 (\overline{q} - 2X_L) + \theta_H \beta_H^2 (\overline{q} - X_L) = \lambda_L \beta_L^2 (\overline{q} - X_L)$$

$$\frac{\partial L}{\partial m_L} = 0 \Longrightarrow (1 - \alpha) = \lambda_L - \theta_H \Longrightarrow \lambda_L = 1$$

By the individual rationality constraint of the low type, $m_L = \frac{1}{2}\beta_L^2 (\overline{q} - X_L)^2$, and by the incentive compatibility constraint of the high type, $m_H = m_L + \frac{1}{2}\beta_H^2 [(\overline{q} - X_H)^2 - (\overline{q} - X_L)]$. Replacing $(1 - \alpha)$ by $\lambda_L - \theta_H$ in $\frac{\partial L}{\partial X_L} = 0$ yields

$$X_L = \frac{\alpha(\beta_H^2 - \beta_L^2)\bar{q}}{\alpha(\beta_H^2 - \beta_L^2) + (1-\alpha)\beta_L^2} > 0$$

$$m_L = \frac{1}{2}\beta_L^2\bar{q}^2 \left[\frac{(1-\alpha)\beta_L^2}{\alpha(\beta_H^2 - \beta_L^2) + (1-\alpha)\beta_L^2} \right]^2$$

We thus have $X_H = 0$ and $X_L > 0$. Noncash payments are thus optimal even in the absence of wealth constraints. More specifically, by asking for positive noncash payments from the low type, the seller is able to extract rents from the high type and increase m_H. Thus, noncash payments not only serve as a second-best instrument to increase sales revenues when buyers are wealth constrained, but also serve as an optimal screening device even when buyers are not wealth constrained. This result is a priori surprising because one would think that, because of the ex post moral hazard problem, making the buyer a full residual claimant on the asset would always be optimal. This assumption is true when ability is observable, as we saw previously, but is not the case once there is asymmetric information about ability. This is a new application of the classical adverse selection trade-off between efficiency and rent extraction: there is no distortion at the top ($X_H = 0$), but incentives of the low type are distorted so as to extract rents from the high type.

One wonders whether the reason for the optimality of noncash payments is that there is no other instrument for screening, as is the case, for example, in auctions where the probability of selling is used as an additional screening device. Maskin (1991) was the first to model auctions with noncash bids. Let us look at second-price sealed-bid auctions, restricting the analysis to that of efficient auctions. We look only at truthful mechanisms and can thus think of auctions as bidders announcing their type and the seller specifying (m_i, X_i), and the probability of selling as a function of the announcement of the type. As we look at efficient auctions, a higher type wins with probability 1 when faced with a lower type and with probability $\frac{1}{2}$ when faced with the same type.

In an auction with cash and noncash payments where we assume that the noncash bids and monetary payments are independent of the identity of the other bidder, $X_{HH} = X_{HL} = X_H$, $X_{LL} = X_L$, $m_{HH} = m_{HL} = m_H$, $m_{LL} = m_L$, the seller solves

$$\max_{m_H, m_L} \alpha(2-\alpha)\left(\beta_H e_H^* X_H + m_H\right) + (1-\alpha)^2 \left(\beta_L e_L^* X_L + m_L\right)$$

subject to

$$m_H \leq M$$
$$m_L \leq M$$
$$\beta_i e_i^*(\bar{q} - X_i) - m_i - \frac{e_i^{*2}}{2} \geq 0, \qquad i = H; L$$

$$\left(\frac{\alpha}{2} + 1 - \alpha\right)\left[\beta_H e_{H|H}^*(\bar{q} - X_H) - m_H - \frac{e_{H|H}^{*2}}{2}\right] \geq \frac{1-\alpha}{2}\left[\beta_H e_{L|H}^*(\bar{q} - X_L) - m_L - \frac{e_{L|H}^{*2}}{2}\right]$$

$$\frac{1-\alpha}{2}\left[\beta_L e_{L|L}^*(\bar{q} - X_L) - m_L - \frac{e_{L|L}^{*2}}{2}\right] \geq \left(\frac{\alpha}{2} + 1 - \alpha\right)\left[\beta_L e_{H|L}^*(\bar{q} - X_H) - m_L - \frac{e_{H|L}^{*2}}{2}\right]$$

We restrict the analysis to the case where M is large so that the budget constraints are not binding. First-order conditions yield

$$\frac{\partial L}{\partial X_H} = 0 \Longrightarrow \alpha(2 - \alpha)(\overline{q} - 2X_H) = \theta_H(2 - \alpha)(\overline{q} - X_H)$$

$$\frac{\partial L}{\partial m_H} = 0 \Longrightarrow \alpha(2 - \alpha) = (2 - \alpha)\theta_H \Longrightarrow X_H = 0$$

$$\frac{\partial L}{\partial X_L} = 0 \Longrightarrow (1 - \alpha)^2 \beta_L^2(\overline{q} - 2X_L) + \theta_H(1 - \alpha)\beta_H^2(\overline{q} - X_L) = \lambda_L \beta_L^2(\overline{q} - X_L)$$

$$\frac{\partial L}{\partial m_L} = 0 \Longrightarrow (1 - \alpha)^2 = \lambda_L - \theta_H(1 - \alpha) \Longrightarrow \lambda_L = 1 - \alpha$$

Replacing $(1 - \alpha)^2$ by $\lambda_L - \theta_H(1 - \alpha)$ in $\frac{\partial L}{\partial X_L} = 0$ yields

$$X_L = \frac{\alpha(\beta_H^2 - \beta_L^2)\overline{q}}{\alpha(\beta_H^2 - \beta_L^2) + (1 - \alpha)\beta_L^2} > 0$$

$$m_L = \frac{\beta_L^2}{2}(\overline{q} - X_L)^2$$

Using the incentive-compatibility constraint,

$$m_H = \frac{\beta_H^2}{2}\overline{q}^2 - \frac{1 - \alpha}{2 - \alpha}\left[\frac{\beta_H^2}{2}(\overline{q} - X_L)^2 - m_L\right]$$

Note that this expression is larger than $m_H = \frac{\beta_H^2}{2}\overline{q}^2 - \left[\frac{\beta_H^2}{2}(\overline{q} - X_L)^2 - m_L\right]$, the cash payment in the case of sales to a single buyer, since $\frac{1-\alpha}{2-\alpha} < 1$.

We thus see that positive noncash bids for the low type still appear in the optimal efficient auction. Moreover, higher cash payments can be obtained from the high type. Noncash payments thus serve as an additional screening device to extract rents from the high-ability type. Indeed, an alternative way of extracting rents from the high-ability type would be to use as an instrument the probability to sell to a low type competing against a low type. Since we are looking at efficient auctions, noncash payments remain optimal even when wealth constraints are nonbinding.

The debate on privatization methods in Central and Eastern Europe has put forward questions of what are the optimal sales contracts under asymmetric information and wealth constraints. These questions have led us to consider the role of noncash bids and to the idea that noncash payments are optimal, even in the absence of wealth constraints. This idea has potentially broad applications. For example, in the context of bankruptcy reforms, it has been objected that noncash bids are unnecessary if there are perfect capital markets. The Bolton, Pivetta, and Roland (1997) model shows that this objection is not valid. Because of the screening motive, noncash payments are optimal even in a world where individuals can borrow freely.

10.3   EMPIRICAL EVIDENCE

There is by now a very extensive empirical literature on the effects of the form of privatization on enterprise performance. We describe briefly the results of the main papers comparing the effects of privatization forms.

Before doing so, it is interesting to note that initial empirical studies on enterprise behavior found that the main difference in behavior was between existing enterprises (SOEs and privatized) and new enterprises (see, e.g., Konings, Lehmann, and Schaffer, 1996; Konings, 1997; Bilsen and Konings, 1997). In effect, the so-called de novo enterprises displayed better measures of performance, such as productivity growth, controlling for factors such as enterprise size and capital intensity. However, such exercises are not easy because of a potential sample selection bias. The new enterprises are generally those that survived an early competitive process. This selection bias tends to overstate their performance compared to existing state enterprises.

Another problem is the endogeneity problem when analyzing the effect of ownership form on enterprise performance by regressing the latter on the former. Causality may indeed run the other way with performance determining ownership change, the better enterprises being privatized first, for example, or the better enterprises being privatized primarily to insiders who have superior information about the firm. This is a serious problem, and the Gupta, Ham, and Svejnar (1999) paper cited in Chapter 2 has provided solid evidence in the case of the Czech Republic that the more profitable firms do get privatized first. Only a few studies have tried to tackle this endogeneity problem.

Barberis and colleagues (1996) have provided a neat empirical analysis of retail shops in Russia. Their study aims at providing evidence on the relative importance of the two channels mentioned earlier in this chapter through which privatization improves efficiency: (1) more efficient matching between managers and assets and (2) better incentives. Restructuring is measured by capital renovation, layoffs, and changes in suppliers. They found that measures of restructuring occurred significantly less often when the shop was privatized to owners than when there were new owners who were different from incumbent management. These findings suggest that the matching of managerial skills with assets is empirically more important than improvements in incentives for incumbent management. In this study, incentives as measured by the size of the manager's ownership stake were found to have less effect than the replacement of management. They made use of the instrumental variable approach to control for the endogeneity problem using the method of privatization as an instrument. Though the study is interesting and well done, evidence on Russian shops is of course limited evidence on the effects of privatization, especially on the privatization of large firms.

Earle and Estrin (1997) have done a detailed study of privatization in Russia, surveying 300 enterprises after the completion of mass privatization in mid-1994. They found first that the state remained a dominant owner (with a stake of over 40 percent of shares) in 38 percent of firms surveyed (firms are weighted by employment). Firms with a dominant private owner were overwhelmingly privatized to insiders (more than 70 percent). As measure of restructuring performance they use both a composite index of eleven variables and labor productivity. Using different specifications, the general findings from OLS regressions are that private ownership has a small positive impact on enterprise performance. The impact is large in cases of insider (managerial) ownership and of ownership by investment funds but insignificant with other forms of outside ownership. They then correct for endogeneity (the better firms being selected for privatization) also using as instrument the privatization method. The main difference obtained in the instrumental variable approach is that outside ownership has a significant impact except for dispersed ownership, which has a negative impact on enterprise performance. The difference between the instrumental variable and the OLS approach thus suggests that the better firms were privatized to managers and the weaker ones to outside owners. However, the performance measures relate to the period immediately after privatization, and further studies on Russia are needed, especially in the light of subsequent events such as the generalization of barter and important increases in payment arrears.

Of particular interest is the comparative study by Frydman and colleagues (1999). They used panel survey data for 209 midsize manufacturing firms (with between 100 and 1,500 employees) in the Czech Republic, Hungary, and Poland in the fall of 1994. The ownership structure of the sample was roughly 25 percent insider owned, 25 percent foreign owned, 20 percent ownership by investment funds, and the remaining 15 percent dominantly state owned. Their dependent variables are the growth rates of enterprise revenue, employment, productivity, and unit costs. They use a fixed effect estimation. This approach can take care of the potential endogeneity problem only if one assumes that the selection effects do not change over time. They found that outsider privatization had a positive impact on revenue and productivity growth and that insider privatization helped to reduce layoffs. Among outside owners, foreign ownership contributes significantly to revenue and employment growth, while ownership by domestic financial firms and large minority state ownership lead to increased revenue and productivity growth. The latter result is a priori astonishing and suggests state passivity in those firms. The effect of the second-largest owner mirrors quite closely effects found for the largest private owner. Note that ownership transferred to domestic outsiders as individuals has no effect on performance. Privatization has no effect on cost cutting. This last result suggests that privatization is more important for strategic restructuring than for defensive restructuring and that the latter can occur before privatization, in line with the analysis of the previous chapter.

Using the same data set, Frydman and colleagues (in press) showed that measures of major product restructuring have an important positive impact on revenue growth for outsider-owned firms but not for insider-owned and state firms. Interestingly, this impact remains strong even in outsider-privatized firms where management was not replaced. More broadly, the results of these last two papers confirm the importance of the distinction elaborated by Grosfeld and Roland (1997) between defensive and strategic restructuring. Defensive restructuring takes place in privatized enterprises as well as in SOEs. However, strategic restructuring as measured by revenue growth is affected by ownership. Outsider-privatized firms perform significantly better than SOEs or insider-privatized firms from the point of view of strategic restructuring.

Grosfeld and Nivet (1997a, 1997b) have looked at the impact of defensive and strategic restructuring in a large sample of Polish firms (see also Chapter 9) up to 1994. They find that privatized firms invest significantly more and grow faster, confirming the effect of privatization on strategic restructuring. They do not distinguish between different types of privatization, but in their sample privatization occurred through sales to strategic investors.

Marcincin and van Wijbergen (1997) found that in the Czech Republic firms privatized entirely through vouchers tended to be of lower initial quality than firms privatized through sales or partial sales. They found that privatization to outsiders had a positive though small impact on performance and that, after controlling for the selection effect, firms privatized entirely via vouchers had weaker performance.

Weiss and Nikitin (1998) also analyzed privatization in the Czech Republic. They found that concentrated outside ownership has an effect on changes in enterprise performance only in the case of outside ownership other than the investment funds. This result comes out even stronger if one regresses changes in performance against changes in ownership composition. The latter eliminates any initial selection effect but is a noisy measure of control, as a dominant owner may reduce his ownership stake after having secured control over a firm. They attribute partly the lack of performance of ownership by investment funds to the perverse corporate governance arrangements and to the asset stripping that has been taking place ("tunneling") exploiting the lack of protection of minority shareholders.

Prasnikar and Svejnar (1998) used data from Slovenia to test whether asset stripping had been taking place. They tested whether managers of SOEs who are also owners of private firms underinvested in the former and found this was not the case. They found that outside ownership has a positive effect on investment behavior but none on wage-setting behavior. This finding suggests that privatization has not reduced the bargaining power of workers inside the firms.

Lizal and Svejnar (1997) use micro data on 3,000 medium and large industrial firms in the Czech Republic between 1992 and 1995 to analyze strategic restructuring and the investment behavior of firms depending on their ownership status. They find that foreign companies tend to invest the most and cooperative firms the least. Private joint-stock companies tend to invest more than state-owned joint-stock companies. However, private/limited liability companies invested relatively little, while state-owned/limited liability companies invested more than domestic private firms in 1994 and 1995.

The 1999 EBRD Transition Report has produced preliminary evidence on the broader rent-seeking environment of privatization by examining the link between state governance, the degree of state capture, and the results of privatization. A business survey was used to get an indirect measure of the capture of the state by powerful business interests. Firms were asked whether the sale to private interests of parliamentary votes or presidential decrees had an impact on their business. In Russia, Moldova, Ukraine, and Azerbaijan, more than 40 percent of firms felt a significant impact from the sale of government legislation, whereas in Uzbekistan and Slovenia, fewer than 10 percent of firms report a significant impact. There are thus "high-capture" and "low-capture" countries. Moreover, the influence on government appears to be concentrated in a small number of firms. In general, fewer than 5 percent of firms surveyed reported that they have a significant influence on policymaking. There is a negative correlation between the degree of capture, as measured by the degree of response to the question on the impact of sale of legislation, and a general measure of governance that measures the effectiveness, as perceived by business firms, of state governance in areas of regulation, taxation, inflation, policy instability, physical infrastructure, and law and order. Even more interestingly, it is found that the effect of privatization on the quality of governance differs depending on the degree of capture of government: in low-capture states, progress in large-scale privatization is associated with a better quality of state governance, whereas in high-capture states, progress in privatization is associated with a lower quality of governance! The latter group includes Azerbaijan, Ukraine, Romania, Croatia, Bulgaria, Moldova, Kyrgyzstan, Georgia, and Russia.

Overall, the evidence so far on transition economies does tend to confirm prior analyses of the economic effects of privatization, namely, that privatization in former socialist economies can contribute to the enhancement of enterprise performance provided sound corporate governance arrangements are put in place. It is thus not true that any form of privatization is always better than state ownership. In particular, insider privatization in Central Europe and privatization to investment funds in the Czech Republic show disappointing results, and dispersed outside ownership can even cause performance to deteriorate.

The empirical literature tends to show the importance of using the privatization process to achieve a better matching of managerial skills with assets. Many of these analyses, however, were conducted a very short period after the completion of privatization. Empirical analysis over an extended time period will improve our understanding of the policies followed. Comparative analyses across countries like those of Frydman and colleagues (1999) are very useful in assessing the overall process. Further research is needed to better assess the impact of the specific privatization policies followed in the various countries, controlling for country-specific characteristics. Such cross-country analysis is also needed to understand not only the impact of specific privatization methods but also the impact of the legal, financial, and political environment. Empirical research is also needed to understand the channels of hardening of budget constraints through privatization methods. Has insider privatization, for example, contributed to harden budget constraints, and in what way?

The empirical literature on privatization in transition economies is important for economics in general because it tells us a lot about the corporate governance of firms, their relation to government, and the specific channels through which economic efficiency is enhanced at the micro level.

CHAPTER 11

INCENTIVES WITHIN GOVERNMENT BUREAUCRACY

In Chapter 8 we analyzed the coordination problems of law enforcement, yielding multiplicity of equilibria, including possible collapse of government. We also analyzed some institutional mechanisms that make it possible to prevent collapse in government. In this chapter we take a complementary, more microeconomic approach to the topic of Chapter 8 and look at the incentives of government agents or agencies within the general organization of government in transition economies.

This is a very important issue. As seen in Chapter 8, government collapse does not allow property rights to be secured, a first-order effect in transition. However, violation of private property rights originates often, sometimes most often, in predatory behavior by government agents who abuse their power to regulate, to deliver licenses and permits, to inspect, and so on. Government agents instructed to implement a reform may oppose it and sabotage implementation passively or actively because they see the reforms as a threat to their own interests. It would be illusory to believe that economic reforms can simply be implemented by decree from above if these reforms face general hostility by the government administration. In Part I we analyzed ways to overcome political constraints to the adoption and implementation of reform. However, it is still a distinct issue to give government agents incentives that are sufficiently aligned with economic efficiency.

This issue of incentives within government has been much overlooked in transition debates in Eastern Europe. To many radical reformers in Eastern Europe, the priority was to privatize the bulk of SOEs and to reduce the size of government. They overlooked the danger of abuse of power by individual government bureaucrats in a generally delinquent state structure and the deleterious effects of such abuse on market development and entry of new private firms. Shleifer and Vishny (1997), for example, showed that bribe taking in Russia is like the double-marginalization problem in industrial organization: uncoordinated and sequential bribe taking by various government bureaucrats and agencies leads to a bribe tax that is greater than that of a corrupt government where bribes are decided centrally.

China provides some of the most interesting lessons from the transition experience from the point of view of incentives within government. China's experience is unique in the sense that privatization was an ideological taboo until very recently, and still partly is today. Nevertheless, China has experienced a tremendous growth since reforms started in 1978. GNP grew at an average of 9.5 percent per year between 1979 and 1998 compared to an average of 6.1 percent between 1953 and 1978 (Hussain, Stern, and Stiglitz, 1999). Most of that growth came from the development of the nonstate sector and especially from the so-called township and village enterprises (TVEs). The development of TVEs, like many other developments in China, is a completely spontaneous development and was not the result of any deliberate policy of the Chinese government. Between 1978 and 1993 the TVEs share of national industrial output went from 9 to 36 percent (Che and Qian, 1998b). TVEs started to develop very fast after the launch of agricultural reform, yielding a growth of rural industrial output of 21 percent between 1978 and 1985, and maintaining rapid growth throughout the 1990s (Naughton, 1995). Indeed, decollectivization allowed not only for spectacular growth in agricultural output from 1978 onward (see McMillan, Whalley, and Zhu, 1989; Lin, 1992), but also released an important proportion of the workforce from the land. Between 1979 and 1997 the share of farm labor in total labor dropped from 71 to 47 percent. Not only was entry of TVEs spectacular because of the excess labor force released by agricultural reform, but the performance of the sector is also one of the major successes of Chinese reforms. Early research by Svejnar (1990) found that productive efficiency in TVEs was not lower than in private firms and that TVEs learned quickly to operate without hoarding labor. The big question in China, therefore, is why such spectacular successes with TVEs have been achieved despite the absence of privatization and despite the absence of a genuine private sector alongside the state sector.

In this chapter we highlight some of the responses that have been put forward in the transition literature to answer that question. To do so, one needs to look at how the organization of government structures the incentives of particular government bureaucrats, at different levels of government. The main thread that goes through this chapter is decentralization of government. We saw in Chapter 2 that the organization of Chinese planning along provincial lines, analogous to the M-form in business organizations, played an important role in allowing for local experiments with reform, which lowered the cost of experimentation. Here we look at other aspects of decentralization in relation to incentives that are directly relevant for understanding transition in China and that also carry more general lessons for other transition countries, and even beyond.

First of all, the decentralization of government has allowed for forms of competition between local governments. Competition between governments is not necessarily good from the welfare point of view because of the externalities involved. However, in the context of transition, competition between governments may help to accelerate the reform process and even change their incentives in the direction of more efficiency. For example, liberalization by some regions may be followed by liberalization from other regions if mobility of goods cannot easily be prevented (recall our discussion in Chapter 6). Fiscal competition, to attract foreign and private capital, can change the incentives of local governments in the direction of more efficiency. In section 11.1, we show how fiscal competition can be used to harden budget constraints, in the absence of privatization. This discussion leads us to predict that SOEs under the supervision of lower-level governments would face better incentives than SOEs supervised by central government.

Mutatis mutandis, the same argument can be applied broadly to the small countries in Central Europe. For example, as already mentioned in Chapter 2, Poland, Hungary, and the Czech Republic were, from the beginning of transition, engaged in an implicit competition to be the "most advanced" country in transition with the hope of thereby attracting foreign investment to their country rather than to a "competitor" country.[1]

Second, decentralization of government along regional lines rather than along functional lines can also improve the incentives of government bureaucrats. The idea, explored by Maskin, Qian, and Xu (in press) and discussed in section 11.2, relies on the fact that aggregation of government tasks by region (M-form) rather than by function (U-form) allows better exploitation of yardstick competition when aggregation of government performance by region yields a more precise measure of performance than aggregation along functional lines.

Third, incentives of various government levels can be strongly affected by the public finance arrangements in the country. We will see in section 11.3 that the Chinese public finance arrangements give local authorities correct incentives for tax collection but also incentives to support economic growth and the nonstate sector. In contrast, in Russia the public finance arrangements encourage local governments to be predatory toward private business.

Section 11.4 deals with the TVE phenomenon. Indeed, important improvements in enterprise incentives have taken place in China despite the absence of privatization programs. Most of these improvements have taken place in the township and village enterprises, which are not privately owned but started booming after the beginning of the reform process (see, e.g., Weitzman and Xu, 1993; Bolton, 1995; and D. Li, 1995). The development of the TVEs can be seen as an original response to the specific Chinese institutional context where private property rights are not protected and where the rule of law is not established, in the absence of a democratic government. This experience shows all the more the importance of the organization of government and how specific arrangements in the organization of government can align the interests of government bureaucrats with the development of markets and of growth.

11.1   FEDERALISM AND THE HARDENING OF BUDGET CONSTRAINTS

The model of Qian and Roland (1998) takes as its basis the modified version of the Dewatripont-Maskin model with moral hazard discussed in Chapter 9 and embeds it in a public finance setup. The economy is composed of N identical regions, which can

[1] *This competition was omnipresent early in transition. The Hungarians boasted constantly that they had the most early experience with reforms and with dealing with foreign firms. The Czechs boasted that they had the most rapid privatization program, while the Poles boasted of having started with shock therapy in 1990 before anyone else. The following anecdote is telling: I remember in late 1993 talking in Budapest to Hungarian economists coming back from a meeting in Brussels. They were upset because the Poles had come up with figures for the share of the private sector (de novo plus privatized firms) that were higher than the other countries. I heard the following comment: "Let us adopt the Polish broad definition of the private sector and show that we have the largest private sector."*

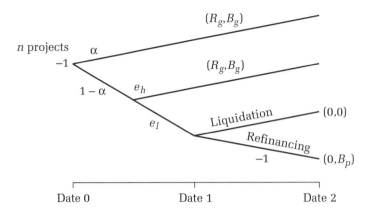

FIGURE 11.1 THE SOFT-BUDGET-CONSTRAINT GAME BETWEEN A GOVERNMENT AND AN SOE

be viewed as Chinese provinces or lower-level governments. There is thus one central government and N local governments.

Figure 11.1, which is nearly identical to Figure 9.5, shows the timing of the basic game between a government authority and the enterprises under its jurisdiction. At date 0, there are n (n large) SOEs having a project in place. As in Chapter 9, there is a proportion α of good projects and a proportion $(1 - \alpha)$ of poor projects. There is asymmetric information on the project type. Good projects yield, at date 1, a taxable return of R_g and a nonverifiable (nontaxable) private benefit B_g accruing to management and workers of the SOE. Poor projects yield the same outcome (R_g, B_g) only if high effort e_h is put in the project. One can interpret high effort as restructuring efforts. Private benefit B_g is assumed to be net of effort. However, if low effort e_l is chosen, then the project yields $(0, 0)$ at date 1. In that case, the government authority has the choice between either terminating the project, leaving it at outcome $(0, 0)$, or bailing it out by injecting a subsidy of 1. In that case, the outcome will be (R_p, B_p) at date 2. For simplicity, it is assumed that $R_p = 0$. The important assumption is that $B_p > B_g > 0$. This means that a manager with a poor project prefers to put up low effort rather than high effort if he knows he can expect a bailout, and vice versa he will have an incentive to restructure if he expects to be terminated. For simplicity, there is no discounting.

The only difference with the Dewatripont-Maskin framework is that the adverse selection problem of submitting a project is replaced with a moral-hazard problem of providing effort. The basic sequential structure is nevertheless the same, as there is the ex post choice of bailing out a project or not, with this choice influencing the ex ante choice of management in the direction of more or less efficiency.[2]

11.1.1 SOFT BUDGET CONSTRAINTS UNDER CENTRALIZED GOVERNMENT

This sequential structure is now embedded in a richer public finance setup. At date 1 nonstate enterprises invest capital K_i in region i with a technology represented by the production function $f(K_i, I_i)$, where I_i represents public infrastructure investment in region i financed from the government budget at date 1. The production function is assumed to have standard properties:

$$f_K(K_i, I_i) > 0, \quad f_I(K_i, I_i) > 0, \quad f_{KK}(K_i, I_i) < 0, \quad f_{II}(K_i, I_i) < 0, \quad f_{KI}(K_i, I_i) > 0 \qquad \text{(11.1)}$$

The most important assumption is that public infrastructure investment raises the marginal productivity of nonstate capital. Nonstate capital can be interpreted either as foreign capital or as domestic nonstate capital. In what follows, we will use the interpretation of foreign capital. As this is a model involving fiscal competition, it is assumed for analytical simplicity that the total amount of capital $K = \sum_{i=1}^{N} K_i$ is fixed but that there is perfect capital mobility across regions, implying that the return on capital must be equalized across regions:

$$f_K(K_i, I_i) = f_K(K_j, I_j) \qquad \text{(11.2)}$$

Let us now look at the government budget at date 1. Tax revenues T_i come exclusively from state enterprises. It is assumed that all verifiable revenues of SOEs are taxed away.[3] Nonstate capital is assumed not to be taxed, a reasonable assumption in the case of China.[4] On the expenditure side, the budget is used for three purposes: bailout subsidies S_i, public infrastructure investment I_i, and local public goods z_i. The budget can be written in the following form:

$$T_i - S_i = E_i = I_i + z_i \qquad \text{(11.3)}$$

If budget constraints are hard, then firms with poor projects choose high effort and we have $E_i^H = nR_g$, and if budget constraints are soft, low effort will be chosen and we have $E_i^S = \alpha nR_g - (1-\alpha)n$. It is clear that $E_i^H > E_i^S$.

Local government in region i is assumed to maximize welfare W_i, and central government maximizes $W = \sum_i W_i$. The population in each region consists of two groups: employees in SOEs and employees working in foreign firms. The total private benefits of the latter are denoted $x(K_i, I_i) = f(K_i, I_i) - K_i f_K(K_i, I_i)$, where $x(K_i, I_i)$ is assumed to be an increasing and concave function of I_i. Total private benefits of employees in SOEs are denoted y_i and are equal to nB_g in case of hard budget constraints and to $\alpha nB_g + (1-\alpha)nB_p$ in case of soft budget constraints. We define W_i as the sum of rents obtained by employees in the private and public sectors plus the utility derived from local public goods:

$$W_i = x(K_i, I_i) + y_i + u(z_i) \qquad \text{(11.4)}$$

where $u(z_i)$ is a concave utility function of local public goods.

Let us first look at government decisions under centralization. It seeks to choose I_i, S_i, and z_i so as to maximize equation (11.4) subject to equation (11.3). If the government

[3] Qian and Roland (1998) have a somewhat richer setup where they derive this assumption endogenously.

[4] Qian and Roland (1998) also develop the analysis for the case where nonstate capital is taxed.

could commit to terminate poor projects, then there would be no subsidies, and I_i and z_i would be chosen optimally so that

$$\frac{\partial x(K_i, I_i)}{\partial I_i} = u'(z_i) \tag{11.5}$$

$$I_i + z_i = E_i^H = nR_g$$

Noting I_i^{FB}, the first-best level of infrastructure investment solution to equation (11.5), and I_i^C, the level of I_i solving

$$\frac{\partial x(K_i, I_i)}{\partial I_i} = u'(z_i) \tag{11.6}$$

$$I_i + z_i = E_i^S = \alpha nR_g - (1 - \alpha)n$$

then under centralization there will be a soft budget constraint and no hard budget constraint if

$$B_p > \frac{\partial x(K_i, I_i^C)}{\partial I_i} \tag{11.7}$$

Indeed, given the objective function W, the cost of not bailing out is B_p, whereas the benefit is $u'(z_i) = \frac{\partial x(K_i, I_i)}{\partial I_i}$. The ex post cost from not bailing out is thus higher than the ex post benefit. Note also that as $E_i^H > E_i^S$ and as $x(K_i, I_i)$ and $u(z_i)$ are concave, we will have $I_i^C < I_i^{FB}$ and $\frac{\partial x(K_i, I_i^C)}{\partial I_i} > \frac{\partial x(K_i, I_i^{FB})}{\partial I_i}$. As $B_p > \frac{\partial x(K_i, I_i^{FB})}{\partial I_i}$, there cannot be a hard budget constraint, since the government would gain ex post from bailing out SOEs with poor projects.

11.1.2   The Hardening Effect of Fiscal Decentralization

Under the same assumptions as before, let us now look at the case of decentralization where local governments collect all tax revenues from their region and are fully responsible for public expenditures in their region. Local governments now maximize W_i. However, under decentralization local governments can compete with each other. In particular, they will compete with each other in trying to attract foreign capital to their region. In doing so, they will not internalize the externalities they impose on other regions.

Note indeed that by increasing the level of public infrastructure investment in region i, the authorities of that region attract capital to their region and away from other regions:

$$f_{KK}(K_i, I_i) < 0 \text{ and } f_{KI}(K_i, I_i) > 0 \implies \frac{dK_i}{dI_i} > 0 \text{ and } \frac{dK_j}{dI_i} < 0$$

Indeed, by total differentiation of equation (11.2) we get

$$f_{KK}(K_i, I_i)\frac{dK_i}{dI_i} + f_{KI}(K_i, I_i) = f_{KK}(K_j, I_j)\frac{dK_j}{dI_i}$$

Using the fact that $K = \sum_{i=1}^{N} K_i$, we have $\frac{dK_i}{dI_i} + \sum_{j \neq i} \frac{dK_j}{dI_i} = 0$. Assuming initially that $I_i^* = I_j$ for all j, we have $\frac{dK_i}{dI_i} = -(n-1)\frac{dK_j}{dI_i}$. By making the adequate replacements, the result immediately follows.

Fiscal competition between regions to attract capital is of course a zero-sum game given the fact that capital is fixed. Nevertheless, its incentive effects are interesting. Because of the fiscal competition, the first-order condition for local government i becomes

$$\frac{\partial x(K_i, I_i)}{\partial I_i} + \frac{\partial x(K_i, I_i)}{\partial K_i}\frac{dK_i}{dI_i} = u'(z_i) \tag{11.8}$$

For hard budget constraints to obtain, we must have I_i^D and z_i^D be a solution to equation (11.8) subject to $I_i + z_i = E_i^H$ and at the same time have

$$\frac{\partial x(K_i, I_i^D)}{\partial I_i} + \frac{\partial x(K_i, I_i^D)}{\partial K_i}\frac{dK_i}{dI_i} > B_p > \frac{\partial x(K_i, I_i^C)}{\partial I_i} \tag{11.9}$$

As we see, the left-hand side indicates the marginal benefit from infrastructure investment to the local government or the opportunity cost of bailing out SOEs. If fiscal competition is strong enough, that is, if $\frac{\partial x(K_i, I_i^D)}{\partial K_i}\frac{dK_i}{dI_i}$ is big enough, then fiscal competition can harden budget constraints by increasing strongly the marginal benefit of infrastructure investment to the region as compared to the marginal benefit for the country as a whole. The allocative distortion of fiscal competition can thus be used to correct the inefficiency related to the soft budget constraint. Note that for hard budget constraints to prevail, we must have $z_i^D < z_i^C$ despite the fact that hard budget constraints lead to a higher government budget $E_i^H > E_i^S$. Indeed, equations (11.6) and (11.8) imply that $u'(z_i^D) > B_p > u'(z_i^C)$, which by concavity of $u(z_i)$ implies that $z_i^D < z_i^C$. The threshold of local public goods below which hard budget constraints will obtain is $\underline{z} = u'^{-1}(B_p)$.

Decentralization of government thus implies a trade-off. On one hand, there is a distortion toward excess infrastructure investment, but on the other hand, there may be harder budget constraints that increase government revenues and may potentially increase W_i. Figure 11.2 shows the welfare trade-off.

Fiscal decentralization may thus make it possible to solve the lack of commitment to refrain from bailing out SOEs. Note that the commitment to decentralization is itself self-enforced. Indeed, after observing the allocative choices of local governments at date 1, the central government would find it impossible to bail out enterprises because revenues would already have been spent. At the same time the central government would have no incentives to recentralize ex ante if expected welfare is higher under decentralization than under centralization.

11.1.3   PARTIAL DECENTRALIZATION: FISCAL AND MONETARY POLICY

Qian and Roland (1998) extend the model in several ways. First, they analyze the effect of partial decentralization where central government keeps some revenues that it can redistribute in the form of earmarked grants to local governments. This case is interesting because it allows us to look at the case of soft budget constraints of local governments.

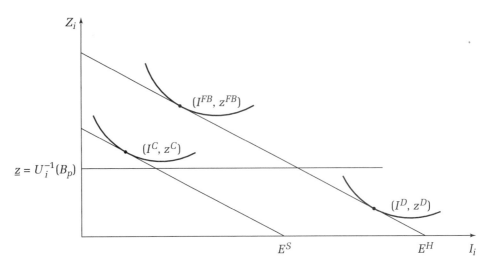

FIGURE 11.2 THE WELFARE TRADE-OFF OF FISCAL DECENTRALIZATION: HARDER BUDGET CONSTRAINTS BUT AN ALLOCATIVE DISTORTION IN PUBLIC GOOD PROVISION

When there is only partial decentralization, then local governments can compete for grants, that is, try to get a larger grant than other local governments. They can do so by distorting their expenditure decisions if they can receive grants ex post. In that case, they may distort their expenditures toward even more infrastructure investment so as to try to attract more grants for governments. Such competition for grants is again a zero-sum game but still may lead to hard budget constraints for SOEs despite the fact that budget constraints of local governments are soft!

The softness of budget constraints of local governments is somewhat different than in the usual Dewatripont-Maskin sense. Indeed, first of all, the softness of budget constraints is only an off-equilibrium event. Only if all local governments kept their allocative decisions fixed could a local government extend its budget, that is, attract a larger grant from central government. In equilibrium, since regions are equal, they all distort their allocative decisions equally and receive equal grants.

This mechanism is the same as the one analyzed by Wang (1991). In his model decentralization is seen as increased autonomy given to enterprises. Enterprises receive from the central planner fixed investment and circulating capital, which are combined in a Cobb-Douglas production function. With increased autonomy, enterprises can decide how to allocate funds between fixed investment and circulating capital. Enterprises will then strategically distort the use of funds by allocating all funds to circulating capital in the hope of attracting more funds from the central government for fixed investment. The lesson is that more enterprise autonomy, but not complete autonomy, can lead to a softening of budget constraints, on one hand, because it gives more room for strategic distortions to obtain funds, but on the other hand, because the autonomy is only partial and enterprises still depend on government funding.

Qian and Roland also extend the model to analyze interaction between fiscal and monetary policy. If the grants from central government are financed from increasing the money supply in an accommodating way, that is, if decisions on earmarked grants are made after the allocative decisions of local governments, then hard budget constraints of SOEs may still be obtained. However, this approach will always result in higher inflation than under a regime of fiscal and monetary centralization where SOEs have soft budget constraints.[5] The reason is that the allocative distortions by local governments increase the marginal benefit of inflation for central government, leading to a higher equilibrium inflation level.

Interestingly, in a situation where there is an ex ante commitment to monetary creation and seignoriage allocation between regions and where local governments have full control over the use of revenues, including allocated seignoriage, hard budget constraints of SOEs go together with a lower inflation rate than under fiscal and monetary centralization. Indeed, the expectation that local governments will distort their expenditures reduces the marginal benefit of inflation and thus the equilibrium level of inflation. The conflict of interest between the central monetary authority and the local governments thus leads to less inflation. This can be seen as a "checks and balance" effect or a "separation of powers" effect.[6]

A pathological case is that of fiscal and monetary decentralization. Monetary decentralization means that local governments have the power to print money. This is a rare situation, but it has occurred in Brazil, in the former Soviet Union after the fall of communism, and de facto in China in the late 1980s when local governments had the power to force the local branches of the central bank to extend credit and print money. In such cases, high inflation results (and thus also soft budget constraints) because there is a tragedy-of-the-commons situation: local governments impose on other regions a share of the inflationary costs of the increase in money supply in their region while they reap all the benefits.

11.1.4   COMPARATIVE STATICS: SOEs versus TVEs

Comparative statics on the same model can shed light on why township and village enterprises (TVEs), owned by lower-level localities, may have harder budget constraints than SOEs, owned by higher-level regional authorities (Qian and Roland, 1996). For simplicity, we omit infrastructure investment from the model. The condition for a soft budget constraint is then $B_p > u'\{n[\alpha R_g - (1 - \alpha)]\}$. The budget constraint will be hardened if B_p is lowered so that $B_p < u'(nR_g)$. If we interpret B_p as rents workers can get depending on labor market conditions, then one can argue that such rents are lower in TVEs than in SOEs. Indeed, labor market competition is stronger in rural areas, and hiring and firing rules are more flexible. Moreover, employees in SOEs are subject to welfare regulations entitling them to receive health and disability insurance, pensions, and the like according to national standards. Such regulations do not exist for TVEs (Walder, 1995). On top of that, as a legacy from central planning, employees in SOEs receive all sorts of services from their enterprise (housing, day care, meals, medical services, and so on). This is not the case for TVEs.

[5] If there are soft budget constraints under fiscal centralization, the additional financial source of money creation increases total financial means. Given the concavity of $x(K_i, I_i)$, condition (11.7) is even more likely to hold.

[6] For an analysis of checks and balances and separation of powers in a democracy where legislators and executive are subject to electoral accountability, see Persson, Roland, and Tabellini (1997).

TVEs tend to be much smaller in size than SOEs. The soft-budget-constraint syndrome is often associated with big enterprises and the "too big to fail" motive. Assume that enterprises have a variable size L. Let $F(L)$ be the cumulative density function measuring the proportion of firms from size 0 to L. Let $C(L)$ be the cost borne by the government when an enterprise of size L is closed down. Assume $C(L)$ to be a convex function. This convexity may be due to layoff externalities: the more people are laid off, the higher the probability of social unrest. It may also be due to other reasons, such as congestion effects on the labor market resulting from high unemployment levels. If B_p measures rents per workers of staying in the enterprise, then we can define a size L^* such that

$$B_p + \frac{C(L^*)}{L^*} = u'[n\{F(L^*)R_g + [1 - F(L^*)]\alpha R_g - (1 - \alpha)\}] \tag{11.10}$$

The left-hand side represents the net benefit per employee of bailing out en enterprise, whereas the right-hand side represents the cost per employee of bailout. Because of the convexity of $C(L)$, enterprises with size below L^* will have hard budget constraints, and enterprises with size above L^* with poor projects will have soft budget constraints.

TVEs are under the jurisdiction of local governments. The local governments thus tend to have relatively few TVEs under their jurisdiction compared to the number of SOEs under the jurisdiction of larger regional governments. With a smaller number of enterprises, the opportunities for cross-subsidization from good to poor projects become smaller, and this fact tends to harden budget constraints. Assume thus that n is small but larger than 2. Call p the probability of an enterprise with a poor project choosing high effort in a symmetric mixed-strategy equilibrium. Assume the government will refinance all projects as long as it can generate enough revenue, and assume that $R_g > n - 1$ so that revenue from one good project can refinance $n - 1$ projects. Out of $n - 1$ projects, the probability of having at least one good project or one poor project with high effort is $1 - (1 - \alpha)^{n-1}(1 - p)^{n-2}$. In a mixed-strategy equilibrium, p is chosen such that an enterprise with a poor project is indifferent between choosing high or low effort:

$$[1 - (1 - \alpha)^{n-1}(1 - p)^{n-2}]B_p = B_g$$

One sees immediately that $\frac{dp}{dn} = [\ln(1 - \alpha) + \ln(1 - p)]\frac{1-p}{n-2}$, which is negative. A reduction in n thus hardens budget constraints.

All these straightforward extensions tend to show that TVEs are more likely to have hard budget constraints than SOEs.

11.1.5 EMPIRICAL EVIDENCE AND APPLICATIONS

The discussion of the model of this section follows closely some of the features of Chinese transition and the decentralization of its government structures. In 1994 local expenditures represented 60 percent of government expenditures in China. The corresponding figure is 34 percent in industrialized countries and 22 percent in developing countries (World Bank, 1996).[7] During the 1980s, SOEs supervised by local governments accounted for about three-quarters of state industrial output.

[7] *One should of course be cautious in comparing these figures, since China is the most populous country in the world.*

D. Li (1997), in his study of enterprise behavior (which we used in Chapter 9) found that SOEs with directors appointed by local governments were more likely to reduce workers' wages and bonuses in case of poor performance (net output and profits) than directors appointed by central governments, thus suggesting that supervision of SOEs by local governments leads to a hardening of budget constraints as compared to supervision by central government. The evidence by Anderson, Korsun, and Murrell (1997) on Mongolia, also cited in Chapter 9, showed that local government ownership, unlike central government ownership, did not tend to soften budget constraints, controlling for obvious characteristics such as the size of firms. This finding suggests that the hardening effect of decentralization of government goes beyond China.

Between 1994 and 1997 local governments took important restructuring initiatives with respect to the SOEs under their supervision. These initiatives took the form of massive layoffs or of privatization. In 1996 and 1997 more than 10 million workers per year were laid off. By 1996 counties such as Yibin of Sichuan, Shunde of Guangdong, and Zhusheng of Shandong had privatized their enterprises. By 1997 more than half of the SOEs under local supervision had been privatized.

Fiscal competition has been present in China, especially in infrastructure investment, where complaints about duplication have been voiced regularly in the Chinese press and among academics (see, e.g., Wong, 1991). Broadman and Sun (1997) show that the level of infrastructure development plays a significant role in attracting foreign direct investment across provinces.

China's monetary institutions have changed greatly in recent years along lines close to this model. Before 1993 there were episodes of either near-complete monetary decentralization or very accommodating monetary policy (see Qian and Weingast, 1996). Before 1994, 70 percent of the central bank's loans to state banks were made by the central bank's local branches, which were heavily influenced by the local governments. Since 1993, China has recentralized its monetary authority, and the central bank has ended any accommodating policy toward local governments. When Zhu Rongji became governor of the central bank, he put the local branches of the bank under the sole supervision of the headquarters. Moreover, the new central bank law of 1995 made the central bank more independent of government. Furthermore, in 1998 the thirty provincial branches of the central bank were replaced with nine cross-province regional branches, as in the U.S. Federal Reserve system. As a result of this recentralization, inflation has declined drastically, from over 20 percent in 1993 to about 2 percent in 1997.

Although the model is specific to China, it is clear that it applies to other contexts. It illustrates more generally the commitment effects of fiscal competition. This issue is important in the context of European unification where, since the introduction of the euro, the question of the adequate level of fiscal centralization or decentralization has been on the agenda. It is also important in the context of the United States, where there is renewed interest in questions of federalism. More generally, the use of game theory in models of fiscal federalism permits the capture of strategic behavior of government agencies, a feature that was absent in the pre-game-theoretic literature on fiscal federalism.

11.2   FEDERALISM AND YARDSTICK COMPETITION

There is another advantage of federalism that can play a useful role in transition (but also in broader contexts), namely, the possibility of using yardstick competition (Lazear and Rosen, 1981; Holmström, 1982; Nalebuff and Stiglitz, 1983; Shleifer, 1985) within a federal government structure.

This idea was put forward by Maskin, Qian, and Xu (in press). They start from the observation that yardstick competition has always been used more extensively in China than in the Soviet Union. Whereas in the latter aggregate plan fulfillment (or underfulfillment) by a given economics ministry was the main indicator of success (or failure), in China relative performance evaluation has been used extensively and is used in the reform process. Provinces, cities, counties, townships, and villages are continually ranked in various dimensions: growth, foreign investment, profits, implementation of reforms, and so on. For example, in the transition process, the central government has explicitly pursued a policy of encouraging regions to "get rich first." Rankings based on these various dimensions are published officially in government statistical reports and also in the mass media. Such rankings play an important role in evaluating the performance of government officials and of determining their career advancement.

Maskin, Qian, and Xu argue that yardstick competition can be used more easily when performance is aggregated along regional lines, as in the Chinese M-form organization, rather than along functional lines, as in the Soviet U-form (see the discussion in Chapter 2 on the M-form and the U-form in experimentation with reforms). Comparing two regions having each a whole array of activities and sectors appears easier than comparing two different functional ministries, such as the steel ministry and the textile industry. This approach seems easier because there may be less noisiness in comparing performances of regions than in comparing performances of sectors. If this is the case, yardstick competition can be more effective in providing incentives to bureaucrats when the government is organized along regional lines as in a federal state rather than along functional lines as in a centralized unitary state.

To see this point, let us take a much simplified version of the model of Maskin, Qian, and Xu. Assume that there are two regions A and B and two industries 1 and 2. Assume that the performance of region r has the following form:

$$R_r = e_r + \varepsilon_r \tag{11.11}$$

where e_r denotes effort by the bureaucrat managing region r and ε_r denotes a shock to regional performance. As usual in moral-hazard models, we assume that the effort of the manager is not directly observable, so that incentive schemes can be made contingent only on the observable performance R_r. It is assumed that ε_A and ε_B are jointly normally distributed with $E(\varepsilon_r) = 0$ and variances σ_A^2 and σ_B^2 and covariance σ_{AB}.

Similarly, assume that performance of industry i is given by

$$R_i = e_i + \varepsilon_i \tag{11.12}$$

where e_i denotes the effort of the head of ministry i and ε_i the industry shock. Similarly, ε_1 and ε_2 are jointly normally distributed with $E(\varepsilon_i) = 0$ and variances σ_1^2 and σ_1^2 and covariance σ_{12}.

In a federal government, when there is yardstick competition, the utility of regional bureaucrat r is given by

$$U[w(R_A, R_B)] - g(e_r) \tag{11.13}$$

where U is a concave function of a remuneration scheme $w(R_A, R_B)$ that depends on the performance of both regions, and where $g(e)$ is the disutility of effort, for which it is assumed that $g' > 0, g'' > 0$, and $g''' > 0$.

Define similarly the utility of a bureaucrat heading a functional ministry under yardstick competition in a unitary state where government administration is organized along functional lines:

$$U[w(R_1, R_2)] - g(e_i) \tag{11.14}$$

To see in which organizational form better incentives can be provided, one must look at the conditional variances that are relevant when analyzing yardstick competition. Thus if

$$\text{var}(\varepsilon_A \mid \varepsilon_B) < \text{var}(\varepsilon_1 \mid \varepsilon_2) \tag{11.15}$$

then one can show that manager A can be provided better incentives than manager 1. Moreover, if the following conditions hold, both managers A and B can be given better incentives than managers 1 and 2:

$$\min\{\text{var}(\varepsilon_A \mid \varepsilon_B), \text{var}(\varepsilon_B \mid \varepsilon_A)\} < \min\{\text{var}(\varepsilon_1 \mid \varepsilon_2), \text{var}(\varepsilon_2 \mid \varepsilon_1)\} \tag{11.16}$$
$$\max\{\text{var}(\varepsilon_A \mid \varepsilon_B), \text{var}(\varepsilon_B \mid \varepsilon_A)\} < \max\{\text{var}(\varepsilon_1 \mid \varepsilon_2), \text{var}(\varepsilon_2 \mid \varepsilon_1)\}$$

While the proposition can be proved in quite general terms, one gets more intuition by deriving it for a model with specific functional forms.

Assume that managers have an exponential utility function. Thus for manager r in a federal state we have

$$U[w_r(R_A, R_B)] = -e^{-rw_r(R_A, R_B)} \tag{11.17}$$

and the utility of a manager i in a unitary state is defined analogously. Moreover, let us restrict ourselves to linear incentive schemes. In a federal state we have

$$w_A(R_A, R_B) = a_A + b_A R_A + c_A R_B \tag{11.18}$$
$$w_B(R_A, R_B) = a_B + b_B R_A + c_B R_B$$

Linear incentive schemes for managers of industry in a unitary state can be defined analogously:

$$w_1(R_1, R_1) = a_1 + b_1 R_1 + c_2 R_2 \tag{11.19}$$
$$w_2(R_1, R_2) = a_2 + b_2 R_A + c_2 R_B$$

The form of the utility function gives us a constant absolute risk aversion r. Using the certainty equivalent expression $E(w_r) - \frac{1}{2}r \, \text{var}(w_r)$ for $U[w_r(R_A, R_B)]$, for manager r, we can express $U[w_r(R_A, R_B)] - g(e_r)$ in the following way:

$$a_r + b_r e_A + c_r e_B - g(e_r) - \tfrac{1}{2}r(b_r^2 \sigma_A^2 + c_r^2 \sigma_B^2 + 2b_r c_r \sigma_{AB}) \tag{11.20}$$

We can derive similar expressions for managers i.

Let us for now concentrate on managers A and B in a federal state. We assume the principal is risk neutral and maximizes the payoff of managers A and B net of incentive payments:

$$(1 - b_A - b_B)e_A + (1 - c_A - c_B)e_B - a_A - a_B$$

An efficient contract maximizes the sum of payoffs of the managers and the principal:

$$\max_{e_r, b_r, c_r} \ e_A - g(e_A) - \tfrac{1}{2}r(b_A^2 \sigma_A^2 + c_A^2 \sigma_B^2 + 2b_A c_A \sigma_{AB}) \tag{11.21}$$

$$+ \ e_B - g(e_B) - \tfrac{1}{2}r(b_B^2 \sigma_A^2 + c_B^2 \sigma_B^2 + 2b_B c_B \sigma_{AB})$$

The first-best level of effort e_r for manager r if effort were observable would be given by

$$1 = g'(e_r) \tag{11.22}$$

However, since effort is not observable, managers A and B will always choose their effort level so as to maximize expression (11.20) yielding first-order conditions

$$b_A = g'(e_A) \tag{11.23}$$

$$c_B = g'(e_B)$$

The optimal second-best contract thus maximizes expression (11.21) subject to the incentive constraints given by equation (11.23). Using $b_A = g'(e_A)$ to replace b_A in expression (11.21), the first-order conditions for e_A and c_A are, respectively,

$$1 - g'(e_A) = r[g'(e_A)\sigma_A^2 + c_A \sigma_{AB}]g''(e_A) \tag{11.24}$$

$$c_A = -g'(e_A)\frac{\sigma_{AB}}{\sigma_B^2} \tag{11.25}$$

Plugging in the expression for c_A in equation (11.24), the optimal effort for a manager is implicitly given by

$$1 - g'(e_A) = rg'(e_A)g''(e_A)\left(\sigma_A^2 - \frac{\sigma_{AB}}{\sigma_B^2}\right) \tag{11.26}$$

Now, given that ε_A and ε_B are jointly normally distributed with covariance σ_{AB}, it follows that

$$\text{var}(\varepsilon_A \mid \varepsilon_B) = \sigma_A^2 - \frac{\sigma_{AB}}{\sigma_B^2}$$

Denoting $\text{var}(\varepsilon_A \mid \varepsilon_B)$ by V_{AB} and differentiating equation (11.26) with respect to V_{AB} and e_A, we have

$$\frac{de_A}{dV_{AB}} = \frac{-2g'g''}{g'' + rV_{AB}(g''^2 + g'g''')} < 0 \qquad (11.27)$$

A higher conditional variance will thus yield lower incentives. *Mutatis mutandis,* using the same exercise for all managers leading to equations (11.26) and (11.27), which are analogous to derive because they differ only in their conditional variance, if conditions (11.16) hold, then managers A and B can be given better incentives than managers 1 and 2.

Maskin, Qian, and Xu (in press) give evidence based on data from 520 Chinese SOEs between 1986 and 1991 to estimate industry-specific and region-specific shocks and find that conditional variances of regional shocks tend to be smaller than the conditional variances of industrial shocks, confirming empirically that yardstick competition can work better in comparing regions than in comparing industries. They also give econometric evidence of the use of yardstick competition in the Chinese bureaucracy: an increase in the relative economic ranking of a region enhances the representation of that region (and thus its bureaucrats) in the Central Committee of the Chinese Communist Party.

The model in this section is complementary to the one in the previous sections. In the latter, factor mobility made it possible to rely on competition between regions to improve the incentives of local governments. In the model in this section, mobility is not needed, but we have another form of competition in the form of yardstick competition that can be used to improve the incentives of government officials.

Note that the model could be adapted to a democratic framework where government officials are held accountable by voters. Yardstick competition can play a role in disciplining elected officials. This would be an interesting extension to consider.

11.3 CHINESE FEDERALISM VERSUS RUSSIA

In 1980 a very interesting fiscal reform was introduced in China. Lower-level governments were held responsible for collecting taxes. According to a long-term contract, they then had to remit a lump sum fixed in the contract to the higher-level government. Local governments thus became in principle fully residual claimants on their taxes. This was not the only revenue-sharing scheme in place, but most fiscal-sharing schemes between provinces and the center were either strongly degressive or made some provinces and cities fully residual claimants on any increase in tax revenues. Moreover, so-called extrabudgetary revenues of provinces (including, among other things, profits from SOEs) were not shared with higher-level governments (Qian and Weingast, 1996). In the Chinese public finance arrangements, the sums remitted to the upper-level government are used mostly for the needs of central government and are not redistributed to local governments to any degree. Local governments thus have relatively hard budget constraints.

This is also a system in which local governments have an incentive to maximize tax revenues and thus have incentives that are better aligned with economic efficiency.[8]

Jin, Qian, and Weingast (1999) have provided some econometric estimates of the Chinese fiscal federalism and its incentive effects. They first find that there is a strong correlation between budgetary revenue and expenditure of provinces and nearly a one-to-one relation between provincial extrabudgetary revenue and expenditure. This means that at the margin any increase in provincial revenue is translated into additional provincial expenditures. However, they also find evidence of a slight ratchet effect: one yuan in increased provincial revenue leads to 0.24 yuan higher remittances to central government the next year. Nevertheless, this ratchet effect was much stronger prior to the fiscal reform, on the order of 80 percent! Also, they find evidence of ex post readjustments to the ex ante fiscal contracting scheme, with some provinces paying extra remittances and others receiving extra funds. These ex post readjustments weaken incentives but are relatively limited (around 7 percent in the early 1990s) and have been declining over time. They also find that fiscal incentives, in the form of higher contractual marginal retention rates of tax revenues by provinces, have a positive effect on investment by local government and on reform in the state sector (as measured by a higher share of contract workers in total state employment or a higher share of bonuses in total wage payments).

The Russian public finance arrangements stand in stark contrast to the Chinese ones. Instead of fixed long-term contracts, there are annual negotiations between local governments and the center to determine the amount of tax sharing and transfers from central government. Local governments thus rely much more on redistribution from central government for their expenditures, and this reliance makes them much more prone to the soft-budget-constraint syndrome. Cities' own revenues in 1997 constituted less than a fifth of their total budgetary revenues (Zhuravskaya, 1999). However, local governments are not residual claimants on collected taxes. Berkowitz and Li (in press) even model the Russian public finance system as an example of the "tragedy of the commons" where tax-sharing arrangements lead to excessive and predatory taxation by different government levels, in turn leading the private sector to hide revenues and stay in the unofficial sector. This "overgrazing" effect put forward by Berkowitz and Li (1997) represents probably the most important flaw in Russian public finance.

Zhuravskaya (1999) has produced econometric evidence on Russian public finance based on a data set from thirty-five large cities in twenty-nine regions of the Russian Federation between 1992 and 1997. She finds that any increase in their own revenues by local governments tends to be offset by a nearly one-to-one decrease in shared revenues. Moreover, weaker fiscal incentives (a negative correlation between shared revenues and their own revenues) tend, everything else equal, to cause a decrease in private sector growth, as well as spending on education and health. There is also a negative impact on the quality of health, as measured by infant mortality, and on education in the form of reduced evening school attendance by children due to crowded schools. The latter result can be interpreted in line with the results from section 11.1. Given that there is redistribution to local governments, the latter have an incentive to distort their

[8] *Obviously, maximizing revenues is different from maximizing social welfare. However, local governments that are residual claimants on tax revenues have more interest in maximizing the tax base than local governments subject to tax-sharing schemes.*

expenditures in such a way as to try to attract more grants. One way of extracting more revenues from higher-level government is to neglect health and education.

Treisman (1999c) and Shleifer and Treisman (2000) show that the dramatic decline in tax revenue in Russia and the deterioration in tax administration can be related to the perverse incentives created by these tax-sharing arrangements.

The contrasting evidence between China and Russia shows the importance of government reform in the transition process. For obvious political reasons, privatization has been delayed in China, but fiscal decentralization has helped to align the incentives of government authorities with economic efficiency. Russia, however, has followed the standard IMF–World Bank recommendations of liberalization, privatization, and stabilization, though with less success in the last. The absence of reform in the direction of sound public finance arrangements perpetuates softening of budget constraints of local governments and misaligns their interests with those of economic efficiency, thereby strongly reducing the expected positive effects of privatization.

11.4 UNDERSTANDING TOWNSHIP AND VILLAGE ENTERPRISES

An especially characteristic feature of Chinese transition is the phenomenon of TVEs. Even though private firms are allowed, their development is less spectacular than that of TVEs. In 1993 the private sector accounted for only 15 percent of industrial output in China, while TVEs accounted for 27 percent of industrial output and nearly two-thirds of the share of the nonstate sector in industrial output.

Contrary to what some observers had initially thought, TVEs are not private enterprises in disguise. They are genuinely owned by local governments that exercise their control rights (Che and Qian, 1998a). Even though managers of TVEs have considerable autonomy in their day-to-day operations, community governments play an active role in decisions on investment and finance, the selection of managers, and the use of after-tax profits for public expenditures. A challenge for researchers is thus to understand the spectacular growth and performance of TVEs given their ownership structure.

Che and Qian (1998b) came up with a theory based on the absence of the rule of law in China. The absence of the rule of law is seen as an obstacle to the development of a private sector because of the government's power to prey on the income of private firms. The latter are thus inclined to restrict their activities to those where income is mostly unobservable. In particular, this tendency restricts choices of technology to activities that are less capital-intensive and that can be based to a maximum degree on cash transactions. Even though managers in TVEs may have fewer incentives than private owners, the fact that TVEs produce local public goods that benefit the central government directly or indirectly (like law enforcement, basic public health maintenance, infrastructure, and so on) gives the central government fewer incentives to prey on TVEs. The latter are thus less inclined to hide revenues from the central government and are thus more free in their choice of technology. We saw in the model by Qian and Roland (1998) that it is important to differentiate between the behavior of local and central governments. Here we have another example. The local government can be preyed upon by central government but has partly aligned interests with it. Ownership by local government, however, gives the enterprise manager incentives that it would not have under centralized state control. The analysis is another application of the incomplete contract framework of Grossman, Hart, and Moore where the allocation of control rights plays a crucial role. The idea that TVEs play a useful role in limiting predation from central government is also expressed by Chang and Wang (1994) and D. Li (1996).

Consider a business project that lasts for two periods operated by a manager. Assume that the total first-period return is a concave function of effort provided by the manager: $R_1 = R_1(a)$ with a convex cost of effort $D(a)$. We assume that $R_1(0) > 0$ and $D(0) = 0$. Assume that the second-period return depends on the provision of local public goods by local government: $R_2 = eh(G)$ where G is total expenditure on public goods and $h(G)$ is an increasing concave function satisfying Inada conditions. The public good can be thought of, for example, as provision of transport facilities and infrastructure that allow an increase in the sales of TVE output in cities. The effectiveness of public expenditure depends on unobservable effort e provided by the local government. For simplicity, assume e takes two values: $e_l = 0$ and $e_h = e > 0$, having a cost of effort 0 and C, respectively. It is assumed that in the first period a choice can be made by the owner of the business project to hide a proportion q of R_1 so that only $(1 - q)R_1$ is observable, but this comes at a cost, so that only $\alpha(q)R_1$ can be appropriated by the owner where $\alpha(q)$ is concave with $\alpha(0) = 0$ and $\alpha'(q) < 1$. The maximum hiding is at $\overline{q} < 1$ for which $\alpha'(\overline{q}) = 0$. It is assumed that the second-period return has a fixed observable component $(1 - \lambda)$ so that λR_2 is made unobservable by the owner and $(1 - \lambda)R_2$ is observable. It is assumed that $\lambda < \frac{1}{2}$ but is strictly positive. Only observable revenue can be taxed away. The sources of local government expenditure G are remittances T by central government from first-period taxation to the local government and contributions t by the owner of the business project:

$$G = T + t$$

The timing is as follows: In the beginning of the first period, q is decided by the owner of the business and a is decided by the manager. After R_1 is realized, T and t are decided. Then effort by local government is decided, and R_2 is realized.

Before looking at different kinds of ownership, let us first characterize the first best from the point of view of a social planner. This is the solution to

$$\max_{a,T} R_1(a) - D(a) - G + \delta[eh(G) - C] \tag{11.28}$$

subject to

$$0 \leq G \leq R_1(a)$$

where δ is the discount rate. First-order conditions are

$$(1+\mu)R_1'(a) = D'(a) \tag{11.29}$$

$$1 + \mu = \delta e h'(G)$$

$$\mu[R_1(a) - G] = 0$$

where μ is the multiplier associated with the constraint $G \leq R_1(a)$.

It is assumed that revenue-based contracts cannot be enforceable and that the central government can prey on all observable revenues.

Compare three forms of ownership: private ownership by the manager and ownership by central or local government. In the model, ownership gives control rights over q and income rights on the unobservable part of income in both periods.

Under private ownership, the manager will choose to hide a maximum of revenue: $q = \overline{q}$. He will have fewer incentives than under the first best, since his marginal benefit of effort is only $\alpha(\overline{q})R_1'(a)$ instead of $(1+\mu)R_1'(a)$. Since the second-period return R_2 will accrue in proportion λ to the owner and in proportion $(1-\lambda)$ to the central government, the local government has no incentives to provide local public goods and thus receives no revenue either from central government or from the private enterprise: $T = t = 0$. There is thus a double inefficiency related to the absence of the rule of law: (1) there is inefficient revenue hiding by the private firm, and (2) local government does not have incentives for providing local public goods. In a sense, this case is close to the Russian case with private ownership but predation by a higher government level (often the level of regional governors) leading to extreme hiding by private firms and deficiency of public good provision by lower-level government.

Under ownership by the central government, there will be no revenue hiding ($q = 0$), but both the manager and local government will have no incentive ($a = 0$, $e = 0$), and no expenditures will be channeled to local government. This case is the closest to the traditional socialist economy.

The interesting case is that of ownership by local government. Two main results are interesting to derive. First of all, the central government has less incentive to prey on local governments than on private enterprise because it benefits from the local public goods provided by the latter. Second, the local government has an incentive to strictly hide less revenue than a private firm.

For the local government to have incentives to provide effort in public goods provision, it must be the case that the return to local government exceeds its cost:

$$\lambda e h(G) > C \tag{11.30}$$

Turning now to the manager, since he does not get any unobservable income, he has no incentive to put up effort. Thus, $a = 0$.

In the beginning of the second period, for q given, the central government will choose T to solve

$$\max_{T} \ (1-q)R_1(0) - T + \delta(1-\lambda)eh(t+T) \tag{11.31}$$

subject to

$$T \le (1 - q)R_1(0)$$
$$T \ge 0, \quad t \text{ given}$$

Since T are remittances to the local government, $(1 - q)R_1(0) - T$ represents revenue preyed upon by the central government. The higher the T, the lower the level of endogenous predation by central government. Simultaneously, the local government will choose t to maximize the following:

$$\max_t \ \alpha(q)R_1(0) - t + \delta\lambda eh(t + T) \tag{11.32}$$

subject to

$$t \le \alpha(q)R_1(0)$$
$$\lambda eh(G) > C$$
$$t \ge 0, \quad T \text{ given}$$

There is an inefficiency because local public expenditures are financed with voluntary contributions from both central and local government. That joint contribution system will lead to underfinancing.

Nevertheless, there is public good provision in equilibrium. Call $T^* \equiv \arg \max\{\delta(1 - \lambda)eh(T) - T\}$, that is, the optimal unconstrained choice of T by central government in case local government has contributed $t = 0$. Call likewise $t^* = \arg \max\{\delta\lambda eh(t) - t\}$, that is, the optimal unconstrained choice of local government if $T = 0$. Because of Inada conditions, $T^* > 0$ and $t^* > 0$. Assume $\lambda eh(\min[T^*, (1 - q)R_1(0)]) > C$. In that case, the incentive constraint of local government for public good provision is satisfied since $\min[T^*, (1 - q)R_1(0)] \ge G$. Note also that, since it must always be the case that $G \ge \min\{T^*, (1 - q)R_1(0), t^*, \alpha(q)R_1(0)\}$, we will always have $G > 0$.

If T were not strictly positive, from condition (11.31) it must be that $\delta(1 - \lambda)eh'(t + T) - 1 < 0$, since there would then be a corner solution. However, since $G > 0$, from condition (11.32) we must have $\delta\lambda eh'(t + T) - 1 \ge 0$ [with strict inequality if $t = \alpha(q)R_1(0)$]. Since $\lambda < \frac{1}{2}$, however, it is impossible to have $\delta\lambda eh'(t + T) - 1 \ge 0 > \delta(1 - \lambda)eh'(t + T) - 1$. We thus must have $T > 0$. We thus see that there is less predation by central government on local government than on private enterprise. This result is related to the congruence of interests between both government levels because they both benefit from the local public good.

Let us now work backward to the choice of q in the first period by local government. Assume that $T^* > (1 - \overline{q})R_1(0)$. Then we will have $T = (1 - \overline{q})R_1(0)$. Let $t(q)$ be the maximizer of

$$V(q) = \alpha(q)R_1(0) - t(q) + \delta\lambda eh[t(q) + (1 - q)R_1(0)]$$

subject to

$$t(q) \le \alpha(q)R_1(0)$$
$$t(q) \ge 0$$

By the generalized envelope theorem, thus making use of $\frac{dt}{dq} = 0$, we have

$$\frac{dV}{dq} = \alpha'(q)R_1(0) - \delta\lambda eh'[t(q) + (1-q)R_1(0)]R_1(0) + \xi\alpha'(q)R_1(0)$$

where ξ is the Lagrangian associated with the constraint $t(q) \leq \alpha(q)R_1(0)$. Since $\alpha'(\overline{q}) = 0$, $\frac{dV}{dq} < 0$ evaluated at $\overline{q}$. It is therefore profitable to reduce q below $\overline{q}$.

We thus see that there is less revenue hiding under local-government ownership. Therefore, local government may be induced to choose a more efficient technology than private enterprises.

The results by Che and Qian provide an explanation for the faster development of TVEs than private enterprises in China in the absence of the rule of law. Enterprises owned by local governments have more secured property rights because of partial alignment of interests with that of central government, owing to their role in the provision of local public goods. In 1992, 40 percent of the after-tax profits of TVEs were used for local public expenditures. In an econometric study Jin and Qian (1998) found that the higher the share of TVEs relative to private enterprises in rural nonfarm enterprises, the higher the revenue shares of both the national governments and township and village governments, after controlling for per capita income and other variables, thus showing that both the central and local governments benefit from local government ownership.

TVEs can thus be seen as an original organizational response to the failure of the state to commit to refrain from preying on private enterprises.

THE SOFT BUDGET CONSTRAINT AND FINANCIAL TRANSITION

We saw in Chapter 9 that soft budget constraints were a fundamental incentive issue under socialism and that budget constraints of firms can be hardened with privatization when enterprises are no longer financed by the government. However, we also saw in Chapter 10 that soft budget constraints of enterprises may still persist after their privatization, in particular in the context of insider privatization, under conditions where rent seeking can be more profitable than restructuring to insider owners. Privatization is thus not enough to eliminate the soft-budget-constraint problem.

Table 12.1 shows the budgetary subsidies received by enterprises in selected transition economies from Central and Eastern Europe. Subsidies to enterprises are not necessarily a measure of soft budget constraints. An unprofitable enterprise may receive government grants, for example, to sell goods at a prespecified low price that is below marginal cost. In that case, its budget constraint can be hard if it remains within the spending limits specified by its revenue and the government grant. We thus cannot equate subsidies with soft budget constraints. Nevertheless, given the past history of soft budget constraints in government–firm relationships, one can presume a rather strong correlation between softness of budget constraints and the extent of subsidies. Two things should be noticed in Table 12.1. First of all, the size of budgetary subsidies is rather low in most transition economies, given that under socialism they were in the 25 percent range. Subsidies were cut rather drastically early in transition and have been reduced further in a gradual way since then. This fact is not surprising, since such cuts were a standard recommendation of IMF-led macrostabilization programs. Second, subsidies were still important in Russia and Ukraine in 1998, when they represented a two to three times larger share of GDP than in other countries. This difference suggests that soft budget constraints are still a major problem in those countries. Interestingly, Russia went much further than Ukraine in its privatization program. More than 70 percent of Russian GDP is now produced by the private sector, whereas in Ukraine, the share of the private sector was still only around 55 percent in 1998. Nevertheless, the share of

Table 12.1 Budgetary Subsidies in Central and Eastern Europe (percent of GDP)

	1991	1992	1993	1994	1995	1996	1997
Poland	5	3.2	2.2	3.3	2.9	2.5	
Hungary	5.7	4	3.8	4.5	3.8	3.9	3.2
Czech Republic				3	2.6	2.2	2.4
Slovenia		2.5	2.1	1.6	1.6	1.2	1.3
Slovakia		4	3.9	3.2	2.8	2.4	
Bulgaria	2	1.8	2.9	1.3	1.2	0.8	0.8
Romania				3.8	4.1	4.3	2.6
Russia						7.9	8.2
Ukraine					7.5	5.9	6.4

Source: *EBRD* Transition Report *(1999).*

Table 12.2 Flow and Stock of Annual Tax Arrears in Central and Eastern Europe (percent of GDP)

	Annual Flows				Stock (end year)			
	1993	1994	1995	1996	1993	1994	1995	1996
Poland	1–2	0–1			7–9	5–7		
Hungary	1.2	0.7			6.9	7.5		
Czech Republic	1–2				3–4			
Estonia		0.6				5.7		
Lithuania		1			3.7	4.4		
Romania	1.5	3.1			1.5	4.6		
Russia		2.1	1.4	7.3	1.5	4	5.2	12

Source: *Schaffer (1998).*

budgetary subsidies to enterprises in both countries remains higher than in other transition economies.

More direct evidence of persistence of soft budget constraints is given by tax arrears. Tolerance of tax arrears is a more direct manifestation of soft budget constraints. As can be seen in Table 12.2 drawn from Schaffer (1998), there is a rising stock of tax arrears in several transition countries with significant annual flows. Notice the big jump in tax arrears in Russia in 1996.

TABLE 12.3   BANK CREDIT TO THE PRIVATE SECTOR IN CENTRAL AND EASTERN EUROPE (PERCENT OF GDP)

	1990	1991	1992	1993	1994	1995	1996	1997	1998
Poland		10.9	11.4	12.2	12	12.7	15.9	18.1	20.6
Hungary	46.3	38.8	33.2	28.2	26.2	22.3	21.7	23.4	22.8
Czech Republic				50.8	57.8	58.1	55.9	66.3	60.1
Slovenia		34.9	23.3	22.1	22.5	27.5	28.8	28.6	32.5
Slovakia				32.1	24.3	27.8	32	44.2	
Bulgaria		7.2	5.8	3.7	3.8	21.1	35.6	12.6	14.2
Romania							11.4	8.5	12.8
Russia				11.8	12.1	8.5	7.2	8.7	12.7
Ukraine			3.2	1.4	4.6	1.5	1.4	2.5	7.6

Source: *EBRD* Transition Report *(1999)*.

The persistence of soft budget constraints after privatization is in a way not surprising, since soft budget constraints are also present in advanced capitalist economies. The Dewatripont and Maskin (1995) model introduced in Chapter 9 helps us to understand why the soft budget constraint can still be present in bank–enterprise relationships even when banks behave in a profit-maximizing way. So, even after privatization, when strategic restructuring of firms depends on outside finance, and in particular on bank finance, the soft-budget-constraint problem can remain. The more challenging question is why we do not observe more soft budget constraints in the real world, since it is a problem inherent to the sunk-cost nature of investments in a firm.

Table 12.3 shows the importance of bank credit to the private sector for selected transition economies from Central and Eastern Europe. Notice the important variation across time and across countries. Interpreting these figures from the point of view of hardening of budget constraints is not easy. A low volume of credit can be an indication of several things. It can be an indication of a low level of intermediation in the economy. Budget constraints can be hard, but they can also be soft if enterprises have other sources of soft finance like tax arrears, for example. A low volume of lending can also be the indication of a credit squeeze, which can be interpreted as a hardening of budget constraints. But, as we will see in this chapter, it is possible to have coexistence of a credit crunch and soft budget constraints with the bailing out of certain firms crowding out finance to new projects. A high volume of credit can similarly be interpreted as an indication of a high level of intermediation and liquidity provision but also of soft budget constraints.

The size of the bad loans held by banks in selected transition economies from Central and Eastern Europe shown in Table 12.4 gives us a better idea of the extent of soft budget constraints. The size of bad loans increased in Poland and Hungary in the

T**ABLE** 12.4 T**HE** S**HARE OF** N**ONPERFORMING** B**ANK** L**OANS IN** C**ENTRAL AND** E**ASTERN** E**UROPE**
(**AS A PERCENT OF TOTAL LOANS**)

	1991	1992	1993	1994	1995	1996	1997	1998
Poland	16.5	26.8	36.4	34.7	23.9	14.7	11.5	11.5
Hungary	9.4	20.7	25.6	30.2	10.3	7.2	3.6	5.9
Czech Republic	2.7	19.3	22.1	35.8	32.7	28.1	26.5	26.7
Slovenia				22	13.2	14.3	12.5	11.5
Slovakia			12.2	30.3	41.3	31.8	33.4	44.3
Bulgaria			6.6	6.8	12.6	14.6	12.9	
Romania				18.5	37.9	48	57	34.2
Russia					5.9	5.1	3.5	4.6

Source: *Anderson and Kegels (1997)*, EBRD Transition Report *(1999)*.

first years of transition but has decreased since 1995. A similar pattern emerges for the Czech Republic except that the level of bad loans remains higher. Early in transition, macroeconomic stabilization programs led to drastic cuts in budgetary subsidies, and bank finance then became an important channel of soft budget constraints as soft bank credits replaced subsidies. However, this shift inevitably led to increases in the share of bad loans held by banks. Measures were then taken in various countries to take care of the bad loan problem. The widely publicized Polish program to deal with bad loans included bank recapitalization made conditional on the restructuring of bad loans by means of debt-equity swaps and other procedures. Banks proved very reluctant to exchange debt for equity, but the "bank conciliation" procedure proved a very popular way to restructure debts. That procedure required agreement of only 50 percent of the creditors for a restructuring plan. In effect, many smaller creditors like suppliers lost a lot under that procedure, but it had the positive effect of encouraging the banks to be active in dealing with their bad loan problem (see Belka, 1994, for a discussion of the Polish loan-restructuring program). Hungary went through several consecutive bank recapitalizations between 1991 and 1994 before its bad loan problem improved. In the Czech Republic the bad loan problem was addressed by establishing a state-owned "hospital" bank, the Konsolidačni Banka, to take bad loans from banks with the objective of restructuring them centrally through the hospital bank. In countries like Romania and Slovakia the bad loan problem was still very serious as of 1998. In Bulgaria and Russia it appeared less important, but the level of banking intermediation was still far lower than in the more advanced transition economies.

Table 12.5 gives the evolution of the number of banks, including foreign banks, in selected countries from Central and Eastern Europe. Foreign banks are mostly present in Hungary, Poland, and Russia. While the monobanks from socialism were dismantled,

TABLE 12.5 NUMBER OF BANKS IN CENTRAL AND EASTERN EUROPE (FOREIGN-OWNED BANKS IN PARENTHESES)

	1990	1991	1992	1993	1994	1995	1996	1997	1998
Poland	32(11)			87(10)	82(11)	81(18)	81(25)	83(29)	83(31)
Hungary		35(8)	35(12)	40(15)	43(17)	42(21)	41(25)	41(30)	40(27)
Czech Republic				45(12)	55(12)	55(13)	53(13)	50(14)	45(13)
Slovenia		40(1)	45(2)	45(5)	44(6)	41(6)	36(4)	34(4)	34(3)
Slovakia				18(3)	19(4)	25(9)	24(9)	25(9)	24(8)
Bulgaria	67	75	79	41	40(1)	41(3)	42(3)	28(7)	
Romania					20(3)	24(6)	31(8)	33(11)	36(16)
Russia						2,295(19)	2,029(23)	1,697(26)	1,476(29)
Ukraine			133	211	228(1)	230(1)	229(6)	227(12)	

Source: *EBRD* Transition Report (*1999*).

countries differ in the concentration of the banking sector. Russia has a large number of banks, even relative to the size of the country, whereas Slovakia has a relatively small number of banks. Here, an important transition-specific question to ask is to what extent banking decentralization and a large number of small banks are good or not from the point of view of soft budget constraints.

Overall, we see that soft budget constraints can persist and do persist after privatization. In understanding how to deal with soft budget constraints, we thus need to go further in the analysis than we did in Chapter 9. We need to ask what specific institutional solutions can be found that lead to hardening the budget constraints of firms after privatization. Answering this question is the objective of section 12.1.

We first show that decentralization of banking is an important mechanism to harden budget constraints. The main idea is that having multiple creditors increases the costs of bailing out firms ex post because of the conflicts of interests between different creditors at the renegotiation stage. The higher ex post cost of bailouts leads to hardened budget constraints, improved incentives, and ex ante efficiency. The idea of adding some ex post inefficiency to improve ex ante efficiency is one of the most important ideas in research in corporate finance of the last decade. Note the parallel between the advantages of decentralized banking with the advantages of decentralization of government discussed in Chapter 11. Second, we show how restructuring with redeployment of assets can contribute to hardening of budget constraints. Without restructuring, chains of insolvency among SOEs can form with insolvency from bad firms spilling over to good firms, creating a "too many to fail" problem that leads to generalized bailouts. This "too many to fail" problem can then only be solved after enterprise restructuring and the creation of new business links. Third, we show the importance of entry of a dynamic new private sector in hardening budget constraints of existing firms. When the quality of projects from the new private sector is high enough, banks will lose incentives to bail out existing projects, even when the net benefit of refinancing can be relatively high. Fourth, we show how investments by banks in screening technology can enhance the general quality of the pool of new loans, which can also contribute to hardening budget constraints of existing enterprises.

Some of the institutional solutions discussed in dealing with soft budget constraints of firms are partly specific to transition, such as how to untangle interconnected chains of trade arrears, but others, such as the decentralization of banking, the role of entry, and screening, have a more general message that is valid beyond transition.

Soft budget constraints of firms remain particularly pervasive when banks themselves are subject to soft budget constraints and can expect bailouts by government. The issue of dealing with the soft budget constraints of banks is analyzed in section 12.2. Early analysts of the bad loan problem had emphasized the need for bank recapitalization to solve the bad loan problem (Begg and Portes, 1993) and also to give banks correct incentives (Mitchell, 1993). At the same time, analysts acknowledged that such recapitalization could only occur once, since otherwise expectations of future bailouts would seriously dampen banks' incentives. Accumulation of bad loans indeed strengthens pressures to bail out banks, and expectations of bailouts give fewer incentives to banks to avoid accumulation of bank loans. Generalized soft budget constraints in the economy can thus perpetuate.

Several important policy questions have been raised in that framework: Under what conditions can soft budget constraints of banks be prevented? What should be the extent of necessary recapitalization to prevent future repeated bailouts? What should be the role, if any, of hospital banks to which bad loans of commercial banks are transferred, as in the Czech Republic? How should bank regulation give incentives to banks to refrain from covering bad loans so that regulators can get early enough signals of distress in the banking sector? These questions are analyzed in section 12.2, where we look at models of interaction between firms, banks, and the government.

One of the messages that come out of the models analyzed is that initial recapitalization and reserve ratios must be big enough to prevent the soft budget constraints of banks. The initial level of recapitalization and of bank reserves must be bigger, the lower is the quality of the general loan portfolio. These solutions are clearly costly for transition economies, but these costs are necessary to prevent soft budget constraints of banks. Monitoring and tough bank regulations can be a substitute but are also costly. The hospital bank solution can help to improve substantially the loan portfolios of banks even if hospital banks cannot enforce hard budget constraints. One must then also devise pricing schemes for the sale of bad loans to hospital banks that give banks an incentive to accurately report the level of their bad loan problems and to avoid both underreporting and overreporting.

Section 12.4 describes early empirical evidence on the issues dealt with in this chapter.

12.1 DEALING WITH SOFT BUDGET CONSTRAINTS OF FIRMS

We reintroduce the Dewatripont-Maskin model in its moral-hazard version used in Chapters 9 and 11. This will be the basic model we will use throughout the chapter. We start with a bank–firm relation instead of a government–firm relation. In the beginning of period 1, firms draw n projects (normalized to 1 without loss of generality) and submit them to the bank. Projects are of two types, either good in proportion α or poor in proportion $(1 - \alpha)$. Project types are unknown to the bank ex ante, and all have a start-up cost of 1 monetary unit. At the end of period 1, good projects yield a gross monetary, and taxable, return of R_g and deliver private benefits $B_g > 0$ to the firm's management. Poor projects yield nothing after one period unless the manager of the firm exerts high effort. If he does, then the project also delivers a verifiable return of R_g and a private benefit B_g net of effort. When no effort has been exerted and a poor project has delivered nothing after one period, it can then either be liquidated, in which case the bank gets a liquidation value L and the manager gets 0, or be refinanced by injection of an additional unit of funds. In the latter case, the bank gets a return of R_p at the end of the second period, and the manager gets a private benefit of $B_p > 0$. As in the models of Chapters 9 and 11, throughout the chapter we assume no time discounting. It is also assumed that $B_p > B_g > 0$, so that the manager of a bad project prefers to exert effort if he expects liquidation but will prefer not to exert effort if he expects to be refinanced.

In Chapter 9 we saw that if the government cares about social welfare, that is, cares about the sum of profits and private benefits, then there will be soft budget constraints if the ex post net return to refinancing exceeds the returns to liquidation: $R_p + B_p - 1 > L + B_g$. However, when the firm is financed by the bank, the condition for soft budget constraints is stronger, since the bank only cares about its profit and does not internalize the interests of management: $R_p - 1 > L$. Soft budget constraints are inefficient if $R_p < 2$, since the bank only partly recovers its total investment in the project. The total expected net return to lending is then $\alpha(R_g - 1) + (1 - \alpha)(R_p - 2)$. For lending to take place, the expected net return must be positive. Parameter α, the proportion of good loans, plays an important role in that respect. The lower is α, the higher are the efficiency losses from soft budget constraints. When α falls below $\alpha^B = \frac{2 - R_p}{R_g - R_p + 1}$, lending basically stops because it has a negative expected return. In what follows, we will assume that $\alpha > \alpha^B$.

Transfer of lending activities to profit-maximizing banks may thus lead to some hardening of budget constraints under conditions where $R_p - 1 < L < R_p + B_p - B_l - 1$. However, transferring lending activities to private profit-maximizing banks may *not necessarily lead to hardening budget constraints*. There may still be soft budget constraints under conditions where $L < R_p - 1$, that is, when the ex post value of bailing out a poor project exceeds the liquidation value or the collateral value. What is important to note is that when deciding whether or not to refinance, the initial investment in the firm is a sunk cost and does not enter into the decision. This is the key insight of Dewatripont and Maskin: soft budget constraints may occur even with a profit-maximizing bank because the sunk-cost nature of the initial investment creates a wedge between the ex ante return of a poor project and the ex post return to refinancing it. A profit-maximizing bank may thus end up bailing out a project ex post even though it is inefficient to do so from the ex ante point of view.

This simple model shows that the soft budget constraint problem may thus persist after banking reform (that is, when banks are profit maximizing), and even after the privatization of firms, in particular if the liquidation value L is low enough. The liquidation value is related to the level of collateral; in transition economies collateral is scarce, partly because of the absence of private wealth under socialism, partly because of poorly functioning markets for liquidated assets. Consequently, soft budget constraints in banks should be a relevant problem in these economies.

We can even go one step further. The model predicts soft budget constraints to be a widespread phenomenon because the existence of sunk costs drives a wedge between ex ante efficiency and ex post efficiency. We should thus observe soft budget constraints as a very general phenomenon. Judging from the empirical evidence, soft budget constraints are not as pervasive as suggested by this analysis. We will see why in the following sections.

12.1.1 DECENTRALIZED BANKING

In the context of this model, the main mechanism for endogenously hardening budget constraints is the decentralization of credit.

12.1.1.1 Refinancing under Liquidity Constraints

Dewatripont and Maskin (1995) show that if refinancing requires funds from an outside bank, inefficiencies in bargaining between banks may make refinancing less attractive by reducing R_p.

The idea is that the bank that makes the initial loan is small and does not have the additional unit of funds to refinance a poor project. It must then require funding by an additional creditor. However, the initial creditor is assumed to have an informational advantage over the new creditor in monitoring the project. This creates an agency problem between the new creditor and the initial creditor, which leads to a reduction of the return from refinancing, thus making liquidation more attractive, thereby credibly hardening the budget constraint of the firm.

Assume thus that the continuation value of poor projects depends on an effort level e to be exerted by the initial creditor. Specifically, assume that the financial return of a poor project that is refinanced is either 0 or $\bar{R}_p$, and that the probability of $\bar{R}_p$ is e. Finally, assume e to be private information to the initial creditor, who incurs effort cost $\Psi(e)$, assumed to be increasing and convex in e.

In this case, centralization of credit means that the initial creditor will also be the one refinancing a bad firm, so that the chosen effort level e^* will fully internalize the benefit of monitoring:

$$R_p^C = \max_e \left\{ e\,\bar{R}_p - \Psi(e) \right\} \tag{12.1}$$

with first-order condition

$$\bar{R}_p = \Psi'(e^*) \tag{12.2}$$

that is, equalizing the marginal benefit of effort and its marginal cost.

Under decentralization, instead, the initial creditor is short of money, and refinancing has to be performed by a new creditor who has not observed monitoring effort. Given an expected effort $\hat{e}$ and assuming perfect competition among new creditors, the refinancing contract will involve one unit of funds from the new creditor with a promise of repayment of $1/\hat{e}$ deducted from $\bar{R}_p$ whenever the poor project ends up being "successful" (since, by assumption, no resources are available if the project is unsuccessful). Indeed, given the expectation $\hat{e}$, which is also the probability that the new creditor gets repaid, his expected return is $\hat{e} \cdot \frac{1}{\hat{e}} = 1$ given the Bertrand competition between new creditors. Given $\hat{e}$, the effort level privately chosen by the first creditor will lead to

$$R_p^D = \max_e \left\{ e \left\{ \bar{R}_p - \frac{1}{\hat{e}} \right\} - \Psi(e) \right\} \tag{12.3}$$

The first-order condition is

$$\bar{R}_p - \frac{1}{\hat{e}} = \Psi'\left(e^{**}\right) \tag{12.4}$$

As one sees, the marginal benefit of effort is lower than under decentralization, since in case the return is $\bar{R}_p$, $\frac{1}{\hat{e}}$ must be paid to the new creditor. Taking into account that in equilibrium $\hat{e} = e^{**}$ and given the convexity of $\Psi(e)$, one sees immediately from the comparison of equations (12.2) and (12.4) that $e^{**} < e^{*}$, and the associated continuation value of the project R_p^D is lower than R_p^C. If $R_p^D < 1 < R_p^C$, then decentralization of credit, as defined previously, hardens the budget constraint of the firm.[1]

The meaning of decentralization in the Dewatripont-Maskin model relates to the fact that the initial lender is liquidity constrained and cannot refinance a poor project out of its own funds. The model applies to projects with large indivisibilities where multiple financiers may be necessary to provide the funding. However, decentralization does not necessarily imply liquidity constraints. Taken literally, the Dewatripont-Maskin model would imply that projects with large indivisibilities (large factories, big construction projects, bridges and other infrastructure investment, and the like) are subject to harder budget constraints than projects with few or no indivisibilities, everything else equal.

12.1.1.2   Conflicts of Interest between Banks

A model showing that liquidity constraints are not necessary for decentralization of credit to harden budget constraints is due to Huang and Xu (1998). They assume that projects are financed by multiple investors who have conflicts of interests with respect to the reorganization strategy that is to be implemented when a project is refinanced.

Assume that there are two investors A and B, each putting one-half unit of funds in each project. At the refinancing stage, they also each put one-half. However, there are two possible strategies to restructure a poor project, strategy a and strategy b. After refinancing the project, investor A (resp. B) receives a private signal s_A (resp. s_B) about the right reorganization strategy. Each signal s_J can be either low or high and is picked up on $[\underline{s}, \overline{s}]$. Each strategy may benefit each bank differently. Return $R_p^{jJ}(j = a, b; J = A, B)$ of strategy j to bank J includes the financial return but also the private benefit of strategy j to bank J. This definition of return is thus broader than in the Dewatripont-Maskin model. The most obvious way to think of the private benefit to a bank in this context is to consider that there are spillovers from the restructuring strategy to other lenders of the bank.[2] For example, some restructuring strategies may reinforce synergies between the clients or shareholders of a given bank but have no effect or possibly negative effects on clients or shareholders of the other bank. This is also a natural way to think about conflicts of interests between banks (see Huang and Xu, 1998, for a broader discussion and examples).

It is thus assumed that bank A (resp. B) benefits more from a higher signal under strategy a (resp. b) than under strategy b (resp. a), that is, for any $s^h > s^l$. Formally, this assumption means

[1] Note that, in this setup, if R_p^D is greater than one, decentralization of credit is worse than centralization, since refinancing of bad projects is not prevented, but occurs with inefficiently low monitoring. If one allows endogenous creditor size in a market economy, however, it is possible to show that, in this case, a market economy will simply replicate the centralized financing pattern: in equilibrium creditors will have sufficient resources to perform the refinancing themselves (see Dewatripont and Maskin, 1995).

[2] We will see more on spillovers in section 12.1.2.

$$R_p^{aA}(s_A^h, s_B) - R_p^{aA}(s_A^l, s_B) > R_p^{bA}(s_A^h, s_B) - R_p^{bA}(s_A^l, s_B) > 0 \qquad (12.5)$$

$$R_p^{bB}(s_A, s_B^h) - R_p^{bB}(s_A, s_B^l) > R_p^{aB}(s_A, s_B^h) - R_p^{aB}(s_A, s_B^l) > 0$$

However, it is assumed that the total return to both banks $R_p^j = R_p^{jA} + R_p^{jB}$ is such that only strategy a is ex post jointly profitable when $s_A < s_B$ and only strategy b is ex post jointly profitable when $s_B < s_A$:

$$R_p^a > 1 > R_p^b \qquad \text{when} \qquad s_A < s_B \qquad (12.6)$$

$$R_p^b > 1 > R_p^a \qquad \text{when} \qquad s_B < s_A$$

It is also assumed that randomizing between both strategies is not profitable:

$$\Pr(s_A < s_B)R_p^a + [1 - \Pr(s_A < s_B)]R_p^b < 1 \qquad (12.7)$$

We immediately see that there is a conflict between efficiency and incentives. Indeed, an increase in signal s_B increases the likelihood that strategy a is efficient. At the same time, it makes strategy b more beneficial to bank B. This conflict creates an incentive problem because there is asymmetric information on signals received.

Since randomizing is assumed not to be profitable and information is crucial to determine the profitability of refinancing, the two banks must find ways to communicate and extract information from each other if they consider refinancing. On the basis of the revealed signals, they will decide their reorganization strategy, $q(s_A, s_B)$ or $1 - q(s_A, s_B) \in [0, 1]$, that is, the probability of choosing strategy a or b, respectively. Call $T(s_A, s_B)$ a transfer from A to B inducing the latter to reveal its true signal. This transfer must satisfy incentive-compatibility constraints. For any signal $s_A = s^*$, in case $s_B = s_B^h > s^*$, $T(s_A, s_B)$ must be such that the sum of the transfer and the expected return to bank B will be higher than if a wrong signal $s_B^l < s^*$ is reported:

$$q(s_A, s_B^h)R_p^{aB}(s_A, s_B^h) + [1 - q(s_A, s_B^h)]R_p^{bB}(s_A, s_B^h) + T(s_A, s_B^h) \qquad (12.8)$$

$$\geq q(s_A, s_B^l)R_p^{aB}(s_A, s_B^h) + [1 - q(s_A, s_B^l)]R_p^{bB}(s_A, s_B^h) + T(s_A, s_B^l)$$

Similarly, we have the incentive-compatibility constraint for s_B^l:

$$q(s_A, s_B^l)R_p^{aB}(s_A, s_B^l) + [1 - q(s_A, s_B^l)]R_p^{bB}(s_A, s_B^l) + T(s_A, s_B^l) \qquad (12.9)$$

$$\geq q(s_A, s_B^h)R_p^{aB}(s_A, s_B^l) + [1 - q(s_A, s_B^h)]R_p^{bB}(s_A, s_B^l) + T(s_A, s_B^h)$$

Developing the inequalities for $T(s_A, s_B^h) - T(s_A, s_B^l)$ in constraints (12.8) and (12.9), one derives

$$[q(s_A, s_B^l) - q(s_A, s_B^h)][R_p^{aB}(s_A, s_B^l) - R_p^{bB}(s_A, s_B^l)]$$

$$\geq T(s_A, s_B^h) - T(s_A, s_B^l)$$

$$\geq [q(s_A, s_B^l) - q(s_A, s_B^h)][R_p^{aB}(s_A, s_B^h) - R_p^{bB}(s_A, s_B^h)]$$

Given that $R_p^{bB}(s_A, s_B^h) - R_p^{bB}(s_A, s_B^l) > R_p^{aB}(s_A, s_B^h) - R_p^{aB}(s_A, s_B^l)$ by condition (12.5), $q(s_A, s_B^l) \geq q(s_A, s_B^h)$; that is, $q(s_A, s_B)$ should be nonincreasing in s_B to preserve incentive compatibility. However, we see from condition (12.6) that when s_B increases and shifts from $s_B < s_A$ to $s_B > s_A$, efficiency can only be increased by increasing $q(s_A, s_B)$, that is, the probability of choosing strategy a. For both to be satisfied simultaneously, we must then have $q(s_A, s_B)$ constant with respect to s_B. By repeating the whole argument for transfers from B to A, $q(s_A, s_B)$ must also be constant with respect to s_A. No constant q can then do better than $q = \Pr(s_A < s_B)$. But we know from condition (12.7) that refinancing cannot then be profitable. Decentralization of credit thus leads to hard budget constraints.

The intuition of the Huang-Xu model is that there is a conflict between efficiency and incentives. If s_B increases, then strategy a is more likely to be efficient, but bank B's payoff from using strategy b increases with s_B. Therefore, it will be prepared to reveal its true signal only if a higher s_B does not lead to a lower $q(s_A, s_B)$. Incentive compatibility thus conflicts directly with efficiency.

12.1.1.3 Other Models

In a model related to the Huang-Xu model, due to Povel (1995), the hardening of budget constraints is also a result of decentralized finance. Here the ex post inefficiency between the investors is due to a war of attrition. An agreement on a restructuring plan is necessary to refinance a poor project. Valuation by each bank of the continuation value of the project is private information, and each of the two banks tries to convince the other to write down a larger fraction of its claims. While the two banks are busy bargaining, the expected ex post value of refinancing the project declines.[3] If bargaining delays are long enough, then refinancing of poor projects is not profitable.

The general insight behind these results is that decentralized finance may lead to externalities that reduce the attractiveness of refinancing. This suggests that bond or equity finance will typically involve a harder budget constraint than bank finance, a point also stressed by von Thadden (1995). Other models explaining why the multiplicity of creditors can change refinancing outcomes include Bolton and Scharfstein (1996), Berglöf and von Thadden (1994), Dewatripont and Tirole (1994a), and Hart and Moore (1995).

12.1.1.4 Soft Budget Constraints and the East Asian Crisis

Huang and Xu apply the insight about the hardening of budget constraints under decentralized banking to shed light on the East Asian crisis. They note that the Korean *chaebols* were subject to centralized financing and were suffering from lack of financial discipline and soft budget constraints. In contrast, Taiwan's economy was characterized by dispersed financial institutions and decentralized banking. Taiwan suffered much less from the East Asian crisis even though it was also attacked by speculators. By embedding the soft-budget-constraint model in a larger model including bank runs, Huang and Xu can account both for the "East Asian miracle" and its cri-

[3] *The precise assumption is that there is a probability at each moment in time that the information that rescue negotiations are taking place leaks out to the public, thereby making the rescue impossible or ineffective.*

sis. The idea is that in an economy where innovation consists mainly in imitation and the proportion of poor projects is rather low, a fact which can be interpreted as a lower uncertainty of projects, then there will be high bank liquidity and high growth, but when the uncertainty increases above a certain level, bank runs may occur in an economy with soft budget constraints but not in an economy with hard budget constraints. The reason is that soft budget constraints cause deterioration in the quality of the information on bank loans. This bad quality of information increases the general cost of borrowing on the interbank lending market, which usually serves as a counterweight to bank runs. Therefore, soft budget constraints may lead to contagious bank runs.[4]

Interestingly, transparency on the interbank lending market is not a result of good or bad regulation, a point often made on the debate on the East Asian crisis, but is an endogenous outcome related to the degree of centralization or decentralization of credit, a point that had not been made in the debate.

12.1.1.5 Hard Budget Constraints and Short-Termism

Though a hard budget constraint has positive incentive effects, it can also induce short-termism among good entrepreneurs, as shown by von Thadden (1995) and Dewatripont and Maskin (1995). Specifically, introduce into the Dewatripont-Maskin model the ability for entrepreneurs with good projects to choose between a quick outcome that yields R_g and B_g after one period and a slow outcome that yields 0 after one period but a gross financial return $R_s > 2$ and a positive private benefit B_s if refinanced. These slow projects thus have a positive net present value, but at the end of period 1 they cannot be distinguished from the bad projects.

Under centralization, there will be soft budget constraints for poor projects, but those with good projects will also be refinanced. Under decentralization, since good slow projects cannot be distinguished from poor projects, there will be hard budget constraints but no refinancing of good slow projects if $\alpha R_s + (1 - \alpha)R_p^D < 1$. Decentralization is then not necessarily better than centralization from the welfare point of view or even from the point of view of returns to bank financing. Indeed, under a short-termist hard-budget-constraint equilibrium with decentralized banking, the net return to loans is $R_g - 1$. Under centralized banking with soft budget constraints but better liquidity provision for good projects, the net return to lending is $\alpha R_s + (1 - \alpha)(R_p^C - 1) - 1$. The latter will dominate if $\alpha R_s + (1 - \alpha)(R_p^C - 1) > R_g$. The hard budget constraint equilibrium can thus induce "short-termist" behavior that more than offsets the gain from deterring bad long-term projects from being started.[5]

This discussion sheds light on the comparison between financial systems. In particular, it rationalizes the idea that a market-oriented system, as in Anglo-Saxon countries, can be short-termist (Corbett, 1987) compared to the Japanese (or German) bank-based system, which provides more long-run finance and liquidity to firms (Aoki, 1990; Hoshi, Kashyap, and Scharfstein, 1992). However, the latter system also suffers from comparatively soft budget constraints.

[4] *The precise mechanism is a standard adverse selection one: Banks with higher than average quality of loans will prefer to face an early bank run rather than a future liquidation because of a high cost of borrowing when the proportion of poor projects is high enough. These effects may become magnified with expectations of liquidations, triggering more bank runs and increasing the cost of borrowing, eventually leading to a collapse of the banking system.*

[5] *The original Dewatripont and Maskin (1995) model endogenizes the size of banks.*

12.1.2 TRADE ARREARS AND RESTRUCTURING WITH REDEPLOYMENT

We introduce interactions between firms to explore the issue of trade arrears between firms and its relationship to soft budget constraints. Trade arrears were an important phenomenon in the beginning of transition and still are in the former Soviet Union. After price liberalization, many firms became insolvent and could not pay their suppliers, so that payment arrears began to accumulate. De facto, many suppliers were lending to their clients. These trade arrears effectively worsened the financial situation of good firms, which were themselves brought in a difficult financial situation. These spillover effects can create a "too many to fail" problem for banks, forcing them to bail out bad loans in order to prevent a generalized insolvency of firms that could put banks themselves in a difficult position (on the effects of the magnitude of arrears, see Daianu, 1998). In many countries this problem subsided as the government refrained from intervention and levels of interenterprise credits stabilized (see Schaffer, 1998), but several transition economies, notably Russia, Bulgaria, and Romania, have experienced partial government bailouts of interenterprise arrears leading to expectations of future capital infusions, implying a continued soft budget constraint of enterprises.

We model enterprise arrears by incorporating a simplified version of the model by Perotti (1993) in the model of this chapter. We show that when enterprises are linked together by chains of trade credit, budget constraints can be softened because the liquidation of some firms would economically damage more healthy firms up to a point where bailing out bad firms appears to be a lesser evil compared to a tough liquidation policy. Hardening budget constraints can then be noncredible (see also Coricelli and Milesi-Ferretti, 1993, for a similar idea). However, if enterprise restructuring leads to breaking the old business links and to the redeployment of business activities, then budget constraints can be hardened because the liquidation of bad firms will have fewer spillover effects on healthy firms.

Call θ the proportion of firms with poor projects that exert high effort and restructure. This form of restructuring may be seen as defensive restructuring, since, unlike strategic restructuring, it does not require outside investment. Among those firms that do not restructure, let λ be the proportion of projects that the bank decides to liquidate. Thus, $(1 - \alpha)(1 - \theta)\lambda$ projects get liquidated. To capture the possibility of interaction between projects, assume that healthy firms—that is, firms with good projects or firms that have restructured—have supplier–customer relationships with firms with poor projects. We thus modify the basic soft-budget-constraint model by assuming that the gross return to loans in those firms decreases in relation ω to the proportion of liquidated projects in the total number of good and restructured projects. Thus the liquidation of some firms because of their insolvency may affect the financial situation of other firms. As a consequence of this assumption, the return to both the good and restructured projects is $R_g - \frac{\omega(1-\alpha)(1-\theta)\lambda}{\alpha+(1-\alpha)\theta}$.

These interactions between firms due to the trade arrears of insolvent firms give rise to a problem for the bank. A "tough" liquidation policy may spill over to healthy firms, causing their financial situation to deteriorate and, eventually, worsening the bank's own situation.

The bank's expected profit as a function of θ and λ is then given by

$$\Pi(\lambda, \theta) = [\alpha + (1 - \alpha)\theta]R_g - \omega(1 - \alpha)(1 - \theta)\lambda + (1 - \alpha)(1 - \theta)[\lambda L + (1 - \lambda)(R_p - 1)]$$

(12.10)

where λ is chosen by the banks after firms' choice of θ. Otherwise, the timing is the same as in the basic soft-budget-constraint model.

We can rewrite $\Pi(\lambda, \theta)$ as

$$\Pi(\lambda, \theta) = [\alpha + (1 - \alpha)\theta]R_g + (1 - \alpha)(1 - \theta)[\lambda(L - \omega) + (1 - \lambda)(R_p - 1)]$$

(12.11)

The negative spillover of liquidation of bad loans on good loans has the effect of reducing the liquidation value of a loan for the bank from L to $L - \omega$. Looking at the bank's ex post incentive to refinance or to liquidate, it follows immediately that if $\omega > L + 1 - R_p$, then firms have soft budget constraints, and if $\omega < L + 1 - R_p$, then they have hard budget constraints. The basic message is that the stronger the trade links between firms with different projects, the softer the bank will tend to be in order to avoid spillover effects from a tough but self-defeating liquidation policy. By bailing out firms, banks make it possible for them to pay their suppliers who have healthy projects.

The model can be extended to obtain multiple equilibria, and in particular a "too many to fail" result with multiple equilibria, as in Perotti's analysis. Assume now that firms that exert effort and restructure reduce their trade links with traditional state-owned enterprises by doing so. We call this process *restructuring with redeployment*. In effect, ω, instead of being a constant, is then assumed to be a strictly decreasing and differentiable function of θ, $\omega(\theta)$ with $\frac{d\omega}{d\theta} < 0$.

Take equation (12.11) with $\omega(\theta)$ replacing ω. Taking the derivative of $\Pi(\lambda, \theta)$ with respect to λ yields $(1 - \alpha)(1 - \theta)[L - \omega(\theta) - R_p + 1]$. If $\omega(1) < L + 1 - R_p < \omega(0)$, there exists a value θ^* for which $L - \omega(\theta^*) - R_p + 1 = 0$. Since $\frac{d\omega}{d\theta} < 0$, above θ^* the bank will strictly prefer to liquidate. Below θ^* it will strictly prefer to refinance. Firms thus face a coordination problem: the only two pure Nash equilibria of this coordination game are either no restructuring or full restructuring: $\theta = 0$ or $\theta = 1$. Indeed, firms prefer to restructure whenever $B_g > (1 - \lambda)B_p$. For all $\theta < \theta^*$, the bank will prefer to refinance. Hence, $\lambda = 0$. Therefore, for any $\theta \in [0, \theta^*)$, because $B_g > B_p$, firms will be better off by not restructuring at all, and thus $\theta = 0$. We thus have, on one hand, an equilibrium where firms do not restructure and banks refinance. On the other hand, for all $\theta > \theta^*$, the bank will prefer to liquidate, and thus $\lambda = 1$. For any $\theta \in (\theta^*, 1)$ because $B_g > 0$, firms will individually prefer to fully restructure, and thus $\theta = 1$.[6] There will thus be another equilibrium where all firms restructure and the bank would liquidate a non-restructured project.

The interesting insight here is that the marginal benefit of liquidation of a given firm $[L - \omega(\theta) - R_p + 1]$ increases with the extent of restructuring. When firms restructure, it becomes credible for the bank to liquidate ex post, and this credibility leads to hardening of budget constraints. However, when firms do not restructure, the marginal benefit of

---

[6] *If $\theta = \theta^*$, then the bank is indifferent between any $\lambda \in [0, 1]$. For θ^* to be an equilibrium, λ^* must be such that $B_g = (1 - \lambda^*)B_p$.*

liquidation is the lowest or its cost the highest. Therefore, the bank will have an incentive to be soft.

To summarize, the additional source for soft budget constraints analyzed here is the dependency between firms of the old state sector and a lack of restructuring driven by expectations of bailout under conditions of low restructuring.

Note that this model can be linked directly to the output-fall models of Chapter 7. There we saw that an immediate redeployment of business links following liberalization led to an output fall. It would be interesting to extend the present model to take into account the macroeconomic effects of redeployment. It would also be interesting to extend the model to analyze policies that allow a gradual breaking up of old business links so as to minimize the output fall while hardening budget constraints. This is certainly a topic for further research.

12.1.3   ENTRY

We now turn to another extension of the basic soft-budget-constraint model based on Berglöf and Roland (1997). In particular, we study the effect of entry and the competition between old loans to poor projects seeking refinance on one hand and new loans on the other hand. The only change is the addition of another period to the model, specifically a period 0 before period 1. We assume that, at the beginning of period 0, the bank finances a unit mass of projects. Enterprises with poor projects decide during that period on their effort level, given their expectation of future bailout. At the beginning of period 1, the bank faces the problem of using the proceeds from period-0 investment either to finance new projects or to refinance poor projects. We assume that the supply of new projects is perfectly elastic so that there are more new projects than funds to finance them.

An important difference compared to the basic model is that the proportion of good projects in period 1, denoted β, is not necessarily the same as the proportion α of good projects in period 0 because of the entry of new projects. New entry is a characteristic aspect of transition; there is no reason to believe that the quality of projects is the same during the early phases of transition as it was under socialism. Enterprises with poor projects financed in $t = 1$ decide on their effort level during period 1. We assume that at the beginning of period 2, no new projects are generated. The only decision for the bank is whether or not to refinance poor projects using revenues generated by the investments in period 1. If projects are refinanced, they generate revenues during period 2, which is terminal. The timing of the game is given in Figure 12.1.

Given that $2 > R_p > 1$, the bank has an incentive to refinance poor projects in period 2, and enterprises with poor projects know they have soft budget constraints and thus choose low effort in period 1. The expected net return to a new project financed in period 1 is then $\beta(R_g - 1) + (1 - \beta)(R_p - 2)$.

12.1.3.1   Competition from New Projects

It is instructive to contrast the decision of the bank in period 2 that we have sketched (which represents the standard soft-budget-constraint model) with its decision in period 1. Then, the bank can choose to allocate its revenues between the refinancing of existing projects and the funding of new projects. The bank's choice in period 1 determines

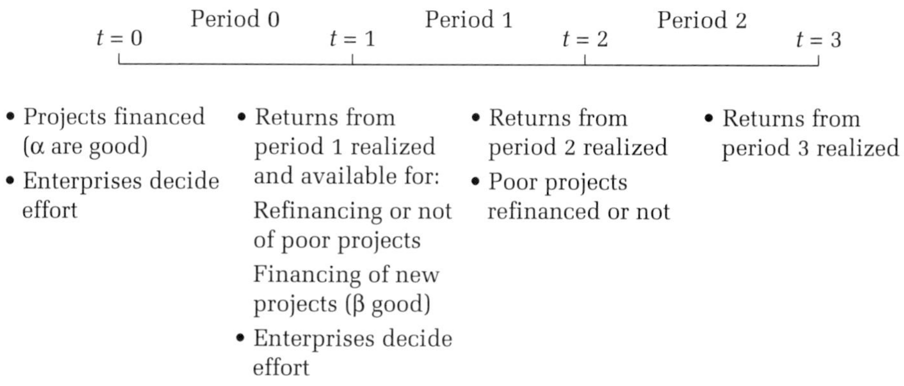

	Period 0		Period 1		Period 2	
$t = 0$		$t = 1$		$t = 2$		$t = 3$

- Projects financed (α are good)
- Enterprises decide effort

- Returns from period 1 realized and available for:
  Refinancing or not of poor projects
  Financing of new projects (β good)
- Enterprises decide effort

- Returns from period 2 realized
- Poor projects refinanced or not

- Returns from period 3 realized

FIGURE 12.1 ENTRY AND THE HARDENING OF BUDGET CONSTRAINTS

whether the budget constraints of enterprises with poor projects funded in period 0 are hard or soft, and this result in turn affects the enterprise's incentives in period 0. Indeed, if the bank prefers to put all its revenues from period-0 loans into new lending, enterprises are better off choosing high effort in period 0 as long as $B_g > 0$. However, given the assumption that $B_p > B_g$, enterprises will always prefer low effort if they expect to be refinanced.[7] If the bank prefers to refinance existing projects before making new loans, enterprises will thus choose low effort. Now, comparing the expected net return to the bank from new lending $\beta(R_g - 1) + (1 - \beta)(R_p - 2)$ and the expected net return from refinancing $R_p - 1$, and given that the supply of new projects is perfectly elastic, there will be hard budget constraints if

$$\beta(R_g - 1) + (1 - \beta)(R_p - 2) > R_p - 1 \tag{12.12}$$

and soft budget constraints otherwise. The direction of the inequality depends very much on β, the proportion of good projects in period 1. There will thus be hard budget constraints if

$$\beta > \widehat{\beta} = \frac{1}{R_g - R_p + 1} \tag{12.13}$$

and soft budget constraints otherwise.

Condition (12.13) has an intuitive explanation. The higher the proportion of good projects β in the entire cohort of new entrants to be financed at $t = 1$, the higher the difference between the return on good projects and the return to refinancing of poor projects (that is, the higher $R_g - R_p$), the more likely budget constraints are to be hard. A low quality of average loan projects and a low variance in returns between good and poor projects will soften budget constraints. Indeed, banks will prefer to recover money on bad loans rather than to finance new projects (many of which are likely to be poor projects) if they expect to receive insufficient compensation from good new projects. By contrast, when projects are of high enough average quality, hard budget constraints will obtain.

[7] This condition must be changed if, when the firm chooses high effort in period 0, it draws with a positive probability a project that is selected in period 1.

12.1.3.2 Soft Budget Constraints in Transition versus Those in Advanced Market Economies

The preceding results shed possible light on the persistence of soft budget constraints in transition economies as compared to advanced industrialized economies. In transition economies, the quality of new enterprise projects was likely to be low, compared to advanced industrialized economies, given the absence of recent past experience of entrepreneurialism. At the same time, entry allows us to understand why the soft budget constraint phenomenon is not more generalized in advanced industrialized economies. Indeed, the nature of sunk costs of existing loans advanced is quite general and does not relate exclusively to phenomena in transition economies. As stated in Chapter 9, it is thus a puzzle why we don't observe more soft budget constraints in banking sectors of all economies. The Berglöf and Roland model proposes an answer: Banks may prefer funding new loans to refinancing old projects if the quality of new projects is high enough; hence, competition from other projects serves as a credible commitment to terminate loans on poor projects.

12.1.3.3 Coexistence of Credit Crunch and Soft Budget Constraints

An immediate corollary to the analysis is that fewer new projects are financed in period 1 if enterprises have soft budget constraints. Comparing the funds available in period 1 for new projects, R_g under hard budget constraints and $[\alpha R_g - (1-\alpha)]$ under soft budget constraints, it is clear that $[\alpha R_g - (1-\alpha)] < R_g$. The lower the quality α of old loans, the bigger the credit crunch under soft budget constraints. This result is interesting because, early in the transition period, findings by Dittus (1994) that banks had cut drastically the allocation of credit to enterprises led to the conclusion—perhaps premature—that banks had hardened the budget constraints of enterprises. The model here shows not only that soft budget constraints and credit crunches are not necessarily inconsistent, but that soft budget constraints can coexist and even lead to a credit crunch with respect to new loans.

12.1.3.4 Financial Systems and the Speed of Adoption of Technological Change

There is another corollary to the analysis developed by Dewatripont and Roland (in press) that goes beyond the experience of transition and that is related to the preceding discussion on the differences between financial systems in market economies. We have shown above that decentralized banking can harden budget constraints but also lead to short-termist behavior by failing to provide liquidity for good slow projects. Things are somewhat different if we integrate that analysis in the Berglöf and Roland (1997) model. Assume, to make the comparison simple between centralization and decentralization, that there is one exogenous unit of funds available both at $t = 0$ and at $t = 1$ and that new projects arising at $t = 1$ are homogeneous and have a return R_n. There will then be refinancing and soft budget constraints under centralization and no refinancing and hard budget constraints under decentralization if

$$(1 - \alpha)R_p^D < R_n - \alpha R_s < (1 - \alpha)R_p^C \tag{12.14}$$

where, as seen previously, R_s is the return on good slow projects, and R_p^D and R_p^C are the returns to poor projects under decentralization and centralization, respectively.

In this case, the trade-off between centralization and decentralization is not only one between hard budget constraints and short-termism. There is now an additional cost to soft budget constraints, namely, the loss of finance of new and potentially more innovative projects. Indeed, under condition (12.14), under centralization, there will be no funds available for financing the new projects, whereas there will be $(1 + R_g)$ funds available under decentralization. This lack of funds for new projects will create an inefficiency if $R_n - \alpha R_s \in [(1 - \alpha)R_p^C - 1, (1 - \alpha)R_p^C]$. In that case, the ex ante return to new projects at $t = 1$ is higher than the ex ante return on projects from $t = 0$, but the old projects get refinanced, including the ex ante unprofitable ones, because their expected continuation value is higher than the ex ante return on new projects.

These differences again shed light on the difference between the "bank-oriented" economies of Germany and Japan and the "market-oriented" United States as far as the finance of firms is concerned. In the 1980s analysts were stressing the role of financial discipline on firms in the United States but were lamenting their "short-termism" relative to Japan and Germany. At that point, many people thought the bank-oriented system was superior. This opinion was reflected in the preceding discussion of the Dewatripont-Maskin (1995) and von Thadden (1995) models. Recently, however, people have been stressing the ability of the U.S. financial system to fund new firms, allowing them to expand fast. This is seen as a key of the perceived U.S. superiority. If the financial system is slow to adapt to technological change (influencing the probability of emergence of profitable new projects), a more "stable" bank-oriented economy with long-run risk taking can thus begin to be outperformed by a more "flexible" market-oriented economy dedicated to short-run projects when technological progress suddenly accelerates.

12.1.4 CHANGES IN SCREENING TECHNOLOGY

Let us now turn back to the Berglöf and Roland (1997) model. The model can be used to show that investments in screening activities, allowing the bank to avoid financing some of the poor projects, will lead to an increase in β and may thus have the effect of hardening budget constraints. Interestingly, in contrast to the results of Dewatripont and Maskin, smaller banks may be softer than bigger banks. Indeed, because of economies of scale, small banks may have to refrain from screening, whereas large banks can afford the fixed investments in screening activities.

Take the same framework as in the preceding subsection, and think of screening as an activity that improves the quality of the supply of projects, that is, that raises the share β of good projects at $t = 1$. In other words, banks can influence the process by which projects are generated. For example, firms may supply better projects because banks screen more closely before providing finance or because banks are actively involved in the firm.[8] More specifically, assume a screening investment made at $t = 0$ with the following technology $\sigma + \phi(\beta - \beta_0)$, where σ is a fixed-cost component and $\phi(\beta - \beta_0)$ a variable-cost component with the function $\phi(\beta - \beta_0)$ increasing and convex in β. It is

[8] *Early monitoring of the firm's effort before the refinancing decision would basically have the same effects.*

assumed that $\phi(\beta - \beta_0) = 0$ if β is maintained at its initial level β_0 without screening but is greater than 0 for higher levels of β.

For banks to engage in screening, they must have the funds and the incentives to do so. We assume that without investment in screening, soft budget constraints would obtain, that is, that $\beta_0 < \widehat{\beta} = \frac{1}{R_g - R_p + 1}$. The question is thus to analyze the conditions under which investment in screening will take place and lead to hard budget constraints.

The level of minimum screening costs necessary to obtain hard budget constraints is given by $\sigma + \phi(\widehat{\beta} - \beta_0)$. For hard budget constraints to obtain, the investment in screening must be profitable enough compared to a situation with soft budget constraints. Call C_0 the initial capital of the bank at $t = 0$. Under hard budget constraints, the optimal level of screening will lead to $\beta_H > \widehat{\beta}$ and to a total return

$$\Pi(\beta_H) = [\beta_H R_g + (1 - \beta_H)(R_p - 1)]R_g\{C_0 - [\sigma + \phi(\beta_H - \beta_0)]\} - C_0 \tag{12.15}$$

such that the marginal benefit of increasing β will be equal to its marginal cost

$$(R_g - R_p + 1)R_g\{C_0 - [\sigma + \phi(\beta_H - \beta_0)]\} \tag{12.16}$$
$$= [\beta_H R_g + (1 - \beta_H)(R_p - 1)]R_g\phi'(\beta_H - \beta_0)$$

Under soft budget constraints, the optimal level of screening will lead to $\beta_S < \widehat{\beta}$ and a total return

$$\Pi(\beta_S) = [\beta_S R_g + (1 - \beta_S)(R_p - 1)][\alpha R_g - (1 - \alpha) + (1 - \alpha)R_p]\{C_0 - [\sigma + \phi(\beta_S - \beta_0)]\} - C_0$$

such that the marginal benefit of increasing β will be equal to its marginal cost

$$(R_g - R_p + 1)[\alpha R_g - (1 - \alpha)]\{C_0 - [\sigma + \phi(\beta_H - \beta_0)]\} \tag{12.17}$$
$$= [\beta_S R_g + (1 - \beta_S)(R_p - 1)][\alpha R_g - (1 - \alpha) + (1 - \alpha)R_p]\phi'(\beta_S - \beta_0)$$

In case an interior solution to equation (12.17) does not exist, then there will be no screening, and the total return will be

$$\Pi(\beta_0) = [\beta_0 R_g + (1 - \beta_0)(R_p - 1)][\alpha R_g - (1 - \alpha) + (1 - \alpha)R_p]C_0 - C_0 \tag{12.18}$$

It is then easy to see that larger banks will tend to impose harder budget constraints. Indeed, note from equations (12.16) and (12.17) that the marginal benefit of screening (the left-hand side of the equations) increases with C_0 but not the marginal cost of screening (the right-hand side). An increase in C_0 will thus tend to increase β_S above $\widehat{\beta}$ and will also increase β_H. Note finally that $\Pi(\beta_H) - \Pi(\beta_S)$ and $\Pi(\beta_H) - \Pi(\beta_0)$ both increase with C_0. There is thus a threshold level of C_0 above which it is optimal for banks to invest in screening so as to secure hard budget constraints.

This result is interesting because, contrary to Dewatripont and Maskin (1995) where a small size of banks is necessary to generate hard budget constraints, in this model a large size of financial institutions leads to hard budget constraints because it allows for more investment in screening technology. Schnitzer (1999) also builds a model emphasizing the benefits of screening in larger banks in transition economies and pointing to the negative effects on the quality of loans of too much competition between too many small banks.

So far we have assumed that monitoring takes place prior to any refinancing decision, but monitoring could also be made contingent on refinance, in which case it actually increases the relative profitability of refinancing, and thus softens firms' budget constraints just as in the Dewatripont-Maskin model. If there are economies of scope between screening and monitoring activities, in the extreme case if fixed investments in screening also allow monitoring, then there is a trade-off between the gains from screening and the reduced credibility not to monitor ex post. Banks could then rationally choose to refrain from investing in screening.

12.2   DEALING WITH SOFT BUDGET CONSTRAINTS OF BANKS

Now, we make the analysis of soft budget constraints and banking in transition more complex by adding another tier to the analysis—a game between the government and banks. The government may be tempted to bail out banks under certain conditions. Banks have indeed been bailed out in several transition economies. Hungary, for example, experienced four bailouts in as many years. Bulgaria went through a major recapitalization of its entire banking sector. Bailouts of banks affect their incentives to harden the budget constraints of enterprises. In other words, the soft budget constraints of banks may lead to soft budget constraints for firms.

The analysis of soft budget constraints of banks substantially enriches our understanding of the soft-budget-constraint phenomenon. Indeed, one now has interactions between three tiers of agents instead of two. The cause of soft budget constraints of firms will not necessarily be the wedge between the ex ante and ex post returns to lending anymore.

In section 12.2.1 we will see that banks may be soft toward enterprises even when no refinancing is involved but loans are only rolled over. Here, the reason the bank may be soft is that it does not internalize all the costs and benefits of refinancing. This will be the case in particular if the government is tempted to recapitalize banks with a negative net position ex post. Initial capitalization or monitoring of banks by regulators may help to change the banks' incentives to harden the budget constraints of firms.

In section 12.2.2 banks may be soft toward firms even if they have no intrinsic interest in refinancing bad loans. However, they may be in a position to exploit government's willingness to bail out firms and to extract subsidies from government so that they bear only part of the costs of refinancing while reaping the monetary benefits. This will be especially the case if banks are poorly capitalized and their pool of loans is of bad quality. There also, initial recapitalization can change the banks' incentives. Interestingly, the setting up of a hospital bank that takes away from the bank a proportion of its bad loans may also change the banks' incentive toward enterprises and discourage their incentive to seek rents by extracting subsidies from government.

12.2.1 BANK PASSIVITY AND GAMBLING FOR RESURRECTION

We start the analysis by incorporating a simplified version of the basic model of bank passivity or softness due to Mitchell (1997). We look at a model where the bank knows that the government will intervene ex post to bail out an unprofitable bank. This knowledge creates incentives for "gambling for resurrection" by not liquidating bad projects. Indeed, while the bank benefits from the upside of such a decision, it does not suffer from the downside. This behavior increases the likelihood of ex post bailout of the bank. The government must thus intervene ex ante to prevent such gambling behavior either by monitoring of banks or by an adequate initial capitalization.

12.2.1.1 The Trade-off between Better Monitoring and Ex Post Recapitalization

Take the basic bank–firm model of section 12.1 and make the following modifications. Assume that when a poor project is refinanced, there is a probability q that it generates return R_p for the bank and a probability $(1 - q)$ that it generates a liquidation value $L_s < L$. A positive net return from refinancing is thus not assured, contrary to the basic soft-budget-constraint model. Refinancing may actually reduce the liquidation value of the firm. In both cases, however, the project yields private benefits B_p.[9] The firm's incentives thus remain unchanged, but the bank's incentives may change, depending on its relationship with the government.

We thus add on top of the game between the bank and enterprises a game between the government and the bank. The government can decide to monitor the bank to detect whether, as a creditor, it is active in filing for bankruptcy, that is, whether it chooses to liquidate poor projects or tries to remain passive. The reason the bank may want to remain passive is that limited liability shelters it from the downside risk of refinancing bad projects. Indeed, it does not pay for the deterioration in the liquidation value of a project from L to L_s but benefits from the upside. In other words, the bank may choose to "gamble for resurrection." The government must decide ex ante on a detection probability D at a cost $C(D)$ assumed to be a convex function of D. Detection takes place after the bank decides whether to refinance or not. If the bank is detected being passive, the government can fire the management of the bank. To make this threat credible, it is assumed that the government can commit to firing management, for example, by writing this power into the bankruptcy law.

The timing of the game is as follows. In period 1 the government decides on D and spends $C(D)$. The bank lends to finance projects, and enterprises with poor projects decide on their effort level. In period 2 returns are observed and the bank decides whether to be active or passive, that is, whether to liquidate or not, and chooses a level of activity $a \in [0, 1]$. Directly afterward, the government monitors and fires passive bank managers. At the end of the period, the government recapitalizes banks by injecting capital K in an amount that is to be determined endogenously. Because of deposit insurance, a negative

[9] *Note that one does not need to assume that refinancing takes place. The model may be simply reinterpreted by assuming that the bank can decide to roll the loan over as in Mitchell (1997), leading to $R_p - 1$ with probability q or to $L_s - 1$ with probability $(1 - q)$.*

Period 1	Period 2

- Government decides D and spends $C(D)$
- Banks lend
- Enterprises decide effort level

- Returns observed
- Banks decide to be active or passive
- Government fires managers detected to be passive

- Government recapitalizes bank with negative net position

FIGURE 12.2 THE TIMING OF THE GAME OF BANK PASSIVITY

net position of the bank must be covered by the government. The government thus faces a trade-off between costs of detection and costs of ex post recapitalization. Figure 12.2 shows the timing of the game.

The government's optimization problem is to minimize $C(D) + K$ subject to the constraint that at the end of period 2 the sum of K and the bank's net position is nonnegative.[10]

The bank's payoff is $\max\{0, \Pi\} + \rho$ where Π is the net return from lending and ρ is the private benefit of managing the bank. The net return from lending may be negative, but the bank's losses will be covered. Thus, $K = \max\{-\Pi, 0\}$, and bank management loses ρ if it is fired. Firing management does not change the bank's financial position. By assumption, when passivity is detected, it is too late to undo the bank's refinancing decision.

Even though we have a three-tier hierarchy, the analysis can concentrate on the government–bank relationship. Indeed, enterprise behavior is easy to characterize. It is obvious to see that firms have soft budget constraints if and only if $(1 - a)B_p \geq B_g$.

Given that $B_p \geq B_g$, firms will thus have hard budget constraints only if the bank is sufficiently active. They will have soft budget constraints otherwise. However, firm behavior affects the financial position of the bank. If firms have hard budget constraints, the bank's payoff will be

$$-1 + R_g + \rho \tag{12.19}$$

If firms do not exert effort, then the bank's payoff is

$$a[\max\{-1 + \alpha R_g + (1 - \alpha)L, 0\} + \rho] + (1 - a)(1 - D)\{q[\alpha R_g + (1 - \alpha)(R_p - 1) - 1] + \rho\} \tag{12.20}$$

With probability q passive banks are lucky, in which case they get the returns from the good loans αR_g and the net returns from refinancing $(1 - \alpha)(R_p - 1)$ minus the initial credit expenditure of 1. With probability $(1 - q)$ they are unlucky with refinancing and realize they ended up throwing good money after bad. Their position then becomes

10 Note that the objective function of government is not equivalent to social welfare. However, efficiency enters directly by way of the concern for recapitalization. Bank passivity and the soft budget constraints of firms create the need for recapitalization costs that the government wants to avoid.

$\alpha R_g + (1 - \alpha)(L_s - 1) - 1$, which can be negative if α is not too big and L_s is sufficiently small. The government's payoff when firms have soft budget constraints is

$$- C(D) - a \max\{0, 1 - \alpha R_g - (1 - \alpha)L\} \tag{12.21}$$
$$- (1 - a) \max\{0, [1 - q][1 - \alpha R_g + (1 - \alpha)(1 - L_s)]\}$$

The amount of recapitalization depends directly on a, not on D, but a itself depends on D. If firms have hard budget constraints, the government's payoff is $-C(D^H)$.

We assume that $1 - \alpha R_g + (1 - \alpha)(1 - L_s) > 0$, so that recapitalization is necessary when banks are passive. To simplify the analysis we also assume that $1 - \alpha R_g - (1 - \alpha)L < 0$, that is, that the bank does not need to be recapitalized when it is active.[11] The more important assumption is that $L_s - 1 < L$, so that the government payoff increases with bank activity.

With $D \geq 0$, the bank will prefer $a = 1$ if

$$-1 + \alpha R_g + (1 - \alpha)L + \rho > (1 - D)\{q[\alpha R_g + (1 - \alpha)(R_p - 1) - 1] + \rho\} \tag{12.22}$$

which is equivalent to

$$D > \tilde{D} = \frac{(1 - \alpha)[q(R_p - 1) - L] - (1 - q)(\alpha R_g - 1)}{q[\alpha R_g + (1 - \alpha)(R_p - 1) - 1] + \rho} \tag{12.23}$$

The banks' decision is thus mainly based on the expected benefits of gambling for resurrection given the existence of deposit insurance and the potential punishment of being fired if caught being passive.

Note first that for any $D < \tilde{D}$, banks choose $a = 0$. The government's optimal choice in that range is then $D = 0$. As soon as $D = \tilde{D}$, banks choose $a = 1$. The government then never gains from choosing $D > \tilde{D}$. The government's choice is binary: whether to incur cost $C(\tilde{D})$, leading to hard budget constraints and no recapitalization, or not to monitor banks, thereby accepting soft budget constraints of firms and recapitalization of banks ex post. Hard budget constraints will thus obtain if $C(\tilde{D}) < (1 - q)[1 - \alpha R_g + (1 - \alpha)(1 - L_s)]$. Otherwise budget constraints will be soft.

Note that $\frac{d\tilde{D}}{d\rho} < 0$, so that the higher the private benefit of bank management, the lower the detection probability necessary to dissuade the bank management from gambling for resurrection. This is the incentive effect related to the threat of being fired. Note also that $\frac{d\tilde{D}}{d\alpha} < 0$. The higher is α, the higher is the bank's loss from good loans in case of recapitalization and the lower the net expected gain from refinancing of bad loans.

Whether hard budget constraints obtain or not thus depends on the costs of effective monitoring versus the potential costs of recapitalization. As expected, the cost of recapitalization decreases with α. In transition economies both the costs of monitoring and those of recapitalization are expected to be high. However, if the cost of recapitalization is sufficiently important, the government will want to eliminate soft budget constraints in banking.

[11] See Mitchell (1997) for a complete analysis of the different cases.

12.2.1.2 Monitoring versus Initial Capitalization

An alternative solution to investing in $\widetilde{D}$ is for the government to directly reduce the incentives for banks to engage in gambling for resurrection by injecting capital equal to C up front at an opportunity cost of government funds, denoted $\lambda(C)$. The minimum level of capital infusion $\widetilde{C}$ necessary to preclude the bank from gambling for bailout is given by

$$\widetilde{C} - 1 + \alpha R_g + (1 - \alpha)L + \rho = q[\alpha R_g + (1 - \alpha)(R_p - 1) - 1 + \widetilde{C}] + \rho \tag{12.24}$$

where the left-hand side is the return from being active, and the right-hand side is the return from being passive. Banks will strictly prefer to be active for

$$C > \widetilde{C} = \frac{1 - \alpha}{1 - q}\left[q(R_p - 1) - L\right] - (\alpha R_g - 1) \tag{12.25}$$

The question remains whether such a policy can be in the interest of government. Ex ante capitalization will never be in the interest of the government if $\widetilde{C} + \lambda(\widetilde{C}) > K$. As can be easily seen, when q increases, $\widetilde{C}$ increases and $K = (1 - q)[1 - \alpha R_g + (1 - \alpha)(1 - L_s)]$ decreases so that $\widetilde{C}$ may be bigger than K. However, $\widetilde{C}$ may be much smaller than K for low levels of q. Under those conditions, when $\widetilde{C} + \lambda(\widetilde{C}) < C(\widetilde{D})$, initial recapitalization achieves hard budget constraints at a lower cost than monitoring. Note also that $\widetilde{C}$ decreases with α. Again, the lower the quality of the pool of loans, the more expensive it is to induce the bank not to be soft toward firms.

This subsection has shown that soft budget constraints can arise in enterprises even when refinancing of poor projects per se is not optimal. In that sense, the cause of soft budget constraints of enterprises here is not the wedge between the ex ante and ex post return to lending, and the model departs from the Dewatripont-Maskin framework. Refinancing enterprises with poor projects, however, is ex post optimal for the bank; otherwise it would not decide to do it. The cause of soft budget constraints, however, is the fact that the bank does not internalize all the costs and benefits of refinancing because the government will intervene to recapitalize it ex post. Protection against downside risk may lead the bank to gamble for resurrection by rolling over credits and avoiding liquidation; in this sense insurance leads to creditor passivity and soft budget constraints. Naturally, this behavior is more likely when banks are poorly capitalized and the cost of monitoring them is high. Better monitoring and high enough initial capitalization are instruments to prevent bank passivity.

12.2.1.3 Bank Passivity and Bankruptcy

Bank passivity may be enhanced if bankruptcy laws are inadequate. In 1998, according to the EBRD annual *Transition Report,* only Hungary, Poland, and Estonia had effective bankruptcy proceedings. In all other transition economies, bankruptcy law was either partly or seriously incomplete or only partly enforced. Among the more advanced transition economies, Mitchell (1998) has compared the bankruptcy experience in Hungary and the Czech Republic. The Czech bankruptcy law was passed in October 1991 but came into effect only in April 1993. As discussed in earlier chapters, there was a deliberate

TABLE 12.6 BANKRUPTCY FILINGS AND DECLARATIONS IN THE CZECH REPUBLIC AND HUNGARY

	1992	1993	1994	1995	1996
Czech Republic:					
Bankruptcy filings	—	1,098	1,816	2,393	2,996
Bankruptcy declarations	—	60	288	480	719
Hungary:					
Bankruptcy filings	18,229	8,229	5,900	6,461	7,477
Bankruptcy declarations (liquidation or reorganization)	4,727	3,480	2,563	2,827	3,092

Source: *Mitchell (1998).*

move to achieve mass privatization while delaying firm restructuring. In contrast, the new Hungarian bankruptcy law of 1992 started with a bang. It included the "hara-kiri" clause triggering automatic bankruptcy procedures for firms with any liability overdue by more than 90 days. This triggered a huge number of bankruptcy filings that literally clogged the courts. As can be seen from Table 12.6, less than 25 percent of filings led to bankruptcy declaration (either in the form of liquidation or reorganization), whereas in subsequent years the percentage was clearly higher. The law was amended in mid-1993. Czech bankruptcy law is more costly to creditors. For a filing to be initiated, at least two creditors must have claims on the debtor. The procedure is long, and there is a long lag between the date of filing and the opening of a bankruptcy procedure by the court. Creditors have little legal protection against asset stripping by debtors.

Table 12.6 demonstrates a big difference in the bankruptcy experience between the two countries. In Hungary bankruptcy filings were reduced after the change in the law and have remained relatively stable. In the Czech Republic it was only gradually that the number of filings increased. A big difference between the two countries remains the low ratio of bankruptcy declarations as a proportion of filings in the Czech Republic (around 20 percent in 1995 and 1996) compared to Hungary (above 40 percent).

12.2.2 RENT SEEKING BY BANKS

In the previous section banks gambled because they were insured against downside risks. However, banks can also trigger bailouts or, more generally, extract rents from the government. They can do so by exploiting the softness of government. Indeed, the government, unlike the banks, cares not only about the verifiable revenues but also about the private benefits of employees. These types of games between governments and banks are an important feature of transition (for an interesting discussion, see Anderson and Kegels (1997).[12] In this section we analyze such a game along the lines developed in Berglöf and Roland (1995).

[12] *Perotti (1993) had already emphasized how deposit guarantees by the government can encourage banks to be soft toward firms.*

The most important modification of the basic model developed in section 2.2 is the assumption that the bank is not interested in refinancing per se, that is,

$$L > R_p - 1 \tag{12.26}$$

This small alteration of the model is conceptually another important departure from the basic framework of Dewatripont and Maskin (1995), in which softness stems from the fact that previous investments are sunk costs at the time of the refinancing decision. In the following, softness arises because banks can extract subsidies from the government.

12.2.2.1 Initial Capitalization and Reserve Requirements

Assume that at $t = 0$, the government capitalizes the banking sector by injecting an initial capital of 1 in the bank at a cost of $1 + \lambda(1)$ (where the latter represents the distortionary costs associated with its financing). A unit mass of projects can be financed by the bank, but the bank may choose to finance only k projects and keep reserves $E = 1 - k$. At $t = 1$, the time of refinancing, the government can give a subsidy S at a cost $S + \lambda(S)$. The subsidy to the bank is paid after a verifiable commitment from the bank that it will bail out firms. By assumption, the government cannot recover the returns from refinancing; its only instrument is to inject capital. However, since the government maximizes the total welfare—that is, the welfare of both banks and firms—it is willing to pay the subsidy ex post if the social benefit from refinancing exceeds its cost:

$$(1 - \alpha)k(R_p + B_p - 1) > S + \lambda(S) \tag{12.27}$$

The government is willing to inject money to finance all projects ex ante because the net expected benefit to government is bigger than the expected cost:

$$\alpha(R_g + B_g) + (1 - \alpha)(R_p + B_p - 1) - 1 \geq 1 + \lambda(1) + 1 - \alpha - \alpha R_g + \lambda(1 - \alpha - \alpha R_g) \tag{12.28}$$

Moreover, the bank's liquidity position can be observed perfectly by the government. The subsidy will cover the extra liquidity needed to bail out the poor projects exactly, that is,

$$S = k[(1 - \alpha) - \alpha R_g] - (1 - k) \tag{12.29}$$

where $(1 - \alpha)k$ is the cost of refinancing, $\alpha k R_g$ is the verifiable revenues generated by the good projects, and $(1 - k)$ is the initial capital contribution by the government net of the investment. Banks will be interested in obtaining a subsidy if the gain from this subsidy is greater than the loss due to the refinancing obligation:

$$S - (1 - \alpha)k(1 + L - R_p) \geq 0 \tag{12.30}$$

Condition (12.30) is thus a necessary condition for the firms to have soft budget constraints. What is the interest of the bank in such an operation? Without subsidy, it has no interest in refinancing firms. However, since it receives the returns from refinancing, if the government bears a sufficiently large part of the cost of refinancing, the bank may reap net gains from these subsidies.

The first question we ask is, If $k = 1$, will budget constraints be soft or hard? Using conditions (12.29) and (12.30), we see that banks will be interested in asking for a subsidy if

$$(1 - \alpha) - \alpha R_g \geq (1 - \alpha)(1 + L - R_p) \Longleftrightarrow \alpha \leq \alpha^H = \frac{R_p - L}{R_p - L + R_g} \tag{12.31}$$

Again, a necessary condition for soft budget constraints is for the proportion of good projects to be low enough. The reason is the following: Even though a lower α increases the loss from refinancing, it increases the subsidy even more when $R_p - L > 0$. Indeed, when $\alpha \longrightarrow 0$, the subsidy tends toward 1, whereas the loss from refinancing tends toward $1 + L - R_p$, which is less than 1 when $R_p - L > 0$. In that extreme case, the refinancing is done entirely by the government, and the bank reaps the gross benefit $R_p - L$ from refinancing. In the following, we assume $R_p - L > 0$, so that soft budget constraints may occur with low α.

Precisely, in case $\alpha < \alpha^H$, the bank may set aside (or be forced to set aside) reserves $E = 1 - k$ and finance only k projects. The more reserves the bank has, the less it will be interested in rent seeking. The bank will be indifferent between hard and soft behavior if

$$S = (1 - \alpha)k - \alpha k R_g - E = (1 - \alpha)k(1 + L - R_p) \tag{12.32}$$

which implies reserves

$$E = k[(R_p - L) - \alpha(R_p + R_g - L)]$$

Given an initial capital infusion of 1, the bank faces the following trade-off: It can opt for either soft budget constraints and a bailout or hard budget constraints and choose $k < 1$ so as to credibly commit not to seek a bailout.

In case of soft budget constraints the profit of the bank is

$$\Pi_s = (1 - k) + k[\alpha R_g - (1 - \alpha)] + S + (1 - \alpha)k R_p = (1 - \alpha)k R_p \tag{12.33}$$

given the definition of S.

Clearly, $\frac{d\Pi_s}{dk} > 0$, so that $k = 1$, implying

$$\Pi_S = (1 - \alpha)R_p \tag{12.34}$$

When budget constraints are hard, bank profit is

$$\Pi_H = k(R_g - 1) \tag{12.35}$$

To ensure hard budget constraints, the bank will need to determine k^H such that, for α given

$$k^H = \frac{1}{1 + (R_p - L) - \alpha(R_p + R_g - L)} \tag{12.36}$$

Since $\frac{dk}{d\alpha} > 0$, the lower the quality of projects α, the higher the level of reserves needed to ensure hard budget constraints.

Hard budget constraints obtained by setting such minimum reserves yield higher profits to the bank if the following inequality is satisfied:

$$\frac{(R_g - 1)}{1 + (R_p - L) - \alpha(R_p + R_g - L)} > (1 - \alpha)R_p$$

which is equivalent to

$$(R_g - 1) > (1 - \alpha)R_p[1 + (R_p - L) - \alpha(R_p + R_g - L)] \tag{12.37}$$

For $\alpha = 1$, it is clear that this inequality is satisfied. For $\alpha = 0$, given that $R_p - L < 1$ and $1 + R_p - L < 2$, it is not obvious that $R_g - 1 > 2R_p$. So we may have $\Pi_H < \Pi_S$ for low α. The right-hand side of the inequality, $(1 - \alpha)R_p[1 + (R_p - L) - \alpha(R_p + R_g - L)]$, is a convex curve declining in α. With higher levels of α, one is thus more assured that hard budget constraints will obtain.

For the bank, being hard yields higher returns but on fewer projects because of the reserve requirements.

What then is optimal for the government? Under soft budget constraints its payoff is

$$-[1 + \lambda(1)] - [1 - \alpha - \alpha R_g + \lambda(1 - \alpha - \alpha R_g)] + \alpha B_g + (1 - \alpha)(R_p + B_p) \tag{12.38}$$

and under hard budget constraints it is

$$-\{1 + (R_p - L) - \alpha(R_p + R_g - L) + \lambda[1 + (R_p - L) - \alpha(R_p + R_g - L)]\} + (R_g + B_g) \tag{12.39}$$

Evaluating the difference between conditions (12.39) and (12.38) at $\alpha = 0$ and $\alpha = 1$ shows that both hard- and soft-budget-constraint equilibria can be preferred depending on parameter values. Obviously, the payoffs to hard budget constraints increase in the liquidation value L.

12.2.2.2 Partial Transfers of Bad Loans to a Hospital Bank

So far we have assumed implicitly that the government cannot observe the quality of bank portfolios, but can only observe the overall proportion of good and bad projects and the bank's liquidity. If the government could identify the bad loans in bank portfolios, it could withdraw bad loans from the bank and refinance them, for example, by transferring loans to a specialized government institution. Such hospital agencies have been set up in many transition economies to clean up bank portfolios and to avoid subsidizing the bank for refinancing bad projects. Withdrawing all the bad loans would be more costly for the government than a bailout in terms of subsidies. Indeed, when all bad loans are transferred to the hospital agency, the cost in terms of subsidies is always higher: $(1 - \alpha) > (1 - \alpha) - \alpha R_g$. The reason is that the government will have to pay the full cost of refinancing, not just the shortfall after the bank's own funds have been used as in a bailout.

Assume instead that only h projects are transferred to the hospital bank. The subsidy to the bank will now be

$$S(h) = (1 - \alpha) - h - \alpha R_g \qquad \qquad \textbf{(12.40)}$$

In essence, the government should withdraw an amount sufficient to make rent seeking unprofitable for the bank. In order to discourage the bank from rent seeking, it must be that

$$S(h) - (1 - \alpha)h(1 - R_p) \leq (1 - \alpha)L$$

which is equivalent to

$$h \geq \frac{(1 - \alpha)(1 - L) + \alpha R_g}{1 + (1 - \alpha)(1 - R_p)} \qquad \qquad \textbf{(12.41)}$$

The government will thus set $h = \frac{(1-\alpha)(1-L)+\alpha R_g}{1+(1-\alpha)(1-R_p)}$ to get hard budget constraints. As expected, the share of loans that must be transferred to the hospital agency decreases in liquidation value and increases in the verifiable revenues from both good and poor projects.

To summarize, we have seen that sufficient ex ante capitalization of the bank can eliminate its incentive to extract subsidies from the government to bail out money-losing firms. Another instrument is the creation of a hospital bank to make such rent seeking unprofitable by taking away from the bank a sufficient amount of bad loans to achieve this purpose.

12.3 INCENTIVES TO REVEAL BAD DEBTS

In the analysis of the previous subsection, the government can perfectly observe the bank's liquidity position when the latter decides to engage in rent-seeking activity. In reality, asymmetric information can be an important problem, and banks may have incentives either to exaggerate or to underreport the amount of bad debts. This issue is partly orthogonal to the issue of soft budget constraints. It was treated first by Mitchell (1995) and subsequently by Aghion, Bolton, and Fries (1996).

Indeed, different policies for dealing with bad loans on the balance sheets of banks may create incentives for the latter not to reveal the amount of its bad debts, as shown by Mitchell (1995). In particular, she shows that policies combining some form of recapitalization with punitive measures toward bank management may lead banks to hide or underestimate the amount of bad loans. In contrast, Aghion, Bolton, and Fries (1996) show that policies that amount to simple recapitalization to compensate for bad debts may give an incentive to banks to exaggerate the extent of their bad debts. How to induce banks to reveal the extent of their bad debts without distortion is thus an important question. One way of obtaining this information is by devising a scheme combining partial recapitalization with a transfer of bad debts to a hospital bank. The pricing of loans, however, must then be devised in such a way as to induce banks to accurately reveal the extent of their bad loans.

In what follows we present the Aghion, Bolton, and Fries model within the framework used in this chapter. Firms play a passive role in this model as we concentrate on the relation between the bank and the firm. We thus abstract from moral hazard used in the previous sections and also from a soft-budget-constraint problem between the firm and the bank.[13] Parameter α represents the proportion of loans yielding an early return R_g. A proportion $(1 - \alpha)$ yields no return after one period, but among those loans there is a proportion q that, when being rolled over, yields in period 2 a return of $R_p > 0$ and a proportion $1 - q$ of loans that yields a return of 0. When a loan is liquidated instead of being rolled over, it yields L with $0 < L < R_p$. It is thus optimal for the bank to roll over the proportion q of loans and to liquidate the other $1 - q$ so as to obtain the liquidation value. It is assumed that $R_g > R_p > 1$ but that $qR_p + (1 - q)L < 1$, that is, that the expected return on bad loans is negative.

Assume that α, the proportion of good loans on the balance sheets of banks, cannot be observed by the government. It is assumed that α can take two possible values, α_1 and α_2, with respective probability μ_1 and μ_2. It is assumed that $\alpha_1 > \alpha_2 \geq 0$. Depending on the value of α, the bank's net position, taking into account an initial finance of 1, is defined as

$$\Pi_i = \alpha R_g + (1 - \alpha)[qR_p + (1 - q)L] - 1 \tag{12.42}$$

We assume that $\Pi_1 = 0 > \Pi_2$. The fraction of liquidated loans in each state if the bank acts truthfully is $\phi_i = (1 - q)(1 - \alpha_i)$. However, it is assumed that the government can only observe the number of liquidated loans and thus make its recapitalization R dependent on the bank's liquidation policy. The bank can thus play on ϕ_i to distort its liquidation decisions. The payoff of the bank management is assumed to be $\Pi_i + R$ if management stays in place and 0 otherwise. Government would like to maximize the continuation value of firms net of any excess recapitalization. Continuation values of firms are defined as

$$V_i = [\alpha_i q + (1 - \alpha_i) \min\{q, \widehat{q}_i\}]R_p + (1 - \alpha_i)(1 - \widehat{q}_i)L \tag{12.43}$$

where $\widehat{q}_i$ is a choice variable of banks. Under excess continuation, with $\widehat{q}_i > q$, the return will be $qR_p + (1 - q)L$ minus a loss of $(\widehat{q}_i - q)L$ that is due to the failure to reap the liquidation value on the proportion $(\widehat{q}_i - q)$. Under excess liquidation, with $\widehat{q}_i < q$, there will be a loss of $(q - \widehat{q}_i)(R_p - L)$ that is due to the excess liquidation on the proportion $(q - \widehat{q}_i)$.

Excess recapitalization would take place if Π_1 is realized and the bank pretends that it is in state Π_2. In that case, even though the bank's position remains positive and would thus not require recapitalization, it may attract funds from the government by following a policy of excess liquidation. The deadweight loss of excess recapitalization is defined by $\lambda[\mu_1(\Pi_1 - \Pi_2)]$.

Let us first look at the effects of a "tough" recapitalization policy whereby management is dismissed if it announces $\Pi_i < 0$. In this case, it will have an incentive to announce Π_1 when Π_2 occurs and to liquidate less than necessary. Indeed, in state 2, it will liquidate a fraction $\phi_1 = (1 - \widehat{q}_1)(1 - \alpha_2) \equiv (1 - q)(1 - \alpha_1)$. Since $\alpha_1 > \alpha_2$, one will have $\widehat{q}_1 > q$, and there will be excess continuation.

Let us now look at the effect of "soft" recapitalization policies where management is immune from dismissal and can even derive benefits from excess recapitalization. Here, in state 1, it will have an incentive to announce Π_2 that will lead to excess liquidation. Indeed, in state 1, it will liquidate a fraction $\phi_2 = (1 - \widehat{q}_2)(1 - \alpha_1) \equiv (1 - q)(1 - \alpha_2)$, thus with $\widehat{q}_2 < q$ and a deadweight loss of $\lambda[\mu_1(\Pi_1 - \Pi_2)]$.

From the welfare point of view, the expected loss from a tough policy will be $\mu_2(1 - q)\frac{\alpha_1 - \alpha_2}{1 - \alpha_2}L$, whereas the expected loss from a soft policy of recapitalization will be $\mu_1[(1 - q)\frac{\alpha_1 - \alpha_2}{1 - \alpha_1}(R_p - L) + \lambda(\Pi_1 - \Pi_2)]$. When μ_1 is high, that is, when the economy is believed to be in a rather good situation, then a tough policy is better, whereas when the economy is believed to be in crisis, that is, when μ_2 is high, then a soft policy is better.

If we introduce the possibility of a hospital bank as a policy instrument as in the Berglöf-Roland (1995) model, we must ask under what conditions the bank will have an incentive to get rid of its bad loans. In other words, what price should the bank be paid to transfer its loans to a hospital bank? Call that price t. Clearly, we must have $t < R_g$ in order not to give the bank an incentive to sell its performing loans. However, with $t = 1$, the bank will sell its bad loans at their initial face value but still make a positive profit from the return on the good loans. A cheaper price would be one where in state 2 the bank is made to break even. Here, t would be the solution to $\alpha_2 R_g + (1 - \alpha_2)q R_p + (1 - \alpha_2)(1 - q)t = 1$. However, even in this case, in state 1, the bank's net position would still be positive. On average, it will thus have a positive net worth.

The cheapest transfer price that is still incentive compatible (in the sense that it induces the bank to transfer only the loans it should liquidate) is a nonlinear transfer price. This nonlinear transfer price will be t_L for a fraction $\overline{m}$ of the bank's portfolio and a price t_H above that.

What characteristics must that pricing scheme have? First of all, in order to avoid overreporting of nonperforming loans, one must have

$$t_H \leq R_p \tag{12.44}$$

Second, the payoff from selling the nonperforming loans to the government in state 1 should not be higher than the payoff from liquidation in that state in order to deter firms from selling their loans to the government in that state:

$$(\phi_1 - \overline{m})t_H + \overline{m}t_L \leq \phi_1 L \tag{12.45}$$

Third, the transfer scheme must allow the recapitalization of a bank in state 2:

$$\alpha_2 R_g + (1 - \alpha_2)q R_p + (\phi_2 - \overline{m})t_H + \overline{m}t_L \geq 1 \tag{12.46}$$

Constraints (12.45) and (12.46) are not linearly independent, so that, if a solution exists, it is not unique. Using both constraints, one gets

$$(\phi_2 - \phi_1)t_H \geq 1 - \phi_1 L - \alpha_2 R_g - (1 - \alpha_2)q R_p \tag{12.47}$$

If constraints (12.44) and (12.47) are mutually compatible, a solution exists. One solution then involves choosing $t_H = R_p$ and $t_L = 0$; then, from constraint (12.45), we obtain $\overline{m} = \phi_1 \frac{R_p - L}{R_p}$.

To summarize, a nonlinear transfer scheme can be the cheapest way to recapitalize banks without distorting their incentives. The intuition is that by setting a low price for a fraction of the loan portfolio, it is possible to discourage the bank from selling its loans in state 1, while the higher price for the rest of the portfolio can be calculated so as to allow the bank to break even in state 2, provided that price is not so high that the bank would want to sell the "good part" of its nonperforming loans.

12.4   THE EMPIRICAL LITERATURE

The empirical literature on how and to what extent financial transition and banking reforms have led to a hardening of budget constraints in firms in transition economies is still at an early stage.

The partial and indirect evidence that exists suggests that there has been substantial hardening in some countries and that the problem of softness has remained important in other countries.

Bonin and Schaffer (1995) have analyzed data covering all medium and large nonfinancial firms in Hungary in 1992 and found that net bank financing to money-losing firms (using 1991 operating profits) was actually negative. They note that net bank financing was also negative for profitable firms, a possible indication of a generalized credit crunch. A similar analysis by Gao and Schaffer (1998) for China shows that unprofitable firms had much more access to bank credit. Figure 12.3 shows an interesting contrast between China and Hungary. The horizontal axis measures the ratio of profits to assets for a sample of firms in 1990 in China and for a sample of firms in 1992 in Hungary. The vertical axis gives a measure of net bank financing of firms one year later (1991 in China, 1993 in Hungary) defined by the increment in bank debt, net of interest costs in relation to the firm's assets. On the one hand, one sees in China that there are a great many firms in the upper-left quadrant, that is, money-losing firms receiving bank finance, whereas that quadrant is much more empty in Hungary. On the other hand, there are more firms that have negative bank financing in Hungary, including firms with positive profitability, suggesting some possible excess tightness in credit provision.

Pinto and van Wijnbergen (1995) analyzed balance-sheet and survey data from Polish SOEs. Whereas they found that prior to 1992 there was a negative correlation between profitability and access to bank credit, this correlation broke down after the banking reform of 1992. While such an analysis is indicative of changes in lending behavior, it does not disentangle supply and demand effects.

Kotzeva and Perotti (1995), using survey data on Bulgaria, found evidence that trade credit taking place between enterprises was based on expectations of a collective bailout, in the spirit of the Perotti (1993) model. Perotti and Carare (1997), using a sample of Romanian SOEs between 1991 and 1994, found evidence of substantial softening of

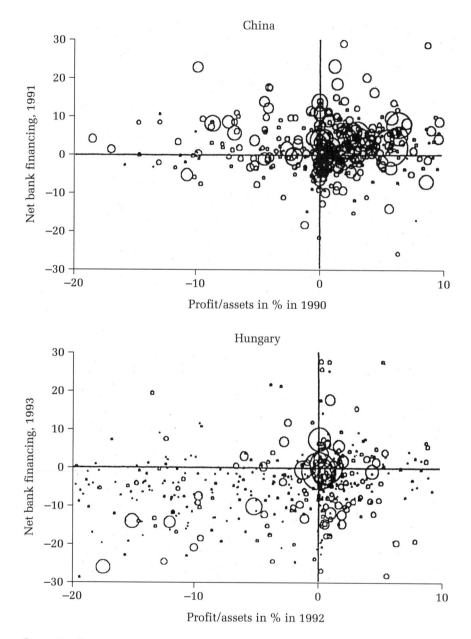

FIGURE 12.3   PROFITABILITY AND NET BANK FINANCING IN HUNGARY AND CHINA

Source: *Gao and Schaffer (1998).*

budget constraints in Romania in the form of an increasing correlation between the stock of financial arrears and bank lending, showing that bank credit was directed increasingly toward larger, less profitable firms with larger trade and bank arrears.

Other empirical papers ask questions that are not directly related to the issue of soft budget constraints and address other questions such as the investment behavior or the access to credit of new private firms.

Lizal and Svejnar's (1997) analysis of investment behavior among medium and large firms in the Czech Republic shows that investment follows the neoclassical/ accelerator specification linking investment to lagged production. Moreover, this specification dominates one based on credit rationing where investment depends on internal funds, proxied by lagged profit. It is only for smaller private firms and cooperatives that the latter specification comes out significant. The effect of profits on investment is negative in 1993, insignificant in 1994, and positive in 1995. These estimates may pick up some soft-budget-constraint effect earlier on, but the authors do not address the soft-budget-constraint problem. Overall, the evidence suggests that firms did not in general face credit rationing for their investment, with the exception of cooperatives and smaller firms. In contrast, a similar exercise on Slovenia by Prasnikar and Svejnar (1998) leads to the conclusion that most firms were credit constrained during the early to mid-1990s.

Bratkowski, Grosfeld, and Rostowski (in press), use a survey of 281 Czech, Hungarian, and Polish newly established small private firms. They find that new private firms have access to bank finance rather early on in their life. Their research shows that there is less credit rationing for new firms than one might have thought initially given the relative inexperience of banks. The relative absence of credit rationing is due to the fact that banks are given enough collateral.

A similar finding emerges from the research by Johnson, McMillan, and Woodruff (1999b) on Poland, Slovakia, Romania, Russia, and Ukraine. They also concentrate on start-ups and find that supply of credit is not an important constraint for firms. They find that the most important problem is a lack of demand for investment funds resulting from insecurity of property rights (see Chapters 9 and 11). They analyze the determinants of reinvestment rates of profits and the determinants of loans. They find that measures of insecurity of property rights have a significant negative effect on the reinvestment rates of profits (except for spinoffs of privatized firms!). They then look at the supply and demand for loans. They also find that collateral has an important impact on the ability to secure loans but that firms with more unused internal funds receive fewer loans. This finding tends to show that there is a demand effect: firms that perceive that they face more insecurity of property rights reinvest fewer profits and demand fewer loans. Interestingly, they find that a lower profit rate increases the probability of receiving a loan. This result may pick up some soft-budget-constraint effects.

In general, one must be cautious when interpreting the results of the analysis of access to credit. Indeed, there tends to be a "survivor bias" to the extent that successful firms stay in the sample while unsuccessful ones do not, and entrepreneurs who were refused any access to credit are not included either.

Much work still needs to be done to come up with unambiguous measures of soft budget constraints and with measures of hardening. Comparative analysis across countries using comparable data should also prove very helpful in understanding the source of hardening of budget constraints in transition economies.

12.5   CONCLUSION TO PART THREE

Let us briefly summarize the main issues analyzed in this last part of the book.

In Chapter 9 we analyzed the incentive issues in the government–firm relationship under socialism. Inefficiencies in the behavior of SOEs stem both from excessive government intervention in firms and from rent-seeking behavior of firms to obtain softer budget constraints. Excessive intervention in firms can be related to objectives that deviate from efficiency, but it can also be related to the absence of government commitment. Whereas the government acts as the third party in court to enforce commitment in contracts between private parties, government commitment is in general more difficult to achieve. This absence of commitment is an important source of inefficiency and leads to the ratchet effect: firms that fear their incentive schemes will be "ratcheted up" tend to maintain inefficient slack. Under socialism, ratchet effects and soft budget constraints reinforced each other, since the government was tempted to ratchet up incentive schemes of more efficient firms and to prey on them in order to bail out less efficient firms. The inefficient firms also did not exert enough effort because they expected to be bailed out, and good firms exerted less effort because of the ratchet effect. The combination of the ratchet effect and soft budget constraints thus led to generalized inefficiency.

The ratchet effect can be eliminated by breaking the government's monopsony over the managerial labor market and by providing enough outside options for managerial careers. This purpose is achieved as soon as a sufficiently large private sector emerges. It may also be accomplished if government is sufficiently decentralized, as in a federal state where states compete with each other to attract good managers. Other forms of government intervention and soft budget constraints are more difficult to eliminate in the transition, since they also exist in market economies. Privatization helps to reduce government intervention in firms to the extent that it increases the costs of such intervention: private firms need to be paid more in order to agree to fulfill objectives that deviate from their profit objective because control over assets gives them greater outside options than those of managers in SOEs. The higher the profit opportunities in private firms, the more costly state intervention becomes. Privatization also helps to reduce soft budget constraints. A private investor like a bank will only bail out a firm if the monetary benefit from refinancing exceeds the cost, whereas the government will take into account other benefits from refinancing such as social welfare. Demonopolization is also an important instrument for hardening budget constraints because entry and excess capacity in a competitive sector reduce the social costs of liquidation and thus generate credibility for hardening budget constraints.

In Chapter 10 we went further in our exploration of privatization policies by comparing the effect of the different privatization policies implemented in various countries on efficiency and the restructuring of firms. In terms of restructuring outcomes, the various privatization policies are much less apart than in terms of transfer of ownership. A policy of fast giveaway may encompass all (or a majority of) SOEs, whereas a policy of gradual sales will only concern the better firms. However, quick defensive restructuring outcomes will tend to be observed only in the better firms, under both policies. Indeed, privatization to insiders tends to lead to entrenchment of the latter. Insiders will tend to block sales to more efficient outside owners and to continue lobbying for subsidies and soft budget constraints rather than to restructure. Moreover, the problem of access to outside funds for strategic restructuring is not solved by mass privatization. The empirical evidence suggests that the extent of defensive restructuring is independent of the form of ownership and corporate governance, whereas outside ownership is important for strategic restructuring and for putting in place more efficient management.

Apart from the effects on enterprise restructuring, policies of mass privatization may contribute to a deterioration of the public finance problem in transition economies through the loss of government wealth and thereby may jeopardize macroeconomic equilibrium. More importantly, the actual experience of mass privatization in the Czech Republic and in Russia suggests that possibly inefficient institutional lock-ins may be created by mass privatization whereby the powerful interest groups created by mass privatization are able to capture the state and block reforms aimed toward more enforcement of tax collection, more transparent financial and prudential regulations, effective implementation of bankruptcy rules, and so on. These lock-ins can also be the source of major political instability in the future.

In Chapter 11 we analyzed changes in incentives within government administration. Changes in the organization and incentives of government agents are as important as privatization because a private sector cannot develop successfully if surrounded by a government administration whose interests are not at least partially aligned with market development. The transition experience is especially interesting from that point of view. In Russia the bulk of SOEs were privatized quickly, but the reform of government administration was neglected. In China privatization was an absolute taboo until recently, but spontaneous changes took place within the organization of government that had a favorable effect on market reform. In particular, the far-reaching decentralization of government in China created forms of competition like fiscal competition that can be considered to have a favorable effect on reforms in the context of transition, even though in general the welfare effects of fiscal competition are ambiguous in a second-best world. Moreover, yardstick competition between regions also strengthens incentives of government officials in a federal state.

The fiscal federalism arrangements in China are particularly interesting because fiscal contracts between lower-level and higher-level government are close to optimal incentive contracts whereby lower-level governments are fully residual claimants of marginal tax revenues. This fact creates a partial alignment of interests of local government with the development of the private sector. In Russia, in contrast, an important part of any increase in tax revenue is taken away from lower-level governments, and they get bailed out in case of a shortfall in tax revenues. No incentives exist for local government to develop the private sector, and government officials do not suffer the negative consequences of predation on the private sector.

Again in China, the development of township and village enterprises (TVEs) constitutes an interesting development in the context of the absence of the rule of law. TVEs provide both private and public goods. This fact reduces the incentives of higher-level government to prey on TVEs, in turn reducing the incentives of TVEs to hide revenues. We know that hiding revenues to avoid predation on revenues is a major source of inefficiency in the development of the private sector in Russia.

In Chapter 12 we have looked in greater detail at how budget constraints of firms can be hardened after privatization and how soft budget constraints of banks can be avoided. Several institutional mechanisms play an important role in hardening budget constraints of firms. We examined in particular the role of decentralization of banking, the effect of restructuring with redeployment of activity toward new business links to avoid chains of insolvency and "too big to fail" effects, the importance of the dynamism of entry by the new private sector, and the importance of investing in improvements in screening technology. Budget constraints of firms can remain soft if banks themselves have soft budget constraints. We have analyzed the role of banking regulation, of initial bank capitalization, and of hospital banks in preventing soft budget constraints of banks, whether the cause of the latter is related to "gambling for resurrection" motives or to rent-seeking motives toward government.

This last part of the book was very rich in results. What should we emphasize? Rather than picking out one or two specific results, I would like to insist on the importance for the behavior of agents of the specific institutional environments in which these agents operate, be they SOEs, private firms, or government agencies. The use of noncooperative game models, as in industrial organization, corporate finance, or political economy, allows us to derive much finer predictions than verbal theorizing and to go much deeper in the analysis than simple dichotomies like private and public ownership. Such models are clearly useful in trying to understand the differences in performance among privatized firms depending on the privatization method (which ultimately determines the corporate governance arrangements of those firms for a sufficiently long period). This approach also helps one to understand circumstances under which budget constraints are more or less hard or more or less soft. It is also relevant if we want to understand how the specific organization of government, along with the incentives it creates, structures the attitude of government officials toward the private sector.

This methodological insistence on the relevance of the specific institutional environment in which agents operate and on the details of that environment, as formulated in extensive form games, seems obvious for those trained in modern microeconomics. The surprises of transition, like the disappointing outcomes of insider privatization, asset stripping after mass privatization, the persistence of soft budget constraints, the early restructuring of SOEs, the success of Chinese TVEs, or the differences in attitude of government agencies in various countries toward private sector development, show that this is the relevant level of analysis.

The finer level of analysis given by extensive form models depicting the institutional environment under which agents operate also means that, while giving better predictions, the predictions of theory depend to a great extent on the specific model chosen. What then are the relevant models? Ultimately, the test of many of these models is empirical. For example, in some of the models reviewed a small size of banks is good for hardening budget constraints because of the ex post efficiencies it creates between multiple creditors at the renegotiation stage. However, we have also seen that a larger size of banks may allow investment in better screening technologies, which helps to shift the bank's preference from refinancing existing loans to financing new projects. Only empirical research can determine which effect dominates. Similarly, only empirical research will tell us what the main mechanisms for softening or hardening of budget constraints are.

Many questions still need further research. One important question is to acquire a better understanding of government ownership. That issue was addressed with the Hart, Shleifer, and Vishny (1997) model, but one needs to go further in the analysis and to analyze the political-economy and institutional channels through which state ownership leads to different behavior and performance than private ownership.

One important issue on which further work is needed is the previously mentioned issue of the possible lock-ins that mass privatization may create. That issue was not at all present in early debates on privatization, but the Russian and the Czech experiences suggest that mass privatization has led to a very fast concentration of economic power in the hands of a small minority that may have become strong enough to block further reforms that could endanger the rents it gained from mass privatization. In the introduction of the book, we mentioned the importance of path dependency created by events taking place in extraordinary periods of change. Both theoretical work and empirical work are needed to gain a better understanding of that question and to put it in historical perspective.

CHAPTER 13

SYNTHESIZING LESSONS FROM TRANSITION

In this concluding chapter, I would like to wrap up some of the lessons we can draw on the basis of the preceding chapters. More than ten years after the fall of the Berlin Wall and the beginning of research on transition, it is time to take stock of what a large body of research on transition has taught us about the transition process. Transition is not yet over. In the summer of 1999 the media were full of reports on corruption and money laundering at the highest levels in Russia. Headline stories abounded about the United States having "lost" Russia, about how that huge country became a kleptocracy instead of a democracy. Beyond the excitement inherent in media stories, it is not exaggerated to state that at the beginning of the twenty-first century the uncertainty about the future of Russia is probably as strong as it was ten years ago. Even in the future, when transition completely belongs to history, we know that the judgment of history will never be definitive. Many lessons from transition will remain controversial for a long time. Nevertheless, many important lessons have been learned compared to how we thought about transition ten years ago. Many of these lessons are humbling for policymakers and researchers, one more reason to spell them out.

In section 13.1, I will try to synthesize, on the basis of the twelve preceding chapters, what we have learned about the transition process from ten years of research in the economics of transition. I will not attempt to summarize the book, as summaries are provided at the end of each of the three parts. Instead, I will try to provide a synthesis of what we have learned from transition, which issues are still controversial, and which ones need further research.

In section 13.2, in line with the goal of this book, I will recall some of the lessons of transition for economics in general and take stock of some of the main spillovers for economics of the research on transition.

13.1   WHAT HAVE WE LEARNED ABOUT TRANSITION?

In order to organize the discussion, I will start with a simplified and schematic presentation of the differences between the two main visions of transition that have crystallized from the beginning of the transition process and that shaped both policy recommendations and research programs.

The first vision of transition is the *Washington consensus*. I will call the second one the *evolutionary-institutionalist perspective*. One could label the former the big-bang or the shock-therapy view, and the latter the gradualist or incrementalist view, but these labels are too narrow in focus because they mainly emphasize the speed of reforms, whereas, as we will see, there are many more dimensions than speed that are involved in both visions. This broadening of the focus since the beginning of transition is the object of a consensus among researchers working on transition on both sides. Moreover, issues of speed have remained relatively controversial, whereas there has been an important convergence of views among researchers on other dimensions in the direction of the "evolutionary-institutionalist perspective." The choice of this label refers both to the major emphasis given to the importance of institutions for successful capitalist development, and *mutatis mutandis* for a successful transition, and to a strong emphasis on the dynamics and the global momentum of institutional change.

The presentation that follows is certainly schematic and incomplete. Most researchers would not fully recognize their own vision of transition in either category, and there has also been an important degree of convergence over time in many of the dimensions that I will evoke. Nevertheless, the schematic typology is a useful starting point for a synthesis on transition.

13.1.1   THE WASHINGTON CONSENSUS VERSUS THE EVOLUTIONARY-INSTITUTIONALIST PERSPECTIVE

The "Washington consensus" view on transition was clearly dominant in the beginning of the transition process in Central and Eastern Europe. It has shaped policy recommendations from international financial organizations and has been supported and endorsed by famous economists from the best universities in the world. It has influenced to a large degree economic policy in most transition economies, with the very large exception of China, which has followed its own transition path in a very pragmatic way. Intellectually, it is rooted in a combination of (1) standard neoclassical price theory, (2) standard macroeconomics and experience of stabilization policy, and (3) a broad body of knowledge in comparative economic systems emphasizing both the complementarity of the constitutive institutions of economic systems and the disappointing experiences with partial reform in Central and Eastern Europe.

The evolutionary-institutionalist perspective has had more support in academic circles than in international policy circles. It was clearly a minority view in the beginning of transition but has gained more and more support over time in the light of the transition experience. It emphasizes strongly the success of the Chinese transition experience, which has followed none of the recommendations of the Washington-consensus vision and poses a challenge to it. Intellectually, it is rooted in (1) the institutionalist perspective given by modern microeconomic theory and its methodology shaped by the development of noncooperative game theory, (2) themes of the evolutionary approach to economics (see, e.g., Murrell, 1992), and (3) a philosophical skepticism, influenced by Hayek and Popper, with a strong emphasis on our relative ignorance of economic and social systems and their transformation, an emphasis on the uncertainty associated with societal engineering, and a strong aversion toward any kind of Bolshevik-style campaigning in large-scale institutional transformation.

Table 13.1 gives a summary and simplified presentation of these two opposed visions (see also typologies in Murrell, 1992, and Stiglitz, in press). Following the order of the book, we emphasize first the political economy of reforms and reform strategies, and then allocative changes and governance changes. Most, though not all, issues were taken up rather thoroughly in the book. Some of the differences listed in the table are less important and less acute, but others are more important.

A fundamental difference between the visions is the attitude toward uncertainty that we already emphasized in Chapter 1. The Washington consensus emphasizes that reform will deliver sure efficiency gains. It contains a strong faith in societal engineering. The idea behind this view is that the economics of reform is well understood. Since the initial situation is characterized by fundamental inefficiencies and since economic theory predicts that transition will deliver sure efficiency gains, then these reforms should be implemented with faith that the efficiency gains will be reaped. We know that capitalism as experienced in the United States or Europe has been proved successful, so it is simply a matter of copying the better models. In contrast, the evolutionary-institutionalist perspective emphasizes the aggregate uncertainty of transition outcomes. Even in trying to copy the better models, things may go wrong. Our understanding of these large-scale changes is still rudimentary, and nothing guarantees that there will not be huge unexpected and undesired outcomes. Moreover, there are a huge number of coordination problems to be solved among economic agents. Among the vast multiplicity of equilibria implied, we do not know in advance which one will be selected and why.

This important difference in starting points has implications for reform strategies. For the Washington consensus, the political economy emphasis is to use early windows of opportunity or periods of "exceptional politics" to push reforms through as fast as possible and to create irreversibility. In the evolutionary-institutionalist perspective, the latter strategy may be dangerous and lock whole countries in situations of inefficient economic outcomes that are hard to reverse. Such outcomes may break social cohesion and generate important political instability. The emphasis is rather on ensuring continuous and growing support for reforms among the population. This implies, as seen in Chapter 2, a stronger emphasis on a gradual approach to reforms, relying on the flexibility of experimentation, with an adequate sequencing of reforms, to possibly reverse reforms that do not work and try other ones.

The Washington consensus rejects in general any partial reform. The idea is that any partial reform will create rents for given groups that will be threatened by further reforms.

TABLE 13.1 A SIMPLIFIED PRESENTATION OF THE TWO DIFFERENT VISIONS OF TRANSITION

	Washington Consensus	Evolutionary-Institutionalist Perspective
1. The political economy of reforms and reform strategies		
Attitude toward uncertainty	Insistence on sure efficiency gains; faith in societal engineering	Insistence on aggregate uncertainty; skepticism toward societal engineering
Political economy emphasis	Use of window of opportunity to create irreversibility	Ensuring continuous and growing support for reforms
View of partial reforms	Creating rents that block further reform progress	Dependent on sequencing: can either create momentum or stall reform process
View of reform complementarities	Of absolute importance. Necessity to jump-start the market economy by simultaneous introduction of all main reforms	Very important but comprehensiveness of initial reforms not necessary provided initial reforms can create momentum for further reforms. Transitional institutions can develop and evolve gradually toward more perfect institutions.
Main support group for reforms	Owners of privatized enterprises	Middle class and new private sector
Focus of reforms	Liberalization, stabilization, privatization	Creation of institutional underpinnings of markets to encourage strong entrepreneurial entry
Attitude toward institutional change	Emphasis on adoption of laws	Comprehensive: legal and financial change, law enforcement, reform of organization of government, development of self-enforcing social norms
Attitude toward initial conditions	Creation of tabula rasa conditions by breaking existing communist state structure	Using existing institutions to prevent economic disruption and social unrest while developing new institutions

TABLE 13.1 (CONTINUED)

	Washington Consensus	Evolutionary-Institutionalist Perspective
2. Allocative changes		
Main view of markets and liberalization	Markets will develop spontaneously provided government does not intervene; supply and demand as focus of analysis	Importance of institutional underpinnings needed to enhance market growth: minimum legal and contracting environment, law enforcement, political stability, building of business networks and long-term partnerships; contracting agents and their institutional environment as unit of analysis
Main attitude toward inefficient SOEs	Aggressive closing down	Containment and politically feasible downsizing. Rely on evolutionary development of private sector to shrink state sector.
Main view of government	Weakening it as much as possible to prevent intervention in markets	Role of government in law enforcement and in securing property rights.
3. Governance changes		
Focus of privatization	Fast transfer of ownership in private hands via mass privatization to break government power and jump-start market economy. Faith in market to ensure efficient resale.	Emphasis on organic development of private sector. Emphasis on sales to outsiders to achieve efficient transfer of ownership from the start.
Main emphasis of government reform	Shrinking the size of government	Reform in the organization of government so as to align as much as possible the interests of government bureaucrats with the development of markets.
Hardening budget constraints	Exogenous policy choice that depends on political will	Endogenous outcome of institutional changes

Therefore, partial reforms create constituencies that will tend to oppose further reform, whereas this will not be the case with a comprehensive introduction of reforms. The evolutionary-institutionalist view is less pessimistic about partial reform. All depends on the sequencing of reforms. Whereas some partial reforms may indeed lead to stalling of the reform process and even to unnecessary reversal, starting with other partial reforms may create momentum for further reform. This will be the case especially when reform complementarities are important.

For the Washington consensus, complementarities in reform are of absolute importance and are an overriding argument for a big bang approach whereby all reforms are introduced in a simultaneous and comprehensive way.[1] For the evolutionary-institutionalist perspective, complementarities, while clearly important, are not an overriding argument as long as sequencing of reforms can be used to create momentum for further reforms. Though there is a general emphasis on the importance of institutions, it is not viewed as necessary, and sometimes not viewed as possible, to directly introduce the "best practice" institutions in the world. The evolutionary perspective implies that transitional institutions can develop that are adequate to the initial conditions but can evolve gradually toward more perfect institutions. Here also, flexibility is important to prevent a lock-in in inefficient institutions that are hard to change.

A more minor point of difference, but nevertheless one with possible wide-ranging practical consequences, is a difference in emphasis on the main support groups for reform. The Washington consensus emphasizes less the need to gain political support for reforms, but to the extent that it does, it tends to emphasize the importance of the support from the owners of privatized enterprises. The idea is that fast mass privatization creates constituencies among insiders and among those who benefit most from mass privatization to block any reversal. Since the owners of privatized enterprises are a minority and are not likely to be median voters in elections, the emphasis is mainly on creating powerful lobbies for capitalism through mass privatization. The emphasis is thus clearly on interest-group politics. The evolutionary-institutionalist perspective pays more attention to the attitudes of voters and to electoral politics, developed in Chapters 3 and 4. There the emphasis is more on the need to rely on a broad group of small entrepreneurs and the middle class that emerges from the entry of new enterprises both in urban areas and in the countryside. The idea is that the middle class always plays an important role in democracies, since voters of that group are more likely to be pivotal in elections. This also explains a greater care for social cohesion and a fear of excessive inequalities that are likely to create more pressures for redistribution and may generate political instability.

Let us now turn to issues related to the substance of reforms and their focus. Here also, there are nonnegligible differences in vision. First of all, the "Washington consensus" view on transition is based on the trinity "liberalization, stabilization, privatization." At the start of this new millennium, few serious economists dispute the need to liberalize, stabilize, and privatize. There is not much dispute either about the advantages of using shock therapy as a stabilization method when it is politically feasible. For the evolutionary-institutionalist perspective, the emphasis is more on the creation of the

---

[1] *Note that if this view is taken seriously, then partial reform cannot stall the reform process over time. We have noted this inconsistency in Chapter 2.*

institutional underpinnings of markets to encourage a vigorous process of entry, competition, and exit. The idea is that liberalization, privatization, and even stabilization will not necessarily deliver the desired outcomes in the absence of such institutional underpinnings and may lead to unpleasant surprises.

While the Washington consensus insists less on institutions, it would be wrong to state that it neglects them. However, the emphasis is more on the adoption of adequate laws to secure private property, rights of shareholders and creditors, absence of corruption, and so forth. The evolutionary-institutionalist perspective takes a more comprehensive view of institutional conditions. These include not only legal and financial change but also conditions of law enforcement, reform of the organization of government, and the development of self-enforcing social norms that foster entrepreneurship, trust, and respect for legality and commitment. The evolutionary-institutionalist perspective has sometimes been derided by statements according to which it recommends that perfect institutions should be introduced first before implementing any liberalization or privatization. As stated earlier, this is not the case. The evolutionary attitude toward institutions implies that minimum institutions underpinning market development must be present from the beginning because these define the rules of the game and thus place restrictions on undesired kinds of individual behavior and reduce uncertainty. Adequate institutions must develop through trial and error and must evolve over time toward more perfect institutions. The latter cannot be introduced overnight, precisely because institutions are not simply a set of laws.

Related to the latter question is the attitude toward the initial conditions of reform. The Washington consensus emphasizes the need to create tabula rasa conditions by breaking as rapidly and as thoroughly as possible the existing communist state structure. The logic is one of "cavalry attack" or Bolshevik-style campaign to break any possible resistance to and sabotage of reforms by the conservative communists of the former *nomenklatura.* The rhetoric uses revolutionary metaphors, and comparisons are often made between postcommunist transition and the French revolution (see, e.g., Sachs, Woo, and Yang, 1999). This emphasis is very strong. Early in transition, most experts on socialist economies were pushed aside and declared "obsolete" by the shock therapists. Many of these new transition experts stated repeatedly that knowledge of the former system is a liability and ignorance an asset in understanding transition. This tabula rasa view has found its most accomplished implementation in East Germany, where the old system was thoroughly broken up at high speed while West German experts came to build their own institutions on the ashes of the old system. As usual, German *Gründlichkeit* was at work. In contrast, the evolutionary-institutionalist perspective shies away from a revolutionary, Jacobin, or Bolshevik-style approach to transition. It emphasizes the need to use the existing institutions to prevent economic disruption and social unrest while developing new institutions. Here, we have an area where both sides put a strong emphasis on institutions, but the Washington consensus insists on an uncompromising approach and the absolute need to thoroughly destroy past institutions and directly put in place the best imaginable institutions.

On allocative changes, the topic of Part Two, the two views differ in their main view of markets and liberalization. The Washington consensus emphasizes that markets will develop spontaneously provided there is price flexibility and the government does not intervene in markets. Markets (supply and demand) are the main focus of analysis (see Chapter 6), and the main implicit theoretical tool guiding this vision is price theory and general equilibrium theory. The evolutionary-institutionalist perspective relies much less on standard market analysis and emphasizes the institutional underpinnings of markets and the effect they may have on the speed of growth of markets and entrepreneurial activity. Contracts and the relations between contracting agents are the focus of analysis (see Chapter 7). Therefore, a strong emphasis is put on the general environment of contracting: the minimum legal environment, security of property rights and law enforcement, political stability, the development of business and market networks facilitating search, the development of specific investments in long-term business relationships, and so on.

A less important difference, though not without consequence, is the one on attitudes toward inefficient SOEs. Early in transition the Washington consensus developed a hostile view toward SOEs, emphasizing the need for fast privatization to prevent asset stripping and the need to close down unprofitable plants and firms as fast as possible. Again, it is in East Germany that this approach was implemented the most thoroughly. The evolutionary-institutionalist perspective is less aggressive and takes an attitude of containment and gradual downsizing and hardening of budget constraints, taking into account political constraints. The emphasis is more on developing a strong new private sector to attract workers away from the state sector and to let it shrink gradually over time.

The main view of government in transition developed by the Washington consensus is that of the necessity of weakening government as much as possible to "depoliticize" the economy and to prevent intervention in markets. The evolutionary-institutionalist perspective emphasizes the importance of government in enforcing the law and security of property rights. In particular, adequate government infrastructure (police, courts) is needed to ensure that the rules of the market game are followed. Among other things, it is important to fight organized crime and racketeering (see Chapter 8). It is also important to enforce an adequate competition policy to prevent monopolization.

Turning now to governance changes, the topic of Part Three, the two visions differ in their focus on privatization policy. The Washington consensus emphasizes the need for a fast transfer of ownership into private hands through mass privatization to break government power and to jump-start the market economy. Speed is of the essence. The idea is that any privatization is always better than maintaining government ownership, so that the benefits of rapid privatization outweigh the costs in terms of possible misallocation of assets to private individuals and groups. There is also a strong emphasis on developing stock markets so that efficient resale of assets can take place after privatization. In contrast, the evolutionary-institutionalist perspective in general puts less emphasis on the importance of rapid privatization of large SOEs. There is a broader view of privatization of the economy with the organic development of the private sector as its main element. In terms of privatization of large enterprises, the emphasis is on competitive sales to outsiders to ensure efficient transfer of ownership from the start. There is great skepticism with respect to the possibility of efficient resales given the necessarily rudimentary development of financial institutions and markets at the beginning of transition. These must necessarily evolve over time and cannot be jump-started. There is also great skepticism with respect to the possibility of overnight development of entrepreneurial skills among the beneficiaries of mass privatization, by the sheer act of that transfer.

In terms of emphasis on reform of the organization of government, the Washington consensus attaches less importance to this question and emphasizes mainly the need to shrink the size of government. The evolutionary-institutionalist perspective goes further than the simple dimension of government size and emphasizes changes in incentives of government bureaucrats. Since government, government agencies, and government officials can prey on markets and the private sector and since they can be captured by such interest groups as monopolies and Mafias, it is important to implement reforms in the organization of government so as to align as much as possible the interests of government bureaucrats with the development of markets. The idea is that markets and the private sector cannot develop in an environment of government hostility. Therefore, adequate reform of government administration is needed to create more congruent interests between the private sector and government bureaucrats (see the analysis of Chapter 11).

In terms of hardening budget constraints, a dimension that has appeared more and more important with the transition experience and that we discussed at length in Part Three, there are also conceptual differences. For the Washington consensus, hardening budget constraints is mainly an exogenous policy choice that depends on the political will of policymakers. For the evolutionary-institutionalist perspective, soft budget constraints are related to a commitment problem. Because of this commitment problem, exhortations to harden budget constraints may not be credible. Hardening budget constraints must be an endogenous outcome of institutional changes set up to create credibility for hardening.

While we have emphasized the differences between the two visions, the Washington consensus and the evolutionary-institutionalist perspective, it is important to note that these are certainly not visions that are diametrically opposed. Both aim at introducing a successful market economy based on private ownership. There is thus no fundamental difference in terms of goals. Nevertheless, these differences in vision reflect differences in the approach to economic analysis and in understanding the fundamental institutions of capitalism. These differences in analysis lead to differences in policy emphasis in several important dimensions.

13.1.2 A BROAD ASSESSMENT

Taking a broad view of the transition experience, it would seem on the surface that the following general assessment can be made: Central European countries that started transition early, that are growing again, and that now face the prospect of entry into the European Union can be broadly seen as a success of the Washington consensus, whereas the Russian experience can be basically seen as an illustration of the shortcomings of that view. In contrast, the success of Chinese transition cannot be attributed to the Washington consensus but can be seen as a confirmation of the evolutionary-institutionalist perspective.

Such a broad assessment is not the consensus of the profession but would seem to be an a priori no-nonsense characterization. Clearly, however, we cannot content ourselves with broad and superficial generalizations and must go into detail concerning the various dimensions to indicate what we have learned, in which areas research has led to broad consensus views, in which areas controversies remain important, and in which areas research has been relatively neglected.

13.1.2.1 The Political Economy of Reform and Reform Strategies

In terms of the attitude toward uncertainty, I would claim that the facts have vindicated the evolutionary-institutionalist perspective and proved the Washington consensus to be wrong. A simple look at the differences in performance between the transition countries (see Chapter 1) shows wide variation in the evolution of output, between the strong growth of the Chinese economy, the U-shaped output evolution in Central Europe, and the continuous decline in many former Soviet Union countries. One can always come up with *ex post* explanations for the observed evolutions in the various countries and trace them to wrong or incomplete policies or lack of comprehensiveness of reforms. Such an attitude is not acceptable for at least two reasons. First, policies are endogenous and not exogenous and depend on political constraints. It is thus a bit vain to lament incompleteness of reforms without taking into account existing political constraints. Second, the policies strongly endorsed by the advocates of the Washington consensus led in several dimensions to important surprises and unexpected outcomes. This is the case for the significant output fall after liberalization. It was not predicted. Another unexpected outcome was the asset stripping following mass privatization in Russia and the Czech Republic. Also on the downside, the development of the Mafia, the strong increase in the size of the hidden economy countries of the former Soviet Union, and the resistance of large Russian enterprises to tax collection were not predicted either. On the upside, the development of TVEs in China was also an unexpected corollary of decollectivization. To be sure, most of these events were not predicted by the advocates of the evolutionary-institutionalist perspective either. Nevertheless, the importance of these large unexpected outcomes shows the relevance of the emphasis on aggregate uncertainty. It is finally important to note that an important convergence has been taking place gradually among researchers working on transition, certainly in the academic community, on the importance of aggregate uncertainty.

In terms of the political economy emphasis, the picture is more mixed. The Central European experience broadly appears to vindicate the Washington consensus. The Chinese experience broadly appears to vindicate the evolutionary-institutionalist perspective. In a way, this result should not be seen as a surprise. While there is clearly a difference of emphasis between the two visions, the theory developed in Chapter 2 can make sense of both observations on the basis of the basic trade-off involved in the political economy of reforms: sequencing of reforms strategy can relax the *ex ante* political constraints and gradually build constituencies for further reform, and thus enhance political feasibility, while big bang can ensure more irreversibility of reforms in cases where there is a window of opportunity—that is, where *ex ante* political constraints are less important. However, it is important to note that aggregate uncertainty is an important assumption in that theory. From that point of view, I would claim that the Russian experience shows the downside of the Washington consensus because of its neglect of aggregate uncertainty. A window of opportunity was used to implement mass privatization, and this was done so as to create irreversibility of reform. However, the relative irreversibility created has locked the Russian economy in an inefficient situation where interest groups who gained most from mass privatization (the famous oligarchs) have become so powerful as to block further reform such as tax reform, government reform, stronger law enforcement, and stronger security of property rights.

This turn of events in Russia tends to suggest that the political economy view relying mainly on the support of owners of privatized enterprises was seriously one-sided. Not only did this lead to phenomena of capture and relative lock-in, but also, in the long run, the fact that a great majority of the population has suffered from the transition so far and resents the strong concentration of wealth created by a privatization process viewed as illegitimate and corrupt is worrying both for political stability and continuation of reforms.

On the effects of partial reform, I would claim that the Chinese experience vindicates the evolutionary-institutionalist perspective that sequencing of reforms does not necessarily stall reform progress but can be used to create momentum for further reform. As seen in Part One, the successes of decollectivization made it possible to create momentum for reform in the state sector. While the Chinese reform process has had its ups and downs, its periods of fast progress and periods of stagnation in reform, the general momentum has continued until today. Insufficient attention, however, has been given to this issue of partial reform and the conditions under which it creates momentum or on the contrary creates vested interests that block further reform. While the models in Part One were relatively abstract and general, one needs political economic models with more flesh to understand better the economic and political dynamics of sequencing.

One lesson that emerges from the transition experience is that the political constraints to reform have been less strong in Central Europe, especially in the countries close to Germany, than in the former Soviet Union. Yegor Gaidar did not have the support that Leszek Balcerowicz and Vaclav Klaus had in Poland and the Czech Republic. Even when former communist coalitions came to power in Central Europe, they did not question the direction of reform, only its speed and its redistributive aspects. Why this striking difference in the importance of political constraints to reform? Clearly further research is needed to answer that question.

In Roland (1997), I suggested that the geopolitical factor has played an important role, a factor that was underestimated at the beginning of transition, certainly by myself. Economists trying to understand transition have generally had the vision of transition as a shift toward democracy and the market. If we take some historical distance, we can see that transition also represents a very important geopolitical move, that is, the shift of Central Europe and the Baltic states to the West. To important parts of populations in those countries, the single most important factor about transition is the change from the status of a satellite country of the Soviet empire to that of a country belonging to the Western block or even to the European Union. Transition represents a unique historical opportunity for several nations to get strongly anchored in Western Europe. Not only is this "anchorage" to the European Union desired by nations of Central Europe, but it also focuses expectations and gives credibility to the political and economic process of transition. Entry into the European Union implies adopting the political and economic system of the West. The potential reward of belonging to the club of Western nations makes it more worthwhile to undergo the cost of transition and thus to accept it more easily. Moreover, the geopolitical factor increases the perceived cost of a policy reversal because it implies the risk of being left out of the Western club, a perspective that many in Central Europe would view as disastrous.

As we saw in Chapter 8, this geopolitical factor may be strong enough as a focal point to explain why countries from Central Europe did not suffer from the type of government collapse, anarchy, and general diffusion of criminality, inside and outside government, that Russia and other countries from the former Soviet Union have been facing. The ability to enforce the law and to protect property rights seems to be a first-order effect in explaining why Central Europe recovered from their output fall while Russia and other countries not facing the prospect of entry to the European Union experienced a continuous decline of output (again see Chapter 8).

The geopolitical factor in Central European countries was reinforced by a "transition tournament" between the Czech, Hungarian, and Polish governments where each pretended to be the most advanced transition country in the hope of being the first to enter the European Union and also of attracting the bulk of foreign direct investment (FDI) to the region. The incentives related to the "prize" of such a tournament are strong enough for countries of that size to create credibility for economic transformation. Countries that entered the transition race later, like Bulgaria and Romania, have little hope of catching up with the more advanced countries or even of pretending to do so, and thus fewer possibilities of attracting FDI.

To understand the strength of the geopolitical factor, compare the situation of Central European countries to that of Russia, where this factor is absent. By contrast to Central Europe, where transition is seen as a liberation from the Soviet empire and as access to the Western club of nations, transition is viewed in Russia as a traumatic experience by important parts of the population. Transition represents indeed the loss, not only of the Soviet empire, but also of territories like Ukraine or the Baltic states that already belonged to tsarist Russia. Not only does this loss mean a wound to Russian nationalist pride, but it implies uncertainty for the families of those who have relatives among the millions of Russians living in the former Soviet republics and who became "immigrants" in former Soviet territories, often with the status of "second-class" citizen. The trauma of the loss of superpower status, similar in a way to the trauma of Germany after World War I, could be, to a certain extent, compensated for by economic gains from transition. Unfortunately, these have not materialized so far for the majority of Russians.

No entry of Russia in the EU is expected nor especially desired. The large size of the country implies that the impact of foreign direct investment is likely to be more diluted, thereby reducing the incentives to participate in "transition tournaments." It is thus no wonder that resistance to transition proved much harder in the former Soviet Union, as witnessed by the greater difficulties in hardening budget constraints of enterprises or in adopting stabilization measures. Nor is it clear that no major policy reversal will take place or is expected to take place.

If we believe the geopolitical factor played a big role in Central Europe, then it would be seriously flawed to compare transition in Central Europe and Russia without taking this factor into account. To understand the effect of political constraints on the transition process, it is better to look at the experience of large countries that must achieve the transition process by their own efforts without counting too much on outside help. The comparison between Russia and China is of relevance there.

If the hypothesis of the geopolitical factor allows us to explain the stronger resistance to reform or weaker support in Russia and countries of the former Soviet Union, it also implies that, everything else equal, the cost of reversal of transition policies is much higher in Central European countries than in Russia and in the former Soviet Union. In that sense, the perceived sense of haste that existed in Central Europe to implement reforms fast to achieve irreversibility may have been exaggerated.[2]

Finally, it is important to recall that the whole analysis of political constraints developed in Part One assumed that the economic outcome of reforms was independent of the speed of their introduction. We saw in Parts Two and Three that this assumption is not accurate. The speed of liberalization and privatization does have important efficiency and distributive implications. More importantly, the outcomes of liberalization and privatization teach us something about the two perspectives.

13.1.2.2 Allocative Changes and the Role of Institutions

With hindsight, I would claim that the outcome of liberalization vindicates the evolutionary-institutionalist perspective and that, on the basis of the transition experience, this is the consensus view that has been developing in the academic community. The important output fall that occurred after price liberalization in Central and Eastern Europe was not predicted. Standard textbook economics based on supply and demand at best would have predicted a low supply response to liberalization, but not a negative one! In the beginning, the debate on the output fall was inspired mainly by the Washington consensus centered on macroeconomic policies, asking questions such as whether stabilization had been too harsh or not. When Russia liberalized but failed to stabilize and nevertheless experienced an output fall, it was clear that new answers were needed. As seen in Part Two, two transition-specific answers have come up so far and have not yet been refuted. One is the traditional double marginalization idea from the industrial organization literature. To the extent that central planning created monopoly-like structures without real substitutes across firms and to the extent that import competition does not play that role, liberalization induces a cascade of price increases and output contraction along supply chains. The other, newer idea, is that of disorganization. This view takes

---

[2] One should not forget, however, that reform programs in Central Europe were started under Gorbachev's regime when the possibility of a successful conservative communist coup to halt reforms was not excluded. At such a time, implementing reforms rapidly in order to increase the costs of their reversal in case of a conservative Soviet backlash could make sense.

seriously the idea that markets have not yet been created when liberalization occurs. Because of bargaining inefficiencies or a combination of investment specificity and search frictions related to the prior absence of markets, existing output chains may suffer from acute disruption where the efficiency gains reaped when producers exit the chain do not compensate the disruption losses for the other producers in the output chain. The ensuing macroeconomic fall in GDP and welfare losses can be very important. These models are de facto inspired by the evolutionary-institutionalist perspective.

The relevance of the evolutionary-institutionalist perspective appears even more clear if we address the question of whether the output fall was an inevitable by-product of liberalization. Here, the Chinese experience is again helpful because it gives a negative answer to that question. A transition-specific institution has been created to prevent the output fall associated with liberalization: it is dual-track liberalization. Dual-track liberalization has several interesting properties. Prices are liberalized at the margin, so that the market information obtained from price liberalization is the same as what would obtain under full price liberalization. In the absence of preexisting markets, the most interesting properties of the dual track are that (1) it allows, by construction, the achieving of Pareto-improving gains from liberalization, a property which is interesting from the political economy point of view because it is a way of overcoming potential resistance to price liberalization, as a result of its distributive effects, and (2) also by construction, it makes it possible to prevent the output fall by maintaining past contractual obligations from the plan. It is in a way surprising to observe not only that the dual-track approach had not been proposed by academic economists in the context of transition but also that it took several years before economists started to understand the advantages of the dual-track system. While the dual track has worked well in China, further research is needed to understand some important aspects of the dual track such as how it can be enforced credibly and prevent the ratchet effect. Research may also help us understand why dual-track liberalization was not applied in Eastern Europe and the former Soviet Union.

If we ignore politics, it is possible to argue that dual-track liberalization could have been applied in the context of CMEA trade. The CMEA breakdown (as well as the breakup of the Soviet Union) has been considered the single most important explanatory factor for the general fall of output in the region (see, e.g., Rodrik, 1992), but it has generally been perceived as an exogenous shock. The breakdown of CMEA, however, was not exogenous but endogenous. It was decided in early 1990 when the Czechoslovak and Polish governments insisted on regaining their freedom of export with respect to CMEA agreements. The Soviets at that time responded by insisting that imports from the Soviet Union would from 1991 onward be paid at world prices and in hard currency. From the economic point of view, it would have been better, and possible, to implement a version of the dual-track system between former CMEA countries to avoid the strong trade disruption of 1991. However, here again politics and the geopolitical factor played an important role. Individual Central European countries wanted to leave the Soviet bloc as quickly as possible and be the first to knock at the door of the European Union. The CMEA breakdown was thus an economic consequence of the political will prevailing in Central European countries to leave the Soviet bloc.

One may argue that the dual-track approach could not have been implemented in the former Soviet Union and in Russia because of the government collapse that followed the implosion of communism after the failed putsch of 1991. However, as seen in Chapter 8, the dual-track system itself can be seen as an instrument to prevent government collapse in a credible way. Again, careful research is needed to understand whether or not conditions existed to implement the dual-track system itself, and mostly to enforce it credibly.

Another area where the evolutionary-institutionalist perspective is vindicated and where a consensus view has been developing fast within the academic community, albeit with strong differences in emphasis, relates to the effects of government collapse, mainly in many former Soviet countries. Government collapse was not an important concern to the Washington consensus. The concern was mainly to cut down the size of government and to "get the state out of the economy." Government collapse would have been seen as a second-best option where markets would emerge at full speed but there might be too few public goods, a lesser evil compared to the evils of communism. The emergence of organized crime, its predatory racketeering activities, and Mafia-related internal corruption of government have had deleterious effects on private sector growth. Again, this evolution was not predicted and was strongly underestimated. As of today, many analysts still see the Mafia mainly as a suboptimal contract enforcement agency.

Also, the more comprehensive view of institutions of the evolutionary-institutionalist perspective seems to be vindicated given the experience of government collapse. While it is always possible to claim for each transition country that there were shortcomings in the legal framework, one cannot claim that legal reform was neglected in Russia. Many important laws were adopted, often with the help of prominent scholars, be it corporate law, commercial law, or financial regulations. Nevertheless, law enforcement is a real problem and confidence in courts is lower than in Central Europe. The adequate social norms for a market economy have not yet emerged, and the level of business trust remains low (see Chapter 8).

13.1.2.3 Governance Changes

The experience with privatization also tends to vindicate the evolutionary-institutionalist perspective against the Washington consensus. The view according to which speed was of the essence in privatization in order to stop asset stripping by incumbent managers has been refuted by reality as many managers in SOEs did show early signs of restructuring. The doomsday predictions about the consequences of a rate of speed that is too low did not materialize in countries like Poland and Hungary where privatization took place in a gradual way. The prediction of generalized asset stripping was wrong. As we saw in Chapter 9, it made sense for good managers to try to attract private investors and to engage in early defensive restructuring for that purpose. Also, as discussed in Chapter 10, both theory and evidence show the importance of using privatization to achieve efficient matching of managers and assets. Insider privatization did not achieve that objective. Not surprisingly, insider privatization did not in general lead to significant improvement in performance, whereas adherents of the Washington consensus claimed that any privatization was always better than no privatization. Moreover, theories discussed in Chapter 10 suggest that the vested interests created by insider privatization may have made ulterior privatization more difficult to achieve and may also have maintained or aggravated the soft-budget-constraint syndrome in firms privatized to insiders. This soft-budget-constraint syndrome more usually takes the form of tax arrears. Further research should determine the extent to which the combination of free distribution of assets and tax erosion in Russia has reinforced tendencies toward government collapse.

In China we have seen the emergence of a very original institution, the TVEs owned by township and village governments. The Washington consensus cannot make sense of TVEs, except to claim that they are pseudoprivate enterprises, which we know is not the case. The theories developed in Chapter 11 suggest that TVEs operate under conditions of hard budget constraints that are very important for efficiency and also that, because of the public goods they help to create in their activity, they are more protected from government predation than private firms in China.

The Chinese experience where privatization remained taboo until recently also shows the importance of reform in the organization of government with the decentralization of government and the development of different forms of competition between local governments that can be made to work in favor of market development. Also, the fiscal federalism arrangements that make local governments residual claimants on any increase in the tax base create partial alignment of interests of bureaucrats with the development of markets and entrepreneurship.

In Russia reform of the organization of government was relatively neglected as the main focus of reform was implementation of mass privatization. With hindsight, reform of government with the purpose of building stable constituencies for reform should have been a priority of reform sequencing in Russia. The unexpected collapse of communism in 1991 created a formidable opportunity to create a democratic constitution with appropriate separation of powers and checks and balances between branches of government as well as between the center and provinces. Legitimate and accountable institutions coming out of a constitutional process would have helped to build more solid constituencies for reform and create a government structure with legitimate authority. There is no clear view among researchers about what should be the best constitution for Russia. In the light of the discussion of Chapter 11 on fiscal federalism, further devolution of power from the center to the regions and fiscal decentralization are part of the solution. Since legitimacy is fundamental, the appropriate constitution should not necessarily result from a blueprint but must be the result of a serious consensus-building deliberative process, as was the case with the successful democratic transition in Spain. As of today, government reform is still a priority in Russia, but the initial aspirations toward democracy have been strongly dampened by the turmoil of transition under Yeltsin.

A final difference we will mention between the Washington consensus and the evolutionary-institutionalist perspective concerns the question of soft budget constraints. Here the dominant thought was that hardening budget constraints was only a matter of exogenous choice by policymakers without thinking about the institutional factors or the factors in the environment of firms that contributed to credibly harden the budget constraint of firms: privatization, demonopolization, government reform, banking reform, and the like. The subsistence of soft budget constraints in different forms even in the advanced transition countries shows that hardening budget constraints is not just a matter of political will but a matter of devising institutional mechanisms that create credibility for hardening. Although there has been quite a body of theoretical work on soft budget constraints, empirical work on the issue is only beginning and should be a priority in research.

Despite the lack of direct empirical tests, the general evidence on enterprise behavior suggests a difference in enterprise behavior with a rapid hardening of budget constraints in the accession countries and persistence of soft budget constraints in most other countries. Here again, the geopolitical factor may have played an important role in shaping expectations early on in accession countries. Further research should give us a clearer picture of the hardening of budget constraints.

The broad assessment developed here tends to show, on the basis of the transition experience, that the evolutionary-institutionalist perspective is more complete and adequate than the Washington consensus. It is deliberately that I use the terms "more complete and adequate" because, as stated previously, the two views share a common goal. Nevertheless, differences in approach can lead to important differences in policy recommendations and outcomes.

There is today an increasing consensus among professional economists that the "Washington consensus" view with the so-called trinity of transition (liberalization, stabilization, privatization) is a misguided recipe for a successful transition. While professional economists do not deny the need to liberalize, stabilize, and privatize, they increasingly recognize that these policies cannot achieve their goals without the existence of appropriate institutional underpinnings of capitalism. In practice, there has been within the academic continuity a growing convergence, if not consensus, toward the evolutionary-institutionalist perspective,[3] and I thought it useful, at the end of this book, to spell out the main ingredients of the evolutionary-institutionalist perspective in contrast to the Washington consensus. To repeat, I presented these two visions as they have crystallized over time. In the beginning of transition, controversies focused nearly exclusively on the speed of transition, an issue that is very important both from the point of view of political economy, allocative changes, and also governance changes but that clearly does not form the whole picture.

While the preceding discussion has attempted to propose a synthesis of the main lessons of transition, an important word of caution is necessary, in line with the evolutionary-institutionalist perspective. Although the theories exposed in this book can contribute to shedding light on the transition processes, there is always a considerable distance between theory and complex reality. Therefore, particular caution is necessary when drawing policy conclusions. While general policy conclusions can be

[3] *It is interesting to note, from this point of view, that at the Fifth Nobel Symposium in Economics devoted to the economics of transition, out of six sessions, only one was devoted to macroeconomic developments, while there were five sessions on institutions, with three devoted to the organization of government and two to contracts.*

drawn from theory and empirical research on transition—the point is of course valid beyond transition—there is still a long distance between general policy conclusions drawn from economic analysis and direct policy recommendations. We can draw general lessons from the economic failures of transition in Russia, for example, but it is still a quite different matter to draw a complete and convincing counterfactual of how things could have evolved and bifurcated at precise moments in time, given the conditions of decisionmaking.

Also, while there is a move away from the Washington consensus toward the evolutionary-institutionalist perspective, many research questions in the latter program remain open. We mentioned at the end of Part One the issue of the effect of specific political institutions on political constraints. We also need a better understanding of the effects of public ownership under alternative institutional setups, as well as a better understanding of the effect of different institutions on the breeding and spreading of corruption. We have mentioned the necessity to better understand the dynamics of an institution like the dual track and the dynamics of institutional change toward greater momentum or toward inefficient lock-in. On the empirical front, a great many questions still remain also, such as a better understanding of the channels of law enforcement and more direct measurements of soft budget constraints. One needs to test various existing models of political economy and in particular the models put forward in this book. Finally, I would like to draw attention to two areas which, with hindsight, have appeared important for transition, but on which relatively little research has been done. The first one relates to inequality of wealth and income. Though the increase in inequality of income and wealth was predicted, the patterns of inequality increase are quite different across countries. Garner and Terrell (1998), for example, found that in the Czech Republic and in Slovakia, redistributive transfers by government acted strongly to correct the increase in inequality induced by market reform. Interestingly, Commander, Tolstopiatenko, and Yemtsov (1999) found that in Russia government expenditures and transfers tended to further increase inequality. How can we explain these differences? What are the political and economic effects of the increase in inequality in transition economies? While this is a general question for economics (Persson and Tabellini, 1994), it is particularly relevant in the case of transition. In particular, one would like to go beyond the median voter model and understand better the political channels through which an increase in inequality affects political decisionmaking: the relative role of electoral politics and special interest politics, the policy and political coalition formation process, and so on. The second theme is that of social behavior, social norms, and social capital. The question of social norms is a general and important question for social science, and this is an area that has been underresearched by economists, at least in the transition process. An obvious route of investigation that has not been used in formal analysis of transition processes so far, at least to my knowledge, is the use of evolutionary game models. Within the evolutionary-institutionalist perspective, this seems a natural route to take given the usefulness of evolutionary game theory in selecting equilibria.

13.2   WHAT HAS ECONOMICS LEARNED
FROM TRANSITION?

After having tried to brush a broad synthesis of some of the main lessons of the transition process so far, I would like briefly to ponder the impact and potential impact of transition research on economics in general.

The main impact has been to reinforce the institutionalist perspective in economics, a move that has also developed independently within economics with the use of noncooperative game theory and extensive form games. The negative surprises with the Washington consensus (output fall, government collapse, bad surprises from mass privatization) and the positive experience of Chinese transition have further contributed to a change of focus in the way to think about economics, emphasizing the importance of the various institutions underpinning a successful capitalist economy. If anything, the experience of transition shows that policies of liberalization, stabilization, and privatization that are not grounded in adequate institutions may not deliver successful outcomes. Instead of delivering growth and prosperity, they may deliver stealing, corruption, racketeering, and economic decline. Thus there is a shift of emphasis from markets and price theory to contracting and the legal, social, and political environment of contracting. Transition has not only helped to reinforce this change of focus in economic thinking, but it has also renewed interest in thinking about the interplay and complementarities between the various constitutive institutions of capitalism.

Research on transition has not only reinforced the existing institutionalist perspective, but has also started to explore new and difficult domains such as the dynamics of institutional change in an evolutionary perspective. It has also emphasized the importance of political support for given institutions and how institutions may evolve with the momentum of the interaction between the politics and economics of institutional change. Stable political support for given institutions is important to create stable expectations and stable economic behavior that in turn may strengthen political support.

Much of the research done on transition has applications that go well beyond the specific transition context.

Issues about the political economy of reform brought up in the transition literature and discussed in Part One apply to other contexts such as European integration or reforms in Latin America where issues of speed and sequencing, complementarities between reforms, and momentum effects play an important role. Further research should examine the effects of differences in political regimes on reform patterns. While the politics of mass privatization is unique to transition, models of the politics of privatization can explain political motives for the underpricing of shares of privatized firms by right-wing governments concerned about securing constituencies for reelection.

While dual-track liberalization is an original institution that has emerged in the context of Chinese transition to implement Pareto-improving liberalization, its principles apply to other kinds of reform in other countries: labor market reform, pension reform, and the like. The dual-track approach may find applications in internal labor market practices and wage-setting behavior in firms. The main unresolved question in research on the dual-track principle, and in practice the most likely stumbling block for implementation of the dual-track type of reform, is the question of government commitment either not to renege on maintaining rents through the old institutions or not to renege on reducing the span of the new market track. This is clearly an issue for further research.

The analysis of liberalization and the output fall also applies to all situations of unexpected liberalization such as the liberalization of capital markets in emerging market economies. The analysis of how particular institutional setups allow us to solve coordination problems related to law enforcement obviously has application not only to transition economies.

Many of the incentive issues of transition discussed in Part Three, like the ratchet effect or the soft budget constraint, of course have very general applications. The discussion of institutional mechanisms to solve these incentive problems also goes far beyond transition. The issue of the managerial labor market and outside options for civil servants, for example, is relevant to all countries.

The economics of the soft budget constraint constitutes an important addition to the body of economics and has very general and important applications, from issues of bank bailouts (the S&L crisis in the United States in the 1980s, other banking crises as in Sweden in the early 1990s) to understanding the East Asian crisis. This kind of research also contributes to a better understanding of the capitalist system where forms of soft budget constraints are present. The analysis of institutional mechanisms that harden budget constraints also goes beyond the experience of transition to such problems as the role of federalism, decentralization of banking, and banking reform and regulation.

We hope that this book will help further cross-fertilization between research on the economics of transition and economics in general.

REFERENCES

Aghion, P., and O. Blanchard. (1994). "On the Speed of Transition in Central Europe." *National Bureau for Economic Research Macroeconomics Annual*:283–319.

Aghion, P., and O. Blanchard. (1998). "On Privatization Methods in Eastern Europe and Their Implications." *Economics of Transition,* 6(1): 87–99.

Aghion, P., O. Blanchard, and R. Burgess. (1994). "The Behaviour of State Firms in Eastern Europe Pre-privatization." *European Economic Review,* 38:1327–1349.

Aghion, P., and P. Bolton. (1991). "Government Domestic Debt and the Risk of Default: A Political Economy Model of the Strategic Role of Debt." In R. Dornbusch and R. Draghi (eds.), *Debt Management: Theory and History,* 315–344. Cambridge, UK: Cambridge University Press.

Aghion, P., and P. Bolton. (1992). "An Incomplete Contract Approach to Bankruptcy and the Financial Structure of the Firm." *Review of Economic Studies,* 59(3): 473–494.

Aghion, P., P. Bolton, and S. Fries. (1996). "Financial Restructuring in Transition Economies," mimeo, European Bank for Reconstruction and Development.

Aghion, P., and R. Burgess. (1993). "Financing in Eastern Europe and the Former Soviet Union: Issues and Institutional Support." In D. K. Das, (ed.), *International Finance: Contemporary Issues,* 101–124. London and New York: Routledge.

Aghion, P., M. Dewatripont, and P. Rey. (1999). "Competition, Financial Discipline and Growth." *Review of Economic Studies,* 66(4): 825–852.

Akerlof, G., A. Rose, J. Yellen and H. Hessenius. (1991). "East Germany in From the Cold: The Economic Aftermath of Currency Union." *Brookings Papers on Economic Activity,* 0(1): 1–87.

Alesina, A. (1988). "Credibility and Policy Convergence in a Two-Party System with Rational Voters." *American Economic Review,* 78(4): 496–805.

Alesina, A., and E. Spolaore. (1997). "On the Number and Size of Nations." *Quarterly Journal of Economics,* 112(4): 1027–1056.

Alesina, A., E. Spolaore, and R. Wacziarg. (1997). "Economic Integration and Political Disintegration." National Bureau for Economic Research Working Paper: 6163.

Alesina, A., and G. Tabellini. (1990). "A Positive Theory of Fiscal Deficits and Government Debt." *Review of Economic Studies,* 57(3): 403–414.

Alexeev, M. (1999)."Privatization and the Distribution of Wealth in Russia." *Economics of Transition,* 7:449–465.

Altomonte, C. (1998). "FDI in the CEEC's and the Theory of Real Options: An Empirical Assessment." Leuven Institute for Social and Economic Studies Discussion Paper No. 76.

Anderson, J. H., G. Korsun, and P. Murrell. (1997). "Which Enterprises (Believe They) Have Soft Budgets after Mass Privatization? Evidence on the Effects of Ownership and Decentralization in Mongolia." Mimeo, University of Maryland.

Anderson, R., and C. Kegels. (1997). *Transition Banking: The Financial Development of Central and Eastern Europe.* Oxford, UK: Oxford University Press.

Aoki, M. (1995). An Evolving Diversity of Organizational Mode and Its Implications for Transitional Economies." *Journal of Japanese and International Economies,* 10:330–353.

Arrow, K. J., and L. Hurwicz. (1960). "Decentralization and Computation in Resource Allocation." In R. Pfouts (ed.), *Essays in Economics and Econometrics.* Chapel Hill: University of North Carolina Press.

Åslund, A. (1991). "Principles of Privatization." In L. Csaba (ed.), *Systemic Change and Stabilization in Eastern Europe,* 17–31. Aldershot: Dartmouth.

Åslund, A. (1994). "Lessons of the First Four Years of Systemic Change in Eastern Europe." *Journal of Comparative Economics,* 19:22–38.

Åslund, A. (1995). *How Russia Became a Market Economy.* Washington, DC: Brookings Institution.

Åslund, A., P. Boone, and S. Johnson. (1996). "How to Stabilize: Lessons from Post-Communist Countries." *Brookings Papers on Economic Activity,* 1:217–313.

Atkeson, A., and P. J. Kehoe. (1996). "Social Insurance and Transition." *International Economic Review,* 37:377–402.

Atkeson, A., and P. J. Kehoe. (1997). "Industry Evolution and Transition: A Neoclassical Benchmark." National Bureau for Economic Research Working Paper: 6005.

Aumann, R. (1976). "Agreeing to Disagree." *Annals of Statistics,* 4:1236–1239.

Bai, C., D. Li, and Y. Wang. (1998). "Enterprise Productivity and Efficiency: When Is Up Really Down?" *Journal of Comparative Economics,* 24(2): 265–280.

Bai, C., D. Li, Y. Qian, and Y. Wang. (1999). "Anonymous Banking and Financial Repression: How Does China's Reform Limit Government Predation without Reducing Its Revenue?" Mimeo, Stanford University.

Bain, J. A., J. B. Miller, J. R. Thornton, and M. Keren. (1987). "The Ratchet, Tautness and Managerial Behaviour in Soviet-Type Economies." *European Economic Review,* 31:1173–1202.

Balcerowicz, L. (1995). *Socialism, Capitalism, Transformation.* Budapest: Central European University Press.

Baldwin, R. E. (1995). *Towards an Integrated Europe.* Center for Economic Policy Research, London.

Barberis, N., M. Boycko, A. Shleifer, and N. Tsukanova. (1996). "How Does Privatization Work? Evidence from the Russian Shops." *Journal of Political Economy,* 104(4): 764–790.

Bardhan, P., and Roemer, J. (1992). *Market Socialism,* Oxford, UK: Oxford University Press.

Barone, E. (1908). "The Ministry of Production in a Collectivist State." English translation in Hayek (1935): 245–290.

Basu, S., S. Estrin, and J. Svejnar. (1994). "Employment and Wage Behavior of Enterprises under Communism and in Transition: Evidence from Central Europe and Russia." Mimeo, McGill University.

Bauer, T. (1978). "Investment Cycles in Planned Economies." *Acta Oeconomica,* 21(3): 243–260.

Begg, D., and R. Portes. (1993). "Enterprise Debt and Economic Transformation: Financial Restructuring in Central and Eastern Europe." In C. Mayer and X. Vives (eds.), *Capital Markets and Financial Intermediation,* 230–254. Cambridge, UK: Cambridge University Press.

Belka, M. (1994). "Financial Restructuring of Banks and Enterprises: The Polish Solution." Paper presented at the Center for Economic Policy Research conference on Bad Enterprise Debts in Central and Eastern Europe, Budapest.

Belka M., S. Krajewski, and B. Pinto. (1993). "Transforming State Enterprises in Poland." *Brookings Papers on Economic Activity,* 0(1): 213–261.

Bennett, J., and H. Dixon. (1995). "Macroeconomic Equilibrium and Reform in a Transitional Economy." *European Economic Review,* 39(8): 1465–1485.

Berg, A., and O. Blanchard. (1994). "Stabilization and Transition in Poland, 1990–1991." In O. Blanchard, K. Froot, and J. Sachs (eds.), *The Transition in Eastern Europe,* 1:51–92. Chicago: National Bureau for Economic Research and University of Chicago Press.

Berg, A., and J. Sachs. (1992). "Structural Adjustment and International Trade in Eastern Europe: The Case of Poland." *Economic Policy,* 14:117–174.

Berglöf, E., and G. Roland. (1995). "Bank Restructuring and Soft Budget Constraints in Financial Transition." *Journal of the Japanese and International Economies* 9:354–375.

Berglöf, E., and G. Roland. (1997). "Soft Budget Constraints and Credit Crunches in Financial Transition." *European Economic Review,* 41(3–5): 807–818.

Berglöf, E., and E. L. von Thadden. (1994). "Short-Term vs. Long-Term Interests: Capital Structure with Multiple Investors." *Quarterly Journal of Economics,* 109:1055–1084.

Berkowitz, D. (1996). "On the Persistence of Rationing Following Liberalization: A Theory for Economies in Transition." *European Economic Review,* 40(6): 1259–1280.

Berkowitz, D. (1997). "Regional Income and Secession: Center-Periphery Relations in Emerging Market Economies." *Regional Science and Urban Economics,* 27(1): 17–45.

Berkowitz, D., and D. N. DeJong. (1999). "Russia's Internal Borders." *Regional Science and Urban Economics* (5): 633–649.

Berkowitz, D., and W. Li. (In press). "Tax Rights in Transition Economies: A Tragedy of the Commons?" *Journal of Public Economics.*

Berle, A., and G. Means. (1932). *The Modern Corporation and Private Property.* New York: Macmillan.

Berliner, J. (1952). "The Informal Organization of the Soviet Firm." *Quarterly Journal of Economics,* 66:342–365.

Bertocchi, G., and M. Spagat. (1997). "Structural Uncertainty and Subsidy Removal for Economies in Transition." *European Economic Review* 41(9): 1709–1733.

Besley, T., and S. Coate. (1997). "An Economic Model of Representative Democracy." *Quarterly Journal of Economics,* 112:85–114.

Bhaduri, A., K. Laski, and F. Levcik. (1993). "Transition from the Command to the Market System: What Went Wrong and What to Do for Now?" Mimeo, Vienna Institute for Comparative Economic Studies.

Biais, B., and E. Perotti. (1998). "Machiavellian Underpricing." Mimeo, Institut d'Economie Industrielle.

Bilsen, V., and J. Konings. (1997). "Job Creation, Job Destruction and Growth of Newly Established, Privatized and State-Owned Enterprises in Transition Economies: Survey Evidence from Bulgaria, Hungary and Romania." William Davidson Institute Working Paper No. 106.

Birman, I. (1978). "From the Achieved Level." *Soviet Studies,* 30(2): 153–172.

Black, B., R. Kraakman, and A. Tarassova. (1999). "Russian Privatization and Corporate Governance: What Went Wrong?" Mimeo, Stanford Law School.

Blanchard, O. (1997). *The Economics of Transition in Eastern Europe.* Oxford, UK: Clarendon Lectures, Oxford University Press.

Blanchard, O., R. Dornbusch, P. Krugman, R. Layard, and L. Summers. (1991). *Reform in Eastern Europe.* Cambridge, MA: MIT Press.

Blanchard, O., and M. Kremer. (1997). "Disorganization." *Quarterly Journal of Economics,* 112(4): 1091–1126.

Blanchard, O., and R. Layard. (1990). "Economic Reform in Poland." *Center for Research on Communist Economies:* 63–83.

Blinder, A. S. (1987). *Hard Heads, Soft Hearts.* Reading, MA: Addison-Wesley.

Boeri, T. (1999). "Transition with Supply of Labor." Paper presented at the Fifth Nobel Symposium in Economics on the Economics of Transition, September.

Boeri, T. (In press). *Structural Change, Reallocation and Income Support.* Oxford, UK: Oxford University Press.

Bolton, P. (1995). "Privatization and the Separation of Ownership and Control: Lessons from Chinese Enterprise Reforms." *Economics of Transition,* 3:1–12.

Bolton, P., F. Pivetta, and G. Roland. (1997). "Optimal Sale of Assets: The Role of Noncash Bids." Mimeo, European Center for Advances Research in Economics and Statistics, Université Libre de Bruxelles.

Bolton, P., and G. Roland. (1992). "Privatization in Central and Eastern Europe." *Economic Policy,* 15:276–309.

Bolton, P., and G. Roland. (1996). "Distributional Conflicts, Factor Mobility and Political Integration." *American Economic Review, Papers and Proceedings,* 86:99-102.

Bolton, P., and G. Roland. (1997). "The Breakup of Nations: A Political Economy Analysis." *Quarterly Journal of Economics,* 112(4): 1057–1090.

Bolton, P., and D. Scharfstein. (1996). "Optimal Debt Structure and the Number of Creditors." *Journal of Political Economy,* 104(1): 1–25.

Bonin, J. P., and M. E. Schaffer. (1995). "Banks, Firms, Bad Debts and Bankruptcy in Hungary, 1991–94." London School of Economics, Center for Economic Performance Discussion Paper: 234.

Bortolotti, B., M. Fantini, and D. Siniscalco. (1999). "Privatization and Institutions: A Cross Country Analysis." Mimeo, Fondazione Mattei.

Bouin, O., and I. Grosfeld. (1995). "Crédibilité des réformes et ajustement des entreprises en Pologne et République Tchèque." *Revue Economique,* 46(3): 775–786.

Boycko, M. (1992). "When Higher Incomes Reduce Welfare: Queues, Labor Supply, and Macroeconomic Equilibrium in Socialist Economies." *Quarterly Journal of Economics,* 107: 907–920.

Boycko, M., A. Shleifer, and R. Vishny. (1995). *Privatizing Russia.* Cambridge, MA: MIT Press.

Bratkowski, A., I. Grosfeld, and J. Rostowski. (2000). "Investment and Finance in De Novo Private Firms: Empirical Results from the Czech Republic, Hungary and Poland." *Economics of Transition,* 8(1): 101–116.

Broadman, H., and X. Sun. (1997). "Distribution of Foreign Direct Investment in China." World Bank Working Paper: 1720.

Brown, A., B. W. Ickes, and R. Ryterman. (1994). "The Myth of Monopoly: A New View of Industrial Structure in Russia." World Bank Policy Research Paper: 1331.

Brus, W., and K. Laski. (1989). *From Marx to the Market.* Oxford, UK: Oxford University Press.

Buchanan, J., and R. J. Faith. (1987). "Secession and the Limits to Taxation: Towards a Theory of Internal Exit." *American Economic Review,* 77(5): 1023–1031.

Burda, M. (1993). "Unemployment, Labour Markets and Structural Change in Eastern Europe." *Economic Policy,* 16:101–138.

Butterfield, J. (1990). "Devolution in Decision-Making and Organizational Change in Soviet Agriculture," in W. Moskoff (ed.), *Perestroika in the Countryside,* 19–46. New York: M. E. Sharpe.

Byrd, W. A. (1987). "The Impact of the Two-Tier Plan/Market System in Chinese Industry." *Journal of Comparative Economics,* 11:295–308.

Byrd, W. A. (1989). "Plan and Market in the Chinese Economy: A Simple General Equilibrium Model." *Journal of Comparative Economics,* 13:177–204.

Byrd, W. A. (1991). *The Market Mechanism and Economic Reforms in China.* New York: M. E. Sharpe.

Byrd, W. A., and L. Qingsong. (1990). *China's Rural Industry. Structure, Development, and Reform.* Oxford, UK: Oxford University Press.

Caillaud, B., R. Guesnerie, P. Rey, and J. Tirole. (1988). "Government Intervention in Production and Incentives Theory: A Review of Recent Contributions." *Rand Journal of Economics,* 19(1): 1–26.

Calvo, G., and F. Coricelli. (1992). "Stabilizing a Previously Centrally Planned Economy: Poland 1990." *Economic Policy,* 14:175–208.

Campos, N. (2000). "Never Around Noon: On the Nature and Causes of the Transition Shadow." Center for Economic Research and Graduate Education Discussion Paper: 1999–19.

Carlin, W., and C. Mayer. (1992). "Restructuring Enterprises in Eastern Europe." *Economic Policy,* 15:311–346.

Carlin, W., J. Van Reenen, and T. Wolfe. (1995). "Enterprise Restructuring in the Transition: An Analytical Survey of the Case Study Evidence from Central and Eastern Europe." *Economics of Transition,* 3(4): 427–458.

Casella, A., and J. S. Feinstein. (1990). "Public Goods in Trade: On the Formation of Markets and Political Jurisdictions." Mimeo, Hoover Institution.

Castanheira, M., and G. Roland. (2000). "The Optimal Speed of Transition: A General Equilibrium Analysis." *International Economic Review,* 41(1): 219–239.

Chadha, B., and F. Coricelli. (1994). "Fiscal Constraints and the Speed of Transition." Center for Economic Policy Research Discussion Paper: 993.

Chandler, A., Jr. (1962). *Strategy and Structure.* New York: Doubleday.

Chang, C., and Y. Wang. (1994). "The Nature of the Township Enterprises." *Journal of Comparative Economics,* 19:434–452.

Chawluk, T., and R. Cross. (1997). "Measures of Shortage and Monetary Overhang in the Polish Economy." *Review of Economics and Statistics:* 105–115.

Che, J., and Y. Qian. (1998a). "Institutional Environment, Community Government, and Corporate Governance: Understanding China's Township-Village Enterprises." *Journal of Law, Economics and Organization,* 14(1): 1–23.

Che, J., and Y. Qian. (1998b). "Insecure Property Rights and Government Ownership of Firms." *Quarterly Journal of Economics,* 113(2): 467–496.

Commander, S., and I. Dolinskaya. (1999). "Non-Monetary Transacting: Its Origins and Effects in Russia." Mimeo, European Bank for Reconstruction and Development.

Commander, S., and C. Mummsen. (1999). "Understanding Barter in Russia." European Bank for Reconstruction and Development Working Paper: 37.

Commander, S., A. Tolstopiatenko, and R. Yemtsov. (1999). "Channels of Redistribution: Inequality and Poverty in the Russian Transition." *Economics of Transition,* 7(2): 411–447.

Corbett, J. (1987). "International Perspectives on Financing: Evidence from Japan." *Oxford Review of Economic Policy,* 3:30–55.

Coricelli, F. (1995). "Fiscal Constraints, Reform Strategies and the Speed of Transition: The Case of Central-Eastern Europe." Mimeo, University of Siena.

Coricelli, F., and G.-M. Milesi-Ferretti. (1993). "On the Credibility of 'Big Bang' Programs: A Note on Wage Claims and Soft Budget Constraints in Economies in Transition." *European Economic Review,* 37(2–3): 387–395.

Crémer, H., M. Marchand, and J.-F. Thisse. (1989). "The Public Firm as an Instrument for Regulating an Oligopolistic Market." *Oxford Economic Papers,* 41(2): 283–301.

Daianu, D. (1998). *Transformation of the Economy as a Real Process.* Aldershot: Ashgate.

Debande, O., and G. Friebel. (1995). "Privatization, Employment and Managerial Decision-Taking." Mimeo, European Center for Advances Research in Economics and Statistics, Université Libre de Bruxelles.

Dehejia, V. (1995). "Will Gradualism Work When Shock Therapy Doesn't?" Mimeo, Columbia University.

Demougin, D., and H.-W. Sinn. (1992). "Privatization, Risk-Taking, and the Communist Firm." *Journal of Public Economics,* 55(2): 203–231.

Dervis, K., and T. Condon. (1994). "Hungary—Partial Successes and Remaining Challenges: The Emergence of a 'Gradualist' Success Story?" In O. Blanchard, J. Kenneth, A. Froot, and J. D. Sachs (eds.), *The Transition in Eastern Europe,* 123–149. Chicago and London: University of Chicago Press.

Dewatripont, M., F. Giavazzi, J. von Hagen, I. Harden, T. Persson, H. Rosenthal, A. Sapir, and G. Tabellini. (1995). *Flexible Integration: Toward a More Effective and Democratic Europe.* Monitoring European Integration Series No. 6. London: Center for Economic Policy Research.

Dewatripont, M., I. Jewitt, and J. Tirole. (1999a). "The Economics of Career Concerns. Part II: Part I: Comparing Information Structures." *Review of Economic Studies,* 66(1): 183–198.

Dewatripont, M., I. Jewitt, and J. Tirole. (1999b). "The Economics of Career Concerns. Part II: Application to Missions and Accountability of Government Agencies." *Review of Economic Studies,* 66(1): 199–217.

Dewatripont, M., and E. Maskin. (1995). "Credit and Efficiency in Centralized and Decentralized Economies." *Review of Economic Studies,* 62:541–555.

Dewatripont, M., and G. Roland. (1992a). "Economic Reform and Dynamic Political Constraints." *Review of Economic Studies,* 59:703–730.

Dewatripont, M., and G. Roland. (1992b). "The Virtues of Gradualism and Legitimacy in the Transition to a Market Economy." *Economic Journal,* 102:291–300.

Dewatripont, M., and G. Roland. (1995). "The Design of Reform Packages under Uncertainty." *American Economic Review,* 85:1207–1223.

Dewatripont, M., and G. Roland. (1997). "Transition as a Process of Large Scale Institutional Change." In D. Kreps and K. Wallis (eds.), *Advances in Economic Theory,* 2: 240–278. Cambridge, UK: Cambridge University Press.

Dewatripont, M., and G. Roland. (In press). "Soft Budget Constraints, Transition and Financial Systems." *Journal of Institutional and Theoretical Economics.*

Dewatripont, M., and J. Tirole. (1994a). "A Theory of Debt and Equity: Diversity of Securities and Manager-Shareholder Congruence." *Quarterly Journal of Economics,* 109(4): 1027–1054.

Dewatripont, M., and J. Tirole. (1994b). *The Prudential Regulation of Banks.* Cambridge, MA: MIT Press.

Dittus, P. S. (1994). "Corporate Governance in Central Europe: The Role of Banks." Bank of International Settlements, *Economic Papers:* 42.

Dixit, A. (1996). *The Making of Economic Policy: A Transaction Cost Politics Perspective.* Munich Lectures in Economics. Cambridge, MA: MIT Press.

Dixit, A., and R. Pindyck. (1994). *Investment under Uncertainty.* Princeton: Princeton University Press.

Dollar, D., and B. Ljunggren. (1997). "Vietnam." In P. Desai (ed.), *Going Global,* 439–471. Cambridge, MA: MIT Press.

Earle, J. S., and S. Estrin. (1997). "After Voucher Privatization: The Structure of Corporate Ownership in Russian Manufacturing Industry." Center for Economic Policy Research Discussion Paper: 1736.

Earle, J., and S. Gehlbach. (1999). "Privatization Policy Design and Popular Support for Reform in the Czech Republic." Mimeo, Stockholm Institute for Transition Economics.

Easterly, W., and P. Vieira-da-Cunha. (1994). "Financing the Storm: Macroeconomic Crisis in Russia." *Economics of Transition,* 2(4): 443–465.

Ellerman, D. (1998). "Voucher Privatization with Investment Funds: An Institutional Analysis." World Bank Policy Research Paper: 1924.

Engel, C., and J. H. Rogers. (1996). "How Wide is the Border?" *American Economic Review,* 86:1112–1125.

Estrin, S., M. Schaffer, and I. J. Singh. (1992). "Enterprise Adjustment in Transition Economies: Czechoslovakia, Hungary and Poland." World Bank Research Paper: 27.

European Bank for Reconstruction and Development (1995–1999). *Transition Report.* London: European Bank for Reconstruction and Development.

Faggio, G., and J. Konings. (1999). "Gross Job Flows and Firm Growth in Transition Countries: Evidence Using Firm Level Data on Five Countries." Center for Economic Polcity Research Discussion Paper: 2261.

Fama, E. (1980). "Agency Problems and the Theory of the Firm." *Journal of Political Economy,* 88:288–307.

Fernandez, R., and D. Rodrik. (1991). "Resistance to Reform: Status Quo Bias in the Presence of Individual-Specific Uncertainty." *American Economic Review,* 81:1146–1155.

Fidrmuc, J. (1998a). "Political Support for Reforms: Economics of Voting in Transition Countries." *European Economic Review* (forthcoming).

Fidrmuc, J. (1998b). "Economics of Voting in Post-communist Countries." *Electoral Studies* (forthcoming).

Fidrmuc, J. (1998c). "Stochastic Shocks and Incentives for (Dis)integration." Center for Economic Policy Research Discussion Paper: 2104.

Fingleton, J., E. Fox, D. Neven, and P. Seabright. (1996). *Competition Policy and the Transformation of Central Europe.* London: Center for Economic Policy Research.

Fischer, S., and A. Gelb. (1991). "The Process of Economic Transformation." *Journal of Economic Perspectives,* 5:91–106.

Freixas, X., R. Guesnerie, and J. Tirole. (1985). "Planning under Incomplete Information and the Ratchet Effect." *Review of Economic Studies,* 52:173–191.

Friebel, G. (2000). "Bureaucracies in Russian Voucher Privatization." *Economics of Transition,* 8(1): 37–58.

Friebel, G., and S. Guriev. (1998). "Why Russian Workers Do Not Move: Attachment of Workers Through In-Kind Payments." Mimeo, Russian European Center for Economic Policy.

Friedman, E., and S. Johnson. (1996). "Complementarities and Optimal Reform." Mimeo, Duke University.

Friedman, E., S. Johnson, D. Kaufmann, and P. Zoido-Lobaton. (1999). "Dodging the Grabbing Hand: The Determinants of Unofficial Activity in 69 Countries." Paper presented at the Fifth Nobel Symposium in Economics: The Economics of Transition, Stockholm.

Frydman, R., C. Gray, M. Hessel, and A. Rapaczynski. (1999). "When Does Privatization Work? The Impact of Private Ownership on Corporate Performance in the Transition Economies." *Quarterly Journal of Economics,* 114(4): 1153–1192.

Frydman, R., and A. Rapaczynski. (1994). *Privatization in Eastern Europe: Is the State Withering Away?* London: Central European University Press.

Frydman, R., A. Rapaczynski, and J. Earle. (1993). *The Privatization Process in Central Europe.* London: Central European University Press.

Frye, T., and A. Shleifer. (1997). "The Invisible Hand and the Grabbing Hand." *American Economic Review,* 87(2): 354–358.

Gaddy, C., and B. Ickes. (1998). "To Restructure or Not to Restructure: Informal Activities and Enterprise Behavior in Transition." Mimeo, Pennsylvania State University.

Gao, S., and M. E. Schaffer. (1998). "Financial Discipline in the Enterprise Sector in Transition Countries: How Does China Compare?" Center for Economic Reform and Transition Discussion Paper: 98/1, Heriott-Watt University, Edinburgh.

Garner, T., and K. Terrell. (1998). "A Gini Decomposition Analysis of Inequality in the Czech and Slovak Republics during the Transition." *Economics of Transition,* 6(1): 23–46.

Gates, S., P. Milgrom, and J. Roberts. (1993). "Complementarities in the Transition from Socialism: A Firm-Level Analysis." Mimeo, Stanford University.

Gatsios, K. (1992). "Privatization in Hungary: Past, Present and Future." Center for Economic Policy Research Discussion Paper: 642.

Gavin, M. (1993). "Unemployment, Labor Markets and Structural Change in Eastern Europe." Mimeo, Columbia University.

Goldfeld, S., and R. Quandt. (1988). "Budget Constraints, Bailouts and the Firm under Central Planning." *Journal of Comparative Economics,* 12(4): 502–520.

Goldfeld, S., and R. Quandt. (1990). "Output Targets, the Soft Budget Constraint and the Firm under Central Planning." *Journal of Economic Behavior and Organization,* 14(2): 205–222.

Gomulka, S. (1992). "The Causes of Recession Following Stabilization." *Comparative Economic Studies,* 33(2): 71–89.

Gordon, R. H., C.-E. Bai, and D. D. Li. (1999). "Efficiency Losses from Tax Distortions vs. Government Control." *European Economic Review,* 43(4–6): 1095–1103.

Grafe, C., and C. Wyplosz. (1997). "The Real Exchange Rate in Transition Economies." Center for Economic Policy Research Discussion Paper: 1773.

Granick, D. (1990). *Chinese State Enterprises: A Regional Property Rights Analysis,* Chicago and London: University of Chicago Press.

Granville, B. (1995). *The Success of Russian Economic Reforms.* London: Royal Institute of International Affairs.

Gros, D., and A. Steinherr. (1995). *Winds of Change: Economic Transition in Central and Eastern Europe.* London: Longman.

Grosfeld, I. (1987). "Modeling Planners' Investment Behavior: Poland, 1956–1981." *Journal of Comparative Economics,* 11(2): 180–191.

Grosfeld, I. (1990). "Prospects for Privatization in Poland." *European Economy,* 43:149–159.

Grosfeld, I., and J.-F. Nivet. (1997a). "Firms' Heterogeneity in Transition: Evidence from a Polish Dataset." William Davidson Institute Working Paper: 47.

Grosfeld, I., and J.-F. Nivet. (1997b). "Wage and Investment Behaviour in Transition: Evidence from a Polish Panel Data Set." Center for Economic Policy Research Discussion Paper: 1726.

Grosfeld, I., and G. Roland. (1997). "Defensive and Strategic Restructuring in Central European Enterprises." *Journal of Transforming Economies and Societies,* 3(4): 21–46.

Grossman, S., and O. Hart. (1980). "Takeover Bids, the Free-Rider Problem and the Theory of Corporation." *Bell Journal of Economics,* 11:42–64.

Grossman, S., and O. Hart. (1982). "Corporate Financial Structure and Managerial Incentives." In J. McCall (ed.), *The Economics of Information and Uncertainty,* 103–137. Chicago: University of Chicago Press.

Grossman, S., and O. Hart. (1986). "The Costs and Benefits of Ownership: A Theory of Vertical and Lateral Integration." *Journal of Political Economy,* 94:691–719.

Groves, T., Y. Hong, J. McMillan, and B. Naughton. (1994). "Autonomy and Incentives in Chinese State Enterprises." *Quarterly Journal of Economics,* 109(1): 183–209.

Groves, T., Y. Hong, J. McMillan, and B. Naughton. (1995). "China's Evolving Managerial Labor Market." *Journal of Political Economy,* 103(4): 873–892.

Gul, F., H. Sonnenschein, and R. Wilson. (1986). "Foundations of Dynamic Monopoly and the Coase Conjecture." *Journal of Economic Theory,* 39:155–190.

Gupta, N., J. Ham, and J. Svejnar. (1999). "Priorities and Sequencing in Privatization: Theory and Evidence from the Czech Republic." Mimeo, University of Pittsburgh.

Ham, J., J. Svejnar, and K. Terrell. (1998). "Unemployment and the Social Safety Net during the Transition to a Market Economy: Evidence from Czech and Slovak Men." *American Economic Review,* 88(5): 1117–1142.

Hare, P., and T. Revesz. (1992). "Hungary's Transition to a Market Economy: The Case Against a 'Big-Bang.'" *Economic Policy,* 14:227–264.

Hart, O. (1983). "The Market Mechanism as an Incentive Scheme." *Bell Journal of Economics,* 14(2): 366–382.

Hart, O., and J. Moore. (1990). "Property Rights and the Nature of the Firm." *Journal of Political Economy,* 98:1119–1158.

Hart, O., and J. Moore. (1994). "A Theory of Debt Based on the Inalienability of Human Capital." *Quarterly Journal of Economics*, 109(4): 841–879.

Hart, O., and J. Moore. (1995). "Debt and Seniority: An Analysis of the Role of Hard Claims in Constraining Management." *American Economic Review*, 85(3): 567–585.

Hart, O., and J. Moore. (1998). "Default and Renegotiation: A Dynamic Model of Debt." *Quarterly Journal of Economics*, 113(1): 1–41.

Hart, O., and J. Moore. (1999). "On the Design of Hierarchies: Coordination versus Specialization." Mimeo, London School of Economics.

Hart, O., A. Shleifer, and R. W. Vishny. (1997). "The Proper Scope of Government: Theory and an Application to Prisons." *Quarterly Journal of Economics*, 112(4): 1127–1161.

Hart, O., and J. Tirole. (1988). "Contract Renegotiation and Coasian Dynamics." *Review of Economic Studies*, 55:509–540.

Hayashi, F. (1982). "Tobin's Marginal and Average *q:* A Neoclassical Interpretation." *Econometrica*, 50:213–224.

Hayek, F. A. von. (1935). *Collectivist Economic Planning.* London: Routledge.

Hayek, F. (1945). "The Use of Knowledge in Society." *American Economic Review*, 35:519–530.

Hayri, A. (1997). "Shrinking Firms, Bureaucracies, and Welfare Programmes: Reform under Political Constraints." *Economic-Systems*, 21(2): 127–149.

Hellman, J. (1998). "Winners Take All: The Politics of Partial Reform in Postcommunist Transition." *World Politics*, 50(2): 203–234.

Hellwig, M. (1991). "Banking, Financial Intermediation and Corporate Finance." In A. Giovannini and C. Mayer (eds.), *European Financial Integration*, 35–63. Cambridge, UK: Cambridge University Press.

Hillman, A., E. Katz, and J. Rosenberg. (1987). "Workers as Insurance: Anticipated Government Assistance and Factor Demand." *Oxford Economic Papers*, 39(4): 813–820.

Holmström, B. (1982). "Moral Hazard in Teams." *Bell Journal of Economics*, 13(2): 324–340.

Hoshi, T., A. Kashyap, and D. Scharfstein. (1992). "The Choice between Public and Private Debt: An Examination of Post-Regulation Corporate Finance in Japan." Mimeo, University of California, San Diego.

Huang, H., and C. Xu. (1998). "Financial Institutions, Contagious Risks and Financial Crises." Mimeo, London School of Economics.

Hussain, A., N. Stern, and J. Stiglitz. (1999). "Chinese Reforms from a Comparative Perspective." Paper presented at the Fourth Annual International Conference on Transition Economics, Beijing, July 22–25.

Ickes, B. (1990). "Do Socialist Countries Suffer a Common Business Cycle?" *Review of Economics and Statistics,* 72(3): 397–405.

Jackson, M., and A. Repkine. (1997). "A Comparison of Structural Changes among Branches of Industry in Seven Transition Countries." Leuven Institute for Social and Economic Studies Working Paper: 64.

Jensen, M. (1986). "Agency Costs of Free Cash-Flow, Corporate Finance, and Takeovers." *American Economic Review* (Papers and Proceedings), 76(2): 323–329.

Jin, H., and Y. Qian. (1998). "Public vs. Private Ownership of Firms: Evidence from Rural China." *Quarterly Journal of Economics,* 113(3): 773–808.

Jin, H., Y. Qian, and B. Weingast. (1999). "Regional Decentralization and Fiscal Incentives: Federalism, Chinese Style." Mimeo, Stanford University.

Johnson, S., D. Kaufmann, and A. Shleifer. (1998). "The Unofficial Economy in Transition." *Brookings Papers on Economic Activity,* 2:159–239.

Johnson, S., D. Kaufmann, J. McMillan, and C. Woodruff. (1999). "Why Do Firms Hide? Bribes and Unofficial Activity after Communism." Paper presented at the Fifth Nobel Symposium in Economics: The Economics of Transition, Stockholm, September 10–12.

Johnson, S., J. McMillan, and C. Woodruff. (1999a). "Contract Enforcement in Transition." Paper presented at the Fifth Nobel Symposium in Economics: The Economics of Transition, Stockholm, September 10–12.

Johnson, S., J. McMillan, and C. Woodruff. (1999b). "Property Rights, Finance and Entrepreneurship." Mimeo, MIT.

Johnson, S., J. McMillan, and C. Woodruff. (1999c). "Entrepreneurs and the Ordering of Institutional Reform: Poland, Slovakia, Romania, Russia and Ukraine Compared." Mimeo, MIT.

Jones, S., W. Megginson, R. Nash, and J. Netter. (1997). "Share Issue Privatizations as Financial Means to Political and Economic Ends." Mimeo, University of Georgia.

Joskow, P. L., R. Schmalensee, and N. Tsukanova. (1994). "Competition Policy in Russia during and after Privatization." *Brookings Papers on Economic Activity, Microeconomics:* 301–381.

Keren, M., J. B. Miller, and J. R. Thornton. (1983). "The Ratchet: A Dynamic Managerial Incentive Model of the Soviet Enterprise." *Journal of Comparative Economics,* 7:347–367.

Kiguel, M., and N. Liviatan. (1992). "The Business Cycle Associated with Exchange Rate Based Stabilization." *World Bank Economic Review*, 6(2): 279–305.

King, R. G., and S. T. Rebelo. (1993). "Transitional Dynamics and Economic Growth in the Neoclassical Model." *American Economic Review*, 83(4): 908–931.

Konings, J. (1997). "Firm Growth and Ownership in Transition Economies." *Economics Letters*, 55(3): 413–418.

Konings, J., H. Lehmann, and M. Schaffer. (1996). "Job Creation and Job Destruction in a Transition Economy: Ownership, Firm Size and Gross Job Flows in Polish Manufacturing, 1988–91." *Labour Economics*, 3(3): 299–317.

Konings, J., and P. Walsh. (1999). "Disorganization in the Process of Transition: Firm-Level Evidence from Ukraine." *Economics of Transition*, 7(1): 29–46.

Kornai, J. (1971). *Anti-equilibrium.* Amsterdam: North Holland.

Kornai, J. (1980). *Economics of Shortage.* Amsterdam: North Holland.

Kornai, J. (1990). *The Road to a Free Economy.* New York: Norton.

Kornai, J. (1992). *The Socialist System: The Political Economy of Communism.* Oxford, UK: Oxford University Press.

Kornai, J. (1993). "Transformational Recession: A General Phenomenon Examined through the Example of Hungary's Development." *Economie Appliquée*, 46(2): 181–227.

Kornai, J. (1995). *Highways and Byways: Studies on Reform and Post-Communist Transition.* Cambridge, MA, and London: MIT Press.

Kornai, J. (1998). *From Socialism to Capitalism.* London: Center for Post-Collectivist Studies.

Kornai, J. (1999). "Hardening the Budget Constraint: The Experience of Post-Socialist Countries." Collegium Budapest Discussion Paper Series: 59.

Kornai, J., and T. Liptak. (1965). "Two-Level Planning." *Econometrica*, 33:141–169.

Kornai, J., and J. Weibull. (1983). "Paternalism, Buyers' and Sellers' Market." *Mathematical Social Sciences*, 7(2): 153–169.

Kotrba, J., and J. Svejnar. (1994). "Rapid Multifaceted Privatization: Experience of the Czech and Slovak Republics." *Most*, 4(2): 147–185.

Kotzeva, M., and E. Perotti. (1995). "Exogenous and Opportunistic Financial Arrears: Evidence from a Survey of Bulgarian State Managers." Mimeo, Central European University.

Kremer, M., and E. Maskin. (1996). "Wage Inequality and Segregation by Skill." National Bureau for Economic Research Working Paper: 5718.

Kydland, F., and E. C. Prescott. (1982). "Time to Build and Aggregate Fluctuations." *Econometrica,* 50(6): 1345–1370.

Laffont, J.-J., and J. Tirole. (1988). "The Dynamics of Incentive Contracts." *Econometrica,* 51:1153–1175.

Laffont, J.-J., and J. Tirole. (1993). *A Theory of Incentives in Regulation and Procurement.* Cambridge, MA: MIT Press.

Lange, O. (1938). "On the Economic Theory of Socialism." In B. E. Lippincott (ed.), *On the Economic Theory of Socialism,* 55–143. Minneapolis: University of Minnesota Press.

Lankes, H.-P., and A. Venables. (1996). "Foreign Direct Investment in Economic Transition: The Changing Pattern of Investment." *Economics of Transition,* 4:331–370.

La Porta, R., F. Lopez-de-Silanes, A. Shleifer, and R. Vishny. (1999). "The Quality of Government." Mimeo, Harvard University.

Lau, L., Y. Qian, and G. Roland. (1997). "Pareto-Improving Economic Reforms through Dual-Track Liberalization." *Economics Letters,* 55(2): 285–292.

Lau, L., Y. Qian, and G. Roland. (2000). "Reform without Losers: An Interpretation of China's Dual-Track Approach to Reforms." *Journal of Political Economy,* 108(1): 120–163.

Lawrence, C., and R. Z. Lawrence. (1985). "Manufacturing Wage Dispersion: An End Game Interpretation." *Brookings Papers on Economic Activity,* 0(1): 47–106.

Layard, R., and J. Parker. (1996). *The Coming Russian Boom: A Guide to New Markets and Politics.* New York: Simon and Schuster, Free Press.

Lazear, E., and S. Rosen. (1981). "Rank-Order Tournaments as Optimum Labor Contracts." *Journal of Political Economy,* 89(5): 841–864.

Lewis, T. R., R. Feenstra, and R. Ware. (1990). "Eliminating Price Supports: A Political Economy Perspective." *Journal of Public Economics,* 40:150–186.

Li, D. D. (1992). "Public Ownership as a Sufficient Condition for the Soft Budget Constraint." University of Michigan Working Paper.

Li, D. D. (1995). "A Theory of Ambiguous Property Rights in Transition Economies." Mimeo, University of Michigan.

Li, D. D. (1996). "Government Control during Transition: Theory and Evidence from China." Mimeo, University of Michigan.

Li, D. D., and M. Liang. (1998). "Causes of the Soft Budget Constraint: Evidence on Three Explanations." *Journal of Comparative Economics,* 26(1): 104–116.

Li, W. (1997). "The Impact of the Chinese Reform on the Performance of Chinese State-Owned Enterprises, 1980–89." *Journal of Political Economy,* 105(5): 1080–1106.

Li, W. (1999). "A Tale of Two Reforms." *RAND Journal of Economics,* 30(1): 120–136.

Lin, J. Y. (1992). "Rural Reforms and Agricultural Growth in China." *American Economic Review,* 82(1): 34–51.

Lipset, S., and G. Lenz. (1999). "Corruption Cultures and Markets." Mimeo, George Mason University.

Lipton, D., and J. Sachs. (1990a). "Creating a Market Economy in Eastern Europe: The Case of Poland." *Brookings Papers on Economic Activity,* 1:75–133.

Lipton, D., and J. Sachs. (1990b). "Privatization in Eastern Europe: The Case of Poland." *Brookings Papers on Economic Activity,* 2:293–361.

Litwack, J. (1993). "Coordination, Incentives and the Ratchet Effect." *Rand Journal of Economics,* 24(2): 271–285.

Litwack, J., and Y. Qian. (1998). "Balanced or Unbalanced Development: Special Economic Zones as Catalysts for Transition." *Journal of Comparative Economics,* 26(1): 117–141.

Lizal, L., and J. Svejnar. (1997). "Enterprise Investment during the Transition: Evidence from Czech Panel Data." Working Paper No. 60, William Davidson Institute.

Macaulay, S. (1963). "Non-Contractual Relationships in Business: A Preliminary Study." *American Sociological Review,* 37:318–321.

Malinvaud, E. (1967). "Decentralized Procedures for Planning." In E. Malinvaud and M. O. L. Bacharach (eds.), *Activity Analysis in the Theory of Growth and Planning.* London: Macmillan.

Manne, H. G. (1966). *Insider Trading and the Stock Market.* New York: Free Press.

Manove, M. (1971). "A Model of Soviet-Type Economic Planning." *American Economic Review,* 61:390–406.

Marcincin, A., and S. van Wijnbergen. (1997). "The Impact of Czech Privatization Methods on Enterprise Performance Incorporating Initial Selection-Bias Correction." *Economics of Transition,* 5(2): 289–304.

Marin, D., and M. Schnitzer. (1999). "Disorganization and Financial Collapse." Mimeo, University of Munich.

Martinelli, C., and M. Tommasi. (1997). "Sequencing of Reforms in the Presence of Political Constraints." *Economics and Politics,* 9(2): 115–132.

Maskin, E. (1991). "Auctions and Privatization." Mimeo, Harvard University.

Maskin, E., Y. Qian, and C. Xu. (In press). "Incentives, Information and Organizational Form." *Review of Economic Studies.*

Maskin, E., and J. Tirole. (1999). "Unforeseen Contingencies and Incomplete Contracts." *Review of Economic Studies,* 66(1): 83–114.

Mauro, P. (1995). "Corruption and Growth." *Quarterly Journal of Economics,* 110(3): 681–712.

Mayer, C. (1988). "New Issues in Corporate Finance." *European Economic Review,* 32:1167–1189.

McKelvey, R. D. (1976). "Intransitivities in Multidimensional Voting Models and Some Implications for Agenda Control." *Journal of Economic Theory,* 12:472–482.

McKinnon, R. (1991). *The Order of Economic Liberalization.* Baltimore: John Hopkins University Press.

McMillan, J., and B. Naughton. (1992). "How to Reform a Planned Economy: Lessons from China." *Oxford Review of Economic Policy,* 8:130–143.

McMillan, J., J. Whalley, and L. Zhu. (1989). "The Impact of China's Economic Reforms on Agricultural Productivity Growth." *Journal of Political Economy,* 97(4): 781–807.

McMillan, J., and C. Woodruff. (1999a). "Dispute Prevention without Courts in Vietnam." *Journal of Law, Economics and Organization,* 15(3): 637–658.

McMillan, J., and C. Woodruff. (1999b). "Interfirm Relationships and Informal Credit in Vietnam." *Quarterly Journal of Economics,* 114(4): 1285–1320.

Mehlum, H. (In press). "Speed of Adjustment and Self-Fulfilling Failure of Economic Reform." *Journal of International Economics.*

Mihalyi, P. (1992). *Socialist Investment Cycles: Analysis in Retrospect.* London: Kluwer Academic.

Milanovic, B. (1998). *Income, Inequality, and Poverty during the Transition from Planned to Market Economy.* World Bank Regional and Sectoral Studies, Washington, DC.

Milanovic, B. (1999). "Explaining the Increase in Inequality during the Transition." Mimeo, World Bank.

Milesi-Ferretti, G. M., and E. Spolaore. (1994). "How Cynical Can an Incumbent Be? Strategic Policy in a Model of Government Spending." *Journal of Public Economics,* 55(1): 21–40.

Milgrom, P., and J. Roberts. (1992). *Economics, Organization and Management.* Englewood Cliffs, NJ: Prentice Hall.

Mitchell, J. (1993). "Creditor Passivity and Bankruptcy: Implications for Economic Reform." In C. Mayer and X. Vives (eds.), *Capital Markets and Financial Intermediation,* 197–224. Cambridge, UK: Cambridge University Press.

Mitchell, J. (1995). "Cancelling, Transferring or Repaying Bad Debt: Cleaning Banks' Balance Sheets in Economies in Transition." Mimeo, Cornell University.

Mitchell, J. (1997). "Strategic Creditor Passivity, Regulation, and Bank Bailouts." London School of Economics, Center for Economic Performance Discussion Paper: 1780.

Mitchell, J. (1998). "Bankruptcy Experience in Hungary and the Czech Republic." Mimeo, European Center for Advances Research in Economics and Statistics, Université Libre de Bruxelles.

Montias, J. M. (1962). "On the Consistency and Efficiency of Central Plans." *Review of Economic Studies,* 29:280–290.

Moore, B., Jr. (1966). *Social Origins of Dictatorship and Democracy.* Boston: Beacon Press.

Morduch, J., and T. Sicular. (1999)."Politics, Growth and Inequality: Does It Pay to Join the Party?" Mimeo, Princeton University.

Moskoff, W. (1984). *Labor and Leisure in the Soviet Union.* London: Macmillan.

Munich, D., J. Svejnar, and K. Terrell. (1998). "The Worker-Firm Matching in Transition Economies: (Why) Are the Czechs More Successful Than Others?" William Davidson Institute Working Paper: 107.

Murphy, K., A. Shleifer, and R. Vishny. (1992). "The Transition to a Market Economy: Pitfalls of Partial Reform." *Quarterly Journal of Economics,* 107:889–906.

Murrell, P. (1992). "Evolution in Economics and in the Economic Reform of the Centrally Planned Economies." In C. Clague and G. Raisser (eds.), *The Emergence of Market Economies in Eastern Europe,* 35–53. Cambridge, UK: Blackwell.

Mussa, M. (1978). "Dynamic Adjustment in the Heckscher-Ohlin-Samuelson Model." *Journal of Political Economy,* 86:775–791.

Mussa, M. (1986). "The Adjustment Process and the Timing of Trade Liberalization." In A. Chokin and D. Papageorgiou (eds.), *Economic Reform in Developing Countries,* 68–124. Oxford, UK: Basil Blackwell.

Nalebuff, B., and J. Stiglitz. (1983). "Prizes and Incentives: Towards a General Theory of Compensation and Competition." *Bell Journal of Economics,* 14(1): 21–43.

Naughton, B. (1995). *Growing out of the Plan.* Cambridge, UK: Cambridge University Press.

North, D. (1990). *Institutions, Institutional Changes and Economic Performance.* Cambridge, UK: Cambridge University Press.

North, D., and B. Weingast. (1989). "Constitutions and Commitment: Evolutions of Institutions Governing Public Choice." *Journal of Economic History,* 49:803–832.

Nove, A. (1958). "The Problems of 'Success Indicators' in Soviet Industry." *Economica:* 1–13.

Nove, A. (1980). *The Soviet Economic System,* 2nd ed. Boston: Allen and Unwin.

Okoliczanyi, K. (1991). "Privatization Drive Slackens." *Radio Free Europe Report,* Oct. 25.

Perotti, E. (1993). "Bank Lending in Transition Economies." *Journal of Banking and Finance,* 17:1021–1032.

Perotti, E. (1995). "Credible Privatization." *American Economic Review,* 85(4): 847–859.

Perotti, E. (1998). "Inertial Credit and Opportunistic Arrears in Transition." *European Economic Review,* 42:1703–1725.

Perotti, E., and O. Carare. (1997). "The Evolution of Bank Credit Quality in Transition Theory and Evidence from Romania." Center for Economic Policy Research Discussion Paper: 97/02, Heriott-Watt University, Edinburgh.

Perotti, E., and P. van Oijen. (1999). "Privatization, Political Risk and Stock Market Development." Center for Economic Policy Research Discussion Paper: 2243.

Persson, T., G. Roland, and G. Tabellini. (1997). "Separation of Powers and Political Accountability." *Quarterly Journal of Economics,* 112(4): 1163–1202.

Persson, T., G. Roland, and G. Tabellini. (In press). "Comparative Politics and Public Finance." *Journal of Political Economy.*

Persson, T., and Svensson, L. (1989). "Why a Stubborn Conservative Would Run a Deficit: Policy with Time-Inconsistent Preferences." *Quarterly Journal of Economics,* 104:325–346.

Persson, T., and G. Tabellini. (1994). "Is Inequality Harmful for Growth?" *American Economic Review,* 84(3): 600–621.

Pinto, B., M. Belka, and S. Krajewski. (1993). "Transforming State Enterprises in Poland." *Brookings Papers on Economic Activity,* 1:213–270.

Pinto, B., and S. van Wijnbergen. (1995). "Ownership and Corporate Control in Poland: Why State Firms Defied the Odds." Center for Economic Policy Research Discussion Paper: 127.

Pissarides, F., M. Singer, and J. Svejnar. (1996). "Small and Medium Size Enterprises in Transition, Evidence from Bulgaria and Russia." Mimeo, European Bank for Reconstruction and Development, London.

Polishchuk, L. (1999). "Distribution of Assets and Credibility of Property Rights." Mimeo, University of Maryland and New Economic School, Moscow.

Portes, R. (1990). "Introduction to Economic Transformation of Hungary and Poland." *European Economy,* 43:11–18.

Portes, R. (1991). "The Path of Reform in Central and Eastern Europe: An Introduction." *European Economy,* Special Issue, 2:3–15.

Portes, R., R. Quandt, D. Winter, and S. Yeo. (1987). "Macroeconomic Planning and Disequilibrium: Estimates for Poland, 1955–1980." *Econometrica,* 55(1): 19–41.

Portes, R., and D. Winter. (1980). "Disequilibrium Estimates for Consumption Goods Markets in Centrally Planned Economies." *Review of Economic Studies,* 47(1): 137–159.

Povel, P. (1995). "Multiple Banking as a Commitment Not to Rescue." Mimeo, European Center for Advances Research in Economics and Statistics, Université Libre de Bruxelles.

Powell, R. P. (1977). "Plan Execution and the Workability of Soviet Planning." *Journal of Comparative Economics,* 1(1): 51–76.

Prasnikar, J., V. Prasnikar, D. Mihaljek, and J. Svejnar. (1994). "Behavior of Participatory Firms in Yugoslavia: Lessons for Transforming Economies." *Review of Economics and Statistics,* 76(4): 728–741.

Prasnikar, J., and J. Svejnar. (1998). "Investment and Wages during the Transition: Evidence from Slovene Firms." William Davidson Institute Working Paper: 184.

Qian, Y. (1994). "A Theory of Shortage in Socialist Economies Based on the Soft Budget Constraint." *American Economic Review,* 84:145–156.

Qian, Y. (In press). "The Institutional Foundations of China's Market Transition." In B. Pleskovic and J. Stiglitz (eds.), *Proceedings of the World Bank's Annual Conference on Development Economics, 1999.* World Bank.

Qian, Y., and G. Roland. (1995). "Government Paternalism and Predation: A Theory of Enterprise Incentives under Socialism and Transition." Work in progress.

Qian, Y., and G. Roland. (1996). "The Soft Budget Constraint in China." *Japan and the World Economy,* 8(1): 207–223.

Qian, Y., and G. Roland. (1998). "Federalism and the Soft Budget Constraint." *American Economic Review,* 88(5): 1143–1162.

Qian, Y., G. Roland, and C. Xu. (1998). "Coordinating Changes in M-form and U-form Organizations," Mimeo, European Center for Advances Research in Economics and Statistics, Université Libre de Bruxelles.

Qian, Y., G. Roland, and C. Xu. (1999). "Why Is China Different from Eastern Europe? Perspectives from Organization Theory." *European Economic Review,* 43(46): 1085–1094.

Qian Y., and B. Weingast. (1996). "China's Transition to Markets: Market-Preserving Federalism, Chinese Style." *Journal of Policy Reform,* 1:149–185.

Qian, Y., and C. Xu. (1993). "Why China's Economic Reforms Differ: The M-Form Hierarchy and Entry/Expansion of the Non-State Sector." *Economics of Transition,* 1:135–170.

Qian, Y., and C. Xu. (1998). "Innovation and Bureaucracy under Soft and Hard Budget Constraints." *Review of Economic Studies,* 65(1): 151–164.

Repkin, A., and P. Walsh. (1999). "Evidence of European Trade and Investment U-Shaping Industrial Output in Bulgaria, Hungary, Poland and Romania." Mimeo, Leuven Institute for Social and Economic Studies.

Rivière, A. (1997). "Scale and Size Effects in the Political Economy of Separation and Integration." Mimeo, European Center for Advances Research in Economics and Statistics, Université Libre de Bruxelles.

Rodrik, D. (1991). "Policy Uncertainty and Private Investment in Developing Countries." *Journal of Development Economics,* 36(2): 229–242.

Rodrik, D. (1992). "Political Economy and Development Policy." *European Economic Review* (Papers and Proceedings), 36(2): 329–336.

Rodrik, D. (1994). "Foreign Trade in Eastern Europe's Transition: Early Results." In O. Blanchard, K. Froot, and J. Sachs (eds.), *The Transition in Eastern Europe,* 2:319–356. Chicago: National Bureau for Economic Research and Chicago University Press.

Rodrik, D. (1995). "The Dynamics of Political Support for Reforms in Economies in Transition." *Journal of the Japanese and International Economies,* 9(4): 403–425.

Rodrik, D. (1999). "Institutions for High-Quality Growth: What They Are and How to Acquire Them." Paper prepared for the IMF Conference on Second Generation Reforms, Nov. 8–9, 1999, Washington, DC.

Roland, G. (1987). "Investment Growth Fluctuations in the USSR: An Econometric Analysis." *Journal of Comparative Economics,* 11(3): 192–206.

Roland, G. (1988). *Economie politique du système soviétique.* Paris: L'Harmattan.

Roland, G. (1990). "Complexity, Bounded Rationality and Equilibrium: The Soviet-Type Case." *Journal of Comparative Economics,* 14(3): 401–424.

Roland, G. (1991). "Political Economy of Sequencing Tactics in the Transition Period." In L. Csaba (ed.), *Systemic Change and Stabilization in Eastern Europe*, 47–64. Aldershot: Dartmouth.

Roland, G. (1994). "The Role of Political Constraints in Transition Strategies." *Economics of Transition*, 2(1): 27–41.

Roland, G. (1997). "Political Constraints and the Transition Experience." In S. Zecchini (ed.), *Lessons from the Economic Transition*, 169–188. Dordrecht: Kluwer.

Roland, G., and K. Sekkat. (1992). "Market Socialism and the Managerial Labor Market." In P. Bardhan and J. Roemer (eds.), *Market Socialism*, 204–215. Oxford, UK: Oxford University Press.

Roland, G., and K. Sekkat. (In press). "Managerial Career Concerns, Privatization and Restructuring in Transition Economies." *European Economic Review*.

Roland, G., and A. Szafarz. (1990). "The Ratchet Effect and the Planner's Expectations." *European Economic Review*, 34: 1079–1088.

Roland, G., and T. Verdier. (1994). "Privatization in Eastern Europe: Irreversibility and Critical Mass Effects." *Journal of Public Economics*, 54: 161–183.

Roland, G., and T. Verdier. (1999a). "Transition and the Output Fall." *Economics of Transition*, 7(1): 1–28.

Roland, G., and T. Verdier. (1999b). "Law Enforcement and Transition." Mimeo, European Center for Advances Research in Economics and Statistics, Université Libre de Bruxelles.

Romer, T., and H. Rosenthal. (1979). "Bureaucrats vs. Voters: On the Political Economy of Resource Allocation by Direct Democracy." *Quarterly Journal of Economics*, 93:563–587.

Rosati, D. (1994). "Output Decline during Transition from Plan to Market." *Economics of Transition*, 2(4): 419–442.

Ruggerone, L. (1996). "Unemployment and Inflationary Finance Dynamics at the Early Stages of Transition." *Economic Journal*, 106(435): 483–494.

Rutowski, M., and S. Sinha. (1995). "Employment Flows and Sectoral Shifts during the Transition Shock in Post-Socialist Countries." Mimeo, World Bank.

Sachs, J. (1993). *Poland's Jump to the Market Economy*. Lionel Robbins Lectures. Cambridge, MA, and London: MIT Press.

Sachs, J., and W. Woo. (1992). "Structural Factors in the Economic Reforms of China, Eastern Europe, and the Former Soviet Union." *Economic Policy*, 9(18): 101–145.

Sachs, J., W. Woo, and X. Yang. (1999). "Economic Reforms and Constitutional Transition." Mimeo, Harvard University.

Sah, R. K. (1987). "Queues, Rations, and Market: Comparisons of Outcomes for the Poor and the Rich." *American Economic Review,* 77(1): 69–77.

Sappington, D., and J. Stiglitz. (1987). "Privatization, Information and Incentives." *Journal of Policy Analysis and Management,* 6:567–582.

Savvateev, A. (1998). "Production and Rent-Seeking Behavior." Working Paper, New Economic School, Moscow.

Schaffer, M. (1989). "The Credible Commitment Problem in the Center–Enterprise Relationship." *Journal of Comparative Economics,* 13:359–382.

Schaffer, M. (1998). "Do Firms in Transition Economies Have Soft Budget Constraints? A Reconsideration of Concepts and Evidence." *Journal of Comparative Economics,* 26(1): 80–103.

Schaffer, M., and G. Turley. (1999). "Effective vs. Statutory Taxation: Measuring Effective Tax Administration in Transition Countries." Mimeo, Center for Economic Reform and Transition, Heriott-Watt University, Edinburgh.

Scharfstein, D. (1988). "The Disciplinary Role of Takeovers." *Review of Economic Studies,* 55:185–200.

Schmidt, K. (1995). "The Costs and Benefits of Privatization: An Incomplete Contracts Approach." Mimeo, University of Bonn.

Schmidt, K. (2000). "The Political Economy of Mass Privatization and the Risk of Expropriation." *European Economic Review,* 44(2): 393–421.

Schmidt, K., and M. Schnitzer. (1993). "Privatization and Management Incentives in the Transition Period in Eastern Europe." *Journal of Comparative Economics,* 17:264–287.

Schneider, F., and D. Enste. (1998). "Increasing Shadow Economies All Over the World: Fiction or Reality? A Survey of the Global Evidence of Its Size and of Its Impact from 1970 to 1995." Mimeo, University of Linz.

Schnitzer, M. (1999). "Enterprise Restructuring and Bank Competition in Transition Economies." *Economics of Transition,* 7(1): 133–155.

Segal, I. (1998). "Monopoly and Soft Budget Constraints." *Rand Journal of Economics,* 29(3): 596–609.

Segal, I. (1999). "Complexity and Renegotiation: A Foundation for Incomplete Contracts." *Review of Economic Studies,* 66(1): 57–82.

Shapiro, C., and R. D. Willig. (1990). "Economic Rationales for the Scope of Privatization." In E. N. Suleiman, and J. Waterbury (eds.), *The Political Economy of Public Sector Reform and Privatization,* 55–87. Boulder, CO, and London: Westview Press.

Shleifer, A. (1985). "A Theory of Yardstick Competition." *Rand Journal of Economics,* 16(3): 319–327.

Shleifer, A., and D. Treisman. (2000). *Without a Map: Political Tactics and Economic Reform in Russia.* Cambridge, MA: MIT Press.

Shleifer, A., and R. Vishny. (1992). "Pervasive Shortages under Socialism." *Rand Journal of Economics,* 23(2): 237–246.

Shleifer, A., and R. Vishny. (1994). "Politicians and Firms." *Quarterly Journal of Economics,* 109: 995–1025.

Shleifer, A., and R. Vishny. (1997). "Corruption." *,Quarterly Journal of Economics,* 108(3): 599–617.

Sicular, T. (1988). "Plan and Market in China's Agricultural Commerce." *Journal of Political Economy,* 96(2): 283–307.

Simonovits, A. (1991). "Investments, Starts, and Cycles in Socialist Economies: A Mathematical Model." *Journal of Comparative Economics,* 15(3): 460–475.

Sinn, H.-W., and G. Sinn. (1993). *Jumpstart.* Cambridge, MA: MIT Press.

Sonin, C. (1999). "Inequality, Property Rights Protection, and Economic Growth in Transition Economics." Mimeo, Russian European Center for Economic Policy.

Sorm, V., and K. Terrell. (1999). "A Comparative Look at Labor Mobility in the Czech Republic: Where Have All the Workers Gone?" Center for Economic Policy Research Discussion Paper: 2263.

Staniszkis, J. (1991). *Dynamics of the Breakthrough in Eastern Europe.* Berkeley, CA: Berkeley University Press.

Stiglitz, J. (In press). "Whither Reform? Ten Years of the Transition." In B. Pleskovic and J. Stiglitz (eds.), *Proceedings of the World Bank's Annual Conference on Development Economics, 1999.* World Bank.

Sussman, O., and J. Zeira. (1994). "The Economics of Transition: Some Theoretical Issues." Mimeo, Hebrew University of Jerusalem.

Svejnar, J. (1989). "A Framework for the Economic Transformation of Czechoslovakia." *PlanEcon Report,* 5(52): 1–18.

Svejnar, J. (1990). "Productive Efficiency and Employment." In W. A. Byrd and L. Qingsong, *China's Rural Industry: Structure, Development, and Reform,* 243–254. Oxford, UK: Oxford University Press.

Svejnar, J., D. Munich, and K. Terrell. (1997). "The Worker-Firm Matching in the Transition: (Why) Are the Czechs More Successful Than Others?" William Davidson Institute Working Paper: 107.

Tobin, J. (1969). "A General Equilibrium Approach to Monetary Theory." *Journal of Money, Credit and Banking,* 1(1): 15–29.

Treisman, D. (1996). "The Politics of Intergovernmental Transfers in Post-Soviet Russia." *British Journal of Political Science,* 26:299–335.

Treisman, D. (1999a). "The Causes of Corruption: A Cross-National Study." Paper presented at the Fifth Nobel Symposium in Economics: The Economics of Transition, Stockholm.

Treisman, D. (1999b). "Decentralization and Corruption: Why Are Federal States Perceived to Be More Corrupt?" Mimeo, University of California, Los Angeles.

Treisman, D. (1999c). "Russia's Tax Crisis: Explaining Falling Revenues in a Transitional Economy." *Economics and Politics,* 11(2): 165–169.

Van Atta, D. (1993a). "Russian Agriculture between Plan and Market." In D. van Atta (ed.), *The "Farmer Threat,"* 9–24. Boulder, CO: Westview Press.

Van Atta, D. (1993b). "The Return of Individual Farming in Russia." In D. van Atta (ed.), *The "Farmer Threat,"* 71–95. Boulder, CO: Westview Press.

van Wijnbergen, S. (1992). "Intertemporal Speculation, Shortages and the Political Economy of Price Reform." *Economic Journal,* 102:1395–1406.

von Mises, L. (1920). "Economic Calculation in the Socialist Commonwealth." English translation in Hayek (1935): 87–130.

von Thadden, E. L. (1995). "Bank Finance and Long Term Investment." *Review of Economic Studies,* 62:557–575.

Walder, A. (1995). "China's Transitional Economy: Interpreting Its Significance." *China Quarterly,* 144:963–979.

Wang, Y. (1991). "Economic Reform, Fixed Capital Investment Expansion and Inflation: A Behaviour Model Based on the Chinese Experience." *China Economic Review,* 2(1): 3–27.

Wei, S.-J. (1991). "To Divide or to Unite: A Theory of Secessions." Mimeo, Harvard University.

Wei, S.-J. (1993). "Gradualism vs. Big Bang: Speed and Sustainability of Reforms." Mimeo, Harvard University.

Wei, S.-J. (1997). "How Taxing Is Corruption on International Investors?" National Bureau for Economic Research Working Paper: 6030.

Wei, S.-J. (1998). "Corruption in Economic Development: Economic Grease, Minor Annoyance or Major Obstacle." Mimeo, Kennedy School, Harvard University.

Weingast, B. (1995). "The Economic Role of Political Institutions: Market-Preserving Federalism and Economic Growth." *Journal of Economics, Law and Organization,* 11:1–31.

Weingast, B. R. (1997). "The Political Foundations of Democracy and the Rule of Law." *American Political Science Review,* 91(2): 245–263.

Weiss, A., and G. Nikitin. (1998). "Performance of Czech Companies by Ownership Structures." Mimeo, Boston University.

Weitzman, M. (1970). "Iterative Multi-Level Planning with Production Targets." *Econometrica,* 38:50–65.

Weitzman, M. (1974). "Prices vs. Quantities." *Review of Economic Studies,* 41(3): 477–491.

Weitzman, M. (1980). "The Ratchet Principle and Performance Incentives." *Bell Journal of Economics,* 11:302–308.

Weitzman, M. (1991). "Price Distortion and Shortage Deformation, or What Happened to the Soap?" *American Economic Review,* 81(3): 401–414.

Weitzman, M., and C. Xu. (1993). "Chinese Township and Village Enterprises as Vaguely Defined Cooperatives." *Journal of Comparative Economics,* 18:121–145.

Williamson, O. (1975). *Markets and Hierarchies.* New York: Free Press.

Williamson, O. (1985). *The Economic Institutions of Capitalism.* New York: Free Press.

Winiecki, J. (1991). "The Inevitability of a Fall in Output in the Early Stages of Transition to the Market: Theoretical Underpinnings." *Soviet Studies,* 43(4): 669–676.

Wong, C. (1991). "Central-Local Relations in an Era of Fiscal Decline: The Paradox of Fiscal Decentralization in Post-Mao China." *China Quarterly:* 691–715.

Woo, W. (1994). "The Art of Reforming Centrally Planned Economies: Comparing China, Poland and Russia." *Journal of Comparative Economics,* (3): 276–308.

World Bank. (1996). *From Plan to Market: World Development Report.* Washington, DC: World Bank.

Zhuravskaya, E. V. (1999). "Incentives to Provide Local Public Goods: Fiscal Federalism, Russian Style." Mimeo, Russian European Center for Economic Policy.

Author Index

SUBJECT INDEX